THE CANADIAN CHALLENGE

Don Quinlan • Doug Baldwin • Rick Mahoney • Kevin Reed

OXFORD
UNIVERSITY PRESS

OXFORD
UNIVERSITY PRESS

70 Wynford Drive, Don Mills, Ontario M3C 1J9
www.oupcanada.com

Oxford University Press is a department of the
University of Oxford.

It furthers the University's objective of excellence in research,
scholarship, and education by publishing worldwide in

Oxford   New York

*Auckland   Cape Town   Dar es Salaam   Hong Kong   Karachi
Kuala Lumpur   Madrid   Melbourne   Mexico City   Nairobi
New Delhi   Shanghai   Taipei   Toronto*

With offices in

*Argentina   Austria   Brazil   Chile   Czech Republic   France   Greece
Guatemala   Hungary   Italy   Japan   Poland   Portugal   Singapore
South Korea   Switzerland   Thailand   Turkey   Ukraine   Vietnam*

Oxford is a registered trade mark of Oxford University Press
in the UK and in certain other countries

Published in Canada
by Oxford University Press

Copyright © Oxford University Press Canada 2008

The moral rights of the author have been asserted

ISBN 978-0-19-543156-8

Database right Oxford University Press (maker)

First published 2008

3 4 – 11 10 09

Printed and bound in Canada

The publisher has endeavoured to meet or exceed industry
standards in the manufacturing of this textbook. The spine and
endpapers of this sewn book have been reinforced for extra binding
strength, and the cover material is a premium polymer-reinforced
material designed to provide long life and withstand daily classroom
use. The text pages have been printed on Forest Stewardship Council
certified paper, harvested from a responsibly managed forest, which
contains a minimum of 10% post-consumer waste.

ENVIRONMENTAL BENEFITS STATEMENT

Oxford University Press Canada saved the
following resources by printing the pages of this book
on chlorine free paper made with 10%
post-consumer waste.

TREES	WATER	ENERGY	SOLID WASTE	GREENHOUSE GASES
38 FULLY GROWN	13,965 GALLONS	27 MILLION BTUs	1,798 POUNDS	3,380 POUNDS

Calculations based on research by Environmental Defense and the Paper Task Force.
Manufactured at Friesens Corporation.

Acknowledgments from the Authors

The authors would like to recognize the splendid efforts of the Oxford
editorial and production team who enabled us to meet the many "challenges" of such a complex text.

Thanks to David Stover, President, Oxford University Press
Canada; Anna Stambolic, VP and Director, Education Division; Linda
Masci Linton, Executive Editor, Education Division; Arlene Miller,
Production Editor; and Elaine Aboud, Editor. We offer a very special
thank you to Loralee Case for her patience, excellence, insight, and
complete dedication to this project.

Dedications

To Peter Lawley, a wonderful teacher, a fellow Oxford
author, and a great friend.   –Don Quinlan

To my five grandchildren Riley, Cole, Chase, Ella,
and Georgia.   –Doug Baldwin

To the staff and students in the Social Sciences department
at York Mills CI for allowing me to look forward to coming
to school each day—and Cathie, Katie, Jacob, Danny, and
Andrew for making it a bigger pleasure to come home.
            –Rick Mahoney

To my parents, Jim and Louise, for their boundless love
and support, and to my wife, Lisa, for her patience and
kindness.   –Kevin Reed

Acknowledgements

Oxford University Press wishes to thank the dedicated
team of reviewers who provided advice and expertise
throughout the development process:

Theresa Fitzpatrick Meikle, Curriculum Consultant,
   Literacy/Student Success, Intermediate/Senior English,
   York Region District School Board, The Centre for
   Leadership and Learning
Kenneth Garlick, Vincent Massey Secondary School,
   Greater Essex County District School Board
Sherida Hassanali, Equity Officer, Nova Scotia Barristers'
   Society, and Professor of Education, Mount Saint
   Vincent University
Zainab Jamal, Marc Garneau Collegiate Institute, Toronto
   District School Board
Rocky Landon, Bayridge Secondary School, Limestone
   District School Board
Ian Pettigrew, Instructional Coordinator, Social Studies,
   History and Geography, Canadian and World Studies,
   Social Sciences and Humanities, H.J.A. Brown
   Education Centre, Peel District School Board
Shane Pisani, St. John Catholic High School, Catholic
   District School Board of Eastern Board
Pina Sacco, Department Head, Canadian and World
   Studies, St. Augustine Catholic High School, York
   Catholic District School Board
Matthew Tran-Adams, Parkdale Collegiate Institute,
   Toronto District School Board

In addition, we wish to thank Loralee Case, Lead
Developmental Editor; Elaine Aboud, Developmental
Editor; Alex Schultz, Developmental Editor; Arlene Miller,
Production Editor; Aniko Szocs, Copy Editor; Deborah
Sun de la Cruz and Janice Evans, Photo Researchers and
Permissions, Sherill Chapman, Cover and Text Design, and
ArtPlus Ltd., Layout and Art.

Cover images: top, l-r *The Stretcher-bearer Party* by Cyril
Barraud, 19710261-0019, Beaverbrook Collection of War
Art, ©Canadian War Museum; ©Bettmann/CORBIS;
Dept. of National Defence/Library and Archives Canada/
PA-145516, **bottom, l-r** ©Reuters/CORBIS; Ceremony to
mark the 60th anniversary of Canadian Citizenship, ©Office
of the Secretary to the Governor General of Canada 2007,
photo: MCpl Issa Paré, February 16, 2007. Reproduced
with the permission of the Office of the Secretary to the
Governor General; Jana Chytilova/Ottawa Citizen;
Shamanizing #1 by Aoudla Pudlat, ©Aoudla Pudlat,
Courtesy Galerie Vincent, Ottawa.

Since this page cannot accommodate all copyright notices,
pages 468–472 are considered extensions of this page.

Every possible effort has been made to trace the original
source of text and visual material contained in this book.
Where the attempt has been unsuccessful, the publisher
would be pleased to hear from copyright holders to rectify
any errors or omissions.

Contents

 Go the *The Canadian Challenge* online resource centre.

Features in *The Canadian Challenge*

Personalities

Communities

Map Study

Issues

Skill Path:
Writing a Research Essay

Success in school often depends on how well you find and present information and express your point of view. During this course—in fact, throughout your life—you may be called upon to process information, make decisions, and present your ideas. To present information in a research essay in a clear and logical way, follow these steps:

STEP 1: Choose a Topic

Before you can begin to write a research essay, you have to choose a topic. Focus on only one specific aspect of a topic. For example, in writing a research essay during your work with *The Canadian Challenge*, you would first narrow down your topic to one aspect of Canadian history, such as Aboriginal peoples or Québec. Then you would narrow it down further to a specific topic, such as Aboriginal peoples and land claims or the rise of Québécois nationalism.

STEP 2: Conduct Your Research

Use a variety of sources to find information on your research topic, including newspapers, magazines, books, encyclopedias, government documents, and Internet sites. Carefully read and evaluate the information you find. Print, photocopy, or take notes of useful information. (See the Skill Path: Making Effective Notes, page 63.) Bookmark your favourite Internet sites. As you gather your sources, be sure to include complete bibliographic information so you can cite your sources. (See the Skill Path: Documenting Your Sources, page 288.)

STEP 3: State Your Thesis

Once you have become familiar with your topic, do some critical thinking to formulate your thesis statement. Then state your thesis clearly in one sentence. Your thesis statement should summarize your point of view about the topic and should tell your audience what the purpose of your essay is. (See the Skill Path: Formulating a Thesis Statement, page 187.)

STEP 4: Prepare an Outline

A good outline is the key to a successful research essay. The outline is a way to organize your ideas logically before you start to write. Begin your outline with an introduction. This is where you clearly present your thesis statement and the purpose of your research essay. The main body of your research essay follows the introduction. This is where you present your arguments to support your thesis statement. You should use three supporting arguments to support every position you take. Begin with a strong argument. Then build your case with a second, stronger argument. Save your strongest argument for last as you make your final point.

INTRODUCTION
- First paragraph: Introduce the topic and state your thesis statement.

MAIN BODY
- Second paragraph: *First argument*
  Fact to support it
  Fact to support it
  Fact to support it
- Third paragraph: *Second argument*
  Fact to support it
  Fact to support it
  Fact to support it
- Fourth paragraph: *Third argument*
  Fact to support it
  Fact to support it
  Fact to support it

CONCLUSION
- Fifth paragraph: Summarize the information and restate your thesis statement.

STEP 5: Analyze Your Information

Once you are satisfied with your outline, analyze your research information critically. (See the Skill Path: Using Primary and Secondary Sources, page 27.) Double-check the accuracy of your information and make sure it is accurate and up-to-date. Determine what information is relevant to your essay. Do not include any information that is irrelevant or that you do not understand. Be sure to acknowledge any ideas or quotations that you have borrowed from your sources.

The following Skill Paths may help you analyze your information: Identifying Cause-and-Effect Relationships, page 87; Recognizing and Analyzing Bias in Sources, page 136; Analyzing and Interpreting Political Cartoons, page 153; Analyzing and Interpreting Visual Evidence, page 172; Analyzing Different Perspectives, page 252; and Keeping Up with the News, page 419.

STEP 6: Write a First Draft

To write the first draft of your essay, begin with the first topic in your outline. Record all of the relevant information for this topic on note cards or in word-processing files. Organize your information in the order you wish to present it. Use a code or different-colours to categorize your information according to your outline. Then write your first draft for this topic. Repeat the process for all of the topics in your outline.

STEP 7: Prepare Your Final Essay

Once you have drafted your essay, read it carefully for content errors and double-check for accuracy. If necessary, adjust or reorganize your outline and essay. Stay focused on the purpose of your essay. Then check your essay to make sure there are no spelling or grammar mistakes. Exchange your essay with a partner and proofread each other's work.

STEP 8: Evaluate Your Work

To get a fresh perspective on your essay, set it aside for a few days. Then reread it and evaluate it by asking yourself the following questions:
* Is my thesis statement clear?
* Did I follow my outline?
* Did I present my arguments in a logical order?
* Do my arguments support my thesis?
* Have I proven my thesis with strong supporting arguments?
* Are there any revisions that would improve my essay?
* Have I clearly cited all of my sources?

Use the answers to these questions as the basis for a final edit of your essay.

Refer to the Table of Contents for a complete list of all Skill Paths in this textbook.

Looking Back
Canada in the Early Twentieth Century

The Dawn of a New Era

The dawn of the twentieth century marked the beginning of a new era. Canada was experiencing unprecedented social, political, and economic changes. **Immigration**, **urbanization**, and **industrialization** were creating both exciting opportunities and great challenges. Immigrants from non-British countries were settling in the West. Their arrival revealed deep feelings of intolerance in Canadian society. There were great inequalities across the country, too—between rich and poor, business and labour, men and women. Aboriginal peoples and people of Asian and African heritage were denied equal rights. Yet it was also a time of optimism. The prime minister, Sir Wilfrid Laurier, proclaimed that the twentieth century belonged to Canada.

Conflicting Identities

Prior to the First World War, Canada was gradually emerging from the shadows of British **colonial** rule. Canada was a self-governing nation, yet it was not a completely independent one. Although Canada controlled its domestic affairs, Britain still determined its foreign policy. As a result, ties to Britain remained strong, at least throughout much of English Canada.

One of the country's greatest challenges was balancing the different perspectives on the Canadian identity. Laurier envisioned a society based on respect and tolerance between French and English Canadians. Achieving this

harmony proved difficult, however, as the interests of British **imperialists** in English Canada clashed with those of French Canadian **nationalists** in Québec. In the West, most new immigrants were neither English nor French. Their arrival in Canada added another dimension to the Canadian identity as the country began to evolve into a **multicultural** nation.

Different Perspectives

Aboriginal peoples were the first to live on the land that had become Canada. For thousands of years, their traditional lands had defined their identities. By the early twentieth century, however, they had lost most of these lands. Isolated by **racist** and discriminatory policies, the First Peoples struggled not only to maintain their identities, but to ensure their survival. As Canada searched for its national identity, their voices were unheard.

In English Canada in the years before the First World War, imperialism was the dominant form of **nationalism**. The majority of English Canadians considered Canada to be a British country, bound together by history and culture. They took pride in being part of the **British Empire**. Their sense of belonging to and participating in a great world power bolstered their sense of identity. Many English Canadians hoped Canada would gain greater influence over Britain's imperial policies and supported spreading British ideas of justice and democracy around the world.

Reading Strategy

Before you begin reading this textbook, think about what you already know about Canada's reputation in the world. Do you think Canada's image is mainly positive or negative? Why do you think so? As you explore Canada's history since 1914, try to make connections by thinking about events that may have contributed to this reputation.

"This land is our soul. And it is upon the souls of thousands of people that this country has been formed."

–Chief George Manuel, leader of the National Indian Brotherhood, 1975

"There is no antagonism … between Canadianism and imperialism. The one is but the expansion of the other. To be a true Canadian … is to place yourself in harmony with the spirit of the empire, with its love of liberty, with its resolute defence of its rights … with its disposition to deal even-handed justice to its subjects, irrespective of race and creed."

–Ontario Premier George Ross, the *London Advertiser*, 28 September 1900

Peleg Franklin Brownell is regarded as one of Canada's first **Impressionists**. He introduced rich colours into Canadian painting in works such as in the detail of this one, called *Street Scene*. What is your impression of this scene. What is your opinion of the way this artist presented his work?

Support for Britain and imperialism was cultivated in schools, where teachers taught students to express their loyalty to the Empire. What British symbols are evident in this Alberta classroom in 1910?

"A free Anglo–French Confederacy ... united by bonds of ... kinship with Great Britain and France, of two great nations from which it had derived its races, its civilization, and its thoughts, and offering to ... the world a friendly rival ... to the expanding civilization of the United States, would become one of the greatest contributions to humanity."

–Québécois nationalist Henri Bourassa, to the Canadian Club of Ottawa, 18 December 1912

French Canadians rejected imperialism. They believed it would lead to involvement in foreign wars that did not concern Canada. Closer ties to the global British Empire would make French Canadians an even smaller minority and would reduce their power here at home. They wanted Canada to determine its own foreign policy and become an independent nation within the British Empire. Their feelings of nationalism were exclusively Canadian, built on the foundations of the country's French and English heritage.

Imperial Rivalries

In the first decade of the twentieth century, the United States had challenged Germany's economic supremacy as it emerged as the world's fastest-growing industrial economy. Britain, once the richest and most powerful country on earth, had fallen to a distant third. By 1909, Britain's naval supremacy was being challenged, too. The British believed the German navy was planning to build the most powerful fleet of battleships the world had ever seen. Britain feared that Germany's growing naval strength threatened its military and economic power.

Conflicting Viewpoints

To keep pace with Germany, Britain asked Canada and its other colonies to contribute money to build bigger and better warships for the British navy. If Laurier agreed, as English Canadians demanded he do, he would offend French Canadians, who opposed any involvement in Europe's conflicts. Laurier proposed a compromise. Canada would create its own navy of five cruisers and six destroyers. The navy would be under Canadian control, but in times of war—and with Parliament's approval—the ships could be at Britain's disposal.

The compromise failed to satisfy either side. French Canadians accused Laurier of giving in to British demands. English Canadians were embarrassed by what they called a "tin-pot navy" consisting of a few outdated ships. The controversy contributed to the defeat of Laurier's government in 1911. Three years later, on the eve of the First World War, Canada had neither contributed to the British navy nor built a viable navy of its own.

The Prospect of War

Meanwhile, the great powers of Europe continued to manoeuvre for economic and political supremacy. Over the years, a complex network of open and secret **alliances** had emerged. As political tensions mounted, the prospect of war loomed large on the horizon. By 1914, Canada's role in the British Empire would be called into question again as the country went to war to defend Britain in the "war to end all wars."

"Laurier imposes on us a costly navy, which will serve no purpose except to kill our own sons in the wars of England. Laurier forces me today to choose between him and the country. I choose the country."

–Henri Bourassa, November 1911

"I am branded in Québec as a traitor to the French, and in Ontario as a traitor to the English … In Québec I am attacked as an imperialist and in Ontario as an anti-imperialist. I am neither. I am a Canadian."

–Prime Minister Wilfrid Laurier, November 1911

 **Reading Strategy**

Before you continue reading, preview the textbook and examine how it is organized. Become familiar with the common features that appear in this book. Look for headings, subheadings, photographs, maps, and captions, along with the unique features of this book: Profiles in Power, Personalities, Communities, Issues, Sign of the Times, Skill Path, and Thinking Like a Historian.

In 1910, the first ships of the Royal Canadian Navy (RCN) were commissioned. The *Rainbow* (shown here) and the *Niobe* were Canada's only offensive warships.

Thinking Like a Historian

Throughout this textbook, you will be performing a variety of tasks associated with historical thinking. They include analyzing, questioning, examining, researching, interpreting, predicting, evaluating, and concluding. As you perform these tasks, you will be developing the skills, strategies, and attitudes of a historian. You will then have the opportunity to apply these skills and strategies to a framework for historical thinking as you investigate history using the following concepts. You will also find many of these skills will be useful in your personal life as well as in your future career.

Establishing Historical Significance

Essential Question: As a historian, how do you determine why certain events, trends, and issues from the past—and not others—are still important today?

History is the study of the past. As a historian, however, it is impossible to study *everything* that happened in the past. How do you decide what is historically significant? People's perspectives of a person, issue, or event may determine whether they perceive it to be historically significant or not. What is historically significant to one group may be insignificant to another. Gender, culture, race, religion, wealth—even where people live—may influence their perspectives on issues, events, and people. A country as geographically, economically, culturally, and racially diverse as Canada has many different perspectives on the past. As a historian, to help you determine their historical significance, you need to consider two key questions:

- Did the issue, event, or person result in significant change for a large number of people over the long term?
- Did the issue, event, or person reveal a long-standing or emerging issue for a group of people?

Using Primary Source Evidence

Essential Question: As a historian, how do you find, select, and interpret different sources of information?

A historian's knowledge of the past is based on evidence. There are many different kinds of evidence. They include written records, oral histories, physical remains, and artifacts. Examining a source to find evidence is different from simply looking for information. When you look for evidence, you need to ask the right questions:

- What is it?
- Who created it?
- What was the purpose?
- What was the time and place?
- What does the evidence reveal?

Identifying Continuity and Change

Essential Question: As a historian, how do you recognize how things have changed or stayed the same over time?

Continuity and change are interrelated. Change does not usually happen as the result of a single event. More often, it is the result of a series of events spread out over time. Some changes happen more quickly than others. Sometimes change is for the better. Sometimes it is not. To identify continuity and change, as a historian you need to compare different points in time. Remember to look closely. Even when some things change, other things remain the same. Think about the following questions as you identify patterns of continuity and change:

- What is the chronology of events—that is, in what order did things take place?
- In what ways did things change over time?
- Were the changes obvious or subtle?
- In what ways did things stay the same?

Analyzing Cause and Consequence

Essential Question: As a historian, how do you analyze how and why certain circumstances and actions led to certain consequences?

Throughout history, individuals and groups have promoted, shaped, and resisted change. The long-term causes that lead to change may be motivated or influenced by deeply held beliefs or widespread social or economic conditions. The short-term causes are particular events stemming from these conditions that cause individuals or groups to take action. When you are making connections between causes and their consequences, ask yourself the following questions:

- What were the long-term causes of this event?
- What short-term actions triggered the event?
- What were the consequences? Which consequences were intended? Which were not?

Developing Historical Perspective

Essential Question: As a historian, how do you understand the different social, cultural, intellectual, and emotional factors that shaped people's lives and actions?

It is difficult to think about past events from the perspective of another time and place. As a historian, you need to develop **historical empathy**—that is, you need to develop an understanding of the social, cultural, intellectual, and emotional factors that shaped people's lives and actions during that time. To help you develop empathy, ask yourself the following questions:

- What evidence is there to suggest why individuals or groups of people acted the way they did?
- What different perspectives did people have about this issue or event?

Making Moral Judgments about the Past

Essential Question: As a historian, how do you make moral judgments about actions that took place in the past?

While examining all meaningful and significant issues, events, and people from the past, historians must pass moral judgments. Making moral judgments helps us learn from the past and prepares

us to make better decisions in the future. As a historian, ask yourself the following questions to help you make moral judgments about the past:

- What were the typical social values and attitudes of the time?
- How did the perspectives of the people involved reflect these values and attitudes?
- What moral lessons can we learn from these actions?
- Which causes and consequences were most significant or important?

NOTE: These concepts of historical thinking are adapted from Peter Seixas, "Benchmarks of Historical Thinking: A Framework for Assessment in Canada," The Centre for the Study of Historical Consciousness, The University of British Columbia, April 2006.

You, the Historian

As you embark on your investigation of Canada's history since the beginning of the First World War, you can begin to develop the *skills* and *strategies* of a historian by completing the following activities:

1. As a class, brainstorm some of the ways you, as a historian, can decide if an event is significant. Start by thinking about events at your school or in your own lives. Decide which are significant and which are not, and why.

2. Think about what you already know about Canada's past. What issues, people, and events stand out in your mind as being especially important? Why do you think they are more important than others?

3. How do you think the *skills* of a historian may be useful to you, not only as a student of history, but in your personal life?

The Globe and Mail

CANADA DECLARES WAR!

amation Issued Following Solid Vote in Parliam

saw Defenders Hurl Enemy Back on City's Frin

mans Raid French Positions Under Heavy Ba

r-Offensive zis Believed Preparation

POLES HOLD UNDER NAZI ONSLAUGHT

Proclamation of War

Dominion Comm To Stand With B In Fight Against

Chapter 1:	The War to End All Wars
Chapter 2:	The Boom Years
Chapter 3:	The Dirty Thirties
Chapter 4:	The Second World War

IN FOCUS

In 1900, Canadians were optimistic about the future. Few would have predicted that the first half of the century would produce some of the most tumultuous years in Canada's history. By 1914, the nation was embroiled in the First World War. In its aftermath, Canadians experienced growth and prosperity. The good times did not last, however. In 1929, Canada and much of the world were plunged into a decade of economic despair. Only the Second World War ended the economic nightmare.

As you explore these defining moments in forging the Canadian identity, focus on the following questions:

- How did the First World War shape the Canadian identity?
- What impact did the boom to bust cycle of the 1920s and 1930s have on Canadians?
- How did the Second World War contribute to Canada's evolving identity?
- What identity had Canada created for itself on the world stage by the middle of the century?

Pegi Nichol MacLeod's work reflected what it was like to be a woman during the Second World War. The detail of this painting, *Untitled (WRCNs in Dining Room)*, shows women in the navy. How would you describe the artist's work?

The War to End All Wars

Figure 1.1 The First World War was a titanic struggle fought by countries around the world. Vimy Ridge was Canada's greatest victory during the long and bloody war. However, the ghosts of Vimy haunted Canadian unity during and after the war. When the guns finally fell silent on 11 November 1918, Canadians were facing a new and troubling world order. What feelings do you have when you look at the detail of this painting? What does the image suggest about the war?

Chapter at a Glance

Thinking Ahead

Canada has earned a reputation as a peaceful country that helps other countries around the world. Many Canadians are proud of our reputation as peacekeepers. However, Canada also has a long military history earned on global battlefields with the loss of much Canadian blood. In this chapter, you'll find out about Canada's role in the First World War. As you explore this role, consider the following key questions:

- Should Canada have entered the First World War?
- What impact did the war have on Canada?
- Who were the heroes of the war?
- What was the most important result of the war for Canada?
- Was the outcome of the war worth Canada's participation?
- How do Canadians today view this event?

Profile in Power:

Robert Laird Borden

"I believe the time has come when the authority of the state should be invoked to provide reinforcements necessary to sustain the gallant men at the front who have held the line for months, who have proved themselves more than a match for the best troops that the enemy could send against them, and who are fighting in France and Belgium that Canada may live in the future."

—Robert Borden introducing conscription to the House of Commons, 18 May 1917

Figure 1.2 Robert Laird Borden (1854–1937)

In December 1912, Robert Borden stood in the House of Commons to make an important speech. When Borden sat down, he missed his chair and fell to the floor with a loud thump, breaking his glasses in the fall. Imagine how he must have felt in this situation! Eight years later, when Borden retired from politics, no one was laughing. Borden's efforts during the First World War made him one of Canada's most successful prime ministers.

Borden's father and grandfather were farmers in Grand Pré, Nova Scotia. Borden, however, found farming "extremely disagreeable." Education became his avenue to a different life. His mother taught him to read and write. He later attended a private school where he learned discipline, hard work, patience, and to have a sense of humour.

Borden taught school for several years before he decided to become a lawyer. He joined a Halifax law firm in 1874, where he did well and moved up in the firm. In 1896, he was elected to the House of Commons. When Charles Tupper resigned after losing the 1900 election to Wilfrid Laurier's Liberals, the Conservatives turned to Borden to lead their party. He was reluctant. "I have not either the experience or the qualifications which would enable me to successfully lead the party," Borden wrote. However, out of a sense of duty to the country, he accepted the position. After losing to Laurier in the 1904 and 1908 elections, Borden finally became prime minister in 1911. When Great Britain declared war on Germany three years later, Borden said he did not think that the fighting would amount to very much.

Canada was unprepared for war. Canadian factories were not equipped to produce guns, bullets, tanks, or other military equipment. Canada's army was poorly equipped and just over 3000 men strong. The entire country and its economy had to be readied for war. This put an enormous weight on Borden's shoulders. He began to show symptoms of nervous strain. Wartime issues such as **conscription** and **internment** camps led to death threats against Borden, forcing him to travel with bodyguards.

As the war dragged on into 1917 and casualties mounted, Borden began to feel increasing pressure to adopt conscription—forcing eligible young males to enlist in the military. This pressure had been building for more than a year, especially from English Canadians who believed that French Canadians were not doing their part. On the other hand, French Canadians did not feel welcome in an army where materials and instructions were often entirely in English. On 17 May 1917, Borden told his party that he was ready to adopt conscription.

Borden believed that he was indispensable to the war effort. "Our first duty," he said, "is to win at any cost…" He gave police sweeping powers to round up immigrants considered disloyal and to place potentially dangerous German, Austrian, and Ukrainian immigrants in internment camps. Borden also denied them the right to vote.

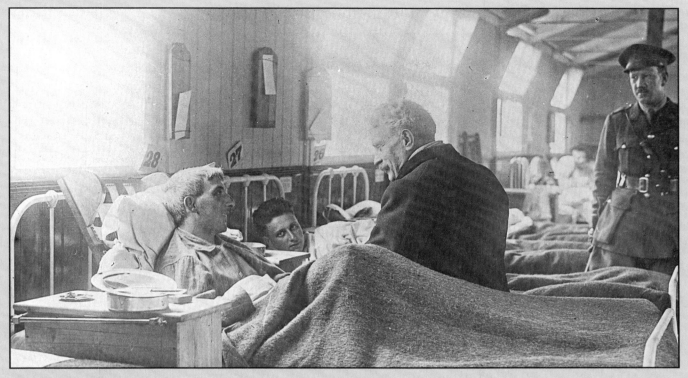

Figure 1.3 Prime Minister Borden talks with a wounded soldier in 1917. His visits to the front lines convinced him that conscription would have to be imposed, regardless of the political consequences. How might Borden's observations at the front lines have influenced him?

The war took every ounce of Borden's energy. At its conclusion, doctors advised him to quit politics immediately. On 10 July 1920, Arthur Meighen became Canada's next prime minister. Borden presented Meighen with his lucky charm, a shamrock that had been presented to him during the 1911 election campaign. He carried it in his pocketbook throughout that election and again in 1917.

Borden died on 10 June 1937. His most lasting contributions were managing Canada's war effort and expanding Canada's autonomy from Great Britain.

Responding

1. In your view, what were Robert Borden's basic strengths as prime minister?
2. What do you think would be most difficult about being a Canadian prime minister in wartime? Explain your response.

War!

While the young country of Canada was enjoying the summer of 1914, the old countries of Europe were heading toward a terrible conflict.

Causes of the War

On 28 June 1914, a royal couple were victims in a fatal shooting in Sarajevo. In the small corner of the Austro-Hungarian Empire, someone had thrown a bomb at their limousine. Archduke Franz Ferdinand had bravely pushed the bomb away. Neither he nor his wife, Archduchess Sophia, had been hurt in the explosion. However, as the royal motorcade continued, the couple was attacked again. A young man stepped out from the shadows of a house and threw himself onto their vehicle. He pointed a pistol. Within minutes, the heir to the Austrian throne and his wife lay dead. Gavrilo

Princip, the teenaged assassin, was a member of a Serbian extremist group called the Black Hand.

The First World War was not simply caused by this one brutal assassination. Rather, Princip's bullets were the spark that set off the final explosion on the road to war. For years, the world—and Europe in particular—had been plagued by forces such as **militarism**, nationalism, and imperialism. Together they provided the framework for the First World War.

Europe in 1914

In 1914, the major European powers were Germany, Great Britain, France, Russia, Italy, and Austria-Hungary. They were wealthy and militarily powerful. They were also bitterly divided and competitive. Some had extensive empires spread across the globe.

By 1914, these powers had divided themselves into two great military alliances: the **Triple Entente** (Britain,

Figure 1.4 Archduke Ferdinand and Archduchess Sophia shortly before their murder. Princip's bullets would soon lead to an all-out war that would claim tens of millions of lives and forever alter the twentieth century. How might a world war permanently change a country such as Canada?

France, and Russia) and the **Triple Alliance** (Germany, Austria-Hungary, and Italy). Both alliances were prepared to go to war to defend their interests. Thus, a conflict between two countries could easily expand to include all the major European powers and their empires. The stage for confrontation had been prepared by increasing militarism, nationalism, and imperialism.

Militarism

Increasingly, European countries had come to trust in military might as the answer to resolving conflicts. A weapons race had turned Europe into an armed camp. Armies were larger and the race to build military strength was feverish. In particular, a naval race based on the all-powerful dreadnought heightened tensions between England and Germany.

Economic Rivalry

Many countries were beginning to flex their muscles after the success of the Industrial Revolution. New factories produced more goods than countries could absorb. Modern technologies helped create new weapons of increasingly destructive power. Countries competed for materials and markets for their booming industries.

Nationalism

Many European countries were extremely nationalistic. This often led to contempt for other countries and the desire to win against them. Burning competition extended to the creation of vast empires spanning the globe. To extreme nationalists, war was the ultimate competition in which countries tested each other.

Imperialism

As you discovered in Looking Back, the imperial powers of Europe were competing to expand their nations through the founding of colonies or the conquering of territories around the globe. Both Africa and Asia were the targets of European expansion and imperialism. This mad scramble for more people, resources, wealth, and glory created much tension among the major powers of Europe. Several earlier conflicts had almost led to open war. The stage was being set for an explosion.

Reading Strategy

Start keeping a personal glossary in which you note and define any unfamiliar terms or concepts you come across in this text. To help you find the meaning of a word, read the entire paragraph and look for clues in the text that might explain its meaning.

Figure 1.5   The dreadnought, or "fear nothing," a type of heavily armoured battleship, was first built by the British. Germany soon joined Britain in a deadly naval race to launch more of these powerful warships. In the past, Britain had asked for Canada's help in this race for naval power. What impact might an arms race have on the outbreak of war?

"It is our duty to let Great Britain know and to let the friends and foes of Great Britain know, that there is in Canada but one mind and one heart and that all Canadians are behind the Mother Country."

—Former Prime Minister Wilfrid Laurier, 1914

Flashpoint: The Balkan Powder Keg

It was in the Balkans where the final spark would ignite a wider war. This was an area of Europe where many wars had been fought. It was called the "Balkan Powder Keg" because it was so potentially explosive and needed only a match to set the troubled region completely ablaze.

Great powers such as Russia, Germany, and Austria-Hungary had interests there. Nationalism was rampant. The Austrian province of Bosnia had recently been added to the Austrian Empire. It was home to Serbs, some of whom wished to unite with Serbia, across the border.

The assassination of the Austrian archduke, the heir to the throne, sparked an explosion. When Austria-Hungary demanded that Serbia allow its troops to enter Serbia to search for other extremists, Serbia refused and turned to Russia for help. Germany pledged to support Austria-Hungary, and Russia turned to France. The alliances drove blindly down the road to war. When German troops struck France through neutral Belgium, Britain entered the war. The First World War had begun.

The Canadian Connection

In 1914, most Canadians could not find Serbia on a map. Although Archduke Ferdinand's assassination was newsworthy and tragic, few Canadians understood what it meant. However, Canada was a proud and loyal member of the British Empire. Canada's relations with foreign powers were in the hands of Great Britain. When Britain was at war, Canada was automatically at war, but Canada could determine the extent and nature of its effort.

While many Canadians were keen to follow Britain to the battlefields of Europe, few understood the background causes of the war. Many felt that Britain was in the right and Germany was at fault.

So without much thinking or real debate, the young country advanced into the unknown. Canadians eagerly joined a war that they had absolutely no role in causing or declaring. They would, however, play a great part in fighting the war. They would also soon know the pain and price of war.

Challenge and Response

1. How were Principip's bullets the "spark" that led to the First World War?
2. Use a concept web to show the major longer-term causes of the war.
3. How could Canada, which was so far away from Europe, be drawn into the conflict?
4. Should Canada have supported the war? In a chart, list reasons for, and against, supporting the war. Write a concluding statement. You may want to revise your chart and statement as you work through the chapter.

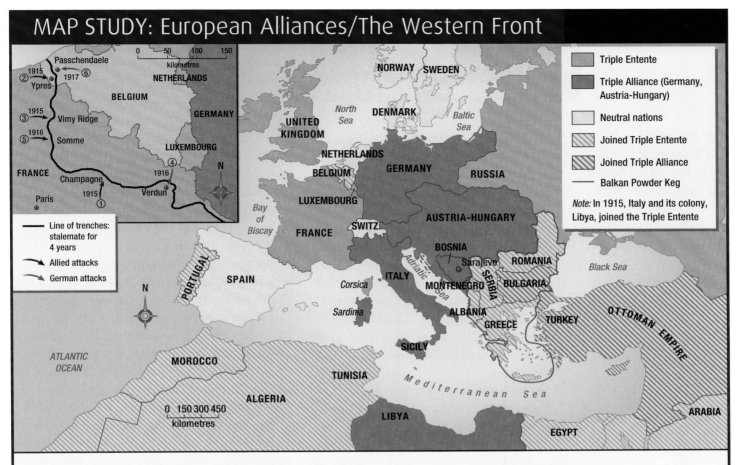

Source: Don Quinlan, et al., *Twentieth Century Viewpoints*, 2nd edition, (Don Mills: Oxford University Press, 2003), 37, 48.

Figure 1.6 The main map shows the alliances in Europe in 1914 as well as the location of the Balkan Powder Keg. The inset map shows some of Canada's major battle sites along the Western Front between 1914 and 1918.

The countries of Europe formed two powerful alliances: the Triple Entente and the Triple Alliance. The threat of eventual war spurred countries to form military agreements and even secret treaties. Many of these countries also controlled vast overseas empires that were brought into the conflict. Within Europe, the Balkans was a region of considerable turmoil and had endured several recent nationalist wars. Both Austria-Hungary and Russia had ambitions in the region. When they clashed they brought in their allies, who then called on their empires. The world was soon at war.

The trenches of the **Western Front** snaked across western Europe. Canadian soldiers played an important role in the fighting along this front. They were considered excellent attack troops, as you will find out later in the chapter.

Analysis and Response
1. In your opinion, which alliance enjoyed the strongest geographic position? Why?
2. How could conflict in the Balkans lead to a wider war?
3. In which country did Canadian troops do most of their fighting?

Over There: Ypres, the Somme, and Vimy

"We should be unworthy of the blood that runs in our veins if we sought to avoid an inevitable conflict."

–Prime Minister Borden, to the House of Commons, 1914

In 1914, Canada's army totalled a mere 3000 men. Nevertheless, Prime Minister Borden and his cabinet decided to support Britain wholeheartedly. Most Canadians were quite happy to join the **Allied** forces. In fact, plans were put in motion to establish a Canadian Expeditionary Force (CEF) even before Britain requested one. This enthusiastic support of British war aims would cost Canada billions of dollars and tens of thousands of lives. It would gain Canadians pride and international recognition. It would also tragically divide Canadians for years.

As men rushed to join the army, particularly those Canadians who had been born in Britain, Sir Sam Hughes, the minister of Militia and Defence in Borden's cabinet, was given the task of assembling the CEF. Within one week, 10 000 men volunteered. Within two months, 30 000 volunteers enlisted and were equipped, trained, and shipped off to Britain for more training. Many soldiers felt the war would be over by Christmas 1914. They were eager to go off to Europe as quickly as possible.

By September 23, the first ships were steaming for Britain cramped with half-trained, but enthusiastic, troops. They spent a wet, cold winter in Britain undergoing more training under the watchful and often critical eye of British commanders. Canadians were often viewed by the British as untrainable and unsuitable soldiers. They were slow to salute the British officers and had little respect for their British trainers. They were, however, physically fit and keen to fight. Sam Hughes resisted all attempts to break up the Canadians and put them into existing British units.

Prejudice

The CEF reflected Canada's racial attitudes and prejudices in the early twentieth century. Canadians of all backgrounds volunteered to do their patriotic duty and fight for Canada. They were not all treated equally, however. People of Aboriginal, African, and Asian heritage faced hostility and discrimination that reflected the intolerance of all "non-British" people during the war. French Canadians who enlisted encountered a British-dominated army that showed little respect or concern for their language and culture. Women were prohibited from joining the armed forces, although many volunteered to work overseas as nurses and ambulance drivers (see page 23). Canadians of Italian, Jewish, Chinese, and Japanese heritage who enlisted for combat duty often found themselves assigned to labour battalions instead. Although Canadians of all backgrounds showed their patriotism and loyalty to Canada, their contributions were not recognized.

No. 2 Construction Battalion

Canadians of African heritage faced hostility and prejudice, even as they expressed their patriotism by volunteering to fight for Canada. Many military leaders believed the war was a "white man's war." They were reluctant to accept African Canadian recruits. However, the death toll on the front lines and the persistent lobbying of leaders in the African Canadian community convinced the government to change its position. Soldiers of African-Canadian heritage were allowed to join the CEF in a non-combat role if

PERSONALITIES

Francis Pegahmagabow: The "Deadliest Shot"

Most Aboriginal soldiers could have cited treaty provisions and stayed out of the war. However, 4000 served in the conflict. They were among the most highly skilled riflemen. Snipers usually worked in pairs (one shooting while the other found targets and protected their position), often far from other soldiers. They got very close to enemy trenches to practise their deadly trade. At least 50 decorations were awarded to Aboriginal soldiers for their bravery and courage during the war.

Figure 1.7 Francis Pegahmagabow is Canada's most decorated Aboriginal soldier and a member of Canada's Native Hall of Fame.

recognition for his courage and bravery. He later had a successful career as an Aboriginal leader and spokesperson for the rights of the Wasauksing First Nation. Pegahmagabow was the inspiration for Elijah Weesageechak, the main character in *Three Day Road*, a novel about the First World War. Francis Pegahmagabow died in 1952.

"Pegahmagabow was one of those rare Canadian soldiers who enlisted in 1914 and fought to the end of the war. Throughout his service at the front, he became Canada's premier sniper of the war."

–Canadian Museum of Civilization

Francis Pegahmagabow, of the Wasauksing First Nation near Parry Sound, Ontario, was credited with 400 hits. He was considered to be the deadliest shot in any army on the Western Front. He survived pneumonia, a serious leg wound, and gassings. Like many Aboriginal fighters, he carried a medicine bag as protection and believed it saved his life during the war. When the war ended, he suffered both physically and emotionally.

After the war, Pegahmagabow, like so many of his Aboriginal comrades, was given fewer benefits than white soldiers and received very little

"On his return he [Francis Pegahmagabow] was required to bear arms of a different nature. His fight was to improve the living conditions of the [First Nations] of Canada."

–Merle Pegahmagabow, grandson

Although Aboriginal soldiers distinguished themselves in both world wars, it took many years before they were formally recognized for their efforts. Finally, in June 2001, the Aboriginal Soldiers Monument was unveiled in Ottawa. It honours Aboriginal men and women who served in the First and Second World Wars, the Korean War, and **peacekeeping** operations.

Responding

1. What skills did Francis Pegahmagabow have that were highly valued and led to several medals?
2. Why do you think it took so long for Canada to recognize the contributions of Aboriginal soldiers?

Reading Strategy

After you read a quotation, take note of who the speaker is by checking the source line. This information will help you put the quotation in context. Notice that there are two types of margin quotations in this book—one from noted authorities and the other from young people. What features set these two types of quotations apart from each other?

they could gather enough men to form a segregated battalion.

In response, in July 1916, hundreds of soldiers of African-Canadian heritage formed the No. 2 Construction Battalion. After training in Nova Scotia, they deployed overseas, where they dug trenches for the troops training in England. Later, they went to France, where they worked in logging and shipping operations, repaired roads, and distributed supplies. All of the officers of the all-African Canadian battalion were white, however, except for the chaplain, Captain William White. He was the first commissioned officer of African heritage in the Canadian armed forces and the only one in the British Empire during the war.

Eventually, some African Canadian soldiers broke through the racial barriers and joined the front-line combat units. Later in this section, you will learn

of the courage of one African Canadian soldier, Jeremiah Jones, at Vimy Ridge. His commanding officer recommended Jones for the Distinguished Conduct Medal for his heroism, but military authorities refused to acknowledge the heroism of African Canadian soldiers or honour their patriotism with medals.

The Western Front

A bristling line of trenches and fortifications stretched nearly 1000 kilometres across Europe, with Allied forces facing German and Austro-Hungarian forces. This was called the Western Front. It soon became a nightmarish landscape of mud, craters, barbed wire, blood, and bone.

Troops hurled themselves against an enemy dug-in, or foxhole, in heavily protected trenches stretching back for kilometres. Enduring bombing, artillery, underground mines, and machine-gun fire, casualties quickly rose into the millions. On the first day of the Battle of the Somme, 57 470 members of the British army were killed, wounded, or missing in the mud. It is not surprising that the killing zone between the lines was called **no man's land**.

Ypres, 1915

The Canadians entered the front lines in February 1915. They soon took up positions in the trenches near the small Belgian town of Ypres. Their war was about to erupt. As bad as trench warfare was, Canadians would face a new, more terrible, element in their first major battle. On 22 April 1915, the front lines near Ypres witnessed the use of poison gas (one of the century's first weapons of mass destruction, or WMD)—another technological breakthrough in modern warfare. Along a front of 6.5 kilometres, 165 tonnes of deadly chlorine gas were released

Figure 1.8 "Has there ever been anything more terrible, in the history of war, than the trenches? What set trench warfare apart from all the other ways men have tortured each other was the length of time spent in one miserable place. They stayed in the trenches for weeks, months, years, living in squalor with disease and lice till they were killed or maimed, making no progress in a war that made no sense." –Robert Fulford, 10 October 1992. What might be Fulford's reasons for saying that the war "made no sense"?

from over 5730 canisters. The German army 100 000 strong came in behind to smash the Allied lines, including the Canadian division.

The gas was deadly—soldiers reeled at their posts, choking and rolling about "like mad dogs in their death agonies." When French troops retreated, the Allied line was broken. German soldiers headed into the gap in the Allied line. When the gas hit the Canadian lines, the troops had no gas masks, even though an attack had been expected. Soldiers urinated in their handkerchiefs and held them over their faces to neutralize the effect of the gas. Canadian forces courageously extended their own lines and closed the gap.

However, Ypres did not fall. The bitter fighting resulted in atrocities on all sides including this event recorded by a Canadian soldier:

"Our rifles were jammed and the only machine gun that remained had been clogged with mud ... then the enemy broke into the trench further along and started bombing their way toward us. One of our officers ... ordered us to surrender and we threw up our hands ... Though we held our hands aloft and were now unarmed, the cold-blooded crew started to wipe us out. Three of our men were bayonetted before an officer arrived and saved the rest of us. Even then, our rough captors struck us with their rifle butts and kicked some of our men who were unfortunate enough to be laid out with wounds."

–Private W.C., quoted in J.C. McWilliams and R.J. Steel, *Gas! The Battle for Ypres 1915* (St. Catharines: Vanwell Press, 1985), 121–122.

When the guns fell silent, the Canadians had held the Allied line. They paid for their victory with 6000 casualties. They earned the respect of both ally and foe and earned four Victoria Crosses. Allied Supreme Commander Marshal Foch called the Canadian stand "the finest act in the war." As General Arthur Currie noted, "The untried amateur soldiers suddenly became transformed into a skilful body of veterans."

The Somme, 1916

The Battle of the Somme was designed as the "big push" that would destroy the German lines, bringing a swift and victorious end to the war. Instead, it resulted in 623 907 Allied deaths and 660 000 German deaths. The Germans called it *Das Blutbad* (the bloodbath). On 1 July 1916, the first day of the battle, British forces took 57 540 casualties in a few hours. Among those lives lost were young men from Newfoundland. They died in a mini-battle at Beaumont Hamel within the vast slaughter of the Somme battlefield.

Vimy, 1917: Birth of a Nation

In 1867, Canada became a dominion but, for some observers, it actually became a country during a terrible battle in April 1917. The Allied military leaders were slowly learning that sending troops of men "over the top" to be slaughtered as they stumbled toward enemy machine gunners and barbed wire was not going to bring victory. It was getting harder and harder to find new recruits willing to die on the killing fields of Europe. The slaughter of the Somme demanded a new approach to the war.

Using tunnellers, engineers, and railway troops, Canadian forces led by General Arthur Currie transformed the terrain. Currie helped develop a new strategy to tackle the endless massacre of soldiers along the Western Front. He insisted that his soldiers be

"The effects of the successful gas attack were horrible. I am not pleased with the idea of poisoning men. Of course, the entire world will rage about it first and then imitate us. All the dead lie on their backs, with clenched fists; the whole field is yellow."

–Rudolph Binding, German officer, quoted in *Gas! The Battle for Ypres 1915*

"After the battle of Ypres, Canada sat in a different position in the eyes of Belgium and France. The name Canada was a word symbolizing thankfulness and bravery due to the effort of the 1st Division in the battle of Ypres."

–Jason Bessey, Canadian Youth Overseas

"All of my friends have either been killed or wounded ... For miles around, corpses completely cover up the ground ... When one of my friends was killed at my side, I saw red: some Germans raised their arms in surrender, but it was too late for them. I will remember that all my life."

–Sergeant Frank Maheux, in *A People's History of Canada*

Learn more about Canada's battles in the First World War

"From dugouts, shell holes, and trenches, men sprang into action, fell into artillery formations and advanced to the ridge—every division of the Corps moved forward together. It was Canada from the Atlantic to the Pacific on parade. I thought then, and I think today, that in those few minutes, I witnessed the birth of a nation."

–Brigadier General Alex Ross, in D.E. McIntyre, *Canada at Vimy*, 1967

"I believe the Battle of Vimy Ridge to be one of the greatest battles of World War I because Canadians won the battle by themselves and a lot of guns, prisoners and land were taken on that day."

–Brent Le Coure, Canadian Youth Overseas

carefully trained and thoroughly prepared for battle, rather than mindlessly, but bravely, charging across battlefields. His methods would prove their value in the overwhelming victory at Vimy.

The preparations included building 11 underground tunnels to move troops secretly and safely and an underground city with 34 kilometres of wiring and 1770 kilometres of telephone cable. Models were built and the troops were informed on the features of their targets. This would be no blind dash for the other side. As well, the enemy was weakened with a barrage, or bombardment, of great accuracy. This was aided by aerial reconnaissance (a military survey of enemy territory). The Germans called this shelling the "week of suffering."

In earlier battles, the enemy generally had a good idea of when an attack was to be launched. After a punishing barrage, soldiers emerged from their dugouts and readied their weapons for the attack that was likely to come. Because soldiers often advanced in massed lines as they tried to cross over broken ground and barbed wire, they were usually mowed down.

This time, Canadians used a new tactic called the "creeping barrage." In this type of attack, the artillery continued to fire even as the Canadians left their trenches. The goal was to hurl shells just ahead of the advancing forces. In this way, enemy soldiers were forced to stay in their dugouts and keep their heads down. This meant soldiers on the ground and the artillery troops had to have perfect discipline, training, and timing. The hope was that, while the enemy huddled deep, Canadian forces would be on top of them before they could organize resist-

ance. Obviously, errors would be disastrous for the advancing troops who could be killed by friendly fire.

By the first week of April, all was ready. When the Canadians did finally unleash their attack, it was in a bitter snowstorm on 9 April 1917.

The timing and training paid off. In the snow and bombardment, 40 000 Canadians sped from their trenches and overwhelmed the German forces. Within hours, most troops had reached their positions. In two days, German forces retreated from the ridge. The victory was staggering. The Canadian forces had taken more guns, ground, and prisoners than any previous British attack. The Canadians won four

Figure 1.9 "I threw a hand bomb right into the nest and killed about seven of them. I was going to throw another bomb when they threw up their hands and called for mercy." –Jeremiah Jones. Jones marched the remaining members of the German machine-gun nest to his lines. He carried their deadly weapon and gave it to his commanding officer.

What do you think about the author's contention that Canada became a country during this terrible battle?

Victoria Crosses for their gallantry under fire. As well, a new sense of Canadian identity was forged in the firestorm of Vimy.

Ten thousand, or 1 out of 10 who fought that day, were casualties, including 3600 dead. The troops lost in these desperate battles were not being replaced—as the losses were not being matched by new volunteers. More soldiers were needed to replace those who had fallen. Everyone realized that this war offered death and dismemberment rather than easy glory. How to replace the losses was destined to bitterly divide the country born so bravely on Vimy Ridge.

The Bluebirds

More than 3000 Canadian women served overseas on the battlefield as nursing sisters. Called "bluebirds" because of their blue uniforms, these women were part of the CEF. In 1914, their average age was 24.

They experienced the horror of war first-hand and worked under terrible conditions to ease suffering and heal soldiers' wounds. They had to deal with injuries unknown before the war. The high mortality rate of patients was a painful part of serving in a war that produced huge casualties on a daily basis. Although many bluebirds had seen death before, few had ever faced the loss of so many patients—many of whom were young men barely out of their teens.

Bluebirds often served in casualty clearing stations close to the front lines. At times, the front lines shifted quickly—the nursing sisters came under fire and lost their lives as well. In one attack, three bluebirds were killed in the deliberate bombing of a hospital in Étaples, France. Some bluebirds died from shelling, some died from disease, and others died when a hospital ship was torpedoed. In total, 46 of Canada's nurses lost their lives in the war.

Learn more about the bluebirds

Challenge and Response

1. What evidence is there that Canada responded quickly to Britain's call for help?
2. Why were the early battles so costly in terms of lives?
3. What new battle tactics were successfully employed at Vimy?
4. Do you think that the victory at Vimy was worth the toll it took? Explain.
5. Do Canadians today accept such high casualty figures for their soldiers? Explain your response.
6. How did women participate overseas in the First World War? Explain your opinion of this role.

The Air and Sea Wars

Learn more about the air and sea wars

Canada had no air force before or during the First World War. The Royal Canadian Air Force was not organized until 1924. However, about 20 000 Canadian airmen, pilots, mechanics, and gunners served with British forces. They were a large part of the Allied victory in the war.

When war broke out, Canada's "tin-pot navy" consisted of 350 sailors and two aging warships, the *Niobe* and the *Rainbow*—one for each coast! By 1918, this skeletal force had mushroomed to 112 warships staffed by 5500 officers and men. In addition, 8000 Canadians served with the Royal Navy.

The War in the Air

Trench warfare offered no glory. Young men, most in their late teens or early twenties, flocked to the air force. Pilots fought in leading-edge war machines, received better food and pay, wore smart uniforms, and slept in warm beds at night. They paid a high price for their glory. For new pilots on the Western Front, lifespan was measured in weeks. They called the air service the "suicide service." Half of the casualties were a result of mechanical failure. Parachutes were unavailable until the end of the war. The great fear of pilots, who termed their planes "flying coffins," was to be hit and go down in a "flamer."

> "There won't be any 'after the war' for a fighter pilot."
>
> –Raoul Lufbery, French-American pilot

War on the High Seas

Control of the sea lanes was vital to Allied victory. Although the German surface navy was no match for the Royal Navy, Germany excelled at submarine warfare. It built 400 submarines, or U-boats, which were brutally effective in sinking Allied ships. At one point, Britain was reduced to six weeks of food, and one-quarter of ships leaving British ports were sunk.

Men, munitions, food, and other war materials had to be transported overseas from Canada. With British leadership and Canadian support, heavily guarded convoys steamed from Halifax to Europe. The Canadian Patrol Service protected shipping and sought out submarines. The Patrol Service was quite effective—only three steamers and about twenty-four fishing boats were lost in Canadian waters during the war. Mine-laying, heavier depth charges, heavily armed convoys, and zigzagging helped defeat the U-boat threat. More than half of the German U-boats were sunk or captured.

Death Ship

Halifax was a booming city during the First World War. The port was the chief transport link between Canada and Europe. Ships from all over the world came to Halifax to transport goods to the war zone.

On 6 December 1917, the horror of war was transported to the citizens and sailors of Halifax. Two Allied ships collided in the busy harbour. One, the *Mont Blanc*, carried a deadly cargo of 2000 tonnes of TNT and other explosives. The ship caught fire, drifted, and blew up in a roaring explosion that was heard 300 kilometres away. In one blinding flash, large sections of the city were levelled. When the buildings collapsed, fires broke out. People were buried in the rubble. Some were blinded, while others burned to death in the inferno. This explosion was to be the greatest human-made explosion in history until the atomic bomb was dropped in 1945.

Canadian Fighter Pilots

In the whirling dogfights in the skies above the European battlefields, young Canadian pilots excelled at this new but deadly form of warfare. Canadian pilots accounted for 127 aces, or pilots who registered at least 5 "kills." In fact, there were 127 Canadian aces who shot down 1500 enemy aircraft. Canada had 4 pilots with over 50 kills, more than any other country in the war. By 1918, 40 per cent of Royal Air Force pilots were Canadian.

Figure 1.10 This romantic view of war in the air masked the fact that combat was deadly. Why might the artist have portrayed air combat in this way?

Billy Bishop

Billy Bishop is Canada's best-known pilot in the First World War. Bishop's 200 dogfights and 72 kills made him the greatest ace in the British Empire. He won the Victoria Cross for a feat of incredible courage. He had longed to directly attack a German airfield—something that had not yet been done. Early one morning he left his base and set out to attack the enemy deep behind their lines. When his bullet-ridden plane limped home, he had shot down three enemy aircraft in his daring solo attack. On his last day at the front, he was credited with five kills.

Billy Barker

Barker was considered by other pilots to be the deadliest pilot alive. He started flying after only 55 minutes of instruction. He had 53 kills to his credit and also earned the Victoria Cross. His exploits earned him more medals than any other Canadian. His last air battle was his most glorious but almost killed him and left him permanently injured. After shooting down a German observation plane, Barker found himself facing nearly 60 German aircraft. He decided to attack. He hit two more planes before being wounded and he shot down another attacker before being wounded yet again. He somehow managed to steer his plane over his own trenches and barely survived a crash landing.

Raymond Collishaw

With 60 kills, Raymond Collishaw was Canada's second-highest ace. He was the first pilot to claim six victories in a single day. In 1917, when the *Luftwaffe* (German air force) dominated the skies, Collishaw organized an all-Canadian squadron named Black Flight for their habit of painting their planes in black.

Black Flight specialized in daring head-on attacks. Collishaw shot down 14 planes in the first 15 days of June. Collishaw was also fortunate. Twice in three days, he was shot down but managed to walk away from total wrecks.

Responding

1. What evidence suggests the importance of the role that Canadian pilots played in the war in the air?
2. What appear to have been the most important characteristics of Canadian aces?
3. Which of these pilots do you think is most memorable? Why?

"The last sight on earth for hundreds of people was a flash of light, brighter, greater, more dazzling than the sun. An instant later they were dead or blind."

–Robert Macneil, *Burden of Desire*, 1992

The toll included nearly 2000 dead, 9000 injured, and 1630 buildings destroyed. Almost 6000 people lost their homes, and 25 000 others lost roofs, walls, windows, heat, or water. To make matters worse, a blizzard ravaged the city, making rescue work almost impossible. In hours, however, aid was on its way from neighbouring towns. Within two days, a ship from Boston arrived with over $300 000 worth of relief supplies. Thirty million dollars was collected from around the world to help rebuild the city and assist the survivors. American generosity is still commemorated today with the gift of a special Christmas tree shipped from Nova Scotia to Boston.

Figure 1.11 Over 10 % of the population was homeless after the explosion. The working-class sections of Halifax were particularly hard hit. Why do you think these sections experienced the worst destruction?

 **Learn more about the Halifax Explosion**

Challenge and Response

1. What were the positive and negative aspects of being a pilot?
2. What was the U-boat threat and how was it countered?
3. How did the Halifax Explosion bring the war home to Canada?

Skill Path:
Using Primary and Secondary Sources

Historians typically categorize information into two types: primary and secondary sources. In this Skill Path, you will learn to distinguish between these two types of information, and learn how to use them effectively.

STEP 1: Identify Primary and Secondary Sources

Primary sources are first-hand reports created by people who witnessed or participated in the events. They usually date from the period of time being researched. Examples of primary sources include

- artifacts
- autobiographies
- blogs
- clothing
- diaries
- eyewitness accounts
- films
- government documents
- journals
- letters
- maps
- music
- news reports from the scene
- oral interviews
- paintings
- photographs
- speeches
- statistics
- video and DVD recordings

Secondary sources are accounts of events created by people who did not witness the events. Examples of secondary sources include

- books and textbooks
- documentaries
- encyclopedias
- essays
- newspaper editorials and articles

STEP 2: Determine Your Purpose

Historians use primary and secondary sources for different purposes. They use primary sources to find out what people were thinking during the time period being studied. They also use these sources to capture the spirit of the times. For example, quotations from letters or diaries allow historians to understand people's feelings, while photographs and paintings give them some sense of what the world looked like in another place and time.

Historians use secondary sources to research the accumulated knowledge of a subject. Textbooks and encyclopedias allow them to see the big picture of an event or a time period. Historical works give them the opportunity to find out how other historians view a subject.

STEP 3: Select Appropriate Resources

When you conduct research, try to find examples of both primary and secondary sources. Each type will reveal different aspects of the event or person you are studying. You will probably use secondary sources to understand the overall picture and primary sources add weight to your research. Use primary sources as evidence for the points you are making. They will also help bring your work to life by connecting with the people who lived through the historical events you are describing.

STEP 4: Practise Your Skill

1. Determine whether each of the following is a primary or secondary source. Each one refers to the Halifax Explosion of December 1917.
   a) a picture of Halifax after the explosion
   b) a newspaper report of the explosion written at the time by someone in Halifax
   c) a newspaper report of the explosion written by someone not in Halifax
   d) an interview with a survivor of the explosion
   e) a list of statistics showing the injuries and deaths in the explosion
   f) an encyclopedia article on the explosion
   g) your history textbook's account of the explosion
   h) a documentary film about the explosion
   i) a memoir written years after the explosion by someone who lived through it
   j) a poem written about the explosion by a grandchild of a survivor
2. Look through this chapter and find examples of primary sources.

Total War

Reading Strategy

When you look at photographs and paintings, examine the details of the foreground, middle ground, and background. What in particular catches your attention? Why? What do you think is the intention of the photographer or artist?

The First World War was the first "total" war of the twentieth century. It was total because it involved the efforts, energies, and passions of almost everyone. Although most experts felt that the war in Europe would last only a few months, it was destined to last over four years. It resulted in the highest death toll of any war in history, before or since. Civilians were targeted as well as soldiers. Barbaric attacks, indiscriminate killing of prisoners, and the unleashing of terrible weapons became a regular feature of this war.

Every effort was made to secure victory. Vast armies of citizen soldiers replaced the elite professional armies of the past. Home fronts were enlisted to support the battle front. Everyone could participate in the final victory. Women, diverse groups, children, senior citizens, those in poor health—all

had a role to play. In this war for "civilization," no resource was left unused.

Propaganda

It is said that in war, truth becomes the first casualty. All countries rushed to present their views of events. Victories were praised and casualties downplayed. The enemy was accused of being a cruel animal. Governments printed and distributed posters urging their citizens to enlist and support the war effort.

In Canada, at the start of the war, Max Aitken organized a successful propaganda machine to promote the Allied position. He was particularly interested in making sure that the United States entered the war on the Allied side, which it finally did in 1917.

Aitken organized the publishing of articles, books, and pictures that supported the Allied cause. He financed a special Canadian War Memorials Fund to employ artists to paint the battlefields for the home front and future generations.

New Weapons

War often drives scientific research and technological innovation as enemies try to find any means for gaining victory. Most of the technological advances in the First World War resulted in even more deadly and efficient weapons:

- *Tanks.* This term was the British code word for an armoured chariot-type weapon. Its firepower, steel plates, and caterpillar tracks made it the ideal weapon to cross no man's land. After many failures, the tank proved its worth in 1917 and spearheaded the Allied advances until the end of the war.
- *Poison gas.* First used unsuccessfully by Allied forces, gas was a key element in the German attack at Ypres. Although banned by

Figure 1.12 This dramatic image of men courageously going "over the top" is actually a rehearsed and staged picture. It is an example of propaganda. Do you think this photo accurately reflects the nature of the battlefields of the First World War? Explain.

international treaty, armies were quite willing to use this weapon to gain ground. Gas was particularly unreliable because a change in wind direction would send it right back over the user's own lines. Chlorine, mustard, and phosgene gases were most widely used. They often resulted in asphyxiation and internal and external burning. Soon all troops were supplied with gas masks to meet this threat.

- *Zeppelins.* These dirigibles, or blimps, were used to fly high over enemy towns and drop bombs. German Zeppelins successfully bombed Britain on several occasions. This random slaughter of the civilian population was to become characteristic of warfare in the new century. Canadian flyers were particularly skilled at attacking Zeppelins and accounted for 50 per cent of Zeppelin kills. Planes flying higher and using fire-producing bullets turned these hydrogen-filled airships into raging infernos.

- *U-boats.* This submarine vessel was perfected in the First World War and was used with deadly results. Germany had the largest submarine fleet—over 400 ships. Allied forces finally defeated the U-boat with new types of mines, depth charges, and Q-ships (ships disguised as vulnerable targets but able to quickly attack submarines when they came to the surface).

- *Machine guns.* These deadly weapons probably accounted for most of the casualties in trench warfare. They were steadily refined and improved during the war. Closely packed advancing men were easy prey for the spray of hundreds of rounds per minute. In combination with barbed wire two metres high, they made attacks on opposing trenches a suicide mission. In the air war, machine guns were fitted with a special mechanism to allow bullets to pass through propellers. This created the possibility for tens of thousands of deadly aerial dogfights.

Spies

Both sides used spies during the war. Propaganda posters made everyone alert to the danger of "loose lips." At first, the Halifax Explosion was thought to have been the work of spies and saboteurs. Germany's plots to enlist Mexico against the United States and to blow up Canada's Welland Canal kept everyone on edge at home. If caught, spies were treated harshly.

Challenge and Response

1. Why is the First World War often seen as a "total" war?
2. In your view, what was the deadliest of the new weapons? Discuss your ideas in a small group.
3. Do you think wars today are more or less bloody? Explain your position in one or two paragraphs.

Division on the Home Front

War often brings out both the best and the worst in people and countries. Canadians were no exception during the First World War. Much of the country was united as never before, making courageous and generous sacrifices in the war effort. On the other hand, the pressure of war encouraged intolerance, prejudice, and greed. Canada was both proudly united and bitterly divided from 1914 to 1918.

The War Effort at Home

Canadians who did not fight overseas were still able to contribute to the war effort in various ways. Rationing freed up supplies for soldiers overseas. Buying **Victory Bonds** helped pay for the war. Canadians also got used to a range of government controls designed to guarantee victory. These included:

- *Censorship.* Books, magazines, newspapers, and even postcards from the front lines were censored by the government. For example, some of the most gruesome pictures of the Halifax Explosion were not released until years later.
- *Income tax.* This tax on the income of a person or business was a truly revolutionary measure. It might never have been accepted had it not been presented as a "temporary" measure necessary to win victory.
- *Debt.* Canada's debt (money owed by the government) as a result of the war rose from $463 million in 1913 to $2.46 billion in 1918. At one point, the war was costing Canada over $1 million a day.
- *War production.* Canadians, especially women, worked long hours in difficult, sometimes dangerous,

Figure 1.13 In addition to their huge contribution on the battle front, Canadians also generated vast quantities of materials such as weapons and munitions for the war effort. Many factories relied almost solely on female labour, particularly for work that required dexterity and patience. For some women, it was the first time that they had received payment for their labour. What impact do you think this had on women and society in general?

conditions to produce record amounts of food, war materials, and general supplies.

Not all Canadians supported the war effort itself. Some groups of **pacifists** protested Canadian involvement. Mennonites, Hutterites, and **conscientious objectors** protested the war and conscription on moral grounds. They believed that killing was simply wrong. Even families were divided over the war. For example, the Canadian Women's Peace Party was led by Laura Hughes, a niece of Sam Hughes, minister of Militia and Defence.

"If women in war factories stopped for 20 minutes, we should lose the war."

–French general Joseph Joffre

The Enemy Within

When war broke out in 1914, Canada was on its way to becoming the diverse society it is today. The Laurier years had seen a tremendous wave of new immigrants who had been attracted by Canada's vast open spaces. Within days of the outbreak of hostilities, many of the people Canada had so eagerly courted were seen as **enemy aliens**. They were now subject to injustice and discrimination. As war fever turned into hysteria, many Canadians wanted to strike out at new Canadians from Germany and Austria-Hungary. Many peoples, such as Ukrainians, had come to Canada to escape the bonds of the German and Austrian Empires. They were shocked to find themselves targeted by their adopted country.

Panicked Canadians demanded that people from the territories of these empires be controlled. In 1914, Parliament passed the **War Measures Act**. The Act allowed for the registration and internment of anyone considered a threat to Canada. It was used to imprison Canadians of German and Slavic descent. This resulted in the forcible internment of 8579 people, including 156 children, in 24 camps across Canada. The majority were forced to do hard labour in remote areas. Some of the internees helped build Canada's first national parks. Those who tried to escape or protest their imprisonment were dealt with harshly. In at least one camp in northern Ontario, full-scale conflict broke out.

Internment is a sad chapter in Canada's history. It reveals how patriotic zeal can quickly turn to prejudice. The internees had done nothing wrong. They had committed no crimes. Their only "crime" was to have been born in empires now locked in mortal combat with their adopted country. A North-west Mounted Police report later noted that "the closest investigation has not revealed the slightest trace of organization or concerted movement amongst the alien enemies."

Conscription

By 1917, Canada's role in the war had expanded dramatically. The First Division of the CEF had increased to four divisions. Fewer and fewer men were volunteering for a likely death in no man's land. More and more families were unwilling to sacrifice yet another young man. Nevertheless, when Prime Minister Borden returned from a tour of the European battlefields, he was determined to ensure the existence of Canadian forces overseas.

The answer, though brutal, seemed simple. Canada would have to conscript soldiers for overseas duty. If battlefield losses could not be replaced, it was clear that the CEF would have to be disbanded. The remaining men would have to serve in other Allied units. Conscription in Canada, however, faced particular challenges:

- At the outset of the war, Borden had clearly promised no conscription for overseas service.
- Canadians were divided on the question of conscription. Some felt it was their patriotic duty, while others disagreed with this position.
- Canada had already contributed generously in men, food, supplies, and money. Some Canadians felt the country had done its duty.
- Increasingly, the wholesale butchery on the battlefields led Canadians to question the value of the war. They complained that their civilian and military leaders did not value their lives. Stories of wartime profiteering (making an unfair profit on essential goods during times of emergency)

"It had been a long war. Canadians had lived with the constant fear of invasion, or sabotage, by a fifth column operating inside the country. At times the battle front seemed to be the home front."

–Roger Sarty and John G. Armstrong, "Defending the Home Front," *Horizon Canada*, 1986

"There has not been and there will not be compulsion or conscription. Freely and voluntarily, the manhood of Canada stands ready to fight beyond the seas."

–Prime Minister Borden, 1914

"To me it is as clear as the day that if we defeat conscription we cannot possibly get the last available man and fulfill our promise to Britain."

–the Reverend S.D. Chown, church leader, 1917

 Learn more about the conscription crisis

"Was conscription needed? Troop reserves were low, but few conscripts actually made it overseas. At the time of enaction, conscription was seen as the only recourse. Quite simply, conscription was disastrous for Canada. It tore apart the fragile unity of the English and French in Canada, to which even today, we still see the effects."

–Randy Byrne,
Morell Regional
High School, 2003

by unscrupulous business people further dampened their enthusiasm for a war without end.

Borden's Approach

Prime Minister Borden decided that the CEF deserved to be replenished. Canada had come too far to withdraw from the war now. He knew that decisive battles lay ahead. He wanted conscripts if the volunteers did not come. He also realized that the issue was divisive at a time when Canada needed unity. The course of action he took was:

- Borden first approached Liberal leader Wilfrid Laurier with a plan for a Union government. When Laurier refused, Borden then successfully appealed to several leading English-speaking Liberals to join this government.
- In July 1917, Parliament passed the Military Service Act, making conscription for overseas service the law. There were protests and even riots in Québec.
- Borden's Conservative government attempted to influence the results of the 1917 election to ensure that conscription would stay in force:
  - The Military Voters Act gave the vote to male and female members of the armed services. For the first time in Canadian history, women could vote in federal elections. Borden was sure that those already in the armed forces would elect his government because it had introduced conscription.
  - The Wartime Elections Act extended the vote to mothers, daughters, wives, and sisters of men serving overseas. These new voters would also likely support Borden's policies because their relatives were already overseas and desperately

needed reinforcement and relief. This law enraged Borden's opponents because it also denied the vote to conscientious objectors and those naturalized Canadians (about 30 000 voters) born in enemy countries. This act effectively stacked the upcoming election in Borden's favour.

The Khaki Election

The election of 1917 was dubbed the "khaki election" because it was a wartime election fought over conscription. (Khaki was the greenish-brown colour of the soldiers' uniforms.) The election tore at the heart and soul of Canada. Election meetings were full of tirades; sometimes riots broke out. The French were accused of being cowards and of supporting Germany. The English were seen as Prussian dictators. Borden's attempts to "rig" the vote created long-term bitterness.

The Unionists won 153 seats but only 3 in Québec. On the other hand, Laurier's Liberals won 82 seats, 62 in Québec. The country was bitterly divided along language lines.

Even though conscription passed and Borden was re-elected, conscripting soldiers overseas was not easy. In Ontario, 12 750 of the first 118 128 conscripts applied for exemption. In Québec, the figure was 115 507 of 117 104. In the end, 100 000 were successfully conscripted, but only 50 000 made it overseas and only 25 000 actually got to the front lines before the war ended.

Women: A New Political Force

Another divisive issue both before and during the war was the political rights of women. Before the outbreak of war, women could neither vote nor hold office in Canada. Educational, social,

ISSUES

The Conscription Debate

The issue: What was the impact of conscription on Canada during the First World War?

Compulsory military service, or conscription, shattered Canadian unity during the First World War. Forcing men to kill or be killed against their will is perhaps the ultimate power for a government to have. As millions of Allied troops were being killed, disabled, or wounded, it became increasingly difficult to find replacements. By 1917, most Allied governments had imposed conscription policies on their citizens.

After the battle at Vimy Ridge, the issue had become critical for Canada. Most of the early recruits had been born in Britain and were keen to fight for their home country. However, native-born Canadians were less willing to die on a European battlefield. Many farmers were also opposed to conscription because they and their sons were needed to manage the farms and produce the food for the soldiers overseas.

French Canadians were most unwilling to volunteer. Many viewed the war as a British war and found the Canadian army to be an unfriendly British institution. Feeling no loyalty to France (the country that they felt had abandoned them), and even less to Britain (the country that had once ruled them), many French Canadians believed the war was not Canada's concern. Their ongoing struggle to protect their language rights made them even less willing to fight for *les anglais*. By war's end, only 13 000 of 500 000 volunteers were French-speaking. Conscription and the election of 1917 unleashed a bitter storm in Canada.

"What England needs most are not soldiers, but bread, meat, and potatoes."

–Henri Bourassa, Québec politician

"All citizens are liable to military service for the defence of their country, and I conceive that the battle for Canadian liberty and autonomy is being fought today on the fields of France and Belgium. If the war should end in defeat, Canada, in all the years to come, would be under the shadow of German military domination."

–Sir Robert Borden

"Is it not true that the main reason advocated for conscription—not so much publicly as privately, not shouted but whispered—is that Québec must be made to do [its] part, and French Canadians forced to enlist compulsorily since they did not enlist voluntarily?"

–Sir Wilfrid Laurier, leader of the Opposition and former prime minister

"It is the exact truth. All Canadians who want to fight conscription … must have the courage to say and repeat everywhere: 'No conscription! No enlistment! Canada has done enough.'"

–Henri Bourassa

"I oppose this bill because it has in it the seeds of discord and disunion."

–Sir Wilfrid Laurier

"To shirkers at home, nothing but hisses are due. I never want to take the hand of any man who is physically fit and has not volunteered to come to the front."

–Canon Frederick Scott, chaplain, First Division of the Canadian Corps

Responding

1. With which of the above comments do you agree/disagree? Explain your choices.
2. Which of these comments do you think would have been most harmful to Canadian unity? Why?
3. In a chart, list what you think are the major arguments for, and against, conscription.

and employment opportunities were quite limited. Although women's suffrage, or the right to vote, had been debated for some time, progress was slow. One result of having no political power was that women had few legal rights or protections.

The First World War provided an opportunity for women to display their true value and to gain the political rights granted to men. During the war, a small group of women campaigned for peace. The Canadian Women's Peace Party criticized the impact and cost of the war.

The war had drained Canada of young able-bodied men. Women quickly and skilfully moved into roles usually reserved for men. At home, they managed the family farm, kept the family together, and made important decisions. Jobs once denied to them were now open to women. Women excelled in factory work, particularly in the production of war materials.

The esteem and independence that come from paid work were empowering.

Socially, they played leading roles in relief organizations and fundraising campaigns. They endured the demands of rationing and the loss or injury of loved ones. Considering the quality of their efforts, it became more and more difficult to deny women the vote.

In 1916, under pressure from women and some men, the three Prairie provinces extended the vote to women. The manner in which Prime Minister Borden gave certain women the right to vote in federal elections was criticized by some Canadians. He had promised to extend the vote to all Canadian women who were over 21 and British subjects. He did so in 1918. By 1920, women could seek election to the House of Commons. However, it was some time before most Canadians —men and women—were comfortable with political equality for women.

Challenge and Response

1. How did the war divide Canadians?
2. Would you support conscription in a future conflict? Explain your position in a brief oral presentation.
3. Using primary and secondary sources, conduct research to find out why women in the Prairie provinces were the first to gain the right to vote in provincial elections. Then write a paper in which you present your findings.

Sign of the Times

WARTIME MUSIC

Listening to and playing music was a popular pastime during the war. Most middle-class families owned a piano. They often gathered around it to sing. Naturally, the war was a popular musical theme. There were songs about patriotism and heroism, about sad partings and happy reunions.

Figure 1.14 Gitz Rice was a soldier wounded at Vimy Ridge. He wrote songs about life at the front. His song "He Will Always Remember the Little Things You Do" encouraged women to support the war effort. Gordon V. Thompson's "I Want to Kiss Daddy Good Night" was another popular song.

WHY AIN'T YOU IN THE ARMY?

Figure 1.15 Specially trained teachers instructed cadets like these in the St. Mary's Cadet Corps in 1917. Students were trained in such things as infantry drills and rifle exercises. Young men who had almost finished high school were encouraged to enlist and serve their country overseas.

Young men who did not enlist faced pressure to do so.

"It was rather annoying to go out at all because the men in uniform, when you would walk down the street, they'd come and tap you on the shoulder and say 'Why ain't you in the army?'"

–Martin Colby, quoted in *The Great War and Canadian Society: An Oral History* (Toronto: New Hogtown Press, 1978), 103.

"Young girls were going along and they would meet what looked like a pretty good able-bodied man and they'd pin something white on them—called them a coward in other words, because they weren't in that army. 'What are you doing in civilian clothes when all my brothers are in the army?' That sort of thing."

–Robert Swan, quoted in *The Great War and Canadian Society: An Oral History* (Toronto: New Hogtown Press, 1978), 93.

Responding

1. What role do you think music plays during times of war?
2. How do you and your peers feel about military service today?

The Long March to Victory

As the war dragged on into its third year, neither side had made any significant gains. Even the great battle at Vimy Ridge had not opened up the path to decisive victory. In desperation, the generals sent more and more troops "over the top."

Passchendaele, 1917

General Douglas Haig was the commander of all British forces, including Canadian troops. In 1917, he ordered an assault at Passchendaele in Belgium. Following months of bombardment, the fields were a sea of mud that sucked living men below the surface. After gaining little ground, Haig refused to withdraw. He ordered the same men who had won so brilliantly at Vimy to lead a final assault on Passchendaele. General Arthur Currie objected, saying it would be a slaughter, but he was forced to follow orders. Canadians fought mud, mustard gas,

and machine guns in a hopeless struggle. Though they seized the town, they suffered 15 000 casualties before being ordered to retreat. In spite of horrendous costs and obstacles, the Canadian forces met their objectives.

The slaughter of the battle was so bad that Prime Minister Borden told the British prime minister, "Mr. Prime Minister, I want to tell you that if there is a repetition of the battle of Passchendaele, not a Canadian soldier will leave the shores of Canada as long as the Canadian people entrust the government of Canada to my hands."

The months after Vimy had brought rapid change. In November 1917, Russia fell to internal revolution and eventually pulled out of the war. By 1918, the Russians had given up a large amount of territory and signed a peace treaty with Germany. For the first time, German forces could now be concentrated on one front—the Western Front. As the Allies braced themselves for one more onslaught, the United States finally entered the war on the Allied side. In 1918, German forces launched a massive assault on the Allied lines. It seemed as if final victory was in their hands. The allies regrouped after almost crumbling under the German onslaught.

The Hundred Days, 1918

In 1918, the tide of war finally began to turn in the Allies' favour. The anti-submarine campaign had won control of the seas. The British blockade of Germany was slowly starving that country of food and the raw materials needed for the war. With the entry of the United States, the Allies now had a powerful, fresh member in their alliance. Soon American troops and supplies were pouring across the Atlantic. After one last offensive in

Figure 1.16 The muddy wasteland of Passchendaele sucked up weapons and men. One general wondered, "Good God, did we really send men to fight in that?" Why might General Haig have insisted that his troops attack Passchendaele, despite the odds?

1918, Germany began suffering great losses. Canadian forces participated in a sweep known as the "Hundred Days" that finally broke the back of the German military effort.

On 8 August 1918, Canadian forces supported by tanks and aircraft smashed into German lines. The Allies drove ahead for 13 kilometres, a far cry from the earlier gains of 91 metres at a time. German officers called it "the black day of the German army." For six weeks, Canadians served as the leaders of the 130 kilometres Allied advance. It was to be the last great offensive of the war. Canadians seized 31 527 prisoners, 623 artillery pieces, and 2842 machine guns. These gains were paid for with blood: 45 830 casualties.

By November 11, the war was over. As the **armistice** took effect, the cost of the war appeared staggering in human terms. Nearly one-third of Canadian soldiers were casualties. A small country had sacrificed 66 655 dead and 173 000 wounded. There was little to cheer about other than a final end to the horror of war.

The Treaty of Versailles

On 11 November 1918, an armistice was signed that finally brought the war to an end. Attention now shifted to the struggle to build a lasting peace. The 32 victorious countries met at the Palace of Versailles in France.

For the victors, particularly Britain and France, revenge was a central motive. They also wanted to ensure that Germany could never again rise to such a powerful position in Europe. The defeated were eager to get the best terms possible. They too had suffered horribly in four years of war.

In the end, a peace treaty was negotiated. In general, the terms were dictated by the victors. For the losers,

Germany in particular, the treaty was difficult to accept. Many even argued that it was better to continue fighting than accept such a humiliating document. However, the treaty was signed in 1919, and the world hoped that the First World War had been "the war to end wars."

Terms of the Treaty

The final treaty was supposed to be a framework for a lasting peace and for protection from future German aggression.

Territories
- Germany was forced to accept the independence of Austria, Czechoslovakia, and Poland.
- Germany gave up all its overseas colonies.
- Germany lost about 12 per cent of its pre-war territory to various neighbouring powers.
- France took back the lost territory of Alsace-Lorraine.
- France gained control of the Saar coal region for 15 years.

The Military
- Germany's western border with France was to be demilitarized.
- The German army was reduced to 100 000 troops with no tanks or heavy artillery.
- The German air force was disbanded.
- The German navy was reduced.

Reparations
- Germany was expected to pay damages of about $32 billion to Great Britain, France, and Belgium for losses during the war.

War Guilt
- Germany was forced to accept full responsibility for causing the war.

> "The war was over. Princip's bullet had caused some 67 million men to don uniforms and go to fight. One in every six of these men was killed. Of the remainder, approximately half were wounded. On the Western Front alone, more than 4 million had died in their ditches."
>
> –Stephen O'Shea, *Back to the Front*, 1996

> "Obtain what mercy you can, but for God's sake make peace!"
>
> –Germany's instructions to armistice negotiators

MAP STUDY: Europe After the First World War

Source: Don Quinlan, et al., *Twentieth Century Viewpoints*, 2nd edition, (Don Mills: Oxford University Press, 2003), 60.

Figure 1.17 The First World War resulted in a new map of Europe. Compare this map with the map of pre-war Europe on page 17.

Analysis and Response

1. What changes on the map do you think are most significant? Why?
2. Do you think these territorial changes reduced or increased the chance of another war? Explain.
3. If you had been part of the Canadian delegation at Versailles, what territorial changes would you have suggested? Why?

Reading Strategy

Maps are a visual way of providing information. When reading a map, start by looking at the title to find what the map is about. Then look for and read the caption, legend, labels, arrows, and other details.

The League of Nations

Another result that came out of the Treaty of Versailles was the creation of a new international body, the **League of Nations**. Canada was an eager member of this new organization, which promised to end the evil of war. By 1919, Canada was a very different country in a new and dangerous world. In Prime Minister Borden's words: "The world has drifted far from its old anchorage and no man can with certainty prophesy what the outcome will be."

Challenge and Response

1. Use a flowchart to indicate the events that helped to turn the tide against German forces.
2. What role did Canadians play in the dying days of the war?
3. Discuss why there was so little to cheer about when the guns fell silent.
4. Do you think the Treaty of Versailles was fair? Present your opinion in a newspaper editorial.
5. How do you think the Germans might have viewed this treaty? Give reasons for your answer.

A "New" Country

The Canada that emerged bloodied but victorious from the ashes of the First World War was in many ways a new country. Canada's growth from colony to nationhood had come at a terrible cost to the lives of young men and women. The country was uneasy and divided. The road to nationhood had been rocky and winding. However, the achievements were many:

- Canadians had fought as a united force under Canadian leadership.
- Canada had demanded and received a seat at the Imperial War Cabinet.
- Following the war, Canada received a seat at the Peace Conference and signed the Treaty of Versailles on its own.
- Canada joined the League of Nations as an independent country.

But were these achievements worth the price? Canada had suffered losses far in excess of its size as a country—eight million inhabitants at the time:

- During the war, 628 736 Canadians served in the Canadian army.
- Twenty-two per cent of Canadians (138 166 people) serving overseas were wounded.
- Ten per cent, or 66 573, were killed.

"Having fought so well and having contributed so generously, Canada was no longer a colony in fact or in image, Canada was a nation among the others and worthy of every honour to be accorded a nation-state."

–J.L. Finlay and D.N. Sprague, *The Structure of Canadian History*, 1989

"Canada had also lost its optimism. Fifteen years earlier, Prime Minister Wilfrid Laurier had promised that the 20th century would be Canada's, just as the 19th had been that of the United States. In 1919, that vision lay as dead as the former prime minister."

–R. Douglas Francis, Richard Jones, and Donald B. Smith, *Destinies: Canadian History Since Confederation*, 1996

Figure 1.18 This 1918 painting by Maurice Cullen is titled *Dead Horse and Rider in a Trench*. What does it suggest about the First World War? Do you think it is an accurate portrayal of the war? Explain.

"Their role was to offer their lives. Ours is to Remember."

–Remembrance Day message

Learn more about the Spanish Flu

"Lest We Forget"

The war finally ended at the 11th hour of the 11th day of the 11th month of 1918. Since that time, the citizens of the 30 warring countries take time to remember the ultimate tragedy and sacrifice of war on November 11, at 11 A.M.

Spanish Flu

In 1918–1919, another, and even more deadly killer rose out of the devastation of the war. The Spanish Flu was a deadly **pandemic** that killed between 20 and 40 million people around the world. The flu was transported to Canada and many other countries on board crowded troop ships carrying soldiers home from war. Out of 9 million Canadians, approximately 2 million contracted the disease. Eventually, 50 000 died.

A New World Order

When the war ended, the world's political landscape had changed. The old order had disappeared as monarchies and empires had fallen across Europe. The power of the British Empire was fading as it slowly moved towards a commonwealth of equals. In the aftermath of war, Canada was ready to redefine its role in the new world order.

Challenge and Response

1. Discuss what lessons young historians might learn from the history of the First World War.
2. Do you think young people today would be willing to volunteer for war? If so, under what circumstances? Would you volunteer? Give reasons to support your response.

Thinking Like a Historian:
Asking Historical Questions

Essential Question: As a historian, how do you find, select, and interpret different sources of information?

Historians constantly read and evaluate primary sources and the works of other historians. As they do so, they ask questions to check their understanding and evaluate the accuracy and credibility of what they read.

During this course, you will learn about factors you need to keep in mind when finding and selecting primary sources. You will also learn strategies for analyzing and evaluating the point of view of these sources. For now, you will consider the types of questions you might ask yourself while reading primary sources in order to check and enhance your understanding.

FACTUAL. These questions explore the facts of an event or issue to provide you with background information.
Examples:
- What does the term *female suffrage* mean?
- What were the provisions of the Treaty of Versailles?

CAUSAL. These questions ask you to explore the causes of an event or issue.
Examples:
- Why did Canada go to war in 1914?
- Why did Parliament pass the War Measures Act in 1914?

COMPARATIVE. These questions ask you to compare two or more events or issues to look for common patterns or significant differences.
Examples:
- What similarities and differences are there among militarism, nationalism, and imperialism?
- How did Canadian women's roles change after the outbreak of the First World War?

SPECULATIVE. These questions speculate on possible alternative outcomes of an event or issue.
Examples:
- What might have happened if Canada had not introduced conscription in 1917?
- What might have happened if the Allies had been defeated in the First World War?

Formulating and then answering these types of questions will improve your understanding of historical events and issues.

You, the Historian

1. Select a section in this chapter and then create an example of each type of question (Factual, Causal, Comparative, or Speculative) based on the information in that section. Be prepared to share your questions and answers with your peers.

Chapter 2

The Boom Years

Figure 2.1 The 1920s are often portrayed as an era of freedom, fast times, and prosperity. What do you see when you look at this image? How has the image of women changed from that of earlier decades? What does this image suggest about young women in the 1920s? What does it suggest about the era itself?

City of Toronto Archives, Fonds 1244, Item 48.7

Chapter at a Glance

Thinking Ahead

At the end of the Great War, Canadian troops returned to a vastly changed country. The early years of the 1920s brought considerable labour strife and unemployment. By mid-decade, the economy had improved. Jobs were plentiful. Money and credit flowed freely, and the pent-up passions of the war years brought a freer, more creative society that seemed to thrive on innovation. Yet the revolution in art, fashion, and popular culture masked serious economic and social problems that erupted at the end of the dizzying decade. As you explore this chapter, consider the following key questions:

- What kind of Canada did Canadian soldiers discover on their return from war?
- What was the significance of the Winnipeg General Strike?
- What were the main features of Canadian society in the 1920s?
- How was a new Canadian identity being shaped during this period?

Profile in Power:

William Lyon Mackenzie King

"In matters between Canada and other countries, Canada should arrange her own affairs."

–Mackenzie King, House of Commons, 21 April 1921

Figure 2.2 William Lyon Mackenzie King (1874–1950)

"We do not believe that isolation in world affairs is possible for Canada. No happening of any magnitude abroad is without its repercussions on our fortunes and our future."

–Mackenzie King, House of Commons, 18 June 1936

"It is what we prevent, rather than what we do, that counts most in Government." This remark by Prime Minister William Lyon Mackenzie King sums up the secret of his success. He did not have an exciting image. He gave no mesmerizing speeches. He supported few radical policies. Yet Mackenzie King was perhaps Canada's most successful prime minister. At age 18, he wrote in his diary, "Surely I have some great work to accomplish before I die." It seems that he did. In 1999, 14 out of 25 Canadian scholars ranked King as Canada's greatest prime minister.

King's grandfathers both fought in the 1837 Rebellion of Upper Canada. His maternal father, William Lyon Mackenzie, led the rebellion. His paternal grandfather was an officer in the army that opposed the rebels. His mother spent many hours telling her son about his famous grandfather. Her stories inspired King to serve his country.

As a student, King joined a debating club, where he developed an interest in politics. As a student at the University of Toronto, he wrote for the university newspaper. He was working on his Ph.D. at Harvard University in 1900 when he was offered a position in the Canadian Department of Labour. King accepted, believing that the opportunity offered him a chance to carry on his grandfather's legacy of public service.

Figure 2.3 Until the Liberal Party convention of 1919, party leaders were chosen behind closed doors by the party's senators and MPs. King was the first political leader to be elected by his party. What impact might this fact have had on his leadership?

In 1908, King won a seat as a Liberal Member of Parliament and served as the minister of Labour under Sir Wilfrid Laurier. When the Liberals were defeated in 1911, however, Mackenzie King went to the United States, where he became a labour consultant for the Rockefeller Foundation.

When King returned to Canada, he ran unsuccessfully in the election of 1917. He was one of the few English-Canadian candidates to support Laurier's opposition to conscription. When Laurier died in 1919, King succeeded him as Liberal Party leader, with the support of French Canadians who remembered he had stood by Laurier during the conscription debate.

In 1921, King easily defeated Conservative leader Arthur Meighen to become Canada's prime minister. Throughout the 1920s, he worked to gain greater independence from Britain. Because Canada was still a **colony**, Britain controlled its political and economic relations with other countries. At the 1923 and 1926 Imperial Conferences between Britain and its colonies, King campaigned for the rights of the colonies to control their own **foreign policies**.

In the election of 1925, the Liberals won fewer seats than the Conservatives. However, they managed to stay in power with the support of the Progressive Party, an agricultural protest party. King remained as prime minister until the Progressives threatened to withdraw their support in response to a scandal in the Customs Department. The Governor General then asked the Conservative leader, Arthur Meighen, to form a government. However, Meighen's new government was quickly defeated and another election was held in 1926. This time, King and the Liberals were returned to office with a majority. They remained in power until 1930, when the Conservatives won a solid majority.

King remained leader of the Opposition for five years, until 1935 when the Liberals were returned to office with a record majority. King remained as prime minister until 1948. You will learn more about this period in the life of William Lyon Mackenzie King in the Profile in Power feature in Chapter 4.

Responding

1. How might Mackenzie King's background have prepared him for the role of prime minister?
2. Why do you think King felt it was important for Canada to take charge of its own foreign policy?

A Different Canada

Reading Strategy

Before you start reading this section, recall what you learned in Chapter 1 about how the First World War changed the lives of Canadians.

After the victory parades and memorial services, a different Canada emerged after the war. When the soldiers returned to Canada, both they and their country had forever changed. The young soldiers endured horrible memories of slaughter and death. Hoping for better times, in the early years of the 1920s, they found only poverty and disappointment.

Urbanization

In 1921, for the first time, more of Canada's almost nine million people lived in urban areas than in rural areas.

Montréal remained the largest urban centre, followed by Toronto and Winnipeg. In the West, Vancouver, Victoria, Regina, Saskatoon, Edmonton, and Calgary had each grown to over 25 000 people. The following factors contributed to this growth:

- Fewer workers were needed on farms because of mechanized farm machinery. As a result, farm workers migrated to the cities.
- In the cities, factories had hired more workers during the war to produce wartime industrial goods.
- The lure of city life had drawn people from rural Canada.

After 1924, an economic boom spurred greater **industrialization**. Toronto and Montréal grew by 33 per cent and Vancouver surpassed Winnipeg in population. People flocked to such towns as Windsor, Oshawa, and Walkerville to work in automobile factories. Skyscrapers began to dot the skylines of major cities. The growing use of automobiles promoted the growth of suburbs.

The Royal York Hotel in Toronto symbolized the new era. When it opened in 1929, it was the tallest building in the British Commonwealth. The hotel included a 12-bed hospital, a bank, a library, 10 ornate elevators, a glass-enclosed roof garden, and a concert hall.

The Population

Canada was a young country. More than half the population was less than 30 years old. The average family was large. More than half of Canada's families had three or more children; 12 per cent had more than five children.

Politics and Regional Protest

In July 1920, Arthur Meighen became prime minister following Robert Borden's resignation. Meighen inherited

Figure 2.4 The Royal York Hotel became known as a city within a city. It was 28 floors of splendour, opulence, and mechanical genius. Each of the 1048 rooms had a radio and private bathroom. The switchboard was 20 metres long and required 35 telephone operators.

the reins of a country torn apart by strikes, unemployment, inflation, and regional divisions.

Québec

The war and the conscription crisis had left a feeling of bitterness in Québec. After the 1917 election, there were no French-Canadian Conservative MPs. Alienated from the rest of Canada, many French Canadians formed their own trade unions, farmers' parties, and **co-operatives**.

Continuing economic problems drove many French Canadians to the larger cities or to the United States for work. To slow this tide, the Québec government encouraged American **capitalists** to invest in the province, particularly in its natural resources. Lured by economic incentives and a cheap work force, American money fuelled the growth of mining, pulp and paper, and hydroelectricity in the province. Not everyone agreed with American investment. Henri Bourassa, a Québec politician, complained that the government was selling the province's "jewels."

Another group believed that the only way French Canadians could survive as a people with their own culture was to separate from Canada. In the pages of his influential journal *L'Action française*, professor and priest Abbé Lionel Groulx warned that French-Canadian culture was in danger. The only way to "become masters in our own house," he said, was to take control of Québec's natural resources and large industries.

The Maritimes

The Maritime provinces also felt alienated from the rest of the country. The decline in demand for fish and coal put added strains on the region's economy. Many large companies, such as the Bank of Nova Scotia, had already moved to Central Canada. Those that remained wanted the federal government to reverse policies that they believed hurt their chances of survival. Railway freight rates, which had doubled since the end of the war, made it too expensive to ship goods to Central Canada. **Tariffs** favoured the growth of manufacturing companies in Central Canada. The resulting unemployment forced thousands of young people to leave the Maritimes.

The Maritime Rights Movement tried to use regional co-operation to force the federal government to solve the area's economic problems. In particular, it wanted lower tariffs, larger federal **subsidies**, and reduced freight rates. In 1926, Prime Minister Mackenzie King created a Royal Commission to investigate the situation—and to quiet the region. Although the Commission supported the demands of the Maritime Rights Movement, King made only minor changes. The West now had a larger population than the Maritimes and thus more seats in Parliament. Consequently, King favoured Western grievances over Eastern concerns.

Farmers and the West

Before the 1917 election, Borden had promised that farmers' sons would not be conscripted, only to break that promise. Following the war, the world market for wheat collapsed and many prairie farmers were desperately short of cash. Farmers had been encouraged to mechanize during the war in order to increase production. Now they faced large debts. They claimed that high tariffs pushed up the prices of farm machinery and consumer goods at their expense.

"[Lionel Groulx] offered … a nationalism that combined a renewed sense of the importance of the Québec government, a quest for economic emancipation, … and a firm belief that … loyalty to tradition, both religious and cultural, was the key to an exciting future."

–Pierre Trépanier, *The Oxford Companion to Canadian History*, 2004

"The [Maritime Rights] Movement helped foster a regional consciousness and sense of identity. It did not secure any significantly different approach in federal government policies."

–David Kilgour, former member of Parliament, Edmonton-Beaumont

> "We as farmers are downtrodden by every other class. We have grovelled and been ground into the dirt; we are determined that this shall not be. We will organize for our protection; we will nourish ourselves and gain strength, and then we shall strike out in our might and overthrow our enemies."
>
> –Henry Wise Wood, leader of the United Farmers of Alberta

Learn more about the Progressive Party

When Borden and Meighen did not lower tariffs, many farmers gave up on the old parties. They believed that Ontario and Québec controlled politics and the economy for the majority of their populations' benefit. As a result, farmers began to organize to defend their interests.

Farmers in almost very province established their own political parties, some with great success:

- In 1919, the United Farmers of Ontario captured 56 seats and formed a **minority government**.
- Two years later, the United Farmers of Alberta captured the provincial government.
- In 1922, the United Farmers of Manitoba formed the government in that province.
- Thomas Crerar, a former member of Borden's Cabinet, established the Progressive Party in 1920 to fight for farmers' rights at the federal level. Based in Alberta, Manitoba, Saskatchewan, and rural Ontario, it was the first significant third federal party in Canadian history.

In the 1921 election, Mackenzie King's Liberals won almost all the seats in Québec, much of the Maritimes, and a large portion of Ontario. Two Independent Labour MPs were also elected, including J.S. Woodsworth and Abraham Heaps in Winnipeg. The Progressive Party captured 65 seats.

In the next few years, King spent much of his energies trying to win over the Progressives, whom he considered "Liberals in a hurry."

The Progressive Party

With the second largest number of seats, the Progressives were entitled to form the official opposition. However, party members were divided on policies and principles, so the Conservative Party formed the Opposition instead. The Progressives wanted the people to have more control over their representatives and advocated policies such as **recall** and **referendums**.

In the 1925 election, the Progressives lost almost all their Ontario seats but were moderately successful in the West. Since neither the Liberal nor the Conservative parties won a majority of the seats, the Progressive Party now held considerable power. Although Mackenzie King won fewer seats than Arthur Meighen, he convinced the Progressives to support his Liberal Party. Thus King became prime minister of Canada's first minority government.

In another election the following year, most Progressive voters returned to the Liberal Party, allowing King to form a majority government. To remain in power, King courted the support of the Labour MPs by passing the Old Age Pensions Act in 1927.

Challenge and Response

1. What evidence is there that many regions in Canada were dissatisfied with the federal government?
2. Do you think that the concepts of recall and referendum would be useful in Canadian politics today? Write an editorial in which you explain your views.

Arthur Meighen

Figure 2.5 Arthur Meighen (1874–1960)

Arthur Meighen was born in Ontario in 1874. He was elected to Parliament as a Conservative MP in 1908. He succeeded Robert Borden as prime minister in 1920, but was defeated by King in 1921.

In the next election in 1925, the Conservatives won the most seats, but King formed an alliance with the Progressive Party to hold on to power. When the alliance collapsed, Meighen became prime minister. He quickly lost a vote of confidence, however, and was defeated in 1926.

Meighen's intellect may have appealed to voters' minds, but Meighen himself never appealed to their hearts. After returning to politics as Conservative leader in 1941, he was defeated in a by-election in 1942. Meighen then retired from public life.

Mackenzie King and Canadian Independence

The cost of the First World War in human lives left many Canadians wary of further involvement in international affairs. However, Canada was still a British colony. Great Britain controlled Canada's economic and political relations with other countries. Mackenzie King was determined to change this situation. He believed that most Canadians did not want to get involved in another European war. He also wanted to avoid being dragged into a war that would again divide English and French Canada and might lead to the defeat of his government. Like the United States, which decided not to join the League of Nations, King took an **isolationist** stance.

The Chanak Crisis, 1922

The Chanak Crisis was the first step in this direction. In October 1922, Turkish troops threatened British troops stationed near Chanak on the Dardanelles (a narrow strait between Europe and Turkey). In response, the British government asked its colonies for military support. It released this request to the press before asking the Dominion leaders. To King, this was a return to the old days when Canadian politicians had to find out about British foreign policy in the newspapers.

Instead of agreeing, as Canadian prime ministers were expected to do, King refused to send troops. He said that the Canadian Parliament would have to decide. Arthur Meighen, the Conservative leader, disagreed. He felt that Canada should stand by Britain. By the time the issue had been debated in Parliament, the war was over. But,

" … it is not right to take this country into another European war, [and] I shall resist to the uttermost."

–Mackenzie King, diary entry, September 1922

MAP STUDY: The Chanak Crisis

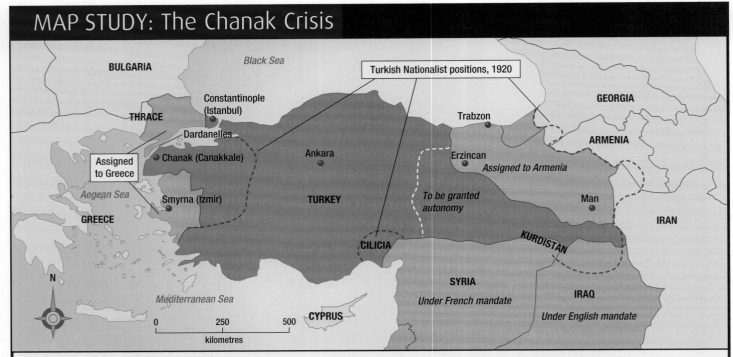

Source: Dr. Andrew Andersen.

Figure 2.6 This map shows Turkey after the Treaty of Sèvres. In Asia, Turkey lost present-day Iraq, Kurdistan, Palestine (which became a British **mandate**), Syria, Lebanon (which became a French mandate), and, among other areas, Armenia. In Europe, Turkey lost parts of Thrace and some Aegean islands. The Dardanelles was demilitarized and controlled by an international body.

Following the First World War, the Allies (excluding Russia and the United States) forced the Ottoman Empire (Turkey) to sign the Treaty of Sèvres in 1920. The treaty destroyed Turkey as a national state and was rejected by the new Turkish government. Turkish nationals threatened British and French troops stationed in the region. Britain was prepared to fight. It expected Canada and other members of the Commonwealth to join them. Conflict was averted when an agreement was reached on 11 October 1922. The crisis had blown over, but the incident left King suspicious of British intentions in controlling Canada's foreign policy.

Analysis and Response

1. Why would the Dardanelles be such an important strategic location?
2. What role, if any, should Canada have played in the Chanak Crisis? Create a PMI chart to assess this issue. Identify the positive (Plus) and negative (Minus) aspects, and record any information that is neither positive nor negative as "Interesting." Based on the results of your PMI, develop a position on the issue.

Plus	Minus	Interesting Information

King had made his point—Parliament would decide what role Canada would play in foreign affairs. This was the beginning of the end of Canada automatically agreeing to British requests.

The Halibut Treaty, 1923

In March 1923, Canada and the United States signed a treaty covering the protection of the Pacific halibut fishery. At King's insistence, the treaty was signed by the Canadian Fisheries minister, with no counter-signature by the British ambassador in Washington. The British government protested but gave in when King threatened to appoint a Canadian diplomatic representative in Washington. Even though the treaty was not approved by the U.S. Senate, it set a precedent for Canada's authority to sign treaties independent of Britain.

The Imperial Conference, 1923

King attended the Imperial Conference determined to resist British efforts to establish a centralized foreign policy for all the Dominions. Although the British foreign secretary considered King "obstinate, tiresome, and stupid," King succeeded. The final report noted that foreign policy decisions "are necessarily subject to the actions of the Governments and Parliaments of the various portions of the Empire."

Constitutional Crisis, 1926

In 1925, the economy was doing well and King decided to call an election. This decision turned out to be a mistake. The Liberals won only 99 seats. The Conservatives captured 116 seats. The Progressives took 24 seats. No party held a majority.

Most people, including Governor General Lord Byng, thought that King should resign and allow Arthur Meighen to become prime minister. King refused to resign. He hoped that the Progressive Party would support him. A government scandal in the Customs Department ruined King's plans. When the prime minister fired the minister responsible for the scandal and then appointed him to the Senate, Arthur Meighen saw his chance to force King to resign. Before Parliament could criticize the government, King asked Byng to dissolve Parliament and call an election. When Byng refused, King asked him to consult the British government. Byng again refused and the constitutional crisis began.

Arthur Meighen then became the prime minister on Byng's request. Within a week, Meighen lost a **non-confidence vote**. This time, when the prime minister requested dissolution of Parliament and an election, Byng agreed. King was returned to office with a majority in 1926. Meighen resigned as Conservative leader and was replaced by R.B. Bennett.

Traditionally, the position of Governor General had represented both the British monarch and the British government. In the election campaign, King argued that Byng had been wrong to refuse the prime minister's request for an election. King posed as the champion of Canadian independence with such slogans as "Is Canada a (locally autonomous) Dominion, or a (subservient) Crown Colony?" This constitutional issue distracted voters from the Customs scandal. When he came to power for the second time, King tried to redefine the role of the Governor General as a representative

Learn more about Canada's role in world and Commonwealth affairs

"If Meighen seeks to carry on I believe he will not go far. Our chances of winning out in a general election are good. I feel I am right, and so am happy may God guide me in every step."

–Mackenzie King, diary entry, 1926

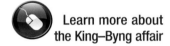

Learn more about the King–Byng affair

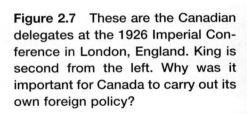

of the monarch and not the British government—meaning that the Governor General should not ignore the advice of the elected government.

The Imperial Conference, 1926

The 1926 Imperial Conference saw further recognition of Dominion **autonomy**. King drafted what became known as the Balfour Declaration, which updated the relationship between Britain and the Dominions. Canada was now free to make its own foreign policy decisions.

King was also successful in redefining the Governor General's powers. The Canadian government would now communicate directly with the British government rather than through the Governor General. In 1928, Britain appointed a High Commissioner to Canada for this purpose. King established **legations** in the United States (1926), France (1928), and Japan (1929) to carry out Canada's foreign policy. Likewise, American, French, and Japanese legations were sent to Ottawa.

Canada also had to expand its foreign service in Ottawa, where there were only three staff members in the Department of External Affairs. In the late 1920s, young, highly qualified candidates such as future prime minister Lester Pearson were recruited.

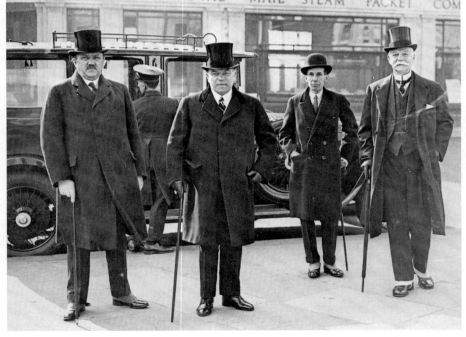

Figure 2.7 These are the Canadian delegates at the 1926 Imperial Conference in London, England. King is second from the left. Why was it important for Canada to carry out its own foreign policy?

Challenge and Response

1. What major steps did Mackenzie King take from 1922 to 1926 to establish a more independent Canadian foreign policy? Rank order these steps from most to least important. Be prepared to explain your choices.
2. Who would you have supported in the 1926 constitutional crisis— King or Byng? Why?

Labour Unrest

The First World War had deepened the divisions between workers and employers. **Inflation** had increased faster than wages, doubling the cost of living and reducing people's buying power. While soldiers were dying overseas fighting for their country, some employers had made huge profits supplying the armed forces. Now, thousands of returning soldiers could not find work.

People who had jobs joined unions to fight for better pay and working conditions. When employers were unsympathetic, unions went on strike. The number of strikes doubled between 1917 and 1919 as labour unrest spread across Canada. However, employers were often able to get court injunctions to prevent the workers from striking or picketing. If that did not work, owners hired non-union strikebreakers to replace the strikers.

One Big Union

In March 1919, union delegates from across Western Canada gathered in Calgary to create a large union to fight for workers' rights. Unlike the Ontario-dominated Trades and Labour Council that organized workers by individual crafts (such as carpenters and shoemakers), the One Big Union (OBU) included trained and untrained workers in the same union. The OBU advocated the use of the general strike. It reasoned that if all business activities were stopped, employers would have to grant workers' demands.

The federal government sent undercover police officers to the Calgary meetings. When the officers reported that the OBU had praised the recent communist revolution in Russia and had used "radical" sounding phrases, government officials feared the worst.

The Winnipeg General Strike

Resentment among the working class had been growing in Winnipeg for several years. Unions complained that the **Establishment** supported employers over workers. In the spring of 1919, the Winnipeg metal and building trades began negotiations with their employers. In addition to the usual demands for higher wages and an eight-hour workday, the unions demanded the right to **collective bargaining**—to negotiate on behalf of their members rather than each worker negotiating for him or herself. When the employers refused to negotiate with the unions, approximately 30 000 people walked out in a general strike on 15 May 1919.

As the strike spread from industry to industry, Winnipeg shut down. Mail delivery, streetcar and taxi service, newspapers, garbage collection, telephone service, gasoline pumps, and milk delivery came to a halt. Most restaurants and retail stores closed. Union leaders asked the police to remain on duty. The workers formed a Central Strike Committee to oversee the conduct of the strike. It held mass meetings and published the *Strike Bulletin* on a daily basis to update the workers.

The Committee issued permits for essential services such as milk delivery and electric power. Permit cards in store windows and on the side of delivery carts read "Permitted by Authority of the Strike Committee." The city's elite viewed these signs as an indication that the city was in the grips of a revolution.

The Citizens' Committee of 1000 was created to end the strike and run the city until then. Most members of

> "You may have a titled aristocracy and a moneyed aristocracy, but there is only one true aristocracy in any community, in my opinion, and that is the aristocracy of labour."
>
> –A.A. Heaps, Labour Party MP, House of Commons, 14 February 1929

"The leaders of the general strike are all revolutionists of varying degrees and types, from crazy idealists to ordinary thieves."

–Arthur Meighen

"In fact, it has nothing to do with revolution. It is an attempt to meet a very pressing and immediate need."

–J.S. Woodsworth, strike leader

the Committee (made up of some of Winnipeg's wealthiest manufacturers, lawyers, bankers, and politicians) opposed the unions as a matter of principle. The Citizens' Committee declared that the strike was a communist conspiracy. It fired the police and replaced them with 2000 "specials," armed with baseball bats. The Committee published its own newspaper, the *Citizen*, to discredit the strikers. Although the leaders of the strike were primarily British in origin, the *Citizen* portrayed them as "dangerous foreigners" and "enemy aliens."

As word of the strike spread across the country, sympathy strikes were held in more than 30 centres, including Regina, Toronto, Calgary, and Edmonton. With Winnipeg attracting international attention and business at

a standstill, the federal government intervened. Several Cabinet ministers met with the Citizens' Committee. Federal employees were ordered back to work. Ottawa quickly **amended** the Immigration Act so that British-born immigrants could be deported and expanded the definition of **sedition** to make it easier to arrest the strike leaders. On June 17, eight members of the Strike Committee were arrested and charged with seditious conspiracy. Protests erupted across Canada. In Winnipeg, a mass rally was planned for June 21. Winnipeg mayor Charles Gray warned that "foreigners" who participated could "expect immediate deportation to Russia or wherever they come from," and banned "open-air meetings, either in parks, streets or public places…"

Figure 2.8 Bloody Saturday brought an end to the Winnipeg Strike. How might knowing that the streetcar company had resumed service that day change a person's opinion of this scene? Why did the Strike Committee want to prevent this type of violence?

Despite these acts of intimidation, the strike continued. Thousands of people gathered downtown to protest the arrest of the strike leaders. The strike leaders tried to avoid violence, but the crowd became rowdy, pulling a streetcar off its tracks and setting it on fire. The mayor called on the North West Mounted Police to disperse the crowds. Armed with baseball bats, the police galloped into the crowd. The protestors showered them with stones, bricks, and pieces of concrete. Shots were fired. One man was killed and 30 were injured. Soon the army was also on the streets, patrolling with machine guns mounted on their vehicles. This event, known as "Bloody Saturday," broke the strike. On June 26, fearing more violence, the strike leaders declared an end to the strike, six weeks after it had started.

Impact of the Strike

In the short run, the strike was a disaster for the workers. Several leaders were sentenced to jail. Many men who returned to work were forced to sign "yellow-dog contracts," forbidding them from joining a union or taking part in union activities. Workers considered to be troublemakers were barred from returning to their jobs.

Charges of communism allowed employers to discredit union organizers. In Québec, the Catholic Church established its own trade union to prevent radical activities. The crushing of the Winnipeg General Strike demoralized workers across the country. It would be another generation before the labour movement regained its strength.

However, the strike did ignite labour's political consciousness. In 1920, several strike leaders were elected to the Manitoba legislature. In 1921, social activist and labour leader J.S. Woodsworth was elected to the House of Commons.

Learn more about labour history and the Winnipeg General Strike

Challenge and Response

1. Use a flowchart to show what you think were the most significant causes, events, and consequences of the Winnipeg General Strike.
2. To what extent was the Winnipeg General Strike a failure or a success for the workers? Create a written or an oral submission on this issue for an imaginary "Royal Commission on Labour Disputes" established to address labour concerns. Be sure that your position is well supported.
3. How would you describe conditions between employers and workers in Canada today? Provide some specific examples.

PERSONALITIES

James Shaver Woodsworth: "A Saintly Politician"

James Shaver Woodsworth was born in Ontario in 1874. He grew up in Manitoba, where he became a Methodist minister. In 1907, he became the superintendent of the Winnipeg Methodist city mission. He witnessed first-hand the injustice and poverty within Winnipeg's new industrial society. In his books *Strangers Within Our Gates* and *My Neighbour*, Woodsworth described the suffering of working-class immigrants and criticized the unsympathetic policies and practices of governments and employers.

In 1917, Woodsworth was fired from the mission for criticizing the government's wartime policies. In 1918, he resigned from the Methodist Church, which he accused of being more concerned with money than with those in need. He placed his religious faith in the **social gospel** movement that called for widespread religious renewal to create a more just and equitable society.

Woodsworth moved to the Pacific coast where he became a dock worker. He helped organize the Federated Labour Party of British Columbia and became a regular speaker at labour meetings. In 1919, on a speaking tour of Western Canada, Woodsworth found himself in the middle of the Winnipeg General Strike, where he was arrested, but never charged, for supporting the strikers.

Figure 2.9
As an MP, J.S. Woodsworth was a tireless advocate for farmers, labourers, and immigrants.

In 1921, Woodsworth was elected to the House of Commons as a Labour MP. In 1926, he and another Labour Party MP, A.A. Heaps, supported Prime Minister King's minority government in return for King's promise to create an old-age pension plan. Woodsworth's ultimate triumph, however, was in 1933 when he founded and became leader of Canada's first socialist party, the Co-operative Commonwealth Federation (CCF)—known today as the New Democratic Party.

"[T]he Government exists to provide for the needs of the people, and when it comes to choice between profits and property rights on the one hand and human welfare on the other, there should be no hesitation whatsoever in saying that we are going to place the human welfare consideration first and let property rights and financial interests fare as best they may."

Source: J.S. Woodsworth,
quoted in "Building democracy—J.S. Woodsworth".

 Learn more about J.S. Woodsworth

Responding

1. What evidence do you see of Woodsworth's influence in Canadian social policies today?
2. People often referred to Woodsworth as a "saintly" man. Do you think this label is justified? Explain your response.

Technology and Invention

The 1920s was an era of innovation and discovery—from improved telephone service and radio broadcasting to the discovery of insulin.

Telephones

At the beginning of the decade, only 25 per cent of Canadian homes had a telephone. To operate these phones, the dialer had to crank the generator in a clockwise direction. The mouthpiece was separated from the earphone. To phone long distance, it was necessary to ring up an operator. During the decade, telephone technology improved rapidly. The first regular dial telephone (without the crank) appeared in Toronto in 1924. Three years later, people could buy telephones that combined the mouthpiece and earphone. By the end of the decade, about 75 per cent of Canadian homes had telephones.

Air Travel

Air travel was an extraordinary experience at the time. After the war, Canadian fighter pilots were eager to continue flying. Some flew across the country, performing daring stunts at county fairs. Others became bush pilots and ferried oil and mining prospectors and their supplies to remote areas. In 1924, the government created the Royal Canadian Air Force to conduct surveys, patrol for forest fires, and watch out for smugglers. Three years later, the post office hired pilots to fly mail into remote areas. By 1927, small carrier planes were flying people from city to city.

The Discovery of Insulin

In the early 1900s, the only treatments for diabetes were starvation diets and strict exercise regimens. As a result, thousands of people with diabetes faced blindness, limb amputations, and death. People with diabetes were unable to absorb sugar and starch from the bloodstream because they were missing an important hormone called insulin. Dr. Frederick Banting had devoted much of his time to studying the disease. He believed that if he could isolate insulin in animals, he could use it to treat people with diabetes.

In October 1920, Banting convinced Professor J.R.R. Macleod at the University of Toronto to give him a research lab and one of his brightest medical students, Charles Best, as an assistant. Banting and Best conducted hundreds of experiments using laboratory dogs. Macleod assigned chemist James Collip to develop a method for making animal insulin safe for humans.

In January 1922, the serum underwent its first human trial when Banting injected insulin into 14-year-old Leonard Thompson. Thompson, who had been suffering from diabetes for three years, weighed only 30 kilograms. After the injection, his blood sugar levels dropped and he gained strength. In further testing, all of the patients made similar recoveries. For the first time, people with diabetes could lower their blood sugar levels and live longer, healthier lives. It was one of the most revolutionary discoveries in medical science.

"Insulin was discovered in Canada because of a combination of serendipity, improvements in blood sugar monitoring, and the fact that a world-class research capacity had been developed at the University of Toronto. Two of the early patients, who had come within days of death, outlived all the members of the discovery team."

–Michael Bliss, *The Oxford Companion to Canadian History*, 2004

The first radios contained a small piece of quartz crystal. Listeners located stations by moving a thin wire over the crystal's surface. In May 1920, XWA in Montréal carried the first Canadian broadcast. By the end of 1922, radio stations had been established in Vancouver, Edmonton, and Winnipeg. That year, Montréal's CJBC was perhaps the first French radio station in the world.

Canadian National Railways (CNR) used wireless radios to communicate between trains. In 1924, CNR launched CKCH in Ottawa. The next year, Edward S. Rogers revolutionized the radio industry when he invented the world's first alternating current (AC) radio tube. This enabled radios to be powered by ordinary household electricity rather than by batteries that needed constant recharging.

Initially, radios were status symbols. A good radio cost as much as a car. In the evenings, families gathered around the radio. By 1929, there were 60 radio stations in Canada and approximately one-third of Canadian households owned a radio. The previous year, the King government had appointed Sir John Aird to chair a Royal Commission to consider the future of broadcasting and the government's role in the field. The Aird Report recommended that a government board operate a coast-to-coast radio system—the Canadian Radio Broadcasting Commission (the forerunner of the Canadian Broadcasting Corporation, or the CBC).

Figure 2.10 In 1923, Macleod and Banting were awarded the Nobel Prize for Physiology and Medicine. They shared the $40 000 prize money with Best and Collip. Banting (right) and Best sold the patent rights to insulin to the University of Toronto for $1 so that everyone would benefit from their discovery.

Radio

The radio made the world seem smaller. It provided inexpensive entertainment. It ended isolation. It brought families together to listen to the latest news, sports, music, or drama. It was remarkable!

Challenge and Response

1. In your opinion, what was the most significant innovation during the 1920s? Explain your choice clearly.
2. Compare the role of radio in the 1920s with the role that it plays in Canadian society today.

A Booming Economy

During the early decades of the 1920s, few could have predicted the booming economy that lay ahead. In 1923, unemployment was at 17 per cent. Inflation was eating up people's life's saving. Exports to war-ravaged Europe were on the decline. It appeared to be a gloomy economic forecast.

Natural Resources

In 1924, however, the economy began to improve. Canada's abundant supply of forests, minerals, water, and fertile land fuelled this economic growth.

Agriculture

The Prairie provinces enjoyed bumper wheat crops from 1925 to 1928. As agricultural prices climbed higher, farmers invested their profits by buying trucks, harvesters, and other equipment. In many areas, farmers organized wheat pools and co-operatives to help market their wheat, cattle, and dairy products.

Pulp and Paper

Supplying newsprint to the United States became Canada's second largest industry. From Nova Scotia to British Columbia, vast forests of spruce, pine, and poplar trees were cut down to supply the growing newspaper and magazine business south of the border. By mid-decade, Canada was the world's largest supplier of newsprint. The major producers of pulp and paper were Québec, Ontario, and British Columbia. Six companies controlled 86 per cent of the Canadian market.

Mining

The Canadian Shield yielded large deposits of nickel, copper, gold, silver, lead, and zinc. In 1929, mines in Sudbury produced 80 per cent of the world's nickel. Copper flowed out of the mines at Noranda, Québec, and Flin Flon, Manitoba. Zinc and lead were unearthed from one of the world's largest mines in Kimberley, BC. The demand for these and other metals steadily increased as more and more automobiles and electric appliances appeared on the market.

Energy

The tremendous growth in the automobile industry increased the demand for gasoline and oil, which were also used for heating and cooking. In 1924, "black gold" was found in Turner Valley, south of Calgary. Alberta was soon providing 90 per cent of Canada's petroleum exports.

The huge amount of power required for mining and smelting (extracting metal from ore by melting) led to a dramatic increase in the production of hydroelectricity. In addition to Niagara Falls, fast-flowing rivers such as the Saguenay and the Saint-Maurice in Québec were harnessed. Canada became the second-largest producer of hydroelectric power.

Consumer Goods

By the mid-1920s, a mood of gaiety and optimism had set in. People found jobs and began to buy consumer items. There was now a large variety of new consumer goods to choose from: electric stoves, refrigerators, and vacuum cleaners, cars, toothpaste, radios, and sliced bread. The growth of cheap electricity brought new comforts for middle- and upper-income Canadians. Every magazine carried ads for products made by General Electric, Westinghouse, Kodak, and Hoover. Large chain stores such as Dominion, Loblaws, Woolworth's, and Eaton's sold groceries, fashions, phonographs, radios, wristwatches, and hair dryers.

"As public awareness of the immense economic, social, and political ramifications of hydro-electric development increased in the early 20th century, most provincial governments enacted legislation nationalizing private electric companies, thereby ensuring that the benefits of hydro power flowed to their taxpayers rather than to utility owners."

–Keith R. Fleming, *The Oxford Companion to Canadian History*, 2004

MAP STUDY: Canada's Production by Province, 1920s

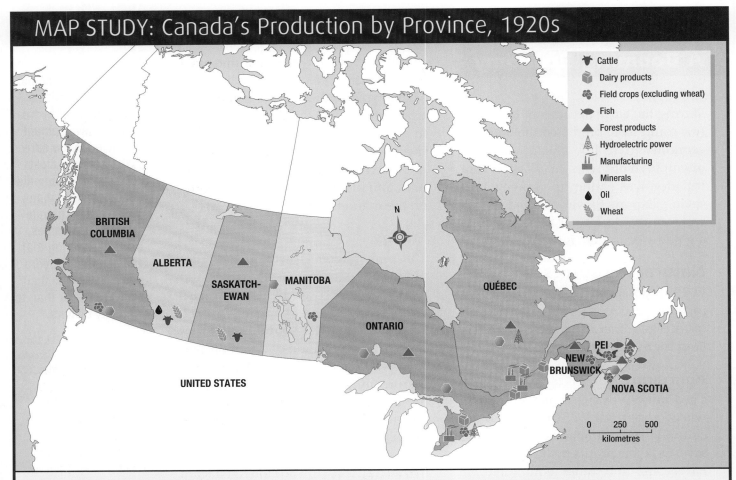

Figure 2.11 This map shows the production of Canada's main resources by province only in the 1920s. Newfoundland and Labrador did not join Confederation until 1949.

By the mid-1920s, Canada's economy was experiencing a high rate of growth—even higher than that in the United States. The Prairie provinces were developing a wheat-based economy. Industrial activity and manufacturing were expanding in Central Canada. Across the Canadian Shield, new resource industries were emerging. These resources fuelled an expanding export trade, particularly with the United States. Throughout the decade, Canada became a growing supplier on world markets of food, forest products, and metals. The leading export was wheat, which in 1929 accounted for 32 per cent of the country's total exports.

Analysis and Response

1. Compare Canadian production by province in the 1920s with that of Canada today. What similarities and differences do you find? What might account for these similarities and differences?

2. Use a PMI chart to assess the positive and negative aspects of having a single country, such as the United States, as such an important trading partner.

3. Conduct research to find out if the United States is still a major importer of Canadian products. Explain your findings. What other nations are important to Canada today?

The Automobile

By the 1920s, the automobile had revolutionized society. Cars changed people's lifestyles. They allowed friends and family to visit more often. They enabled farmers to come to town to sell their crops and buy consumer goods. They made travelling to summer cottages possible. They also had a profound impact on the physical patterns of cities, allowing them to spread farther out from the urban centres. In 1920, 1 in every 22 Canadians owned a car. At the end of the decade, this figure was 1 in every 8.5.

Economic Impact

The automobile had a major impact on the economy. By 1929, more than 16 000 workers had jobs assembling cars. Oshawa, Windsor, and Walkerville were thriving automobile manufacturing centres. Thousands of other workers manufactured tires and auto parts. The rising demand for materials such as rubber, iron, leather, asphalt, lead,

gasoline, paint, tin, and glass boosted these industries. Every town had an automobile dealership, gas stations, and repair shops. The growing number of car accidents also led to expanded police forces. New roads required engineers and labourers. Motels and roadside restaurants multiplied. American tourists, most of whom came by car, added more than $300 million to the Canadian economy in 1929.

Canada became the second-largest automobile manufacturer in the world. At one time, about 70 companies, many of them Canadian, sold cars in Canada. Soon, however, the Canadian companies were absorbed by American firms. By 1926, only one Canadian car company remained. By 1929, two-thirds of all cars sold in Canada were manufactured by Ford, General Motors, or Chrysler.

Foreign Investment

To finance their growth, companies raised money by offering bonds or **shares**.

> "I resent their presence, I wanted to think that there was one place in the world where the strident honk-honk of a car horn could never jar on the scented air."
>
> –Lucy Maud Montgomery, author, on the automobile coming to PEI

> "Automobile technology has been a prime factor in the social and economic transformation of modern Canadian society. The automobile industry is a bellwether for the economy as a whole. The very shape of our cities, our neighbourhoods, and even our dwellings has been dictated by the presence of the automobile."
>
> –Douglas Leighton, *The Oxford Companion to Canadian History*, 2004

Figure 2.12 This was an assembly line at a Canadian car factory about 1925. By 1926, 55 of Canada's 70 auto and auto parts factories were located in Windsor. Locate Windsor on a map. Why do you think Windsor was the automobile capital of Canada?

"At this rate, American capital will soon run Canada and Canadians. … It's the direct result of the folly of our wartime spending spree. We wanted to play the part of a grand nation: we've gone bankrupt to save 'civilization' and 'democracy.' We are now at the mercy of our neighbours."

–Henri Bourassa, Québec politician, *Le Devoir*, 1925

Foreign Capital Invested in Canada, 1900–1930

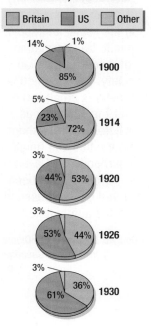

Source: J. Bradley Cruxton and W. Douglas Wilson, *Spotlight Canada*, 4th edition (Don Mills: Oxford University Press Canada, 2000), 153.

Figure 2.13 These pie graphs show foreign capital invested in Canada between 1900 and 1930. During which period did American investments increase most rapidly? Why?

The First World War changed investment patterns in Canada. Earlier, British financiers had invested in Canada by buying bonds. Unlike shares, bonds do not involve ownership but provide guaranteed **interest** payments. American investors preferred to buy shares in natural resource companies. By 1930, American firms controlled 20 per cent of Canada's industries, rising to 40 per cent in such key sectors as mining, smelting, and petroleum. As Figure 2.13 illustrates, American investments surpassed Britain's by 1926.

To avoid paying tariffs on goods they exported to Canada, some American companies established **branch plants** in Canada. Although these firms were run by American managers and returned profits to the home office, they produced "made in Canada" goods and thus avoided paying tariffs. By the end of the decade, Americans owned 82 per cent of Canada's auto production, 68 per cent of the electronics industry, 64 per cent of rubber, 42 per cent of machinery, and 41 per cent of chemical production. Economically, Canada was becoming tied to the United States. Serious concern about foreign investment lay many years in the future.

The Bust

The tremendous economic growth convinced almost everyone that good times were here to stay. Canada's **stock markets** were booming. From 1921 to the autumn of 1929, share prices tripled. Every day, the newspapers were full of stories about people making a fortune on the stock market. Each share represented ownership of the company. The amount this share was worth depended on how many people wanted to buy it. The more popular it was, the more it was worth. From 1925 to 1929, it seemed as if every company's shares had increased in value. With secure employment and rising salaries, small and large investors speculated that prices would continue to rise. Billions of dollars were invested in the market as people bought on margin—purchasing stock with a small down payment and borrowing the rest based on the value of the stock as collateral. They expected to pay off their loans by selling the shares at a profit.

Credit was easy to get. Many investors committed their life savings, mortgaged their homes, and cashed in safer investments to make a fast buck in the market. Even banks, wanting to increase profits, speculated dangerously. As you will discover in Chapter 3, however, it all came to a swift end on **Black Tuesday**—the "crash heard around the world."

Challenge and Response

1. Complete a concept web that explores the "Canadian Economy in the 1920s." Start by writing this title in the centre and then generate a web of ideas to explore the topic, developing and relating these ideas. What conclusions can you draw from your web?

2. As a class, discuss the major negative and positive consequences of the automobile industry in Canada since the 1920s.

3. Which economic conditions and issues of the 1920s continue to be important in Canada today? What ones have changed?

Skill Path:
Making Effective Notes

Making notes is an important skill. You need to make notes when you listen to a teacher or student give a presentation, or when you read a textbook. The ability to make effective notes will also help you in your career. In almost every type of work, people need to be able to write down instructions, summarize reports, and record observations.

STEP 1: Understand the Topic

First you have to understand the topic or main idea. This may be identified in the title or the introductory paragraph. Once you know the main idea, you need to identify and record statements that support it. For example, your notes about pages 59 and 61 might look like this:

The Booming Economy in the 1920s
In 1924, the economy began to improve:
- Natural resources drove economic growth.
- Car manufacturing had a major impact on the economy.

You could also use diagrams, drawings, or charts to record your notes. For example, you might record the above notes in a diagram such as the one below:

STEP 2: Categorize the Details

To make effective notes, you need to categorize the most important details. Look for clues that help you focus on these details, such as chapter previews, section heads, and boldface words. Paragraph structure provides clues, as well. Many paragraphs identify the main topic in the first sentence and then support it with examples in the rest of the paragraph. For example, your notes for page 59 might look like this:

Natural Resources
Natural resources fuelled economic growth:
- *Agriculture*—Crop prices rose; farmers reinvested profits in their farms.
- *Pulp and paper*—Canada was the world's largest supplier of newsprint.
- *Mining*—Demand for nickel, copper, gold, silver, and other metals grew.
- *Energy*—Alberta provided 90 per cent of Canada's petroleum exports; Canada was the second-largest producer of hydro-electric power.

You may prefer to record these notes in a diagram like one below:

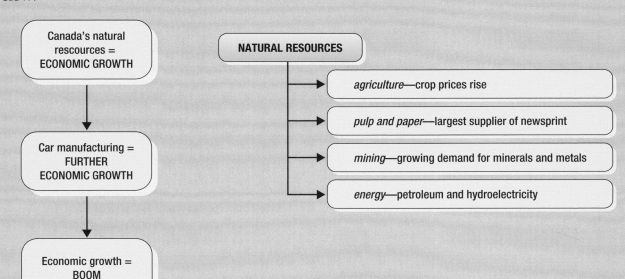

STEP 3: Organize and Summarize the Information

To organize information, you need to select the most relevant material and summarize it in your own words. For example, your notes for page 62 might look like this:

The Bust

From 1921 to 1929, stock prices tripled.
- Investors bought on margin.
- They expected to pay back their loans by selling shares at a profit.
- Credit was easy to get, so people gambled with their savings, homes, and investments.
- Banks engaged in dangerous speculation to increase profits.
- It all ended with the crash on Black Tuesday.

You may wish to record these notes in a diagram similar to the one below:

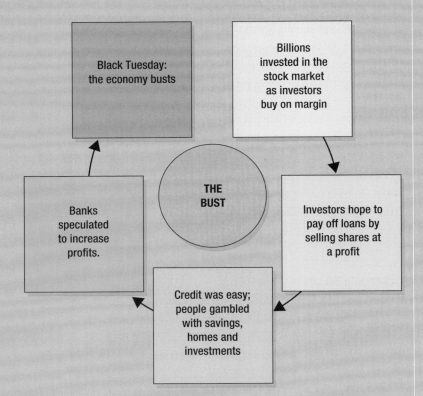

STEP 4: Practise Your Skill

- Practise your note-making skills using the information in other sections of this chapter. You might want to work in groups, with one person making notes on each main section. When you have finished, share your notes with your group.
- Working on your own, select one of the following occupations or choose an occupation of your own. Explain why a person in this occupation would need effective note-making skills:

a) actor
b) doctor
c) history teacher
d) journalist
e) magician
f) police officer
g) restaurant manager
h) safety inspector

A Changing Society

The 1920s brought change in a wide range of social issues including prohibition, the rights of women and Aboriginal peoples, immigration, and secondary-school education.

Prohibition

During the First World War, every province except Québec banned the sale of liquor. In March 1918, the federal government prohibited the manufacture, importation, and transportation of liquor. Prohibition, its supporters argued, saved needed grains for the soldiers. Prohibition became synonymous with patriotism. It was also part of a broad social reform movement aimed at eliminating such behaviour as drinking, smoking, and gambling.

In January 1919, the United States banned the sale, but not the consumption, of alcohol. When Canadian prohibition ended in 1919, provincial laws did not prevent the exportation of liquor. As a result, some Canadians began "rum-running" to the United States. Ontario, with six large distilleries and twenty-nine breweries, benefited from this illegal trade. Distillery owners built their fortunes supplying alcohol to thousands of thirsty Americans. During the 1920s, every province except Prince Edward Island abandoned prohibition in favour of government-run liquor stores.

The Role of Women

Although women had made great strides in the previous decade, including the right to vote, they were still not considered equal to men. A few women persevered to become doctors, dentists, lawyers, school principals, engineers, and company executives. In general,

though, occupations for middle-class women were limited to nursing, journalism, and elementary-school teaching. These jobs were considered good training for mothers-to-be and were seen as less important than traditional male occupations. They also paid considerably less. Other women worked as store clerks, secretaries, or factory workers, making up about 20 per cent of the workforce by the end of the decade.

As soon as a woman got married, she usually stopped working outside the home if the couple could afford it. Women who worked as teachers and civil servants were usually forced to leave their jobs after they married.

Many immigrant women took jobs as domestic servants. Some women were discriminated against because of their heritage. Employers often refused to hire women of Asian and African heritage. Men and women of Japanese and Chinese heritage were barred from entering universities or working in hospitals.

Women and Sports

Figure skating, diving, swimming, and tennis were seen as the only "proper" sports for women. Despite these attitudes, women took part in a wide range of sports including hockey, basketball, baseball, and horse jumping. When the women's Olympic track and field team returned from the 1928 Olympics with two gold medals, a silver, and a bronze, parades were held in Toronto and Montréal. The press estimated that 200 000 people packed Toronto's Union Station and another 100 000 lined the parade route.

Are Women "Persons"?

When Emily Murphy was appointed a judge in Alberta in 1916, a lawyer challenged her right to judge a case

"After a girl has spent four years of her time [at university] and a great deal of her parents' money in equipping herself for a career she is never going to have, the wretched creature goes and gets married, and in a few years has forgotten which is the hypotenuse of a right-angle triangle."

–Stephen Leacock, humorist and McGill University professor, 1922

"On April 24, 1928, … [w]hile acknowledging that the role of women had changed since the BNA Act was written, the [Supreme] Court said the Act was to be interpreted in light of the times in which it was written … Further, the Justices stated that all nouns, pronouns, and adjectives in the BNA Act were masculine, and that was who was meant to govern Canada."

–The Senate of Canada, "Background on the 'Persons' Case"

"The exclusion of women from all public offices is a relic of days more barbarous than ours. And to those who would ask why the word *person* should include females, the obvious answer is, why should it not?"

–Lord Sankey, Lord Chancellor of the Privy Council, 1929

Learn more about the Alberta Five and other prominent Canadian women

"Each day in High School adds $25 to a man's life's earnings."

–*Maclean's*, 1925

because she was a woman. In the eyes of the law, women were not "persons." Although the Supreme Court later ruled that women could be judges, women were not eligible to be senators. The prime minister was responsible for appointing senators. Several women's groups unsuccessfully petitioned Prime Minister Borden to appoint a female senator. During the next eight years, Prime Ministers Meighen and King ignored similar requests. Both argued that the British North America Act of 1867 stated that only "persons" could be appointed, and that women did not qualify as persons.

In 1927, the "Alberta Five"—Emily Murphy, Nellie McClung, Louise McKinney, Henrietta Muir Edwards, and Irene Parlby—challenged the definition of persons in the BNA Act. In 1928, the Supreme Court of Canada ruled against them. Disappointed, but not defeated, the Alberta Five took the case to the Privy Council in England, which was the final appeals court at the time. On 18 October 1929, the Council ruled that women were "persons." It was a resounding victory for all women in Canada.

Education

The 1920s witnessed the beginning of the modern high school in Ontario. New laws required children to remain in school until the age of 16 and prohibited them from working in factories and mines. The new economic prosperity meant more educated workers were needed to fill new job opportunities. Tuition was free, making commercial, technical, and collegiate schools available to children regardless of their family's income. As a result, the number of secondary students and schools multiplied.

Many schools held assemblies each morning. Students sang along with the school orchestra before opening exercises (prayer, the anthem, and announcements). The auditorium became the central feature of high schools. It nurtured school spirit, trained students in public speaking, and taught self-control, orderly habits, consideration for others, and respect for authority.

Extracurricular activities such as athletics, music and drama clubs, and school dances promoted good citizenship. They were meant to provide wholesome alternatives to billiard halls, taverns, and nightclubs. Gender stereotypes continued. Boys dominated student governments and headed newspapers and yearbooks, while girls filled the secretarial or assistant positions.

Immigration and Racism

Canada's immigration policy changed after the First World War. King's government decided to focus on Britain and the United States as sources of immigrants. Between 1919 and 1931, about 1.2 million immigrants arrived in Canada—substantial numbers but well below those of the first decade of the century.

Discrimination continued to influence the government's immigration policy. In 1919, two Protestant religious groups, the Mennonites and the Hutterites, were barred from coming to Canada, along with members of a Christian religious sect from Russia, the Doukhobors. Mennonites were not allowed in again until 1922 and Doukhobors until 1926. In 1928, immigrants from Japan were limited to 150 per year.

Figure 2.14 Much of the best land in Western Canada belonged to the Canadian Pacific Railway and the Canadian National Railways. Both companies pressured King to admit Eastern and Southern European immigrants, which he agreed to do in 1925. Why might these companies have wanted immigrants from Eastern and Southern Europe?

"Canada welcomes men and women of the right type who come to seek their fortune in this broad new land ... [people] of good moral character, and in good health, mentally and physically."

–Immigration pamphlet, circa 1925

 **Reading Strategy**

When reading a table, examine the headings and determine the relationship between them. This will tell you what the table is about. Then examine the figures in each column and look for sequence, patterns, trends, and other details.

The 1923 Chinese Exclusion Act prevented the immigration of almost anyone from China. Only 15 immigrants from China were allowed into Canada between 1923 and 1947. Passed on Dominion Day, this Act was seen by the Chinese Canadian community as the ultimate form of humiliation. For years, the community refused to celebrate Dominion Day and referred to it as "Humiliation Day."

The Ku Klux Klan

The arrival of the Ku Klux Klan (KKK) in the early 1920s revealed the extent of prejudice among many Canadians. In the United States, the Klan targeted people of African-American heritage. In Canada, it targeted Jews in Québec, French Canadians in Saskatchewan, Asians in British Columbia, and all foreigners everywhere else.

Although there were Klan members in Eastern and Central Canada, the KKK was most successful in the West.

| IMMIGRATION TO CANADA, 1920–1929 ||
Year	Number of Immigrants
1920	138 800
1921	91 700
1922	64 200
1923	133 700
1924	124 200
1925	84 900
1926	136 000
1927	158 900
1928	166 800
1929	165 000

Source: Valerie Knowles, *Strangers at Our Gates: Canadian Immigration and Immigration Policy, 1540–1990* (Toronto: Dundurn Press, 1992).

Figure 2.15 This table shows total immigration figures between 1920 and 1929. Between which two years did immigration increase the most? What might be the reason for this increase? Create a graph using these figures. What does the graph illustrate?

"Immigrants that came into Canada ... were considered 'foreigners' because of their race, colour, religion, or their customs. 'Foreigner' also meant different and inferior. These immigrants were allowed into Canada because we needed more people to farm the prairies, work in forests, factories or mines."

–Rebecca Chowen, Morell Regional High School, 2003

"All Indians were superstitious, having strange ideas about nature. They thought that birds, beasts … were like men. Thus an Indian has been known to make a long speech of apology to a wounded bear. Such were the people whom the pioneers of our own race found lording it over the North American continent."

–An example of racist attitudes as published in an Ontario elementary school history text, 1910

"When I got back to school, because I ran away, they were going to give me punishment … They said they were going to give me a real short haircut for my punishment. So my hair was cut really short, almost like a boy's."

–Quoted in Celia Haig-Brown, *Resistance and Renewal: Surviving the Indian Residential School*

Reading Strategy

To help you understand the experiences of residential school students, think about how you would have felt in their place.

In British Columbia, the KKK insisted that the government forbid the immigration of all people of Chinese, Indian, and Japanese heritage and seize the property of Asians already living in Canada. In the Prairies, large crosses were set on fire on hilltops to protest the use of French and other "foreign" languages. The Klan was most powerful in Saskatchewan, where newspapers and church leaders lent their support and convinced the provincial government to abolish the teaching of French in Grade 1.

Many Canadians were outraged, however, at the lies and racism of the KKK. They urged other Canadians to reject their racism and prejudice. By 1930, the KKK had disappeared in Canada.

Aboriginal Peoples

Throughout the decade, Aboriginal peoples struggled to preserve their cultures. Official government policy was to **assimilate** them. Duncan Campbell Scott, head of Indian Affairs in Canada from 1913 to 1932, wrote, "I want to get rid of the Indian problem. Our object is to continue until there is not a single Indian in Canada that has not been absorbed. They are a weird and waning race … ready to break out at any moment in … dances." Scott's beliefs were shared by many Canadians.

Residential Schools

Residential schools were designed to separate First Nations children from their families so they could be more easily assimilated. Children aged seven to fifteen were removed from their homes and forced to live in dormitories far away from their communities. When the children arrived at these schools, they were given new names to replace their given ones, stiff uniforms

in place of their traditional clothing, and European haircuts.

Students were severely punished if they were caught speaking their own languages. In class, no references were made to the history or cultures of First Nations. Music, history, and English reflected only the themes of English and French societies. Teachers were usually poorly trained, and few students received a good education. Discipline was often violent. Some children experienced physical, psychological, and sexual abuse. Many residential schools were built on flat land and in remote areas to make escape difficult. By the end of the 1920s, there were 80 residential schools in Canada.

Aboriginal Rights

In 1920, the Meighen government allowed the Department of Indian Affairs to force "deserving" First Nations people to be **enfranchised**. This meant that they could vote and have all the rights of British citizenship. It also meant that they would no longer have First Nations status or share in treaty rights. Later on, ceremonies associated with many First Nations religions were declared illegal.

First Nations people on reserves struggled to survive. The government wanted them to become farmers, but the land they had been given was often poor. People who left the reserves faced discrimination and were given the worst jobs. Increasingly, non-Aboriginal people began to trap and hunt on First Nations lands. Eventually, the federal government attempted to limit non-resident hunters by tripling hunting and trapping fees.

To protest these conditions, First Nations groups marched on Ottawa several times during the early 1900s.

In 1919, Frederick Loft, a Kanien'kehá:ka [gun-yung-gay-HAH-gah] (Mohawk) veteran from the First World War, organized the League of Indians to provide a united voice for Aboriginal peoples. The League lobbied for

- the vote without giving up First Nations status
- better health and education
- more financial aid
- the right to hunt, fish, and trap on the reserves without interference

In British Columbia, other First Nations organizations pushed for Aboriginal land rights. When they took their demands to Great Britain, Canadian officials prevented them from being heard.

This political activism alarmed the government. Duncan Campbell Scott threatened to enfranchise Loft, thereby depriving him of credibility among Status First Nations peoples. Loft protested strongly and the threat was never carried out. In 1927, the King government made it illegal for Status First Nations to organize politically, raise money to lobby the government for land claims, and retain legal help to pursue claims against the government. By 1930, the government's actions had successfully restrained Aboriginal political activism—for the time being.

"The White man is a much more zealous hunter, covers a greater extent of territory, and takes more fur than the Indian, and is denuding the hunting grounds of the red man to such an extent that it is becoming a serious problem."

–Charles Stewart, minister of the Interior

Learn more about residential schools and about the Statement of Reconciliation published by the federal government in 1998

Challenge and Response

1. In a chart, compare the purposes of education and experiences of high school students in the 1920s with today.
2. Using the steps in this chapter's Skill Path, make notes about immigration and racism in the 1920s. Then discuss your notes with a partner to gain a better understanding of this issue.
3. How might the perspectives of immigrants and Aboriginal peoples have influenced their impressions of the "Roaring Twenties"? Be specific in your answer.
4. Which of the primary source quotations in this section do you find most objectionable in terms of current Canadian values and understandings? Explain your choices.

Lifestyle and Culture

The 1920s brings to mind images of women with bobbed hair, the Charleston, jazz musicians, silent film stars, Model T Fords, and athletes such as Babe Ruth and Howie Morenz.

Music and Dancing

Jazz was the music of the 1920s. Originating with musicians in New Orleans, the sound soon spread across the United States and north to Canada. The most famous jazz musicians were Louis Armstrong, Jelly Roll Morton, and Duke Ellington. As jazz evolved throughout the decade, other musical genres took shape, including blues and swing, which would become more popular in the next decade.

The Jazz Age encouraged daring and energetic dances. Some adults considered them indecent because of their suggestive movements. The Charleston was the most popular dance. The Black Bottom and the Fox Trot were popular as well.

Movies

Silent movies were rarely silent. They were shown with piano or organ accompaniment, sound effects, and subtitles. Live orchestras played at larger theatres, frequently using music written specifically for the film. When "talkies" arrived in Canada in 1927, theatre jobs for musicians disappeared.

Comedy was the most popular type of movie during the era of silent films. The humour was usually slapstick—people got hit on the head, fell into holes, or were smacked in the face with custard pies. Buster Keaton, Laurel and Hardy, and Charlie Chaplin were the most famous comedians.

Figure 2.16 Examine this photograph of a Charleston dance marathon in 1926. Why might some adults have objected to the Charleston? Are there dances today that some adults object to? If so, why?

The newsreel, a collection of short news clips, became a standard part of movie theatre programs, along with short cartoons, a sports reel, and a travelogue. By the end of the decade, thousands of Canadians regularly attended one of the more than 900 movie theatres across Canada.

Canadians in Film

Several Canadians played a major role in early movies. Walter Huston, Norma Shearer, Marie Dressler, Fay Wray, and Mary Pickford were famous Hollywood actors. With his three brothers, Jack Warner founded Warner Brothers Pictures in 1923. The company released the first motion picture with synchronized sound, *The Jazz Singer*, in 1927. Decades later, the company became Time Warner Inc., one of the world's largest media and entertainment companies.

Louis B. Mayer grew up Saint John, New Brunswick. In his late teens, Mayer moved to Boston and then opened his first movie theatre in 1907. Within a few years, he had the largest theatre chain in New England. Several years later, Mayer started his own production company, Louis B. Mayer Pictures. In 1924, it became Metro-Goldwyn-Mayer (MGM).

Professional Sports

Canada was sports crazy in the 1920s. Canadians followed the heroics of such North American athletes as Babe Ruth in baseball, Bobby Jones in golf, Howie Morenz in hockey, and Fanny "Bobbie" Rosenfeld in the 1928 Summer Olympics. The media helped make the 1920s the golden age of sports in Canada. Newspapers promoted all sporting events. Popular magazines such as *Maclean's* ran regular articles. Radio and film created a mass appeal for sports. Cinemas showed films of famous boxing matches and provided highlights of important sporting events prior to the feature film.

Baseball was the most popular summer sport in Canada. Its popularity reflected the growing influence of American culture in Canada. Every community had an amateur baseball team. Toronto won the Little World Series in 1926. The Montreal Royals and the Toronto Maple Leafs played in the International League, a step below the majors.

The National Hockey League was established in 1917. There were five teams: two in Montréal, one in Toronto, one in Ottawa, and one in Québec City. In 1924, the Boston Bruins were the first American team to join the NHL. They were joined by the New York Americans in 1925. By 1926, the NHL had another team in New York (the Rangers), as well as teams in Pittsburgh, Chicago, and Detroit. Although professional hockey was becoming concentrated south of the border, the majority of players were still Canadian.

American Influence on Popular Culture

Sparked by improvements in printing technology, more than 300 American magazines circulated in Canada during the 1920s. The best sellers were *Ladies Home Journal*, *Saturday Evening Post*, and *McCall's Magazine*. For every Canadian magazine printed, eight were imported from the United States. The leading Canadian magazines were *Canadian Home Journal* and *Saturday Night*. Canadians were reading more American books and magazines than Canadian publications. This situation alarmed some Canadians who feared we were losing our culture.

> "If baseball were not already the national pastime of the United States, I suspect we would long ago have declared it ours."
>
> –William Humber, Canadian sports historian

 Learn more about the early history of hockey

> "After 1919, most creative people, whether in painting, writing or music, began to have a guilty feeling that Canada was as yet unwritten, unpainted, unsung … In 1920, there was a job to be done."
>
> –Arthur Lismer, Group of Seven artist

Sign of the Times

THE FLAPPERS

The "flappers" symbolized the 1920s. A typical flapper was a young woman who rejected conventional dress and behaviour. Flappers sometimes offended the older generation because they rebelled against their parents' morals. Before 1920, it was considered shameful to reveal bare skin. Now, ankles, calves, knees, and even backs were exposed. It was a fashion revolution!

Before the 1920s, only wealthy women could afford high fashion. The new styles were less complicated than earlier fashions. This allowed middle-income women to make their own clothes at home. However, the new fashions remained beyond the means of most women with lower incomes.

Figure 2.17 Common dresses were sleeveless or cap-sleeved, scoop-necked, and had no waistline or a dropped waist. Strapped shoes, called Mary Janes, were the preferred style of the 1920s.

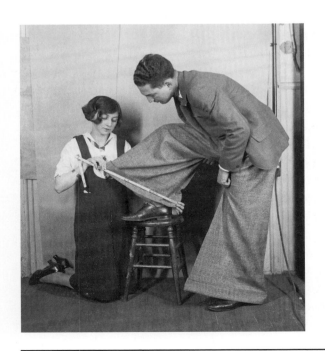

STYLES FOR MEN

Flannel and tweed were popular fabrics for men's clothing. Silk ties in small geometric patterns or diagonal stripes were secured with tiepins. Men's shoes were often two-toned in white and tan or white and black. Black bowler hats often completed the ensemble. Imitating movie star Rudolph Valentino, men parted their hair in the middle and slicked it down for "the patent leather look."

Figure 2.18 By 1925, baggy pants known as Oxford bags (after the students at Oxford University who were the first to wear them) were the style in men's fashion. Oxford bags measured from 56 to 100 cm around the bottom.

EVENING WEAR

Women's evening dresses revealed more of the body. Skirts were still full length, but necklines and backs were low, especially on dresses women wore to speakeasies and nightclubs. Formal eveningwear for men was a tailcoat worn with a top hat.

Figure 2.19 Evening gowns were often made of silk and embroidered with beads. Instead of hats, fancy combs, scarves, and headbands were the trend. The men wore starched white shirts with pleated yokes or bow ties or shirts with white wing collars. Black patent-leather shoes added the finishing touch.

THE BOB

The "boyish look" was fashionable. Flappers wore their hair bobbed—a blunt cut level with the bottom of the ears. The popularity of this shorter hairstyle created a demand for trained hairdressers as beauty parlours sprung up everywhere. The bob was a radical departure from the long hair women had traditionally worn.

Figure 2.20 To emphasize their short hair, women wore cloche hats. The cloche was pulled down over the eyes, so women had to tilt their heads at an angle to see where they were going.

Responding

1. In a T-chart, compare and contrast fashions today with those of the 1920s.
2. What influences are there in today's fashion trends for your generation?
3. How do you respond to fashion trends? How important do you think fashion trends are to your peers? How important do you think fashion should be? Give reasons for your responses.

COMMUNITIES

The Group Of Seven

In 1920, seven young Canadian artists—Arthur Lismer, Franklin Carmichael, Lawren Harris, A.Y. Jackson, Frank Johnston, J.E.H. MacDonald, and Frederick Varley—created a national artistic identity that allowed Canadians to discover the beauty of the Canadian landscape. The Group of Seven, as they called themselves, challenged Canadians to stop looking to Europe for their artistic inspiration and to embrace art created by Canadians that celebrated the beauty of Canada. They travelled to Algonquin Park and Georgian Bay in Ontario and the Laurentians in Québec to capture some of Canada's magnificent landscapes. They used brilliant colours and thickly applied paints to capture sunlight on red sumacs, shimmering blue waters, and white birch trees against backdrops of green and black evergreens.

"An Art must grow and flower in the land before the country will be a real home for its people."
Source: From the Group of Seven's first exhibition catalogue, 1920.

The Group called themselves Canada's national school of painters. Yet in their early years, there were many harsh critics within the artistic establishment. Their work was described as "hot mush," "Hungarian goulash," and just plain "bad taste"! With the support of the National Gallery of Canada, however, the Group's influence quickly spread throughout Canada's artistic community. When Johnston dropped out of the group in 1920, A.J. Casson replaced him. To broaden their artistic base beyond Toronto, the Group then invited other artists to join them, including Montréal's Edwin Holgate and Winnipeg's L.L. FitzGerald. In 1932, the Group of Seven disbanded, satisfied that they had achieved their goal of bringing a uniquely Canadian style to landscape painting.

 Learn more about the Group of Seven

Figure 2.21 Since they often painted together, the styles of the Group of Seven developed along somewhat similar lines. *Above Lake Superior* was painted by Lawren Harris in 1922. How does Harris portray the landscape? What subjects would you paint to represent Canada today?

Responding

1. What are the central features of the art created by the Group of Seven?
2. In what ways did the Group challenge Canadians' views of themselves?
3. Find some art books or websites on the Group of Seven. Then write a critique of their overall style and approach to their work.

The Canadian Authors Association was founded in 1921 to promote nationalism and to convince Canadians to buy Canadian books. *Maclean's* magazine promised to print only Canadian non-fiction writing and to use Canadian spellings. Other Canadian magazines followed. Canadian publishers asked for higher tariffs on American magazines and for lower tariffs on raw materials such as paper and processing equipment to make their publications cheaper to produce. But their efforts failed—few politicians wanted to increase the price of these popular American publications.

By the end of the decade, Canada had 51 radio stations, compared with over 600 stations in the US. The limited range of many Canadian stations meant that some rural areas received no radio signals, while others had their signals drowned out by the more powerful American transmitters. In 1930, about 40 per cent of Canadians received only American stations. Because US stations had a larger market, they could afford to develop more appealing and more varied programs. As a result, some Canadian stations obtained the right to broadcast American programs by becoming affiliates with networks such as NBC and CBS.

Initially, Canada had a thriving feature film industry, with Canadian film crews, casts, and settings. By 1929, however, Famous Players distributed 90 per cent of all feature films in Canada. The immense popularity of American movies was particularly troubling to some Canadians, who worried that American ideas and culture would corrupt young moviegoers.

Challenge and Response

1. Create a word wall that describes pop culture, fashion, music, and movies in the 1920s. What information was completely new to you?
2. Do you think that Canadian culture has become stronger or weaker since the 1920s? Offer specific examples to support your views.
3. Write a paragraph that you think most accurately describes the decade of the 1920s. As the basis of your paragraph, you might wish to choose a word from the word wall you created in question 1.

ISSUES

The "Boom" Years

The issue: To what extent did Canadians benefit from the boom years of the 1920s?

Popular history portrays the 1920s as a time of frivolous fun and economic prosperity following the desolation of the First World War. Young people enjoyed wild dances, fun fashions, and new consumer goods in what many people perceived to be a happy, carefree time.

This picture tells only part of the story, though. Not all Canadians shared in the good times of the "Roaring Twenties." Those who played the stock market and bought the new consumer goods were primarily middle- and upper-income Canadians living in the cities of Central Canada. Elsewhere, other Canadians, including many fishers, trappers, labourers, and immigrants, struggled to earn a decent wage. In 1929, the average annual income of a typical Canadian family was $1200 a year. But according to social workers, a family needed $1430 a year to stay above the poverty level. The chart and the quotations shown here reflect the different viewpoints on the reality of the "boom years."

"Never in our history has our country been in better shape, nor have our people faced the future with greater confidence...No country has made a greater recovery from postwar depression as has Canada, and today there is every reason to believe that the Dominion has embarked on a prolonged era of development and prosperity."

Source: From an editorial in *Saturday Night*, December 1928.

"It is likely that more than half of the Canadian people were never anything but poor between the wars, although they were worse off in the Thirties than before. For these people, the Twenties had not roared."

Source: Michiel Horn, *The Dirty Thirties: Canadians in the Great Depression* (Toronto: Copp Clark, 1972).

The Boom Years: Change	The Boom Years: Continuity
• New inventions made life easier. • The automobile revolutionized society. • New fashion trends challenged conservative norms. • New developments in music, art, and film transformed popular culture.	• Labour unrest continued. • New political parties fought for better conditions for workers, farmers, and immigrants. • Women continued to struggle for equality. • Economic inequalities persisted across Canada's regions.

Figure 2.22 This chart highlights how things changed or stayed the same during the 1920s. What other things might you add to this chart?

Responding

1. What sources would you need to consult to determine the nature of the so-called "boom" of the 1920s?
2. Write a letter to the editor expressing your opinion on the "boom" of the 1920s.
3. Do you consider the time you are living in right now to be one of "boom" or "bust"? Give reasons for your response.

Thinking Like a Historian:
Identifying Continuity and Change

Essential Question: As a historian, how do you recognize how things have changed or stayed the same over time?

The era of the 1920s seems far in the past, yet we are confronting today many of the same issues people faced at that time. One of the common issues for both time periods is the degree of change that people experienced. The changes were social, political, economic, cultural, and technological. Life at the end of the 1920s was much different than it had been at the beginning of the decade.

You, the Historian

1. Examine the editorial cartoons below that date from the 1920s. Then create an organizer like the one below to analyze these primary sources.

Describe the cartoon	What is its central theme or message?	Which aspects of this theme are similar to life today?	Which aspects of this theme are different from life today?	Is the theme more similar or more different from life today?

PROTECT THE CHILDREN
Why not make a clean sweep while at it?

THE HOLIDAY SEASON
What can be more delightful than a day or two off speeding in the fresh country air amidst the restful quiet and beautiful scenery?

Chapter 3

The Dirty Thirties

Figure 3.1 The unemployment created by the Great Depression led to frustration among many Canadians. The economic collapse drove many Canadians into poverty and despair. What does this protest suggest to you about the mood of the decade?

Chapter at a Glance

Thinking Ahead

The 1920s were a time of economic growth and prosperity. In 1929, however, the good times came to an abrupt halt when the stock market crashed. Economic chaos swept across Canada, North America, and much of the world. For the next decade, people around the world faced widespread unemployment and economic despair. There was little governments could do to ease the crisis. Only after 10 years would a crisis of a different kind—a world war—end the **Great Depression**.

In this chapter, you will investigate the Depression and its impact in Canada and the world. As you do, focus on these key questions:

- Which factors were the most significant causes of a prolonged Depression?
- To what extent did the government respond effectively to the economic conditions that emerged during the Depression?
- What impact did the Depression have on Canada and Canadians?
- How did the Depression influence Canadian politics?
- What global factors carried the world into another world war?

Profile in Power:

Richard Bedford (R.B.) Bennett

"In the last five years, great changes have taken place in the world. The old order is gone. We are living in conditions that are new and strange to us. Canada on the dole is like a young and vigorous man in the poorhouse ... I am for reform. And in my mind, reform means government intervention."

—R.B. Bennett, announcing economic reforms, 14 January 1935

Figure 3.2 Richard Bedford Bennett (1870–1947)

Richard Bedford (R.B.) Bennett was born in Hopewell Hill, New Brunswick, in 1870. In his youth, Bennett became a teacher, but he soon decided to pursue a law degree. After graduating, he relocated to Calgary, where he rose to prominence as a corporate lawyer and business leader. Bennett was a firm believer in capitalism and the free enterprise system. He applied these principles to become a self-made millionaire.

In 1911 Bennett was elected to the House of Commons as a Conservative MP. When Prime Minister Robert Borden chose not to give him a position in his Cabinet, Bennett refused to run for re-election in 1917. In 1921, however, the new Conservative prime minister, Arthur Meighen, offered Bennett the position of justice minister if he returned to federal politics. Bennett accepted, but he was defeated in the election. He did not return to the House of Commons until 1925.

When Meighen resigned in 1927, Bennett became the new Conservative leader. By the time he faced his first election as leader, the Great Depression was crippling the country. Bennett promised to end unemployment—"or perish in the attempt." Canadians put their faith in him and chose Bennett as the country's 11th prime minister in August 1930.

Once in office, however, Bennett's policies did little to relieve the misery of the Depression.

As frustration boiled over into anger and social unrest, he took a harsh stand against protestors and strikers who demanded his government do something to ease the economic hardship. Yet his public actions were in stark contrast to his private response to the crisis. He secretly donated large sums of money to charities and sent small sums and gifts to Canadians who wrote to him seeking help.

Bennett's inability to deal with the economic crisis became his political legacy. Yet he was responsible for a number of lasting reforms that affected economic and social welfare in Canada. They included

- creating the Bank of Canada to regulate **monetary policy** (1934)
- establishing the Canadian Wheat Board to regulate wheat prices (1935)
- introducing unemployment benefits (1935)

Bennett lost the election of 1935. He left the prime minister's office a bitter man. In 1938, he resigned as Conservative leader and left Canada. He lived the rest of his life in Britain, where he was a member of the House of Lords until his death in 1947. Before he died, he expressed his wish not to be buried in Canada. Instead, R.B. Bennett rests in Surrey, England—the only Canadian prime minister to be buried abroad.

Figure 3.3 Bennett (shown here campaigning with his sister) came to symbolize the country's economic chaos. Broken-down, horse-drawn cars were called "Bennett buggies." The rundown shacks of the unemployed were called "Bennett burghs." Why do you think people expressed their frustrations on such a personal level?

Responding

1. Why might Bennett have taken a hard line against protestors?
2. Do you think it was fair to blame any one person for the long-term effects of the Depression? Give reasons for your response.

The Great Depression

During the prosperity of the 1920s, many people played the stock market in the hope of getting rich quick. Investors bought stocks at low prices and sold them when prices were high. Many people bought stocks on credit, putting 10 per cent down and borrowing the rest from a broker. When the stocks increased in value, they sold them, paid back their broker, and kept the profits. Then, in 1929, prosperity quickly turned to poverty. What happened to plunge Canada and the world into the worst economic crisis in history?

The Stock Market Crash

The prosperity of the 1920s came to an abrupt halt. On Black Tuesday, 29 October 1929, the stock market crashed in the United States. What lay ahead

Figure 3.4 The stock market crash and the Depression that followed hit industrial nations like the United States, Canada, Britain, Germany, France, and Australia particularly hard. Why do you think this was so?

was the Great Depression and the decade that came to be known as the "Dirty Thirties."

As the value of stocks plummeted, investors panicked as they scrambled to sell their stocks. The more stocks they sold, the lower prices fell. In just a few hours, the value of stocks on the world's major stock exchanges dropped by 50 per cent. Millions of dollars were lost. Thousands of investors went broke. The stock market crash quickly spread to Canada and other countries.

The Causes of the Depression

The collapse of the New York stock market determined the timing of the Great Depression. However, economists still debate the role that other factors played in creating the length and intensity of the economic crisis.

Easy Credit

During the 1920s, businesses borrowed money to expand their operations. As long as prices held, they were able to repay their debts. As prices dropped, though, lenders demanded repayment of their loans. Many companies went broke. As workers lost their jobs, they could not repay their debts. Creditors repossessed people's cars, stoves, refrigerators, farms, and homes.

A Lack of Financial Regulation

In the United States, there was little government regulation of financial services. In the 1920s, banks made investments using depositors' money. When the market crashed, people stampeded to get their savings out of the banks. With their cash reserves empty, many banks went bankrupt. In Canada, there were more financial regulations. As a result, there were no bank failures and fewer Canadians lost all of their savings. Still, the economic crisis deeply affected many Canadians, particularly in the West.

Shrinking Demand

The Canadian economy relied on exporting staples such as wheat, pulp and paper, fish, and minerals. In the 1920s, global demand for these resources led to overproduction and the flooding of world markets. As demand decreased, prices plummeted. This had a devastating impact on the economies of countries like Canada that relied on exports and trade.

Economic Ties

The United States was Canada's most important trading partner. When the Depression crippled the American economy, the effects flooded over into Canada. There were fewer orders for Canadian resources and products. As demand declined, US parent companies shut down their Canadian operations, putting thousands of people out of work. As a result, Canada was probably the second hardest hit country by the Depression after the United States.

Protective Tariffs

Many countries imposed protective tariffs on imported goods to protect their industries from foreign competition. This meant major exporting countries like Canada had fewer markets in which to sell their products.

Getting By

Canada had faced hard times before. Yet nothing prepared Canadians for the hardships of the Depression. At its height, nearly 30 per cent of workers were unemployed. Without money, people bartered for goods and services.

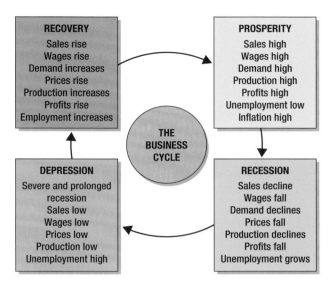

Figure 3.5 The **business cycle** is a natural feature of the free-market system. A depression may follow the second stage of **recession** if the period of economic decline is prolonged and severe. Canada's experience during the Great Depression resulted in significant changes in the role of government in the economy to prevent a similar economic crisis in the future. Do you think it is ever possible to be certain that such a crisis will not happen again? Why or why not?

Families that were unable to pay their rents and mortgages and lost their homes. At the time, there was no unemployment insurance, family allowances, or **universal health care** to help people through the tough times. If they needed help, Canadians turned to their families or to churches and private charities.

Regional Effects

People in all parts of Canada suffered as the Depression tightened its grip. Not all parts of Canada suffered equally, though. The West was one of the hardest hit regions. In the 1920s, the prairies had been one of the most prosperous farming regions in the world. In the 1930s, however, the economic crisis joined with the forces of nature to create desperate times for prairie farmers.

Learn more about Canada's economy

"A recession is when a neighbour has to tighten his belt. A depression is when you have to tighten your own belt. And a panic is when you have no belt to tighten and your pants fall down."

–Politician and activist Tommy Douglas, 1971

MAP STUDY: The Dust Bowl

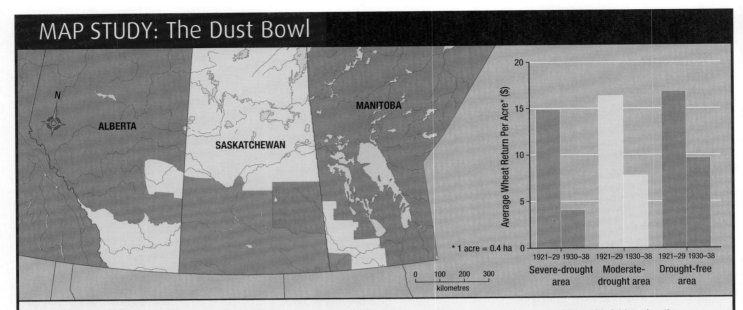

Source: Donald Kerr and Deryck Holdsworth, eds., Geoffrey J. Matthews, maps, *The Historical Atlas of Canada, Volume III: Addressing the Twentieth Century, 1891–1961* (Toronto: University of Toronto Press, 1990).

Figure 3.6 This map shows wheat returns by area across the prairies between 1921 and 1929 and 1930 and 1938.

For thousands of years, the thick grasslands protected prairie soils from the destructive forces of nature. They helped the soil retain its moisture and prevented winds from eroding it. Herds of buffalo grazed on the plains without disturbing this delicate balance of nature. First Nations developed **sustainable economies** that left the natural vegetation intact.

After European settlers converted the prairie grasslands into fertile farmland, the balance of nature shifted. The prairies became vulnerable to the cycles of nature. This had a devastating impact on prairie farmers during the summers of 1929, 1931, and 1933 to 1937. Severe droughts hit southern Alberta and Saskatchewan. Without rain, the crops failed. Topsoil was swept away by hot, dry windstorms that darkened the skies for hundreds of kilometres. Adding to the devastation were plagues of grasshoppers that infested the crops and an epidemic of wheat rust that destroyed the wheat fields.

The Dust Bowl led to the creation of the Prairie Farm Rehabilitation Administration (PFRA) in 1935 to coordinate strategies for reducing soil erosion. Today, the PFRA works with prairie farmers to sustain the agricultural industry and to develop strategies for sharing Canadian knowledge and technologies with the international community.

Analysis and Response

1. Which province experienced the most severe drought? What geographic factors do you think contributed to this?

2. As a class, brainstorm other ways in which human activities adversely affect natural systems. What can people do to reduce these effects?

3. Between 1928 and 1933, average incomes fell 61 per cent in Alberta and 72 per cent in Saskatchewan. Many people had to abandon their farms. Others could not afford to buy farm equipment to harvest what few crops they had. What impact do you think this had on manufacturers in Central Canada?

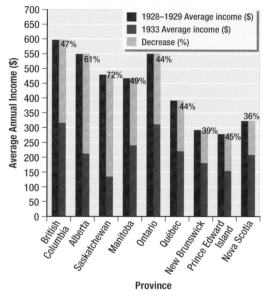

A Comparison of Average Incomes Per Person, 1928–1929 and 1933

Source: Rowell Sirois Report, Book 1: Canada 1867–1939.

Figure 3.7 Average annual incomes per person declined dramatically between 1928–1929 and 1933. This graph shows the average decline per person, by province, during the worst years of the Depression. Which provinces experienced the greatest decline? What overall trends or patterns does the graph reveal?

The Effect on Agriculture

The industrial heartland of southern Ontario and Québec enjoyed the greatest prosperity during the 1920s. When the Depression struck, these regions were not as hard hit as other parts of the country, in part because of tariffs designed to protect domestic industries. Still, the declining fortunes of prairie farmers had a ripple effect on the manufacturing sector. Companies producing farm equipment had to cut back production. This in turn led to layoffs among workers. As unemployment rose, fewer people had money to buy other consumer goods, such as cars and appliances, so production in these sectors fell, too. Then more workers lost their jobs. It was a vicious cycle.

In Atlantic Canada, the contrast between the prosperity of the 1920s and the hardships of the 1930s was less severe. The region had not experienced the same level of prosperity that Western and Central Canada had. Farmers in Atlantic Canada fared better than farmers on the prairies did. They grew a greater variety of crops so they were able to grow enough food to feed their families. Some even had small surpluses to sell. Fewer farmers in the eastern half of the country lost their properties.

The Effect on Resource Industries

Workers in the fishing, timber, and coal industries experienced the full effects of the economic downturn as the global demand for resources dried up. First Nations and Métis peoples who earned their living from fur trapping and fishing felt the impact of the diminishing demand for resources. Newfoundland, which was then an independent dominion of the British Commonwealth, was hit hard by the decline in fish exports, too. The combination of interest and relief payments bankrupted the government and forced Britain to take control of the dominion's economy.

Who Benefited?

A few wealthy Canadians with cash on hand benefited from the Depression. They were able to buy farms, homes, and land at cheap prices and sell them later for huge profits. Many large corporations remained profitable by cutting wages, laying off workers, and reducing production. For the majority of Canadians, however, the Depression meant lower wages—if they had wages at all—and a daily struggle to maintain the necessities of life.

Reading Strategy

When you read a graph, ask yourself the following questions:
- What type of graph is it: a bar, line, pie, or scatter graph?
- What information can I learn from the title, caption, and labels?
- What is the best way to analyze the information?
- What patterns can I identify?

"One of my jobs was to walk over after dark to the garden of the family that looked after the nearest grain elevator ... and steal carrots, radishes, anything that was growing. I never got caught because their dog was friendly. never have a friendly dog in a Depression."

–A young Canadian, in Barry Broadfoot, *Ten Lost Years: 1929–1939*

"These really are good times, but only a few know it."

–American auto manufacturer Henry Ford, March 1931

Challenge and Response

1. In what stage of the business cycle was Canada in the 1920s? In what stage is the country today? Give reasons to support your response.
2. Why were the Prairie provinces the hardest hit during the Depression?
3. How do you think Canada's social programs, such as unemployment insurance and universal health care, would ease the hardships if another depression happened today?

Responding to the Depression

When the Depression began, Prime Minister William Lyon Mackenzie King failed to recognize the magnitude of the economic crisis. Like most politicians of the day, he believed that government had no role to play in the economy. But King was out of touch with the mood of Canadians. They expected their government to do something to end the crisis. When King called an election in 1930, his opponent, Conservative leader R.B. Bennett, promised jobs for all those willing to work and high tariffs to protect Canadian industries. In contrast, King offered no plans for reducing unemployment or jump-starting the ailing economy.

In what may have been the turning point of the campaign, King proclaimed that he would not give a "five-cent piece" to help any Conservative provincial government fight unemployment. On the campaign trail, unemployed workers expressed their outrage at the prime minister's remark by pelting him with wooden nickels. On election day, voters expressed their discontent with King and the Liberals

"With respect to giving monies out of the federal treasury to any Tory government in this country for these alleged unemployment purposes, with these governments situated as they are today, with politics diametrically opposed to those of this government, I would not give them a five-cent piece."

–Prime Minister William Lyon Mackenzie King, House of Commons, 3 April 1930

by giving Bennett and the Conservatives a commanding majority.

Bennett's Response
Once in office, Bennett applied traditional economic policies in an attempt to restore prosperity. After the United States raised its tariffs on imported goods, Bennett kept his election promise and raised tariffs on goods entering Canada. The tariffs offered some protection to the manufacturing sector in central Canada, but they crippled Canada's export trade, which relied on global demand for primary resources. As a result, Canadian exports dropped by 67 per cent. In response, some companies laid off workers; others declared bankruptcy. The unemployment rate skyrocketed. By 1933, over 826 000 people were out of work—not including unemployed fishers and farmers, who were not counted in the unemployment figures.

Seeking Relief
As the Depression continued, resourceful Canadians looked for ways to support themselves. Some became door-to-door salespeople. Others offered to work in exchange for room and board. Some borrowed money from family

Skill Path:
Identifying Cause-and-Effect Relationships

Most events have a cause and an effect. The *cause* is what makes an event happen. The *effect* is the consequences of that event. When you investigate events from the past, you need to use your ability to reason to understand the relationship between causes and their effects.

When you are identifying cause-and-effect relationships, follow these steps to establish connections.

STEP 1: Identify the Facts
Begin by writing down all the facts you have about the event, in the order they took place.

STEP 2: Identify the Causes
Identify the different causes of an event. First, look for the direct or immediate causes. For example, the crash of the New York stock market on 29 October 1929 was a direct cause of the Great Depression. Next, think about the indirect or more distant causes. For example, the ability to obtain easy credit in the 1920s was an indirect or more distant cause.

STEP 3: Identify the Effects
Next, identify the different effects of an event. Make a distinction between short-term and long-term effects. For example, the short-term effect of the stock market crash was that people rushed to sell their stocks. The long-term effect was that the economy was in a desperate slump for the next decade.

STEP 4: Record Patterns
Graphic organizers help you identify patterns in cause-and-effect relationships. Record the information you identified in steps 1 and 2 in an organizer similar to one of the organizers shown on this page. You would use the first organizer to show a simple cause-and-effect relationship. You would use the second one to show events that have more than one cause and effect.

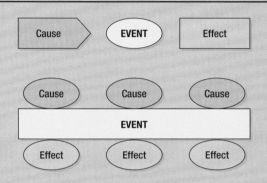

STEP 5: Use Connecting Words and Phrases
Once you have identified cause-and-effect relationships, record your observations in writing. Use words and phrases that connect ideas to demonstrate patterns in the cause-and-effect relationship. For example, "*As a result of* the stock market crash, the economy was sent into a downward spiral that led to the Great Depression." Other connecting words and phrases you might use include the following:

Because . . .
If . . . then . . .
Nevertheless . . .
Since . . .
Therefore . . .
This led to . . .

STEP 6: Practise Your Skill
1. Think about an event in your life recently. Complete an organizer to show the cause of the events and its effects. Then write an explanation of these causes and their effects using connecting words and phrases.
2. Start an organizer highlighting the causes and effects of the Great Depression. You will be adding to it as you work through this chapter.

"What girl with a business training wants to sew or cook, unless it be in her own home, building for the future? We are trained for business. We like it. We need the money, most of all in our youth ... My ambition was to save enough money to travel ... Today the height of my ambition is to keep off the rocks ... We can only live for today. Tomorrow and tomorrow's plans we are obliged to ignore."

–Mary Howlett,
1 January 1934

and friends. Others turned to churches and charities. Some panhandled for spare change. For many, however, it was impossible to meet their basic needs. By 1933, more than 1.4 million Canadians relied on **relief**.

Although the Depression affected everyone to some degree, some groups suffered more than others. Young people, unskilled workers, small business owners, farmers, and working women faced the greatest economic hardships. In the 1930s, it was unacceptable for a woman to take a job away from a man. As a result, men got jobs in traditionally female occupations, such as teaching and secretarial work. The women they replaced were left to do domestic work in the homes of wealthy Canadians.

To qualify for relief, people had to have lived in their town or community for a specific period—usually six months to a year. This meant that thousands of unemployed men who travelled the country in search of work did not qualify. Even if people met the residency requirements, there was a

long list of other conditions, such as turning in their driver's licences and removing telephones from their homes. Most Canadians would have avoided relief had there been any other alternative.

The Impact on Aboriginal Communities

Since the passage of the Indian Act in 1876, the government had tried to assimilate Aboriginal peoples. They encouraged them to get off the land and become part of mainstream Canadian society. Yet when the Depression hit, the government failed to provide the same relief to Aboriginal peoples that it offered other Canadians. Instead, it urged them to return to their traditional ways by living off the land.

The Impact on First Nations

By this time, though, living off the land was no longer an option for many people. Many communities had lost their traditional lands. On the prairies, it was illegal for First Nations to hunt and fish on government lands. Without land, people had lost their hunting and fishing skills, so they were no longer able to provide for themselves.

To save money, the government cut funding to First Nations reserves. Many communities experienced widespread hunger. Malnutrition and disease, such as tuberculosis, reached epidemic proportions.

The Impact on the Inuit

In the North, the federal government began a program to relocate the Inuit of Baffin Island to Devon Island in 1934. Officially, the government wanted the Inuit to move to a location where game and other resources were in

Figure 3.8 The army operated relief projects like this rock excavation project in Round Lake, Ontario, in 1935. Who do you think these projects benefited?

Figure 3.9 In spite of the economic hardships, many people found some comfort among family and friends. These members of the Calgary Ski Club got together for a "hard-times dance" in 1936. In what ways do you think social gatherings helped people cope?

greater supply. Yet the government also wanted to populate isolated northern islands to reinforce Canada's **sovereignty** in the Arctic.

The Inuit had the option of returning to Baffin Island if they were dissatisfied with their relocation. After enduring harsh winter weather and hurricane-force winds for two years, they chose to return home. The relocation to Devon Island, however, was only the first of many attempts to relocate the Inuit.

"I've seen tears in men's eyes, as though they were signing away their manhood, their right to be a husband and sit at the head of the table and carve the roast. It was a very emotional time when a man came in and went up to the counter."

—A relief worker, in Barry Broadfoot, *Ten Lost Years: 1929–1939*

"Oh, I remember them days, them Dirty Thirties. But the missus and I managed to keep the kids fed. That was the thing having a farm. You could always have the seeds and grow your food, and we used to do the hunting or the trapping so we'd have meat. But them folks up there in the city, they didn't have [anything]. Well, neither did we, but we [were] used to not having anything."

—Aboriginal Elder Ike Hill

Challenge and Response

1. Why do you think unemployed workers responded so forcefully to King's "five-cent piece" comment?
2. How would you and your family change the way you spend money if an economic depression happened today? How would your lifestyle change in terms of a) food, b) clothing, c) transportation, d) entertainment, and e) communications? Discuss your ideas with a partner. Then share your ideas with the class.
3. Imagine you are a member of a First Nations or Inuit community. Write a letter to Prime Minister Bennett expressing your views about his government's response to your community's conditions during the Depression.

Learn more about Bennett's response to the Depression and the hardships Canadians experienced

MAP STUDY: Métis Land Settlements in Alberta

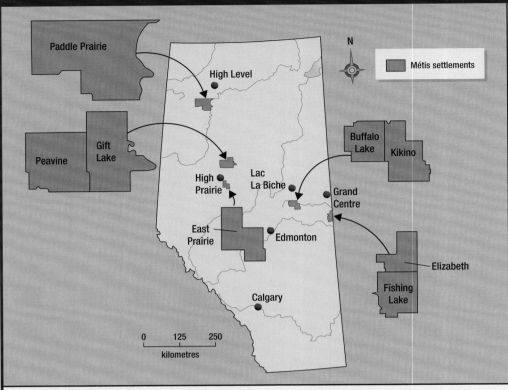

Source: International, Intergovernmental and Aboriginal Relations (IIAR).

Figure 3.10   Alberta is the only province to have passed legislation to provide settlements for the Métis. Of the original 12 Métis settlements, 8 exist in the province today.

Inuit, Métis, and First Nations peoples had few organizations to promote their interests during the Depression. Circumstances were particularly difficult for the Métis. Since the late nineteenth century, they had been Canada's "forgotten people." They had no land of their own and the government did not recognize them as Aboriginal peoples.

In Alberta in 1932, however, two Métis activists, Jim Brady and Malcolm Norris, founded the Association des Métis de l'Alberta to defend the interests of Métis people. They petitioned the Alberta government to recognize Métis land rights and to establish a land base on which viable communities could be built. In response, in 1934 the province created a Royal Commission to look into the question of Métis land claims. The commission refused to acknowledge that the Métis had any right to land. However, it did recommend that the government pass the Métis Population Betterment Act in 1938 to provide land and financial aid to the Métis. The province created 12 settlements where the Métis could lease land from the government. The settlements provided a means for the Métis to gain control of their own destiny. Over the years, they have created strong, self-reliant communities built on the strength of their land and culture.

Analysis and Response

1. Locate the current eight Métis settlements on a map showing the physical features and natural resources of Alberta. To what extent do you think the location of these settlements allows the Métis to practise their traditional lifestyle?

2. To what extent is the fact that many Métis in Alberta live in organized communities an advantage when negotiating land and resource rights with the government? Give reasons for your response.

Writers and Artists

During the Depression, **realism** dominated the arts. Artists and writers focused on social issues that captured the despair and disorder of the Depression. As you read and view these literary and artistic images, think about the ways in which they capture the experiences and attitudes of Canadians during the Depression.

Sinclair Ross: Novelist

Sinclair Ross was born in Saskatchewan in 1908. One of his best-known works is a novel called *As for Me and My House*. The story is set in a fictional town in Saskatchewan during the Depression. It chronicles the lives of Mr and Mrs Bentley and their struggle to overcome the isolation of their prairie home, as seen through the eyes of Mrs Bentley.

Sunday Evening, April 16

"Philip preached well this morning, responding despite himself to the crowded, expectant little schoolhouse. They were a sober, work-roughened congregation. There was strength in their voices when they sang, like the strength and darkness of the soil ... Five years in succession now they've been blown out, dried out, hailed out; and it was as if in the face of so blind and uncaring a universe they were trying to assert themselves, to insist upon their own meaning and importance."

Source: Sinclair Ross, *As for Me and My House*
(Toronto: McClelland & Stewart, 1989), 26.

Charles Comfort: Artist

Figure 3.11 Charles Comfort painted *Young Canadian*, a portrait of his friend, painter Carl Schaefer, in 1932. The hands in the foreground symbolize the man's ability to work, but there is no work for him. How do the subject's facial expressions and body language symbolize the Depression?

Responding

1. What messages are contained in each of these expressions of art?
2. Compare these literary and artistic images with the photographs and information in this chapter. What connections can you make? Present your findings in a Venn diagram.
3. Choose the image from this chapter that you think most effectively conveys the hardships of the Depression. Write a brief rationale explaining why you chose this image.

Reading Strategy

When you read the reflections of individuals, keep in mind that people have different points of view. Be sure to separate the facts from the personal viewpoints.

"The Tory government of R.B. Bennett had decided a role for the single unemployed. They were to be hidden away to become forgotten men, the forgotten generation. How naïve of Mr Bennett. Never were forgotten men more in the public eye."

–Ronald Liversedge, a relief camp worker, Vancouver, June 1935

"It was jail, you know. What else would you call it? ... If you thought the army was bad, then you don't know about one of those camps ... They treated us like dirt. And we weren't. We were up against it, broke, tired, hungry..."

–An 18-year-old relief camp worker

From the Rails to the Camps

Many men left their families and homes in search of work in other parts of the country. Many "rode the rails" on top of boxcars or on the rods beneath the cars. Thousands travelled west. There were no jobs on the prairies, though, so the men continued on to British Columbia. In Vancouver, they overwhelmed relief organizations, churches, and charities. The city asked the federal government to get the men off the streets. In response, the government created relief camps.

Most relief camps were located in remote parts of the country. Over 200 000 single men 18 years of age and older went to live in the camps. Discipline in the camps was very strict—there were rules for everything. The men worked hard, long hours, cutting trees and brush, moving rocks, and building roads, all for just 20 cents a day. They slept on bunk beds in crowded auditoriums and ate greasy soups and watery stews that had often gone bad. Many felt that working in the relief camps was like living in prison.

The bleak life of the camps left many men angry and frustrated. Many began to listen to demands for radical social and economic change expressed by groups like the Communist Party of Canada. In the spring of 1935, thousands of camp workers in British Columbia formed the Relief Camp Worker's Union (RCWU). Their leader was Arthur Evans, a communist labour organizer. The men went on strike demanding better pay, food, clothing, and shelter at the camps. In April and May, the strikers demonstrated in Vancouver. In June, they launched the On-to-Ottawa Trek: over 1600 men aboard freight trains bound for the nation's capital and a confrontation with R.B. Bennett.

The Regina Riot

Bennett was determined to stop the On-to-Ottawa Trek protestors. On June 14, he ordered the police to halt the trains at Regina. He invited Trek leaders to Ottawa, hoping that in their absence the protest in Regina would fizzle out peacefully.

In Ottawa, talks broke down after only an hour. The frustrated men returned to Regina. They gathered in Market Square on July 1 to discuss their next strategy. When Bennett ordered local police to arrest the men, a riot broke out. When it was over, one plain-clothes police officer was dead and several protestors and citizens were injured. Reluctantly, many men returned to the relief camps. It was a victory for Bennett, but at a great cost to his reputation.

Bennett's "New Deal"

Bennett set aside millions of dollars for emergency relief and increased tariffs on imported goods. Yet these measures did little to reverse the country's economic misfortunes. By 1933, the Depression was at its worst. It had created economic hardships that Bennett—or any other politician—was not able to handle. Yet many Canadians blamed Bennett for being indecisive and ineffective.

Meanwhile, in the United States, President Franklin D. Roosevelt launched the New Deal—a series of radical social reforms aimed at providing relief and economic recovery. In January 1935, Bennett announced his own "New Deal." The one-time sup-

Figure 3.12 A Royal Commission investigating the causes of the Regina Riot blamed the incident on the communists. How does this conclusion reflect the fear of communism in the country at the time?

Learn more about the On-to-Ottawa Trek

"They opened the door and out they come beating the [heck] out of us. They chased us all over town. The amount of people I saw with their heads bashed in was terrible, really terrible."

–Trekker Jack Geddes, reflecting on the Regina Riot, 2002

"Why should one expect young, virile people, whether they be men or women, to be content with a life which at best gives food, provides work which may not be interesting, and for which there is no pay, and houses them in camps where all natural living and interest are denied? It is not reasonable to expect that they would be content with such a life, nor would it be healthy for Canada if they were."

–Agnes Macphail, Canada's first female MP, House of Commons, 2 July 1935

porter of unregulated capitalism now argued that the country's economic system needed an overhaul. Bennett promised sweeping new social programs, including unemployment insurance and a minimum wage. Critics charged Bennett with making "a deathbed conversion" in a desperate attempt to win re-election. For many Canadians, it was too late. The Liberal campaign slogan was "King or Chaos!" The voters chose King. The Liberals returned to power with 173 seats compared to 40 for the Conservatives.

King Returns

When King returned to office, he inherited a dismal economy. In the years leading up to the Second World War, he did little to tackle unemployment. However, he did invest money in public works projects and relief programs. Ultimately, however, there would be three more years of ineffective government action before the Second World War sparked the economic boost Canada, and the world, needed to end the Great Depression.

Challenge and Response

1. Write a brief speech or create a poster encouraging men to take part in the On-to-Ottawa Trek.
2. Write an editorial expressing your point of view about the government's decision to arrest the men in Regina.
3. Return to the cause-and-effect organizer you began in the Skill Path on page 87. Add more information to the organizer based on what you have learned in this section.

Reading Strategy

As you read this section on alternative political parties, use a spider organizer to categorize the social, political, and economic philosophies of each one.

 Learn more about the CCF

The Emergence of Political Alternatives

Neither the Liberals nor the Conservatives knew how to fix the economic problems that plagued the country. As a result, one of the effects of the Depression was that many Canadians lost confidence in traditional political parties. Many turned to new regional parties that demanded social and economic reforms.

Figure 3.13 This family took to the road with all of their possessions in search of work. Why do you think some families like this one listened to calls for reform from parties like the CCF?

The Co-operative Commonwealth Federation

In 1932, a small group of reform-minded MPs formed the Co-operative Commonwealth Federation (CCF)—known today as the New Democratic Party. The roots of the CCF were in Western Canada. Led by Winnipeg MP J.S. Woodsworth, the CCF rejected both capitalism and revolutionary communism in favour of **democratic socialism**. In its Regina **Manifesto**, issued in 1933, the CCF blamed the Depression on the capitalist system and introduced a number of socialist policies, including

- public ownership of banks, public utilities, transportation companies, and other major industries
- improved health and social services
- a tax system designed to redistribute wealth

Opponents of the CCF capitalized on the "**Red Scare**" in the West that emerged following the communist revolution in Russia in 1917. They charged that the CCF's platform was "communism in disguise." However, the CCF emphasized that it was committed to democratic social change through the free choice of Canadian voters.

The CCF gained support in the Western provinces. In 1939, it became the official opposition in British Columbia, Saskatchewan, and Manitoba. As you will discover, the CCF would expand its influence in the West and in Ottawa in the coming years.

The Social Credit Party

Like the CCF, the Social Credit Party had its roots in Western Canada. Social Credit was based on an economic theory that proposed the government pay a **social dividend** to every citizen. Consumers would spend the money buying more goods. An increase in demand would lead to an increase in production. This in turn would create more jobs and jump-start the economy.

During the Depression, the idea of a social dividend made sense to many people—especially to an Albertan named William Aberhart. Nicknamed "Bible Bill" because of his strong religious beliefs, Aberhart hosted a popular radio show. He used this forum to preach the idea of Social Credit. He called upon the provincial government to pay every adult in Alberta $25 a month. When he failed to convince the government of the merit of his idea, Aberhart formed the Social Credit Party. In the election of 1935, his new party swept the province, winning 56 out of 63 seats.

Once in power, however, Aberhart had to face political reality: the government simply did not have the money to pay $25 to every Albertan consumer. Aberhart decided to print more money, but the courts ruled that monetary policy was a federal responsibility. Although Aberhart failed to deliver on his promises, the Social Credit Party remained in power in Alberta for 35 years.

The Union Nationale

In the early 1900s, Québécois nationalism had emerged as a powerful force in Québec. By the mid-1930s, nationalism found its place on the political stage as well.

The Liberals had been in power in Québec since 1897. With close ties to the English business community, the government resisted pressure for economic reforms. By the mid-1930s, however, many voters were ready for change. A lawyer named Maurice Duplessis sensed the new political

opportunity at hand. He joined forces with a group of rebellious Liberals to form the Union Nationale.

In the election campaign of 1936, Duplessis focused on corruption in the Liberal government. He promised to defend French language, religion, and culture against English business interests. His campaign strategy worked. The Union Nationale was swept into office. Once in power, however, Duplessis failed to deliver many of his election promises. Instead, he left the economy in the hands of English business interests and passed laws outlawing any labour protests.

The Padlock Law

Claiming that communism was a threat to Québec society, in 1937 the Duplessis government passed the Padlock Law. It gave authorities the power to enter any public or private building to search for and seize communist propaganda. If they found any, they padlocked the building until the owner appeared in court for trial. The Padlock Law left authorities to define communism on their own terms and to determine what was, and was not, communist propaganda. As a result, the law silenced radical political opposition in Québec and kept labour unions weak for 20 years.

Despite the controversies, Duplessis held on to popular support by defending the traditions and values of the French language, religion, and culture. He aggressively defended the province's autonomy by opposing various grants and initiatives from the federal government. In 1948, Duplessis created the Québec flag, the *fleur-de-lys*. In 1954, he introduced a provincial income tax system. Many critics considered the conservative and authoritarian rule of the Duplessis govern-

"We aim to replace the present capitalist system, with its inherent injustice and inhumanity, by a social order from which the domination and exploitation of one class by another will be eliminated … and in which genuine democratic self-government, based on economic equality, will be possible."

–The Regina Manifesto, 1933

"The fact is your advisors are chiefly bankers and lawyers who … think that THE PEOPLE are made for the systems and not the systems for THE PEOPLE."

–William Aberhart, in a letter to Prime Minister Mackenzie King, 1937

Learn more about the history of the Social Credit Party

Learn more about the Union Nationale

ment to be a dark period in Québec's social and intellectual history. Nevertheless, Duplessis's brand of national-ism ensured that his government was elected five times between 1936 and his death in 1959.

Figure 3.14 Demonstrators protested the Padlock Law in Montréal in 1937. Why do you think the Supreme Court ruled the Padlock Law was unconstitutional in 1957?

Challenge and Response

1. a) Use a three-circle Venn diagram to compare and contrast the Co-operative Commonwealth Federation, the Social Credit Party, and the Union Nationale.
   b) Which of the three new parties provided the most practical response to the problems of the Depression? Give reasons for your response.
2. Should people have the right to free speech even if they use it to advocate radical change? Defend your opinion in an editorial or letter to the editor.
3. Return to the cause-and-effect organizer you began earlier in this chapter. Complete the organizer by identifying additional causes and effects of the Great Depression based on what you have learned in this section.

Canadian Culture

During the Depression, many Canadians wanted to escape from life's harsh realities. Entertainment offered them the means to do just that. Movies, radio, books, and magazines all gave people the chance to dream about other people, places, and times.

Radio Comes of Age

In the 1930s, listening to the radio was a diversion all Canadians enjoyed. People gathered around the radio to listen to comedies, dramas, sports, serials, and variety shows. Most of the programs originated in the United States, however. Many Canadians were concerned about the amount of American content on the airwaves. In response, in 1932 Bennett created the Canadian Radio Broadcasting Commission (CRBC) to broadcast Canadian radio programs in French and English and to regulate broadcasting. In 1936, King created the network Canadians know today as the Canadian Broadcasting Corporation (CBC).

Many Canadian-made radio programs copied the formats of popular American shows. They included programs like *The Happy Gang*, which presented lighthearted entertainment with likeable characters, a few laughs, and easy-listening music. Some programs were uniquely Canadian, though. *Hockey Night in Canada* was first broadcast from Toronto's Maple Leaf Gardens in 1931. Since then, *Hockey Night in Canada* has become a weekly Saturday-night ritual for millions of hockey fans across the country.

Musical Trends

The "big band" sound became popular in the 1930s. American performers such

Figure 3.15 Many Canadians listened to news, sports, and entertainment on special radio trains. Why do you think listening to the radio was such a popular pastime during the Depression?

as Jimmy Dorsey and Benny Goodman played to packed halls in Canada's major cities. The CBC provided a forum for artists such as Guy Lombardo and Glenn Miller. Some songs reflected the harsh economic times—"I Can't Give You Anything but Love" and "Brother, Can You Spare a Dime?" Others, such as "Walking in a Winter Wonderland" and "Moonlight Serenade," offered an escape from reality.

Artists of African-American descent began to make their mark in the music world during the 1930s, as well. Singers such as Billie Holiday and Ella Fitzgerald sang both soulful blues and powerful religious songs. Singers and songwriters of African-American descent in the 1930s had a profound influence on the development of modern North American popular music.

Newspapers and Magazines

American publications dominated the magazine industry in Canada. The popular American magazine *Life* consistently outsold Canadian publications

"Hockey was the thing in those days. The big thing. The Toronto Maple Leafs and Foster Hewitt on Saturday nights ... He was better known than the prime minister."

–A young Canadian, in Barry Broadfoot, *Ten Lost Years: 1929–1939*

Learn more about CBC radio broadcasts during the 1930s

such as *Maclean's* and *Chatelaine*. In 1931, Bennett responded to pressure from Canadian publishers for protection from foreign competition by imposing a hefty tariff on US magazines. In four years, sales of Canadian magazines soared by 64 per cent, while American sales slumped 62 per cent. When King returned to office in 1935, however, the tariff was cut as part of a trade agreement with the US, and American magazines quickly regained their market share.

Although most newspapers were Canadian-owned, American press services provided most foreign news coverage. As a result, news stories had an American slant. There was little or no coverage about Canada or Canadians in international current events.

A Media Sensation

Perhaps the most sensational media coverage of the day was in 1934 following the birth of the Dionne Quintuplets. The miracle of the birth and survival of five baby girls in northern Ontario provided welcome relief to Depression-weary people around the world. Newspapers and magazines wrote upbeat stories about the girls' progress. Advertisers used the girls' pictures to sell their products.

The Ontario government saw the media sensation as an opportunity to expand tourism and create much-needed jobs. They removed the girls from their parents' care and placed them in a special facility. "Quintland" became a major tourist attraction, with over three million people coming to gaze at the girls from behind a one-way screen.

Learn more about the Dionne Quintuplets

Figure 3.16　It is estimated that the tourism and media coverage surrounding the Dionne Quintuplets generated $350 million. Although there was a $15-million trust fund set up for the girls, the money mysteriously disappeared. When they turned 21, the Dionne sisters received only $119 000 each. In 1998, the Ontario government formally apologized to the three surviving women and paid them $4 million in compensation.

"Multiple births should not be confused with entertainment, nor should they be an opportunity to sell products. Our lives have been ruined by the exploitation we suffered at the hands of the government of Ontario…"

–Annette, Cécile, and Yvonne Dionne, in a letter to parents of newborn sextuplets, in *Time*, 1 December 1997

Challenge and Response

1. Do you think it is important to have a publicly owned broadcasting system? Give reasons for your response.
2. The most popular magazines during the Depression reported on the lives of the rich and famous. Why do you think these magazines were so popular? Is this type of magazine popular today? Discuss your ideas in class.
3. a) What is your opinion about the way in which the government treated the Dionne Quintuplets? Explain your response.
   b) In what ways does society exploit people today? Explain your response with examples.

Sign of the Times

During the Depression, many young Canadians left their worries behind them at the movies. There was no feature film industry in Canada in the 1930s, but Canadians entertained themselves by watching American films produced in Hollywood. For just 25 cents, you could escape into a fantasy world. In the cities, many young Canadians went to the movies once or twice a month looking for laughter, romance, thrills, and chills!

KING KONG

King Kong (1933) was one of the first horror/adventure films. A movie director meets a young girl stealing an apple during the Depression. He offers her a starring role in his new film, in which a group of filmmakers encounters a giant gorilla named Kong on a mysterious island. They capture Kong and return with him to New York. The film starred Fay Wray, from Cardston, Alberta, as the young woman Kong tries to protect.

Figure 3.17 *King Kong* was a hit for its special effects, including the final scene in which Kong fights off airplanes from the top of the Empire State Building.

THE WIZARD OF OZ

The Wizard of Oz (1939) was ahead of its time. It was a musical fantasy, filmed in colour, about Dorothy and her little dog, Toto. They are whisked away by a tornado from Auntie Em's farm in Kansas to the magical and mysterious kingdom of Oz. Dorothy has many adventures as she tries to reach the Wizard who is supposed to help her get back home.

Figure 3.18 The *Wizard of Oz* introduced viewers to such memorable characters as the Cowardly Lion, the Scarecrow, the Tin Man, and the Wicked Witch of the West.

Responding

1. These movies are Hollywood classics. Why do you think each one was so appealing in the 1930s? Why do you think some movies are able to maintain their appeal across generations?

The Rising Tide of Fascism and Nazism

"Dictatorship is better than revolution."

–Rodrigue Cardinal Villeneuve, archbishop of Québec, May 1935

"We went to Spain because we knew what the people of Spain had gone through, how they had suffered and starved, the same thing we were going through in Canada, and we decided that if at all possible we would get to Spain to help defend democracy and their elected government."

–Perry Hilton, volunteer soldier in the Spanish Civil War, 1936

"From 1936 to 1939, 1546 Canadians left families, jobs, and country to help the Spanish people defend democracy against the rise of fascism ... Despite suffering heavy losses, many of the survivors went on to continue the fight by serving in the Canadian armed forces in WW II."

–Part of the inscription on the memorial plaque to the Mackenzie-Papineau Battalion, Ottawa

North America was not alone in the Great Depression. By 1933, almost 30 per cent of the global workforce was unemployed. The turmoil of the post-war world sparked the initial rise of **fascism**. In 1922, Benito Mussolini took power in Italy in the first fascist **dictatorship** in Europe. By the 1930s, the chaos of the Great Depression provided fuel for other fascist movements in Germany and Spain.

Civil War in Spain

In 1931, Canada gained greater control of its destiny when the British Parliament passed the Statute of Westminster. It gave Canada independence over its foreign policy. King used this new independence to remain neutral in foreign conflicts. When Japan invaded Manchuria in 1931, King refused to support **sanctions** by the League of Nations. When Italy invaded Ethiopia in 1935, King chose not to support actions against Italian aggression.

In 1936, Francisco Franco led a military coup in Spain to overthrow the elected government. The civil war that followed was a battle between fascism and communism. Franco had the support of the fascist leaders, Mussolini and Germany's Adolf Hitler. The ousted government had the support of the communist regime in the Soviet Union.

In Canada, King believed taking sides in the conflict threatened national unity. In Québec, many French Catholics were sympathetic to Franco because he supported Spain's Catholic values and traditions. The Communist Party of Canada, on the other hand, supported

the ousted **left-wing** government. In English Canada, people feared the communist cause might appeal to many frustrated, angry, and unemployed workers. To eliminate Canadian involvement in the conflict, King banned Canadians from fighting in foreign armies. Yet over 1500 Canadians defied the law and took up the fight in Spain.

The Canadians in Spain formed the Mackenzie-Papineau Battalion, or Mac-Paps (named after William Lyon Mackenzie and Louis-Joseph Papineau, the Canadian leaders of the Rebellions of 1837). Half of the battalion died in the fighting. After Franco's army gained victory, the Canadians who survived returned home. For years, history ignored them and the government refused to recognize them as veterans. Only in October 2001 were the Mac-Paps acknowledged with a monument in Ottawa.

Hitler Gains Power

In 1936, concern over the Spanish Civil War quickly subsided as far graver events began to unfold in Europe. Germany had suffered deeply from the Depression, with over six million people unemployed. By the early 1930s, many Germans had grown tired of traditional politics and politicians. The leader of the fascist Nazi Party, Adolf Hitler, promised he would restore full employment. Many Germans desperately wanted to believe him.

In 1933, Hitler succeeded in manipulating his way into power. He moved quickly to gain absolute control over the country by imposing **censorship** to silence political opposition. He banned strikes and unions. He created youth groups to teach young Germans the beliefs of the Nazi Party, including the superiority of the **Aryan** race.

"The great masses of the people ... will more easily fall victim to a big lie than to a small one."

–Adolf Hitler, *Mein Kampf*, 1925

Figure 3.19 The reign of terror against German Jews reached terrifying new heights on 9 November 1938 during Kristallnacht—the night of broken glass. Groups of young Nazis roamed the Jewish quarter of Berlin. They destroyed homes and businesses. They beat and killed innocent people. Why do you think some people are drawn together to persecute others?

In particular, the Nazis believed that Aryans were superior to Jewish people. As a result, Jews became the scapegoat for all of Germany's economic woes as Hitler launched a campaign of persecution against them. Jewish people lost their German citizenship. They could not work in certain professions or marry non-Jews. By 1939, all Jews had to carry identification cards and observe a curfew forbidding them from going out after dark. The Nazis seized Jewish homes, businesses, and valuables. It was a terrifying time for the Jews of Germany. Yet as you will discover in Chapter 4, this was just the beginning of Hitler's plans for all the Jews of Europe.

The Voyage of the *SS St. Louis*

As the persecution escalated, many Jews tried to escape Europe. They boarded ships bound for North and South America. In June 1939, almost 1000 refugees chartered the German ocean liner the *SS St. Louis* and sailed across the Atlantic. The United States, Argentina, Paraguay, Panama, and Cuba all rejected their requests for safe haven. The ship then headed north to Canada. Despite appeals from prominent Canadians, both Jews and non-Jews, King refused to accept the refugees. The *SS St. Louis* returned to Europe. Almost half of its passengers eventually died in Nazi **concentration camps**.

"[Canada's refusal to take the passengers from the *SS St. Louis*] is a large blemish on Canadian history and should be recognized by people today [so] that a mistake like this never happens again."

–Mitchell MacPhee, Morell Regional High School, 2007

ISSUES

Prohibiting Jewish Immigration

The issue: What social and cultural factors influenced Canada's decision to deny Jewish refugees entry into Canada on the eve of the Second World War?

Today, Canada thinks of itself as a safe haven for oppressed peoples. Yet in the 1930s, Canada denied Jewish refugees entry into the country. Between 1933 and 1945, Canada accepted just 4000 Jewish refugees, compared with 200 000 in the United States and 85 000 in Britain.

Why did Canada—a nation of immigrants—refuse to accept Jewish refugees? The Depression reinforced the idea that immigrants took jobs away from Canadians. In 1930, the government banned immigrants from Europe, except for those who could farm or who had family here. The next year, it banned European immigration altogether.

Anti-Semitism was another powerful factor in denying Jews entry into Canada. Cities like Toronto, Montréal, and Winnipeg had thriving Jewish communities. Even so, Jews faced discrimination because their values and lifestyles were different from those of French and English Canadians. During the Depression, these suspicions grew more intense as Jews were among those groups many people perceived as radicals. Jews faced barriers in entering some schools and professions. Some private clubs and associations restricted the membership of Jewish citizens.

These sentiments were widespread across the country, and the prime minister was not about to challenge public opinions. As a result, King's policies reflected these social attitudes, as expressed by the head of Canada's immigration department, Frederick Blair.

"I often think that instead of persecution it would be far better if we more often told them frankly why many of them are unpopular. If they would divest themselves of certain of their habits I am sure they could be just as popular in Canada as our Scandinavians."

Source: Frederick Charles Blair, director of immigration, November 1938.

Not all Canadians were anti-Semitic, though. Many prominent Canadians supported the efforts of the Canadian Jewish Congress to increase public awareness of the plight of European Jews. They urged the government to adopt a more compassionate policy and to open Canada's doors to Jewish refugees. Despite their efforts, however, they could not persuade King to change his government's policy.

"The stories circulating against the Jew are so astounding and contradictory that no thinking person could believe them. In the same breath, the Jew is accused of being a Communist as well as controlling the money bags of the world."

Source: Senator Cairine Wilson, responding to Blair's anti-Semitic comment, November 1938, in Don Gilmour, *Canada: A People's History*, vol. 2, the Canadian Broadcasting Corporation, 2001.

Learn more about Canada's immigration policy during the 1930s

---

Responding

1. Imagine you are a Member of Parliament in 1939. Prepare arguments to present in a speech to persuade the government to reverse its policy and admit Jewish refugees.
2. How can we ensure respect for cultural diversity today? Discuss your ideas as a class.

Cairine Wilson: Canada's First Female Senator

Cairine Wilson was born Cairine Mackay in Montréal in 1885. In 1909, she married Liberal MP Norman Wilson. The couple settled in the French-speaking community of Rockland in eastern Ontario. While raising eight children there, Wilson developed her French-language skills to become fluently bilingual.

After the family moved to Ottawa in 1918, Wilson became a social activist. She supported many liberal causes, including less restrictive divorce laws, family allowances, and government health care.

In 1930, King appointed Wilson, a long-time friend and Liberal, as Canada's first female senator. If King expected Wilson to be a humble political supporter, however, he was wrong. Wilson frequently took stands against King's policies, including his approval of the Munich Agreement. She also took up the cause of Jewish refugees. When the passengers on board the *SS St. Louis* requested safe haven, Wilson urged King to accept them.

"Our leaders continue to subscribe to a concept of anarchy which actually permitted the World War of 1914 and which might well have permitted its repetition in the last few hours ... The new barbarians represented by Germany may now be free to extend to the Black Sea and other continents."

Source: Senator Cairine Wilson, commenting on the Munich Agreement, October 1938, in Don Gilmour, *Canada: A People's History*, vol. 2, the Canadian Broadcasting Corporation, 2001.

Learn more about other Canadian women in politics

After the war, Wilson campaigned to raise public sympathy and support for refugees and displaced persons. As head of the Senate Committee on Immigration and Labour, she promoted a more open immigration and refugee policy. In 1949, she became Canada's first female delegate to the United Nations. Cairine Wilson continued to fight for refugees even as her health began to fail before her death in 1962.

Figure 3.20 In 1930, Cairine Wilson declared: "As women we wish to use our powers to redress existing evils and ... to promote legislation which will benefit the greatest number." How do you think male politicians of the day might have responded to this?

Responding

1. What kind of a role model do you think Wilson was for women of her day? How strong a role model is she for women today? Give reasons for your response.

War on the Horizon

When Hitler came to power in Germany, he was determined to overturn the Treaty of Versailles, which had ended the First World War. He systematically set out to restore and consolidate Germany's power on the continent. In 1935, he began to rearm Germany and rebuild the military. In 1936, he reoccupied the Rhineland, the **demilitarized** zone in Western Germany. In 1938, the Nazi army occupied Austria as part of Hitler's plan to integrate all German-speaking nations. Yet Britain and France did little to stop German aggression. Instead, they adopted a policy of appeasement, making concession after concession to Hitler's demands.

The Munich Agreement

In 1938, Hitler demanded that Germany gain control of the Sudetenland, the German-speaking region of Czecho-slovakia. With Europe on the verge of war, the leaders of Germany, Italy, France, and Britain met in Munich to work out a compromise. Without consulting the Czech government, Britain and France appeased Hitler once again. In September 1938, they signed the Munich Agreement, which allowed Germany to take control of the Sudetenland. In return, Hitler promised to end his campaign to acquire more German-speaking territories. Western leaders accepted him at his word. Yet, as you will discover in Chapter 4, Hitler was not finished with his plans to conquer Europe.

Figure 3.21   King travelled to Germany in 1937. King supported **appeasement**, convinced that Hitler was "a man of deep sincerity" who was determined to avoid war. What message do you think it sends when a Canadian prime minister visits a country that is embroiled in controversy?

Challenge and Response

1. Do you think the federal government should have recognized the Mac-Paps as war veterans when they returned home? Support your answer.
2. Why do you think some Canadians condoned the discrimination against Jews? Give reasons for your response.
3. As a class, rank-order the reasons for countries adopting a policy of appeasement rather than confrontation.

Thinking Like a Historian:
Developing Historical Perspective

Essential Question: As a historian, how do you understand the different social, cultural, intellectual, and emotional contexts that shaped people's lives and actions in the past?

When you are developing historical perspective, you are developing *empathy* for a person from the past. Empathy is not the same as *sympathy*. Sympathy involves emotions—you imagine what a person felt like in a certain situation and you identify with them. Empathy involves evidence that helps you understand the motives and reasons behind a person's thoughts or actions from the different perspectives *at that time*.

The following activity helps you develop historical perspective by analyzing letters written during the Depression. Try to understand the economic, social, cultural, and emotional contexts from the writer's perspective by asking yourself the following questions:
- What does each letter tell me?
- What evidence does each letter contain?
- What does each letter reveal about the person who wrote it and his personal response to the Depression?

Ottawa
March the 4th 1932

"Dear Sir,

I am just writing a few lines to you to see what can be done for us young men of Canada. We are the growing generation of Canada, but with no hopes of a future. Please tell me why is it a single man always gets a refusal when he looks for a job. A married man gets work, & if he does not get work, he gets relief. Yesterday I got a glimpse of a lot of the unemployed. It just made me feel downhearted, to think there is no work for them ... & also no work for myself ... I am wandering the streets like a beggar, with no future ahead..."

Source: From a letter signed R.D. from Ottawa in the papers of R.B. Bennett, in L.M. Grayson and Michael Bliss, eds., *The Wretched of Canada: Letters to R.B. Bennett, 1930–1935* (Toronto: University of Toronto Press, 1976).

Winnipeg, Manitoba

"It is now forty months since I had the pleasure of a pay check. My family are all undernourished, ill clothed and ill sheltered and are in need of Medical Assistance. How long do you think we can carry on under these circumstances? You stated that there would be no one starve in Canada I presume you meant not starve over night but slowly our family amongst thousands of others are doing the same ... I do not believe I am crazy but am reaching the breaking point. My body, my muscles, my brain are like sodden wood crumbling under this strain..."

Source: From a letter signed Charles Grierson in the papers of R.B. Bennett.

You, the Historian

1. What economic, social, cultural, and emotional hardships are evident in these letters?
2. Imagine you are a young Canadian during the Depression. As the oldest child in your family, you want to contribute to your family's income, but you are unable to find a job. Write a letter or diary entry expressing your feelings.

Chapter 4

The Second World War

Figure 4.1 The contributions of Canada's soldiers during the Second World War are honoured at cemeteries and memorials throughout Europe. What lessons can be learned from the experiences of war?

Chapter at a Glance

Thinking Ahead

The Second World War was an even greater global conflict than the First World War had been. It was **total war**, affecting all Canadians either on the battlefield or on the home front. The war transformed the nation economically, politically, socially, and culturally. When the guns finally fell silent in 1945, Canada had earned a new place on the world stage.

As you discover the key events for Canada and Canadians in the Second World War, focus on the following questions:

- What were the key steps on the road to the Second World War?
- What contributions did Canadians make in the war in Europe and in the Pacific?
- In what ways did the Canadian government violate human rights during the war?
- What contributions did Canadians on the home front make to the war effort?
- What impact did the war have on Canada and the world?

Profile in Power:

William Lyon Mackenzie King

"Not necessarily conscription, but conscription if necessary."

Source: Prime Minister William Lyon Mackenzie King,
House of Commons, 7 July 1942.

Figure 4.2 William Lyon
Mackenzie King (1874–1950)

When William Lyon Mackenzie King returned to power in 1935, a crisis was looming in Europe. Hoping to avoid another bloody war, King supported the policy of appeasement toward Germany promoted by Britain and France. Once war came, however, King quickly recalled Parliament and Canada declared war on 10 September 1939.

King played an active role in the wartime strategy sessions with other Allied leaders. His priority was on the home front, though. King was desperate to maintain national unity. He adopted a series of compromises and half measures to accommodate the polarized viewpoints in English and French Canada over the issue of conscription.

After the war, the Liberals won another majority government in 1945. King lost in his own riding of Prince Albert, Saskatchewan, though, forcing him to run in a by-election in Glengarry, Ontario. After 30 years as leader of the Liberal Party and 21 years as prime minister, many members of King's own party began to question whether it was time for him to retire. In 1948, King bowed to the pressure and resigned as prime minister and Liberal leader. He remained in the House of Commons until the election of 1949. Then he retired from public life. His retirement was short-lived as his health quickly failed. On 22 July 1950, King died of pneumonia.

King passed away before he had time to write his memoirs. Throughout his life, though, he had recorded his innermost thoughts and secrets in his personal diaries. In his will, he left instructions to destroy the diaries, except for selected parts he indicated to save. But the parts to save were never identified. Without any memoirs, the diaries became the only record of King's long political career. The government kept the diaries, making them public 50 years after King's death.

The diaries revealed some surprising secrets. Canadians discovered that the prime minister most considered dull and boring was fascinated with the afterlife and the spiritual world. He regularly held seances to communicate with his late mother and other dead relatives and friends. Through his contact with the spirits, he sought reassurances about his political decisions.

William Lyon Mackenzie King is Canada's longest-serving prime minister. Some historians rank him among the country's greatest prime ministers for his success in maintaining national unity and his implementation of social reforms such as unemployment insurance and family allowances. Others argue that he was an uninspiring leader who lacked a clear vision of Canada or any progressive ideas for moving the nation forward. Whichever way Canadians assess him, King remains one of Canada's most intriguing politicians.

Figure 4.3 King (middle) met with US President Franklin Roosevelt (left) and British Prime Minister Winston Churchill (right) in Québec in August 1943. What does this suggest about the importance of Canada's role in the Second World War?

Responding

1. Do you think King was right to be concerned about national unity, even though the country was at war? Explain your response.
2. How do you think Canadians might have reacted had they known about King's fascination with the spiritual world while he was prime minister? How would you have reacted?
3. Do you agree with the decision to make King's diaries public? To what extent should the private lives of political figures remain private? Discuss these questions as a class.

War!

Reading Strategy

Before you begin reading this section, think about what you already know about the events leading up to the Second World War from the previous chapter.

As you discovered in Chapter 3, in the 1930s events in Europe were leading the world to the brink of another war. With growing concern, the League of Nations watched Germany's fascist dictator, Adolf Hitler, extend his power across Europe. In March 1939, Hitler dismissed the Munich Agreement as a "scrap of paper" as the German army invaded Czechoslovakia. The British prime minister, Neville Chamberlain, warned Hitler that Britain was prepared to go to war to prevent Germany from gaining any more territory in Europe.

Hitler had joined forces with the Italian dictator Benito Mussolini to form the **Axis** alliance. At the same time, Germany signed a non-aggression pact with the Soviet Union. The two countries agreed not to take military action against one another for 10 years. Both sides were buying time. Hitler needed time to neutralize the powers of Western Europe. The Soviet leader, Josef Stalin, needed time to rebuild the Soviet army.

Assured that the Soviet Union no longer posed a threat to his ambitions, Hitler launched a swift and devastating *blitzkrieg*, or "lightning war," against Poland on 1 September 1939. German tanks rolled into the country as the air force launched an aerial bombardment. Fear and confusion swept across Poland as German troops stormed in after the tanks and seized control of the country. Britain and France declared war on Germany on 3 September 1939.

Figure 4.4 Hitler was a powerful speaker who drew huge crowds to his public appearances. Why do you think some political leaders are able to attract such widespread public support?

ISSUES

The Road to War

The issue: What was the most important event on the road to war?

1931
Japan invades Manchuria

1933
Germany rearms;
Violates Versailles

1935
Mussolini invades Ethiopia

1936
Germany occupies
the Rhineland

1937
Japan launches war
against China

1938 (March)
Germany occupies Austria

1938 (September)
Munich Agreement
allows Hitler to take over
Sudetenland

1938 (October)
Hitler and Mussolini sign
the Axis Pact to
divide Europe

1939 (March)
Germany occupies
Czechoslovakia

1939 (August)
Germany and the
Soviet Union sign a
non-aggression pact

1939 (September 1)
Germany invades
Poland

1939 (September 3)
Britain and France
declare War

Figure 4.5 The steps leading up to war unfolded over a decade. At each stage, the League of Nations failed to take action against the aggressor.

Throughout the 1930s, a series of events were leading up to the massive and horrific conflict that was the Second World War. Yet as each event unfolded, the League of Nations and the leaders of the most powerful countries in Europe, Britain and France, maintained a policy of appeasement. In the end, however, Hitler broke promise after promise as he extended his power over Europe.

The complex road to war leads to some important questions:

- What was the most important step on the road to war?
- Was there a point at which Western leaders could, or should, have stopped Hitler—or was war inevitable?

Now that you have read about the steps leading to war on the left, read the viewpoints below and respond to the questions that follow.

"The Covenant of the League has been violated … We shall therefore have to climb down, and Hitler has scored. We must swallow this humiliation as best we may, and be prepared to become the laughing stock of Europe."

Source: British diplomat Harold Nicholson after Hitler seized the Rhineland, March 1936.

"We must always demand so much that we can never be satisfied."

Source: Adolf Hitler on his strategy during the Munich Agreement, September 1938.

"It is a total defeat. Czechoslovakia will be swallowed up by the Nazis. And do not suppose that this is the end. This is only the beginning."

Source: Winston Churchill on the Munich Agreement, September 1938.

Responding

1. In your opinion, what was the most important event on the road to war? Do you think war was inevitable? Give reasons for your response.
2. Canada had gained independence over its foreign policy in 1931. As a class, discuss what responsibilities a country has when it has gained the right to independence.

"We stand for the defence of Canada; we stand for co-operation of this country at the side of Great Britain; and if this house will not support us in that policy, it will have to find some other government to assume the responsibilities of the present."

–Prime Minister Mackenzie King, House of Commons, 10 September 1939

Canada Declares War

In the First World War, when Britain declared war, Canada was automatically at war, too. Now that Canada had control over its foreign policy, the government had to decide what responsibility it had to stop Hitler and the spread of fascism in Europe. English Canadians wanted Canada to stand by Britain and do whatever was necessary in the war effort. French Canadians supported a declaration of war, but opposed compulsory military service. Once again, war in Europe threatened national unity here at home.

From a military perspective, Canada was not ready for war. During the Depression, the armed forces had deteriorated. By 1939, there were only 8000 personnel in the army, navy, and air force combined and there were few modern naval ships or military aircraft. Yet King faced growing pressure to join the fight in Europe. This pressure only intensified after a German submarine torpedoed a British passenger ship on September 3, killing over 100 passengers, including a young Canadian girl. Her death became a rallying point for joining the war.

Figure 4.6 Newspapers screamed headlines like these at the outbreak of the Second World War. What powerful words are used to describe the coming of war?

After calling a special sitting of Parliament and holding a vote in the House of Commons, King declared war on Germany on 10 September 1939. It was a historic event in Canadian history—the first time Canada had declared war as an independent nation.

Germany Occupies Europe

The period between September 1939 and May 1940 was known as "the phony war." There was little real combat as both sides built up their armies and arsenals. In the spring of 1940, though, things changed. Germany launched a series of blitzkrieg attacks and quickly occupied Denmark, Norway, the Netherlands, Belgium, and Luxembourg.

France was next. With an army of six million, France had one of the most powerful military forces in the world. The Allies expected French forces to be embroiled in a long and fierce campaign against the German invaders. However, they were unable to stop the rapidly advancing German military machine. Just 10 days after invading the country, Nazi soldiers had pushed all the way to Paris and now occupied the city.

Trapped at Dunkirk

As German troops spread across the country, thousands of British troops raced across the English Channel to help defend France. In May 1940, the German army descended upon the Channel coast at Dunkirk, trapping British and French soldiers on three sides. For the British, the only escape was by sea. For five days, warships, fishing boats, ferries, barges, and rowboats evacuated 300 000 British soldiers from Dunkirk to England. One million French soldiers had only one option, however—to surrender. Within six weeks, France had fallen to the Germans. Britain now stood alone against the Axis powers.

"We shall defend our island, whatever the cost may be. We shall fight on the beaches, we shall fight on the landing-grounds, we shall fight in the fields and in the streets, we shall fight in the hills. We shall never surrender."

–British Prime Minister Winston Churchill, 1940

Challenge and Response

1. What challenges did Canada face in deciding to declare war?
2. During the evacuation at Dunkirk, Britain had to leave behind most of its military hardware. What impact do you think this had on Canada's role as a supplier of military equipment?

The Canadian Forces

Canadians of all backgrounds answered the call to duty in the Second World War. In 1939, half of Canada's population was of British heritage. Many people still had close ties to Britain. As a result, thousands of Canadians of English, Scottish, Irish, and Welsh heritage enthusiastically supported the war.

For more than 200 years, French Canadians had been separated from France politically and culturally. As a result, their feelings of loyalty to France were not as strong as the feelings many English Canadians had for Britain. They certainly felt no loyalty toward the British Empire. Still, many French Canadians volunteered to take part in the liberation of Europe, making up 19 per cent

Figure 4.7   In October 2005, Aboriginal veterans returned to the Canadian War Cemetery at Beny-sur-Mer, France, on an Aboriginal Spiritual Journey. These First Nations ceremonial performers honoured the Aboriginal veterans of the battlefields of Europe.

of the military. Many of the French-speaking volunteers played a valuable role as undercover agents in Nazi-occupied France.

Almost 50 000 Canadian women volunteered for active duty. At first, they were restricted to non-combat roles, working as drivers, radio operators, clerks, and military aids. Gradually, however, they took on roles as mechanics, technicians, and spies. Women were not treated as equals and did not receive the same pay or benefits as men, even when they were doing the same jobs.

Many Canadians enlisted in the armed forces despite the fact that they faced prejudice and discrimination at home. Aboriginal peoples and Canadians of Asian heritage did not have the right to vote and they were not allowed to enlist in the air force or the navy. Still, more than 3000 Aboriginal people, including 72 women, joined the army, even though enlisting meant they lost their **status**. For many, volunteering for duty continued a tradition that had started in the War of 1812 and continued in the First World War. Sons and daughters of veterans of the first war followed their parents' example. Many veterans of the first war who were too old for active duty joined the Veterans Guard and served their country on the home front. When the war was over, however, the contributions of Aboriginal soldiers were ignored. They were denied the rights and benefits other Canadian war veterans had.

In 1940, the Canadian military attempted to ban Canadians of African heritage from enlisting. Although the attempt failed, in the early years of the war, the military rejected many of these volunteers. As the war dragged on, however, more soldiers were needed overseas. In response, the military accepted several thousand Canadian volunteers of African descent. Unlike the First World War, in which they were confined to their own battalions separate from the rest of the military, this time Canadians of African heritage were integrated throughout the army, navy, and air force.

When the war began, Canadians of Chinese and Japanese heritage were discouraged from enlisting.

their patriotism. Many who tried were turned away. Most of those who were accepted served as translators for Japanese prisoners of war and as broadcasters of Allied propaganda.

More than 17 000 Canadians of Jewish faith volunteered for military service—20 per cent of the total Jewish male population in Canada. The actual number of soldiers may have been even higher. Many soldiers of the Jewish faith concealed their religious identity out of fear of the way they would be treated if they were captured by the Nazis.

Figure 4.8 Allan Bundy was a university student from Dartmouth, Nova Scotia. He was accepted into the air force in 1943 after being rejected on racial grounds four years earlier. Why do you think people still volunteered even after they had faced discrimination earlier?

When war in the Pacific broke out, however, the Allies needed interpreters and translators who could speak Japanese, Mandarin, and other Asian languages. As a result, Canada eased its restrictions. Hundreds of Canadians of Chinese descent volunteered. Many of these soldiers served in an elite unit trained to fight in the jungles of Asia. Some worked as spies behind enemy lines. Since Canada was at war with Japan, many Canadians of Japanese heritage wanted to enlist to prove

Figure 4.9 Many war graves of Canadian soldiers are marked with the Jewish Star of David as well as the Canadian maple leaf. How do these symbols honour the soldiers buried here?

Responding

1. Assume the role of a member of one of the groups you have read about here. Write a letter to the prime minister expressing your feelings about your participation in the war.

Years of Crisis

"Hitler knows that he will have to break us in this island or lose the war. If we can stand up to him all Europe may be free and the life of the world may move forward into broad, sunlit uplands; …
Let us therefore brace ourselves to our duty and so bear ourselves that if the British Commonwealth and its Empire lasts for a thousand years, men will still say 'This was their finest hour.'"

–British Prime Minister Winston Churchill, speaking about the forthcoming Battle of Britain in the British House of Commons, 18 June 1940

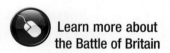
Learn more about the Battle of Britain

In May 1940, the western half of Europe was in Hitler's hands. Only the English Channel and the powerful British navy separated Britain from the new German Empire. Hitler was convinced that Britain had no choice but to seek peace. But Britain's new prime minister, Winston Churchill, had always opposed the policy of appeasement. He was not about to trust Hitler now, nor was he about to discuss any peace agreement. An angry Hitler then set plans in motion to invade Britain.

The Battle of Britain

Hitler planned to bomb Britain into submission and pave the way for a direct invasion. The German *Luftwaffe* (air force) bombarded Britain's airfields, radar installations, factories, and ports. In September, they began bombing London and other major cities in what the British called "the Blitz." Night after night, people huddled in underground bomb shelters, emerging each morning to survey the damage and clean up the wreckage.

Eighty Canadian pilots joined hundreds of pilots from Britain's Royal Air Force (RAF) to repel the attacks and gain control of the skies over Britain and the English Channel. It was a dangerous mission. In the early days, 16 Canadian pilots were killed over the skies of Britain. Over time, however, their success rate improved. When the Battle of Britain was over, Allied pilots had shot down almost 3000 German aircraft while losing only 900 of their own.

Although the fighting raged on in the skies over Britain until May 1941, by October 1940 Hitler knew the Battle of Britain was lost. He postponed plans for an invasion and refocused his attention on the Soviet Union. The Battle of Britain was Germany's first defeat. Although more than 40 000 British men, women, and children died in the Blitz, it was a major victory for Britain. It had prevented Germany from launching a naval invasion against the island nation and had boosted the sagging morale of the British people.

Figure 4.10 In 1941, British Prime Minister Winston Churchill (right) paid a visit to Prime Minister King in Canada. Why do you think it was important for Allied leaders to meet face to face?

MAP STUDY: The Battle of the Atlantic

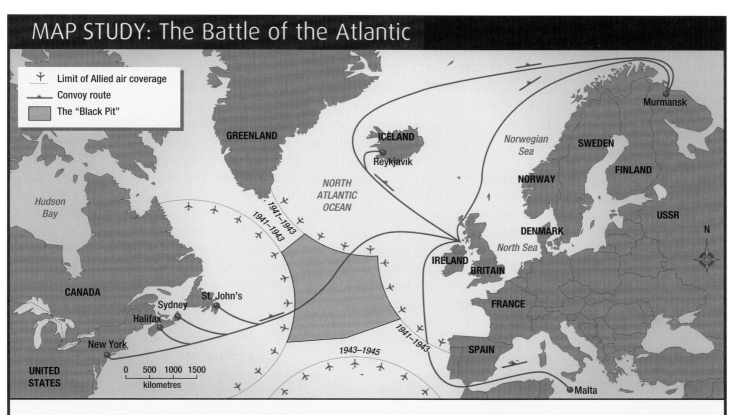

Source: Daniel Francis, et al., *Canadian Issues*, (Don Mills: Oxford University Press Canada, 1998), 159.

Figure 4.11 This map shows the convoy system and the Battle of the Atlantic. The battle built Canada's naval power. When the war began, the Canadian navy consisted of just 11 ships and 20 000 sailors. When it ended, Canada had the third-largest navy in the world, with close to 400 ships and 113 000 personnel, including 7000 women.

The Battle of the Atlantic was a naval operation designed to prevent Canadian and American troops, munitions, and supplies from reaching Britain. The ships crossed the Atlantic in convoys of 50 to 60. A naval destroyer and three or four small, fast ships called corvettes escorted each convoy. The corvettes kept watch for German U-boats prowling the waters.

More than 12 000 **merchant mariners** worked on the convoys. Theirs was a dangerous job. One in ten lost their lives—a death rate five times higher than that of the Royal Canadian Navy (RCN).

Even in Canada's coastal waters, the sailors were at risk. Between spring 1942 and autumn 1944, German subs in the Gulf of St. Lawrence sank 23 ships, killing 340 people. In all, Canada lost 2210 lives and 24 warships in the Battle of the Atlantic.

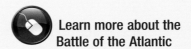

Learn more about the Battle of the Atlantic

Analysis and Response

1. The "Black Pit" was an area in the middle of the Atlantic Ocean where the air force was unable to provide cover for the convoys. Why do you think it was not possible to cover the ships here?
2. Imagine you are a member of the merchant marines during the Battle of the Atlantic. Write a short letter to your family describing your life on board ship.

"We had no protection. We were in a cross-fire from the two high sides of the beach and a frontal fire which covered the whole beach. We were just pinned down. We couldn't walk back, we couldn't get forward, we couldn't go on the sides. We were dead, really, before dying."

–Colonel Dollard Ménard, Les Fusiliers Mont-Royal, veteran of the Battle of Dieppe

"There were pieces of bodies everywhere. The water had turned a sickly pink colour, and the air was filled with the sweet smell of blood and death … There were arms and legs, and boots with feet in them everywhere. The stones were stained with blood and there were men still burning, stuck in the barbed wire with packs of explosives on their backs."

–Jack A. Poolton, Canadian veteran who fought at Dieppe

 Learn more about the Dieppe Raid

War on the Eastern Front

In September 1940, Germany and Italy extended their alliance to include Japan. (The three countries had a secret pact to protect one another in case of invasion by the Soviet Union.) Then, in June 1941, Hitler broke his non-aggression pact and invaded the Soviet Union. Hitler wanted to destroy communism and seize control of the rich natural resources of the USSR, particularly oil. He was confident of another quick victory as German troops overwhelmed an ill-equipped and disorganized Soviet army. Within three months, the Germans had conquered Ukraine and occupied Leningrad (now St. Petersburg). They were now just 20 kilometres from the capital of Moscow.

By 5 December 1941, however, the Germans had stopped in their tracks. The long march through the country's rugged landscape in a bitterly cold winter had left the soldiers exhausted. Then, on December 6, the Soviet Union launched a counterattack. German fortunes were beginning to change. In the spring of 1942, they won some victories but suffered major losses, too. For the next two years, the Soviet and German armies fought some of the fiercest and deadliest battles in history. Slowly, the Soviets began to force German troops to retreat.

Rehearsal for Invasion

By 1942, the Allies were making plans to retake Europe. They decided to test Germany's defenses along the French coast and gather intelligence to see how Germany might respond to a full-scale invasion. They launched a series of quick raids across the English Channel.

Raid on Dieppe

On 19 August 1942, 6100 Allied troops, including 5000 Canadians, landed on the beaches of the French town of Dieppe. But the raid was doomed from the start. A chance encounter with a German convoy on the English Channel had alerted the Germans to the impending raid. As a result, the landing was delayed until daylight. The Allies had lost both the element of surprise and the cover of darkness. As Allied troops scrambled ashore, artillery fire rained down on them from German troops perched on the cliffs above Dieppe. Tanks that were supposed to support the troops sank down in the deep water and on the rocky beach. A steep seawall created a difficult barrier for the soldiers that made it across the beach, leaving them exposed to heavy machine-gun fire.

Most soldiers tried to get back to their ships, but they were open targets. The battle that day lasted for over nine hours. Of the 5000 Canadians who took part, 913 lost their lives, while another 1950 were taken as prisoners of war.

The first major battle for Canadians on the Western Front was a disaster. However, Allied commanders learned some valuable lessons. They decided to push back a full-scale invasion to regain control of Europe from 1943 to 1944 to give them more time to strengthen their forces. They changed their military strategy by deciding to launch a massive aerial strike ahead of the invasion to weaken German defenses. The invasion would take place at less secure areas along the French coast rather than at heavily defended ports like Dieppe.

Figure 4.12 Dieppe was a disaster for the Canadians. It raised many questions about the Allies' ability to effectively plan and execute an invasion. Today, people still debate why it was such a disaster.

Challenge and Response

1. Following the Battle of Britain, Winston Churchill said, "Never in the field of human conflict was so much owed by so many to so few." What do you think he meant? Do you agree with him? Give reasons for your response.

2. Complete a cause-and-effect organizer similar to the one shown here to explain the raid on Dieppe.

Causes of the Raid	Why It Failed	Effects

The Liberation of Europe

"Fresh graves show where some of the fiercest battles have raged. On some, the only indication of whether the grave is friend or foe is a Canadian or German helmet atop a rifle or rough wooden marker. Ahead, the sounds of battle grow louder and fiercer…"

–Lieutenant Charles Sydney Frost, Princess Patricia's Canadian Light Infantry, September 1944

Despite the disaster at Dieppe, the fortunes of war were changing for the Allies. In the Soviet Union, the invading German army had been defeated in the Battle of Stalingrad. German forces were no longer gaining ground. The stage was set for the Allies to begin the fight to take back Europe.

The Italian Campaign

In July 1943, Canadian, British, and American forces launched an assault on the Italian island of Sicily. Tired of war, the Italians offered little resistance to the Allied invaders. By September, the Allies had pushed on to the Italian mainland. The battle for the mainland would be a greater challenge for the Allies, though. They encountered fierce resistance from German soldiers sent in to reinforce the country.

The Battle of Ortona

The biggest test for Canadian troops was the Battle of Ortona. The ancient town on the Adriatic coast was a natural fortress. Its narrow, twisting streets made it impossible for the soldiers to use tanks. Instead, they moved through the town on foot, carefully navigating around the debris left behind after German troops blew up buildings to make the streets impassable.

The Canadians had to take the town house by house, street by street, using a technique called "mouseholing." Soldiers blasted a hole in the outside wall of a house at the end of a street. Then they threw in grenades to clear the room before charging inside and clearing the rest of the house with machine-gun fire. Next, they moved to the attic, blasted a hole in the wall to the adjoining house, and repeated the process all over again.

For a week, the Canadians fought a fierce battle. Finally, two days after Christmas, they succeeded in driving the Germans out of Ortona. The loss of life was staggering—over 2300 officers and soldiers died in the fighting. The techniques the Canadians used at Ortona became the model for urban warfare for the duration of the war. In Italy, the fighting continued until June 1944, when the Allies finally gained control of Rome. In all, more than 90 000 Canadians fought in Italy and 5400 lost their lives.

Figure 4.13 This painting is titled *Via Dolorosa, Ortona* by Charles Comfort. It is the artist's rendition of the battle at Ortona. What does it reveal about the nature of the battle?

Learn more about the Italian campaign and the Battle of Ortona

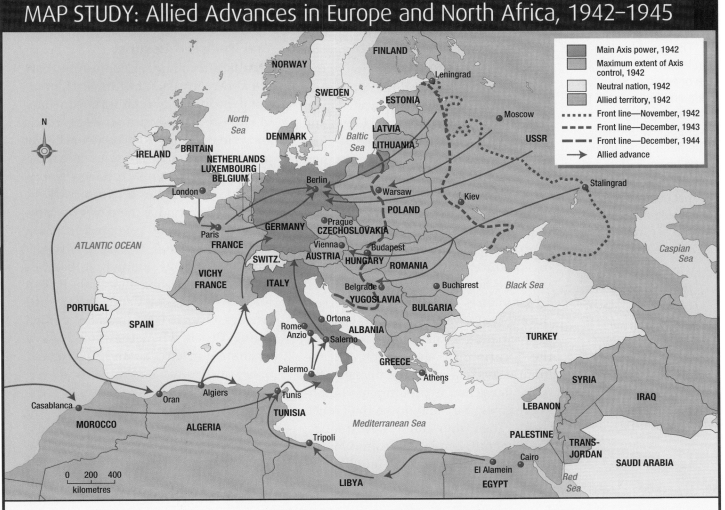

MAP STUDY: Allied Advances in Europe and North Africa, 1942–1945

Legend:
- Main Axis power, 1942
- Maximum extent of Axis control, 1942
- Neutral nation, 1942
- Allied territory, 1942
- Front line—November, 1942
- Front line—December, 1943
- Front line—December, 1944
- Allied advance

Source: Daniel Francis, et al., *Canadian Issues*, (Don Mills: Oxford University Press Canada, 1998), 150.

Figure 4.14 This map shows the occupation of Europe and northern Africa and Allied advances throughout the region between 1942 and 1945.

By the end of 1941, the war in Europe had spread into northern Africa into countries that were once colonies of the imperialist powers of Europe. It was a decidedly different war from the First World War. The days of trench warfare were gone. Modern technology allowed the war to escalate rapidly. Tanks rolled in and occupied vast expanses of enemy territory in just a few days. Aircraft bombarded helpless enemy civilians and soldiers into submission in just a few hours. As a result, the number of civilian casualties was far greater than in previous wars. In fact, the number of wounded and dead civilians in the Second World War far outnumbered the casualties sustained by the military on both sides.

Analysis and Response

1. What does the movement of Allied advances across Europe and northern Africa suggest about the impact on civilian populations?
2. What impact do you think this new type of war had on the resources of the warring countries?

"The great landing in Western Europe is the opening of what we hope and believe will be the decisive phase of the war against Germany. The fighting is certain to be heavy, bitter, and costly. You must not expect early results. We should be prepared for local reverses as well as success."

—Prime Minister
William Lyon Mackenzie
King, 1944

Learn more
about D-Day

D-Day

By the spring of 1944, after almost five years of bloody combat, the Allies were ready to launch their long-awaited invasion of Europe. Code-named Operation Overlord, the invasion involved close to one million British, American, and Canadian troops steaming across the English Channel to storm the beaches of France.

The Allies were determined to keep their plans a secret. They wanted to convince the Germans that their intended target was Pas de Calais, just 50 kilometres from the English coast. But the real invasion was to take place at Normandy to the south. To disguise the location of the attack, in the months leading up to the invasion the Allies launched a preliminary bombing campaign up and down the French coast. Then they built fake planes, landing craft, and tanks around Pas de Calais to mislead German intelligence.

The Invasion Begins

Shortly after midnight on 6 June 1944 the D-Day invasion began. First, paratroopers dropped in behind enemy lines to capture and secure strategic roads and bridges. Then 2000 bombers began pounding German defenses in preparation for thousands of Allied troops to storm the beaches of Normandy.

Sailing in under the cover of darkness, Allied troops prepared to break down the walls of "Fortress Europe." American troops landed at beaches code-named Omaha and Utah. British soldiers landed at Gold and Sword beaches. Over 15 000 Canadians landed at Juno Beach, where they faced heavy machine-gun fire as they navigated their way around landmines scattered on the beach. The casualties for the day were high: 335 Canadian soldiers killed and another 700 wounded.

Still, by the end of the day the Canadians had secured Juno Beach—the only Allied force to achieve its goal on the first day. They had learned the lessons of Dieppe well.

By the end of the first week, over 300 000 Allied soldiers had landed safely on the beaches of Normandy. With the battle now raging on three fronts—east, west, and south—the Germans retreated. Yet they would continue to put up fierce resistance for another year before the Allies could claim victory.

Victory in Europe

Following D-Day, Allied forces pushed the Germans east to the capital city of Berlin. As they crossed the continent, they liberated country after country from their long years of Nazi occupation. In April 1945, Soviet troops were the first to reach Berlin. As they occupied the city, Hitler learned of the fate

Figure 4.15 D-Day was the largest seaborne invasion in history. It involved 700 warships and 4000 landing craft, supported by 11 000 planes providing air cover. Canada provided 110 ships and 33 air squadrons in addition to 30 000 troops. How might the lessons learned at Dieppe have helped the Canadians?

of his ally, Benito Mussolini. He was captured and executed by his own people. To escape a similar fate, Hitler committed suicide in his underground bunker in Berlin on 30 April 1945. His death marked the symbolic end to the war in Europe. A week later, on May 7, Germany surrendered. On 8 May 1945, the Allies celebrated **VE Day**. Across the country, Canadians took to the streets to express their joy and relief that, at last, there was victory in Europe.

> "We often overlook some of the most important Canadians ever: those who fought in the world wars ... There needs to be more done to celebrate these heroes ... We hear all about the great battles that we won ... but we need to see, learn, and hear more about some of the battles that didn't go entirely well ... No matter what the outcome was, we need to honour those who fought and give them the respect that they deserve."
>
> –Andrew Murray, Morell Regional High School, 2007

Figure 4.16 After the Normandy invasion, 175 000 Canadian troops led the liberation of the Netherlands and 7600 Canadians lost their lives. Canada earned the gratitude of the Dutch people. Today, the Dutch still show their gratitude to returning Canadian veterans. Why do you think the Dutch show such respect for the Canadians so many years after the war? Do you think Canadians treat our war veterans with the respect they deserve? Give reasons for your response.

Learn more about the defeat of Germany and the final days of the war

Challenge and Response

1. Why do you think it was important for the Allies to conquer Italy?
2. Create a mind map or other organizer to summarize the different ways Canadians were involved in the war in Europe.

Reading Strategy

Before you begin reading this section, think about what you already know about the Holocaust. Then, as you read the quotations, reflect on the question of individual responsibility when carrying out crimes against humanity.

"The Jews are the eternal enemies of the German people and must be exterminated. All Jews within our grasp are to be destroyed without exception, now, during the war. If we do not succeed in destroying the biological substance of the Jews, the Jews will some day destroy the German people."

–SS Leader Heinrich Himmler on the Nazi's policy toward Jews

"Not far from us, flames were leaping from a ditch, gigantic flames. They were burning something. A lorry drew up at the pit and delivered its load—little children. Babies! Yes, I saw it—saw it with my own eyes ... those children in the flames ... I could not believe it. How could it be possible for them to burn people, children..."

–Elie Wiesel, Auschwitz concentration camp survivor of Hungarian Jewish descent

The Holocaust

In 1942, the Nazis launched the **Final Solution** to what they described as "the Jewish problem." Nazi soldiers rounded up Jewish men, women, and children and shipped them to concentration camps throughout Germany and Poland. The camps became prisons for other "undesirables," such as communists, homosexuals, Roma (Gypsies), and people with mental or physical illnesses.

When the prisoners arrived at the camps, soldiers divided them into two groups. The strongest prisoners went to work in labour camps. The rest went directly to the gas chambers. Men, women, and children were herded into large rooms disguised as showers. Once inside, a deadly gas filled the room. Only then were the innocent victims aware of their fate.

The gas chambers were highly efficient killing machines. It took only a few minutes for thousands of people to die. Afterwards, a special detachment of prisoners had the gruesome task of dragging out the bodies and stripping them of everything, including gold fillings from teeth. Then, they placed the remains in massive ovens for cremation.

Life in the Camps

Those who went to work in the Nazi labour camps worked hard for at least 16 hours a day. They lived in filthy, unheated quarters, with only a bowl of broth and a piece of bread to eat each

Figure 4.17   The death camps were designed to kill the greatest number of people in the shortest amount of time. Auschwitz was one of the most notorious of the camps. The Nazis exterminated more than 6000 people there every day. After the war, the Allies decided to preserve the camps to serve as permanent reminders of the Holocaust. Why is it important to understand what happens when hatred leads to tragedy?

day. Electrified barbed-wire fences surrounded the camps. Armed guards stood in their watchtowers, eager to shoot anyone who stepped out of line. Some prisoners suffered as human guinea pigs as Nazi scientists conducted horrific medical experiments on them.

There was little opportunity to resist the Nazis' brutality. Yet some prisoners fought back in whatever ways they could. Some sabotaged the factories where they worked. Some tried to escape and a few even succeeded. The defiance of a few gave a glimmer of hope to thousands more who suffered through the brutality of the camps.

Liberating the Camps

As Allied forces moved through Europe, they discovered the horrendous secret the Nazis had been hiding. Although there had been rumours of the death camps, few people believed such massive **genocide** could take place in the "enlightened" era of the twentieth century. Now, though, as the Allies liberated the camps, the world witnessed the horror and brutality that happens when hatred overrules humanity.

War Crimes

In all, six million Jews lost their lives at the hands of the Nazis. The atrocities were well documented by the Nazis themselves. They kept meticulous records of the number of prisoners killed in the gas chambers. They recorded the horror of life in the camps in official photographs and films.

After the war, the Allies used this evidence as the basis for charging Nazi leaders with war crimes and crimes against humanity. In 1946, 22 high-ranking Nazis went on trial in a special criminal court in Nuremberg, Germany. It was a historic event. It established for the first time that those who commit atrocities in times of war are responsible for their actions. Soldiers who murdered civilians or herded them into the gas chambers could not deny their personal responsibility by claiming they were following orders.

Of the 22 original defendants at the Nuremberg Trials, 12 received the death penalty. Seven others received prison terms. Three were found not guilty. The trials continued until 1949. Afterwards, the hunt for Nazi war criminals continued. Over the years, many of those in hiding were found and tried, although the majority managed to avoid facing punishment for their crimes.

> "I felt as if I were in another world … What we discovered was anti-Semitism, but above all it showed where the descent into barbarism can lead. This was not a chance mishap, but a systematic death machine, a truly scientific industry of elimination, a hell fabricated with great care."
>
> –René Lévesque, war reporter

> "It took from three to fifteen minutes to kill the people in the death chamber … We knew when the people were dead because their screaming stopped … I estimate that at least 250 000 victims were executed and exterminated [at Auschwitz] by gassing and burning, and at least another half million succumbed to starvation and disease."
>
> –Nazi commandant Rudolf Hoess, from testimony at the Nuremburg Trials, 1946

Challenge and Response

1. Do you think it was important for the Allies to hold the Nazis accountable for war crimes and crimes against humanity? Give reasons for your response.
2. What should countries like Canada do to stop one group of people from committing genocide against another group? Discuss your ideas as a class.
3. Find out more about a contemporary example of genocide. Working with a partner, prepare a report of your findings.

Learn more about the Holocaust and the Nuremberg Trials

War in the Pacific

"Canadian soldiers did an excellent job at Hong Kong, and despite its failure they fought with bravery to the end ... When Canadians fought, they fought with honour ... I am proud to be Canadian because of people like this."

–Wes Unwin,
Port Perry High
School, 2005

 **Learn more about the battle for Hong Kong and Canadian prisoners of war**

Although the United States had provided supplies and munitions to Britain in the war in Europe, officially the US remained neutral. That changed abruptly on 7 December 1941 when Japan launched a surprise attack on the US military base at Pearl Harbor, Hawaii. The United States immediately declared war on Japan. Germany and Italy declared war on the United States. In a matter of hours, the Second World War had mushroomed into another global conflict.

The Battle for Hong Kong

In the fall of 1941, Japanese troops invaded parts of China, where they routinely defeated the poorly equipped Chinese army. Fearing its Pacific colony of Hong Kong would be next, in September 1941 British Prime Minister Winston Churchill asked Canada to send troops to help with defence. It was a controversial request. Many British leaders believed defending the tiny colony was an impossible task. Others argued that sending in reinforcements provided moral support. King agreed to Churchill's request. In November, 2000 soldiers from Québec's Royal Rifles and the Winnipeg Grenadiers arrived in Hong Kong.

On December 7, just hours after the attack on Pearl Harbor, over 50 000 Japanese troops invaded Hong Kong. With only 15 000 troops, the Allies were badly outnumbered. Without an air force or navy, they had little chance of fighting back the Japanese invaders.

Still, they defended the colony as best they could for 17 days before the British commander surrendered on Christmas Day, 1941.

Japanese Occupation

While the battle for Hong Kong was over, the ordeal for the surviving soldiers and civilians had just begun. It was the cultural tradition of Japanese soldiers to fight to the end. They never surrendered—it was considered dishonourable. Therefore, when their enemies surrendered, they did not respect them in the same way as the Allied forces did. When they occupied conquered territories, they held their captives in contempt. They treated both civilians and soldiers with extreme cruelty. In Hong Kong, they set fire to buildings and looted homes. Some soldiers raped and murdered women. Others tortured and killed Allied soldiers and civilians. The atrocities committed the day of the surrender were so horrific that the Allies called the day "Black Christmas."

Soldiers captured as prisoners of war faced harsh treatment, as well. After surrendering in Hong Kong, 1685 Canadians were imprisoned in prisoner-of-war camps. They stayed barely alive on starvation diets. Many were tortured. Some were forced into labour. While 300 Canadians died in the battle for Hong Kong, 267 more died from their treatment in the prison camps. This raised even more questions about the decision to send in Canadian troops on a dangerous mission that most believed they could never win.

ISSUES

Prisoners of War

The issue: What social, cultural, and intellectual factors should govern the ethical treatment of prisoners of war?

During the Second World War, both sides accused one another of committing atrocities, including murder. In 1949, the Geneva Convention was expanded to provide as much protection as possible from the horrors of war for both soldiers and civilians. Violating the rules of the Geneva Convention may constitute either war crimes or crimes against humanity.

As you explore this issue, think about these questions:
- What rights should prisoners of war have?
- What should happen to those who violate these rights?
- At what point does killing the enemy become murder instead of an act of war?

Read the following scenarios. Two describe conditions for prisoners of war during the Second World War. The last one raises questions about prisoners' rights today.

"Eighty prisoners went out. Four of them were recaptured almost at once. The others got away. The Germans turned more than 2000 guards out to search the countryside; ... Finally a group was recaptured and removed to Gestapo headquarters ... They were interrogated for hours. Then came the word that 47 of the boys had been shot. It's nonsense to say it was a second attempt to escape. It is impossible and no one would have tried it ... Our men were deliberately shot. There is no doubt about it ... It was deliberate and it was murder."

Source: RCAF squadron leader R.H. Boulton, Ottawa, 26 June 1942.

"The bodies of 17 German servicemen lie at rest in a small military cemetery on the snowy, windswept hills overlooking the Abitibi River ... Through the uncertain tides of war, their destiny was death in a wild, rugged land, 4000 miles [6437 kilometres] away from home ... Buried in this remote forest plot are German soldiers, sailors, and airmen who died during the Second World War at the Monteith prisoner-of-war camp ... Of the hundreds of men imprisoned at the camp or employed in bush work across the north, only these 17 were left behind. Most of the 17 died from the after-effects of wounds received in battle."

Source: Don Delaplante, "German POW's buried in bleak northern bush." *Globe and Mail*, 12 April 1950.

"As time passes, it grows undeniable that transferring detainees to Afghanistan is a source of shame. Even the Afghan government's own human-rights watchdog concedes that torture is 'a routine part of police procedures' ... Thus, when Canadian soldiers follow standing orders and transfer men to self-confessed torturers, they could be, through no fault of their own, aiding and abetting that offence—which makes them prosecutable for war crimes."

Source: Amir Attaran, professor of law, The University of Ottawa, "Afghan detainees: treat 'em right." *Globe and Mail*, 9 March 2007.

Responding

1. To what extent do you think each of these scenarios violates the rights of prisoners of war? Explain your response.
2. Are there any other situations in the world today in which prisoners of war are denied their rights? Present your findings in an oral or written report, giving evidence to support your position.

The Birth of the Atomic Age

Learn more about the Manhattan Project

> "Within a few days at the latest the power of the atomic bomb will be disclosed ... I feel that we are approaching a moment of terror to mankind, for it means that under the stress of war men have at last not only found but created the Frankenstein which conceivably could destroy the human race."
>
> –Prime Minister William Lyon Mackenzie King, in his diary, 27 July 1945

In 1939, a German-Jewish scientist named Albert Einstein warned the United States that Germany was developing a bomb capable of mass destruction. In response, Roosevelt formed the Manhattan Project—a group of American, Canadian, and other Allied scientists in a top-secret race to produce the world's first atomic bomb. (Canada's involvement also included a laboratory in Montréal, uranium from a mine in the Northwest Territories, and a uranium refinery in Ontario.) In July 1945, the atomic age was born when the Americans successfully tested the first **weapon of mass destruction** in the New Mexico desert.

Soon, the bomb would be put to the real test. By 1945, American forces had succeeded in pushing Japanese troops out of many of the Pacific islands they occupied. Yet their victories had come at the cost of many casualties. Conquering Japan through direct invasion would likely cost the lives of many Allied soldiers—perhaps as many as a million. As a result, newly elected US President Harry Truman chose to end the war using the Americans' newest weapon—the atomic bomb.

The following month, on 6 August 1945, the United States dropped the first of two atomic bombs on Japan. Hiroshima, a city of 340 000 people and an important military and industrial centre, was the first target. As the bomb dropped, a lightning flash burst across the sky. In seconds, a giant mushroom cloud of poisonous gases and smoke hovered over the city. It is estimated that more than 75 000 people were killed instantly. Thousands more died from burns and radiation poisoning in the hours, days, and weeks that followed.

When Japan still refused to surrender, the United States dropped a second bomb on Nagasaki three days later. Another 40 000 people died instantly. On 15 August 1945, Japan surrendered unconditionally. War in the Pacific was over. The effects of the atomic bombs, however, would last for years as over the next decade half a million people died from radiation poisoning.

A New World Order

With the fall of Japan, the Second World War was finally over. In all, over 62 million people had died—an average of one person every three seconds, day and night, for six years. Most of the casualties were innocent civilians caught in a global battle for power and supremacy. The use of the atomic bomb to end the war in the Pacific marked a significant change in the world. It signalled to the Soviet Union—a growing international power in its own right—that the United States was a power to contend with. This set the stage for a new world order as the United States and the Soviet Union became engaged in a battle for world supremacy in the **Cold War**—a new type of war that would divide the world for much of the second half of the twentieth century.

Learn more about the bombing of Hiroshima and Nagasaki

Figure 4.18 Japan had been the target of massive Allied bombing raids that had destroyed cities and killed thousands of people before the US dropped the bombs. On a single day in March 1945 alone, more than 100 000 residents of Tokyo were killed in a bombing raid. Why was the decision to drop the atomic bombs so controversial? What were the ethical and moral implications about using such deadly bombs?

Challenge and Response

1. Do you think the Americans were justified in using atomic bombs on civilian targets? Give reasons for your response.
2. Today's weapons of mass destruction are many times more powerful than the atomic bombs used in the Second World War. In your opinion, can there ever be any justification for using such weapons? Give reasons for your response.

War on the Home Front

When the war began, Canada's closest international ties were with Britain. By the time the war ended, Canada's key international relationship had permanently shifted to the United States as Canada entered into a series of international agreements.

Wartime Agreements

In December 1939, Britain, Australia, New Zealand, and Canada signed the British Commonwealth Air Training Program (BCATP) to train the Commonwealth's air force pilots in the open spaces and relative safety of Canada. The plan created 107 training schools across the country. In all, over 131 000 pilots and crew trained in Canada. The training program was a major factor in the eventual superiority of the Allied air forces during the war.

In 1940, there was growing concern that if Britain fell to the Nazis, North America would be Hitler's next target. In response, the United States and Canada signed the Ogdensburg Agreement. It created the Permanent Joint Board on Defense to coordinate the defence of both countries, which still exists today.

In 1941, the Lend-Lease Act allowed the United States to manufacture war materials and sell, exchange, lease, or lend them to any country it chose. This meant that Britain could obtain military supplies from the US and delay payment. However, if Britain bought more supplies from the United States, it would buy less from Canada. In response, the Hyde Park Agreement ensured the US bought more war sup-

> "I suppose no more significant agreement has ever been signed by the Government of Canada, or signature placed in the name of Canada to a definitely defined obligation in human life and in dollars and cents."
>
> –Prime Minister Mackenzie King, referring to the BCATP agreement, 17 December 1939

plies from Canada and allowed Britain to buy Canadian supplies under the terms of the Lend-Lease Act.

In 1942, the Americans were concerned about a possible Japanese attack on Alaska. If an invasion took place, they needed access to the remote northwestern corner of the continent. The US reached a deal with Canada to build the Alaska Highway through 2500 kilometres of Canadian wilderness from Dawson Creek, British Columbia, to Fairbanks, Alaska.

A Wartime Economy

The Second World War pulled Canada out of the economic crisis of the Depression. Production in all sectors expanded dramatically. Exports soared. To avoid the greed and price fixing of the First World War, King planned to maintain strict government control over the wartime economy.

One of King's most prominent Cabinet ministers, C.D. Howe, was in charge of building the wartime economy. With the help of the nation's business leaders, Howe expanded existing industries and created new ones. The auto industry switched from producing cars to making jeeps and army trucks. Manufacturers of railway cars made tanks instead. The government created 28 **Crown corporations** to produce everything from rubber to airplanes. The size of the federal civil service skyrocketed, from 46 000 in 1939 to 116 000 in 1945.

Doing Their Part

As the Second World War raged overseas, on the home front Canadians did their part to support the war effort. To help raise the billions of dollars needed to finance the war, the government issued Victory Bonds. The bonds were a loan to the government. Canadians who bought them received a written guarantee that the government would repay the money with interest. Over the course of the war, Canada's 11 million people raised $8.8 billion in war bonds.

Rationing

To ensure resources were available for wartime production, Howe established the Wartime Prices and Trade Board (WPTB) to control prices and prevent inflation and to distribute resources. Every man, woman, and child was issued a ration card to buy gasoline, sugar, meat, tea, and other essentials. The cards limited the amount of goods people could buy, but ensured that everyone got their fair share. People needed special permits to buy cars, appliances, rubber tires, and other products. Producing goods for the war was the number one priority. Few Canadians complained, though. After 10 years of the Depression, most people were used to doing without. More importantly, compared to the hardships the people of Europe faced, Canadians knew they were lucky.

Women's Wartime Role

By 1941, the booming wartime economy faced a shortage of workers. In response, the government launched a campaign to recruit women into the paid work force. Before the war, only 21 per cent of women worked outside the home. Now, Canadian women by the thousands signed up to serve their country on the home front.

At first, the recruitment campaign targeted only young, unmarried women. By 1943, however, all women—married

or single, with or without children— were encouraged to do their part. Women worked in all industries and all occupations, as welders, machinists, bus drivers, and munitions workers. In rural areas, women ran the farms in the absence of men fighting overseas. Those women who could not join the paid workforce worked as volunteers, knitting warm scarves and socks for the soldiers and serving coffee and sandwiches at army canteens.

For a time, women's new roles allowed them to improve their social and economic status. They made more money than they had ever made in traditional jobs—but they still made less than the men they replaced. When the war was over, most women gave up their jobs to the returning soldiers as social attitudes toward women slipped back to the traditional views of the pre-war era. Some women, however, resisted returning to their old lives. They planted the seeds of the women's rights movement that would emerge in the decades ahead.

"I think the war played a huge part in changing the lives of women ... Women liked the freedom, and this made women notice they could do jobs just as well as men could ... The women who enlisted in the war haven't received the amount of recognition they deserve."

–Jenna Lewis, Morell Regional High School, 2007

Learn more about the role of women in the Second World War

Figure 4.19
Although there were some government-sponsored daycare centres in Ontario and Québec for women who took jobs in the paid workforce, most women had to find their own childcare solutions. This Mi'kmaq woman brought her child to work with her in the shipyards at Pictou, Nova Scotia. What other challenges do you think women who worked in the labour force faced?

Elsie MacGill: Queen of the Hurricanes

Elsie MacGill was born in Vancouver in 1905. Her mother was a newspaper reporter and suffragist who became the first female judge in British Columbia. She campaigned to improve the lives of women and children and was a strong role model for her daughter Elsie.

"I'm no hero. I was lucky. I got a good education. So my mother was a judge; so what? I didn't think it was any more remarkable for a woman to be a judge than it was for me to be an engineer."

Source: Dr Elsie MacGill, in Stacey Gibson, "Fairly determined." *University of Toronto Magazine*, Spring 2002.

Elsie MacGill was the first woman to receive an electrical engineering degree in Canada. After she graduated in 1927, she worked at an automotive plant in the US. When the company expanded into aircraft production, MacGill enrolled at the University of Michigan, where she became the first woman to earn a master's degree in aeronautical engineering.

Before she was able to launch her career, however, MacGill contracted polio. Doctors told her she would probably spend the rest of her life in a wheelchair, but a determined MacGill taught herself to walk again. In 1934, she resumed her career as an aeronautical engineer. In 1938, she went to work for the Canadian Car and Foundry Company, where she became the world's first female aircraft designer.

During the war, MacGill designed a new airplane for training pilots. It gave student pilots greater visibility and better stability during takeoff and landing. She was responsible for overseeing the production of Hawker Hurricane fighter planes, which were instrumental in the Battle of Britain. At the peak of production, MacGill had more than 4500 people under her supervision.

In 1943, MacGill married William Soulsby, but she kept her family name—a bold move that was almost unheard of in those days. She moved to Toronto, where she opened her own business

Figure 4.20   Elsie MacGill was a symbol of the technological innovations of the wartime economy. This comic, called *Queen of the Hurricanes*, of True Comics was published in 1942 and celebrated MacGill as a wartime hero.

as an aeronautical engineering consultant. Before her death in 1980, MacGill received many honours and awards in recognition of her work and for her commitment to the advancement of women's rights.

Responding

1. What made Elsie MacGill unique?
2. Do you think MacGill was a wartime hero? Give reasons for your response.

Sign of the Times

JOHNNY CANUCK

Young Canadians were reminded of the war even in their leisure time when they read the comics. During the war, comic books were called "Canadian whites" because they were printed in black and white due to a shortage of coloured dyes. Comic books featuring Canadian action heroes played an important role in wartime propaganda.

Figure 4.21 Canadian publishers produced comic books about Canadian action heroes during the war. One of the most popular ones featured a fighting hero named Johnny Canuck—"Canada's Answer to Nazi Oppression", as seen here. This page is from the Number 2 edition, published by Dime Comics in March, 1942.

WARTIME REALITY

In class, teachers taught their students that victory was sure to come as they tried to boost young people's spirits by singing patriotic songs such as "Rule Britannia" and "God Save the King." For some young people in British Columbia, however, the threat of war was all too real as Japanese submarines were detected off the Pacific coast. Rumours of Japanese spies and saboteurs were everywhere.

Figure 4.22 Students in Vancouver practised air raid drills. They had to wear gas masks to prepare for the possibility of a gas attack.

Responding
1. What do you think it was like for students to practise for air raids and gas attacks? In what ways is this similar to school lockdowns today?

"Eiko sleeps in a partitioned stall … This stall was the former home of a pair of stallions … The whole place is impregnated with the smell of ancient manure and maggots … The toilets are just a sheet metal trough, and up till now they did not have partitions or seats … There are 10 showers for 1500 women."

–Muriel Kitagawa, describing the conditions at the holding facility at Hastings Park in Vancouver, April 1942

"Most of the Japanese that were living in BC and the rest of Canada were born here in Canada and had not even seen their native land of Japan … [They] helped to develop the Canadian West … They cared about Canada as much as any other … Canadian."

–Nick Brown, Parkside Collegiate Institute, 2003

Learn more about the treatment of Canadians of Japanese descent

The Internment of Japanese Canadians

The attack on Pearl Harbor and the battle for Hong Kong fuelled long-standing racism against Canadians of Asian heritage in British Columbia. At the time, there was no human rights legislation to protect people from discrimination or unfair persecution. The premier of British Columbia ordered all male Canadians of Japanese heritage between the ages of 18 and 45 to relocate to work camps in the interior of the province. Then, in February 1942, King used the War Measures Act to order all people of Japanese descent living near the BC coast to move to camps in the interior.

Authorities immediately began rounding up people of Japanese descent. At first, they were held in horse stables in Vancouver's Hastings Park, where they were photographed, fingerprinted, and assigned ID numbers. Then they waited days to board trains that transported them to internment camps. Each person could take only one suitcase. The government sold the rest of their possessions, including their homes and properties, without their consent and without compensation. It used the profits to pay for the internment camps.

More than 21 000 people of Japanese descent were relocated into the interior. After the war, they were not allowed to return to the Pacific coast. The government considered deporting all people of Japanese heritage—including second- and third-generation Canadians. The government never followed through, but 4000 people left Canada on their own.

A Public Apology

Today, the treatment of Canadians of Japanese heritage during the war is seen as one of the worst human rights violations in Canada's history. For years, the Japanese Canadian community asked the government to acknowledge that it had violated their rights. In 1988, the government finally issued a formal apology and agreed to pay $21 000 to every evacuee still living. The government also gave millions of dollars to support the Japanese Canadian community and allocated $24 million to establish a Canadian Race Relations Foundation.

Figure 4.23
At the internment camps, the Japanese lived in basic huts, sharing kitchens and bathrooms with other families. There was no electricity or running water. This camp was at Greenwood in the interior of British Columbia.

Hide Hyodo Shimizu: Human Rights Champion

Figure 4.24   Hide Hyodo Shimizu was determined that children in the internment camps would be able to continue their education, so she set up classes for them.

Hide Hyodo was born in Vancouver in 1908. After earning her teaching certificate in 1926, she began teaching a Grade 1 class of students of Japanese heritage in Steveston, BC. Shortly afterwards, the provincial government made it illegal for any more Canadians of Japanese descent to earn their teaching certificates. At the age of 18, Hide Hyodo found herself the only teacher of Japanese heritage in British Columbia.

In 1936, Shimizu joined a four-party delegation, sponsored by the Japanese Canadian Citizens League, on a trip to Ottawa to lobby the government for the right to vote. However, a motion in Parliament supporting voting rights for Canadians of Japanese descent was defeated.

During the evacuation, Shimizu organized school classes at Hastings Park in Vancouver. After she was evacuated to an internment camp, she travelled from camp to camp each month, planning classes and training high-school students to become teachers.

"I was still continuing to teach daily at Steveston, so every other day after school I'd rush from Steveston, and in the long interurban tram ride to Hastings Park, look over the schedule and make assignments for the next two days ... Then I'd have to rush home by curfew time and get ready for my evacuation, too."

Source: Hide Hyodo Shimizu, "School yard memories." the Virtual Museum of Canada.

After the war, she relocated to Toronto, where she married a minister named Kosaburo Shimizu. She spent much of her life volunteering for the church and lobbying the government for compensation for the Japanese Canadian community. In 1982, Shimizu received the Order of Canada in recognition of her efforts for her community during the war. In 1993, the Status of Women Canada honoured Shimizu in a tribute to women who helped shape the history and evolution of Canada. Shimizu died in 1999 at the age of 91.

Responding

1. What characteristics do you think best describe Hide Hyodo Shimizu? Give reasons for your response.
2. To receive the Order of Canada, a person has to demonstrate a "lifetime of distinguished service in or to a particular community, group, or field of activity." In your own words, explain why Shimizu was worthy of this honour.

Skill Path:
Recognizing and Analyzing Bias in Sources

We all have our own preferences, or **biases**. Bias exists when you take into account only one side of an issue or when you use the facts to defend only one point of view.

In history, many of the sources you read are biased. These sources can distort your understanding and unfairly influence your thinking. To get a balanced perspective, you need to seek information from a variety of sources and multiple perspectives. You also have to be able to recognize bias in the sources you use.

STEP 1: Consider the Source of Information
When you read a source of information, ask yourself the following questions:
- What year was it created?
- Is the author an expert in this field?
- Does the author have a personal bias?
- Who was the intended audience?
- What was the social, political, and economic climate at the time?
- Have things happened since then that might make this information outdated or invalid?

Reading Strategy

Read the credentials for your Internet sources carefully. Websites for governments, universities, and organizations like the UN are usually credible sources of information. Websites written by individuals may not be.

STEP 2: Evaluate the Information
There are two types of bias: *explicit* and *implicit*. If bias is explicit, the author states his or her position up front—usually in the opening paragraph or thesis statement. The audience has no doubt about the author's perspective.

Implicit bias is more difficult to detect because it is subtle—that is, the author does not state his or her bias directly. You have to think about the implications of the statement.

Another form of bias is the use of emotionally charged words or phrases that present information in a favourable or unfavourable light. Words that exaggerate or overgeneralize may be biased, too. For example, *never* and *always* are biased words because they are absolute.

STEP 3: Distinguish between Facts and Opinions
Facts are those pieces of information that can be proven. *Opinions* are those pieces of information that are influenced by the author's personal perspectives and biases. It is important to be able to distinguish between the two.

STEP 4: Corroborate the Evidence
If you are unsure whether an author is presenting biased information or inaccurate facts, you need to corroborate the evidence—that is, find other sources of information that either support the facts as presented or prove they are inaccurate.

STEP 5: Practise Your Skill
Browse through some newspaper editorials on current events. Choose one editorial that you think is biased. Then follow the steps in this Skill Path to identify a) the types of bias, and b) the emotionally charged words. If necessary, corroborate the facts. Then write a summary of your findings, with evidence to support your ideas.

 View more World War II propaganda posters

Figure 4.25
Photographs, artwork, political cartoons, and war propaganda may be biased if they reflect the perspectives of the person or organization that created them. What biases are contained in these propaganda posters from the Second World War?

The Conscription Question

During the First World War, the issue of conscription threatened to tear Canada apart. King did not want to revisit the crisis. When the war began, he promised his government would not impose mandatory enlistment for military service overseas.

In 1940, however, as fears grew that the war might reach Canadian shores, King introduced the National Resources Mobilization Act. It required all men to register for military service in Canada. Yet King kept his word that there would be no conscription for overseas service. It was an important concession to French Canadians. Most were willing to defend Canada, but they drew the line at fighting for Britain.

By 1941, however, Germany's success in Europe and the expansion of the war into the Pacific renewed pressure for conscription. In April 1942, King held a **plebiscite** to ask Canadians to release him from his earlier pledge. The results showed how divided Canadians were on conscription: 79 per cent of English Canadians voted Yes while 72 per cent of French Canadians voted No.

Despite the outcome of the plebiscite, King cautiously waited to impose conscription until 1944. By then, the Allies were close to winning the war. But the battle to liberate Europe had taken its toll as casualties were mounting. Some members of King's Cabinet threatened to resign if he failed to act on conscription. In response, in November 1944, King issued an **Order-in-Council** to send 16 000 troops overseas.

Many English Canadians were reassured by King's decision. Others denounced him for wavering over the issue for so long. In Québec, there were protests against the decision. But they were not as forceful as they had been in the First World War. Many French Canadians believed King had listened to them and had avoided conscription for as long as possible.

"The present government believes that conscription of men for overseas service will not be a necessary or an effective step…

–Prime Minister William Lyon Mackenzie King, House of Commons, 8 September 1939

"The reply to the plebiscite must be: No. Why? Because nobody asks to be freed of an obligation if he does not already have the temptation to violate it, and because, of all the promises he has made to the people of Canada, there remains only one which King would prefer not to be obliged to keep: the promise not to conscript men for overseas."

–The manifesto of the Ligue pour la Défense du Canada, April 1942

Challenge and Response

1. Prepare a list identifying 10 things you would ask Canadians to ration if there was rationing in Canada today.
2. How did traditional roles in Canadian society change to support the war effort? How do you think many women felt about leaving their jobs after the war? Give reasons for your response.
3. How do you think King handled the conscription issue? Give reasons to explain your position.
4. In your opinion, are *all* citizens obligated in wartime to serve their country? Discuss your ideas as a class.

The Impact of War

Canada emerged from the Second World War a different nation. More than one million volunteers—almost 10 per cent of Canada's population—had fought for liberty and freedom around the world. The war modernized the Canadian economy as industrial production increased dramatically to support the war effort. After almost two decades of "doing without," Canadians were ready for a spending spree that would launch a postwar economic boom.

The wartime experience focused Canada's attention on human rights. As Canadians discovered the extent of the Holocaust, they had to re-examine their own values, attitudes, and actions. They began to question the role Canada played in sealing the fate of European Jews by refusing to accept Jewish refugees and examine whether the country had overreacted in its distrust of people of Japanese descent. After the war, Canada became a peaceful haven as it opened its doors to refugees and immigrants from the devastated countries of Europe.

Internationally, Canada assumed a new place among the nations of the world. The country emerged as a **middle power** with an increasingly important role to play in world affairs. For the first time in its history, Canada was in a position to make its presence felt in the new world order that emerged in the aftermath of the war.

Challenge and Response

1. In an organizer similar to the one shown here, identify the ways the war changed Canada.

Social Changes	Economic Changes	Political Changes	International Changes

Thinking Like a Historian:
Making Moral Judgments about the Past

Essential Question: As a historian, how do you make moral judgments about actions that took place in the past?

As a historian, you sometimes have to make moral judgments about people, actions, and events that took place in the past. Lessons learned from significant events that happened in the past help us make good decisions about moral issues today. One of the decisions historians make is deciding when governments owe a debt to the memories of these past events.

As you discovered in this chapter, during the Second World War, the government made decisions based on the moral standards of the day. Although today we know that there was no evidence that Canadians of Japanese descent were acting as spies for Japan or posed any other real threat to national security, the government forced them to relocate to internment camps and confiscated and sold their property. After the war, the Japanese-Canadian community wanted the government to acknowledge its mistakes. Although the government refused for over 30 years, the decision to offer an apology and compensation in 1988 set a precedent. This motivated other groups whose rights had been violated in the past to seek a similar acknowledgment.

You, the Historian

1. The following are groups of people in Canada whose human rights have been violated in some way in the past. For each one, do some research to find out how their rights were violated, what compensation they are seeking, and what action the government has taken, if any.

   - Aboriginal peoples (land claims; cultural issues; residential schools)
   - Canadians of Chinese descent
   - other groups who have been interned
   - people infected with serious diseases from tainted blood supplies or contaminated water
   - people wrongly convicted, imprisoned, or deported

2. Based on the information you learned in question 1, work with a group to establish a list of criteria the federal government should use to determine whether an apology and/or compensation is justified. Give reasons to support your ideas.

3. Find out what other groups in Canada are currently seeking compensation for past injustices. Working with a partner, conduct some research on one case. Next, prepare a written or oral report describing the injustice and the compensation the people are seeking from the government. Then use your criteria from question 2 to write a brief argument either for or against their claim.

UNIT 2

Developing the Canadian Identity: 1945–1967

IN FOCUS

In the aftermath of the Second World War, Canada was a self-confident nation ready to meet the challenges and opportunities of the new world order. Internationally, Canada committed itself to a unique role on the world stage as a middle power and peacekeeper. Domestically, Canada experienced remarkable population growth and unprecedented prosperity, fueled by immigration, the baby boom, and the emergence of a new consumer society. As a result, a new sense of Canadian national identity began to emerge between 1945 and 1967.

In this unit, you will explore these years of challenge, change, and growth. As you do, focus on the following questions:

- In what ways did the Canadian identity remain the same in the post-war years?
- How did the Canadian identity change?
- What were the most significant factors that contributed to the development of a unique Canadian identity by the time of the Centennial in 1967?

One of Alex Colville's best-known works is *Horse and Train* (1954). Disaster appears imminent as the horse and train are headed for collision. Can destiny be altered? Discuss this idea as a class.

Chapter 5

Challenges in the Post-war World

Figure 5.1 In 1948, Canada joined Britain and the United States in secret talks to establish a military alliance for their collective security against the Soviet Union. In 1949, they formed the North Atlantic Treaty Organization (NATO) with France, Belgium, the Netherlands, Luxembourg, Denmark, Iceland, Italy, Portugal, and Norway. What other countries are members of NATO today?

Chapter at a Glance

Thinking Ahead

When the Second World War ended, Canadians hoped the world was a safer place. In many ways, it was. There was optimism that the second half of the century would be better than the first half had been. As the tensions of the new Cold War began to reveal themselves, however, there were storm clouds on the horizon. The fear of communism and the threat of nuclear war worried many people in Canada, the United States, and Europe.

As you learn about the global challenges facing Canada in the post-war world, think about the following questions:

- What were the major causes and consequences of the Cold War for Canada?
- What were the significant changes in Canada's foreign policy after the war?
- What were the key military turning points during the Cold War?
- How significant was Canada's role in Cold War hot spots such as Korea and the Suez Canal?

Profile in Power:

Louis Stephen St. Laurent

"When I ask you to support a North Atlantic Treaty, I am simply asking you to pay an insurance premium which will be far, far, less costly than the losses we would face if a new **conflagration** devastated the world."

Source: Prime Minister Louis St. Laurent, CBC Radio, 11 November 1948

Figure 5.2 Louis St. Laurent (1882–1973)

Louis St. Laurent was born in Compton, Québec, in 1882. His father was French. His mother was Irish. St. Laurent grew up speaking French with his father and English with his mother. Only as a teenager did he discover that this was unusual in most families of the day.

St. Laurent attended Laval University, where he graduated with a degree in law. He joined a Québec law firm and for the next 25 years built a thriving law practice. St. Laurent counted many Liberal politicians among his friends, but he had no desire to become one himself. At the age of 59, however, circumstances led him to change his mind.

In 1941, Prime Minister King's justice minister and chief Québec Cabinet minister died. Many Liberal MPs recommended St. Laurent as his replacement. St. Laurent protested that he lacked political experience. Out of patriotic duty, however, he agreed to run in a by-election—but vowed to retire as soon as the war was over.

St. Laurent quickly evolved into a skilled politician. His distinguished appearance and gracious style made him an attractive political candidate. St. Laurent reflected the more relaxed atmosphere of the post-war era. He was also a person with political integrity as he refused to play political games. This earned him the respect not only of members of his own party but of his opponents, too. Canadians admired St. Laurent for his bilingual and bicultural heritage and his ability to communicate with both cultures.

When the war ended, King offered St. Laurent the position of minister of External Affairs. Hoping to shape Canada's new role on the world stage, he agreed to stay on. St. Laurent saw Canada as a middle power and intermediary in world affairs. As a firm believer in **collective security**, he enthusiastically supported the creation of the United Nations (UN) and the North Atlantic Treaty Organization (NATO).

St. Laurent still planned to resign from public life, but when King retired in 1948, once again circumstances dictated another course of action. The Liberals believed St. Laurent was the best choice to replace King. They convinced him to run for the party leadership. He agreed, and in November 1948, Louis St. Laurent became the prime minister of Canada.

During his years in office, St. Laurent continued to shape Canada's new role on the world stage. Under his leadership, Canada emerged as a more significant player in international affairs. In Chapter 6, you will find out how St. Laurent shaped the future of Canada here at home.

Figure 5.3 St. Laurent (here addressing NATO delegates in Ottawa) insisted that NATO's charter include an article calling on members to strengthen democratic institutions internationally.

 Learn more about Louis St. Laurent

Responding

1. Do you think St. Laurent was an ambitious politician? Explain your response.
2. Why do you think St. Laurent insisted on including the article on strengthening democracy in the NATO charter? How do you think this reflected his view of Canada's role on the international stage?

Reading Strategy

Scan this chapter and write down three things that you find interesting.

"From Stettin in the Baltic to Trieste in the Adriatic, an iron curtain has descended across the Continent. Behind that line lie all the capitals of the ancient states of Central and Eastern Europe. Warsaw, Berlin, Prague, Vienna, Budapest, Belgrade, Bucharest, and Sofia; all these famous cities and the populations around them lie in what I might call the Soviet sphere, and all are subject, in one form or another, not only to Soviet influence but to a very high, and in some cases increasing, measure of control from Moscow."

—Former British prime minister Winston Churchill, 5 March 1946

The Cold War

In 1945, the world emerged from six long years of war to find itself faced with a new type of conflict—the Cold War. The post-war world quickly divided into two camps: the world's communist states, led by the Soviet Union, and the world's democratic states, led by the United States. Unlike real war, at first the Cold War did not lead to active aggression between the two new **superpowers**. Instead, the Cold War began with a tense **arms race** that threatened world peace.

Origins of the Cold War

The Cold War was born in Europe in the closing days of the Second World War. The Western Allies, including the United States, Canada, and Britain, liberated the countries of Western Europe, while the Soviet Union liberated the countries of Eastern Europe. The countries of Western Europe adopted democratic governments and set about the task of rebuilding their war-torn countries. The Soviet Union maintained control over Eastern Europe, installing puppet communist governments that would follow Moscow's

directives. The division between East and West prompted former British prime minister Winston Churchill to declare that an **Iron Curtain** had fallen across Europe.

The Spread of Communism

Two vastly different economic and political systems were at the centre of the Cold War. Under communism, the government controlled most of the property and businesses. It restricted individual freedom, including where people lived, worked, and travelled. In the Western democracies, private individuals and companies owned most of the property and businesses. People had the right to live, work, and travel where they chose. As the Soviet Union extended its power and influence throughout Eastern Europe, people in the West grew increasingly concerned about the Soviets' intentions and alarmed that their way of life may be threatened.

In this atmosphere of fear and suspicion, there was a growing concern that communists were around every corner. As you are about to discover in the Personalities feature, one of the first faceoffs in the Cold War happened in Canada in 1945 when a worker in the Soviet Embassy in Ottawa **defected**, taking the secrets of a Soviet spy ring with him.

Figure 5.4 At the Paris Peace Conference after the war, the Allied leaders tried to cooperate. However, the differences between the Soviet Union and the United States and their respective allies were too great. Why is it often difficult for political leaders with different points of view to get along?

Igor Gouzenko: The Man in the Mask

In Canada, one of the most powerful symbols of the Cold War was a Russian defector named Igor Gouzenko. In 1943, Gouzenko came to Canada to work as a **cipher** clerk in the Soviet Embassy. In 1945, he decided to defect rather than return to Moscow.

Gouzenko gathered over 100 documents detailing the secrets of a Soviet spy ring that had infiltrated the highest levels of intelligence, including the Canadian Department of Defence. Even a Canadian MP—Fred Rose, the first and only communist ever elected to Parliament—was on the Soviet payroll. Gouzenko planned to use this information as a bargaining chip as he sought **asylum** in Canada.

"Dangerous living had never appealed to me, and adventure always associated itself with unromantic danger in my mind. But that night of September 5, 1945, during the long walk from Somerset Street to Range Road, I came as close to becoming a hero as I ever will."

Source: Igor Gouzenko, on his departure from the Soviet Embassy, in Igor Gouzenko, *This Was My Choice* (Toronto: J.M. Dent & Sons (Canada) Limited), 1948.

At first, Gouzenko had trouble finding anyone willing to listen to his story. On the day he defected, he attempted to contact officials in the justice department, but their offices were closed. Gouzenko spent the day trying to avoid detection by Soviet agents. But that night, four men from the Soviet Embassy tried to abduct Gouzenko and his family. The police prevented their attempt, but the incident likely helped to convince Canadian authorities to take Gouzenko seriously.

 Learn more about the Gouzenko Affair

Figure 5.5 For many people, spies existed only in the movies, so many Canadians were shocked when they discovered that Soviet spies were operating in Canada. How do you think the spy scandal influenced people's thinking about the Soviet Union and communism?

The leaders of Canada, Britain, France, the United States, China, and the Soviet Union were about to meet to negotiate post-war peace. King was concerned that the spy scandal would hurt the talks, so he was reluctant to act on Gouzenko's information. British intelligence officials persuaded him to change his mind and offer Gouzenko asylum.

After defecting, Gouzenko and his family went into hiding. When he appeared in public, Gouzenko hid his identity by wearing a cloth sack over his head. The press dubbed him "the Man in the Mask." Convinced that he was a target for assassination by Soviet agents, Gouzenko lived the rest of his life under the assumed name of George Brown.

Responding

1. Gouzenko's memoirs became the basis of a movie called *Behind the Iron Curtain*. Why do you think people were so interested in Gouzenko's story?
2. Why do you think the Gouzenko Affair marked a turning point in post-war relations between the West and the Soviet Union?

"I have here in my hand a list of 205 … names that were known to the Secretary of State as being members of the Communist Party and who nevertheless are still working and shaping policy in the State Department."

–US Senator Joseph McCarthy, February 1951

"You can't wash off the poison. How can you fight back against this sort of thing?"

–Herbert Norman, 1951

Communist Paranoia

In the aftermath of Gouzenko's spy revelations, 19 Canadians were arrested and charged with treason. Of those, eleven were found guilty and sentenced to prison. The exposure of the spy ring fuelled fears of communism. In the United States, there was widespread paranoia about communist sympathizers infiltrating American society. US Senator Joseph McCarthy led a congressional committee charged with investigating "un-American activities." The committee targeted actors, writers, journalists, and labour leaders. Many who were called before the committee to answer questions about their politics refused to answer questions or to implicate their friends and colleagues. They were branded as communists. Many were barred from practising their professions. This national obsession with communism ruined the careers of many Americans.

Accusations

McCarthy's accusations extended beyond American borders. The name of Herbert Norman, a Canadian diplomat, was raised in the hearings in 1951. As a university student at Harvard and Cambridge, Norman had associated with a group of left-wing students. Now that he was a diplomat, his former friendships cast doubts about his political beliefs.

Figure 5.6   The McCarthy hearings in the US Congress were televised nationally. Millions of Americans watched the proceedings each day. How do you think this may have influenced people's ideas about communism?

The American accusations led to an investigation of Norman's activities by the RCMP. Canada's minister of External Affairs, Lester B. Pearson, stood by Norman, whose name was finally cleared. But an air of suspicion lingered. In 1956, during the Suez crisis (see page 169), American suspicions resurfaced after Norman was sent to Cairo as Canada's ambassador to Egypt. In March 1957, the US House Un-American Activities Committee again accused him of being a communist. After years of suspicion, it was too much for the diplomat. In April 1957, Norman committed suicide.

Paranoia in Canada

After the Gouzenko Affair, the RCMP created a counter-espionage branch to monitor activities in the Soviet Embassy. In 1951, the government amended the Citizenship Act to allow authorities to revoke the citizenship of naturalized Canadians convicted of "disaffection or disloyalty"—in other words, anyone suspected of being a communist sympathizer.

The government wanted to rid the civil service and the military of anyone it thought was a potential security threat, too. Most of the people the government targeted were suspected of being either communists or gays or lesbians. Since homosexuality was illegal in the 1950s, the government thought Soviet agents might blackmail gays and lesbians into acting as spies. People under suspicion were transferred to less sensitive positions or lost their jobs altogether.

Secret Experiments

Some of the most threatening activity created by communist paranoia took place in a Montréal laboratory. Between

1957 and 1964, the US Central Intelligence Agency (CIA) funded secret brainwashing and mind-control experiments. They wanted to find out to what extent the human brain could be programmed. Dr Ewen Cameron conducted the experiments at McGill University's Allan Memorial Institute. He used his unsuspecting patients as guinea pigs, injecting them with mind-altering drugs, jolting them with electrical shocks, and inducing them into extended periods of sleep. Authorities in both Canada and the United States knew of the experiments. However, they remained a carefully guarded secret kept from the public until the 1970s.

In 2007, one former patient reached an out-of-court settlement with the federal government as compensation for her lifetime of suffering as a result of experiments conducted on her. Other lawsuits were pending.

The Nuclear Threat

In the immediate aftermath of the Second World War, the United States believed it had a monopoly on atomic technology. Therefore, they were surprised and concerned when the Soviet Union tested its first atomic bomb in 1949. The United States was already working on a more powerful bomb than the atomic bombs dropped on Japan. In November 1952, the US tested the world's first hydrogen bomb in the Pacific Ocean. The hydrogen bomb was a thousand times more powerful than the blasts that had rocked Hiroshima and Nagasaki.

The Soviets kept pace, though. In September 1954, they tested their own hydrogen bomb. The fear of nuclear war reached new heights as people realized the total destruction of the planet was

"Never have I violated my oath of secrecy. But how the issues will be obscured and twisted! But I am too tired of it all. The forces against me are too formidable, even for an innocent man, and it is better to go now than to live indefinitely pelted with mud—although so much of it will be quite incorrect and false."

–Herbert Norman, in a suicide note, 4 April 1957

"I had no identity, I had no memory, I'd never existed in the world before."

–A female victim of the experiments at Allan Memorial Institute, 6 January 1998

Figure 5.7 The heat generated by a nuclear blast like this test bomb at Bikini Island in 1946 is hotter than the sun. It melts human skin and vaporizes living things—including people—leaving only their shadows. The pressure wave from the blast creates hurricane-force winds, followed by a massive firestorm that burns everything in its path. Do you think the nuclear arms race acted as a deterrent to open warfare between the two superpowers? Give reasons for your response.

> "If the ... bombs of the 1960s were 2900 times more powerful than Hiroshima, simply imagine what the ... bombs of today would be like."
>
> –Joanna Hildebrand, Valleyview Secondary School, 2003

now possible. Over the years, both sides began stockpiling their nuclear arms. Some military strategists argued that having the ability to retaliate was the strongest **deterrent** against a military attack. Others, however, including many Canadians, opposed the buildup of nuclear arms. Many people openly protested against having nuclear weapons on Canadian soil. (You will learn more about the controversy over nuclear weapons in Chapter 7.)

Civil Defence

A poll conducted in 1951 revealed that 36 per cent of Canadians believed a Soviet attack could happen at any time. To prepare for such a horrific event, the government set up a national civil defence program and developed plans for mass evacuations. Air-raid sirens and fallout shelters appeared in cities across the country. People built underground shelters in their backyards. If a nuclear attack happened, Canadians planned to do whatever they could to survive it.

Figure 5.8 From 1959 to 1961, the federal government built a massive underground shelter under a farmer's field outside Ottawa. It was big enough to house 535 government officials and military personnel in the event of a nuclear attack, with enough supplies to last for 30 days. Today, the Diefenbunker, as it was called, is a museum. How effective do you think a shelter like this would have been in the event of a nuclear attack?

Challenge and Response

1. Compare and contrast the Canadian and American governments' responses to the communist threat. Do you think the fear of communism justified the actions of either government? Give reasons for your response.
2. The hunt to track down communists violated the human rights of many innocent people. Can you think of any situations today in which the governments of Canada or the United States are accused of violating people's human rights? Explain your response.
3. Imagine you are a student in the 1950s. Create a poster or political cartoon expressing your point of view about the nuclear arms race.

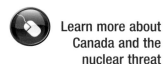

Learn more about
Canada and the
nuclear threat

Canada and the Post-war Economy

> "Canada has already contributed in a very large part to the economic recovery in Europe .... Certainly, we want to ensure markets in England and in Europe, but the stronger the economies of these countries are, the more they will be in a position to oversee their own defence and the more our military security will grow."
>
> –Prime Minister Louis St. Laurent, in a speech to the Canadian Club, Toronto, 27 March 1950

After the war, Canada was looking to expand its economic relations with other countries. One way to create economic ties was through foreign aid programs. As a wealthy nation, Canada felt a humanitarian duty to help less prosperous countries improve or rebuild their quality of life. To achieve this goal, Canada provided financial and technical support through foreign aid. There were political motives in providing foreign aid, as well. Prosperous countries were likely to be more stable— and therefore less likely to embrace communism. Stronger global economic ties also benefited the Canadian economy by opening up markets for Canada's exports.

The Marshall Plan

After the war, the United States was determined to fight the spread of communism in Europe by rebuilding the war-ravaged economies of Western Europe. In June 1947, the US announced a massive aid program known as the Marshall Plan. Canada agreed to contribute to the plan. In the first year, Canada shipped $706 million in goods to war-torn countries in Western Europe. Between 1948 and 1953, Canada and the United States together contributed $13.5 billion worth of supplies to 16 European countries. The massive aid program succeeded in rapidly rebuilding the economies of Western Europe and prevented the Soviet Union from extending its influence beyond its Eastern satellite states.

Figure 5.9   Both William Lyon Mackenzie King (right) and his successor, Louis St. Laurent (left), wanted Canada to play a more active role in world affairs after the war. How do you think the role Canada played in the war may have influenced their decision?

Skill Path:
Analyzing and Interpreting Political Cartoons

Identifying the purpose and meaning in political cartoons is an important skill for history students. It helps you to understand the atmosphere surrounding current and historic issues and events. Some political cartoons poke fun at people and situations. Others use **caricature** and exaggeration to express a point of view. Political cartoons are a visual way of making an editorial statement.

When you analyze a political cartoon, follow these steps:

STEP 1: Find the Facts

Begin by finding the obvious information in the cartoon. Ask yourself the following questions:

- Does the cartoon have a title and/or caption? If so, what does it mean?
- Who are the people depicted in the cartoon?
- What is the setting?
- What action is taking place?
- What objects and symbols are in the cartoon?
- What techniques does the cartoonist use?

STEP 2: Interpret the Message

Once you have identified the people and the setting in the cartoon, think about the cartoonist's point of view. Ask yourself the following questions:

- How has the cartoonist represented the characters in the cartoon?
- Has the cartoonist used stereotypes to portray groups of people?
- To what event or issue does the cartoon refer?
- What is the message in the cartoon? What point of view does it reflect?

STEP 3: Evaluate the Cartoon

Once you understand the cartoon's context and point of view, think about how effective the cartoonist was in conveying his or her message. Ask yourself the following questions:

- Does the cartoonist's message make sense?

- Are the techniques and devices the cartoonist uses to convey his or her point of view effective? Why or why not?
- What could the cartoonist have done differently to make the cartoon more effective?
- Do I agree with the cartoonist's point of view? Why or why not?

STEP 4: Practise Your Skill

1. Analyze and respond to these two political cartoons. Read the caption before you begin.

Figure 5.10 These cartoons express points of view on how the two superpowers viewed each other during the early days of the Cold War. What does the American cartoon say about the Soviet Union's intentions in Europe? What does the Soviet cartoon say about the motives of the US in the Marshall Plan?

"The world would be much the poorer without the quality of internationalism that has been peculiarly Canada's."

–Shridath Ramphal, Secretary-General of the Commonwealth from 1975–1990

"My hope is that they will return to the Commonwealth in due course. There will always be a light in the Commonwealth window."

–Prime Minister John Diefenbaker, speaking about South Africa, 1961

 Learn more about the Commonwealth

The Commonwealth

After the Second World War, Canada's military and economic ties shifted away from Britain and toward the United States. Canada still maintained its British ties through the Commonwealth, however. Membership in the Commonwealth gave Canada the opportunity to define its own role in the global community and to express points of view that were separate and distinct from those of the United States.

Initially, the Commonwealth consisted of Britain, Canada, Australia, New Zealand, South Africa, and the Irish Free State. After the war, however, more British colonies, such as India, Pakistan, Burma (now Myanmar), and Ceylon (now Sri Lanka), gained their independence. Canada supported these countries as they emerged from British colonial rule and acted as an intermediary between the original states of the Commonwealth and its newest members.

The Colombo Plan

In 1950, Canada worked with the other members of the Commonwealth to develop the Colombo Plan. The plan was the equivalent to the US Marshall Plan to aid economies in Europe. It provided financial and technical support to the developing countries of the Commonwealth. Between 1950 and 1970, Canada contributed $2 billion to the plan.

Racial Equality

Canada also played a key role in persuading the Commonwealth to adopt a policy of racial equality. When South Africa became a republic in 1960, it had to reapply for admission to the Commonwealth. Britain supported the application, despite the fact that

Figure 5.11   Today, Canada continues to play a leading role in the Commonwealth. What purpose do you think membership in international organizations has?

South Africa had a policy of **apartheid** that legally made Black South Africans second-class citizens. In 1961, Canada supported India, Malaya (now Malaysia), and Ghana in their demands for racial equality. When the policy was adopted, South Africa withdrew from the Commonwealth. It was readmitted in 1991 after apartheid was abolished and Nelson Mandela became South Africa's first Black president.

The General Agreement on Tariffs and Trade

After the war, there was greater co-operation in world trade. In 1947, Canada joined 22 other countries in signing the General Agreement on Tariffs and Trade (GATT). The agreement was designed to reduce tariffs and stimulate world trade. Under the agreement, if one country gave certain trade privileges to one member nation, it had to give the same privileges to all members.

Canada wanted to participate in the GATT to expand its trading partners and reduce its dependence on trade with the United States. Over the years, the GATT has helped to fuel the growth of the Canadian economy. The United States remains Canada's biggest trading partner, though.

INTERNATIONAL ECONOMIC ORGANIZATIONS		
Organization	**Year**	**Purpose**
The World Bank	1945	To provide aid to countries devastated by the war Continues to provide money for economic development projects
The International Monetary Fund (IMF)	1945	Stabilizes exchange rates and promotes international trade Lends money to countries in debt
The Organisation for Economic Co-operation and Development (OECD)	1961	Promotes economic and social policies for its members

Figure 5.12 After the war, Canada joined other Allied countries as world leaders established a new international monetary system to promote international trade and regulate currency. Today, most countries in the world have connections with these global organizations. In what ways does global trade affect your life?

Challenge and Response

1. Recall what you know about Canada's economic relations with other countries before the Second World War. How did they change after the war?
2. Think about the things you use on a regular basis. Where do they come from? What does this suggest to you about global economic relations today?

Becoming a Middle Power

Despite Canada's impressive contribution to the war, the United States and Britain dominated post-war politics and power in the West. Canada had historic ties to Britain, France, and the United States. First King, and then St. Laurent, wanted to use these connections to influence world affairs.

The United Nations

Even before the Second World War ended, plans were underway to create a new international organization to secure world peace. The Allies agreed that the League of Nations had been a failure. Its policy of imposing political and economic sanctions to avoid conflicts had been ineffective. The organization that replaced it had to have real power to intervene and settle disputes before events escalated to war. Any new international body had to have its own armed forces that could keep enemies apart.

Between April and June 1945, representatives of 51 countries, including Canada, gathered in San Francisco to define the principles of the new organization. In June, they signed the charter that created the United Nations. Its main objectives were
• to ensure collective security by working together to avoid war
• to encourage co-operation among countries
• to defend human rights
• to improve living conditions for people around the world

Reading Strategy

On your own, read the section on the United Nations. As you read, write down a key word from each paragraph that you find interesting. Then, working with a partner, use each word as a cue to summarize this section.

"We, the peoples of the United Nations, determined to save succeeding generations from the scourge of war, which twice in our lifetimes has brought untold sorrow ... do hereby establish an international organization to be known as the United Nations."

–The opening words of the Charter of the United Nations, June 1945

The Universal Declaration of Human Rights

One of the first objectives of the United Nations was to create the Universal Declaration of Human Rights. In 1946, John Humphrey, a Canadian law professor from New Brunswick, became the head of the UN Division for Human Rights. In 1947, Humphrey wrote the original 400-page draft of what would become one of the most important human rights documents in history. After many consultations and revisions, the UN General Assembly unanimously adopted the declaration on 10 December 1948.

The UN and War Refugees

The Second World War devastated Europe physically, economically, and emotionally. During the war, many people fled their homes to escape the Nazis and their allies. Some fled to escape the fighting. Others lost their homes in the bombings and battles. When the war finally ended, many people in Eastern Europe fled to escape communism. In all, almost 20 million people in Europe found themselves homeless. Families lived on the streets, carrying the few possessions they had with them. One of the first challenges facing the United Nations was to provide aid for these war **refugees**.

In 1946, the United Nations established the International Refugee Organization (IRO). Working with the Red Cross, the IRO took over abandoned military bases and prisoner-of-war camps and turned them into refugee shelters. Canada contributed $18 million to the IRO. Many Canadians aided with in the refugee relocations.

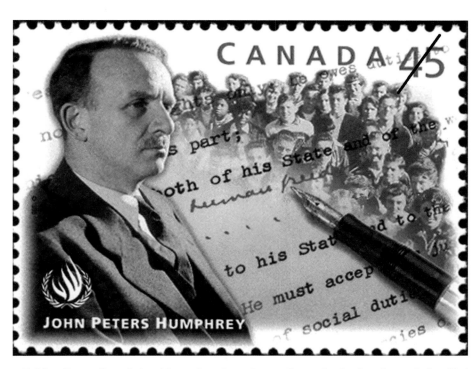

Learn more about the United Nations' Universal Declaration of Human Rights

Figure 5.13 Canadian John Humphrey's role as the principal writer of the Universal Declaration of Human Rights was not fully recognized until the original draft containing his handwritten notes was discovered in 1988. This stamp, issued by Canada Post in October 1988, commemorated the 50th anniversary of the UN adoption of the Declaration. Today, the John Humphrey Centre for Peace and Human Rights promotes universal human rights through teaching and education, particularly among young people. To what extent do you think Canada upholds this commitment to human rights today?

Human Rights

The discovery of the horrors of the Nazi concentration camps focused attention on human rights. The refusal of many countries to offer asylum to Jewish refugees contributed to the massive death toll. The United Nations was determined that such a tragic mistake would never be repeated. Therefore, one of its first priorities was to guarantee all people everywhere the right to seek asylum from persecution in the Universal Declaration of Human Rights.

Refugees in Canada

As you discovered in Chapter 3, Canada had been one of the worst offenders in denying entry to Jewish refugees. As a result, King's government faced growing pressure from humanitarian groups to lift the country's immigration restrictions. In response, Canada dropped some of its discriminatory immigration policies, including those directed toward Jewish refugees. Between 1947 and 1952, more than 186 000 refugees found asylum in Canada.

Since the Second World War, Canada has accepted thousands of refugees from all countries around the world. The Nansen Refugee Award (formerly the Nansen Medal), issued by the United Nations High Commission for Refugees, is the highest honour awarded to individuals and groups for protecting refugees. Canada received this honour in 1986. It is the only country ever to receive the award.

"Everyone has the right to seek and to enjoy in other countries asylum from persecution."

–Article 14, Universal Declaration of Human Rights

"A mix of economic self-interest, international pressure, and humanitarianism led an initially reluctant Canada to participate in a plan to resettled these 'hard-core' refugees ... Welcomed as freedom lovers, but also seen as war casualties who might require costly support, most of Canada's 100 000 [refugees] set about rebuilding their lives while also influencing Canada's Cold War culture."

–Franca Iacovetta, historian, The University of Toronto, 2004

Figure 5.14   In 1956, over 200 000 refugees fled Hungary after the Soviet army moved in to put down an uprising against communist rule. Canada accepted 37 500 Hungarian refugees. Under what circumstances do you think Canada should open its doors to refugees?

Challenge and Response

1. Develop a mind map to illustrate the major elements of Canada's foreign policy after the Second World War.
2. As a class, develop your own charter of rights and responsibilities. Include provisions to deal with harassment by your peers and the right to be different. Use your school's code of conduct to help you.
3. Reread the quotation on this page. In what ways do you think the refugees from Eastern Europe would have influenced the attitudes of Canadians toward the Cold War?

Thérèse Casgrain: Feminist, Reformer, Humanitarian

"The true liberation of women cannot take place without the liberation of men."

Source: Thérèse Casgrain, *A Woman in a Man's World*
(Toronto: McClelland & Stewart, 1972).

Thérèse Forget was born in 1896 in Montréal. At the age of 19, she married Pierre Casgrain, a Liberal politician. She campaigned for the political, social, and economic rights of women. In the 1920s and 1930s, Casgrain had a profound influence on the feminist movement in Québec. One of her most cherished goals was fulfilled after the women of Québec won the right to vote in provincial elections in 1940.

During the Second World War, Casgrain ran, unsuccessfully, as an independent Liberal candidate in the federal election of 1940. After the war, she turned to the Co-operative Commonwealth Federation (CCF), whose social policies more closely reflected her own ideals. In 1951, she became the first woman in Québec to head a political party after she was elected leader of the CCF's Québec wing.

In the post-war years, Casgrain broadened the scope of her human rights campaign to include the rights of Aboriginal peoples, refugees, and other groups. In 1961, Casgrain founded the Québec branch of the Voice of Women, a movement dedicated to world peace. She campaigned against the war in Vietnam while heading an

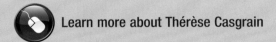
Learn more about Thérèse Casgrain

organization to provide medical aid for the thousands of victims of that war.

In 1966, Casgrain joined other humanitarians in the newly formed Canadian Human Rights Federation. In 1967, the National Council of Jewish Women named Casgrain "Woman of the Century" in Québec for her work promoting human rights for refugees. In 1974, Casgrain became a Companion of the Order of Canada.

In 1970, Casgrain was appointed to the Senate. She sat as an independent for nine months until she reached the **mandatory retirement** age of 75. Having to leave the Senate because of her age inspired Casgrain to campaign for the rights of seniors. She continued to campaign for human rights for all Canadians until her death in 1981.

Figure 5.15 A postage stamp honouring Thérèse Casgrain was issued by Canada Post in April 1985. Today, the Canadian government sponsors the Thérèse Casgrain Volunteer Award for volunteers who campaign for human rights. What do you think young Canadians today can do to support human rights?

Responding
1. What do you think Casgrain meant in the quotation about the liberation of women and men? Give reasons for your response.
2. Do you think that mandatory retirement violates the human rights of older Canadians? Give reasons for your response.

"We in Canada are agreed … that totalitarian communist aggression constitutes a direct and immediate threat to every democratic country, including Canada … The best guarantee of peace today is the creation and preservation by the nations of the Free World … of an overwhelming preponderance of force over any adversary or possible combination of adversaries. This force must not be only military; it must be economic, it must be moral."

–Minister of External Affairs Louis St. Laurent, describing the formation of NATO, 1948

 Learn more about NATO

Military Alliances

As the countries of Europe attempted to rebuild after the war, it appeared that the Iron Curtain that divided the continent was becoming increasingly inflexible. In response, the Allies wanted a peacetime military alliance to defend against potential Soviet aggression.

The Creation of NATO

Prior to the Second World War, most countries, including Canada, practised a policy of **isolationism**. They preferred not to get involved in conflicts that did not concern them. The global power structure changed dramatically after the war and all countries now had to re-evaluate their international commitments. As a result, in April 1949, the Allies joined in the North Atlantic Treaty Organization (NATO). The alliance represented a milestone in international relations. The members of NATO pledged to defend one another in the event of an attack by an enemy nation.

Under the NATO agreement, each member had to contribute troops and equipment to NATO defence forces. Canada agreed to station troops at NATO bases in Europe—the first time Canadian troops had served overseas in peacetime. Canada's NATO commitment also led to a significant increase in military spending—from 1.7 per cent of the country's **Gross National Product** (GNP) in 1947 to 7.6 per cent in 1953.

NATO strengthened Canada's emerging role as a middle power. Through the alliance, Canada had the opportunity to exert its influence in world affairs. Its long-standing relationship with Britain and the United States placed it in an ideal position to act as a mediator in any disagreements over defence policies.

Figure 5.16 NATO leaders, meeting in 1952, wanted to prevent any further Soviet expansion in Europe and to keep Germany in check—even though NATO was a defensive alliance.

MAP STUDY: NATO and the Warsaw Pact

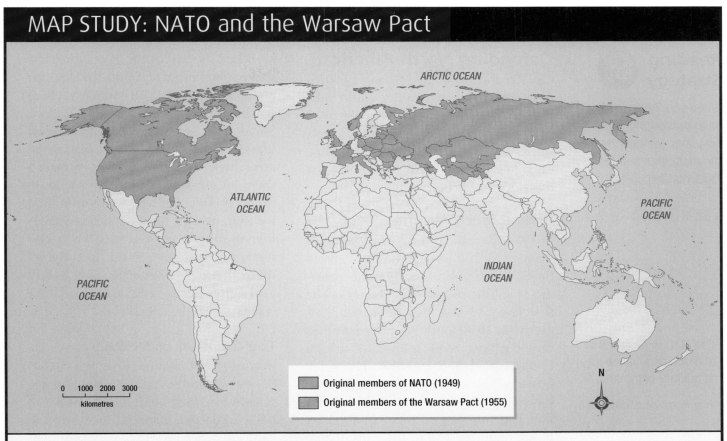

ARCTIC OCEAN

ATLANTIC OCEAN

PACIFIC OCEAN

INDIAN OCEAN

PACIFIC OCEAN

PACIFIC OCEAN

0 1000 2000 3000
kilometres

N

Original members of NATO (1949)
Original members of the Warsaw Pact (1955)

Source: Don Quinlan, et al., *Twentieth Century Viewpoints*, 2nd edition, (Don Mills: Oxford University Press, 2003), 148.

Figure 5.17   This map shows the two major alliances of the Cold War during the 1950s: NATO and the Warsaw Pact.

NATO's primary goal was to stop further Soviet expansion in Europe. The original members of NATO included Canada, the United States, Britain, France, Belgium, the Netherlands, Luxembourg, Denmark, Norway, Iceland, Portugal, and Italy. Greece and Turkey joined in 1952. West Germany joined in 1955. As a precaution, German forces were placed under US control. NATO still exists today.

In 1955, the Soviet Union responded to the formation of NATO by forming an alliance of its own. The Warsaw Pact included all of the satellite countries within the Soviet sphere of influence: Albania, Bulgaria, Czechoslovakia, East Germany, Hungary, Poland, Romania, the Soviet Union, and Yugoslavia. With the fall of the Soviet Union in the late 1980s, the Warsaw Pact was disbanded.

Throughout the Cold War, these two powerful alliances stood their ground in Europe, always threatening—but never engaging—in direct combat.

Analysis and Response

1. Do you think the creation of two powerful alliances prevented another large-scale, global war? Justify your response.
2. Today, NATO has expanded to include 26 members, including Poland, Bulgaria, Romania, and the Czech Republic. Why do you think former members of the Warsaw Pact joined NATO? As a class, speculate on what you think may be the greatest threat to NATO today.

Reading Strategy

When you finish reading each paragraph, make sure that you understand the main idea and the facts that support it.

"NORAD is as much a diplomatic alliance as a military command."

–*Time* magazine, 19 May 1958

Learn more about NORAD

Defending North America

Canada and the United States knew the next international conflict could take place in North America. Any Soviet invasion would likely come from the north, across the Arctic. Therefore, defending Canada's vast northern territory was a top priority for both countries.

Early Radar Warning

In 1954, Canada and the United States agreed to build three radar lines across the Arctic to provide early radar warning of an impending Soviet attack. The first line was the Pinetree Line, completed in 1954. With 33 radar stations, the line cost $450 million of which Canada paid $150 million. The Mid-Canada Line was completed in 1957. It included 98 radar stations. Canada financed this line on its own, at a cost of $250 million. The northernmost line was the Distant Early Warning (DEW) Line. The United States agreed to finance the line, but Canadians, including many Aboriginal peoples, built the line beginning in 1954.

The US, however, ran the radar installations. This establishment of a strong American military presence in the Canadian North had serious implications. Canada had to give up its sovereignty around the radar lines—only the United States could decide who entered the facilities. Canadian reporters had their stories censored by the US military to ensure the "right" message got out. The building of the radar lines also affected the Inuit. For some, the construction and installation of the stations disrupted their resource base. For others, their lives were uprooted as they were relocated to counterbalance the influx of American personnel. (See page 164.)

Although hundreds of millions of dollars were invested in the radar lines, in the end their usefulness was short-lived. In 1957, the Soviets launched the first Sputnik satellite. The rocket that launched Sputnik into orbit could also be used to launch nuclear warheads destined for the United States. The Americans were concerned that the Soviets had taken the lead in the arms race. In response, they replaced their long-range bombers with long-range missiles called intercontinental ballistic missiles, or ICBMs. The Soviets then built their own ICBMs. The radar warning systems could not detect these missiles. Therefore, only a few years after being built, the radar lines were regarded as obsolete.

The Creation of NORAD

In addition to the radar lines, the United States wanted a unified air defence system for North America. In 1956, the US persuaded Canada to form the North American Air Defense Agreement (NORAD). (The name was changed to the North American Aerospace Defense Command in 1981.) Under the agreement, each country maintained its own independent air force. In the event of an attack, however, both air forces would be under joint control, with an American commander and a Canadian second-in-command. Both countries needed time to integrate their air forces, though. As a result, the agreement was not formally signed until 1958.

NORAD had wide-ranging implications for Canada's military autonomy. For the first time, Canada was squarely under the American defence umbrella. The country was now committed to participating in US conflicts even if it did not want to get involved. Canada also had to rely on the American defence industry for its military hardware. All of Canada's existing defence equipment was eventually replaced with American-produced technology. (In Chapter 7, you will learn about some other military and defence controversies.)

Figure 5.18 Soviet citizens gathered to watch ICBMs as they were paraded through Moscow's Red Square. What effect do you think the Soviets wanted to create by these public demonstrations of their military power?

Challenge and Response

1. Reread St. Laurent's quotation about NATO on page 160. What powerful words and phrases does he use? What impact do these have? What gives these words and phrases their power?

2. Canada's commitments to NATO have cost hundreds of millions of dollars in military personnel and equipment. Do you think this investment is worthwhile? Give reasons for your response.

3. Use a T-chart to show the advantages and disadvantages of a common defence policy with the United States.

COMMUNITIES

The Inuit of Inukjuak

While Canada and the United States were developing their military defence system in the Arctic, the government was relocating Inuit communities to the same region. In the fall of 1953, supply ships left the small community of Inukjuak in northern Québec. The ships were bound for Ellesmere and Cornwallis islands 2000 kilometres away in the High Arctic. On board were several Inuit families. The Inuit had agreed to leave their community and relocate after the government assured them that there was good hunting and better economic opportunities. It promised them they could return home after two years. The following excerpts reveal part of the impact the relocation had on the people of the Inukjuak community.

"We were sent away to a place they told us abounded in wildlife. We would never be hungry again, they told us. The Government carried out this move, even though we did not consent to being sent away … In those days, Inuit were not educated and did not understand the meaning of written documents, nor how government worked and operated. We were also not aware of all Canadians' freedom to live where they so chose. We did not know of our right to refuse to be moved to the High Arctic … Since we were not knowledgeable about this, though, our fathers gave in and agreed to move. They mostly feared the awesome authority of the Government."

Source: Markoosie Patsauq,
House of Commons Standing Committee
on Aboriginal Affairs, 19 March 1990.

"We had been promised that our whole group would stay together, that we would not be separated. But when we got near Craig Harbour on Ellesmere Island, the RCMP said to us, half of you have to get off here. We just went into a panic because they had promised that they would not separate us … I remember we were all on the deck of the *C.D. Howe*. All the women started to cry.

And when women start to cry, the dogs join in. It was eerie … The women were crying, the dogs were howling, and the men had to huddle to decide who is going to go where."

Source: John Amagoalik,
House of Commons Standing Committee
on Aboriginal Affairs, 19 March 1990.

"We were landed on a bare shore … It started snowing just as we went about pitching our tents. The autumn had already arrived, it was bitterly cold and already freezing … We could not fetch water from anywhere. We had to melt ice for water, and this was an entirely new burden. Then when winter came, we had to settle into igloos … When spring came, we gathered wood scraps from the dump … Then when summer came around, they started to build houses from the wood from the dump … There was not much to insulate these houses with. They … insulated them with cloth rags … So when we got these houses, they were actually one room shacks with no other rooms. We had stoves, old drum stoves that we made ourselves. There was also a lot of coal discarded at the dump. So we went there to scrounge coal that we would use in our homemade stoves. There was no other light. Old coal was our only source of heat all winter."

Source: Sarah Amagoalik,
House of Commons Standing Committee
on Aboriginal Affairs, 19 March 1990.

"In regard to the promise of caribou, it sounded abundant. But in reality [my father] was restricted to killing one caribou a year …. He was also told of abounding musk oxen. But it turned out to be: If you kill a musk ox, you can be fined $5000.00 or be arrested. This turned out to be an enticement, a lure, and a false one at that."

Source: Unidentified testimony,
House of Commons Standing Committee
on Aboriginal Affairs, 19 March 1990.

Figure 5.19 The Inuit who were relocated lived in substandard housing, like here in Resolute Bay on Cornwallis Island in 1956. They had no schools or medical facilities in their new locations. They had experience hunting caribou and other game, but none hunting polar bears. What impact do you think these changes had on their lives?

Responding
1. What do you think was the hardest part of the relocation for the people of Inukjuak? What would be the hardest part for you if you were in a similar situation?
2. In what ways did the government violate the rights of the Inuit? Could the government carry out a similar relocation today? Explain your response.

ISSUES

Apologizing for Past Actions

The issue: Should Canada issue an apology for its past actions in relocating Inuit peoples?

Relocations like the one that so dramatically affected the Inuit of Inukjuak occurred across the Arctic between 1939 and 1963. Officially, the government claimed the relocations were in the Inuit's best interests. Inuit populations had increased while game resources had declined. The Inuit could no longer live off the land in their home communities. If they did not relocate, they would have to rely on government assistance.

Many Inuit believed there was another motive behind the relocations, however. The Cold War and the need for defence led to a strong American military presence in the North. The Americans had only accepted Canada's sovereignty in the Arctic as part of the DEW Line agreements. The Inuit believed the government relocated them to reinforce Canada's claim to sovereignty.

In the 1970s, the Inuit demanded an apology and compensation for the pain and suffering they endured for more than 20 years. In 1996, the government offered the Inuit $10 million in compensation, but refused to apologize.

"It is the Inuit presence in the North that has given this country its greatest claim to sovereignty to that one-third of Canada's land mass in Labrador, Québec, Nunavut, and the Inuvialuit region of the western Arctic that Inuit call home."

Source: Okalik Eegeesiak,
president of the Inuit Tapiriit Kanatami,
January 1998.

"An apology implies we're apologizing for something we did. Now there's nobody in the government who had anything to do with the relocation at the original time; so I think it might be more appropriate to say there'd be an expression of regret on behalf of the Canadian people."

Source: An official in the Department of Indian and Northern Affairs,
March 1996, "Ethics Updates: Inuit Relocation,"
The University of San Diego, 2001.

"The absence of an apology is like a slap in the face to us. The government is behaving like a criminal who has confessed his crimes but has expressed no remorse."

Source: Inuit leader John Amagoalik, 8 March 1996.

Responding

1. In what ways was the relocation of the Inuit similar to, and different from, the relocation of people of Japanese heritage during the Second World War?

2. Why do you think many Inuit resented the fact that the government refused to apologize in 1996?

3. In January 1998, the federal government issued a statement of reconciliation to all Aboriginal peoples. It apologized for some specific injustices, including residential schools, but it did not specifically apologize for the Inuit relocations. Do you think the government should have apologized for the relocations? Write a letter to your Member of Parliament expressing your point of view.

Cold War Hot Spots

At first, the Cold War was a war of words as the United States and the Soviet Union tried to persuade or pressure countries into their sphere of influence. By 1950, however, Cold War tensions were about to spill over into armed conflicts in other parts of the world. These conflicts would have a major impact on Canada.

The Korean War

The first active combat between the two superpowers took place in Korea in the early 1950s. During the Second World War, Japanese forces occupied Korea. After the war, the Allies divided the Korean peninsula at the 38th parallel. The Soviet Union supported a communist regime in North Korea. The Americans supported a democratic republic in South Korea. For a few years, the two sides maintained an uneasy truce. Then, on 25 June 1950, North Korea launched a massive invasion of South Korea. They had Stalin's support and an arsenal of Soviet weapons at their disposal.

The United States immediately asked the United Nations to condemn North Korea for its aggression. The Americans began gathering support for a multinational "police action" against the North. The Soviet ambassador to the United Nations would have vetoed any condemnation. However, at that time the Soviets were boycotting the UN because of its refusal to recognize the new communist regime in the People's Republic of China. Without the Soviets to block it, the resolution condemning North Korea passed. The UN Security Council demanded that North Korea withdraw its troops.

When it failed to comply, the UN authorized an international military force to drive out the invaders.

Canada's Involvement

Canada was among 16 countries that agreed to take part in the Korean War. Although officially the military response was a UN initiative, the United States headed the force. It marked the first time that Canadian forces had served under US commanders.

Canada agreed to supply three battleships and a squadron from the Royal Canadian Air Force. King was reluctant to send troops, though. After a three-day Cabinet meeting, however, he agreed to call for a voluntary force to go to Korea. Thousands of Canadians responded. The first Canadian troops headed to the Korean peninsula in November 1950.

In the meantime, China had joined the fight in support of North Korea. The addition of hundreds of thousands of Chinese troops began to tip the balance in favour of the North Koreans. In a massive offensive in April 1951, Chinese forces surrounded Canadian and Australian units at Kapyong. The UN forces managed to hold their positions, preventing the Chinese offensive from gaining further ground. The Canadian and Australian units received presidential citations from the United States for their bravery under fire.

Stalemate

For months, the battle lines shifted back and forth. With the two sides locked in a stalemate, the US commander, Douglas MacArthur, urged all-out war—including the use of nuclear weapons. The American president, Harry Truman, refused to take such drastic measures, though, and so the stalemate continued.

Learn more about the Korean War

"I left my hillside battle position to come back to Canada and when I returned almost two years later for a second tour of duty, I was astonished to be assigned to the same hill I had left. The trenches were deeper, the defences and the barbed wire seemed more permanent, and the possibility of military victory was all but forgotten."

–Canadian private D.A. Strickland, 1953

MAP STUDY: Stalemate in Korea

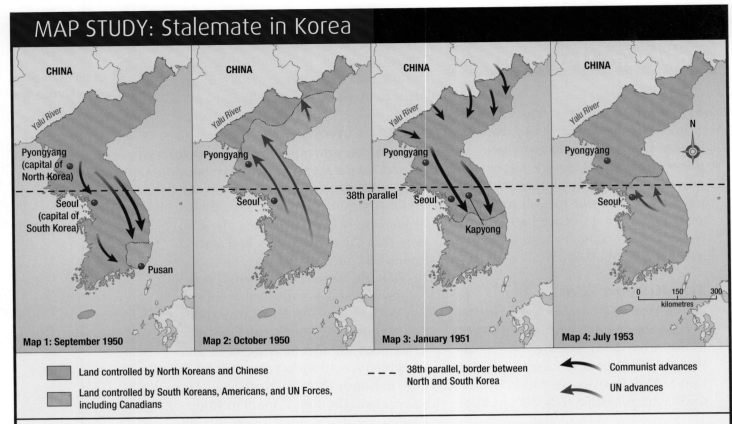

Source: Don Quinlan, et al., *Twentieth Century Viewpoints*, 2nd edition, (Don Mills: Oxford University Press, 2003), 189.

Figure 5.20 These four maps show the military offensives at different stages during the Korean War.

Despite their military power, things did not go well for the UN forces in the early months of the war. In September 1950, the North Korean army had pushed the UN troops back to the southern tip of the peninsula (see map 1). By October 1950, however, UN forces had pushed North Korean and Chinese troops considerably back behind the 38th parallel (see map 2). The see-saw battle continued as the two sides pushed one another up and down the peninsula. By January 1951, the North Koreans had pushed the UN forces back into the southern part of the peninsula (see map 3). When the war finally ended in July 1953, both sides ended up where they had started (see map 4).

Analysis and Response

1. To what city did UN forces retreat at the start of the North Korean invasion of South Korea?
2. Why do you think the UN forces were reluctant to cross the Yalu River?
3. Do you think Canada should have participated in the Korean War? Give reasons for your response.

Although peace talks began in July 1951, sporadic outbursts of fighting continued for two more years. Finally, the two sides declared a **ceasefire** in July 1953. The war ended where it began. North and South Korea remained divided at the 38th parallel. The North remained a communist country; the South remained a democratic republic. It has remained an uneasy truce ever since.

The Consequences of the War

The Korean War was the first major test of the commitment of the United Nations to respond forcefully to international aggression. For the United States, it was an opportunity to demonstrate its military strength and to prove beyond a doubt that it had overtaken Britain as the world's greatest military power.

For Canada, the war marked a turning point in foreign policy. Traditionally, Canada's military commitments had been to Britain. Now, the United States had become Canada's closest military ally. In the future, Canada would use its position as a trusted ally to attempt to moderate what was often aggressive US foreign policy. As would be the case throughout the Cold War, Canada was on the same side as the Americans, even though it did not always agree with them.

The Suez Crisis

Following the war, in 1948 the Western Allies had partitioned the Arab state of Palestine to create a Jewish homeland for Holocaust survivors. As a result, the Middle East had become a hotbed of political tension between Arabs and Israelis. By 1956, a crisis in the region threatened to lead to a major confrontation between the two sides.

At the time, Britain and France controlled the Suez Canal in Egypt. The canal was a vital trade route that joined the Mediterranean Sea to the Red Sea and the Indian Ocean. It was also the key supply route for the Middle East's

Figure 5.21 By the end of the war, 25 000 Canadians had served in Korea; 516 lost their lives. More than two million Koreans died in the fighting. Yet in the end, North and South Korea remained the same as they had been before the war started. Do you think the UN intervention in Korea was justified? Give reasons for your response.

Reading Strategy

After you read a quotation, take note of who the speaker is by checking the source line. This will help you put the quotation in context. Notice that in this text there are two types of margin quotations—one from noted authorities and the other from young people. What sets these two types of quotations apart from one another?

Learn more about the UN Security Council

Figure 5.22 As British and French tanks rolled into Egypt, the invasion created a huge challenge for the United Nations. As members of the Security Council, both countries could use their **veto** power to kill any motions for UN military intervention. How would this undermine efforts to avoid further conflict?

most valuable resource—oil. The Egyptian president, Gamal Abdel Nasser, wanted to free his country from the remnants of colonial rule and to destroy the newly created state of Israel. To do both, he needed money. One way to raise it was to **nationalize** the Suez Canal.

In response, Britain and France threatened to attack Egypt. They lobbied the United States and Canada to join them, but both countries refused. Then Britain and France negotiated a secret agreement with Israel. Israel would invade Egypt. Then Britain and France would issue an ultimatum demanding that Israeli and Egyptian forces leave the region. Israel would agree. Egypt would not. Then Britain and France would launch an intense bombing campaign around the Canal Zone. Nasser's government would fall and the British and

French would regain control of the Suez Canal.

The plan went into action on 29 October 1956 when Israel attacked Egypt. The Soviet Union threatened to launch a nuclear attack against London and Paris if Britain and France did not withdraw. The United States and Canada also demanded that Britain and France withdraw. The world appeared to be teetering on the brink of a third world war.

Canada's Role

International tensions ran high as the United Nations desperately looked for a solution to the crisis. At the time, a future Canadian prime minister, Lester B. Pearson, was secretary of state for External Affairs. After persistent and endless rounds of lobbying, Pearson persuaded the UN General Assembly to organize the world's first international peacekeeping mission. The United Nations ordered all foreign troops out of Egypt. Then it sent in the first UN peacekeeping force to keep the warring sides apart and maintain peace in the region.

Canada's Peacekeeping Role

Canadian General E.L.M. Burns commanded the United Nations Emergency Force (UNEF). However, Egypt rejected the inclusion of Canadian soldiers because their uniforms bore a close resemblance to those of the British forces that had invaded the Canal Zone. Instead, Canadian troops supplied logistical support and aerial reconnaissance personnel.

After the Suez crisis, the United Nations deployed several peacekeeping missions to hot spots around the world. Between 1956 and the late 1980s, Canada took part in every UN peacekeeping mission. For Canada, peacekeeping was a means of meeting some of its objectives as a middle power. Many Canadians viewed peacekeeping as a noble and moral role for Canada to play on the world stage.

Figure 5.23 Pearson's success in averting a confrontation between the superpowers earned him the Nobel Peace Prize. He went to Stockholm in December 1957 to receive the award. To what extent do you think this was an important event for Canada?

"Diplomacy is letting someone else have your way."

—Lester B. Pearson, January 1957

"I am aware that in the work which I have done ... I was the spokesman for Canada and not operating in any personal capacity. Therefore, the award is a tribute to the efforts Canada has made since World War II to bring about peace and better international relations."

—Lester B. Pearson, upon learning he was to receive the Nobel Peace Prize, 12 October 1957

"Canadian troops have been deployed throughout the world as peacekeepers. This is one of the most significant roles of Canadian Forces throughout the world."

—Niall Ohalloran, Dartmouth High School, 2003

Challenge and Response

1. Do you think the United Nations was right to take action after North Korea invaded South Korea? Explain your position in a letter to the editor.

2. How important do you think Pearson's role in the Suez crisis was in establishing Canada's position as a middle power? Explain your response.

3. In your opinion, which Cold War hot spot—Korea or the Suez Canal—posed the greatest threat to world peace? Give reasons for your response.

4. In a survey, Canadians identified peacekeeping (along with hockey and public health care) as one of the most important symbols of Canada. Does Canada's role as peacekeeper today justify its use as a symbol of Canada? Express your point of view in a visual or written presentation.

Skill Path:
Analyzing and Interpreting Visual Evidence

Visual evidence can reveal many clues about past events and other cultures. Visual evidence includes paintings, drawings, and photographs. They can tell you about the clothes people wore, the types of entertainment they enjoyed, and the things that were important to them at a particular time and place.

STEP 1: Study the Evidence

When you analyze visual evidence, you have to look at it closely to see both the big picture and the details it contains. This means you probably have to look at the evidence several times. To help you think about what you are seeing, ask yourself the following questions:

- Does the work have a title or date? If so, what do these tell me?
- What action is taking place?
- Who are the people? What does their relationship to one another appear to be?
- Is there any symbolism in the image? If so, what does it represent?
- What else do I need to know to gain a better understanding of this image?

STEP 2: Identify Bias

Visual evidence has its limits. As a viewer, you see what the artist or photographer wants you to see. A single picture seldom reveals all there is to know about a person or event. Like writers, artists and photographers bring bias to their work. Artists may leave out certain details or add others.

Photographers may centre an image to present a certain point of view. When identifying bias, ask yourself the following questions:

- What message is in the image? Is it positive or negative?
- What is the purpose of the image?
- Who is the intended audience? Does the image reflect or attempt to influence this audience's perspective?
- Has the person who created the image used special effects? If so, how do they affect the accuracy of the image?
- Is there any evidence that conflicts with this view?

STEP 3: Summarize Your Findings

Once you have analyzed the visual evidence and identified any bias, summarize your findings. Describe the image carefully so that your audience can understand your analysis. Point out the main elements in the image first. Then describe the details. If possible, include a copy of the visual evidence so your audience can share your analysis first-hand.

STEP 4: Practise Your Skill

Analyze the visual evidence about the Cold War using the photographs and cartoons in this chapter. First, analyze each image individually. Then look for relationships among the images. What conclusions can you draw about the Cold War by looking at the visual evidence?

Thinking Like a Historian:
Analyzing Cause and Consequences

Essential Question: As a historian, how do you analyze how and why certain circumstances and actions led to certain consequences?

Historians have often considered the reasons for the rapid deterioration in relations between the United States and the Soviet Union in the aftermath of the Second World War. Who was primarily responsible for creating the atmosphere of suspicion and mistrust that led to the Cold War? Were the Americans provoking tensions with the Soviets by demonstrating their military power when they dropped the atomic bombs on Japan? Were the

Americans justified to be concerned about Soviet aggression and expansion in Eastern Europe immediately after the war? What role did Canada play at the time? What role do you think Canada should have played?

To identify the causes of an event like the Cold War, historians have to read and reflect on the words and actions of the participants. Then they make logical connections between these words and actions and the events that subsequently took place to create an accurate picture of the causes of the event.

You, the Historian

1. Review the information in this chapter, including the links on *The Canadian Challenge* website. Create a timeline of events that contributed to the development of the Cold War. Then circle those events that you feel are the most significant. Justify your decisions with your peers.

2 Create a concept web to show the factors that caused the Cold War to intensify. Rank-order which factors you believe to be the most important to the least important, beginning with number 1 to indicate the most important factor.

3. What was Canada's role in contributing to or easing the tensions of the Cold War? In your view, was this the most effective course of action for Canada to play? Give reasons for your response in an essay about Canada and the Cold War.

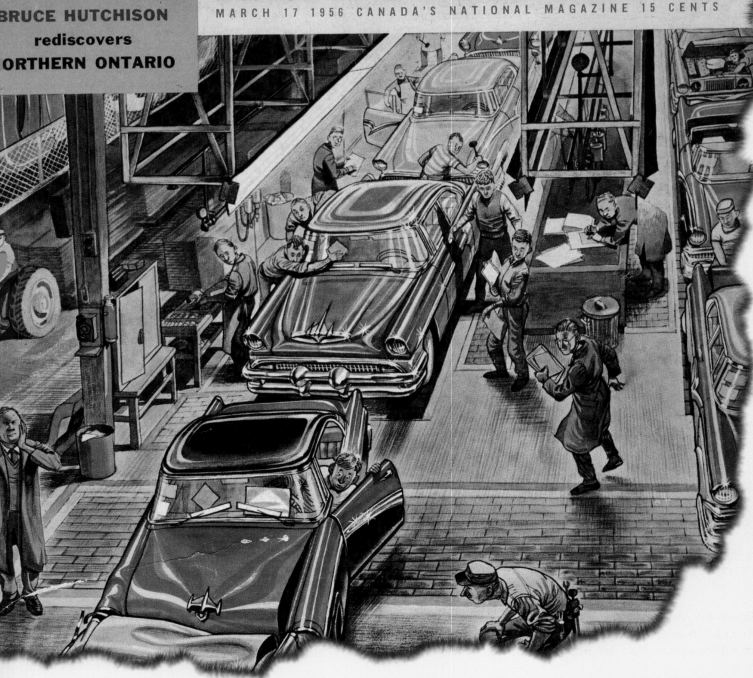

TORONTO
The world's
fastest growing city

BRUCE HUTCHISON
rediscovers
NORTHERN ONTARIO

MACLEAN'S

MARCH 17 1956 CANADA'S NATIONAL MAGAZINE 15 CENTS

Chapter at a Glance

Thinking Ahead

The period between 1945 and 1957 was a time of economic growth and prosperity, symbolized by the emergence of a new consumer society. Governments invested billions of dollars on megaprojects to sustain the growth of industry. The population soared as more couples started families and more immigrants came to Canada. Newfoundland joined the nation as the 10th province, while in Québec a new sense of nationalism was born. Canadians began to express their identity through the arts. Teenagers began to question traditional values. Middle-class families flocked to the new suburbs.

As you explore this period of change, think about these key questions:

- How did Canada's identity change in the 1950s?
- What impact did post-war prosperity have on Canadians?
- How did billion-dollar megaprojects contribute to Canada's growth and prosperity?
- How did Canadian culture evolve in the 1950s?
- What impact did the population explosion have on Canadian society?

Figure 6.1 After the Great Depression and the Second World War, Canadians were ready to enjoy the new prosperity of peacetime. What evidence does this cover of *Maclean's* magazine from 1956 reveal about the prosperity of the post-war era?

Profile in Power:
Louis Stephen St. Laurent

"Our nation was planned as a political partnership of two great races. It was planned by men of vision, of tolerance, as a partnership in which both of the partners would retain their essential characteristics, their religion and their culture."

—Prime Minister Louis St. Laurent, 6 August 1948

Figure 6.2 Louis St. Laurent (1882–1973)

In his first election as Liberal leader in 1949, members of Louis St. Laurent's Liberal Party worried about his public image. Would his quiet, dignified manner appeal to Canadians? On a campaign stop in Manitoba, St. Laurent approached a group of children standing on the railway platform. His natural ease and friendliness quickly charmed the boys and girls. A reporter, noticing the interaction between St. Laurent and the children, predicted "Uncle Louis" would be hard to beat.

The reporter was right. To enhance his public image as a family man, St. Laurent invited the media into his home to take pictures of him with his five grandchildren. His relaxed style reflected the comfortable new mood of the country. St. Laurent promised Canadians that the Liberals would provide them with continued prosperity. Canadians responded by electing him as their prime minister twice, in 1949 and 1953.

Under St. Laurent, Canada launched a series of initiatives designed to promote the welfare of Canadians. He helped to bring Newfoundland and Labrador into Confederation. He opened the doors to greater immigration. He took measures to promote Canadian arts and culture. He initiated the building of a highway across the country and the construction of the St. Lawrence Seaway to create greater access to the markets of Central Canada.

By 1957, however, Canadians began to grow weary of the Liberals' long hold on power. In the election of 1957, St. Laurent won the most votes but his opponent, Conservative John Diefenbaker, won the most seats. Some members of the Liberal Party urged St. Laurent to form a coalition with either the Co-operative Commonwealth Federation or the Social Credit Party. St. Laurent declined, however, believing that Canadians had passed a verdict on his government. His government resigned and in 1958 St. Laurent retired from politics.

Those who served under St. Laurent admired his intellect, decisiveness, and patriotism. Many looked upon him with great personal affection. Canadians never lost their affection for "Uncle Louis," either. He was fondly remembered when he died in Québec City in 1973 at the age of 91.

Responding

1. In your view, what was St. Laurent's greatest contribution as prime minister?
2. How important do you think it is for a politician to have a positive public image?
   Do you think female politicians have to work harder to create a positive public image than male politicians? Give reasons for your response.

Figure 6.3 Louis St. Laurent was the first prime minister to cultivate a media image. What do you think voters might have found appealing about St. Laurent based on this image?

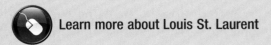 **Learn more about Louis St. Laurent**

Symbols of Independence

After the Second World War, Canada took steps to assert greater independence from Britain. For the first time, Canadians were citizens of Canada. The Supreme Court of Canada became the country's final court of appeal, and a new tradition began of appointing Canadians to fill the position of Governor General of Canada.

Canadian Citizenship

Before the Second World War, Canadians were British subjects. After the war, Canada began to loosen its ties to Britain. The Citizenship Act of 1946 went into effect on 1 January 1947. It defined the country's citizens as Canadians whose primary loyalty was to Canada, not Britain. Canada was the first Commonwealth country to establish citizenship separate from Britain. The government wanted to promote a greater sense of national identity and to put immigrants on equal legal footing with people born in Canada. It was the first post-war step along Canada's continuing road to full independence.

The Citizenship Act
- defined who was a Canadian citizen
- established that immigrants who were 21 could apply for citizenship after living in Canada for five years
- gave men and women equal citizenship status—that is, the citizenship of a wife was no longer determined by the citizenship of her husband
- outlined the conditions under which Canadians lost their citizenship

Flaws in the Act

The new legislation was not without its critics. Some people objected to the fact that it gave special treatment to British subjects. Unlike immigrants from non-Commonwealth countries, British subjects did not have to take the oath of allegiance or take part in a formal swearing-in ceremony to receive citizenship. Nor did the act allow for **dual citizenship**. Canadians who became citizens of another country had to renounce their Canadian citizenship. This had long-lasting consequences for some Canadians.

Between 1947 and the passage of a new Citizenship Act in 1977, provisions in the 1947 act created a generation of "Lost Canadians." They are the children of fathers who left Canada to work in other countries. When the fathers took out citizenship in these countries, they automatically lost their Canadian citizenship. What they did not know was that their children automatically lost their citizenship, as well. Many of these children later returned to Canada, only to discover they were no longer Canadian citizens and could not live in Canada without applying for immigrant status.

These little-known provisions of the act also affected other groups. They include war brides and their children born outside of Canada and "border babies"—babies born across the border in the United States because that is where the closest hospital was. Many babies born to Canadians living outside Canada have no citizenship, either, because their births were not properly registered. Some Canadians even lost their citizenship because they, or their ancestors, were illegitimate at birth.

Experts estimate there are at least 200 000 Lost Canadians in Canada today. For years, many have been petitioning the government to regain their citizenship without success. In May 2007,

"For the national unity of Canada and for the future and greatness of this country ... all of us, new Canadians or old, [must] have a consciousness of a common purpose and common interests as Canadians [so] that all of us are able to say with pride and say with meaning: 'I am a Canadian citizen.'"

–Paul Martin Sr, minister of Health and Welfare, The House of Commons, 22 October 1945

"Canada's Citizenship Act of 1947 was the first in the world to make no distinction between native-born and newcomers."

–Richard Gwyn, *Nationalism with Walls: The Unbearable Lightness of Being Canadian*, 1995

however, the government announced plans to ensure that anyone born or naturalized in Canada on or after 1 January 1947 is a Canadian citizen.

The Supreme Court of Canada

Prior to 1949, the Supreme Court was not Canada's highest court of appeal. Decisions made by the Court were subject to the final authority of the Judicial Committee of the Privy Council in London, which had the power to review—and sometimes overrule—decisions made by Canadian courts. Before the war, there had been plans to abolish this appeals process. Now that the war was over, Canada was determined to make the Supreme Court of Canada truly supreme. In 1949, St. Laurent's government passed a bill ending all appeals to the Privy Council.

When the Supreme Court obtained its independence, it worked to meet the challenges of its new responsibilities. In 1953, the Court ruled on a **civil liberties** case involving a religious group called the Jehovah's Witnesses and the city of Québec. The city had imposed a bylaw banning the distribution of literature by the Jehovah's Witnesses. The Supreme Court ruled that the bylaw was invalid because it interfered with civil rights. It marked the first time in Canada that the Supreme Court determined the legal foundations for the protection of individual rights. It was an important decision. At the time, there was no guarantee of individual rights in Canada's Constitution. The ruling established the Supreme Court's ultimate responsibility to interpret laws and uphold the rights and freedoms of all Canadians.

Figure 6.4 In 1952, a Canadian diplomat and politician named Vincent Massey (shown here on an official visit to the Arctic) became the Governor General of Canada. It marked the first time that Canada, not Britain, appointed the Governor General. It was also the first time that a Canadian was appointed Governor General rather than a male member of the British aristocracy. How have the appointed individuals for Governor General of Canada changed since then?

> "Nothing touched me quite as much as this comment in a Canadian newspaper: 'He made the Crown Canadian.' It was too generous a tribute; but that was what I had tried to do."
>
> –Former Governor General Vincent Massey, 1963

Challenge and Response

1. Find out if the issue of the Lost Canadians has been resolved, and if so, how. Write a brief report of your findings.
2. Why was it important to have the final court of appeal for Canadian legal cases heard in Canada by Canadian judges?
3. Which of the symbols of independence you have read about in this section do you think had the greatest impact on Canada? Give reasons for your response.

Political Changes

After the war, the dream of the Fathers of Confederation became a reality when Newfoundland joined Confederation as the 10th province. Meanwhile, in Québec, a new sense of nationalism was beginning to emerge, while revisions to the Indian Act prompted a renewed activism in Aboriginal communities.

Newfoundland Joins Confederation

The appeal of the welfare state and the politics of the Cold War played an important role in bringing Newfoundland into Confederation after the Second World War. Both Britain and Canada wanted Newfoundland to join the Canadian union. Britain no longer wanted the financial responsibility of its North American colony. Canada wanted to control Newfoundland's natural resources as well as its strategic location on the Atlantic Ocean. With the launching of the nuclear arms race after the war, Newfoundland was a strategic defence location in the North Atlantic.

Newfoundlanders were seeking relief from an uncertain economic future. As you discovered in Chapter 3, during the Depression the colony's economy had collapsed as the global market for fish, lumber, and minerals had dried up. Britain had abolished the island's elected government and replaced it with an appointed Commission of Government. The Second World War had eased the hardships in Newfoundland as both Canada and the United States built naval, air, and army bases on the island. When the war was over, however, it was time to decide the colony's future. In 1946, Britain organized a National Convention to discuss the island's fate. Delegates decided to hold a referendum to let the people of Newfoundland decide what their future should be.

Newfoundlanders Decide

At first, becoming a province of Canada was not even an option. The delegates wanted the people to choose between the status quo and responsible self-government. Britain, however, wanted Newfoundland to join Canada. They found an ally in a man named Joey Smallwood. He launched a petition demanding that Confederation be included as a choice in the referendum. As a result, Newfoundlanders had three options on the referendum ballot:

- to continue with the Commission of Government (which would maintain close ties with Britain)
- to return to a system of responsible self-government and declare independence (which could pull Newfoundland into the American sphere of influence)
- to join Canada

On the first ballot, the Commission of Government received the fewest votes; it was dropped from the second ballot. There were two options left. The main arguments in favour of joining Canada were economic. Newfoundland was not as prosperous as Canada. Incomes and standards of living were much lower. Canada had better support programs and social services for the poor and unemployed. As part of Canada, Newfoundland would improve its international trade.

The main arguments against joining Canada were economic, too. Small businesses were afraid that competition from larger Canadian companies would wipe them out. As a province of

"Newfoundland is the only province of Canada to have freely decided to enter Canada through a referendum."

–Newfoundland premier Brian Peckford, 15 September 1980

Canada, they would have to pay higher income taxes. Which option would Newfoundlanders choose?

On 22 July 1948, Confederation narrowly won. In 1949, Newfoundland became Canada's 10th province.

NEWFOUNDLAND REFERENDUM RESULTS		
Options	First Ballot (%)	Second Ballot (%)
Maintain the Commission of Government	14.3	dropped
Join Confederation	41.1	52.3
Return to responsible self-government	44.6	47.7

Figure 6.5 Only a small percentage of Newfoundlanders voted to maintain the Commission of Government. Why do you think this was not a popular option?

"At midnight on March 31, 1949, that old dream of the Fathers of Confederation finally came true. The oldest settlement in North America became the newest Canadian province and we then understood the meaning of the words 'A mari usque ad mare.'"

–Prime Minister Pierre Trudeau, on the 25th anniversary of Newfoundland joining Confederation, 1 April 1974

 Learn more about Newfoundland and Labrador and Confederation

Figure 6.6 Joey Smallwood signed the agreement making Newfoundland Canada's 10th province on 31 March 1949. Why was this a historic day for Canada?

PERSONALITIES

Joseph "Joey" Smallwood:
A Small Man with Big Ideas

Joseph "Joey" Smallwood was born in the Newfoundland outport of Gambo in 1900, but he grew up in the capital of St. John's. Smallwood left school at the age of 14. He apprenticed as a printer before turning to journalism. As a journalist, Smallwood travelled to New York and London in the 1920s, where he mixed with a circle of left-wing social thinkers. During this time, he developed the skills of writing, debating, and organizing as he pursued his journalism career. Smallwood published historical works about Newfoundland and Labrador and hosted a radio program on Newfoundland history and folklore. In 1941, he edited the *Express*, where he made his negative views on the Commission of Government well known.

Many people have described Joey Smallwood as a small man with big ideas. His biggest idea, of course, was to bring Newfoundland into Confederation. Smallwood advocated joining Canada for many years. In 1949, he succeeded in persuading a small majority of Newfoundlanders to embrace his vision of Newfoundland as Canada's 10th province. When Newfoundland became a province in April 1949, Smallwood became its first premier, a position he retained until 1972.

Figure 6.7 After leaving office, Smallwood published his memoirs, titled *I Chose Canada*, in 1973. He also wrote a three-volume history of the province he loved titled *The Encyclopedia of Newfoundland and Labrador*, published between 1981 and 1991.

As premier, Smallwood was a controversial figure. In 1954, he declared his intention to drag Newfoundlanders "kicking and screaming into the twentieth century." He offered financial incentives to encourage Newfoundlanders in remote outports to relocate to larger centres where there were more services. By 1965, over 100 tiny outposts had disappeared. In their new communities, the people had access to more services, but many were unable to find work. Most felt a profound sense of loss of their communities and resented what they perceived was forced relocation.

Admired by some and despised by others, Smallwood was a powerful and colourful political character who captured the attention of Canadians.

"To convince others, you must first convince yourself. Sheer sincerity can carry an audience."

Source: Newfoundland premier Joey Smallwood, in Richard Gwyn, *Smallwood: The Unlikely Revolutionary* (Toronto: McClelland & Stewart, 1968).

Responding

1. If you had been a Newfoundlander in 1949, how would you have voted in the referendum? Give reasons for your response.

2. Many people call Joey Smallwood one of the founders of Confederation. Do you agree? Give reasons for your response.

A New Québec Nationalism

During the post-war era, the premier of Québec, Maurice Duplessis, focused on the provincial economy and his own hold on power. Social and cultural life was left in the hands of the powerful Roman Catholic Church. Duplessis lured American branch plants to Québec by promising to maintain a tough stand against unions. During a series of long and often violent strikes in the late 1940s, Duplessis repeatedly demonstrated his unwavering refusal to recognize workers' rights.

The Asbestos Strike

The biggest strike of the post-war era in Québec took place at the giant American branch plant Johns-Manville in Asbestos, Québec, in 1949. Workers went on strike demanding that the company offer protection against cancer-causing asbestos dust and increase their wages by 15 cents an hour. In response, the company offered a 5-cent-an-hour pay increase and rejected all of the other union demands.

Since the workers had gone on strike before going to **arbitration**, the strike was declared illegal. The province revoked the union's legal status. In protest, workers in three other asbestos plants walked out in support of the strikers. In all, 5000 Québec workers were on the picket lines. When Johns-Manville brought in replacement workers, the strikers blockaded the road into town. In response, Duplessis ordered more than 200 police officers to move in and crush the strike. Violence broke out. Some strikers were beaten and jailed. Others beat company officials and planted dynamite on company property.

Duplessis was outraged when the Roman Catholic Church supported the strikers. The archbishop of Montréal, Monsignor Joseph Charbonneau, organized food collections for the striking workers and their families. Many journalists also supported the workers. They tried to persuade their audiences to join the fight against Duplessis and his anti-union stand.

The strike dragged on for five months. In the end, the workers gained a 10-cent-an-hour pay increase, but their other demands were rejected. Duplessis was so angry with the Church for supporting the strikers that he arranged to have Monsignor Charbonneau removed from his position by the Vatican.

The Asbestos Strike was the first sign that significant social, economic, and political changes were under way in Québec. A new nationalism was emerging to challenge the status quo and to oppose foreign ownership and the domination of English business interests in Québec's economy. The Asbestos Strike marked the beginning of the Québécois's intention to become *maîtres chez nous* (masters in our own house).

Learn more about Québec in the 1950s

Figure 6.8 The Asbestos Strike was largely a defeat for the unions and a win for the Duplessis government. However, it came to symbolize workers' determination to resist oppression by powerful political and business forces.

Maurice "Rocket" Richard: Québécois Hero

Joseph Henri Maurice Richard was a symbol of the new nationalism in Québec. In 1942, Richard joined the Montreal Canadiens. A year later, he helped bring the Stanley Cup back to Montréal after a 19-year absence. "The Rocket" quickly became a hockey sensation across Canada, but nowhere more so than in Québec.

Richard was the most exciting player in hockey. His ability to score goals at crucial times left fans in awe and admiration. Yet he also had a reputation as a fighter. Richard often found himself in the penalty box or facing fines and suspensions. Many French Canadians believed Richard was penalized for infractions many English players got away with.

On 13 March 1955, a high stick wielded by an opponent struck and cut Richard's head. Richard retaliated by repeatedly hitting the player with his stick. When a linesman stepped in, Richard got into a fight with him. The NHL suspended Richard for the rest of the season. French Canadians charged that the decision was just another example of English Canada asserting its authority over French Canada.

A few days later, the NHL Commissioner attended a game at the Montreal Forum. A riot broke out after more than 10 000 angry Canadiens fans poured into the streets to protest Richard's suspension. To some, the "Richard Riot" was another sign of the new Québécois nationalism.

When "The Rocket" died in May 2000, over 115 000 people filed past his coffin at Montréal's Molson Centre. In tribute, fans draped a Canadiens hockey sweater and the Québec flag over a huge bronze statue of Richard.

Figure 6.9 "Rocket" Richard was *the* hockey player of his generation. He was the first player to score 50 goals in 50 games. Between 1956 and 1960, Richard's explosive speed and scoring heroics led the Montreal Canadiens to five consecutive Stanley Cups.

"There were games when I felt everything I shot would go in. On some nights, if I touched the puck, I knew I would score. We were supposed to win all the time. When we did not win, it was a tragedy to many fans. All they knew was win, win, win."

Source: Maurice Richard, Canoe, 27 May 2000.

Responding

1. Why do you think Maurice Richard was such an important symbol for French Canadians?
2. What qualities do you think it takes to be a sports hero? Choose one current Canadian sports hero and write a brief Personalities feature explaining why this athlete is a Canadian hero.

Revising the Indian Act

More than 6000 Aboriginal soldiers had gone to wars to fight for freedom and democracy yet in their own homeland they were denied these same rights. They did not have full citizenship and they did not have the right to vote. They could not move freely outside of their communities. They did not have the same standard of living or job opportunities as other Canadians had.

In response, in the post-war years Aboriginal groups across Canada grew increasingly political. Faced with an invigorated Aboriginal activism, in 1947 the government announced plans to review and revise the Indian Act. For the first time, First Nations leaders were invited to express their opinions before a Parliamentary committee.

They responded with powerful critiques condemning the government's programs and policies.

First Nations' Demands

Andrew Paull was an influential First Nations leader from British Columbia. In his presentation to the committee, he challenged Canada to give First Nations more autonomy and power. He asked that First Nations peoples be given greater control over their lives, including more power over band governments. He demanded that Aboriginal peoples have the right to vote in federal elections. Paull called on Canada to restore the nation-to-nation relationship it once had with First Nations so they could resolve the issues between them with mutual dignity and respect.

"There exists a growing feeling amongst Indians today that treaty obligations are not being discharged bona fide by the Government of Canada and that the rights of Indians are being curtailed in matters relating to their physical and spiritual development and relating also to their rights over property and with respect to self-government."

–The Indian Association of Alberta, The Archives Society of Alberta, April 1947

Figure 6.10 Tommy Prince (right) was the most decorated Aboriginal soldier in the Second World War. At the Parliamentary hearings in 1947, he spoke on behalf of the Manitoba Indian Association. He called for better housing and roads on reserves, more educational opportunities, and the protection of hunting and fishing rights.

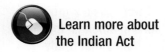
Learn more about the Indian Act

"[The Indian Act] is the only legislation in the world designed for a particular race of people. It was made by Parliament and not by Indian people. Because Parliament is supreme in Canada, it can therefore change the Act without consultation with Indians."

—The Assembly of First Nations

The Government's Response

The revisions to the Indian Act in 1951 eased some of the restrictive and discriminatory policies. It gave First Nations bands more control over their finances and internal affairs. It introduced secret ballots for band elections and allowed women on reserves to vote in these elections. It gave First Nations the freedom to move from reserves without permission, which launched the beginning of a significant migration to urban areas. The Act restored the rights of Aboriginal peoples to practise their traditional dances and celebrations.

Overall, however, the Indian Act remained a means of controlling the lives of First Nations peoples. It still forced thousands of Aboriginal children to attend residential schools. It discriminated against First Nations women by stripping them of their legal status if they married non-First Nations or Non-Status men. The government continued to deny First Nations peoples the right to vote in federal elections. The underlying goal of the Indian Act remained the same—to assimilate Aboriginal cultures in Canada.

A Renewed Activism

For Aboriginal peoples across Canada, the early 1950s marked the beginning of a new campaign to regain their rights in their homeland. Inspired by Aboriginal activists such as Andrew Paull, Tommy Prince, Malcolm Norris, and John Tootoosis, Aboriginal leaders were prepared to take a more confrontational approach with governments to regain their rights.

Challenge and Response

1. Imagine you are preparing to debate the issue of joining Canada with Joey Smallwood. What arguments would you present in favour of responsible self-government? What counter-arguments would you present against joining Canada? Record your ideas in a graphic organizer.
2. Do you think the asbestos workers were justified to strike over health concerns? What responsibilities do you think governments have to protect workers' health? Explain your ideas in a written paragraph.
3. Why do you think the revisions to the Indian Act led to a renewed Aboriginal activism? Discuss your ideas as a class.

Skill Path:
Formulating a Thesis Statement

Reading Strategy

A *topic* is a subject for inquiry. It does not offer an argument, point of view, or opinion. A *thesis statement* is more specific than a topic. It expresses an opinion or point of view that can be argued using evidence.

An important skill you need when you study history is the ability to write a research essay. In a research essay, facts are presented to support an opinion or point of view. For example, a research essay on the symbols of Canadian independence would do more than just describe the symbols. It would present facts to support an opinion about the significance of these symbols as signs of Canada's independence.

Before you can write a research essay, though, you need to formulate a thesis statement. This tells readers what you are trying to prove. To write thesis statements, follow these steps.

STEP 1: Understand Your Topic

Use books, magazines, newspapers, the Internet, and other sources to learn the basic facts and opinions about your topic. Once you have clearly defined your topic, identify three or four main subtopics. As you read, record notes about each one. Think critically about what you have read to make sure you understand the topic.

STEP 2: Formulate a Question

After you understand the topic formulate a question that expresses your opinion or point of view about the topic. For example, a question such as "Did the government violate human rights?" is not a strong question. Instead, you might formulate the following question: "Did the federal government violate the Charter of Rights and Freedoms by refusing to reinstate citizenship to the Lost Canadians?"

STEP 3: State Your Thesis

Once you have decided on a question, you are ready to formulate your thesis statement. State your thesis clearly in a sentence. For example, "The government violated the Charter of Rights and Freedoms when it denied the Lost Canadians the right to regain their citizenship."

STEP 4: Evaluate Your Thesis

Now that you have a thesis statement, use the following criteria to make sure it is sound:
- Is it a statement, not a topic?
- Does the statement express a point of view?
- Does the statement take a clear stand that you can argue?
- Is there evidence to support the statement?

STEP 5: Support Your Thesis

Make sure you have enough evidence to support your thesis statement by double-checking your notes and resources from step 1. Then you are ready to apply your thesis statement to your research essay. (See the Writing a Research Essay Skill Path feature on page viii.)

STEP 6: Practise Your Skill

Read the following statements. Rewrite each one as a thesis statement that reflects your opinion about the topic based on what you have learned so far in this chapter.
- St. Laurent was popular because of his "Uncle Louis" image.
- The Supreme Court of Canada upholds civil liberties.
- Duplessis maintained tight control over Québec unions and workers.
- Revisions to the Indian Act led to a higher level of activism in Aboriginal communities.

Canada's Golden Age

Reading Strategy

As you begin to learn about post-war government policies, recall what you learned about King's government and policies in post World War I in Chapter 2.

After years of hardship and sacrifice during the Depression and the Second World War, Canadians had a new sense of optimism in the post-war years. The government became increasingly involved in the economy as the Liberals adopted the economic philosophy of John Maynard Keynes. The British economist argued that government should play a stabilizing role to control the boom and bust cycles of the economy by spending more money when times were bad and spending less money when times were good. Canada was one of the first Western countries to adopt this economic philosophy.

Shaping the Welfare State

After the war, opinion polls showed that Canadians wanted more protection against poverty and ill health— and they expected the government to provide them with it. Increasingly, Canadians were interested in the social democratic values of the Co-operative Commonwealth Federation (CCF). In response, the Liberals adopted a **social welfare** program to counter the goals of the CCF and satisfy the growing expectations of Canadians. The government introduced a series of social programs designed to provide Canadians with cradle-to-grave protection, including

- family allowances to help mothers provide for their children
- disability pensions for injured military personnel
- financial grants for further education
- homeowners insurance through the Canada Mortgage and Housing Corporation
- funds for provincial hospital insurance plans
- Old Age Security pensions for Canadians over 70

These policies drew support away from the CCF. As a result, the Liberals were re-elected with a small majority in 1945. When King retired as prime minister in 1948, his successor, Louis St. Laurent, continued to shape these social welfare policies.

The New Economy

Unlike the countries of Europe, the war had not devastated Canada, either physically or economically. Wartime industries were able to convert to other types of industries to meet the growing needs of the post-war era. They catered to Canadian consumers who were eager to buy new goods and services.

Signs of economic growth and expansion were evident across the country. The manufacturing sector grew dramatically, as did resource industries such as mining, lumbering, farming, and fishing. The Gross National Product (GNP) rose from $11.9 billion in 1945 to $36.8 billion in 1959. Unemployment was low, averaging just 3 per cent. The possibilities for economic growth seemed unlimited.

The Growth of Unions

To convince voters that the Liberals were as socially progressive as the CCF, the government passed legislation to allow unions to act as bargaining agents in labour disputes. In 1944, the government legalized collective bargaining. After the war, both federal and provincial governments expanded the legal rights of unions. However, they extended their responsibilities, as well. Union leaders had to keep members

"Canada is on the march. It is the land of opportunity. As Canada prospers so will Ontario and so will Metropolitan Toronto. Metropolitan Toronto is the hub and centre of a golden horseshoe of industrial development extending from Oshawa … to Niagara Falls."

–Frederick G. Gardiner, chair, Metropolitan Toronto, 1955

from going on strike while collective bargaining was in progress.

Membership in Canadian unions doubled in the post-war years. As a result, the incomes of many Canadian workers rose as unions negotiated better wages on their behalf. Between 1945 and 1949, the average wage more than doubled, from $32 a week to $73. Prices, on the other hand, rose by only 70 per cent. Employers were willing to pay fair wages to their workers because the workers were also consumers. The more money they had to spend, the better it was for those producing the goods and services. The growth of labour unions helped to distribute wealth to a greater number of Canadians and contributed to the making of a strong middle class.

Learn more about the post-war economy and the forming of the welfare state

Figure 6.11 Canadians had more money to spend than ever before—and spend it they did, on new homes, cars, and appliances. The number of families who were able to buy kitchen appliances skyrocketed in the 1950s. In 1948, fewer than 1 million homes had refrigerators. By 1960, refrigerators were in more than 4 million homes.

"When men would go off to war, women would take over their jobs. They felt both important and wanted ... Then, with the arrival of men coming back from combat, women were let go and men were given their occupations back. Women were expected to stay in the kitchen and be housewives and they were very unappreciated. They were expected to do as their husband said and cater to his every want and need."

–Rachel Machnik, Huron Heights Secondary School, 2003

"Married women were found in female occupational ghettoes, characterized by limited wages and restricted opportunities. Very few were privileged professionals."

–Veronica Strong-Boag, *Journal of Canadian Studies*, Fall 1994

Learn more about women's lives in Canada in the post-war era

Women in the Workforce

After the war, women were under pressure to leave the workplace to make way for returning soldiers. By September 1945, nearly 80 000 women had been laid off by their wartime employers. The participation rate of women in the paid labour force dropped from one-third to one-quarter.

Many observers believed that women would be eager to return to a more traditional way of life. However, many women had enjoyed the opportunities working in the labour force had given them. As a result, by 1951 the number of women entering the labour market began to rise.

For many women, their involvement in the labour force was divided into two phases. Young wives worked until the birth of their first child. Then they left the labour force to raise their families. As their children got older, they then resumed work in the paid labour force.

Women worked primarily in the rapidly expanding service sector as sales clerks, secretaries, nurses, and teachers. Many women worked so that their families could enjoy the growing number of consumer goods that were available to middle-class Canadians. However, in the 1950s, the idea of women working in the paid labour force was still a controversial one, as you will discover in the Issues feature on page 191.

WOMEN'S PARTICIPATION IN THE LABOUR FORCE BY AGE, 1931–2001								
Year	**1931**	**1941**	**1951**	**1961**	**1971**	**1981**	**1991**	**2001**
Age	Percentage							
15–24	33	41	42	41	49	61	65	63
25–34	24	25	24	30	44	66	77	59
35–44	13	16	22	31	44	64	78	60
45–54	13	13	20	33	44	56	70	50
55–64	13	10	14	24	34	42	36	40
Total %	**20**	**21**	**24**	**30**	**39**	**52**	**58**	**54**

Source: Statistics Canada, Table "1 B-2", Labour Force Annual Averages, 71-220-XPB, Reference year 1991.

Figure 6.12 This graph shows the percentage of women in the paid labour force, by age, between 1931 and 2001. What patterns can you identify? Why do you think the trend changed between 1991 and 2001?

Challenge and Response

1. In what ways did the Second World War change the way people saw the role of government in their lives? Express your ideas in a concept web.
2. Why do you think the idea of women working in the paid labour force was controversial in the 1950s? Discuss your ideas as a class.

ISSUES

The Role of Women

The issue: How did middle-class women's response to society's expectations reflect continuity and change in the 1950s?

In the 1950s, there was widespread debate over the role of women. Social conservatives believed women should stay at home and raise their families. They believed that women who joined the workforce were jeopardizing the well-being of their families. Social liberals believed that women could succeed in both roles. They could be responsible wives and mothers as well as effective workers in the paid labour force. The following excerpts reflect these contrasting points of view.

"We are told repeatedly ... that a woman 'owes' it to her husband, her children, and herself to keep her mind alert and active. The theory is that a woman doing two jobs—at home and at the office—is more alive than a woman doing just one job. I've put the theory to the test and I've come to the conclusion that the columnists who advocate it are quite mad."

Source: Anita A. Birt, "Married woman, you're fools to take a job." *Chatelaine* (January 1960): 32.

"Nuts, say I to working wife. She's a quitter and a Judas. She can't cope with a budget, nags her husband for things he can't afford, and hands her kids over to other people to raise. What of the gals who stay at home and make do? There are still a few of us around."

Source: Sheila Stringer Coe, "I won't be a working wife." *Weekend Magazine* (7 July 1957): 35.

"You may work for a while after marriage but when the babies arrive, he'll want you at home ... The young mother who sallies forth to earn luxuries is making two mistakes. She's hurting her husband's ego as a breadwinner and she's neglecting her children when they need her most."

Source: Phyllis Lee Peterson, "Letter to my daughter-in-law," *Chatelaine* (October 1957): 18.

"I think this is a pretty personal decision which every woman who wants to work has to make on the basis of what is good for her family ... I think a woman who wants to work and is prepared to plan can end up being a better wife and mother because of the outside activities—not despite it."

Source: Memo from Rosemary, "How I do my two jobs." *Chatelaine* (May 1954): 4.

The preceding quotations are from Veronica Strong-Boag, "Canada's wage-earning wives and the construction of the middle class, 1945–60." *Journal of Canadian Studies* (Fall 1994).

"If I could change anything, I wouldn't have let the dictates of society as to a 'woman's place' take away my career and ambition ... I wish I had been smart enough not to fall into the all-consuming role of homemaker and mother and followed the emerging female trend towards sharing energies between home and career ... I might have become a more interesting person."

Source: Marilyn Chandler McFadden, in Robert Collins, *You Had To Be There: An Intimate Portrait of the Generation that Survived the Depression, Won the War, and Re-Invented Canada* (Toronto: McClelland & Stewart, 1997), 142.

Responding
1. In a T-chart, highlight the arguments for and against women working outside the home.
2. If you were a woman in the 1950s, how would you have responded to this debate? Give reasons for your response.
3. Outline how you view this debate, now in the twenty-first century.

Billion-Dollar Megaprojects

"We lucky ones, having come through war, are afloat on what one historian will call 'a rapidly mounting wave of prosperity.' Everywhere, the country is ready to build and grow: the St. Lawrence Seaway, the Trans-Canada Highway, the Toronto subway; an ocean of oil in Alberta, aluminum at Kitimat, uranium in northern Saskatchewan, nickel at Thompson, Manitoba, iron ore in the Ungava."

–Robert Collins, *You Had To Be There: An Intimate Portrait of the Generation that Survived the Depression, Won the War, and Re-Invented Canada*, 1997

The post-war years saw Canada launch some of the biggest and most expensive megaprojects in its history. Three projects in particular had a significant impact on the Canadian economy: the Trans-Canada Highway, the Trans-Canada Pipeline, and the St. Lawrence Seaway. There were also huge hydroelectric power projects and lucrative mining opportunities that contributed to economic growth and development across Canada.

The Trans-Canada Highway

In 1949, the federal government passed the Trans-Canada Highway Act as part of a plan to create post-war employment. At the time, Canada had only 16 000 kilometres of paved roads. The highway would provide a continuous link from St. John's, Newfoundland, to Victoria, British Columbia, of over 8000 kilometres of hard-surfaced, two-lane road. Construction costs were to be shared equally between the federal and provincial governments.

The target date for completing the highway was 1956. However, rising construction costs, major engineering challenges through the Rocky Mountains, and different financial priorities of the provinces caused major delays. By 1956, only a small portion of the highway was finished. To speed up the process, Ottawa agreed to increase its share of the financing. Even so, when the Trans-Canada Highway opened in 1962, large parts of the road remained unpaved. It was not until 1966 that the entire route was paved from coast to coast. The Trans-Canada Highway provided an important transportation route for Canadian producers and manufacturers.

The Trans-Canada Pipeline

One of the biggest developments in Canada's resource industries was the discovery of oil at Leduc, Alberta, in 1947. The discovery ushered in a new era of prosperity in the province. Crude oil production in Canada escalated from 8.4 million barrels in 1945 to 84.8 million barrels in 1959.

The discovery of oil in Alberta meant that Canada could now deliver its own supply of oil and gas via pipeline to British Columbia and Central Canada. In 1956, the St. Laurent government announced plans to build a pipeline running 3700 kilometres from Alberta across Canada north of Lake Superior and ending in Montréal.

Private investors, that were mainly American, made a deal with the government to finance the pipeline. However, when the pipeline reached Ontario, more money was needed to complete the project. The government introduced a bill that would provide financing for the rest of the pipeline. The Opposition wanted to debate the bill, but the Liberals were determined to pass it without amendment. They invoked **closure** to end all debate and pass the bill into law as quickly as possible.

Larger Debates

The issue sparked larger debates over two important questions, the first being to what extent should the government help private companies in an attempt to encourage economic development. The government's response was that the industries of Central Canada needed a reliable supply of fuel. Therefore, the pipeline benefited Canadians. Critics charged that if the pipeline was primarily to benefit Canadians, then the government should have built it itself so that the profits went to the taxpayers, not an American corporation.

MAP STUDY: The St. Lawrence Seaway

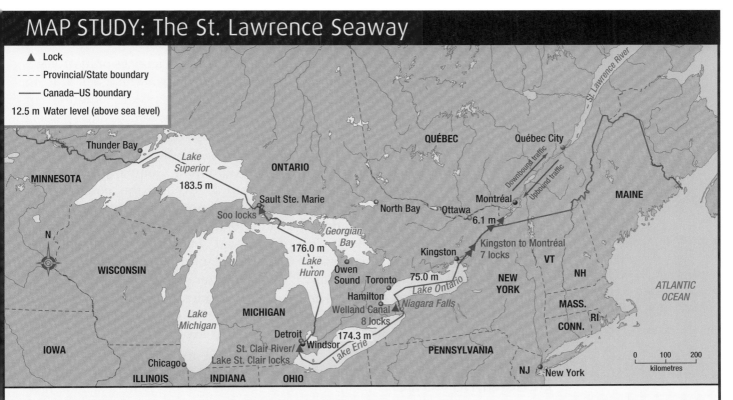

Source: Daniel Francis, et al., *Canadian Issues*, (Don Mills: Oxford University Press, 1998), 198.

Figure 6.13 The building of the St. Lawrence Seaway, with its series of locks to control water levels, was an impressive feat of engineering.

For years, Canada and the United States had discussed plans to expand what would become the St. Lawrence Seaway. With a booming economy and growing trade, there was an urgent need to gain easier access to the large and lucrative consumer markets of Central Canada and the Eastern United States. In the United States, however, the railway companies lobbied the government not to build the Seaway. As a result, in 1951 Canada decided to build the Seaway on its own. Faced with the prospect of having the waterway under Canadian control, in 1954 the Americans changed their minds and joined Canada in the project.

Construction began in 1955. Seven huge locks were created to enable ocean-going vessels to cross rapids along the route between Lake Ontario and Montréal. In the process, farmland, villages, and towns in eastern Ontario were flooded. People in many communities, including First Nations in the territory of Kahnawake, were forced to relocate.

The Seaway officially opened in June 1959. The construction costs were staggering: Canada invested US$330 million, while the US contributed US$133 million. The project provided more than just improved transportation as both countries could now harness the power of the rapids to generate hydroelectric power.

Analysis and Response

1. Why do you think the railway companies opposed building the St. Lawrence Seaway?
2. What impact do you think the relocation of the First Nations of Kahnawake had on their way of life?
3. In what ways did the building of the St. Lawrence Seaway improve transportation in the northern part of North America? How would this have helped the economy?

The second question was whether the government was justified in cutting off democratic debate in the House of Commons. Governments seldom used closure. However, the government argued that the Opposition was stalling on a matter of national importance. Therefore, it was necessary to invoke closure to avoid costly delays in construction of the pipeline. Critics argued that the real reason for invoking closure was simply so the government could get its own way without any review of the terms of the financial agreement. The issue would have repercussions for the Liberals in the election of 1957.

Generating Power

After the war, there was a push to develop hydroelectric power projects in suitable locations across Canada. In British Columbia, the government wanted to create a series of hydroelectric power dams. The goal was to develop the economic potential of resource-rich, but remote and sparsely populated, parts of the province. In the late 1940s, the BC government asked the Aluminum Company of Canada (Alcan) to explore the possibility of building an aluminum smelter in the interior of the province. The project involved building a hydroelectric power plant using the Nechako River as the water source.

Alcan identified Kitimat as the location for the smelter. The company agreed to invest $500 million to complete the project. The costs included the smelter and the power plant as well as a new community with a school, hospital, and recreational facilities for the workers and their families. In return, the BC government turned over a huge area of land and its resource wealth, including parkland and farmland, rivers and lakes, and forests, to Alcan. They reached their agreement without any consultation with the local people or analysis of the impact on the environment.

The Impact on First Nations

The Cheslatta Carrier First Nation had lived in the Nechako River area for thousands of years. They had developed a self-sufficient economy based on local fish, game, and plant life, supplemented by field crops and herds of livestock. A small dam built near the mouth of the Cheslatta River flooded their traditional lands. The people lost their homes and their burial sites were flooded. The Cheslatta had to relocate and adapt to a new way of life. With their ties to the land severed, many people lost their sense of identity and community.

Figure 6.14 In the 1950s, governments did not conduct environmental assessments of huge projects like the power plant at Kemano. What impact do you think projects like this have on the environment?

MAP STUDY: The Nechako-Kemano Diversion

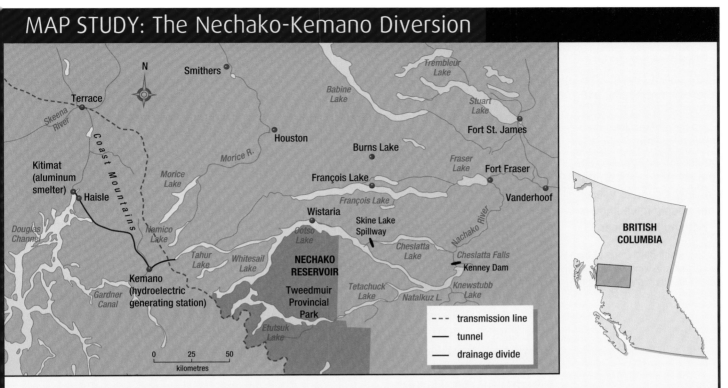

Source: Environment Canada, The National Water Research Institute, http://www.nwri.ca/threats2full/images/ch1_fig1_l.gif.

Figure 6.15 The Nechako watershed is a vast network of rivers and lakes approximately 600 km north of Vancouver. It drains 14 000 km² of north-central British Columbia.

Phase I of the Nechako-Kemano hydroelectric power project began in 1950. The Kemano Dam (Kemano I) was built to redirect the flow of water from the Nechako River westward to Kemano via a tunnel through the Coast Mountains. There, water reaches a vertical drop 16 times higher than Niagara Falls. The water drives generator turbines, then plummets into the Kemano River Basin. Hydroelectricity is then directed to an aluminum smelter in Kitimat via a transmission line.

Kemano I flooded over 800 km² of forest and turned lakes and rivers into a reservoir. The Chinook salmon population was almost wiped out as the water flow was reduced by over 70 per cent. The damage to the environment led First Nations leaders and environmental activists to protest plans to launch the second phase of the project in 1987. As a result, Kemano II was eventually phased out.

Analysis and Response

1. Look at the inset map of British Columbia. What does it tell you about the extent of the water diversion scheme?
2. Do you think the benefits of economic development should outweigh the costs to the environment and to people who live off the land? Express your opinion in a newspaper editorial.

"The dust coated you like flour, it covered our clothes, our heads, our hands. We would sleep on the sacks. No one told us anything about it being dangerous. No one told us about cancer. But over the past 25 years our people have known nothing but cancer."

–Paul Baton, one of the last surviving Dene mine workers, 6 August 1998

Uranium Mining

Uranium was a key ingredient in the making of nuclear weapons. As tensions increased during the Cold War, uranium was in great demand, particularly by the American government.

In the 1950s, Canada became the world's leading exporter of uranium. In 1953, the discovery of uranium near Elliot Lake brought a rush of prosperity to the remote community in northern Ontario. Driven by the American demand for uranium, 11 new mines opened, employing thousands of miners. In 1959, however, the boom came to a crashing halt as the US Atomic Energy Commission ruled that the United States could only buy uranium mined in the US. By 1964, employment in the Elliot Lake mines had plummeted by 80 per cent.

Over the years, the demand for uranium has fluctuated between boom and bust cycles. In the early twenty-first century, the demand for uranium was on the rise once again, providing another opportunity to further develop Canada's uranium industry.

Miners at Risk

In the 1950s, few people knew of the dangers of uranium mining. Contact with radioactive waste can lead to a host of diseases, including cancer. In the 1950s, men from the Dene First Nation worked for a uranium company near their village of Deline, just south of the Arctic Circle in the Northwest Territories. They carried uranium and radium in burlap sacks from the mine down to Great Bear River. The Canadian and American governments knew of the dangers of uranium mining, yet the Dene were never told. As a result, the men were exposed to lethal doses of radioactive waste. The mining company also dumped the waste into lakes and landfills in the Great Bear Lake area. The Dene were unknowingly drinking contaminated water and eating contaminated foods. It was only years later, after many villagers died of cancer, that they became aware of the dangers they had been exposed to.

Challenge and Response

1. In your opinion, which was the most significant megaproject in the post-war era? Give reasons for your response.
2. Do you think that governments should finance foreign companies in building Canadian facilities such as the oil and gas pipeline? Give reasons for your response.
3. Working in a group, role-play a discussion between a representative of the BC government, an official at Alcan, an environmental activist, and a member of the Cheslatta Carrier First Nation over the implementation of Kemano II.

Promoting Canadian Culture

By the 1950s, American culture dominated Canadian radio, television, film, books, art, and music. Canada had few professional arts and cultural organizations to support Canadian artists, writers, and performers. In 1951, the Massey Commission recommended that the government create an independent organization to promote and support the arts in Canada. In response, in 1957, the government established the Canada Council for the Arts.

Home-Grown Culture

The creation of the Council coincided with a burst of artistic expression and activity across Canada. Through its financial grants, the Council played a major role developing theatre and film production. Professional theatre companies opened up in Canada's major cities. However, Canadian playwrights had difficulty persuading theatre directors to stage their productions. Most theatre companies preferred to produce shows by internationally acclaimed playwrights, such as George Bernard Shaw and Tennessee Williams. Still, the new theatres provided opportunities for Canadian actors and technicians to display their talents and skills to Canadian audiences.

The Stratford Festival

In 1953, local residents in Stratford, Ontario, launched the Stratford Shakespeare Festival to produce the works of William Shakespeare and other playwrights. They persuaded a leading British theatre director, Tyrone Guthrie, to become artistic director of the new theatre. Critics predicted the Stratford Shakespeare Festival would last only a few years. Instead, it inspired other theatre companies to open across Canada, including the Shaw Festival in Niagara-on-the-Lake, the only festival in the world dedicated to producing the plays of George Bernard Shaw.

> "The world today needs abundant sources of intellectual and moral energies. Canada wants to be one of those sources, and it has already begun to be one of those sources in several international organizations. With that purpose in mind, we must further develop and enrich our own national soul."
>
> –Prime Minister Louis St. Laurent, announcing the creation of the Canada Council, Ottawa, 12 November 1956

> "I am intensely interested to produce Shakespeare on a stage which might produce the actor-audience relation for which [Shakespeare] wrote—that audience closely racked ROUND the actors... "
>
> –Tyrone Guthrie, British theatre director, 11 May 1952

Figure 6.16 The Festival Theatre is modelled after Shakespeare's own theatre design. Today, the Stratford Shakespeare Festival has an international reputation and attracts audiences from around the world.

"Too many jazz pianists limit themselves to a personal style, a trademark, so to speak. They confine themselves to one type of playing. I believe in using the entire piano as a single instrument capable of expressing every possible musical idea. I have no one style. I play as I feel."

–Oscar Peterson

The Music Scene

In the 1950s, Canadian recording artists had difficulty getting much airplay on Canadian radio stations. Only the CBC devoted any significant time to playing songs by Canadian singers and musicians. However, two talented Canadian musicians, Glenn Gould and Oscar Peterson, gained international attention and acclaim in the 1950s. Gould had a unique style that profoundly affected the way people heard and appreciated music. Peterson is considered by many to be one of the great jazz pianists of all time. In the 1950s, he blended swing and bop to create a unique musical style. Glenn Gould and Oscar Peterson were proof of Canada's growing cultural maturity in the 1950s.

Rock 'n' Roll

No other musical form captured as much in the 1950s as rock and roll. The new music took the Canadian music scene by storm. Its unique sound had its foundation in the rhythm and blues style of musicians in the African-American community. Performers such as Elvis Presley and Bill Haley and the Comets played their versions of rhythm and blues to enthusiastic audiences. For young people, the new music symbolized freedom from their parents' values, which had been born out of the Depression and war. Adults, on the other hand, could not understand the new music's appeal. Many parents were convinced that rock and roll was corrupting their children.

The biggest rock and roll star of them all was Elvis Presley. Elvis performed to packed houses at huge venues such as Toronto's Maple Leaf Gardens. Thousands of teenagers filled the arena to hear Elvis belt out such songs as "Hound Dog" and "Heartbreak Hotel," dancing and swinging his hips to the beat. At the time, many adults found Elvis' stage performances to be too provocative. When Elvis appeared on TV, the cameras had to shoot him from above the waist so as not to offend the sensibilities of the day.

Canada had its own singing stars in the 1950s. A 15-year-old from Ottawa named Paul Anka scored a major hit with the pop song "Diana" in 1957. It sold six million copies and launched an international career that

Figure 6.17 Oscar Peterson (at the piano) developed his talent in the nightclubs of Montréal in the 1940s. In 1972, he received the Order of Canada in recognition of his contribution to Canadian culture.

has spanned decades. With their popular hit "Sh-Boom," the Crew Cuts from Toronto were the first rock and roll band to make a record that sold over a million copies.

Rock and roll was a perfect form of entertainment for the new medium of television. In 1957, *American Bandstand* hit the airwaves, providing a showcase for young musical talent. Teenagers tuned in to see the latest bands or watch their favourites.

In the 1950s, it became popular for Canadian teens to form their own bands and singing groups. They imitated the sounds and songs of their favourite rock and roll stars. Singing rock and roll seemed easy—just mix some light-hearted lyrics with a catchy tune and a good dance beat. Rock and roll provided the perfect backdrop for "rebellious" youth to express themselves.

Television Comes to Canada

When television came to Canada in the early 1950s, it was an instant success. The growth of the television industry was phenomenal. Television sets quickly became as common in Canadian living rooms as sofas and chairs. By the end of 1957, there were over three million TV sets in Canada—about one for every five Canadians.

Figure 6.18 Elvis Presley performing at Maple Leaf Gardens, Toronto, on 2 April 1957. His popularity crossed over into movies. When his films opened in Canada's major cities, female fans pushed past ushers and police to get inside the theatre and find the best seats. What musical stars have that effect on teenagers today?

Since the majority of Canadians lived in the southern part of the country, they were able to pick up US television signals. As a result, most of the TV programs Canadians watched were American, such as *I Love Lucy*, *The Ed Sullivan Show*, and *The Howdy Doody Show*. Television rapidly broadened the influence of American culture throughout Canada.

In 1948, the federal government granted the Canadian Broadcasting Corporation (CBC) an exclusive licence to create a distinctly Canadian television network. In 1952, the first CBC television stations opened in Toronto and Montréal. In 1953, stations opened in Ottawa and Vancouver, followed by stations in Halifax and Winnipeg in 1954. The CBC produced made-in-Canada TV shows that appealed to

Canadians. The CBC aired news programs, public affairs shows, quiz shows, dramas, and comedies. There was something for everyone, including a few American favourites.

Hockey Night in Canada

By far the most popular TV show was *Hockey Night in Canada*. CBC Radio had broadcast the program since 1931. *Hockey Night in Canada* made the leap to television in 1952, bringing the popular hockey broadcaster Foster Hewitt with it. Every Saturday night, millions of Canadian hockey fans across the country gathered around their television sets to watch the game. Probably no other event drew as many people to their TV sets at the same time as *Hockey Night in Canada*. The program helped to secure hockey as part of the Canadian national identity.

Today, Canadians have access to hundreds of television stations, many of which broadcast hockey. As a result, *Hockey Night in Canada* is not as central to the lives of enthusiastic hockey fans as it once was, but it remains a Saturday-night fixture for many Canadians.

Teenagers

In the 1950s, a new word was added to the English vocabulary: *teenagers*. The term had never been used before to describe the generation of young people between the ages of 13 and 19. Teenagers had greater freedom than any generation of young people before them. They also had more money to spend and more ways to spend it—on fashion, music, movies, and magazines. On a typical Saturday night, teenagers in the 1950s went to the movies, the sock hop, or the drive-in restaurant. Teens had lots of leisure time and plenty of money to spend

Figure 6.19 Like teenagers today, the teens of the 1950s expressed themselves through fashion. "Preppies" were neat, tidy, and clean-cut. The girls wore full, rounded skirts often with big appliqués on them. The boys wore neatly pressed shirts and pants. "Greasers" were the rebels of the 1950s. Boys wore their hair greased back, with black leather jackets and boots and blue jeans.

enjoying it. Advertisers were eager to capitalize on the self-indulgent spending habits of the new teenage generation.

Many teenagers were willing to question authority and redefine how they lived their lives. Some boys imitated the style of movie stars like Marlon Brando and James Dean, who made rebelliousness popular in films such as *The Wild One* (1953) and *Rebel Without a Cause* (1955).

Figure 6.20 Teens of the 1950s danced to the new sounds of rock and roll. The television program *American Bandstand* made dances such as the Bop, the Slop, and the Hand Jive popular with teens across North America.

Challenge and Response

1. Do you think American popular culture dominates Canada today? Why or why not?
2. a) To what extent do you think Canadian musicians influence popular culture today?
   b) Choose one popular Canadian musician and write a Personalities feature about this performer.
3. Today, you can watch American television programs from the 1950s on many cable stations or on DVD. Choose one comedy from the 1950s and one comedy from today. Compare and contrast the two programs in a Venn diagram.
4. Why do you think young people were so eager to define themselves differently from their parents? In what ways do teenagers define themselves today?

Sign of the Times

WHAT PEOPLE WATCHED

Can you image a world with no remote controls, no digital television, and no satellite dishes? That is the way it was in the 1950s. Back then, television was new. TV programs were in black and white. Viewers had to move an antenna around trying to pick up one of only a handful of TV stations. You could not watch TV 24 hours a day—most stations were on the air for just a few hours a day.

Figure 6.21 The most popular American television shows in the 1950s included *I Love Lucy*, *Dragnet*, *The Bob Hope Show*, *The Jackie Gleason Show*, *Lassie*, *Father Knows Best*, *The Adventures of Ozzie and Harriet*, and *Captain Kangaroo*. Are you familiar with any of these shows? If so, what is your impression of them?

GLUED TO THE TV!

Students hurried home from school to watch programs like *The Howdy Doody Show*. It was the beginning of a trend. Today, by the time you graduate from high school, you will have spent on average more time watching TV than sitting in a classroom! Think about how much TV you watch in a week.

Figure 6.22 Families began eating their meals in front of their TV sets. This led to the invention of the TV dinner. For under a dollar, you could buy a ready-made dinner, fried chicken, meat loaf, or Salisbury steak, served with potatoes and peas. Just heat and serve!

Responding
1. What are the most popular TV programs in Canada today? Why do you think these programs are so popular?
2. What other media compete with television today?

A Population Explosion

After the war, a flood of immigrants from Europe and the **baby boom** created as young couples married and settled down to raise families led to a population explosion in Canada. This rapid growth in population contributed to Canada's post-war economic growth and prosperity.

Post-war Immigration

During the Depression and the Second World War, immigration to Canada was very low. From 1930 to 1945, an average of just 15 000 people immigrated to Canada each year. After the war, however, the situation changed. As you discovered in Chapter 5, many Europeans were desperate to escape the devastation of their homeland and build new lives in peaceful and prosperous countries like Canada. For its part, to maintain the country's economic prosperity, Canada encouraged immigration from Europe. Although Canada wanted new immigrants, however, immigration policies were designed to preserve the social and cultural status quo. They discriminated against people of African, Arab, and Asian heritage and made it difficult for them to gain entry into Canada.

Most immigrants in the post-war years came either as sponsored relatives or as part of a government-backed labour scheme. The labour scheme required the newcomers to sign contracts agreeing to work for two years as manual labourers in Canada's mines, fisheries, and railways. Women signed on to work as domestic servants. Often, these workers faced discrimination from other Canadians, who remained suspicious about people who were different from themselves. In all, more than 1.7 million immigrants, war brides, and people displaced by the war came to Canada in the 1940s and 1950s. Collectively, they helped transform Canada into a more multicultural nation.

The Baby Boomers

Hard times and uncertain futures during the Depression and the Second World War led to a decline in the birth rate in Canada between 1929 and 1945 as many couples postponed marriage. The decline in immigration also reduced the number of children in Canada. As a result, in the early 1940s, the average age of Canadians was on the rise.

The post-war years reversed that trend, however. After the war, many Canadians had more money than ever before. Family allowances—known as the "baby bonus"—encouraged young couples to have more children. As a result, there was a baby boom. By 1956, children under the age of five accounted for 12.4 per cent of the population, up from 9 per cent in 1941.

The Impact of the Baby Boom

The baby boom has had a profound impact on social and economic institutions in Canada. As the first baby boomers reached school age, the provinces had to scramble to accommodate them. Between 1945 and 1961, school enrolment more than doubled as more than half a million new students entered school each year. School boards had to build hundreds of new schools and hire thousands of new teachers.

The changing economy of the post-war era also placed greater expectations on Canadian students. Many of the new job opportunities required that people have a better education than previous generations. As a result, many baby

> "Canada's immigration policy has undergone great change, while the definition of a good immigrant has gone from being based on your nationality to being based on your personal ability to do as much for the Canadian economy as possible."
>
> –Ryan Jenkins, Huron Heights Secondary School, 2007

 Learn more about immigration to Canada in the post-war years

COMMUNITIES

The War Brides

During and after the Second World War, Canada welcomed thousands of war brides. These young women married Canadian soldiers stationed in Europe. Most war brides came from Britain, but a few thousand came from the Netherlands, Belgium, France, Italy, and Germany. When the war ended, 48 000 war brides and their 22 000 children followed their husbands to Canada.

The journey to Canada was not an easy one. When the war brides left home, there were emotional scenes at train stations and ship docks as the young women said goodbye to their families. Many travelled across the Atlantic on converted luxury liners. Some found the voyage a great adventure. They made new friends and feasted on foods they had not eaten in years because of war rations. Others were homesick and seasick. Their children were restless and bored with life on-board ship. Their mothers were exhausted by the time they docked at Halifax.

Like millions of immigrants before them and since, the war brides entered Canada at Pier 21 in Halifax. From there, they boarded special trains destined for points across the country. As they travelled across Canada, the vastness of their new home fascinated some war brides and overwhelmed others. Many had grown up in the cities of Europe. Those who settled in rural communities were shocked to find wood stoves and outhouses! Still, for most of the war brides, after enduring years of war, they were determined to build new lives in Canada.

"Some [of the war brides] settled down in Canada immediately and never worried about England again. Others never really adjusted to coming here. They'll always have one foot in England and one foot here."

Source: Betty Patriquin, in Barbara Ladouceur and Phyllis Spencer, *Blackouts to Bright Lights* (Vancouver: Ronsdale Press, 1995), 7.

Figure 6.23 When the war brides left Europe, air transportation was not as common as it is today. As a result, many war brides believed they were saying goodbye to their families forever. How do you think this made them feel? How would you have felt?

Responding

1. Many war brides were surprised at how vast Canada was. In what other ways might life in their new homeland have been different for these young women?

boomers stayed in school longer and pursued post-secondary educations. This created the need for more training schools, colleges, and universities across the country.

As the boomers aged, their impact has been felt throughout Canadian society. During the 1960s and 1970s, the number of students entering university skyrocketed. Governments responded by opening new universities. In the 1980s and 1990s, the financial needs of the baby boomers led to new banking and investment services. By the second decade of the twenty-first century, the baby boomers will begin to retire. As they do, the financial costs of an aging population will pass to a much smaller generation of middle-aged Canadian taxpayers.

Reading Strategy

A population pyramid is a common method for showing the population structure of a country. When a pyramid is narrower at the base, wider in the middle and at the top, it means there are more older people than younger people.

Population Pyramids for Canada, 1941–2006

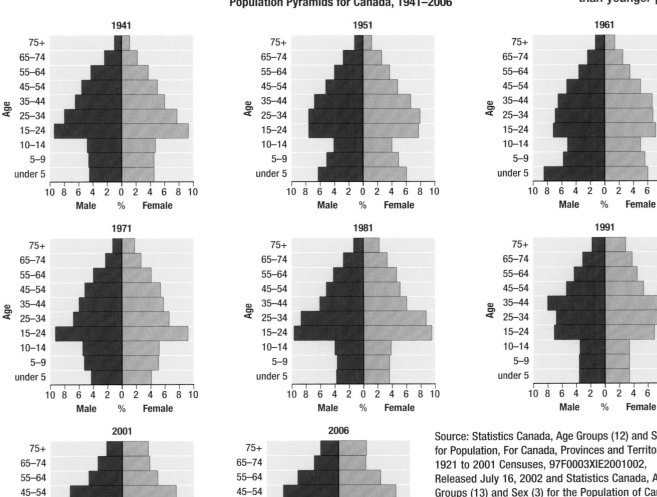

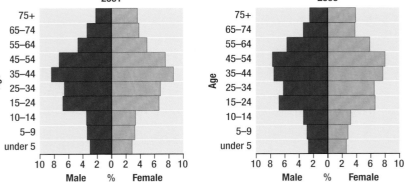

Source: Statistics Canada, Age Groups (12) and Sex (3) for Population, For Canada, Provinces and Territories, 1921 to 2001 Censuses, 97F0003XIE2001002, Released July 16, 2002 and Statistics Canada, Age Groups (13) and Sex (3) for the Population of Canada, Provinces and Territories, 1921 to 2006 Censuses, 97-551-XWE2006005, Released July 17, 2007.

Figure 6.24 These 8 population pyramids show the changes in Canada's demographic makeup between 1941 and 2006. What trends can you identify? Where are the baby boomers on each graph?

Moving to the Suburbs

Cars and houses came to symbolize "the good life" for Canadians in the 1950s. Before 1950, the majority of Canadians lived in rented housing. While a few families owned small homes on small plots of land, only the wealthy could afford large homes with lawns and gardens. The creation of housing neighbourhoods on the outskirts of cities, where land was more affordable, made home ownership accessible to a growing number of Canadians. The growing use of the automobile and an expanding network of roads made it easier for people to live in the suburbs and commute to their jobs in the city. Buying a home became easier when the government introduced the Canada Mortgage and Housing Corporation in 1946, which insured mortgages people obtained from banks.

> "Multiplication by subdivision."
>
> –Frederick G. Gardiner, chair, Metropolitan Toronto, on the growth of subdivisions, 5 December 1999

Figure 6.25 People in the suburbs relied on cars to get to work, run errands, go shopping, and visit friends. The growing traffic problems forced cities to develop more efficient public transportation systems. The first subway line in Canada opened in Toronto in 1954. How important is public transit in Canada today?

Life in the Suburbs

Life in the suburbs emphasized home and family. Gender roles were clearly defined. Social values kept most married women, especially those with children, at home raising their children and managing the household. Fathers worked in the paid labour force to earn money for the family. The suburbs created a stereotypical image of the family made popular on television shows such as *Leave It to Beaver* and *Father Knows Best*. The stern yet loving father was head of the household. The loving and nurturing mother stayed home to look after the children and make sure dinner was on the table. The obedient—and sometimes mischievous—children learned about life from their parents.

Initially, the new suburbs lacked shopping areas, restaurants, theatres, and recreational facilities. People had to go to the city for entertainment or to church and community gatherings to socialize with their neighbours. Increasingly, though, people stayed home to enjoy the newest thing in technology—television. Over time, children began to spend more and more time in front of their TV sets. Television eventually replaced many traditional family activities.

Suburban Consumers

Eventually, large and impersonal supermarkets, department stores, and shopping malls came to the suburbs. They fuelled new levels of consumerism among Canadians who were eager to buy all the goods and services that were available in the 1950s. West Vancouver's Park Royal Shopping Centre, which opened in 1950, was Canada's first open-air shopping mall. In 1953, the Boulevard Shopping Centre in Montréal

Figure 6.26 In 1954, Toronto was the fastest-growing city in North America. New suburbs like Don Mills, the first planned community in Canada, sprang up in all directions. Between 1945 and 1956, a million homes were built across Canada. What impression of the suburbs do you get from this photograph?

marked the beginning of a new era for shoppers. It had covered walkways from bus stops to shops, landscaped parks, and places for weary shoppers to sit and rest. In 1956, the concept of enclosed shopping malls made its debut, with more stores offering even greater shopping choices. Shopping malls have continued to evolve since they made their debut in the 1950s. Today, many shopping malls like Toronto's Eaton Centre and the West Edmonton Mall are complex facilities offering shopping, dining, entertainment, and even hotels.

Challenge and Response

1. What challenges do you think the post-war immigrants faced in Canada? What challenges do you think immigrants face today? Compare your ideas in a Venn diagram.
2. As the baby boomers retire, what jobs and services do you think will become more important? What jobs and services do you think will become less important? Give reasons for your responses.
3. a) If you were to design a suburban neighbourhood, what would your priorities be? List them from the most important to the least important.
   b) Working with a partner, design a layout of your ideal suburban community. Alternatively, you may want to write a promotional brochure outlining the features of your community and the reasons people should want to live there.

 COMMUNITIES

Africville

Some communities in Canada were denied the basic necessities people in the new suburban communities took for granted. One such community was Africville, a small neighbourhood of people of African heritage in Halifax. The community was established by descendants of enslaved Americans in the 1800s. Racial discrimination ensured that Africville became a self-reliant community.

Facilities other Halifax neighbourhoods rejected, such as a prison and a hospital for infectious diseases, ended up on Africville's doorstep. Although the residents of Africville paid municipal taxes, the city failed to provide the community with essential services, such as running water and garbage collection. By the 1950s, Africville had become one of the poorest communities in Canada.

In 1964, the city of Halifax announced an **urban renewal** plan. The land in Africville was **expropriated**. The residents were forced to relocate to public housing projects. Bulldozers rolled over the community, destroying homes and livelihoods. As compensation, the city gave each household $500.

Today, the former residents of Africville hold an annual reunion at Seaview Memorial Park, which marks the site of the original community. In July 2002, the government recognized Africville as a National Historic Site. In 2004, the United Nations urged Canada to pay **reparations** to the residents of Africville, but by 2008, the government had failed to do so.

Figure 6.27 The people founded the Seaview African United Baptist Church in 1849 and opened an elementary school in 1883. Eventually, over 400 people lived in Africville. They developed a rich and vibrant cultural identity centred around church and family.

"Our church meant so much to us. All over the community, we could hear that bell. How it would toll. You could almost hear the words—come to church, come to church. No matter where we go, we always say there will never, never, never be another church like that little Seaview Baptist Church."

Source: Laura Howe, resident of Africville.
Halifax Daily News, 18 December 1991.

 Learn more about Africville

Responding

1. Imagine you are a descendant of a former resident of Africville. Present your case for compensation in a letter to your Member of Parliament.
2. How would you feel if you were forced to leave your community? Discuss your feelings in a small group.

Thinking Like a Historian:
Identifying Continuity and Change

Essential Question: As an historian, how do you recognize how things have changed or stayed the same over time?

Some history books organize past events into periods or eras. This organizes the common issues and events into a time frame that helps to enhance our understanding of the past. Sometimes, however, when we place issues and events into categories it is possible to lose sight of certain aspects of the issue because we are viewing events from a particular point of view.

You, the Historian

In this activity, you are to compare issues and events before and after the Second World War to see the extent to which things changed after the war and the way they stayed the same. You will need to review Chapter 3: The Dirty Thirties to recall what life was like in Canada before the war, as well as Chapter 5: Challenges in the Post-war World to recall how Canada's place in international affairs changed after the war.

1. Complete a graphic organizer similar to the one shown here, recording each element of life in Canada before and after the war.
2. When you have completed the organizer, write a summary of how things changed after the war and how they stayed the same.
3. Next, write a thesis statement expressing your opinion about the changes in Canada after the Second World War.
4. Finally, use your thesis statement as the basis for a research essay on this topic.

	Before the War	After the War
Social		
Cultural		
Political		
Economic		
International		

Competing Visions of Canada

Figure 7.1 From 1957 to 1967, the Progressive Conservative's John Diefenbaker and the Liberal's Lester Pearson battled each other for the leadership of Canada. Their personalities and political styles were distinctly different. When Pearson followed Diefenbaker as prime minister in 1963, Diefenbaker sat as Opposition leader in the House of Commons, challenging the Liberal government at every opportunity.

Chapter at a Glance

Thinking Ahead

From 1935 to 1957, the Liberals were in power in Ottawa. Then, in an election surprise, the Conservatives under new leader John Diefenbaker won a minority government in 1957. The fiery Diefenbaker proved so popular that Canadians handed him a huge majority the following year. When Pearson became prime minister in 1963, he faced the task of guiding Canada through a tumultuous decade.

In this chapter, you will explore the battle for power between Diefenbaker and Pearson and examine the forces that changed Canadian society. As you do, focus on these key questions:

- What significant changes occurred during Diefenbaker's time in office?
- What were the significant changes that occurred during Pearson's time in office?
- What were the major causes and consequences of the Quiet Revolution in Québec?
- What led to the resurgence of Aboriginal artistic expression?
- What impact did young people have on Canadian society?

John George Diefenbaker

"I liken Canada to a garden. A mosaic is a static thing with each element separated and divided from the others. Canada is not that kind of country. Neither is it a 'melting pot' in which the individuality of each element is destroyed in order to produce a new and totally different element. It is rather a garden into which have been transplanted the hardiest and brightest of flowers from many lands, each retaining in its new environment the best of the qualities for which it was loved and prized in its native land."

–John G. Diefenbaker, in Dean Wood, "Multiculturalism: Appreciating our diversity." *Accord* (November–December 1980)

Figure 7.2 John Diefenbaker (1895–1979)

John George Diefenbaker spent his youth moving from town to town before his family finally settled in Saskatoon, Saskatchewan. After graduating from the University of Saskatchewan and serving in the army in World War I, he returned to university to earn a law degree. Diefenbaker proved to be a masterful criminal defence lawyer, utilizing his powerful voice, penetrating stare, and dramatic gestures. His experiences with the law and his exposure to discrimination against immigrants, Aboriginal peoples, and other minorities made **civil rights** a cornerstone of his political ideas.

Diefenbaker was an anti-American, pro-British patriot known for his stirring speeches and his way with words. After becoming a Member of Parliament in 1940, he became one of the Conservatives' most prominent figures. Yet he was rejected twice in bids to become party leader. Finally, in 1956 at the age of 61, Diefenbaker won the leadership he coveted.

Diefenbaker's skills as a leader were put to the test in 1957 when Louis St. Laurent called an election. Most Canadians expected the Liberals to cruise to another victory. To the surprise of many, however, the Conservatives pulled off a stunning upset to form a minority government. Many people credited their success to the new leader, whom they called "the Chief."

After passing some minor legislation, Diefenbaker called a snap election in 1958. The Conservatives' campaign urged voters to "Follow John." Canadians did just that, in unprecedented numbers. The Conservatives won 208 of 265 seats—the biggest landslide in Canadian history.

Diefenbaker granted Aboriginal peoples the right to vote. He improved social programs to provide greater aid to those in need. He abolished racial quotas and opened Canada's doors to immigrants from Asia, Africa, and the Caribbean. He drafted, and his government passed, the Bill of Rights which recognized the rights of all Canadians. Despite these achievements, controversy undermined his term in office. He was uncertain how to handle an ailing economy. He was undecided over Canada's commitment to North American defence. In the election of 1962, the Conservatives' huge majority was reduced to just 116 seats. While they were able to form a minority government, another election quickly followed. In 1963, Canadians returned the Liberals to power with a minority government.

Diefenbaker remained leader of the Conservative Party until 1967 and continued to sit as an MP until his death in 1979. As the funeral train carrying his casket travelled across the prairies, people lined the route to cheer "the Chief" one last time.

Figure 7.3 Under Diefenbaker, Canada experienced a number of "firsts": the first French-Canadian Governor General, the first female federal Cabinet minister, the first federal Cabinet minister of Ukrainian heritage, the first female ambassador, and the first Aboriginal senator. Here, Diefenbaker (centre) is meeting with (from left to right) George Koneak, Shinuktuk, Jean Ayaruak, and Abraham Ogpik in Ottawa in May 1959.

Responding

1. What specific measures did Diefenbaker take to improve the lives of all Canadians?
2. What were the cornerstones of John Diefenbaker's vision of Canada?
3. Do you think that Diefenbaker's commitment to human rights is still evident in Canadian society today? Explain your response.

Dief "the Chief"

The year was 1957. After 22 years in office, many Canadians believed the Liberals had grown arrogant. Still, opinion polls showed the party with a comfortable lead heading into the final days of the election campaign. Therefore, it came as a stunning surprise to almost everyone when the Conservatives ousted the Liberals and formed a minority government.

The election campaign was the first to be seen on the new medium of television. Diefenbaker's energetic style played well on the black-and-white television sets of the country. He denounced the Liberals' old-age pension benefits as too little. He called for a new National Policy aimed at developing the North. He promised to grant subsidies to address the economic challenges facing the Atlantic provinces. His campaign promises demonstrated that the Conservatives were not necessarily conservative when it came to spending. Like the Liberals, they were willing to spend money on social programs.

Six months after the Conservatives' victory in 1957, Diefenbaker called another election. He defeated the Liberals, now led by Lester Pearson, with the largest majority in Canadian history—208 of 265 seats.

The Bill of Rights

John Diefenbaker was of German–Scottish descent. He was deeply aware of the fact that he was the first prime minister who was not of purely British or French heritage. This influenced his desire to protect human rights and create a more inclusive country. As a result, one of his priorities as prime minister was to create a Bill of Rights for all Canadians.

In September 1958, Diefenbaker placed the Bill of Rights before the House of Commons. However, he was unable to get provincial consent to amend the Constitution to include the bill. Therefore, the Bill of Rights became a federal law. Without being enshrined in the Constitution, however, the bill lacked authority in provincial courts.

Still, Diefenbaker persevered and the Bill of Rights was passed on 10 August 1960. It guaranteed the rights and freedoms of all Canadians, including the right to be free from discrimination "by reason of race, national origin, colour,

> "All that is needed ... is an imaginative policy that will open its doors to Canadian initiative and enterprise. We believe in a positive National Policy of development, in contrast with the negative and haphazard one of today. We believe that the welfare of Canada demands the adoption of such a policy, which will develop our natural resources for the maximum benefit of all parts of Canada."
>
> –Prime Minister John Diefenbaker, *John G. Diefenbaker Papers*, XXI, 17, 589

> "I am a Canadian, a free Canadian, free to speak without fear, free to worship God in my own way, freed to stand for what I think right, free to oppose what I believe wrong, free to choose those who shall govern my country. This heritage of freedom I pledge to uphold for myself and all mankind."
>
> –Prime Minister John Diefenbaker, preamble to the Canadian Bill of Rights, 1 July 1960

Party	1957	1958	1962	1963	1965
Liberals	105	48	99	128	131
Progressive Conservatives	112	208	116	93	97
CCF/NDP	25	8	19	17	21
Social Credit	19	0	30	24	5
Other	4	1	1	0	11

Figure 7.4 This table shows the election results from 1957 to 1965 while Diefenbaker was leader of the Progressive Conservative Party. No other government has ever won as large a percentage of seats as the Conservatives did under Diefenbaker in 1958. In your opinion, what are the possible positive and negative consequences of a government with such an overwhelming majority?

religion, or sex." Many historians believed the Bill of Rights was a lofty ideal that ultimately carried little weight. However, Diefenbaker considered it his greatest achievement.

Extending Voting Rights

As a youth, Diefenbaker had witnessed first-hand the widespread discrimination against Aboriginal peoples in Canada. When he came to office, First Nations people were still being denied a fundamental right that all other Canadians enjoyed—the right to vote. If they wanted to vote, they had to give up their status under the Indian Act and become citizens of Canada.

For most First Nations people, losing their status and identity was too high a price to pay for the rights of citizenship.

In 1960, Diefenbaker extended voting rights to First Nations people while allowing them to maintain their official status. Almost 100 years after Canada became a country, the last barrier to voting equality for all Canadians had finally been taken down.

New Immigration Policies

Under Diefenbaker, the government introduced significant changes to Canada's immigration policies. Traditionally, Canada had favoured immigrants from Britain, the United States,

Learn more about the Bill of Rights

"I saw them ill-treated, regarded by the people as a whole as intruders, not invaders, who could never hope to become Canadians. They were second-class citizens."

–John Diefenbaker, CBC Archives, The Canadian Bill of Rights, 16 March 1950

Figure 7.5 First Nations people cast their ballots for the first time in a federal election in 1960. Why do you think they were denied the vote for so long?

Reading Strategy

When you read a passage that includes many dates and figures, you might become distracted by the data. To help improve your comprehension, create a timeline of the key names, dates, and facts in the passage.

France, and other northern European countries. Immigrants from southern Europe, Asia, Africa, and the Caribbean were placed in limited or prohibited categories. Immigration officers had wide discretionary powers over admissions. Individual officers often interpreted the regulations differently and were accused of making arbitrary, and often racist, decisions about who could and could not enter Canada.

In the past, the controversial and politically sensitive nature of immigration had made governments reluctant to revise immigration policy. By the 1960s, the growing recognition of Canada's cultural diversity signalled it was time for a change. In January 1962, the minister of Citizenship and Immigration, Ellen Fairclough, tabled a new set of immigration regulations in Parliament. On the surface, they eliminated racial discrimination from immigration policies by lifting quotas to allow immigration to all continents provided immigrants could demonstrate that they could support themselves and their families. However, discrimination continued in the category of **sponsorship**. The new regulations ruled out sponsorship of immigrants from Asia and Africa, except for close family members.

The policy changes led to a dramatic increase in the number of people immigrating to Canada from Asia, the Caribbean, Latin America, the Middle East, and Africa. Before 1961, almost 90 per cent of Canadian immigrants came from the United States and Europe. By 1971, the number had dropped to 40 per cent. By 1991, the figure was 20 per cent.

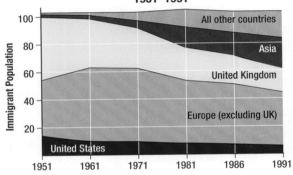

Birthplaces of Canada's Immigrant Population, 1951–1991

Source: Statistics Canada, Native and foreign-born population, 99-517, Volume VII, Part 1, Released in 1965; Statistics Canada, Birthplace, 92-727, Volume 1, Part 3, Released in 1974; Statistics Canada, Population, place of birth, citizenship, period of immigration: Canada, provinces, urban size groups, rural non-farm and rural farm, 92-913, Released in 1984; and Statistics Canada, The Nation: 1996 Census of Population, 93F0020XCB1996004, Released September 18, 1998.

Figure 7.6 Before 1961, only 3% of immigrants were from Asia. By the mid-1970s, the number of European immigrants had decreased significantly while the number of newcomers from Asia and the Middle East comprised almost 50% of all immigrants to Canada each year.

Challenge and Response

1. Read Diefenbaker's second quotation on page 214. What is your opinion? Do his words strike a chord with you today as a Canadian citizen? Give reasons for your response.
2. What is the difference between a right and a freedom? If we have rights, do we also have responsibilities? Give reasons for your response.
3. Why is the granting of voting rights considered an important milestone in the history of Aboriginal peoples in Canada?

Economic and Foreign Policy Woes

In the years following the Second World War, unemployment had remained relatively low at 3 to 4 per cent. By 1957, it had increased to 7 per cent as the country entered a recession. It was the worst economic downturn since the 1930s. Diefenbaker tried to ease the burden by increasing unemployment insurance, cutting taxes, and increasing spending. But he clashed with James Coyne, the outspoken governor of the Bank of Canada, over interest rates. Coyne was more interested in fighting inflation than unemployment and wanted to keep interest rates high. This did little to encourage foreign investment and ensured that unemployment remained high.

In 1960, a group of prominent economists demanded Coyne be dismissed from the Bank. In response, Diefenbaker introduced a bill calling for Coyne's removal. The issue was bitterly debated before Coyne angrily resigned.

At the same time, the Canadian dollar was falling on international **money markets**. In June 1961, the dollar was worth US$1.05. By October, it had plummeted to US$0.96. In May 1962, the government decided to set the **exchange rate** for a Canadian dollar at US$0.925. The decline in the value of the dollar made Canadian goods and services less expensive for foreign consumers, giving a boost to the Canadian economy. Politically, however, the decline in the dollar reinforced the public's perception that Diefenbaker and his government were mismanaging the economy.

Canada and the US

After the Second World War, Canada's most important international ally was the United States. Canada was linked by geography and economics to the United States and by military agreements such as NATO and NORAD. But Canada did not always see eye to eye with the United States. Growing Canadian nationalism and Canada's desire to act as a middle power often left both countries following different paths. This situation was particularly clear during two periods of international tension: the Cuban Missile Crisis in 1962 and the Vietnam War (see page 221).

The Cuban Missile Crisis

In 1959, communist revolutionary Fidel Castro overthrew the dictatorship of Fulgencio Batista in Cuba. In the following years, the United States sought to isolate the country and overthrow Castro's communist government, which gradually allied itself more closely with the Soviet Union. Canada refused to cut its ties with Cuba—much to the frustration of the Americans.

In October 1962, the United States learned that the Soviet Union was stockpiling nuclear missiles in Cuba that could reach the United States.

Figure 7.7 During the election campaign in 1963, the Liberals lashed out at the Conservative government for its poor economic performance. They issued a mock currency known as the "Diefenbuck" worth 92.5 cents. Do you think this depiction of Diefenbaker was a fair and accurate reflection of the Conservatives' economic policy? Provide evidence to support your view.

"The economy did not perform well during the Diefenbaker years, the government seemed to be confused and drifting, and foreign policy, especially defence and nuclear weapons, created all kinds of dilemmas."

–Michael Bliss, "The Prime Ministers of Canada"

Learn more about the Cuban Missile Crisis

MAP STUDY: The Cuban Missile Crisis

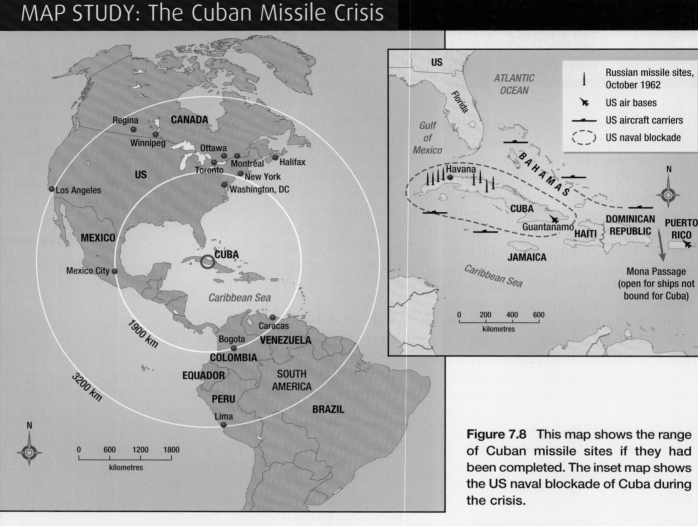

Figure 7.8 This map shows the range of Cuban missile sites if they had been completed. The inset map shows the US naval blockade of Cuba during the crisis.

Source: Don Quinlan, et al., *Twentieth Century Viewpoints*, 2nd edition, (Don Mills: Oxford University Press, 2003), 157.

The 1962 Cuban Missile Crisis was a terrifying event to people around the globe. For Canadians, it was the first time they felt directly threatened by the possibility of a nuclear attack. Schools practised air-raid drills so that students would know what to do in case of a nuclear attack. Cities such as Toronto practised sounding air-raid sirens during the day.

Analysis and Response

1. Which major Canadian cities were within range of the Cuban-based Soviet nuclear missiles?
2. Explain whether you think that the American blockade was the right response. What were the possible consequences of this action?
3. In your opinion, how vulnerable is Canada today to a missile attack? Give reasons for your response.

ISSUES

Grounding the Avro Arrow

The issue: Was Prime Minister Diefenbaker justified in grounding the Avro Arrow?

Under the Liberals, Canada had pledged to develop a military defence jet called the Avro Arrow. However, with costs soaring and few countries interested in buying the aircraft, Diefenbaker cancelled the $12.5-million project. He agreed to buy American-made Bomarc defence nuclear missiles instead.

To the government, the decision made financial sense. But it dealt a crippling blow to the aircraft industry as almost 14 000 workers lost their jobs. Diefenbaker argued that he did not want to fund an industry through federal spending or expand the nuclear arms race. His Liberal opponent, Lester Pearson, called the decision irrational.

"We shall not ... allow the extension of the nuclear family into Canada ... We do not intend to allow the spread of nuclear arms beyond the nations which now have them."

Source: Prime Minister John Diefenbaker, in an election speech, Brockville, Ontario, 1962.

———————————

"This was an aircraft constructed not only by Canadian engineers and the Canadian Air Force but also by the United States. It was classified. It could not have been sold on the open market. I do not see any other solution ... but to turn it to scrap."

Source: Raymond O'Hurley, minister of Defence Production, in Murray Peden, *Fall of an Arrow* (Stittsville: Canada's Wings, 1979), 128.

"There were reasons of defence and economics that could ... justify this decision but none to justify the way it was done. Suddenly ... without any effort to keep together the fine professional team of scientists and engineers ... Diefenbaker pronounced his government's policy [and] ... the decision to scrap the five completed planes and the others half completed so that no museum of science and technology would ever be able to show what we could design and produce."

Source: Lester B. Pearson, *Mike: The Memoirs of Lester B. Pearson*, vol. 3, (Toronto: University of Toronto Press, 1975), 47–48.

———————————

"The unprecedented callous action ... in cancelling the Arrow with immediate resultant loss of 13 000 plus jobs is tantamount to economic treachery."

Source: Peter Podger, business representative of the International Association of Machinists, in Murray Peden, *Fall of an Arrow* (Stittsville: Canada's Wings, 1979), 118.

The controversy did not end there. The Bomarc missiles were effective only when armed with nuclear warheads. But Diefenbaker refused to store the warheads on Canadian soil. Many Canadians questioned why the military had missiles it could not deploy. This issue was a key factor in Diefenbaker's defeat in 1963.

 Learn more about the Avro Arrow

Responding

1. In a T-chart, list reasons for both scrapping and keeping the Arrow. Then examine your T-chart and circle the most compelling reasons on each side. Which side do you support? Give reasons for your response.
2. Many historians believe Diefenbaker made the right decision. Canadian nationalists argue that his decision made Canada dependent on the US for its own defence. What is your opinion? Give reasons to support your position.

"It shall be the policy of this nation to regard any nuclear missile launched from Cuba against any nation in the Western hemisphere as an attack by the Soviet Union on the United States requiring a full retaliatory response upon the Soviet Union."

–President John F. Kennedy in a public address on the Soviet arms buildup in Cuba, 22 October 1962

"[Reconsider] blindly following the US lead, particularly since … President [Kennedy] has not kept the commitment to consult Canada over the impending crisis … If we go along with the US now, we'll be their vassal forever."

–Howard Green, minister of External Affairs, in a plea to the Diefenbaker Cabinet, 1962

The US government took incriminating photographs to the United Nations. The US then placed a naval blockade around Cuba to stop Soviet ships from delivering any more nuclear supplies. The situation became very tense. Nuclear war between the United States and the Soviet Union seemed imminent. As the Americans raised their state of nuclear readiness, they called on Canada to do the same. Canada refused to do so even though public opinion polls showed that 80 per cent of Canadians supported the actions of US President John F. Kennedy.

Prime Minister Diefenbaker argued that "an alert would unduly alarm the people, that we should wait and see what happens…" Diefenbaker and President Kennedy did not see eye to eye. But without Diefenbaker's knowledge, the minister of Defence secretly ordered Canada to go on alert. Although the prime minister eventually agreed to put Canadian forces on alert as the crisis reached its most serious point, Canadian–American relations had been severely strained. After

two weeks of chilling threats and counter-threats, the Soviets finally agreed to dismantle their weapons. While the crisis was now over, it had revealed the strengths and weaknesses of Canada's relationship with the United States.

The Government Falls

When the government called an election in June 1962, few Canadians were surprised that the Conservatives lost their overwhelming majority in the House of Commons. The number of Conservative seats plummeted from 208 to 116—just enough to hang on to power with a minority government.

For Diefenbaker personally, his position as leader of the Progressive Conservative Party was shaky at best. The party was divided and in disarray. By January 1963, many members of the Cabinet had lost confidence in Diefenbaker's ability to govern. There were demands for his resignation. Diefenbaker clung to power, but his government quickly collapsed. The stage was set for another election in April 1963.

Challenge and Response

1. What economic problems did the new Progressive Conservative government face in the late 1950s and early 1960s?
2. Do you think that governments can control economic trends? Give reasons for your response.
3. How do you think Canadians in 1961 might have responded to the quotation by President Kennedy on this page? How might Canadians today view this type of statement by an American president?
4. What might have occurred in Canada had the Cuban Missile Crisis escalated into open conflict between the United States and the Soviet Union?

The Liberals Return to Power

The Liberals, led by Lester Pearson, took advantage of Diefenbaker's reputation for indecision. They campaigned on a promise of "60 Days of Decision." Pearson called for a new flag, better French–English relations, universal health care, and a national pension plan. His promises earned the Liberals 41 per cent of the popular vote in the 1963 election—enough to form a minority government.

Canadian–American Relations

Pearson's victory marked the beginning of better relations with the United States. Unlike Diefenbaker, Pearson had a relaxed friendship with US President John F. Kennedy. Although he was personally opposed to the nuclear arms race, Pearson agreed to accept nuclear warheads for the Bomarc missiles as part of Canada's commitments to NATO and NORAD. He also agreed to arm Canadian troops stationed with NATO forces in Europe. Relations with the United States soon soured again, however, when Lyndon Johnson succeeded Kennedy as president in November 1963 following Kennedy's assassination.

The Vietnam War

The United States had been involved in Vietnamese politics since the mid-1950s. The Americans supported the government of South Vietnam against the communist government of North Vietnam. President Johnson decided to increase American involvement in Vietnam. Starting in 1965, his government sent hundreds of thousands of American troops into South Vietnam to begin bombing North Vietnam in "Operation Rolling Thunder."

While accepting a prestigious World Peace Award in Philadelphia in April 1965, Pearson used the opportunity to urge the United States to halt its bombing of North Vietnam: "[T]here does appear to be at least a possibility that a suspension of such air strikes against North Vietnam, at the right time, might provide the Hanoi authorities with the opportunity, if they wish to take it, to inject some flexibility into their policy without appearing to do so as the direct result of military pressure."

At lunch the next day, Johnson exploded. He shouted at Pearson, scolding the prime minister for publicly criticizing him while Pearson was a guest in his country. The angry confrontation lasted for an hour, with Johnson at one point grabbing Pearson by the lapels of his jacket. Afterwards, the two men went out to meet the press, both smiling and pretending nothing was wrong. Even though the two men parted with a handshake, Pearson was badly shaken and relations between the two leaders never recovered. It was a very low point in Canadian–American relations.

The situation in Vietnam became more and more desperate and public opinion both in Canada and the United States turned against the war. Tens of thousands of American men fled to Canada, either as deserters from the US military or to avoid being **drafted** and sent to Vietnam. For the first time, television showed the horrors of the war and as a result, massive protests were held throughout the United States. Eventually, those protests spilled over into Canada.

> "I haven't much to say except that it has been a very pleasant couple of hours."
>
> –Prime Minister Pearson, addressing the media, 3 April 1965

Learn more about Canada's role in the Vietnam War

Profile in Power:

Lester Bowles Pearson

Figure 7.9 Lester Pearson (1897–1972)

"As the symbol of a new chapter in our national story, our Maple Leaf Flag will become a symbol of that unity in our country without which one cannot grow in strength and purpose; … the unity also that recognizes the contributions and the cultures of many other races … Under this Flag may our youth find new inspiration for loyalty to Canada; for a patriotism based not on any mean or narrow nationalism, but on the deep and equal pride that all Canadians will feel for every part of this good land."

–Lester B. Pearson, speech to the House of Commons, 15 February 1965

Lester Pearson was born in a small town in southern Ontario. In 1915, he volunteered for duty in the First World War but was forced to return to Canada in 1917 after being hit by a bus during a London blackout. "Mike," as he was known to his friends, then enrolled in university, where he became a star baseball and hockey player. After graduating in 1919 and working briefly in a law office, Pearson turned to semi-professional baseball.

Soon Pearson was back at school, enrolling in Oxford University in 1921. He was a good student but an even better athlete. He excelled at rugby, hockey, and lacrosse and earned a spot on Britain's Olympic hockey team in 1922. After earning a master's degree, Pearson returned to Canada in 1923 to teach history at the University of Toronto. In 1928, he was on the road again after joining the Department of External Affairs. He served in many key diplomatic posts, including London and Washington, DC. He was also active in the United Nations, chairing a number of important committees.

In 1948, Pearson embarked on a second career when he entered federal politics and won election to the House of Commons. He served as minister of External Affairs under Prime Minister Louis St. Laurent. Pearson's shining moment in this position came in 1956 when he helped to prevent a world war and created the UN's first peacekeeping mission during the Suez crisis. For his diplomatic skills and powers of persuasion, he received the Nobel Prize for Peace in 1957. He is the only Canadian ever to have received this award.

In 1958, Pearson won the leadership of the Liberal Party. One of his first acts was to demand Diefenbaker's resignation. Diefenbaker called an election instead. Despite Pearson's highly respected international profile, Diefenbaker's superior campaigning skills and personal appeal led the Progressive Conservatives to another victory.

In 1963, Pearson finally defeated Diefenbaker at the polls to form the first of his two minority governments. He campaigned on a promise to create a new flag—one that was distinctly Canadian. A lengthy debate in Parliament over the design of the flag brought the government to a standstill. (You will learn more about this debate in the Issues feature on page 226.) When Pearson died in 1972, his wife, Maryon Pearson, said that the flag was his proudest achievement.

Figure 7.10 To Canadians today, Lester Pearson is perhaps best known for giving Canada the Maple Leaf flag. His determination to give the country its own flag was partly based on his experience after the Suez crisis. The Egyptian president initially refused to allow Canadian soldiers to be part of the UN's peacekeeping force because they carried the Red Ensign, reminding the Egyptians of British invaders. Pearson felt that rejection by another country on this basis was embarrassing for Canada and wanted to ensure that it never happened again.

Responding

1. How might Lester Pearson's diplomatic career have prepared him for his role as prime minister?
2. What does the excerpt from Pearson's February 1965 speech to the House of Commons suggest to you about his attitude toward Canadian unity? What does it suggest about his attitude regarding Canada's international reputation?

WHUT'S THIS ABOUT PICKIN' YOU UP BY THE SCRUFF OF YOUR NECK?

LUCKY IT WASN'T HIS EARS

Figure 7.11 A famous photograph was published showing Lyndon Johnson picking up his dog by its floppy ears. This cartoon compares that incident with the altercation between Johnson and Pearson. To what extent is this an accurate comparison? To what extent are personal relationships important in political matters between heads of states?

"No one would dispute that the 1965 agreement between Canada and the United States ignited a tremendous surge in two-way trade in cars and parts, making possible a[n] ... industry that has lowered costs, increased sales and generally benefited everyone ... On the other hand, it gave us ... a perpetual lobby for subsidies, protection, and other state favours; a whining, grasping, pampered bunch ... which never ceases to use the Auto Pact as the base from which to mount fresh new campaigns for special treatment."

–Andrew Coyne, Canadian journalist, 1997

The war finally ended with the retreat of American forces and the defeat of South Vietnam by North Vietnam in 1975. Although some individual Canadians joined US forces, the government of Canada never agreed with its close neighbour and ally over the Vietnam War.

The Auto Pact

Economic relations between Canada and the United States fared somewhat better than political relations did. The 1950s and 1960s were boom years for Canada's automobile industry. Post-war prosperity led to skyrocketing sales. New highway construction, migration to the suburbs, and a growing economy combined together put more and more Canadians behind the wheel. Although some of the cars Canadians bought were made in Canada, most were imported from the United States. These American-made cars were subject to tariffs designed to protect Canadian car manufacturers. By the 1960s, however, most Canadian automakers had disappeared or had been bought out by American companies. The tariffs created a barrier between two separate markets, with Canadians paying 30 per cent more than Americans for the same car.

In 1965, the Liberal government signed an agreement with the United States. The Auto Pact eliminated tariffs in the auto industry. Canadians would now be able to buy cars at lower prices. The flow of cars and car parts across the border was made easier, as well. The Pact protected the jobs of thousands of Canadian auto workers. But critics argued that the Canadian automobile industry was still dominated by the "Big Three" American automakers—General Motors, Ford, and Chrysler—and that all of the senior positions and design decisions remained in the United States.

Overall, most economists agreed that the deal was good for the Canadian economy. Within two years, employment in the auto industry skyrocketed by 27 per cent, new investment was up by $500 million, and exports to the United States increased tenfold. At the time, it was the most significant international trade deal in the history of Canadian–American relations.

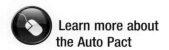

Learn more about the Auto Pact

Challenge and Response

1. Why do think Prime Minister Pearson was against the United States' bombing of North Vietnam?

2. Do you think Pearson was out of line during his speech in Philadelphia when he suggested that the United States should suspend its bombing of North Vietnam? Explain your reasoning.

3. Use a PMI chart to outline the positive, negative, and interesting aspects of the Auto Pact. What conclusions can you draw from your chart?

4. In your opinion, is Canada's relationship with the United States still as important as it was in the eras of Diefenbaker and Pearson? Explain.

Redefining Canada

Although the Liberals never formed a majority government under Lester Pearson, they succeeded in passing legislation that strengthened Canada's **social safety net**.

- In 1965, Pearson introduced the Canada Pension Plan. This was a mandatory investment fund that deducted wages from employee's paycheques and redistributed them in the form of a retirement pension.

- In 1967, Pearson launched the Royal Commission on the Status of Women after women's groups demanded equal rights.

- In 1968, Pearson adopted the public health care system founded by Tommy Douglas in Saskatchewan when he introduced national medicare. The federal government contributed 50 per cent of the costs while the provinces were given the power to manage their own systems.

- Pearson put a temporary hold on **capital punishment**, effectively banning all executions of convicted criminals in Canada. (Capital punishment was formally abolished in 1976.)

- Under Pearson, new labour laws established a minimum wage, the eight-hour workday, and the forty-hour work week and made it mandatory for employers to provide a minimum of two weeks' paid vacation to their full-time employees.

Many of the social programs Pearson implemented continue to define Canada today. In 2004, Pearson was chosen as one of the top 10 greatest Canadians in the CBC's *Greatest Canadian* contest.

Expo '67: Canada Celebrates!

In 1967, Canada turned 100. The government celebrated with a year-long birthday bash. The Centennial Train, carrying displays about Canadian history and culture, toured the country. Communities from coast to coast joined in with their own Centennial projects—from new skating rinks to libraries to statues. Canadian musician

Reading Strategy

Before you start reading an Issues feature, think about where you stand on the issue based on your background knowledge. After you have read the feature, think about whether your new knowledge supports your original position or changes your point of view.

ISSUES

The Great Canadian Flag Debate

The issue: To what extent does the Canadian flag represent Canada's national identity?

In 1964, Canadians became embroiled in a long and bitter debate over a new national flag. The Red Ensign, consisting of the British Union Jack in one corner and Canada's coat of arms in the other, had served as the country's unofficial flag. Pearson wanted to create a distinctly Canadian flag—one that had no colonial or cultural symbolism attached to it. In June 1964, he unveiled his proposal: a cluster of three red maple leaves on a white background, with blue bars on either side. The leaves symbolized Canada's founding peoples—the First Peoples, the French, and the British—while the blue panels represented the oceans on the east and west coasts. Diefenbaker was outraged, demanding that Britain be honoured on the new flag.

The debate dragged on in the House of Commons for six months. A committee of members from all parties took on the task of finding an acceptable design. They chose a red maple leaf on a white background with red bars on either side. Yet Diefenbaker continued his protest. He launched a **filibuster** that brought the House of Commons to a standstill.

After hundreds of speeches, even members of Diefenbaker's own party had had enough. They asked the government to force a vote: 163 members voted in favour of the flag; 78 voted against it. On 15 February 1965, Canada's new flag was officially unfurled.

> "I believe that today a flag designed around the Maple Leaf will symbolize and be a true reflection of the new Canada."
>
> Source: Prime Minister Lester Pearson introducing the new flag at a Canadian Legion meeting in Winnipeg, 17 May 1963.

> "The Pearson flag is a meaningless flag. There is no recognition of history; no indication of the existence of French and English Canada; ... It is a flag without a past, without history, without honour and without pride."
>
> Source: Former prime minister John Diefenbaker, quoted in Rick Archbold, *I Stand for Canada: The Story of the Maple Leaf Flag* (Toronto: MacFarlane, Walter & Ross, 2002).

You don't see red ensigns muckin' up the lawns like this!

Figure 7.12 Even political cartoonists got in on the flag debate. What is this cartoonist's message? How effective is it?

Responding

1. Why would some people have wanted to keep the Red Ensign? Who might have wanted a distinctly Canadian flag? Why?
2. How does the maple leaf suggest that Canadians find at least part of our national identity in our geography? Do you think the maple leaf is an appropriate symbol for the Canadian flag? Explain your response.

Tommy Douglas: The Greatest Canadian

PERSONALITIES

Tommy Douglas was born into a family of Scottish immigrants in Winnipeg. At the age of 10, he was hospitalized with a bone infection. A series of operations failed to heal the infection, but his family could not afford to see a specialist. Doctors told them the only option was to amputate. Fortunately, a visiting surgeon offered to operate for free if his students were allowed to observe. The surgery saved Douglas's leg—and perhaps his life. His ordeal was the inspiration behind his quest for universal health care in Canada.

As a young man, Douglas dabbled in different professions before he became a Baptist minister in 1924. In 1935, he was elected as an MP for the Co-operative Commonwealth Federation (CCF). After nine years in the House of Commons, Douglas won the leadership of the provincial CCF in Saskatchewan. In 1944, he led his party to a landslide victory in the province, winning 47 of 53 seats.

In 1947, Douglas took the first step towards universal health care by introducing public hospital insurance in Saskatchewan. For a premium of five dollars a year, every person in the province would receive hospital care when needed. What the premiums did not cover the government would pay. In 1959, Douglas announced a complete health insurance plan that included payment of doctors' fees. However, doctors bitterly opposed the plan. The day after it came into effect on 1 July 1962, 90 per cent of the doctors in Saskatchewan went on strike. The government recruited doctors from other provinces and from Britain to fill the void. The bitter standoff dragged on for 23 days. When

Figure 7.13 Tommy Douglas was an passionate politician and champion of social justice. When he became premier of Saskatchewan in 1944, he became an instant celebrity as leader of North America's first socialist government.

"I made a pledge with myself long before I ever sat in this House in the years when I knew something about what it meant to get health service when you didn't have the money to pay for it. I made a pledge with myself that some day, if I ever had anything to do with it, people would be able to get health services, just as they are able to get educational services as an inalienable right..."

Source: Tommy Douglas, speech to the Saskatchewan legislature, 1954.

it was over, the doctors won some minor concessions, but they had no choice but to accept medicare.

Douglas predicted that medicare would be adopted across the country within a decade. He was right. In 1966, the Pearson government introduced national health care for all Canadians. After being elected leader of the national New Democratic Party, the successor of the CCF, in 1961, Douglas continued to promote his socialist policies. The Liberals and Conservatives began to adopt his progressive social ideas—once considered radical—as their own.

"For more than 50 years, his staunch devotion to social causes, rousing powers of speech, and pugnacious charm made Tommy C. Douglas an unstoppable political force."

Source: "Tommy Douglas: The greatest of them all." CBC, 2007.

Responding

1. In 2005, over a million Canadians took part in a CBC television program to choose the "Greatest Canadian." The winner was Tommy Douglas. Explain why you agree or disagree with this choice.

Learn more about Expo '67

Figure 7.14 Expo '67 boasted a shiny new monorail to transport visitors around the ultra-modern site. How might a world's fair benefit a country like Canada? What might the drawbacks have been?

> "This was the greatest thing we have ever done as a nation and surely the modernization of Canada—of its skylines, of its styles, of its institutions—will be dated from this occasion and from this fair."
>
> –Peter C. Newman, *Toronto Star*, 28 April 1967

> "Expo has done more for Canada's self-confidence than anything within memory … 'We're on the map,' a friend told me. 'They know who we are in New York now.' … Others go even further, demanding an alarmingly high emotional return from what is, after all, only a world's fair. A good one, maybe even the most enjoyable one ever. However, within it there lies merely the stuff of a future nostalgic musical, not the myth out of which a nation is forged."
>
> –Mordecai Richler, Canadian author, 1968

Bobby Gimby wrote a special song called "CA-NA-DA" that became the Centennial's anthem.

The centrepiece of the celebration was the world's fair known as Expo '67 in Montréal. Ninety countries participated, organizing shows and exhibits on two islands in the St. Lawrence River created especially for the event. A new subway shuttled over 50 million visitors to the islands.

Expo '67 made headlines around the world. Many world leaders visited Montréal that summer, including French President Charles de Gaulle. Everywhere de Gaulle went huge crowds of Québécois gathered to hear him speak. For most Canadians, however, he injected a sour note in the national celebrations when he declared the battle cry of Québec separatists *"Vive Montréal! Vive le Québec! Vive le Québec libre!"* (Long live Montréal! Long live Québec! Long live a free Québec!) from the balcony of Montréal's city hall.

De Gaulle's proclamation was seen not only as interference in Canada's internal affairs, but also as a slap in the face of the federal government. Pearson was so angry that he refused to meet with the French president. De Gaulle was forced to cancel a trip to Ottawa and abruptly return to France.

Despite the controversy, Expo '67 unleashed a new feeling of national pride and confidence. Many Canadians discovered they had more in common with one another than they thought. For some, Expo's success marked Canada's coming of age as a country.

Challenge and Response

1. How did Pearson strengthen Canada's social safety net? How important do you think these measures are in Canadian society today?
2. Do you think Pearson deserved to be named one of the top 10 Canadians in the CBC's *Greatest Canadian* contest? Why or why not?
3. Newman and Richler expressed different opinions about the impact of Expo '67 on Canada's nationhood. Hold a class debate on this issue. Refer to the *Skill Path* on page 236.

Québec and Canada

In the 1960s, dissatisfaction over Québec's place in Canada was on the rise. Prime Minister Pearson wanted to focus on the strained relationship between Québec and Ottawa and to control the development of Québécois nationalism and **separatism**. In 1963, he appointed the Royal Commission on Bilingualism and Biculturalism to examine the growing crisis. At a federal–provincial conference in 1964, he attempted to find a formula that would allow Canada to amend its Constitution and give the provinces greater powers. However, his efforts failed after Québec premier Jean Lesage refused to support the plan.

Québec was still a priority after Pearson was re-elected with a second minority government in 1965. He recruited three leading Québec activists to join the federal government and help staunch the separatist tide in Québec:

- Jean Marchand, a prominent labour leader
- Gérard Pelletier, editor of *La Presse*
- Pierre Elliott Trudeau, a law professor and one of the founders of the influential journal *Cité Libre*

Marchand, Pelletier, and Trudeau—known in the media as "the three wise men"—joined Pearson's Cabinet. When he announced his retirement in 1968, Pearson worked quietly behind the scenes to choose his successor—Pierre Elliott Trudeau.

The Quiet Revolution

For generations, political and religious leaders in Québec had protected French culture by embracing French-Canadian traditions. Québécois society favoured rural life over urban, religion

over the state, and isolationism over engagement with the wider world. Maurice Duplessis, the domineering premier of Québec from 1944 until his death in 1959, had kept a tight rein on these traditions. Economically, American and English-Canadian business interests owned and operated most Québec industries and maintained English as the language of the workplace.

After his death, the party Duplessis had led, the Union Nationale, lost the election in 1960 to the Québec Liberal Party. The Liberals' campaign slogan was *Il faut que ça change* (Things have to change). Under the leadership of Jean Lesage, the Liberals promised to end the corruption and **patronage** that had characterized the Duplessis government. Their victory marked the start of a stunning transformation in Québec society on all fronts—political, social, cultural, and industrial. They called it *La Révolution tranquille* (the Quiet Revolution). Although the Quiet Revolution occurred in the 1960s, the attack on the society of the past had

"Canada, without being fully conscious of the fact, is passing through the greatest crisis in its history."

–Interim report of the Royal Commission on Bilingualism and Biculturalism, 1965

"National unity does not imply subordination in any way of provincial rights or the alienation of provincial authority. It does require a government at the centre strong enough to serve Canada as a whole; and its full realization demands a strong Canadian identity with the national spirit and pride that will sustain and strengthen it."

–Prime Minister Lester Pearson, 15 October 1964

Figure 7.15 This historic photograph shows Pierre Elliott Trudeau, John Turner, Prime Minister Pearson, and Jean Chrétien following a Cabinet shuffle in 1967. Each of these men served as prime minister of Canada during the last 40 years of the 20th century and into the 2000s. What does this suggest to you about the political impact that the Liberal Party had on Canadian politics during those years?

"Bludgeoning the present and the future to death with the past is finished."

–Le Refus global

"Our generation is much too preoccupied with the future to centre its interest on the past."

–Julien Chouinard, Maclean's, 6 April 1963

Learn more about the Quiet Revolution

actually begun with the publication of a manifesto called *Le Refus global* (Total Refusal) by a group of artists and intellectuals in 1948. Led by abstract artist Paul-Émile Borduas, the group called for Québec society to overcome its attachment to Roman Catholicism, the French language, and the idealization of rural life.

The Transformation of Québécois Society

The Québec government urged the Québécois to reject their status as second-class citizens in their own province and to take control of their destiny to become *maîtres chez nous* (masters in our own house). Under Lesage, the government established a stronger French presence in the province's economy. It took over several private power companies to create Hydro-Québec, a publicly owned hydroelectric company. Investment agencies were set up to help finance Québécois business initiatives. A French

Language Office was established to promote the use of French in business.

The government also took control of the province's social services—restricting the role played by the Roman Catholic Church. To improve health care, the province built new hospitals and introduced a provincial hospital insurance plan. It created government departments to oversee cultural affairs and federal–provincial relations. The province also took responsibility for education away from the Roman Catholic and Protestant Churches and created a ministry of Education. Mandatory school attendance was extended until the age of 16. The *collège d'enseignement général et professionnel* (CEGEP) system, a two-year, pre-university program, was introduced to improve the quality of education across the province.

Events in Québec had a significant impact on the rest of the country. Québec demanded more powers and more money from the federal government. The provinces gained the power to levy their own taxes. They were given the right to opt out of national social programs and create their own provincial counterparts. Québec withdrew from the federal pension plan and created its own provincial plan. In total, the province opted out of 29 federal-provincial cost-sharing projects in an effort to assert its provincial rights.

Artists of all genres contributed to a new sense of Québec nationalism. In

Figure 7.16 The Manic-2 Generating Station in Manicouagan, Québec, was completed in 1967. Why do you think hydroelectric power became one of the symbols of pride during the Quiet Revolution?

the theatre, playwrights such as Michel Tremblay used *joual* (Québécois slang) to draw attention to the lives of working-class people in the cities. His 1969 play *Les Belles-soeurs*, with its all-female cast of characters, focused on Québec working-class women. In music, Gilles Vigneault captured Québec's growing nationalism with songs such as "Mon Pays," which became the anthem of the separatist movement.

Although the changes in Québec were rapid, not everyone agreed on how far they should go. Some saw Québec as a unique province and the homeland for French-speaking peoples in North America. They wanted a more assertive Québec within Confederation, with special status to protect and encourage French language and culture. Others believed Québec needed to exert greater influence over government in Ottawa by sending top-quality candidates to the House of Commons. Other Québécois wanted a separate nation. While the people of Québec were debating their future, they were debating the future of Canada, too. "What does Québec want?" became a common question. Finding an answer would become a central challenge in Canadian political life in the coming decades.

Terrorism Comes to Canada

During the Quiet Revolution, some Québécois began to embrace the idea of Québec separating from Canada to become an independent state. Most separatists wanted to work for change peacefully through the political system. However, a few separatists were impatient and chose to work for change outside the law.

Canadians were used to news reports about acts of terrorism. Bombings, kidnappings, and assassinations happened with regularity—in other parts of the world. In the 1960s, however, it was discovered that Canadians were not immune to terrorism.

In 1963, the Front de libération du Québec (FLQ) launched a campaign of terror in Québec. This small group of extremists carried out a string of bombings and bank robberies, mainly in Montréal. Between 1963 and 1970, the FLQ committed over 200 violent acts that killed several people. They targeted symbols of the English business establishment and the federal government. Bombs were placed in mailboxes in Montréal's affluent, largely English, Westmount district. The FLQ exploded bombs in the Montréal Stock Exchange and at McGill University. They threatened the life of Queen Elizabeth II in advance of a royal visit to Canada. By 1970, 23 members of the FLQ were in jail. However, as you will discover in Chapter 8, their greatest act of terrorism was yet to come.

> "Since I naturally owe my first allegiance to French Canada, before the Dominion, I must ask myself the question: which of two choices will permit French Canadians to attain the fullest development—Confederation, in which they will be a shrinking minority doomed to subjection?—or the independence of Québec, their true native land, which will make them masters of their own destiny?"
>
> –M. Chaput, *Why I Am a Separatist*, 1961

> "In a little while the English, the federalists, the exploiters, the toadies of the occupiers, the lackeys of imperialism—all of those who betray the workers and the Québec nation—will fear for their lives!"
>
> –An FLQ communiqué, March 1969

Challenge and Response

1. Why might Pearson have thought that the appointment of Marchand, Pelletier, and Trudeau to Cabinet positions would help control the rise of separatism in Québec?

2. Use a concept web to illustrate the course of action taken by the Lesage government and the Québécois to realize the goal of *maîtres chez nous*. Refer to the Skill Path on page 240.

Aboriginal Peoples in Canada

"The aspirations of Native Canada [are not] unique; around the world in countries claimed by colonial empires, indigenous peoples are gaining momentum in struggles to protect their way of life. Liberation movements, civil rights movements, and Aboriginal rights movements have been the hallmark of the latter part of the 20th century."

–Tim Schoulis, John Olthuis, and Diane Engelstad, "The basic dilemma: Sovereignty or assimilation", 1992

"We Haida were surrounded by art. Art was one with the culture. Art was our only written language. It documented our progress as a people, it documented the histories of the families. Throughout our history, it has been the art that has kept our spirit alive."

–Robert Davidson, in *Eagle of the Dawn*, 1993

During the 1960s, Aboriginal peoples in Canada began to demand their rights. They were inspired in part by indigenous peoples in Asia and Africa who had formed movements to sever their colonial ties and regain their sovereignty. Through collective political action, Aboriginal peoples around the world were making their voices heard.

First Nations people gained the right to vote in 1960. While this was an important milestone, it did little to improve the social and economic conditions for Aboriginal peoples. They still experienced much higher levels of poverty, illness, and other social problems than did other Canadians.

In 1964, Pearson implemented a Parliamentary committee to investigate the social, economic, political, and educational needs of Aboriginal peoples. In 1966, the Hawthorn Report condemned assimilation of Aboriginal peoples—a position opposite of 100 years of government policy in Canada. It recommended that Aboriginal people become "citizens plus." This meant that, in addition to the rights of Canadian citizenship, Aboriginal people had additional rights, including treaty rights. It recommended that the Department of Indian Affairs take action to ensure social and economic equality for Aboriginal peoples through new programs. These recommendations reflected a radical shift in thinking about the relationship between the government and Aboriginal peoples.

Cultural Revival: The Resurgence of Aboriginal Art

Traditionally, art played an important role in Aboriginal societies. Objects were handmade and decorated with designs that told of family histories and spiritual beliefs. Art was both decorative and practical. Tools and clothing often reflected a people's artistic values.

By the beginning of the twentieth century, many ancient art traditions had declined or been lost. Attempts to assimilate Aboriginal peoples, including banning many ceremonies, reduced the number of works that artists created. As these artistic treasures disappeared, so did the skills needed to create them. Still, a few artists struggled to keep the ancient ways alive.

The new era of political activism coincided with a resurgence in Aboriginal cultural expression. People began teaching themselves the artistic symbols and traditions of the past, and blending these with modern techniques

Figure 7.17 Haida artist Bill Reid was a prominent artist in the cultural revival. Like many Aboriginal artists, he taught himself the artistic principles and techniques of the Haida by studying the works of his grandfather and other artists. Reid created this famous sculpture, called *Raven and the First Men*, in 1980. It depicts the creation story of how Raven created the Haida First Nation.

George Manuel: Champion of Aboriginal Rights

George Manuel was born in 1921 into the Secwepemc [SUHK-wep-muhk] Nation in south-central British Columbia. As chief of the Secwepemc Nation in the 1950s, Manuel believed the best way to improve the lives of First Nations peoples was to unite them under one organization. In 1958, he travelled around BC promoting unity. In 1959, he became president of the North American Indian Brotherhood of British Columbia and served as National Chief of the Assembly of First Nations from 1970 to 1976.

Manuel believed that people held the power to shape their own futures. This belief defined his leadership. In order for Aboriginal societies to bring about positive changes, the people had to work together.

"At this point in our struggle for survival, the Indian peoples of North America are entitled to declare a victory. We have survived. If others have also prospered on our land, let it stand as a sign between us that the Mother Earth can be good to all her children without confusing one with another. It is a myth of European warfare that one man's victory requires another's defeat."

Source: George Manuel, *The Fourth World: An Indian Reality* (Toronto: Collier-Macmillan, 1974).

Figure 7.18 "George Manuel spoke for many when he concluded that Aboriginal people in North America live in a 'fourth world'—sharing the experience of colonization with the third world, but different as Aboriginal peoples, a minority in their own homeland, governed by the laws and institutions of settler governments." –Indian and Northern Affairs Canada

Manuel worked for Aboriginal peoples across Canada and indigenous peoples around the world. In 1975, he became the first president of the World Council of Indigenous Peoples. Between 1975 and 1981, he travelled the world meeting indigenous peoples and their leaders. He realized that the Aboriginal peoples of Canada had much in common with other indigenous nations, including their world view and spirituality and their fight to gain rights in the face of adversity. Manuel was instrumental in bringing about the UN's Universal Declaration of the Rights of Indigenous Peoples.

Manuel was honoured many times for his work, including his appointment as an Officer of the Order of Canada. He died in 1989, but his legacy lives on today.

Responding
1. Do you agree with Manuel that the idea of "one man's victory requires another's defeat" was a myth? Give reasons for your response.
2. Are there individuals in your own community who are role models for positive change? Describe how they inspire others.

The Artists of Cape Dorset

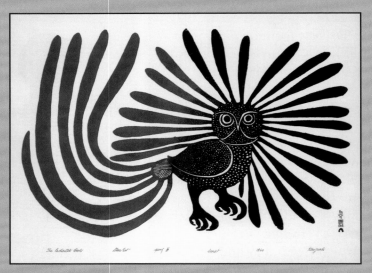

Figure 7.19 Kenojuak Ashevak was one of the first artists in the Co-operative to gain international acclaim and success. This print produced in 1960, called *The Enchanted Owl*, has appeared on a Canadian stamp. The original print sold for $58 000, the highest price ever paid for an Inuit print. Ashevak was awarded the Order of Canada in 1967.

Traditionally, art was a way for the Inuit to survive in the harsh Arctic environment. In the 1950s, however, Inuit art began to evolve into a thriving artistic enterprise. In 1959, the West Baffin Eskimo Co-operative was formed to spearhead the production of Inuit art. Since then, it has brought the unique work of Inuit artists to the attention of the world.

The Co-operative is centred in the tiny community of Cape Dorset, Nunavut, on the southwestern tip of Baffin Island. Of the residents, 25 per cent of them work in the arts. This makes Cape Dorset—or *Kinngait* in the Inuktitut language—the most artistic community in Canada.

The Co-operative promotes awareness and appreciation of Inuit fine art through its stone sculptures, graphic arts, and other artistic pieces. The residents of the community own the Co-operative. The works created by the artists are marketed through Dorset Fine Arts. In 1978, the Co-operative opened a showroom in downtown Toronto. It sells the graphics and sculptures to galleries specializing in Inuit art around the world. Today, people travel from around the world to visit the Co-operative and meet the artists.

Figure 7.20 Pitseolak Ashoona was another of the early Inuit artists to gain international recognition. Her work, including this piece called *Summer Camp Scene* (1974), depicted the traditional Inuit way of life. Her art is displayed in many important galleries, including the National Gallery of Canada. Ashoona was awarded the Order of Canada in 2007.

 Learn more about Cape Dorset's artists

"I wish I was born in the past. I would know [things] in the traditional way. But I'm not from the past. I didn't see any igloo in my life. Only today, Ski-Doo, Honda, House."

Source: Annie Pootoogook, *Toronto Star*, 17 February 2007.

Figure 7.21 Annie Pootoogook comes from a long line of Inuit artists. Her mother, Napachie Pootoogook, is a famous artist, and her grandmother was Pitseolak Ashoona. Pootoogook represents the new generation of Cape Dorset artists. Unlike her predecessors, whose work focused on legends, animals, hunting, and fishing, Pootoogook's art, like this one titled *Playing Super Nintendo* (2004), reflects the reality of life and technology in modern Inuit communities.

Responding

1. What are your impressions of Inuit art from these images?
2. Compare the work of the earlier Cape Dorset artists with that of Annie Pootoogook. How would you describe the differences? Which do you prefer? Why?

and technologies. They passed down their knowledge and experiences to new generations of artists. For example, Norval Morrisseau, a member of the Anishinabe First Nation, was largely self-taught. He created a new school of art known as the Woodlands style. This technique uses dark outlines radiating from or connecting to objects to show symbolic links between the characters in the painting. Morrisseau's 1962 art exhibition in Toronto was a phenomenal success. Every painting was sold on the first night.

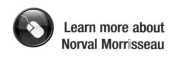

Learn more about Norval Morrisseau

Challenge and Response

1. What factors led to increased political activism among Aboriginal peoples?
2. How did the Hawthorn Report redefine the relationship between the government and Aboriginal peoples?
3. How might the loss of cultural traditions have affected Aboriginal societies?
4. Why do you think Aboriginal peoples want to repatriate art treasures that were taken from them?

Skill Path:
Participating Effectively in Debates and Discussions

In a history class, you may be asked to investigate an issue by discussing or debating it. In a debate, students are arranged in teams. One team argues in favour of a position and the other team argues against it. The teams use logical arguments and cite examples to make their case. They also try to refute the position of the opposing team. Issues can also be explored in a discussion that draws out opinions from the class. The moderator may ask questions to clarify students' positions. Students may also respond to the arguments raised by other members of the class. In any debate or discussion, however, it is important to follow these steps.

STEP 1: Determine Your Position

The issues addressed in historical discussions and debates are often complex and controversial. It is important to read about the issue and take time to reflect on it before deciding how you feel about it. To help you, create a T-chart listing the arguments for and against a particular position. In a debate, the position is stated in the affirmative, for example, "Be it resolved that the Canadian flag accurately represents our national identity." Then the two sides argue for or against this position.

STEP 2: Prepare Your Case

Once you have determined your position on an issue, you will need to collect evidence to support it. Write down your arguments to help you remember what you want to say. Arrange your ideas logically and choose appropriate language to effectively express your point of view. You can consult your notes briefly as you speak, but you should not read directly from them.

STEP 3: State Your Opinion

To state your opinion effectively, you should
- speak clearly and concisely
- begin with a clear statement of your opinion
- modulate your voice to emphasize key points
- look at the audience or opposing team while speaking
- repeat keywords or phrases to keep the audience focused on your argument
- conclude your speech by summarizing your main points

STEP 4: Respond to Others

Listen carefully to the arguments put forward by members of the opposing team and your own team. As you listen, make notes to remind yourself of the speaker's arguments. You will need to refer to these later on as you refute the argument of the opposing side.

STEP 5: Practise Your Skill

Working in five groups, debate one of the following issues:
- Canada should continue to ban capital punishment.
- Canada should have built the Avro Arrow.
- John Diefenbaker was a better prime minister than Lester Pearson.
- Canadian women still do not enjoy full equality with Canadian men.
- Québec will eventually separate from Canada.

Each group should divide itself into two sub-groups—one representing the pro side, the other the con side. Each group should present its arguments to the class. One student should act as the moderator to ensure that the debate proceeds smoothly.

Changing Times

In the 1960s, the new age of television was changing the way young people viewed the world. Every night from the comfort of their living rooms, they could now watch the events that would come to define the era, such as the Quiet Revolution in Québec and the **civil rights movement** in the United States. As they did, they began to question the **status quo** and to reject the Establishment and the values and attitudes of their parents' generation. Young people rebelled against society as they protested the Cold War, the Vietnam War, and the nuclear arms race. They demanded an end to the injustices and discrimination that made women and diverse groups second-class citizens.

In the early 1960s, Diefenbaker's government distributed pamphlets informing Canadians of their rights under the new Bill of Rights. Young Canadians began to assert their rights as individuals, including the right to dress and wear their hair the way they wanted. No longer could businesses, universities, and schools impose strict dress codes. "Doing your own thing" became the norm.

The Status of Women

At the beginning of the decade, men were the primary wage earners and most women stayed home to raise their children. Fewer than one in five women worked outside the home, usually in occupations that were considered "female"—for example, as nurses, teachers, or secretaries. They received lower wages than men, even if they were doing the same work. In fact, women were treated unequal to men in all aspects of life—social, political, legal, and cultural.

By the mid-1960s, women were becoming increasingly dissatisfied with the status quo. Social expectations about family size and lifestyles were changing. The arrival of the birth control pill gave women more control over reproduction and lifestyle choices. Across the country, women's groups campaigned for equal rights, equal job opportunities, and an end to discrimination based on gender. They sought equal pay legislation, paid maternity leave, and an end to women being shut out of the upper levels of management and government. These groups also worked to address issues such as sexual exploitation and the establishment of rape crisis centres and homes for battered women.

In 1966, 32 women's groups established the Committee for the Equality of Women (CEW) under the leadership of Laura Sabia. Together with the Fédération des femmes du Québec, the CEW successfully lobbied for a Royal Commission on the Status of Women. When the Pearson government stalled, Sabia threatened to "lead an uprising of Canadian women." The Commission was set up in February 1967 and headed by Florence Bird, a broadcaster and journalist. Beginning in the spring of 1968, public hearings were held across the country—468 briefs were presented and 1000 letters were sent describing the issues that affected Canadian women. The Commission submitted its report to the House of Commons in December 1970. Its 167 recommendations resulted in the following:

- The National Action Committee on the Status of Women was established in 1971 to "create a favourable climate for equality of opportunity for the women of Canada." It was initially headed by Laura Sabia.

 **Reading Strategy**

One way to remember new terms such as *status quo* is to use them as soon as and as often as you can. Write a few sentences using the term, or discuss what the term means. Remember to record the term in your personal glossary.

"Television brought the brutality of war into the comfort of the living room. Vietnam was lost in the living rooms of America—not on the battlefields of Vietnam."

–Marshall McLuhan, 1975

"In the late 1960s, feminism was emerging in Québec, but it was very, very interlinked with all the other social movements at the time, the nationalist question, the trade union movement. The slogan of the women's liberation movement was, 'There can be no liberation of Québec without women's liberation, and no women's liberation without the liberation of Québec.'"

–Monique Simard, Québec union activist

 Learn more about the Royal Commission on the Status of Women

PERSONALITIES

Marshall McLuhan: Communications Pioneer

In the 1960s, Marshall McLuhan revolutionized the way people thought about media and culture. Born in Edmonton, McLuhan studied in Manitoba and England before becoming a professor of English literature at the University of Toronto.

McLuhan believed that media produced a certain way of thinking and a certain kind of society. For example, print media (books, newspapers, and magazines) are linear. They require the reader to read one letter after another and one word after another in order to make sense of the information. The emphasis in print media is on the logical progression of ideas. This in turn affects the kind of information that it presents.

Electronic media (radio, television, and the Internet), on the other hand, are visual. Although visual images are constructed, the emphasis is not on logical arguments but on emotional statements. Therefore, television is better at presenting us with emotional stories rather than logical arguments. Since electronic media differ from print media, their messages differ as well. Therefore, the means we use to communicate is just as important as the information we convey.

McLuhan also offered his insights into modern technology, which has eliminated the concept of distance. He foresaw that, as television signals bounced around the world, they would draw everyone into the same community of images, creating what he called the **global village**.

Figure 7.22 "The *Economist* and other magazines that once disdained Canada's intellectual comet now routinely refer to McLuhan in discussions of the meaning of new media." –McLuhan
Why do you think these magazines criticized McLuhan's ideas in the past?

"The medium is the message."

Source: Marshall McLuhan, 30 July 1959, first published in *Understanding Media* (New York: McGraw Hill, 1964).

"The new electronic independence recreates the world in the image of a global village."

Source: Marshall McLuhan, *The Gutenberg Galaxy*, (Toronto: University of Toronto Press, 1962).

McLuhan believed that world cultures would slowly begin to blend into one another, becoming more alike as they experienced the same media and absorbed the same information. He theorized that distinct national identities would dissolve as the distances created by geography succumbed to the instant interactions created by technology.

"He died in 1980 … more than a decade before the creation of the Internet … If only he were alive today! What heaven the present moment would have been for him! How he would have loved the Web!"

Source: Author Tom Wolfe, writing about McLuhan in *Forbes* magazine, "The all-in-one global village", November 1999.

Responding

1. Do you agree with McLuhan that the way in which information is presented is as important as the message it conveys? Why or why not?
2. McLuhan coined the term *global village*. To what extent do you think this reflects the world today? To what extent are you involved in the global village?

- A portfolio for the Status of Women in the federal Cabinet was created in 1971.
- The Canadian Advisory Council on the Status of Women was created in 1973.
- Several federal statutes were amended to eliminate sections that were discriminatory to women. For example, the Canadian Labour Code was amended in 1971 to ensure women equal wages with men if they were employed in the same industrial establishment "performing, under the same or similar working conditions, the same or similar work on jobs requiring the same or similar skill, effort, and responsibility."

While the Royal Commission on the Status of Women drew attention to women's social position and recommended changes to eliminate sexual inequality through social policy, several of the issues women faced in the 1960s continue today. For example, a Statistics Canada study released in June 2007 found that university-educated women in their twenties earned 18 per cent less than men from 1991 to 2001. This was only a slight improvement from 1991, when women earned 20 per cent less than men.

The Emergence of the Counterculture

The emerging **counterculture** was reflected in the music of the 1960s generation. Canadian folk music experienced a revival in coffee houses and taverns in places such as Yorkville—the youth hangout of the 1960s in Toronto. With its tradition of social commentary, folk music symbolized the new social consciousness. Influenced by its American counterpart, Canadian folk music expressed the protests, fears, and hopes of the younger generation. With themes based on truth and sincerity, the music addressed the issues and values of the day. It appealed to many Canadians because it fostered national identity and expressed hope for solutions to society's problems. As the 1960s progressed, the counterculture would leave its imprint on North American society.

"The need for responsible and knowledgeable women at the policy-making level of Government is imperative. Just as long as women apathetically abdicate their grave responsibility to help formulate legislation, we will continue to have the discriminatory legislation that takes women a lifetime to eradicate."

–Laura Sabia, 1968

"What I learned from feminism was that women's place had as much to do with the social and economic system as it had to do with race … I also believed that … the battle against racism would be fought more effectively by women and men standing side by side as equals, rather than by an unbalanced, lopsided team of unequal partners."

–Rosemary Brown, *Being Brown: A Very Public Life*, 1989

Challenge and Response

1. Why did young people in the 1960s reject the values and traditions of their parents' generation? To what extent is this true of young people today? Explain.
2. In a Venn diagram, indicate the issues that women faced in the 1960s, issues they face today, and issues that are common to both eras.
3. What changes that originated in the 1960s are still evident in Canada today?

Learn more about the 1960s counterculture

Skill Path:
Creating Concept Webs

In the Skill Path for Chapter 2, you learned how to make effective notes in order to summarize and simplify information. Creating concept webs is another method you can use to structure and simplify information. A concept web is used to show how different factors are connected to one central idea or an issue. It is made up of a series of cells, each containing a category of information. Directional arrows indicate relationships between the cells.

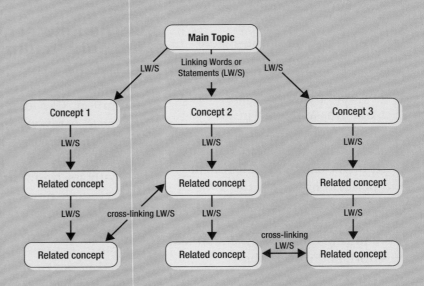

STEP 1: Determine the Purpose of Your Concept Web

Concepts webs can be used to
- develop an understanding of a topic
- explore new information on a topic
- access prior knowledge
- gather new knowledge and information
- share knowledge and information

STEP 2: Develop a Rough Concept Web

Once you have determined the purpose and topic of your concept web, follow this process:
- Focus on your topic and then identify related keywords or phrases. These are your concepts.
- Determine how the concepts relate to one another.
- Write the main topic in a circle or box at the top of a sheet of paper.
- Indicate your concepts in a series of ovals or rectangles underneath the main topic. You can use nouns, verbs, labelled drawings, or symbols.
- Draw connecting lines with arrows between your concepts to indicate relationships.
- Label the connecting lines with linking words or statements.
- Use point-form notes, symbols, and different colours to help you organize your ideas.

STEP 3: Create Your Final Draft

Once you are satisfied that your rough concept web is complete, create your final draft using coloured pencils, markers, or computer software.

STEP 4: Practise Your Skill

Use a concept web to illustrate one of the following:
- Diefenbaker's economic and foreign policies and the collapse of his government in 1963
- Québec's place in Canada and the Quiet Revolution
- Aboriginal activism and the resurgence of Aboriginal art

 # Thinking Like a Historian:
Asking Historical Questions

Essential Question: As a historian, how do you find, select, and interpret different sources of information?

In the 1990s, a group of Canadian historians and political scientists rated all of Canada's prime ministers. They rated William Lyon Mackenzie King as a great prime minister. Pearson was rated a "high average," while Diefenbaker received only an "average" rating.

You, the Historian

Diefenbaker faced off against Pearson in four elections. Three of them resulted in minority governments. This suggests that Canadians were not completely satisfied with either leader. In this activity, you will compare the effectiveness of these two prime ministers using information from the text and the web links.

1. Complete an organizer like the one shown here to compare what you believe are the strengths and weaknesses and political successes and failures of both prime ministers.

2. Rank-order the criteria below from most important (1) to least important (3). Explain your choices.
3. In small groups, share and discuss your conclusions.
4. In a brief position paper, state your opinion about who was the more effective prime minister—Diefenbaker or Pearson. Use specific evidence.

Rank	Criteria		John Diefenbaker	Lester Pearson
	Personality	strengths		
		weaknesses		
	Domestic Policy	successes		
		failures		
	Foreign Policy	successes		
		failures		

IN FOCUS

In the 1970s and 1980s, Canada faced many challenges. Separatism challenged the political union. Terrorism challenged the country's sense of security. Women challenged traditional roles and responsibilities. Aboriginal peoples challenged the nature of Aboriginal–Canadian relations. Multiculturalism challenged traditional views of society. Immigrants challenged Canadians to create unity through diversity. Environmental issues challenged Canadians' awareness of the way we live our lives.

Internationally, Canada's relations drifted away from Europe toward other parts of the world. At times, Canadian leaders moved closer to our powerful American neighbour. At other times, they forged a more independent path.

In this unit, you will discover how the roots of modern-day Canada were planted in the 1970s and 1980s. As you do, think about the following questions:

- What challenges did Canadians face?
- What impact did these challenges have on the Canadian identity?
- How successful was Canada in dealing with these challenges?
- In what ways is Canada today different from Canada in the 1960s?

This detail of an art image by Daphne Odjig, called *Rebirth of a Culture* (1979), celebrates the survival of disappearing Aboriginal communities. How does this painting reflect its title?

Chapter 8

The Pursuit of the Just Society

Figure 8.1   Pierre Elliott Trudeau has had a lasting impact on Canadian society. What do you know about him?

Chapter at a Glance

Thinking Ahead

Imagine a prime minister doing backflips off a diving board or being chased by young women like a rock star! In the late 1960s, that was exactly the kind of man who became Canada's prime minister. The baby boomers were growing up in the new counterculture of the sixties. Young people were demanding change. Trudeau tapped into this youthful energy. In 1968, Canadians of all ages swept him into the prime minister's office.

In this chapter, you will look at the challenges and changes that transformed Canadian society during the late 1960s and in the 1970s. As you do, focus on these key questions:

- What challenges to Canadian unity did Québec present?
- How did women transform Canadian society?
- In what ways did Aboriginal peoples begin to redefine their place in Canada?
- How did multiculturalism shape the Canadian identity?
- What economic and environmental challenges did Canada face?

Profile in Power:

Pierre Elliott Trudeau

"We believe in two official languages and in a pluralist society not merely as a political necessity but as an enrichment. We want to live in a country in which French Canadians can choose to live among English Canadians and English Canadians can choose to live among French Canadians without abandoning their cultural heritage."

–Prime Minister Pierre Trudeau, introducing the Official Languages Act, House of Commons, 17 October 1968

Figure 8.2 Pierre Elliott Trudeau (1919–2000)

Pierre Elliott Trudeau was born into a wealthy Montréal family. His father was a successful French-Canadian business person. His mother was of Scottish descent. Both parents were bilingual. As a child, Trudeau learned to speak effortlessly in both languages.

After attending law school in Montréal in the 1940s, Trudeau studied at Harvard and the London School of Economics after the Second World War. In the 1950s, he founded *Cité Libre*, a magazine of social commentary he used to express his opposition to Québec's ruling elite.

During the Quiet Revolution, Trudeau criticized the new brand of Québécois nationalism. He wanted a renewed federation in which French and English Canada were full and equal partners. To achieve this goal, in 1965 Trudeau and two close colleagues, Jean Marchand and Gérard Pelletier, joined the federal Liberal Party.

After being elected to the House of Commons, Trudeau quickly rose up the party ranks. As minister of Justice in 1967, he embraced the changing values and attitudes of Canadians. He liberalized laws on divorce and abortion and decriminalized homosexuality.

When Lester Pearson retired in 1968, the Liberals elected Trudeau as their new leader. Trudeau's charisma, intelligence, and wit captivated many Canadians. He shattered the traditional image of politicians. He drove himself to work on Parliament Hill in a flashy sports car, wearing sandals and a cape. He dated famous celebrities. He slid down the banister in the House of Commons. He pirouetted behind the back of Queen Elizabeth II. Behind this public persona, however, was a shy and private man who preferred the solitude of canoeing in the Québec wilderness to the glare of the media.

Trudeau had a vision of a Canada in which all Canadians were equal. He made bilingualism and multiculturalism official government policies. He opened Canada's doors to immigrants from around the world. He gave new opportunities to many Canadians who had long been denied a voice.

Economically, however, Trudeau faced a number of challenges. Foreign ownership of Canadian businesses led to new economic policies that outraged Americans and angered many Canadians. Inflation, unemployment, and double-digit interest rates created an economic crisis that led many Canadians to lose confidence in Trudeau's leadership.

For better or for worse, however, between 1968 and 1980, Trudeau captured the attention of the nation and often of the world. In 1980, after losing the federal election, he announced his retirement. As you will discover in Chapter 9, however, Pierre Trudeau's political career was far from over.

Figure 8.3 They called it *Trudeaumania*—a cross between political enthusiasm and rock-star frenzy during the 1968 federal political campaign. What impression does this give you of Pierre Trudeau?

Responding
1. In your opinion, what made Trudeau different from the other prime ministers you have read about in this book?
2. Why do you think Trudeau appealed to so many Canadians in 1968? Do you think he would appeal to Canadians today? Give reasons for your response.
3. Do you think campaign style is as important as campaign issues? Discuss this idea as it relates to Trudeaumania as a class.

Reading Strategy

Throughout this book, there are two types of margin quotations—one from noted authorities and the other from young Canadians. After you read a quotation, remember to take note of who the speaker is by checking the source line. This will help you put the speaker's comments in context.

"Most of the people who deal with the government of Canada speak only one language. It is because everyone in the country is not expected to speak both languages, and never will be, that the federal government must be able to speak to Canadians in either French or English wherever there are enough French speakers or English speakers to justify it."

–Prime Minister Pierre Trudeau, statement on the Official Languages Act, July 1969

A Question of Language

Pierre Trudeau was a passionate federalist who firmly believed that Québec's place in North America was within Canada. One of the priorities on Trudeau's political agenda was to forge a new relationship between French and English Canada.

The Official Languages Act

In 1963, Prime Minister Lester Pearson created the Royal Commission on Bilingualism and Biculturalism. When it issued its report in 1969, the Commission declared that there was a crisis in French–English relations. French Canadians felt alienated from the rest of Canada, largely because their language was not equal to English in other parts of the country. They felt they belonged in Québec, but not in Canada.

To create equality between French and English, the Commission made three major recommendations:

- make the services of the federal government more widely available in French across the country
- open the federal civil service equally to French and English Canadians
- improve and expand the teaching of French as a second language

To meet these objectives, Trudeau introduced the Official Languages Act in 1969. It gave equal status to the French and English languages and made Canada an officially bilingual nation.

The Official Languages Act angered some English-speaking Canadians. Many claimed the government was trying to "shove French down our throats." Some thought the Act gave French-speaking Canadians preferential treatment. Others complained about the cost of providing French services in parts of the country where few people spoke French. Some English Canadians misunderstood the Act, believing that official bilingualism meant that *all* Canadians had to be bilingual.

Bill 22: Making French Mandatory

Selling the Official Languages Act became more difficult after the Liberal government in Québec under Robert Bourassa passed Bill 22 in 1974. Preserving the French language had become a major concern for Québec's political leaders. The birth rate among French Canadians was low, while the immigrant

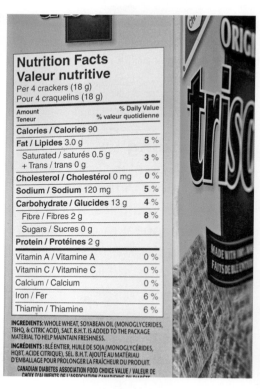

Figure 8.4 The Official Languages Act requires that the labels on all packaging in Canada be in both French and English. What are the positive and negative aspects of the Act?

population was growing. Many immigrants who settled in Québec preferred to learn English rather than French. Many sent their children to English-language schools. To address these problems, the government introduced legislation to preserve and strengthen the French language in Québec.

Bill 22 made French the only official language in the province. It required that

- all official documents and contracts be written in French
- businesses communicate with their employees in French
- all public signs be in French (although other languages could also be used)
- students be educated in a language other than French (including English) only if they were already fluent in French

Predictably, many English-speaking Canadians and immigrants felt that Bill 22 went too far. Many Québécois nationalists felt it did not go far enough. Bill 22 also provided another argument for those who opposed the Official Languages Act. Why, they asked, should Canada expand the use of French while Québec was restricting the use of English?

Bill 101: Prohibiting the Use of English

The debate over bilingualism heated up again in 1977 after Québec's new separatist government, led by René Lévesque, introduced Bill l01, known as the Charter of the French Language. Bill 101 strengthened Bill 22 by adding more regulations. With few exceptions, it effectively banned the use of English in government and business in the province. The legislation also introduced strict measures to enforce the new laws.

Failure to comply resulted in fines of up to $500 for individuals and $2000 for businesses.

Bill 101 divided Canadians, both inside and outside Québec. While many Québécois and some English-speaking Quebeckers supported Bill 101, others protested it as a violation of human rights. In response, many people and businesses left Québec, including many of Canada's major banks and insurance companies, which moved their head offices from Montréal to Toronto.

Legal Challenges

Those who viewed Bill 101 as an assault on their human rights challenged it in the courts. In 1984, the Supreme Court of Canada struck down the clause requiring at least one parent to have attended an English elementary school in Québec in order for a child to attend an English school. In 1988, the Supreme Court also struck down the clause that required signs to be in French only, although it

BILL 101 HIGHLIGHTS

Education
All students had to attend French-language schools unless at least one parent had been educated in an English school in Québec.

Business
All commercial outside signs had to be in French only. Workers could not be forced to speak any language other than French.

Government
French was the only official language in Québec. All laws of the province were in French.

"I am a French Canadian. I speak French at home, even with my father (who's not Francophone). I went to a French-Canadian elementary school and am now attending a secondary school ... Outside Québec, the only way French can survive is with its schools as other institutions do not exist ... and federal institutions are only bilingual in façade (ever try to get served in French at Canada Post or other federal institutions outside Québec?)

–David Newman, 2002

Figure 8.5 This illustration highlights the main points of the Charter of the French Language. Why do you think Québécois identity is so deeply rooted in the French language?

"In practice ... the Canadian government actively promotes enforced bilingualism in nine provinces, and tolerates enforced French-only unilingualism in Québec. This is a complete change of course from the country-wide bilingualism envisioned by Pierre Trudeau when he first came to office."

–Scott Reid,
Lament for a Notion: The Life and Death of Canada's Bilingual Dream,
1993

"Québécois nationalism is not a characteristic of French Canadians in Alberta. We are frightened of Québec nationalism and fight hard against it. However, we understand it because we also need to preserve our language and culture and unique identity. The difference between us and the Québécois is that we live the struggle as individuals, where the Québécois live it as a province. For us, it is up close and personal."

–France Levasseur-Ouimet,
professor emeritus, the University of Alberta, 2005

Learn more about francophone communities across Canada

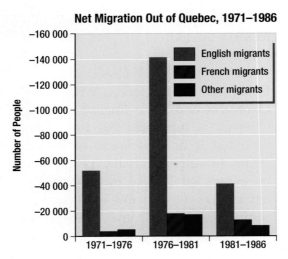

Net Migration Out of Quebec, 1971–1986

Source: Statistics Canada, Languages in Canada (Focus on Canada Series: Analytical Products: 1991 Census of Population), 96-313-XPE, Released August 4, 1994; p. 56 and p. 83.

Figure 8.6 Bill 22 caused many people and corporations to leave Québec. After Bill 101, the number of people leaving the province skyrocketed. Why do you think English Canadians left Québec? Why do you think French Canadians left? Why would people whose first language was not French or English leave? What impact do you think this had on Québec's economy?

gave the province the right to require that French signs be more visible.

In 1999, a Québec court ruled that the province could not continue to restrict the use of languages other than French on commercial signs unless it could prove a real threat to the French language. The Québec Superior Court overturned that decision in 2000. Since then, there have been other court challenges to Québec's language laws, particularly as they pertain to education. Although some have resulted in changes to the laws, they have upheld the province's right to protect the French language.

Francophone Communities outside Québec

If the Québécois needed laws to protect the French language within their own province, what were the chances of the French language surviving in communities outside Québec? Although there were many vibrant francophone communities across Canada, many people believed it was only a matter of time before they would disappear into English Canada. With each generation, more and more French-speaking children learned to speak English, either through their schools or society. As adults, many French-speaking Canadians married English-speaking spouses. Often, the language spoken at home and the language spoken by their children was English rather than French. One of the goals of official bilingualism was to offer support to French-speaking communities and help them to maintain their cultural identities.

Challenge and Response

1. Do you think that preserving the French language justifies restricting individual rights? Discuss this question as a class.
2. Reread the quotation by France Levasseur-Ouimet on this page. In what ways are the experiences of francophones living in Québec different from those living outside the province?

Francophone Communities

Francophones in Ontario

Ontario has the largest French-speaking population outside Québec. More than 485 000 people—about 5 per cent of the population—speak French as their first language. Another 82 300 identify French as one of their primary languages.

Language rights and education have always been an issue for French-speaking Ontarians. It was not until 1968 that francophone students had the right to receive an education in their own language. Since then, there have been many French-language school boards set up across the province. Although Ontario is not officially bilingual, the province has designated that certain communities must receive provincial services in both French and English.

Figure 8.7 Gaétan Gervais, a history professor at Laurentian University, and a group of his students designed the *Franco-Ontarien* flag in 1975. The fleur-de-lys represents their French origins. The trillium symbolizes their Ontario roots.

Francophones in New Brunswick

New Brunswick is Canada's only officially bilingual province. Its 250 000 French-speaking people make up 33 per cent of the population. Although they live and work with their English-speaking neighbours, they successfully maintain their French language, traditions, culture, and identity.

Like other francophone communities, the French-speaking people of New Brunswick have fought for their language and education rights. In 1969, the province passed the Official Languages Act, which made the province officially bilingual

and created a bilingual school system. In 1979, the French language gained equal status with English and guaranteed all government services in both languages. In 1993, New Brunswick's bilingual status became part of the Constitution.

Figure 8.8 Most francophones in New Brunswick can trace their roots back to the Acadians. The Acadian flag, created in 1884, combines the French tricolour with a gold star.

Francophones in Manitoba

The Manitoba Act of 1870 guaranteed publicly funded French-language schools and the use of both French and English in government. In 1890, however, the Manitoba Schools Act created an English-only public school system and made English the only language of government. Almost 90 years later, the Supreme Court ruled that the Manitoba Schools Act was unconstitutional. It declared all of Manitoba's laws to be illegal because they were not translated into French.

In 1993, the Supreme Court declared that francophones in Manitoba had the right to be educated in their own language. Manitoba created a French-language school division in 1994, thereby ending a 100-year struggle for equal rights.

Figure 8.9 The flag of the Franco-Manitoban community was created in 1980. The red band represents the Red River. The yellow band represents wheat. The green plant emblem is the letter *F* placed back to back to represent the French identity of the 54 000 francophones in Manitoba.

Responding

1. Why do you think language rights have been such a divisive issue in Canada?
2. Do you think Ontario should become officially bilingual? Give reasons for your point of view.

Skill Path:
Analyzing Different Perspectives

Reading Strategy

A *perspective* is different from a *point of view*. A point of view reflects a person's opinion about something, based on his or her own *personal* experiences. A perspective reflects a people's world view, based on their *collective* experiences.

STEP 1: Conduct Research

Before you think about different perspectives, conduct some research to find out the facts about the topic or issue. For example, to find information about the history of Canada, you can turn to history books and to encyclopedias.

STEP 2: Identify Different Perspectives

Once you have the facts, you need to do further research to find out who was involved in the issue or event and who was affected by it. To do this, you need to consult specific sources. For example, if you wanted to find different perspectives on issues in Canadian history, you might look at textbooks like this one or history books that focus on specific topics, such as French–English relations. As you do your research, list people and groups who may have relevant perspectives about the issue.

STEP 3: Find Quotations

You may be able to uncover different perspectives in written materials, such as journals, newspaper articles, and legal documents, or on the Internet. For example, Trudeau's quotation on page 248 explains the perspective of his government in introducing the Official Languages Act.

Another way to uncover perspectives is to go to reliable and respected sources, such as an Elder, an activist, or someone directly involved in an issue or event. Be sure that the quotations give you the group's perspective, though, and not one person's personal point of view.

STEP 4: Analyze the Perspectives

Once you have obtained quotations, analyze them to understand the different perspectives. Ask yourself these questions:
- What does the quotation mean?
- What evidence does the speaker present to support his or her message or point of view?
- Do the facts support the evidence? If not, in what ways does the source challenge the facts?

Then compare the different perspectives to determine similarities and differences.

STEP 5: Practise Your Skill

Practise analyzing different perspectives using these two excerpts about official bilingualism.

"It is not about providing special benefits to any group in society, or forcing Canadians to learn a second language; nor is it about making Canada bilingual from coast to coast. Rather, it is about federal institutions serving all citizens with the respect and courtesy they deserve, in the official language they feel most comfortable using, wherever there is significant demand."

Source: Office of the Commissioner of Official Languages, 1993.

"The continued decline of French outside Québec and of English inside the province serves as proof that efforts to build a bilingual nation have been an exercise in futility … it would have been easier for the Canadian government to legislatively move the Rocky Mountains to Québec than to save the isolated French-language communities scattered in their shadow, or to stop the erosion of English communities in Québec's Gaspé Peninsula and the Eastern Townships."

Source: Scott Reid, *Lament for a Notion: The Life and Death of Canada's Bilingual Dream* (Vancouver: Arsenal Pulp Press, 1994).

The October Crisis

As you discovered in Chapter 7, terrorism came to Canada in the 1960s. By 1970, the FLQ was set to resort to new and more dramatic tactics. On 5 October 1970, a small FLQ cell kidnapped James Cross, the British trade commissioner. They threatened to kill him unless the government met their demands. At the top of their list was the release of 23 people imprisoned for terrorist activities. But they also wanted their manifesto broadcast to the public. Hoping to buy some time to find Cross, authorities agreed.

"Just Watch Me"

The FLQ had given authorities 48 hours to meet their demands. On October 10, the Québec government announced it would not release any prisoners. Instead, they offered the kidnappers safe passage out of Canada in exchange for Cross's return. Just minutes later, however, the crisis escalated as another FLQ cell abducted the Québec labour minister, Pierre Laporte.

Panic swept across the province. Québec premier Robert Bourassa and members of his Cabinet took up refuge in a hotel, surrounded by tight security. Laporte wrote a letter pleading for his life. Meanwhile, some Québécois nationalists demonstrated their support for the FLQ in a rally in Montréal. More than 3000 people raised their fists chanting "FLQ! FLQ!" Most did not support their terrorist tactics. But they agreed with their perspective on the balance of power in Québec.

Canada's leaders disagreed on how to handle the crisis. Some wanted the government to talk with the kidnappers. But Trudeau refused to negotiate with terrorists. Bourassa urged Trudeau to send the army into Québec to maintain law and order. Trudeau did not want it to appear that he was using the powers of the federal government to crack down on separatism, though. He insisted that Québec officials submit a written request. Once he received it, Trudeau ordered Canadian soldiers into the streets of Québec City, Montréal, and Ottawa.

The War Measures Act

On October 16, Trudeau invoked the War Measures Act to deal with a state of "apprehended insurrection" in Québec. The Act gave the government extraordinary powers. Police could arrest anyone suspected of belonging to—or sympathizing with—the FLQ, without a warrant. Québec police

Figure 8.10 As armoured tanks and soldiers in full combat gear roamed the streets, Canada looked more like a police state than a democracy. How would you feel if soldiers patrolled the streets of your community?

"The Front de Libération du Québec wants the total independence of Quebeckers, united in a free society, purged forever of the clique of voracious sharks, the patronizing 'big bosses' and their henchmen who have made Québec their hunting preserve for 'cheap labour' and unscrupulous exploitation … Long live Free Québec."

–The FLQ manifesto, *Montreal Gazette*, 9 October 1970

Trudeau: "Yes, well there are a lot of bleeding hearts around who just don't like to see people with helmets and guns. All I can say is, go on and bleed, but it is more important to keep law and order in the society than to be worried about weak-kneed people who don't like the looks of [an army].

Reporter: At any cost? How far would you go with that?

Trudeau: Well, just watch me."

–Prime Minister Pierre Trudeau and CBC reporter Tim Ralfe, Parliament Hill, 13 October 1970

Learn more about the October Crisis

"I feel like I am writing the most important letter I have ever written … You have the power of life and death over me. I depend on you and I thank you for it."

–In a letter from Pierre Laporte to Québec premier Robert Bourassa, 11 October 1970

"The government, I submit, is using a sledgehammer to crack a peanut."

–NDP leader Tommy Douglas, reacting to the use of the War Measures Act, October 1970

"Anyone can play Monday morning quarterback. What would have happened without the special measures, no one will ever know. In history, the past conditional tense explains nothing."

–Secretary of State Gérard Pelletier, responding to the comment by Tommy Douglas

responded swiftly. Within hours, raids across the province had resulted in the arrest of 465 people, although in the end few were ever charged or convicted. Critics later charged that the raids had been an extreme reaction to the crisis.

The Crisis Ends

The day after Trudeau invoked the War Measures Act, police found Pierre Laporte's body stashed in the trunk of an abandoned car. Whatever support the FLQ had among Québécois nationalists quickly vanished.

Yet while Laporte's fate was sealed, the ordeal continued for James Cross. For weeks, no one knew of his fate. Finally, after 53 days in captivity, police located Cross and his kidnappers in a Montréal apartment on 4 December 1970. In exchange for Cross' release, his five kidnappers received safe passage to Cuba. Then, on December 28, four men—Paul Rose, his brother Jacques, Francis Simard, and Bernard Lortie—were arrested and charged with the murder of Pierre Laporte. In

January 1971, Canadian soldiers withdrew from Québec. The October Crisis was finally over.

Debating the War Measures Act

After the October Crisis, Trudeau's popularity soared to record heights. Polls showed that 89 per cent of English Canadians and 86 per cent of French Canadians approved of the way he handled it. Still, the decision to invoke the War Measures Act was a controversial one. In the aftermath, authorities discovered that the FLQ was not the highly organized and powerful terrorist group they believed it to be. In reality, the FLQ consisted of a handful of radicals operating in small, independent cells. They never posed any real threat of insurrection or rebellion. Yet the October Crisis opened the eyes of many Canadians to the depth of feeling Québécois had about their place in Canada. It set the stage for a new era of negotiations over French language and sovereignty in Canada.

Challenge and Response

1. Reread the excerpt from the FLQ manifesto on page 253. What words and phrases reflect an *us* versus *them* mentality?
2. Create a T-chart outlining the pros and cons of invoking the War Measures Act during the October Crisis.
3. Reread Tommy Douglas's quotation on this page. What did he mean when he compared the War Measures Act to "using a sledgehammer to crack a peanut"? Do you agree? Give reasons for your response.
4. How does the government's response to the terrorism of the October Crisis compare with the response of other governments to terrorism in the world today? Discuss your ideas as a class.

Social Justice for All

In 1968, equality was an elusive dream for many people in Canada. In politics and public life, minorities were dramatically under-represented in all levels of government. For example, no woman had ever been the Speaker of the House of Commons, or served as Governor General, or been appointed a chief justice. No Inuit person had served in the Senate. No Aboriginal person had been a Cabinet minister or a lieutenant-governor. In the **Just Society** Trudeau envisioned, all Canadians would have equal opportunities.

Women's Rights

As you discovered in Chapter 7, in the 1960s women's rights activists demanded that Prime Minister Pearson establish the Royal Commission on the Status of Women. Its report in December 1970 contained 167 recommendations, including the following:

- creating a federal agency to continue the work of the Commission
- providing daycare services for women who work outside the home
- prohibiting discrimination on the basis of gender or marital status
- paying unemployment benefits to working women on maternity leave
- establishing wages based on skills and responsibilities rather than gender

The report set the stage for a new era in women's rights. Trudeau created a portfolio for the Status of Women in the Cabinet in 1971. In 1973, he established the Advisory Council on the Status of Women to monitor the progress in implementing the report's recommendations.

The Status of Women

While the women's movement had begun to evolve in the 1950s and 1960s, in the 1970s it intensified. Women from all social, cultural, and economic backgrounds began to challenge the stereotypes and double standards that characterized Canadian society. Given the diversity of Canadian society, they did not always agree on the nature of their problems and the best way to resolve them. Collectively, however, they agreed that they were no longer going to be subordinate to men. In 1973, a coalition of diverse women's groups from across the country joined to form the National Action Committee on the Status of Women (NAC). Its purpose was to lobby the government on such issues as child care, poverty, health, immigration, and violence against women.

Women in the Workplace

One of the priorities of the women's movement was to close the wage gap between men and women. They demanded better educational opportunities for females and new initiatives in education, including eliminating sexism and stereotypes in textbooks and encouraging females to enroll in subjects traditionally dominated by males.

Women also demanded **affirmative action** in the workplace. Many employers introduced programs designed to create a better balance of males and females in all job categories. By the end of the decade, women had started to move up the corporate ladder and to gain greater access to male-dominated professions. These trailblazers inspired a new generation of young women to explore new and exciting career opportunities. But there was still a glass

"For where is the justice in a country in which an individual has the freedom to be totally fulfilled, but where inequality denies him the means?"

–Pierre Trudeau, in *Towards a Just Society*, 1990

"The Just Society that Trudeau proposed ... was to become a response to a democratic and prosperous society's wakening aspirations for greater equality for all its people, including minorities like ... Aboriginal peoples, youth, the elderly, and ethnic groups, not to mention that majority so often treated as a minority—women."

–Senator Jacques Hébert, in *Towards a Just Society*, 1990

Learn more about the Royal Commission on the Status of Women

"We propose to take responsibility for effecting change in the status of women in Canada. We believe that improvement in the status of women can most effectively come about through initiatives taken by women themselves and supported by government."

–Laura Sabia, in "Herstory: NAC's first twenty-five years", February 1972

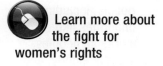

Learn more about the fight for women's rights

Figure 8.11 In 1972, Rosemary Brown became the first female of African heritage to win a seat in the British Columbia legislature. Brown came to Canada from Jamaica in the 1950s as a university student. The racial intolerance she encountered inspired her to become an activist for social and political equality for all Canadians. In 1975, Brown ran for the federal leadership of the New Democratic Party, losing to Ed Broadbent.

ceiling—the invisible barrier that kept women from reaching the highest levels of business and industry.

Women in Politics

Before 1970, women were largely unrepresented in politics. Only 67 women had ever been elected to the House of Commons or to any provincial legislature, compared with 6778 men. In the 1970s, however, women began to take their place on the political stage. In 1972, the election of Jeanne Sauvé to the House of Commons marked the beginning of her distinguished political career. In the 1970s, women made their greatest headway in provincial politics. In 1974, 14 women sat in provincial legislatures: 6 in British Columbia, 3 in Ontario, 2 in Alberta, and 1 each in Québec, New Brunswick, and Prince Edward Island.

Aboriginal Peoples

In the 1970s, life for Aboriginal peoples in Canada was anything but just. Decades of prejudice, discrimination, misunderstanding, and neglect had secured Aboriginal peoples' place at the lowest level of Canadian society. Things began to change in the 1960s, though. The movement toward **decolonization** by oppressed peoples in Africa and Asia encouraged oppressed peoples in the developing world to also take action. By 1970, Aboriginal peoples in Canada were ready to demand justice and equality.

The White Paper

The catalyst for action was the unveiling of the White Paper by the Trudeau government in 1969. It maintained that to create equality in a Just Society, Aboriginal peoples should be treated the same as all other Canadians. Special status under the Indian Act was a form of legal discrimination. Aboriginal peoples received services such as health care and education through the federal government rather than the provinces. If Aboriginal peoples received services from the same source as other Canadians, they would have equality.

The White Paper recommended
- abolishing the Indian Act
- eliminating the Department of Indian Affairs
- abolishing reserve lands and terminating treaties
- transferring responsibility for Aboriginal services to the provinces

PERSONALITIES

Jeanne Sauvé: A Woman of "Firsts"

Jeanne Sauvé was born Jeanne Mathilde Benoît in Prud'homme, Saskatchewan, in 1922. She attended university in Ottawa, where she became active in youth issues—an interest she maintained throughout her life. In 1948, she married Maurice Sauvé. The couple moved to Europe, where Sauvé studied in London and Paris. Later, she became the assistant to the Director of the Youth Secretariat of UNESCO. After returning to Canada, Sauvé embarked on a 20-year career as a freelance journalist in 1952.

"There's no doubt that we've got to work twice as hard as a man."

Source: Jeanne Sauvé in a CBC radio interview, 1974.

Trudeau recruited Sauvé to run for office. In 1972, she was one of only five women elected to the House of Commons. Sauvé was the first Québec woman appointed to the federal Cabinet when she became minister of Science and Technology. She went on to hold other Cabinet positions, including minister of the Environment from 1974 to 1975 and minister of Communications from 1975 to 1979.

In 1980, Sauvé broke down another barrier by becoming the first female Speaker of the House of Commons, a position she held until 1983. After leaving politics, Trudeau appointed Sauvé Canada's twenty-third Governor General in 1984, marking another historic first for women. As Governor General, Sauvé focused on the themes of peace, national unity, and youth.

Figure 8.12 Jeanne Sauvé began her career as a popular radio broadcaster and is shown here as Speaker of the House of Commons.

When her term expired in 1990, she established the Jeanne Sauvé Foundation to help young adults develop their potential and skills. Through the Sauvé Scholars program, young university graduates attend an eight-month program at Montréal's McGill University, where they work with journalists, politicians, and leaders in business, education, and the arts.

After an impressive career as a journalist, politician, and trailblazer, Jeanne Sauvé died in Montréal on 26 January 1993.

Responding

1. Is Sauvé a role model for young women today? Give reasons for your response.

"We view this as a policy designed to divest us of our Aboriginal, residential, and statutory rights. If we accept this policy, and in the process lose our rights and our lands, we become willing partners in cultural genocide. This we cannot do."

–A statement on the White Paper by the National Indian Brotherhood, 1969

"The new Indian policy ... is a thinly disguised program of extermination through assimilation. For the Indian to survive, says the government in effect, he must become a good little brown white man."

–Harold Cardinal, *The Unjust Society: The Tragedy of Canada's Indians*, 1969

NO! to the White Paper

The White Paper angered Aboriginal peoples. They saw it as another effort to assimilate them and deny them their basic rights. Once again, the government had made decisions about their future without consulting them. The National Indian Brotherhood (now the Assembly of First Nations) rejected the White Paper, as did the Indian Association of Alberta. One of its leaders, Harold Cardinal, took the leading role in creating a counter-proposal known as the Red Paper. Its demands included

- maintaining special status to ensure the survival of First Nations cultures
- providing access to the same services as other Canadians
- recognizing the First Peoples as "citizens plus" with unique and inalienable rights

The Trudeau government was unprepared for the forcefulness of the opposition. It withdrew the White Paper, but failed to offer another framework for negotiating Aboriginal peoples' place in a Just Society.

Fighting Discrimination in the Indian Act

One of the long-standing controversies in Aboriginal affairs was the discriminatory policies against women contained in the Indian Act. Under the act, if a First Nations woman married a Non-Status or a non-First Nations man, she lost her status rights. Her children lost their rights, as well. Yet the same standard did not apply to First Nations men. They kept their status rights regardless of whom they married.

For years, First Nations women protested this discrimination. In the early 1970s, two First Nations women's organizations, Indian Rights for Indian Women and the National Native

Figure 8.13   Harold Cardinal's book *The Unjust Society: The Tragedy of Canada's Indians* was a scathing attack on the Canadian government's policy toward Aboriginal peoples. What message does the image used on the cover of the book convey?

Women's Association, launched a campaign to change the law. With the support of non-Aboriginal women's groups, including the National Action Committee and the Voice of Women, they conducted sit-ins and marches and appealed the law through the courts. In 1973, however, the Supreme Court issued a crushing blow when it ruled that the Indian Act did not discriminate because it treated all First Nations women the same.

In 1979, Sandra Lovelace, a Wolastoqewiyik [wah-LAHS-tah-gweh-wee-yeeg] (Maliseet) woman from New Brunswick, took her case to the United Nations Human Rights Committee. In 1981, it found that Canada's Indian Act violated the International Covenant on Civil and Political Rights. In spite of the UN's ruling, however, the government did not amend the Indian Act until 1985 to give First Nations women and their children equal rights with First Nations men.

"Canada's history has proven the contempt toward the First Nations people. Our society needs to recognize the two hundred years of injustice and do something about it."

–Kristin Evans, Huron Heights Secondary School, 2003

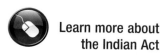

Learn more about the Indian Act

Figure 8.14 The National Action Committee on the Status of Women wanted to draw the public's attention to the Supreme Court's decision that the Indian Act did not discriminate against women. It declared 12 October 1973 a national day of mourning for human rights. How effective do you think protests like these are in promoting human rights?

Challenge and Response

1. In your own words, write a definition of a Just Society.
2. Write an editorial or create a political cartoon that reflects your point of view about one of the issues discussed in this section.
3. What evidence is there that women and Aboriginal peoples still do not have full equality in Canada today? Express your point of view in a class discussion.

MAP STUDY: The James Bay Power Project

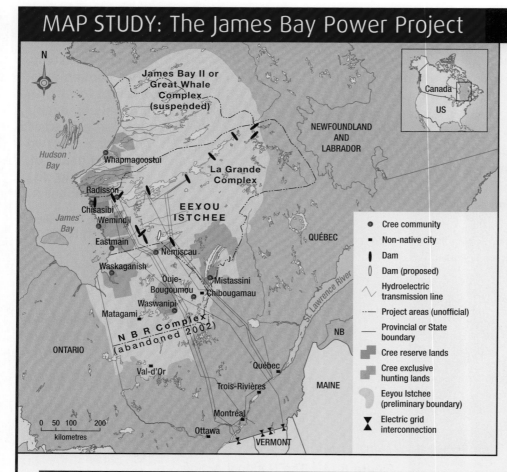

Source: Locations of dams, hydroelectric lines and corridors, Hydro-Québec 2003; Cree Territory and Lands 2003. Map by Glenn B. Garner 2008.

Figure 8.15 This map shows the location and extent of the James Bay Power Project. In 1989, Québec announced plans for James Bay II. Most of the power was to be sold to Vermont and New York. Alarmed at the environmental damage and the killing of wildlife created by James Bay I, Cree Grand Chief Matthew Coon Come persuaded the Americans to cancel their deal with Hydro Québec. The government cancelled James Bay II in 1995.

In April 1971, Québec announced plans to build a hydroelectric power project in northern Québec. The province planned to flood 10 000 km² of Aboriginal lands and build eight hydroelectric dams to harness the energy of the rivers that drained into James Bay.

The announcement came as a shock to the 5000 Eeyouch (Cree) and 3500 Inuit who lived in northern Québec. They relied on fishing, hunting, and trapping for their survival. Massive flooding of their lands would destroy their way of life.

Both groups lobbied for their political, economic, and land rights. The Inuit formed the Inuit Tapirisat (now the Inuit Tapiriit Kanatami), while the Eeyouch formed the Grand Council of the Crees (Eeyou Istchee). Together, they filed an injunction to stop construction. Media coverage

and the reluctance to get embroiled in a long legal battle convinced the government to negotiate.

In 1975, the James Bay and Northern Quebec Agreement became the first modern Aboriginal land claims settlement. The Eeyouch and Inuit received

- $225 million payable over 25 years
- ownership of 5500 km² of land
- exclusive hunting, fishing, and trapping rights over 125 000 km² of land
- self-government within their own communities

Although it was a landmark agreement for Aboriginal peoples, the power project has had long-term negative consequences for the environment. Some lands have been flooded completely. Elsewhere, the water flow has dropped by 90 per cent. The water is undrinkable.

Responding

1. Why do you think the James Bay Agreement was an important landmark for Aboriginal peoples? Give reasons for your response.

Multiculturalism

Trudeau envisioned a country in which many different cultures would not only live together peacefully, but also maintain their cultural identities. In 1971, he formally recognized the diverse nature of Canadian society by adopting multiculturalism as an official government policy—the first country in the world to do so. The government pledged to pursue four basic objectives:

- to assist groups to carry on their own cultural practices and activities
- to assist cultural groups to overcome any barriers to their participation in any aspect of Canadian life
- to promote relations between all cultural groups
- to help immigrants learn either French or English to become full participants in Canadian society

Multiculturalism represented a new direction for Canada. It demonstrated that the government formally recognized the rights and distinct identities of the many different cultures that call

Figure 8.16 Canada became more culturally diverse in the 1970s. Cities like Toronto, Vancouver, and Montréal attracted immigrants from all over the world. Why do you think most immigrants settled in urban centres rather than in rural areas?

Canada home. Multiculturalism did not eliminate prejudice, racism, and discrimination. However, it reinforced the view that all Canadians had the right to fair and equal treatment. The policy of multiculturalism became the basis for new laws guaranteeing equal access to jobs, housing, and education.

"When I think of being Canadian, I think of multiculturalism. It makes me feel united with everyone else because I am not spotted as different because everyone is different ... My friends are from all around—black, Chinese, Indian. They're mixed."

–John Huynh, born in Toronto to Filipino immigrants, 2007

"Being Canadian is like living inside a tossed salad. It means you can be who you want."

–Rhoda Nimoh, immigrant from Ghana, 2007

Arguments For Multiculturism	Arguments Against Multiculturism
• Multiculturalism makes Canada a model for the world, demonstrating that different cultures can live together peacefully and co-operatively. • Multiculturalism makes Canada a richer, more vibrant, and exciting place to live and enriches our social fabric. • Multiculturalism differentiates us from our American neighbours. The United States assimilates immigrants into the American **melting pot**. In Canada, immigrants become part of a **cultural mosaic**.	• Multiculturalism increases feelings of alienation among French-speaking Canadians because it reduces the strength of the French presence in the Canadian nation. • Encouraging cultural groups to live in close, independent communities has a negative impact on national unity. • Many immigrants want to fit in and their children want to adopt Canadian culture and lifestyle. • Immigrants choose to come to Canada for economic opportunities or to escape persecution, not because of our policy of multiculturalism.

ISSUES

The Pros and Cons of Multiculturalism

The issue: To what extent does multiculturalism promote or discourage social harmony and national unity?

Since 1971, there has been an ongoing debate over multiculturalism. Some Canadians believe it should continue to be the foundation of Canadian society. Others believe multiculturalism is an outdated concept that is no longer compatible with Canada's goals. Some people believe that multiculturalism obscures other important challenges, such as resolving the issues affecting Aboriginal peoples. As you read the following quotations, think about the different points of view they express.

"We must strive to understand the cross-cultural composition around us, learn to appreciate the mosaic of Canada from sea to sea, and from east to west. Let us join in the spirit of respect and dignity for all, thus creating a proud identity..."

Source: Henry Bishop, curator, the Black Cultural Centre,
Dartmouth, Nova Scotia, in Sauvé and Sauvé, *Gateway to Canada*
(Don Mills: Oxford University Press, 1997), 89.

"Culture in Canada is treated as something that 'other' people have—namely non-white, non-English-speaking, numerically in the minority people ... It is French Canadians and Aboriginal peoples ... and non-white immigrants that have culture ... White English Canadians are presented as the neutral backdrop against which 'other' people are different."

Source: Zohra Moosa, "Minding the multicultural gap."
Catalyst (16 March 2007).

"Multiculturalism is not about songs and dances, not about special interest groups. It is an affirmation of the right of those Canadians whose heritage is neither French nor English—40 percent of our population—to be participants in the mainstream of Canadian life...
   Only when cultural difference is accepted and recognized will there be harmony in society."

Source: Lilian To, "Does official multiculturalism unite Canada?"
Vancouver Sun, 10 April 1997.

"Canadian multiculturalism has emphasized difference. In so doing, it has retarded the integration of immigrants into the Canadian mainstream while damaging Canada's national sense of self...
   We need to focus on programs that seek out and emphasize the experiences, values, and dreams we all share as Canadians, whatever our colour, language, religion, ethnicity, or historical grievance."

Source: Neil Bissoondath, "No place like home."
New Internationalist, Issue #305.

"Multiculturalism ... fundamentally alters the relationship between [Aboriginal peoples] and the rest of Canadian society. No longer are they seen as a disadvantaged group which can justly demand restitution for the historic injustices ... Instead, they are just one in a mosaic of various cultural groups, all trying to make their way in Canadian society."

Source: Joshua Hergesheimer, "My country, right not wrong."
Catalyst (15 January 2007).

Responding

1. In your opinion, which speaker has made the strongest case for or against multiculturalism? Why do you think so?
2. Do you agree with the opinion expressed about multiculturalism and Aboriginal peoples? Give reasons for your response.

Immigration and Citizenship

In the 1970s, Trudeau continued his quest for a Just Society by introducing widespread changes to immigration and citizenship policies. The Citizenship Act of 1978 abolished earlier discriminatory policies and established immigration guidelines based on three broad objectives:

- *Humanitarian:* to unite families and provide a safe haven for refugees facing persecution in their own countries
- *Economic:* to provide skilled labour for the Canadian workforce and to encourage economic growth and investment
- *Demographic:* to maintain steady population growth

New Classes of Immigrants

The Immigration Act recognized three classes of immigrants:

- *Family class:* people sponsored by members of their immediate family who are already permanent residents of Canada
- *Economic class:* people applying to come to Canada on their own initiative, admitted on the basis of their skills, the financial resources they are willing to invest, and the needs of the Canadian labour market
- *Refugee class:* people who are persecuted in their home countries

The changes signalled Canada's intent to give its immigration policy a more humanitarian focus.

The changes to immigration policies were controversial. Those who favoured them argued that Canada is a vast country with too few people to maintain the economy. Immigrants bring new ideas and valuable skills. Many fill jobs that Canadians cannot or will not do. Young immigrant workers counter the economic effects of the aging baby boomers. The evidence lies in the fact that Canada is a nation of talented and hard-working immigrants who have helped the country grow and prosper.

Those who opposed the new policies argued that there are not enough jobs for new immigrants and that immigrants take jobs away from people who are already living in Canada. Some immigrants, particularly those in large urban centres, end up relying on social welfare programs and services. Furthermore, widespread immigration erodes Canada's Aboriginal-French-English heritage.

Discrimination

The debate over immigration led to tension and friction for many immigrants. In the mid-1970s, unemployment in Canada was high. Some Canadians used immigrants as scapegoats they could blame for their own misfortunes. Many immigrants had difficulty finding jobs and obtaining housing. Some experienced verbal abuse and even physical violence.

Responding to Discrimination

In the 1970s, many Americans of African heritage, as well as many people from the Caribbean, came to Canada. In response to the prejudice and discrimination they faced, they formed lobby groups such as the Toronto Urban Alliance on Race Relations to fight for social justice and equality.

Immigrants from all cultures fought back in other ways, too. They formed their own newspapers, magazines, and radio and television stations to promote their cultures. They formed lobby groups to make their voices heard.

"Immigrants over the years have looked to Canada for asylum, a haven for those that have needed to regroup with their families, find new jobs, escape persecution in their former country, and for those that have looked for a new start in life."

–Russ Pichora, Huron Heights Secondary School, 2003

Reading Strategy

When you read a graph, ask yourself the following questions:

- What type of graph is it: a bar, line, pie, or scatter graph?
- What can I learn from the title, caption, and labels?
- How does the graph relate to the main text?
- What questions does the graph answer?
- What questions does the graph raise?
- What patterns can I identify?

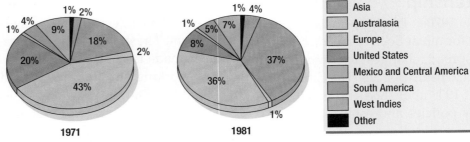

Source: Manpower and Immigration, Immigration Statistics 1971 and 1981. Citizenship and Immigration Canada. Reproduced with the permission of the Minister of Public Works and Government Services Canada, 2007.

Figure 8.17 In 1966, 87% of immigrants came from Europe. By 1970, 50% came from other regions, such as the Caribbean, Asia, and Southeast Asia. By the end of the 1970s, the majority of immigrants were from Africa, Asia, the Caribbean, and Latin America.

Immigrants have fought racist attitudes to ensure that all Canadians live together in reasonable harmony.

Refugees

After 1978, Canada began accepting many refugees. Among the first major group was the Vietnamese "boat people" who were fleeing repression and violence in their homeland. Between 1979 and 1981, more than 60 000 Vietnamese people came to Canada. The government sponsored some of the refugees. Families, charities, and church groups sponsored others. The plight of the Vietnamese refugees highlighted the different perspectives on Canada's new immigration policy. Some Canadians felt compassion and sympathy for the Vietnamese refugees. They believed that Canada had a duty to help displaced persons, both morally and as part of its commitment to the United Nations. Others felt anger and resentment. They believed that many refugees were entering Canada under false claims of refugee status. They were really trying to avoid the long waiting period required to process immigration applications.

Challenge and Response

1. Write a slogan or draw a political cartoon to express your point of view about multiculturalism.
2. How do you think multiculturalism affects the Canadian identity? Express your ideas in a poster, a poem, or another format of your choice.
3. How does Canada's response to the Vietnamese "boat people" compare with its response to Jewish refugees during the Second World War?
4. In your view, what are some of the most pressing immigration issues facing Canada today? Present your ideas in a mind map.

Michael Lee-Chin: Entrepreneur and Philanthropist

PERSONALITIES

"From an early age my mother told me that there were so many of us that if I was to get anything in life I would have to get it myself. So I did."

Source: Michael Lee-Chin, "Get rich slow." *Forbes* (15 April 2002).

Michael Lee-Chin is an immigrant of African-Caribbean and Chinese heritage. He came to Canada from his home of Port Antonio, Jamaica, in 1970 on a scholarship to study civil engineering at McMaster University. As a student, he met and eventually married a Canadian girl of Ukrainian heritage. They returned to Jamaica to live, but later decided to make Canada their permanent home.

In Canada, Lee-Chin embarked on a career in the financial services industry. In 1986, he borrowed money to acquire a company called Advantage Investment Council. He changed the name to AIC Ltd. and quickly transformed it from a $1-million business to an $11-billion empire. Today, Michael Lee-Chin is one of Canada's wealthiest people. He is chair of both AIC and the National Commercial Bank of Jamaica. In 2006, *Forbes* magazine placed him at #365 on its annual Billionaires List. In addition to *Forbes*, the publications *Time*, *Fortune*, *Black Enterprise*, *Canadian Business*, and the *National Post* have all featured stories on Lee-Chin's remarkable rise to fame and fortune.

Lee-Chin is passionate about sharing his success and wealth. In 2004, he created the AIC

Figure 8.18 Michael Lee-Chin was one of nine children. In Jamaica, he began his career working in a tourist hotel and on a cruise ship. Later on in Canada, he worked as a bouncer before turning to investment planning.

Investment Fund to finance projects in the Caribbean. In Jamaica, his companies promote education and provide health services. In Canada, Lee-Chin donates generously to educational institutions, including McMaster University and the University of Toronto. One of his most public and generous acts was a $30-million donation to the Royal Ontario Museum. The money went toward the addition of the Michael Lee-Chin Crystal, which opened in June 2007.

Responding

1. To what extent do you think Michael Lee-Chin is a role model for multiculturalism? To what extent do you think he is a role model for all Canadians?

2. What challenges and hurdles do immigrants face in order to become successful in Canada? Explain your response.

Strengthening the Canadian Identity

During the 1970s, Canadians were bombarded by foreign content—most of it American. They listened to American music, watched American television, and read American books and magazines. As a result, in the 1970s there was a growing trend to revitalize Canadian culture and establish a unique Canadian cultural identity.

Canadian Content

In 1968, the government established the Canadian Radio-Television and Telecommunications Commission (CRTC) to oversee broadcasting in Canada. In 1971, the CRTC introduced Canadian content regulations to ensure that American artists did not dominate Canadian airwaves. The regulations required that 30 per cent of all music played on AM radio stations be Canadian. To qualify as Canadian content, a recording had to meet two of the following criteria:

- song composed by a Canadian
- lyrics written by a Canadian
- song performed by a Canadian
- song recorded in Canada

Critics claimed that regulation would lead to substandard performances. The critics were wrong, though. Greater airtime for Canadian recording artists provided a tremendous opportunity to highlight the country's many talented artists and performers. The Canadian music industry quickly

Figure 8.19   This painting is titled *Scène of Plateau Mont-Royal, Montréal* (1976) by Miyuke Tanobe.

gained an international reputation. The performers of the 1970s and 1980s paved the way for the many Canadian musical superstars known around the world today, such as Avril Lavigne and Nelly Furtado.

The regulations extended to television, too. The number of Canadian television programs increased to meet a 60 per cent content quota in prime time. Among the most popular shows was the television series *The Kids of Degrassi Street*, which first aired in 1979. It led to the spinoffs *Degrassi Junior High*, *Degrassi High*, and *Degrassi: The Next Generation*. The programs gained an international following among young people.

Arts and literature in Canada also flourished during the 1970s. Canadian artists and writers captured the imaginations of readers and earned the praise of critics around the world. Margaret Atwood, Joy Kogawa, and Mordecai Richler were just a few of the many Canadian writers who gained international acclaim. Artists such as Alex Colville, Miyuke Tanobe, and Mary Pratt enriched the artistic world. The resurgence in Aboriginal culture in the 1970s showcased the work of Aboriginal artists, particularly Inuit artists whose work was in demand around the world.

The Canada–Russia Hockey Series

Sports also helped to strengthen the Canadian identity during the 1970s. The first landmark event was the Canada–Soviet Summit Series between the world's two greatest hockey nations in 1972. In the 1960s, the Soviet Union dominated amateur hockey. But many people—especially Canadians— believed the Soviet teams had an unfair advantage. The USSR claimed

its best players were amateurs. In fact, though, they were full-time athletes who earned a living playing hockey. Canada's best players were NHL professionals. Therefore, they were not eligible to play in amateur competitions. In 1972, Canada challenged the Soviet Union to determine which country was *really* the world's greatest hockey nation.

Confident of victory, Canadians watched in shock and disbelief as their team lost the first game in Montréal. By the end of the fourth game in Vancouver, their confidence was shattered. Canada's record was dismal: one win, one tie, and two losses.

Team Canada headed to the USSR to play four more games. In the first game, they lost again. The 3000 hockey-mad Canadians who had travelled with the team to the Soviet Union, however, boosted their spirits with a standing ovation. In the next two games, the Canadians battled the Soviets, winning each game by just a single goal. The two teams now had three wins each. The stage was set for the final showdown.

On the afternoon of September 28, the country came to a standstill. Canadians left work early. Schools suspended classes. Everyone settled in front of a TV to watch the game. As the third period began, things did not look good for Canada. The Soviets had a 5-3 lead. Then Canada scored two goals to tie the game 5-5. The clock ticked down. There was a flurry of activity in front of the Soviet net. Then, with just 34 seconds to go, Paul Henderson scored the winning goal. Canada won the series four games to three.

It was a great victory for Team Canada. But the superior conditioning, rapid skating, accurate passing shots, and precision teamwork of the Soviet

"The Summit Series managed to unify a nation. When Henderson scored the winning goal, it didn't matter what language you spoke or where your ancestors came from. Canada cheered as one."

–Ben Ferriman, York Mills Collegiate Institute, 2007

Figure 8.20 Paul Henderson was the Canadian hero of the series. He scored the winning goals in games 6, 7, and 8.

"The puck comes out to Henderson. He shoots! He scores! Paul Henderson has scored for Canada!"

–Legendary hockey broadcaster Foster Hewitt, CBC Television, 28 September 1972

players proved they were as good as Canada's best. The experience changed the face of hockey in Canada. After the series, the NHL opened its doors to players from the Soviet Union and Eastern Europe.

The Montréal Olympics

In 1976, Canada's national pride surged once again as Montréal welcomed athletes from around the world for the Summer Olympics. Canadian athletes celebrated their best showing at the summer games, winning five silver and six bronze medals. Economic and political issues cast a shadow over the national celebration, though. The mayor of Montréal had promised that taxpayers would not pay a cent to host the games. The money would come from the sale of Olympic coins and stamps and national lottery tickets. However, construction costs skyrocketed out of control and when the games were over, the province of Québec and the city of Montréal were deeply in debt.

Political Controversies

Politically, Trudeau created an international controversy when he refused to allow athletes from Taiwan to compete under the banner of the Republic of China. Canada had officially recognized the People's Republic of China in 1970. Although athletes from the People's Republic were not taking part in the games, Trudeau did not want to alienate the Chinese government by letting the Taiwanese athletes carry the Chinese banner. Many world leaders protested Trudeau's decision, but he refused to back down. The Taiwanese athletes left the country before the games began.

In another political controversy, a group of 26 countries, most from Africa, boycotted the games to protest New Zealand's participation. The New Zealand rugby team had violated a boycott of South Africa by playing a series of games there. South Africa was barred from the Olympics because of its policy of apartheid. The International Olympic Committee (IOC) argued that rugby was not an Olympic sport. Therefore, there was no reason to bar the New Zealand Olympic team. The protesting nations did not agree and they withdrew their athletes from the games.

Figure 8.21   The total cost of the Olympic Games was $3 billion—10 times more than the original budget. The Olympic Stadium was nicknamed "The Big Owe." Do you think the benefits a city and country receive from hosting the Olympics are worth the financial costs? Give reasons for your response.

Challenge and Response

1. What impact did Canadian content regulations have on the music industry? Did they have the same impact on the television industry? Explain your response.

2. "The Summit Series was more than just a sporting event. It was another battle in the Cold War, pitting communism and the collective good against capitalism and the rights of the individual." Discuss this statement as a class.

3. Do you think the Olympics—or any sporting event—is an appropriate stage to carry out political protests? Express your point of view in a newspaper editorial.

Sign of the Times

FLOWER POWER

In Canada, many young people rebelled against the Establishment—their parents, teachers, police, and anyone else who represented law and order. Young people gathered in hippie havens like Yorkville in Toronto preaching their message of peace and love.

Figure 8.22 The hippies' unconventional style denied their middle-class background. They wore their hair long, headbands, beads, and tie-dyed shirts. They expressed their opinions. They explored new religious movements. They embraced sexual freedom. They experimented with drugs.

PEACE

The American involvement in the war in Vietnam was at the centre of the peace movement of the 1960s. Peace medallions became a symbol of young people's opposition to the war.

Figure 8.23 In 1969, Beatle John Lennon and his wife Yoko Ono held a "bed-in" at a hotel in Montréal. They invited reporters into their room, where they talked about peace and love. Lennon later met with Trudeau and gave him "acorns to plant for peace."

Responding
1. What similarities and differences are there between the hippie culture of the 1960s and youth culture today? Present your ideas in a comparison organizer.

Economic Challenges

In 1972, Trudeau won re-election, but this time with only a minority government. After the election, the Liberals governed with the support of the New Democratic Party (NDP). Social programs were an NDP priority. Government spending on these programs was the price the Liberals had to pay for their support. As a result, Trudeau introduced a number of programs, including

- indexing old-age pensions to increase with the cost of living
- increasing unemployment insurance benefits
- introducing benefits for maternity leave through unemployment insurance
- creating a youth employment program

Many people believed increased government spending was necessary to create the Just Society. Others saw it as an attempt to buy the next election at the cost of skyrocketing public debt. This did not seem too important in 1970 when the economy was strong and inflation was steady at 3.7 per cent. By the early 1970s, however, unemployment was on the rise. By 1973, the economy was showing signs of serious trouble. Inflation rose to 7.7 per cent. The price of oil increased from US$2.50 a barrel in 1972 to US$11.50 in 1975. At the same time, government spending and increased demand for goods and services pushed prices higher. Rising prices led unions to negotiate higher wages for employees. Costs were passed on to consumers through higher prices. It was a vicious economic circle.

In the 1974 election campaign, Conservative leader Robert Stanfield promoted wage and price controls as a means of slowing down both inflation and unemployment. Trudeau campaigned against the controls. He argued that Canadian businesses had limited control over prices because so many consumer goods were imported. Trudeau and the Liberals won the election. Afterwards, though, the economy continued its downward spiral.

An About-Face

At first, Trudeau tried to get businesses and unions to co-operate with the government to set economic targets for wages and prices. By 1975, however, he decided to adopt wage and price controls. Trudeau's about-face created a political uproar, even within his own party. The minister of Finance, John Turner, resigned in protest.

Wage and price controls affected 4.2 million Canadians. Union leaders organized protests and demonstrations, including a massive one-day strike by over one million workers on 14 October 1976. The controls held

Reading Strategy

To help you understand difficult passages, read the passage aloud to a partner. Have your partner explain what he or she thinks it means. Then have your partner read the passage aloud to you and explain what you think it means. Together, identify and discuss the main ideas.

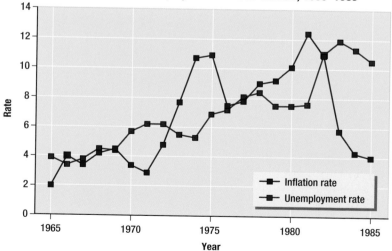

Inflation and Unemployment Rates in Canada, 1965–1985

Source: Statistics Canada CANSIM database http://cansim2.statcan.ca, 326-0002; Human Resources and Social Development Canada, "Applied Research Bulletin —The Canada-US Unemployment Rate Gap" Winter-Spring 1997, Reproduced with the permission of Her Majesty the Queen in Right of Canada 2007.

Figure 8.24 This graph shows the relationship between inflation and unemployment between 1965 and 1985. What patterns can you identify?

"Already … we have surrendered too much ownership and control of our natural resources and our key industries to foreign owners, notably those in the United States. And history has taught us that with economic control inevitably goes political control. This is what colonialism is all about. Indeed, it is sadly ironic that in a world torn asunder by countries who are demanding and winning their independence, our free, independent, and highly developed country should be haunted by the spectre of a colonial or semi-colonial future."

Source: Economic nationalist Walter Gordon, *Toronto Star Weekly*, 1 July 1967

inflation at 7 per cent in 1976, but by 1978, it had rebounded to 9 per cent. By 1980, many workers were demanding greater pay hikes to gain back the ground they had lost in the 1970s.

Who Owns Canada?

During the 1960s and 1970s, many Canadians were concerned about foreign ownership of the Canadian economy. Canada had always relied on foreign investment to finance the country's development. In the early twentieth century, most of this investment came from Britain. By 1960, however, the United States was financing the Canadian economy. By 1972, 99 per cent of Canada's petroleum and coal industries, 95 per cent of its book-publishing industry, 82 per cent of its chemical products industry, and 67 per cent of its mining industry were foreign owned— largely by American interests. No other country in the world had such a high level of foreign ownership.

Between 1968 and 1972, three government reports warned that foreign investment threatened Canadian independence. As a result, the issue of foreign ownership became a politically hot topic. In 1971, a group of **economic nationalists** formed the Committee

for an Independent Canada to lobby the government to restrict foreign ownership.

Controlling Foreign Investment

In response, Trudeau took steps to control foreign investment. In 1971, he established the Canada Development Corporation (CDC) to buy back and manage companies using money from the government and private Canadian investors. Two years later, he created the Foreign Investment Review Agency (FIRA) to approve foreign takeovers of Canadian companies and screen the creation of new companies by foreign owners. In 1975, the Trudeau government established a new petroleum company called Petro-Canada to compete with foreign-owned oil firms.

These agencies had limited powers to stop foreign investment, however. The government feared that any drastic action would hurt the economy. Industrial and business leaders argued that foreign investment was essential to create new industries and jobs and maintain Canada's standard of living. By the 1980s, as the country faced a serious economic downturn, the issue of foreign ownership slipped from the national political agenda.

Challenge and Response

1. To what extent did Trudeau's vision of a Just Society conflict with his economic policies?
2. Reread the quotation by Walter Gordon on this page. What points does he make about foreign ownership? Do you agree with his point of view? Give reasons for your response.
3. As a class, brainstorm a list of economic issues in Canada today. Then, working with a partner, rank-order these issues from most important to least important.

An Environmental Awakening

The environmental movement went hand in hand with the changing social values and attitudes of the late 1960s and early 1970s. Many Canadians began to gain a greater awareness of the damage human activity was doing to the environment.

Environmental Action Groups

In 1969, a new environmental group called Pollution Probe alerted the public to the deadly effects of the insecticide DDT. Runoff from the pesticide was polluting Canada's lakes and rivers and killing fish populations. In turn, the birds that ate the contaminated fish produced eggs with shells so thin the birds crushed them during incubation. Convinced that DDT posed a serious threat to Canada's bird and fish populations, Trudeau banned further use of the insecticide.

In 1970, another emerging environmental group from Vancouver set out to confront the United States over its plans to test nuclear bombs off the coast of Alaska. A small group of protesters planned to sail into the middle of the test site aboard a leaky fishing boat and dare the US military to blow them up. This group of environmentalists called themselves Greenpeace.

In the end, the confrontation never took place. The protesters had to turn back to avoid stormy weather. Yet they attracted so much attention and public support that the US announced it would cease nuclear testing in the North Pacific.

Preventing Arctic Pollution

One of the first environmental challenges for the Trudeau government was safeguarding Arctic waters from pollution. In 1970, the government passed the Arctic Waters Pollution Prevention Act. It claimed a 160-kilometre zone off the Arctic coastline over which Canada would regulate pollution emissions. It prohibited vessels from dumping their waste as they travelled through that area of the Arctic.

Canada claimed it was acting under the United Nations Convention on the Law of the Sea, which gives states the authority to impose pollution laws where year-round ice poses navigational hazards. The United States argued that Arctic waters were international, and therefore, Canada did not have the right to regulate activities there. In reality, Canada had little ability to enforce the law. Many observers saw the act as a means of asserting sovereignty over the Arctic. (You will learn more about Canada and the question of Arctic sovereignty in Chapter 9.)

Learn more about environmental issues

"Our goal is a very simple one: to bring about a confrontation between the people of death and the people of life."

–Greenpeace activist, Vancouver, September 1970

Figure 8.25 The success of Greenpeace campaigns has focused attention on environmental issues not just in Canada but around the world.

Learn more about pollution in the Great Lakes

"We look upon the North as our last frontier. It is natural for us to think of developing it, of subduing the land and extracting its resources to fuel Canada's industry and heat our homes. Our whole inclination is to think of expanding our industrial machine to the limit of our country's frontiers ... But the native peoples say that the North is their home-land. They have lived there for thousands of years. They claim it is their land, and they believe they have a right to say what its future ought to be."

–Tom Berger, *Northern Frontier, Northern Homeland,* 1977

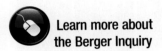

Learn more about the Berger Inquiry

Protecting the Great Lakes

In the 1970s, Lake Erie was on the verge of dying as a buildup of algae killed off fish and made the beaches unusable. Phosphorus from industrial waste, fertilizer runoff, and laundry detergent promoted the growth of the algae. In 1972, Canada and the United States signed the Great Lakes Water Agreement to reduce phosphate emissions in the Great Lakes. They pledged $7.6 billion to upgrade water treatment facilities and to educate farmers about fertilizing options. As a result, phosphorous levels in Lake Erie dropped. The algae disappeared and the fish returned.

The Mackenzie Valley Pipeline

The oil shortage of the early 1970s demonstrated the need to find new fuel sources in North America. There were oil and natural gas deposits along the north coast of Alaska, but it cost too much to transport these resources to southern markets. As the energy crisis worsened, however, a group of Canadian and American companies proposed building a pipeline to carry the gas and oil from Alaska through the Mackenzie River valley in the Northwest Territories to the south. The proposal would be the largest construction project ever undertaken in the North.

Yet what impact would construction of the pipeline have on the fragile Arctic environment and the people who lived there? In 1974, Trudeau established the Mackenzie Valley Pipeline Inquiry to find out. Thomas Berger, a BC Supreme Court judge and former Aboriginal rights lawyer, headed the investigation. He took his show on the road, visiting over 35 communities in Yukon and the Northwest Territories. He held meetings in town halls and Aboriginal lodges to listen to what people had to say about the pipeline and how it would affect their lives. For most northerners, this was the first time the government had bothered to ask them about the issues that affected them.

The Berger Report

Berger delivered his report, titled *Northern Frontier, Northern Homeland,* in May 1977. It pointed out that the North was more than a resource frontier. It was the home of thousands of Aboriginal peoples. Berger concluded that the pipeline would cause serious damage to the fragile northern environment. The influx of outsiders would dramatically disrupt Aboriginal communities. Berger recommended the postponement of the pipeline for at least 10 years to allow time to settle Aboriginal land claims. The government accepted Berger's recommendations. In the end, the Mackenzie Valley Pipeline was never built.

Challenge and Response

1. Do you think environmental groups play a constructive role in the creation of environmental policies? Explain your point of view.
2. What should governments do to protect northern lands and communities in future energy projects? Explain your response.

Northern Peoples

COMMUNITIES

Over 1000 Aboriginal peoples made presentations to the Berger Inquiry. CBC Radio broadcast the proceedings live to give all Canadians the opportunity to listen to the points of view of peoples living in northern communities. The inquiry had a significant impact on the understanding and attitudes other Canadians had toward the North and the Aboriginal peoples who live there.

"To really bring the whole picture into focus, you can describe it as the rape of the northland to satisfy the greed and the needs of southern consumers, and when development of this nature happens, it only destroys; it does not leave any permanent jobs for people who make the North their home. The whole process does not leave very much for us to be proud of, and along with their equipment and technology, they also impose on the northern people their white culture and all its value systems."

Source: Louise Frost, Old Crow, Yukon,
Northern Frontier, Northern Homeland (Ottawa: 1977), 36.

"Now ... it seems like this is the end of a lot of food for us. If they ever drill [for oil] in the Beaufort Sea, if they ever have an accident, nobody really knows how much damage it will make on the Beaufort Sea. Nobody really knows how many fish it will kill, or whales, polar bears, the little whales and the bowheads. These people that did research on the Beaufort Sea will never be able to answer these things. When will the fish and the whales come back?"

Source: Sam Raddi, Inuvik, Northwest Territories,
Northern Frontier, Northern Homeland (Ottawa: 1977), 70.

"To the Indian people our land really is our life. Without our land we cannot—we could no longer exist as people. If our land is destroyed, we too are destroyed. If your people ever take our land you will be taking our life."

Source: Richard Nerysoo, Fort McPherson, Northwest Territories,
Northern Frontier, Northern Homeland (Ottawa: 1977), 94.

Figure 8.26   Justice Berger visited local communities in the North. What are the advantages of conducting a Royal Commission in this way?

Responding

1. What lessons did Canadians learn from the Berger Inquiry?
2. In your opinion, are there ever any circumstances in which it is acceptable to exploit natural resources, regardless of the effect this has on the environment and local communities? Discuss this idea as a class.

Profile in Power:

Charles Joseph Clark

Figure 8.27 Joe Clark (1939–)

In the election of 1979, Joe Clark and the Conservatives campaigned on the slogan "Let's Get Canada Working Again." It was a simple message that appealed to many Canadians who were tired of the Liberals' inability to turn around the failing economy. Clark won a minority government.

Six months later, the Conservatives were defeated in an election. Clark stayed on as leader, but he faced widespread criticism from within his own party. In 1983, he called a leadership convention, and in a tough battle, Clark lost to Brian Mulroney. However, he went on to build a distinguished career in the Mulroney government. Joe Clark retired from politics in 2003.

 Learn more about the career of Joe Clark

Responding

1. In your opinion, what political traits are necessary to sustain a minority government? Give reasons for your response.

Goodbye—But not Farewell

By 1979, Canadians were ready for change. After being defeated by Joe Clark and the Conservatives, Trudeau announced his retirement.

Within six months of Clark's victory, however, the Conservatives faced a critical budget vote. Clark had campaigned on tax cuts to tackle unemployment and to stimulate the economy. Once in office, however, he changed his mind. Instead, he brought in a budget that focused on fighting inflation, including a controversial tax increase on gas.

On the day of the budget vote, Trudeau realized that not all of the Conservative MPs would be in the House of Commons. He pounced on the opportunity to bring down the government. Liberal MPs across the country were called to the House of Commons to vote.

The strategy worked. The Conservatives lost a vote of non-confidence by six votes. The stage was set for another election. The Liberals urged Trudeau to stay on and lead them to one more victory, and he agreed. He had some unfinished business. In Québec, René Lévesque had announced his intention to hold a referendum on independence. Trudeau wanted to lead the federalist fight. His last term in office would turn out to be the busiest and the most significant of his political career.

Challenge and Response

1. Do you think Clark was the architect of his own political defeat? Explain your response.
2. Why was Trudeau so keen to stay on as leader?

Thinking Like a Historian:
Making Moral Judgments about the Past

Essential Question: As a historian, how do you make moral judgments about actions that took place in the past?

Invoking the War Measures Act during the October Crisis remains one of the most controversial political decisions in modern Canadian history. Many historians believe the action was justified given the atmosphere in Canada at the time. Others believe that the government overreacted.

You, the Historian

Read the following excerpt from a speech by Prime Minister Trudeau on 16 October 1970. Then answer the questions that follow.

"If a democratic society is to continue to exist, it must be able to root out the cancer of an armed, revolutionary movement that is bent on destroying the very basis of our freedom. For that reason the Government, following an analysis of the facts, including requests of the Government of Québec and the City of Montréal for urgent action, decided to proclaim the War Measures Act. It did so at 4:00 a.m. this morning, in order to permit the full weight of Government to be brought quickly to bear on all those persons advocating or practicing violence as a means of achieving political ends.

The War Measures Act gives sweeping powers to the Government. It also suspends the operation of the Canadian Bill of Rights. I can assure you that the Government is most reluctant to seek such powers, and did so only when it became crystal clear that the situation could not be controlled unless some extraordinary assistance was made available on an urgent basis.

The authority contained in the Act will permit Governments to deal effectively with the nebulous yet dangerous challenge to society represented by the terrorist organizations. The criminal law as it stands is simply not adequate to deal with systematic terrorism.

The police have therefore been given certain extraordinary powers necessary for the effective detection and elimination of conspiratorial organizations that advocate the use of violence. These organizations, and membership in them, have been declared illegal. The powers include the right to search and arrest without warrant, to detain suspected persons without the necessity of laying specific charges immediately, and to detain persons without bail.

These are strong powers and I find them as distasteful as I am sure do you. They are necessary, however, to permit the police to deal with persons who advocate or promote the violent overthrow of our democratic system..."

Source: Prime Minister Pierre Trudeau, in a national broadcast, CBC Television News, 16 October 1970.

1. What reasons does the prime minister give for imposing the War Measures Act? Which were based on reason? Which were based on emotion?
2. Which groups would likely have supported this decision? Criticized it?
3. What are the most powerful words and phrases Trudeau uses? How effective are they?
4. Imagine you are a student during the October Crisis. Write a letter to the government expressing your support of, or opposition to, invoking the War Measures Act.

Chapter 9

National Unity and International Security

Figure 9.1 Pierre Trudeau and his wife Margaret toured sites in China with the Chinese premier Zhou Enlai in October 1973. Why do you think this was an important trip for the Canadian prime minister? What impact do you think state visits have on relations between countries?

Chapter at a Glance

Thinking Ahead

After winning the 1980 election, a number of urgent issues faced the Trudeau government. This time around, however, Trudeau was determined to do things under his own terms. He focused on four key areas: the Québec referendum, patriating the Constitution, a national energy policy, and international relations. At the same time, social and technological changes were having a profound impact on Canadian society and the world at large.

In this chapter, you will have the opportunity to focus on some of the key events in Canada in the 1970s and 1980s. As you do, think about the following key questions:

- What impact did the quest for Québec sovereignty have on Canada?
- How did Canada's need for greater self-sufficiency in energy influence economic policies?
- What scientific and technological advances challenged and changed Canadian society?
- What impact did Canada have in the global community?

Profile in Power:

Pierre Elliott Trudeau

"Today, at long last, Canada is acquiring full and complete national sovereignty. The Constitution of Canada has come home. The most fundamental law of the land will now be capable of being amended in Canada, without any further recourse to the Parliament of the United Kingdom."

–Prime Minister Pierre Trudeau, Ottawa, 17 April 1982

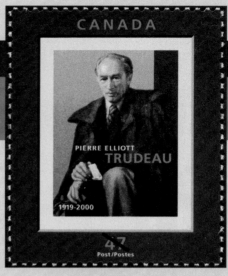

Figure 9.2 Pierre Elliott Trudeau (1919–2000)

After winning the election of 1980, the stage was set for a classic showdown between two old rivals—Pierre Trudeau the federalist and René Lévesque the separatist. Trudeau launched a vigorous campaign to convince Québécois that their future was in Canada. At carefully timed appearances, he gave powerful speeches promising a new partnership between Québec and Canada. It was Trudeau's finest hour. In May 1980, 60 per cent of the people of Québec voted to remain in Canada.

After the referendum, Trudeau set out to live up to his word. His first priority was to bring home the Constitution from Britain. For the next 18 months, he engaged the provincial premiers in a battle of wills as they negotiated a new Canadian Constitution. Finally, after much political manoeuvring, Trudeau and nine of the provincial premiers reached an agreement in November 1981. Only Lévesque failed to sign on. Trudeau had fulfilled his lifelong goal—but without Québec's support. Still, it was a triumphant day on 17 April 1982 when Queen Elizabeth II sat next to Trudeau on Parliament Hill and signed the proclamation that gave the nation a made-in-Canada Constitution.

On 29 February 1984, Trudeau took "a long walk in the snow" as he pondered his future. He had achieved all of his goals. It was time to retire. On June 30, Trudeau formally stepped down as prime minister. He returned to Montréal to practise law. Although he kept a low public profile, behind the scenes he remained a powerful force in Canadian politics. When he spoke out on the issues, Canadians listened. Trudeau's strong opposition to the Meech Lake and Charlottetown accords in the 1980s played a key role in undermining these constitutional initiatives.

In his last years, Trudeau's health declined as he suffered from Parkinson's disease and prostate cancer, and endured the emotional loss of his youngest son who was swept away by an avalanche in British Columbia. When Pierre Elliott Trudeau died on 28 September 2000, there was a huge outpouring of emotion. Canadians across the country stopped to pay their respects to the man who had captured the spirit and imagination of a nation.

Trudeau, the man who sported a red rose as his personal signature, was a towering figure in twentieth-century Canadian politics.

Figure 9.3 Trudeau's funeral was unparalleled in Canadian history. As his casket lay in state on Parliament Hill, 60 000 people filed past. Thousands more lined the railway tracks waving Canadian flags and holding Trudeau's trademark red rose as his funeral train made its way to Montréal. Outside the church, more than 15 000 mourners waited to say goodbye. Why do you think Canadians had such an emotional reaction to Trudeau's death?

Responding

1. Why do you think bringing home Canada's Constitution from Britain was so important to Trudeau?
2. Why do you think Trudeau was still able to influence Canadian politics even out of office?

The Parti Québécois Comes to Power

"Like an adolescent, it wants to be independent. But, by God, it also wants to be paid an allowance by its father."

–Prime Minister Pierre Trudeau, commenting on sovereignty-association, 13 May 1977

During the 1970s, the Parti Québécois (PQ) under René Lévesque gradually gained popular support in Québec. The PQ brought together different groups with a common goal—the peaceful, democratic transition to an independent Québec. Lévesque understood, however, that many Québécois were uneasy about the economic consequences of separation. While 84 per cent wanted a new relationship between Québec and Canada, only 20 per cent favoured outright independence.

Lévesque's solution was **sovereignty-association**. Québec would forge a new partnership with Canada. It would maintain major economic institutions, such as the Canadian currency and banking system and Canada's free trade agreements. But the new nation would make its own laws, charge its own taxes, and have its own citizenship and immigration policies. In the provincial elections of 1970 and 1973, however, the PQ failed to persuade enough voters to embrace Lévesque's version of independence.

In 1976, the PQ found the breakthrough it needed. Corruption and scandal had discredited the Liberal government of Robert Bourassa. The provincial economy was plagued with problems. Tapping into voters' discontent, Lévesque focused on providing the people of Québec with "good government." His strategy worked. On 15 November 1976, Lévesque led the PQ to victory, receiving 41 per cent of the popular vote. But was the PQ's victory a vote for independence—or a vote for better government?

Québec Decides

The Parti Québécois had promised to hold a referendum on the issue of sovereignty-association. Following Trudeau's defeat in 1979, Lévesque saw the perfect opportunity. Instead of the eloquent and determined Québec federalist as his opponent, he would face Joe Clark, the young and inexperienced westerner. In December 1979, Lévesque announced plans for a referendum. As you discovered in Chapter 8, however, Pierre Trudeau's political career was not over. In 1980, he was re-elected prime minister. The stage was set for a showdown between two highly intelligent, articulate, and persuasive political rivals.

Figure 9.4 The issue of Québec sovereignty earned international attention. What message does this *Time* magazine cover convey?

The Referendum Question

Lévesque crafted a carefully worded question for the referendum designed to convince voters that independence would be a slow and cautious process. It asked voters if they agreed to give the Québec government "a mandate to negotiate sovereignty-association with Canada." The question disappointed both federalists and separatists alike. Fierce separatists wanted an outright declaration of independence. Federalists claimed that the question would confuse people into voting for independence without explicitly asking them to do so.

The referendum campaign was hard fought and emotional. Lévesque rallied the "Oui" forces, while Claude Ryan, leader of the Québec Liberal Party, led the "Non" side. Although Ryan had the support of federal politicians from all parties, his greatest ally was Pierre Trudeau. Trudeau accused Lévesque of asking a trick question designed to persuade Québécois to vote for sovereignty-association without any guarantee that Canada would accept such an arrangement. He promised that after a "Non" vote, his government would immediately reopen talks on constitutional reform to satisfy Québec's grievances.

On 20 May 1980, 85 per cent of eligible voters turned out to decide Québec's future. The result was a safe—although not overwhelming—victory for the "Non" side, with almost 60 per cent of the vote. Among French-speaking voters, however, the vote was almost 50-50. For the time being, Pierre Trudeau and the federalists had put off the separatist challenge to Canadian unity.

"The Government of Québec has made public its proposal to negotiate a new agreement with the rest of Canada, based on the equality of nations. This agreement would enable Québec to acquire the exclusive power to make its laws, levy its taxes, and establish relations abroad—in other words, sovereignty—and at the same time to maintain with Canada an economic association, including a common currency. No change in political status resulting from these negotiations will be effected without approval by the people through another referendum. On these terms, do you give the Government of Québec the mandate to negotiate the proposed agreement between Québec and Canada? Yes. No."

–The referendum question, 20 May 1980

Challenge and Response

1. In your opinion, how might the wording of the referendum question have influenced people's decision to support independence?

2. Those who voted "Non" in the referendum tended to be English, new immigrants, older, of lower-income, and less educated. Those who voted "Oui" tended to be French, younger, wealthier, and better educated. Why do you think each group voted the way it did?

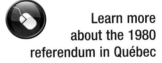

Learn more about the 1980 referendum in Québec

PERSONALITIES

René Lévesque: Champion of Québécois Nationalism

René Lévesque was born in New Brunswick in 1922, but was raised in New Carlisle, a community dominated by wealthy English Canadians, in the Gaspé region of Québec. As a child, he walked past the large and modern English school on his way to the one-room shack that was the French school. Such inequalities between French and English shaped Lévesque's conviction that French Canadians were second-class citizens in their own country.

In the Second World War and the Korean War, Lévesque worked as a war correspondent. He went on to make a name for himself when he sided with striking workers at Radio-Canada, the French branch of the CBC.

In 1960, Lévesque turned to politics, joining the Québec Liberals. After his proposal for sovereignty-association was defeated at a party convention, however, Lévesque abandoned the Liberal Party. In 1968, he formed the separatist Parti Québécois (PQ).

During the 1970s, Lévesque was the most popular politician in Québec. He spoke passionately about Québec in a way that people understood. In 1970, the PQ won almost 25 per cent of the popular vote in its first provincial election. In 1973, the PQ's popular support rose to 30 per cent.

Still, Lévesque failed to persuade the majority of Québec voters to support sovereignty-association. In 1976, he changed strategies by focusing on the economy. Any vote on sovereignty-association, Lévesque promised, would take place in a separate referendum.

Figure 9.5   René Lévesque appealed directly to the hearts of many Québécois. He had a deep connection to their goals and aspirations. How do you think this contributed to his popularity in Québec?

Reassured they could vote for the PQ without necessarily voting for independence, the voters swept Lévesque and the PQ to victory. Independence was no longer the idealistic dream of a fringe group of nationalists. It was a political reality.

"The Independence movement is linked to a universal phenomenon: Québec is at the tail end of the great colonial liberation era which followed the Second World War. If we don't hurry, we're about to miss the boat. Like it or not, we are a colony within Canada."

Source: René Lévesque, *La Presse*, 9 January 1969.

When Lévesque held a referendum on sovereignty-association in 1980, he failed to convince the majority of Québécois to support independence. Although Lévesque and the PQ were re-elected in 1981, in 1985 they were defeated. Two years later, Lévesque died of a heart attack at the age of 65. Today, Québec City and Montréal have major streets named in his honour.

Responding

1. Do you think Lévesque was a successful politician? Give reasons for your response.

Bringing Home the Constitution

With the referendum over, Trudeau set out to live up to his promise of a new relationship between Québec and Canada. His first priority was to **patriate** Canada's Constitution. He had already started the constitutional campaign back in 1971 at a meeting with provincial premiers in Victoria. For a time, it looked as if the prime minister and the premiers had reached an agreement. However, the deal collapsed when Québec's premier, Robert Bourassa, withdrew his support after the Québec media harshly criticized him for not getting enough concessions out of Ottawa.

Almost a decade after the Victoria meeting, in September 1980 Trudeau met once again with the provincial premiers to work out a deal. Trudeau's vision of Canada was of a strong federal state. Any move toward greater decentralization was unacceptable to him. As a result, the talks ended in a stalemate as both sides tried to increase their powers at the expense of the other. After the talks broke down, in October 1980 Trudeau announced plans to proceed unilaterally—the federal government would go on its own to the British Parliament to bring home the Constitution.

Taking It to Court

The provinces decided to fight Trudeau's decision. They asked the Supreme Court to rule on three issues:
- whether the federal government's amending package would have a direct effect on the provinces
- whether it was legal for the government to act unilaterally without the consent of the provinces

- whether the federal government had a moral obligation to win the agreement of the provinces before amending the Constitution

In September 1981, the Supreme Court issued its ruling:
- the amending package would affect the powers of the provinces
- the decision to act unilaterally was legal
- the federal government had a moral obligation to seek the approval of the provinces before amending the Constitution

The third ruling on constitutional convention meant that Trudeau had to negotiate a settlement with the provincial premiers. For their part, the premiers wanted to secure their provincial interests. As a result, all parties agreed to return to the bargaining table.

Negotiations Resume

Negotiations to bring home the Constitution were long and intense. There were so many issues at stake—language rights, natural resources, gender equality, provincial rights—to name just a few.

One of the most contentious issues was the inclusion of an **entrenched** Charter of Rights and Freedoms. Although Diefenbaker had passed a Bill of Rights in 1961, it applied only to areas under federal jurisdiction. Trudeau wanted a charter of rights that would have real impact, both legally and culturally. It would have to be part of the Constitution itself.

Many of the premiers opposed Trudeau's plan, believing it infringed on their powers. They argued that the traditions of the unwritten constitution protected Canadians' rights. Trudeau argued that in the age of big government, the Charter must be

"When you look at the matter coldly, it's clear that there never was a realistic chance of persuading a separatist party to renew the Constitution of Canada. They were in politics to break up Canada, not preserve it."

–Pierre Elliott Trudeau, *Memoirs*, 1993

"[The Charter] seems to really balance the rights of the citizen with the [governing] structure of society. It enables us to pursue our own individual likings without jeopardizing the safety of other people."

–Ashley Muir, Grade 11 student, 2007

"The guarantee in this Charter of certain rights and freedoms shall not be construed as to abrogate or derogate from any aboriginal, treaty or other rights or freedoms that pertain to the aboriginal peoples of Canada including

a) any rights or freedoms that have been recognized by the Royal Proclamation of October 7, 1763; and

b) any rights or freedoms that now exist by way of land claims agreements or may be so acquired."

–The Canadian Charter of Rights and Freedoms, Section 25, 1982

entrenched to ensure the protection of citizens' rights equally at all levels of government.

The Notwithstanding Clause

After intense negotiations, the prime minister reached a deal with nine of the ten premiers in November 1981. The turning point was the inclusion of the **notwithstanding clause**. In return for accepting the Charter of Rights and Freedoms, the provincial premiers insisted that Trudeau include a clause that gave governments the right to pass laws that violated certain Charter rights, providing the law states it is "notwithstanding" a specific provision of the Charter. Believing a weakened charter was better than no charter at all, Trudeau accepted the premiers' proposal.

Only Québec remained on the sidelines. Trudeau knew that the leader of a separatist government in Québec would never agree to a renewed made-in-Canada Constitution. As a result, Lévesque was left out of the final night of negotiations. After Trudeau and the nine premiers reached a deal, Lévesque refused to endorse it.

The Constitution and Aboriginal Peoples

Québec nationalists were not the only Canadians who were dissatisfied with the constitutional agreement. In the

Figure 9.6 Lévesque claimed that the new Constitution was forced on the people of Québec. Trudeau argued that it was not, because he and 72 of the 75 federal MPs representing Québec endorsed the deal. Which argument do you agree with? Give reasons for your response.

original draft of the new Constitution, there was no mention of the rights of Aboriginal peoples. Aboriginal leaders demanded that their rights also be recognized. In response, the prime minister and provincial premiers agreed to recognize existing Aboriginal and treaty rights in the new Constitution. The Charter of Rights and Freedoms also guaranteed that Charter rights cannot interfere with the rights of Aboriginal peoples.

The Constitution Comes Home

The proposed constitutional changes won the approval of both the Canadian and British parliaments. Canada's Constitution was finally coming home. In a simple outdoor ceremony on Parliament Hill on 17 April 1982, Queen Elizabeth II officially signed the new Constitution Act. After 115 years, Canada had finally gained its political independence.

"The First Nations are not a threat to Canada. We do not preach separation. This is our country, from north to south and east to west. It is the only homeland we have. We did not come from anywhere else; we have nowhere else to return to ...

In seeking explicit recognition of our self-government in the Canadian Constitution, we [are] not advocating the dismemberment of our country; rather we envisage the sharing of this land and its bountiful resources based on mutual respect and co-existence ... and based on the recognition of our inherent rights and our distinct societies in Canada."

–Ovide Mercredi, Grand Chief of the Assembly of First Nations, 1982

Figure 9.7 When Queen Elizabeth II and Prime Minister Pierre Trudeau signed the agreement that brought the Constitution back to Canada, representatives from Québec's PQ government refused to attend the ceremony. Do you agree with this decision? Why or why not?

 Learn more about Canada's new Constitution

Challenge and Response

1. Why did Trudeau want to entrench the Charter of Rights and Freedoms in the Constitution? Why did the premiers oppose this?
2. Was it inevitable that René Lévesque would not support the agreement? Give reasons for your response.
3. Reread the quotation by Ovide Mercredi on this page. What points does he make? Give evidence to support your response.

Skill Path:
Documenting Your Sources

Whenever you use someone else's work, you have to give that person credit. Otherwise, you are plagiarizing—taking and using the ideas, words, images, etc., of another person and presenting them as your own. Plagiarism may be intentional or unintentional, but in either case, it is wrong. You can expect consequences if you plagiarize, such as receiving zero on your assignment or being suspended from the course.

Strategies for Avoiding Plagiarism

- Always record all your sources when making notes.
- Document direct quotations, original ideas, or unique lines of thought, arguments, maps, charts, statistics, pictures, diagrams, etc., as well as information that is not widely known in the subject field.
- As much as possible, make notes using your own words. This reduces the chance of copying, enlarges your vocabulary, and ensures deeper comprehension of what you are reading.
- Research widely. Never rely on only a few sources.
- When in doubt, offer a reference. It's better to cite too much than not enough.
- When making notes, use quotation marks and indents and carefully note the exact wording. Some researchers write direct quotations in pen of another colour or in a different font if using a computer.
- When following someone's arguments or line of thinking, indicate this clearly in the text, for example, "According to Lu Wen…" or "as Jane Smith aptly stated…"

Source: Susanne Barclay, Judith Coghill, and Peter Weeks, *Canadian Students' Guide to Language, Literature, and Media* (Don Mills: Oxford University Press, 2001) 335.

STEP 1: Know When to Cite Sources

If something is a fact, there is no need to credit the source. For example, it is a fact that Pierre Trudeau brought Canada's Constitution home from Britain in 1982. Since this is common knowledge, you don't need to credit a source. However, if you rewrite another author's interpretation of events in your own words, you must credit the source.

STEP 2: Record Complete Source Notes

As you conduct your investigation, it is important that you accurately record your sources. This reduces the risk of forgetting where your information came from and making mistakes afterwards. Be sure to include the author, title, place of publication, publisher, date, and all relevant page references.

STEP 3: Cite Footnotes, Endnotes, and Bibliographies

There are different reasons for citing sources. Footnotes and endnotes cite sources for specific quotes and information you have used in your work. Bibliographies identify all the sources you used in preparing your work. The following guidelines will help you know when and how to use footnotes, endnotes, and bibliographies.

Footnotes: Footnotes appear at the bottom of the relevant page. They should never outweigh the main text on the page. Therefore, you should use footnotes for brief references or when only one or two citations are required per page. If you need multiple or lengthy citations, you should set them up as endnotes (see next page). Footnotes should identify the author, title, place of publication, publisher, date, and page reference. For example, if you were to list this textbook as a footnote, the entry would look like this:

[1]Don Quinlan, et al., *The Canadian Challenge* (Don Mills: Oxford University Press, 2008) 100.

Endnotes: Use endnotes in large documents with multiple sources. Endnotes should appear at the back of the document in a section called "Notes." In the written text, list the reference numbers for the endnotes consecutively starting at the beginning of the chapter or document. The numbers in the Notes must correspond to the numbers in the text. In the citation, identify the author, title, place of publication, publisher, date, and page reference. For example, if you were to list this textbook as an endnote, the entry would look like this:

1. See Don Quinlan, et al., *The Canadian Challenge* (Don Mills: Oxford University Press, 2008) 100.

Bibliographies: A bibliography records all the sources you consulted when investigating an issue or event. It appears at the end of the document, after the endnotes. Unless it is brief, the bibliography should be divided into sections based on the type of source—Books, Magazines, Government documents, Videos, etc. Identify the author, title, place of publication, publisher, and date. Organize the titles alphabetically within each section based on the last name of the author. If there is no author, place the entry alphabetically according to the title of the book or article. For example, if you were to list this textbook in a bibliography, the entry would look like this:

Quinlan, Don, et al. *The Canadian Challenge.* Don Mills: Oxford University Press, 2008.

Citing Different Sources of Information

- *Internet sources:* Record the author, title, home page, when the page was last updated, and the URL, or address of the website.

- *Electronic sources (e.g., CD-ROM):* Record the title, type of source, place of publication, publisher, and date.

- *Newspapers:* Record the author, title of the article, name of the newspaper, date, and page reference.

- *Magazines:* Record the author, title of the article, name of the magazine, volume number, date of publication, and page reference.

- *Government publications:* Record the country, government department, title of publication, place of publication, agency, and year.

Check with your teacher as to which style for citing sources is to be used.

STEP 4: Practise Your Skill

1. Find out your school's policy on plagiarism.
2. Visit the library resource centre to do an initial search of sources for one of the following topics related to this chapter:
   - the life of Pierre Elliott Trudeau
   - Trudeau and Québec separatism
   - Trudeau and the Constitution

Find at least five sources from two different media (the Internet, books, magazines, government documents, etc.). Be sure to cite them following the steps in this Skill Path. You may wish to discuss your assignment with a librarian to get a quick and efficient start to your work.

More Economic Challenges

Reading Strategy

Before reading this section, skim the section on the economy in Chapter 8 to recall what you learned about Canada's economic challenges in the 1970s.

"I came into politics to keep Québec in Confederation. Someone else will have to save the West."

–Prime Minister Pierre Trudeau, following the Québec referendum, May 1980

As you discovered in Chapter 8, in the 1970s the industrialized world faced an energy crisis as the oil-producing Arab countries placed an embargo on oil destined for the West. In 1975, Trudeau had attempted to make Canada more self-sufficient in energy by creating Petro-Canada, the government-owned oil company. By 1980, however, as the economic crisis deepened, Trudeau attempted to integrate the country's energy and economic policies.

Western Alienation

The energy issue was a sensitive one between Ottawa and the West, particularly Alberta, which produced most of Canada's oil and gas. Feelings of alienation had escalated in the West throughout the 1970s. On election night on 18 February 1980, westerners' feelings of powerlessness seemed to be confirmed. Even before many west-

ern voters had made it to the polls, the CBC announced that the Liberals had won another majority.

It may have been a majority, but the Liberals won only two seats west of Ontario, both in Manitoba. Trudeau's newest government was clearly a government of Eastern Canada. In the West, the Conservative government in Alberta, led by a powerful premier named Peter Lougheed, was ready for a faceoff with Ottawa. His chance would come in October 1980 when Trudeau announced the National Energy Program.

The National Energy Program

In the early stages of the energy crisis, oil-rich Alberta experienced an economic boom as the province's foreign-owned petroleum companies shipped huge amounts of oil and gas to the United States. It was a different story in Central Canada, though. The energy shortage contributed to an economic crisis in the manufacturing sector.

In October 1980, Trudeau took further steps to ensure greater Canadian control of energy resources. The National Energy Program (NEP) established three main goals to achieve by 1990:

- to establish 50 per cent Canadian ownership of the Canadian oil and gas industry by introducing a tax to fund the expansion of Petro-Canada
- to make Canada self-sufficient in energy by offering Canadian-owned companies incentives to explore for oil and gas in the Arctic
- to create a more equitable distribution of revenue from oil and gas resources by taxing oil production to fund federal programs in other provinces

Figure 9.8 This political cartoon was published on 25 November 1980. Prime Minister Pierre Trudeau, Alberta Premier Peter Lougheed, and Opposition leader Joe Clark are "sitting on the fence" regarding Western separatism.

In addition, the government froze the price of oil to protect consumers from wildly fluctuating oil prices. The NEP was consistent with Trudeau's belief that the country as a whole was more important than its individual parts.

The Reaction to the NEP

The National Energy Program did nothing to improve already strained relations between Canada and the United States. Many Americans believed the NEP was an outright act of anti-Americanism. In retaliation, American oil companies pulled many of their drilling rigs out of Canada and cut back their financial investments in the West. As a result, the economies of the Western provinces experienced an economic downturn.

In 1981, Alberta premier Peter Lougheed announced that Alberta would cut back oil supplies to refineries in Québec and Ontario if Ottawa did not agree to new terms on energy prices and taxes. On March 1, he followed through with his promise. He cut oil production by 100 000 barrels a day. Angry westerners urged Lougheed to cut off the oil supply to Eastern Canada altogether. People pasted bumper stickers on their cars encouraging him to let eastern Canadians "freeze in the dark." Lougheed threatened further cutbacks if Ottawa did not respond to Alberta's demands. In September 1981, Trudeau and Lougheed reached an agreement to give Alberta a greater say in setting oil prices and sharing revenues.

The Effects of the NEP

Despite the protest to the National Energy Program, it had some positive effects. It reduced Canada's dependence on foreign oil and increased Canada's

control of its energy industry from 22 per cent to 41 per cent by 1984. Carmakers focused on producing smaller, more fuel-efficient vehicles. Homeowners practised energy conservation. Canadians began to think about the impact **globalization** had on their daily lives.

However, the primary goal of the NEP was to make Canada self-sufficient in energy resources. By 1982, however, the price of oil began to fall. It continued to do so until 1990. The National Energy Program involved developing the Alberta **tar sands** and exploring for oil and gas in the Arctic. Oil companies would not undertake such costly ventures if prices did not justify their investment. Therefore, as oil prices collapsed, the goals of the National Energy Program were no longer relevant.

The Economic Crisis Grows Worse

Between 1978 and 1983, there were growing signs of more trouble in the Canadian economy. Interest rates were rising. Inflation was in the double digits. Consumer prices were soaring. Workers were laid off. Unemployment was rising. Consumers were spending less. Canadians learned a new term to describe the state of their economy: stagflation—a stagnating economy with a high rate of inflation.

In 1982, Trudeau established the "6 and 5" program. It limited federal employees to a 6 per cent wage increase in the first year and a 5 per cent increase in the following year. The provinces and corporate businesses were encouraged to follow the government's lead. The strategy met with some success as inflation rates fell to 5.8 per cent in 1983 and 4.4 per cent in 1984.

"…The Trudeau government's National Energy Program [was] designed to prevent higher-priced US markets from siphoning off everything Alberta could pump out and to insulate Canada from the worst of world costs."

–Carl Mollins, "The stagnant 70s," *Canadian Business*, August 2003

"Trudeau claimed that the NEP was an instrument of nationalism but, if so, it was more central Canadian than pan-Canadian nationalism. Its goal to provide cheap energy meant that energy-producing provinces…had to sacrifice revenue to fuel the industries of Central Canada."

–Alvin Finkel and Margaret Conrad, *History of the Canadian Peoples*, 2001

Learn more about the National Energy Program

Reading Strategy

When you see numbers in a table, ask yourself the following questions:
- How does the table relate to the main text?
- How does the title connect to the contents?
- What do the footnotes tell me?

KEY ECONOMIC FACTORS, 1978–1983				
Year	Unemployment	Increase in Number of Jobs	Prime Rate*	Inflation Rate
1978	8.3	3.5	9.69	8.9
1979	7.4	4.1	12.90	9.2
1980	7.5	3.0	14.25	10.2
1981	7.5	2.8	19.29	12.5
1982	11.0	−3.3	15.81	10.8
1983	11.9	0.8	11.17	5.8

*Prime rate: The interest rate financial institutions charge their best customers. Most businesses and consumers pay rates higher than prime.

Source: Statistics Canada. 1998. The Canada year book. Statistics Canada Catalogue no. 11-402-XPE. Ottawa.

Figure 9.9 This table shows key economic factors by percentage between 1978 and 1983. In what year did Canada's economy appear to be at its worst?

Inflation Rates of Canada and the United States, 1965–1985

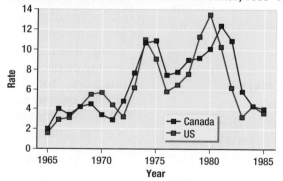

Source: Statistics Canada CANSIM database http://cansim2.statcan.ca, 326-0002; Handbook of Labor Statistics, U.S. Department of Labor, Bureau of Labor Statistics.

Unemployment Rates of Canada and the United States, 1965–1985

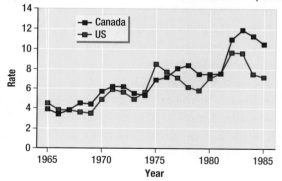

Source: Human Resources and Social Development Canada, "Applied Research Bulletin - Unemployment Rate in Canada and the United States, 1948-1995" Winter-Spring 1997, Reproduced with the permission of Her Majesty the Queen in Right of Canada 2007.

Figure 9.10 These two line graphs highlight inflation rates and unemployment in Canada and the United States between 1965 and 1985. To what extent are the patterns in these graphs similar? To what extent are they different? What do these patterns suggest to you about the nature of economics in industrialized countries?

Challenge and Response

1. Do you think western Canadians were justified in feeling alienated from the government in Ottawa? Give reasons for your response.
2. How did the energy crisis demonstrate the impact globalization has on the lives of Canadians? Are energy prices in Canada still influenced by outside global forces? Discuss your ideas as a class.
3. Do you think the NEP was necessary given the energy crisis of the day? Give reasons for your response.

ISSUES

Exploiting Natural Resources

The issue: Do the benefits of resource exploitation outweigh the risks?

The energy crisis led to a frenzied search for more oil across Canada. One of the new frontiers for oil exploration was the Hibernia oil fields in the open waters of the North Atlantic a few hundred kilometres off the shores of Newfoundland. It was here that Mobil Oil Canada set up the Ocean Ranger, the largest drilling rig of its kind in the world. It loomed 35 storeys high and had a deck the size of two football fields. The rig floated on two giant pontoons resting 24 metres beneath the ocean's surface.

The Ocean Ranger was designed to withstand the stormiest of seas. They said it was unsinkable. Yet on 14 February 1982, the unthinkable happened. A vicious winter storm packing hurricane-force winds battered the rig. Massive waves cresting 18 metres high pounded the platform. One powerful wave blasted through a porthole into the control room, swamping the control panels with sea water. Valves opened on their own, flooding the pontoons. The Ocean Ranger listed to one side. The frantic crew jumped into lifeboats moments before the rig capsized and toppled into the ocean.

When the first search-and-rescue teams reached the scene three hours later, they could see survivors bobbing in the freezing waters. But conditions were so rough the rescuers couldn't reach them. In the end, all 84 crew members—including 67 Canadians—perished.

Figure 9.11 The sinking of the Ocean Ranger was one of Canada's worst maritime disasters. Nothing prepared the people of Newfoundland and Labrador for the magnitude of the tragedy. Of the 84 people who lost their lives, 56 were native Newfoundlanders. Their families received $20 million in compensation from the rig's owner, Mobil Oil.

The tragedy raised some important questions: Why did it happen? Who was to blame? Could the tragedy have been prevented? Do the benefits of oil exploration outweigh the risks?

The Canadian government launched a two-and-a-half-year investigation into the disaster. It concluded that, although the forces of nature were beyond human control, the events that followed were not. The poorly trained crew members were unprepared for the emergency in the control room. There were not enough lifeboats. There were no survival suits to help the crew survive in the frigid waters. The investigation concluded that the Ocean Ranger and its crew could have survived the storm if proper safety procedures and equipment had been in place.

The tragedy prompted the government to implement new safety regulations and better training programs. All oil rigs must have:

- two survival suits on board for each crew member
- a life raft for every crew member
- a standby rescue vessel with fully trained personnel

Since the tragedy, Newfoundland and Labrador has developed technologies and practices that have made it a world leader in training personnel to handle disasters at sea.

 Learn more about the tragedy of the Ocean Ranger

"It was really like being inside an oil drum and someone hit the outside with a baseball bat. When you get out in a big storm like we had the night the Ocean Ranger sank, even the biggest rig or biggest ship doesn't seem so big anymore."

Source: Owen Myers, weather observer at another platform drilling at the Hibernia oil field on 14 February 1982, *CTV News*, 15 February 2007.

"In the wake of this tragedy, advances in technology and training have helped us reduce the risks taken by those who venture out into our oceans. There will always be danger, but there will always be brave men and women willing to meet it."

Source: Scott Simms, Newfoundland MP, *CTV News*, 15 February 2007.

"The legacy of the Ocean Ranger and the 84 lives that were lost is with us everyday in everything we do ... Every decision we make with respect to the offshore is to the backdrop of the Ocean Ranger to ensure that no tragedy like this ever happens again."

Source: Kathy Dunderdale, Newfoundland and Labrador minister of Natural Resources, 14 February 2007.

Responding

1. Why do you think the oil company compensated the victims' families? What other actions do you think should have been taken for the families? Support your answer.

2. Do the benefits of oil exploration in dangerous conditions outweigh the potential dangers? Record your thoughts on this issue in a T-chart. Then discuss your ideas with the class.

Science and Technology: Challenges and Changes

In the 1980s, new scientific challenges and revolutionary technological changes had a profound effect on Canadian society.

The Early Years of HIV/AIDS

In 1981, doctors began reporting rare forms of cancer and life-threatening lung and brain infections, first among some young men in the gay community, then in some hemophiliacs and intravenous drug users. This unknown disease baffled doctors and scientists. Those afflicted with the mystery illness came from all different backgrounds, cultures, and countries. They had one thing in common, though—they were all dying from infections to which most people were immune.

Fear and confusion reigned as researchers struggled to find out what caused the disease and who was at risk. Acquired Immune Deficiency Syndrome (AIDS) did not kill people itself, but it made people's immune systems vulnerable to a host of diseases that could. In 1984, researchers identified the virus that causes AIDS—Human Immunodeficiency Virus, or HIV. They discovered that HIV destroys the immune system, leaving people open to infections. Eventually, HIV leads to AIDS. In the 1980s, HIV/AIDS was a guaranteed death sentence. Anyone was potentially at risk through sexual contact, blood transfusions, or intravenous drug use.

HIV/AIDS in Canada

The first diagnosis of AIDS in Canada was in 1982. The first death was the following year. During the 1980s, the number of reported cases of HIV/AIDS in Canada doubled every six months. By 1988, 1644 people were confirmed to have AIDS; another 30 000 people were infected with HIV. Countries around the world reported similar trends. By the end of the decade, HIV/AIDS had mushroomed from a mysterious illness to a global epidemic. You will learn more about HIV/AIDS and Canada's role in this global health crisis in Chapter 12.

The Information Age

During the 1970s and 1980s, the Information Revolution overtook the Industrial Age. New communications technologies changed the way Canadians lived and worked.

The Computer Age

The invention of the microchip led to the first microcomputer in 1973. Personal computers revolutionized the business world by dramatically changing such things as banking systems, assembly plants, and business offices. At home, people could use personal computers to create documents and play games. The personal computer industry skyrocketed from a $150-million business in 1981 to a $1.18-billion industry in 1985.

Telidon

In 1980, the federal department of communications introduced Telidon. The system connected televisions to remote computer databases using a terminal and telephone lines. The system enabled users to get up-to-the-minute sports scores and weather forecasts as well as do their banking and buy movie tickets. Although Telidon attracted international attention, it failed to live up to expectations.

 Learn more about the AIDS crisis today

PERSONALITIES

Terry Fox: A Courageous Canadian

In 1980, Terry Fox focused Canadians' attention on another deadly disease—cancer. At the age of 18, Terry lost his right leg to bone cancer. While in the hospital recovering from the amputation, he watched children suffering from the disease and committed himself to help find a cure. On 12 April 1980, Terry set out on his Marathon of Hope running across Canada. By the time he reached southern Ontario, Terry was front-page news across the country. Thousands of people turned out to cheer him on and pledge their support. In September 1980, however, doctors discovered Terry's cancer had spread to his lungs. He held a news conference to announce that his Marathon of Hope was over as he returned home to start chemotherapy. Canadians rallied around Terry, showing their support by raising money for cancer research through a variety of fundraisers. On 28 June 1981, however, Terry Fox lost his battle with cancer at the age of 22. Yet, Canadians have not forgotten him. In the CBC's *Greatest Canadian* contest, Terry came in second after the founder of universal health care, Tommy Douglas.

"How many people do something they really believe in? I just wish people would realize that anything's possible if you try. Dreams are made if people try."

Source: Terry Fox, speaking from his hospital bed in Thunder Bay, Ontario, *Globe and Mail*, 4 September 1980.

Figure 9.12   Today, Terry's legacy lives on in the annual Terry Fox Runs held around the world in September. They have raised over $400 million for cancer research. Why do you think people around the world have embraced Terry's mission?

 Learn more about Terry Fox and the Marathon of Hope

Responding

1. Many people believe Terry Fox was a hero. He claimed he was not. How do you define a hero? Does Terry Fox fit your definition? Why or why not?

Sign of the Times

GAY RIGHTS

During the Trudeau era, many young people were politically active. They expressed their points of view in demonstrations, marches, and protests across the country. In the 1970s, many gay and lesbian groups began to demand their rights and to celebrate their diversity.

Figure 9.13 In 1971, gay rights activists presented the We Demand manifesto to Parliament, demanding changes to laws and policies affecting the gay community. In August 1973, the first Gay Pride Week was celebrated nationally across Canada.

Learn more about gay rights and Greenpeace

SAVING THE ENVIRONMENT

Many young people believed that if they worked together they could make a difference. Organizations like Greenpeace drew more and more young people to environmental causes around the world.

Figure 9.14 Greenpeace activists played a leading role in organizing campaigns to protect wildlife. They prevented ships from hunting whales and wrapped themselves around seal pups to prevent seal hunters from clubbing them. The activism led international organizations and some countries to take action to protect and preserve wildlife.

Responding

1. Have you ever participated in a protest or demonstration? If so, what motivated you to take part?
2. In your opinion, what are the most important issues facing Canadians today? Choose one of these issues and present your point of view in a slogan or poster.

The specially designed television cost three times more than a conventional TV set. Users had to pay additional telephone fees to access the system. Although Telidon had some limited commercial success, it never caught on with the public.

An Audiovisual Revolution

Commercially, rapidly changing technology revolutionized audio and video devices. Compact discs producing high-quality sound replaced vinyl LPs. Eight-track recorders gave way to the first personal stereo, the Sony Walkman, the forerunner of MP3 players. Simple home video games evolved into sophisticated systems such as Atari 2600 and Intellivision, the forerunners of Nintendos, PlayStations, and Xboxes. Innovations in audiovisual technology were so rapid it was hard for consumers to keep up.

Space Exploration

The race for space between the world's two superpowers reflected the scope of the new technological age. In the 1970s, the United States launched a series of successful landings on the moon. By the 1980s, the space program had turned to a new kind of mission. This was the space shuttle—a reusable spacecraft that blasts into space like a rocket, but returns to earth like an airplane.

Canada became involved in the space program in 1975 when scientists at SPAR Aerospace developed the Canadarm. The long, robotic arm, which mounts on the exterior of a shuttle, operates by remote control from inside the spacecraft. The Canadarm manipulates heavy objects in space and can lift satellites out of the shuttle's cargo hold and launch them into orbit. It can also retrieve damaged satellites and carry out repairs to shuttles while in space.

Canadians in Space

Canadian astronauts became involved in the US space program in the 1980s. The first Canadian in space was Marc Garneau, an electrical engineer from Québec City. Garneau was one of six Canadians chosen from 4300 applicants for the country's first astronaut training program. He blasted off into space in the *Challenger* space shuttle in October 1984. Since Garneau's first mission, seven other Canadians have been involved in the US space program, including Dr Roberta Bondar, the first Canadian woman in space.

The Debate over Space Exploration

Canada's participation in the space program costs the government hundreds of millions of dollars. This has led to debate over whether the benefits of space exploration outweigh the costs. Is space exploration a wise investment in the future of humankind? Or are the potential scientific benefits too limited to justify the costs? Those who support space exploration argue that Canada achieves international prestige as a technologically advanced country and gains access to leading-edge technologies and scientific research. Opponents claim that the investment of hundreds of millions of dollars diverts money from problems here at home, such as poverty and the environment.

"Space is of great strategic importance in helping the Canadian government reach its stated objective in terms of sovereignty, security, and communication … What we are providing here is an essential service for the citizens of this country. For most Canadians, satellite activity is practically invisible, yet it significantly enriches people's lives."

–Marc Garneau, Canadian astronaut, February 2004

"The more we know about the universe, the more we know about ourselves."

–Chi Cheung, Toronto, BBC News, 10 November 2000

"The money ... could be better spent on dealing with the very real problems ... here on Earth."

–Peter McGuinness, Hamilton, BBC News, 10 November 2000

"Worlds apart. That is what I'd say about the recent talk of space exploration juxtaposed against the reality of lack of affordable living space in the huge expanse of land called Canada..."

–Asaf Rashid, the *Brunswickan*, 21 January 2004

Figure 9.15 The Canadarm was first used on the space shuttle *Columbia* in November 1981. Despite US objections, Canada insisted that the Canadarm display the Canadian logo. Why do you think this was important for Canadians?

Challenge and Response

1. Who should be responsible for educating people about preventing HIV—schools, parents, or medical professionals? Record your ideas in your journal.
2. In your opinion, is space exploration a valid way to spend taxpayers' money? Write a letter to the Canadian Space Agency expressing your point of view.

Canada in the Global Community

> "A country can be influential in the world by the size of its heart and the breadth of its mind, and that's the role Canada can play."
>
> –Prime Minister Pierre Trudeau, CBC Archives, 15 December 1983

In 1970, Trudeau's government set out four main foreign policy objectives:
- to increase spending on foreign aid and development
- to establish diplomatic relations with the People's Republic of China
- to increase Canada's contacts with the countries of the Pacific Rim
- to increase awareness in the international community of Canada's bilingual status

Foreign Aid

In 1968, Trudeau created the Canadian International Development Agency (CIDA) to coordinate all Canadian aid from government sources, religious organizations, and charitable groups. CIDA allocates billions of dollars for

Learn more about CIDC

humanitarian aid, providing money, supplies, and human resources when natural disasters, such as earthquakes, floods, and hurricanes, strike. To create long-term **sustainable development**, CIDA sponsors medical personnel, teachers, farmers, engineers, technicians, and others to help people in developing countries find permanent solutions to their problems.

Distributing Canada's Aid

Canada distributes its foreign aid in three ways:
- *Multilateral aid* is directed to international organizations such as the World Health Organization (WHO), which operate under the support of the United Nations.
- *Bilateral aid* is negotiated between Canada and specific countries on a country-by-country basis.
- *Tied aid* places conditions on funding—usually that the money be spent buying Canadian goods and services. Critics charge that tied aid is self-serving for the donor country and restrictive for the receiving country.

In 1968, then Prime Minster Lester Pearson recommended that every industrial country allocate 0.7 per cent of its **gross national product** (GNP) to foreign aid. Although Trudeau did not reach this target, during his years in office Canada's aid contributions increased from $277 million (0.34 per cent of GNP) in 1969 to $2 billion (0.49 per cent of GNP) in 1984. This made Canada the fifth-largest donor country in the Organisation for Economic Co-operation and Development (OECD).

Figure 9.16 CIDA is involved in at least 100 countries around the world. Its mandate is "to reduce poverty and contribute to a more secure, equitable, and prosperous world."

CIDA Youth Interns

CIDA offers a variety of programs for young Canadians. The International Youth Internship Program provides opportunities for young graduates to volunteer their time working on international development projects. Other youth programs provide Canadian students with the opportunity to express their points of view about international development issues and foreign aid. The following excerpts from the journals of CIDA interns offer perspectives on being a Canadian foreign aid volunteer in the international community.

"Working in Cuba reminded me that the core of any project, the purpose of every reflection, every action, must be the good of humanity. Diving into the depths of Cuba brought me closer to myself and to others, immersing myself in its culture made me love its people, and imbibing its social values gave me hope and made me believe in my fellow human beings."

Source: Leila Benhadjoudja, CIDA intern, Canadian International Development Agency Youth Zone, 23 May 2007.

"International development gives people the chance to act as a bridge ... between peoples, cultures, and ideas. Like any interaction, it's important to respect differences between communities ... International cooperation also allows us to look critically at our own societies, lifestyles, and habits. We can discover how we are socially, politically, and economically interconnected with other parts of the world."

Source: Greg Smythe, CIDA intern, Canadian International Development Agency Youth Zone, November 2004.

 Learn more about CIDA's youth programs

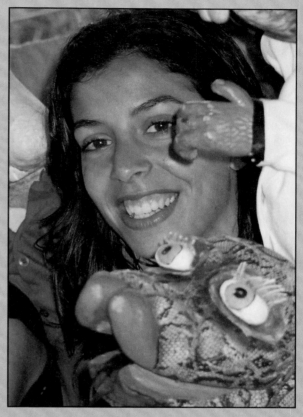

Figure 9.17   Leila Benhadjouda served as a CIDA Youth Volunteer in Cuba.

"What is international development? For me, it is a process of cooperation that allows people to improve their living conditions, to become more independent and self-sufficient...A development project should aim for people not to need it any more... "

Source: Solaine Prince, CIDA intern, Canadian International Development Agency Youth Zone, 23 May 2007.

Responding

1. What are the key messages about international development expressed by these CIDA interns?
2. How do government agencies like CIDA help individuals fulfill their responsibilities as global citizens?

"Living next to you is in some ways like sleeping with an elephant. No matter how friendly and even-tempered is the beast ... one is affected by every twitch and grunt."

–Prime Minister Pierre Trudeau, National Press Club, Washington, DC, 1969

Canadians are divided over the question of foreign aid. Some people believe Canada should not be spending money overseas when there is poverty and unemployment at home. Others argue that foreign aid is a moral obligation of wealthy countries like Canada that also happens to benefit our economy by developing export markets for Canadian products.

The Third Option

Trudeau was keen to redirect Canada's foreign policy. He believed foreign policy should serve Canada's interests first. As a result, Trudeau took cautious steps to distance Canada from American foreign policies.

In 1970, Trudeau commissioned several government studies to review Canadian–American relations. Three options emerged:
- to maintain the current relationship with the United States
- to develop a closer relationship
- to create a more independent relationship

Trudeau chose the so-called Third Option. Canada was about to step out from the shadow of the United States to assert its independence.

Canada and the People's Republic of China

Since 1949, there had been two Chinas in the world: the communist People's Republic of China on the mainland and the Republic of China on the island of Taiwan. Although almost a billion people lived in the People's Republic, in the spirit of the Cold War the United States refused to recognize the country under its new regime. In 1970, Canada broke with the United States and formally recognized the People's Republic of China. It was a clear signal that Canada was pursuing an independent foreign policy, whether the United States liked it or not.

Building a New Relationship with China

Trudeau wanted to take advantage of Canada's new political relationship with China to build an economic relationship. In 1973, he made his first official visit to China. The trip led to a series of trade agreements that opened up the huge Chinese market for Canadian businesses. This made Canada the first Western country to have an extensive trading relationship with China. By 1984, China had become Canada's fourth-largest trading partner.

Figure 9.18 On his first official trip to China, Trudeau met with the Chinese premier, Zhou Enlai. He later met with the head of the Chinese Communist Party, Mao Zedong. In 1973, the United States changed its long-standing policy and recognized the People's Republic of China, too. Do you think Trudeau's initiative may have influenced their decision? Support your answer.

MAP STUDY: The Pacific Rim

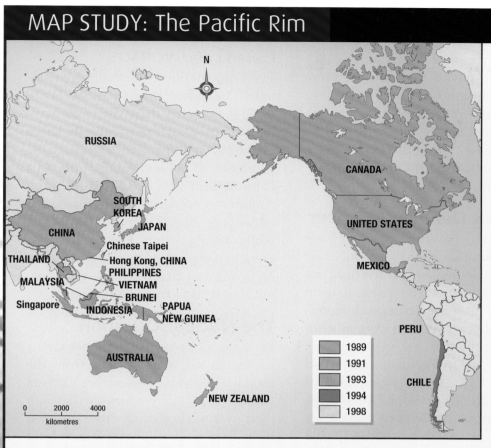

Source: APEC Members website (http://www.dfait-maeci.gc.ca/canada-apec/map-en.asp), Foreign Affairs and International Trade Canada, 2008. Reproduced with the permission of Her Majesty the Queen in Right of Canada, represented by the Minister of Foreign Affairs, 2007.

Figure 9.19 The major political and economic organization in the Pacific region today is the Asia-Pacific Economic Cooperation, known as APEC. The goal of APEC is to provide free and open trade and investment opportunities among its members and to share knowledge and skills to promote growth in the Pacific region. This map shows the member countries of APEC and the years they joined the organization. By 2008, APEC countries had become a powerful force in the global economy.

Trudeau recognized the rising economic power of the Asian economies. He wanted to increase Canada's economic ties with countries such as Japan, South Korea, and Malaysia, which were building strong economies. Most of the goods exported to the Pacific Rim, such as wheat and lumber, were produced in the Western provinces. Increased trade would benefit their economies, which in turn might ease tensions between the Western provinces and Ottawa.

Since the 1970s, successive governments have continued the Trudeau government's initiative to build a closer relationship with the countries of the Pacific Rim. Today, the region is a significant source of immigration and investment for Canada. In return, it provides a vast and growing market for Canadian goods.

Analysis and Response

1. Which three countries do you believe are the most important in the Pacific Rim? Give reasons for your response.
2. Which countries do you think will be the most important to Canada in the future? Why will they be important?
3. What does the growth of APEC suggest to you about the importance of the Trudeau government's pursuit of the "Third Option" in foreign policy? Express your ideas in a short newspaper editorial.

Canada's new relationship with China also paved the way for more Chinese immigrants to come to Canada under a "family reunification" agreement. Chinese citizens who had family already living in Canada were allowed to leave China and immigrate to Canada.

Canada's Defence Alliances

In the 1970s, Trudeau began to have second thoughts about Canada's role in NATO. He questioned the need for Canada to continue to participate in European defence. National sovereignty and peacekeeping were more of a priority.

In the 1970s, Trudeau announced plans to withdraw 50 per cent of Canada's troops stationed in Europe and to freeze the defence budget for NATO. He also announced that Canada's NATO forces would no longer use nuclear weapons. The controversial decision angered Western European leaders. Trudeau quickly realized that in order to improve economic relationships with Europe, he would have to reverse his decision and maintain Canada's commitment to NATO. Between 1975 and 1977, the defence budget for NATO increased and the defence department updated military equipment. However, the amount of money Canada contributed to NATO remained lower than other members of the alliance would have liked.

Canada and NORAD

The Trudeau government also re-evaluated Canada's role in NORAD. In 1972, the defence department dismantled two nuclear-armed missile bases in Québec and Ontario. Critics accused Trudeau of abandoning Canada's commitment to NORAD. Many Americans accused Canada of taking advantage of US defence strategies while offering nothing in return. In 1975, Canada reconfirmed its commitment to NORAD, but proceeded to eliminate nuclear arms from Canadian soil.

The Nuclear Question

By 1984, Canada had eliminated the last of its nuclear weapons from the military. However, elsewhere Canada was helping other countries to develop their own nuclear capabilities. In 1974, India exploded an atomic bomb built with plutonium from a CANDU nuclear reactor. In 1976, Canada agreed to sell a CANDU nuclear reactor to South Korea. Canada continued to export plutonium to the US for use in its nuclear weapons.

Nuclear Testing

In 1983, Trudeau signed a five-year agreement allowing unarmed cruise missile testing in northern Alberta. Outraged by the decision, peace activists protested across the country. Trudeau argued that Canada had to fulfill its defence commitments. The cruise missile tests went ahead in March 1984.

"Canada is passing the buck to the rest of us."

–British Defence Secretary Dennis Healey, commenting on Canada's NATO commitment, 19 September 1969

"It is hardly fair to rely on the Americans to protect the West but to refuse to lend them a hand when the going gets rough. In that sense, the anti-Americanism of some Canadians verges on hypocrisy. They're eager to take refuge under the American umbrella but don't want to help hold it."

–Prime Minister Pierre Trudeau, *Toronto Star*, 10 May 1983

Challenge and Response

1. In what ways did Trudeau's policies demonstrate both co-operation and conflict with the United States? Present your ideas in a mind map or concept web.
2. Do you think Canada's participation in the nuclear industry hurt its credibility when it demanded an end to the arms race? Give reasons for your response.

ISSUES

Arctic Sovereignty

The issue: How important was the issue of Canadian sovereignty in the Arctic in the 1970s to sovereignty claims today?

One of Trudeau's priorities was establishing Canada's sovereignty. One of the first tests of Canada's emerging independence from US policies took place in 1969. An American oil company sent an oil tanker, the *SS Manhattan*, into the Northwest Passage to find a route from the oil fields of Alaska to the US east coast. The incident raised an important political question: Who owns the Arctic?

The United States maintained that the Northwest Passage was an international waterway. Therefore, it was open to ships from all countries. Canada argued that it had sovereignty over Arctic waters, including the Northwest Passage.

Figure 9.20 The Canadian government was angry that the Americans had not asked permission for the *Manhattan* to make the trip through the Arctic. Canada sent the icebreaker *Sir John A. Macdonald* to escort the *Manhattan* and establish its authority in the region.

For Canada, control of Arctic waterways had another implication: if Canada did not control the waters, did it not control the Arctic islands either?

In the end, the supertanker proved to be an impractical method of transporting oil. However, the incident highlighted Canada's concerns about American actions in the Arctic and their impact on Canadian sovereignty. In 1985, another American ship—a US Coast Guard vessel called the *Polar Sea*—made a voyage through the Northwest Passage from Greenland west to Alaska. This time, the Americans informed Canada about their plans, but still insisted they did not need Canada's permission to make the trip. To establish its sovereignty, however, Canada announced it was giving the *Polar Sea* permission to make the journey. The incident demonstrated once again that Canada and the United States remained deeply divided over the issue of Arctic sovereignty.

While Canada and the United States continue to debate the question of Arctic sovereignty, there is a third perspective on the issue. The Inuit argue that they own these lands because they have occupied them for thousands of years. In Canada, this issue is part of ongoing negotiations over Aboriginal land claims. Internationally, however, this may be Canada's strongest claim to the Arctic because the Inuit are Canadian citizens. You will find out more about the issue of Arctic sovereignty in Canada today in Chapter 12.

 Learn more about the debate over Arctic sovereignty

Responding

1. Why would Canada want to establish its sovereignty in the Arctic? Why would the United States disagree with this? Discuss these questions as a class.

2. What message was the United States sending through their symbolic acts with the *SS Manhattan* and the *Polar Sea*? What message did Canada send?

3. Today, global warming threatens to make Arctic waters easier to navigate year-round. Why might this make the issue of Canadian sovereignty in the Arctic even more significant?

The Canadian Rangers

Many Canadians may not be aware that a group of part-time volunteers called the Canadian Rangers is the country's first line of defence in the Arctic. They evolved from a group of Militia Rangers recruited to protect Canada's Pacific coast from Japanese attack during the Second World War. After the war, the Department of Defence disbanded the Militia Rangers and replaced them with the Canadian Rangers.

There are currently over 1500 Canadian Rangers in 56 communities across the North. Most are Inuit and First Nations people who live and work in remote and isolated communities. They are responsible for surveillance and security in the Arctic and remote coastal areas. Their motto is *Vigilans*—"Watchers." They watch for ships, vehicles, and people who are trespassing in Canadian territory, including foreign poachers who come to hunt Canadian polar bears. The Rangers also assist in emergencies, such as air disasters and evacuations.

The Junior Canadian Ranger program is for young people between the ages of 12 and 18. They wear a Ranger-style uniform, but they are not members of the Canadian Forces. Junior Rangers have the opportunity to live off the land and learn about traditional skills and spirituality. They also learn how to administer first aid and navigate through the remote northern wilderness. Junior Rangers benefit from the experiences of the Canadian Rangers and the Elders of northern communities.

Figure 9.21 The Canadian Rangers patrol throughout Canada's North, including the 8000 km stretch between Qausuittuq (Resolute Bay) in Nunavut and Canadian Forces Station Alert—the northernmost, permanently inhabited area in the world.

"It was an important patrol. It was very satisfying doing this for Canada. This is our land."

Source: 21-year-old Ranger Jeff Kuptana, Sachs Harbour, NT, "Trekking on top of the world." www.forces.gc.ca.

"I can't say enough about the Rangers. They are truly the sovereign people of the North. They are our eyes and ears and our guides … Canada owes them a lot."

Source: Major Chris Bergeron, commanding officer, 1st Canadian Ranger Patrol Group, "Patrol overcomes terrain, weather to confirm sovereignty." www.forces.gc.ca.

Responding

1. Think back to what you learned in Chapter 5. Why do you think Canada was concerned about northern security after the Second World War?

2. What are the benefits for Canada having Rangers who are members of the Inuit community patrolling the Arctic? What are the benefits of the Canadian Rangers for northern Inuit communities? Record your ideas in a T-chart.

MAP STUDY: La Francophonie

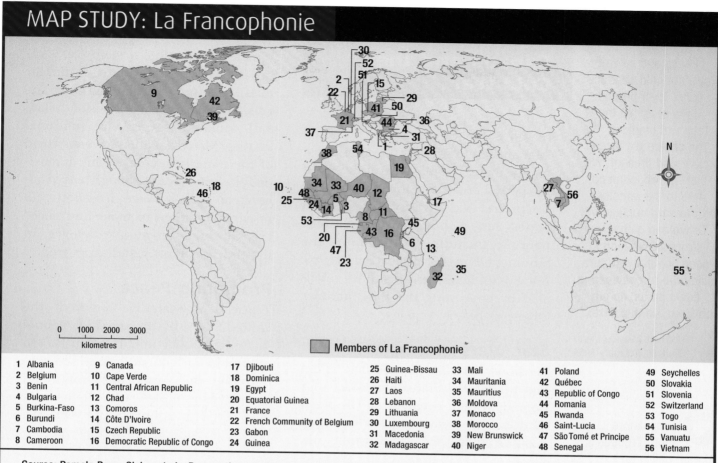

Members of La Francophonie

1 Albania	9 Canada	17 Djibouti	25 Guinea-Bissau	33 Mali	41 Poland	49 Seychelles
2 Belgium	10 Cape Verde	18 Dominica	26 Haiti	34 Mauritania	42 Québec	50 Slovakia
3 Benin	11 Central African Republic	19 Egypt	27 Laos	35 Mauritius	43 Republic of Congo	51 Slovenia
4 Bulgaria	12 Chad	20 Equatorial Guinea	28 Lebanon	36 Moldova	44 Romania	52 Switzerland
5 Burkina-Faso	13 Comoros	21 France	29 Lithuania	37 Monaco	45 Rwanda	53 Togo
6 Burundi	14 Côte D'Ivoire	22 French Community of Belgium	30 Luxembourg	38 Morocco	46 Saint-Lucia	54 Tunisia
7 Cambodia	15 Czech Republic	23 Gabon	31 Macedonia	39 New Brunswick	47 São Tomé et Principe	55 Vanuatu
8 Cameroon	16 Democratic Republic of Congo	24 Guinea	32 Madagascar	40 Niger	48 Senegal	56 Vietnam

Source: Pamela Perry-Globa, et al., *Perspectives on Globalization* (Don Mills: Oxford University Press Canada, 2007), 109.

Figure 9.22 In 2006–2007, there were 200 million francophones worldwide, according to La Francophonie.

One of Trudeau's priorities was to increase global awareness of Canada as a bilingual nation. To achieve this goal, Canada became a founding member of an international organization known as La Francophonie in 1970. Like the Commonwealth, this association of French-speaking countries of the world includes both developed and developing nations. Québec and New Brunswick have special status as participating governments. They are eligible to vote on development issues, but only Canada can vote on political issues.

The overall goal of La Francophonie is to promote French language, culture, and identity around the world. Preserving the French language is a priority in a world dominated by English. La Francophonie successfully lobbied the International Olympic Committee to make all announcements at the Olympic Games in both English and French. La Francophonie also operates TV5, an international television station broadcasting news, sports, and entertainment in French to millions of viewers around the world. La Francophonie encourages wealthy countries to pool their resources to help other countries with sustainable development projects.

 Learn more about La Francophonie

Analysis and Response

1. What patterns can you identify on this map?
2. What valuable relationships do you think members of La Francophonie may form?
3. How does Canada benefit from membership in global organizations like this one?

> "Peace and security are not cold abstractions. Their purpose is to preserve the future of mankind … The choice we face is clear and present. We can … abandon our fate to the mindless drift toward nuclear war. Or we can gather our strength, working in good company, to turn aside the forces bearing down on us, on our children, on this Earth."
>
> –Prime Minister Pierre Trudeau, February 1984

Learn more about Trudeau's foreign policy and peace initiatives

Canada and the Cold War

In 1979, the Soviet Union invaded Afghanistan to support the communist regime there. The move abruptly ended the period of **détente** in the Cold War. To protest the invasion, the United States led a boycott by Western nations, including Canada, of the Summer Olympics in Moscow in 1980. The Soviet Union and its allies retaliated by boycotting the 1984 Summer Olympics in Los Angeles.

Star Wars

Tensions between the Soviet Union and the United States increased after Ronald Reagan became the US president in 1981. Reagan took a hard-line position against the Soviet Union, calling it the "evil empire." In 1983, he announced plans for a Strategic Defense Initiative (SDI), dubbed "Star Wars." The satellite system was supposed to detect and intercept nuclear missiles before they reached their targets. The project cost billions of dollars and violated several international treaties. Many Canadians were critical of the plan, believing it only intensified the arms race. Although tens of billions of dollars were invested, US researchers failed to make any major breakthroughs in missile defence. In the end, Star Wars just disappeared.

Promoting Peace

Trudeau repeatedly angered the United States by his refusal to follow its foreign policy initiatives. In 1973, a motion in Parliament was passed condemning the Americans' continued involvement in the war in Vietnam. In 1976, Trudeau toured South America, paying a visit to Cuba and its communist leader, Fidel Castro—another move that angered the United States. In 1983, Trudeau criticized the United States for supporting repressive regimes in Guatemala, Chile, and El Salvador with known records of extreme human rights violations.

Tragedy in the Air

In September 1983, Soviet fighter planes shot down a Korean Air Lines passenger plane after it went off course into Soviet airspace. The plane crashed into the Sea of Japan, killing all 269 passengers and crew. The Soviet Union claimed it had mistaken the plane for an American spy mission. The United States did not believe it, though. President Reagan called it "a cold-blooded, barbarous attack." Tensions between the American and Soviet governments ran high. Trudeau responded by proposing a peace plan aimed at reducing the number of nuclear weapons in the world. In 1984, Trudeau

Figure 9.23   In 1976, Trudeau succeeded in obtaining Canada's membership in the G7, joining France, Britain, Italy, Germany, Japan, and the United States. The leaders hold annual summits to discuss global issues. Why do you think becoming a member of the G7 was an important step for Canada?

travelled to Western capitals as well as Moscow and Beijing seeking support for his plan. Once again, the United States was angry with Trudeau for taking an independent stand. In the end, Trudeau's peace mission failed, in part because the Americans persuaded their other Western allies that supporting American interests was in their best interest.

At his final meeting with the G7 in London in June 1984, Trudeau pushed his peace initiative one last time. The G7 leaders stopped short of endorsing nuclear disarmament, but they agreed to a more open dialogue with the Soviet Union. For his efforts to ease Cold War tensions, Trudeau received the Albert Einstein Peace Prize in 1984.

Challenge and Response

1. Why did some people believe that the development of programs such as Star Wars increased the chances of nuclear war?
2. Why do you think the G7 leaders were reluctant to support nuclear disarmament? Discuss your ideas as a class.

The End of an Era

Trudeau announced his second—and last—retirement from political life on 29 February 1984. For 16 years, he had been the dominant force in Canadian politics. Only Sir John A. Macdonald and William Lyon Mackenzie King had held office longer. Trudeau achieved the goals he cared about most: bilingualism, multiculturalism, a new Constitution, and the Charter of Rights and Freedoms. He laid the foundations for a more equitable and just society while holding back the surging tide of separatism in Québec.

When he left office, Trudeau's popularity among Canadian voters was in decline. Yet when he died in 2000, public opinion polls showed he was the most popular and respected Canadian politician of the twentieth century. Journalists and broadcasters named Trudeau "the top newsmaker of the century." Canadians chose him as the "PM of the Century." With his uncompromising vision of a bilingual, multicultural, and just society, Pierre Trudeau left his mark on the Canadian landscape.

The Beginning of a New Era

After Trudeau retired in 1984, the Liberals chose former finance minister John Turner as their new leader and prime minister. Turner quickly called an election. It was the first as party leader for both Turner and his chief rival, Conservative leader Brian Mulroney. Turner wanted to disassociate himself from Trudeau's policies. However, he made a critical mistake when he proceeded with a series of **patronage** appointments Trudeau announced before leaving office. The appointments created a backlash across the country.

The turning point in the election campaign came during a televised debate.

Profile in Power:

John Napier Turner

When Trudeau retired in 1984, former Cabinet minister John Turner replaced him as head of the Liberal Party and as Canada's prime minister. From the beginning of his political career, Turner seemed destined for political greatness. But when he quickly called an election after becoming Liberal leader, he had been out of politics for many years, and he appeared awkward and ill at ease. Conservative leader Brian Mulroney, on the other hand, was smooth talking and confident. The Liberals suffered a massive defeat at the polls. John Turner's much-anticipated reign as prime minister came to a crashing end in just 80 days.

Figure 9.24 John Turner (1929–)

Responding

1. Can you think of any other political leaders, either in Canada or elsewhere, who showed great promise but failed to live up to expectations? Discuss your ideas as a class.

A confident and controlled Mulroney demanded that Turner apologize to Canadians for following through with the patronage appointments. Turner weakly replied that he had no choice.

The striking contrast in leadership sealed the fate of the election. The Conservatives won an overwhelming victory, with 211 seats to the Liberals' 40. At the time, it was the worst defeat of a governing party in federal history. A new political era had begun.

Challenge and Response

1. Do you agree with the evaluation of Trudeau as Canada's "top newsmaker of the century" and "PM of the Century"? Express your point of view in a newspaper editorial.

Thinking Like a Historian:
Using Secondary Source Evidence

Essential Question: As a historian, how do you find, select, and interpret different sources of information?

Reading Strategy

Before you begin working on this activity, review the Skill Path on using primary and secondary sources on page 27 of Chapter 1.

You have already discovered that historians rely on primary sources such as speeches, diaries, and legal documents to find evidence to support their work. Often, however, students of history must rely on secondary sources, such as reference books and textbooks to find information about the past.

In his book *Citizen of the World: The Life of Pierre Elliott Trudeau*, Canadian historian John English has summarized the mixed feelings and emotions that Canadians feel toward Trudeau. He describes him as "the prime minister who intrigues, enthralls, and outrages Canadians most." Indeed, many Canadians have great respect for Trudeau and the Just Society he created in Canada. Others think his position on Québec and his economic policies did serious harm to the country.

You, the Historian

In this activity, you will be analyzing the following statement about Trudeau to determine its merit.

"Had Pierre Trudeau left office for the last time in 1979, he would have been remembered as an interesting but unsuccessful prime minister, his time in office a bridge between the liberalism of the 1960s and the neo-conservatism of the 1980s. He would have been a disappointment, rather like John Diefenbaker in his failure to seize the moment and change the country for the better. Yet thanks to a series of political accidents ... Trudeau got that rarest of commodities, a second chance in politics, like Sir John Macdonald in 1878 and Mackenzie King in 1935. Macdonald and King were remembered among Canada's great prime ministers; would Trudeau be the same?"

Source: Robert Bothwell, *The Penguin History of Canada* (Toronto: Penguin Group (Canada), 2006), 461–462.

1. As a class, brainstorm a list of criteria for a "successful" prime minister.
2. a) Review Chapters 8 and 9 to identify Trudeau's accomplishments and failures between 1968 and 1979.
   b) Review the chapters again to identify Trudeau's accomplishments and failures between 1979 and 1984.
   c) What primary source evidence can you find to support your conclusions?
   d) Complete an organizer to compare and contrast your information.
3. Do you think Trudeau was one of Canada's great prime ministers? Write a position paper of 250 words to support your point of view. Alternatively, hold a class debate on the issue.

Chapter 10

New Directions

Figure 10.1 In 1990, South African anti-apartheid activist Nelson Mandela was welcomed to Canada's Parliament by Prime Minister Brian Mulroney and other Members of Parliament. Mulroney was instrumental in bringing an end to apartheid in South Africa. He threatened to sever Canada's diplomatic and economic ties with South Africa if apartheid was not dismantled. Do you think that cutting off ties with a country is an effective way of bringing about reform? Explain.

Chapter at a Glance

Thinking Ahead

After more than 20 years of Liberal government, the Progressive Conservative Party under Brian Mulroney came into power with a landslide election victory in 1984. Mulroney was the first Conservative prime minister in years to lead two consecutive majority governments. However, when he resigned in 1993, he had lost the support of the majority of voters, and his party had divided into regional factions.

In this chapter, you'll explore some of the issues that characterized Brian Mulroney's term in office. As you consider these issues, focus on the following key questions:

- What was Mulroney's vision for Canada?
- What were the arguments for and against free trade?
- What has been the impact of free trade on Canada?
- How did Canada's foreign policy change under Mulroney?
- What economic challenges did Mulroney face?
- What were some of the societal changes that Canada experienced?
- Why did the Meech Lake and Charlottetown accords fail?

Profile in Power:

Martin Brian Mulroney

"Throughout our history, trade has been critical to Canada's livelihood. Now, almost one-third of what we produce is exported. Few countries in the world are so dependent on trade. This trend ultimately threatens the jobs of many Canadians and the living standards of the nation as a whole. We must confront this threat. We must reverse this trend. To do so, we need a better, a fairer, and a more predictable trade relationship with the United States. At stake are more than two million jobs which depend directly on Canadian access to the US market."

–Brian Mulroney, in "First among equals: The prime minister in Canadian life and politics." Library and Archives Canada, 1985

Figure 10.2 Brian Mulroney (1939–)

Like several other prime ministers, Brian Mulroney declared as a teenager that he would become prime minister of Canada. He went on to study political science at St. Francis Xavier University in Antigonish, Nova Scotia, and served as prime minister of the university's model parliament. In 1956, he attended the Progressive Conservative leadership convention as a campus delegate and served as vice-chair of the Youth for Diefenbaker Committee. Mulroney's interest in politics continued as he was studying law at Laval University in Québec.

After graduating from Laval, Mulroney entered a Montréal law firm and specialized in labour relations. As a member of the Cliche Commission on industrial violence in the construction industry, he became well known in Québec. He remained active within the Conservative Party as a fundraiser and organizer.

In 1976, Mulroney ran for the federal leadership of the Progressive Conservative Party but lost to Joe Clark. He ran again in 1983, winning the leadership and then was elected to the House of Commons through a by-election. The defining moment in the 1984 federal election came during the leadership debate with Liberal leader John Turner. Mulroney attacked Turner's support for Pierre Trudeau's **patronage** appointments: "You

had an option, sir, to say no, and you chose to say yes, yes to the old attitudes and the old stories of the Liberal Party." The Conservatives won the greatest majority in Canadian history—211 seats in the House of Commons.

Two initiatives dominated Mulroney's term as prime minister—amending Canada's Constitution and securing a free trade agreement with the United States. The patriation of the Constitution in 1982 had taken place without Québec's consent. In order to persuade Québec to sign the Constitution, Mulroney and the provincial premiers met at Meech Lake outside of Ottawa in April 1987 to discuss changes to the Constitution. However, what Mulroney had hoped would be the triumph of his career, turned into a political nightmare as Canadian public opinion gradually turned against the Meech Lake Accord. In the end, Manitoba and Newfoundland failed to ratify the Accord before the specified deadline. The Charlottetown Accord of 1992 was Mulroney's second attempt at a constitutional agreement. A national referendum was called on this agreement, but it was also ultimately rejected.

Mulroney had better luck in his dealings with the United States. He had good relationships with Presidents Ronald Reagan and George Bush and worked with them on environmental and trade

314

Figure 10.3 Brian Mulroney and Ronald Reagan met in Québec City in March 1985 to discuss the Free Trade Agreement. At a social gala on St. Patrick's Day, the leaders—both of Irish heritage—sang a duet of "When Irish Eyes Are Smiling." Their meeting is now referred to as the "Shamrock Summit." To what extent do you think it is important for the leaders of Canada and the United States to be compatible?

issues. When the Liberal-dominated Canadian Senate refused to ratify the Canada–US Free Trade Agreement (FTA) that Mulroney and Reagan had signed in January 1988, Mulroney called an election. The FTA was the main issue of the campaign. Mulroney argued that free trade with the US was vital in a world that seemed destined to be dominated by regional economic blocs. During the televised leadership debate, John Turner accused Mulroney of selling out Canada with "one signature of a pen." After the Conservatives won another majority, the FTA became law in 1989. In 1992, Mulroney signed the North American Free Trade Agreement (NAFTA) with the US and Mexico. NAFTA came into effect in 1994.

Brian Mulroney resigned from politics in 1993. Since then, he has worked as a lawyer, global entrepreneur, and political speaker.

Responding

1. How did Brian Mulroney's earlier experiences help prepare him to serve as leader of the Progressive Conservative Party and prime minister?
2. As you learned, two initiatives that dominated Mulroney's term as prime minister were constitutional amendment and free trade. To what extent do you think a leader's initiatives are projects of high personal value or responses to political realities?

A New Conservative Government

Reading Strategy

Before reading a chapter, scan through the headings, illustrations, and words in bold type to get an idea of what the chapter is about. This will help you to focus your reading.

Brian Mulroney's election victory was of no surprise to many Canadians. The Liberals had been in power for a long time and their patronage appointments dominated the system. Trudeau was a dynamic politician, but Canadians had grown tired of the economic problems that they associated with the Liberal government. They were looking for change. Internationally, a shift was underway in Western politics as Conservative governments came into power. In Britain, Margaret Thatcher was elected prime minister in 1979. Ronald Reagan was elected president of the United States in 1980. Both leaders supported policies that cut government spending, increased private business involvement in the economy, and reduced government control. In this way, they hoped to address their countries' economic problems. Canadians were interested in exploring a similar approach.

The result was one of the greatest victories in Canadian electoral history. Mulroney's Progressive Conservatives won 211 out of 282 seats, with an impressive 58 out of 75 seats in Québec—a province where historically they had experienced difficulty in winning seats. Voters, especially in Québec, were dissatisfied with the Liberal Party. Mulroney—a dynamic speaker and fluently bilingual business leader from Québec—was able to reap the benefits of that dissatisfaction. He promised to address the reasons why Québec had refused to sign the Constitution in 1982. He also pledged to improve Canada's economy by improving relations with the United States.

Globalization

In Chapter 7, you learned that Canadian communications theorist Marshall McLuhan coined the term *global village* in the 1960s. He used it to describe a world where people who are separated by vast distances communicate through advanced technological communication devices. Computers, the Internet, telephones, satellites, television, and radio have all made the global village a reality today. As a result, people and economies throughout the world have become closely linked. The impact of global events is experienced almost immediately. We now refer to this process as globalization. Canadians are linked through technology with people around the globe on a daily basis. Moreover, our well-being often depends on these connections.

Figure 10.4 Brian Mulroney and his wife Mila acknowledge their supporters following the Conservative's sweeping victory in September 1984. What do you think are the benefits and drawbacks of a government holding such a large majority?

After his election, Mulroney promised to reinvent Canada's image in this increasingly globalized world. He wanted Canada to be seen as a

- free, open-minded, and independent country
- reliable trading partner
- good place to invest and do business
- country of entrepreneurs
- country that honours its commitments to its allies

In a speech to the Economic Club of New York in December 1984, Mulroney explained that his government had "embarked on a fundamental change in economic direction." As he stated it, Canada was "open for business again." To that end, the Mulroney government replaced the Foreign Investment Review Agency with Investment Canada. The organization's purpose was to "encourage and facilitate [foreign] investment" in Canada.

Since 1984, more than 11 000 businesses have been purchased by foreign companies. As you will learn in the next section, the Mulroney government not only opened Canada for business but also signed the Free Trade Agreement with the United States in 1988 and NAFTA with the United States and Mexico in 1992. Since then, the trend has been toward economic globalization with freer trade and open borders.

Canada had long been a member of organizations such as the United Nations, the Commonwealth, and the World Trade Organization (and its predecessor GATT) that supported the process of globalization. Through these organizations, Canada sought to strengthen its position in the world by improving global security and political and trade relationships. Mulroney also looked for new avenues where Canada could develop international relationships. As the world changed during Mulroney's time in power, so did Canada's involvement in global affairs. Later in this chapter, you will learn how the collapse of the communist bloc countries of Eastern Europe in the late 1980s changed how and where Canada focused its international efforts.

Challenge and Response

1. How was the result of Canada's 1984 election similar to political changes in other parts of the world?
2. Mulroney had five points in his vision of how he wanted the world to see Canada. Create a T-chart in your notebook with these headings: "Mulroney's Five Points" and "My View of Canada Today." Under the second heading, write one or two sentences stating the extent to which you believe each point is true today. Provide at least one specific piece of evidence to support each of your views.

International Trade

The process of globalization occurred rapidly during the 1980s and 1990s. One of the trends of globalization was the creation of **trading blocs**. One goal of these trading blocs was to eliminate tariffs between member countries to allow for freer trade.

Modern geographic trading blocs began to take shape in the 1960s with the creation of the European Community in 1965—the forerunner of the European Union—and the Association of Southeast Asian Nations in 1967. During the 1970s, both these trading blocs expanded as other countries within the regions became members. New trading blocs were formed in other regions, for example, the Economic Community of West African States. By the 1980s, North America was one of the few regions of the world that did not have a trade agreement that guaranteed its countries favourable access to markets. In the mid-1980s, Canadians were forced to decide whether they wanted to change this situation.

Freer Trade

In 1983, Brian Mulroney had campaigned against just such an agreement. He seemed to support the belief that entering into a free trade agreement with the United States would not be good for Canada because the Americans' dominant market position would lead to decisions that were mainly in American interests. In 1985, however, the Royal Commission on the Economic Union and Development Prospects of Canada released its report. One of its major recommendations was that Canada establish a free trade agreement with the United States. As a result, in 1985 Mulroney took the advice of the Royal Commission and introduced his intent to negotiate such an agreement with the United States.

The Shamrock Summit

Canada's relations with the United States, especially while Presidents Richard Nixon and Ronald Reagan were in power, had become strained under the leadership of Pierre Trudeau. Both presidents viewed many of his policies as anti-American. As a Conservative, Mulroney had more in common with the Republican president Reagan, and he promised to change Canadian–American relations.

In March 1985, President Reagan visited Canada for the first time since Mulroney had come to power. This first meeting of the two leaders—the Shamrock Summit—set the tone for Canadian and American relations for the rest of Mulroney's term as prime minister. It also became a focal point for people who felt that his relationship with the United States was too cozy. During the Summit, Mulroney and Reagan agreed on some shared military defence programs, including some involvement for Canada in the creation of Reagan's proposed Strategic Defence Initiative. Commonly referred to as "Star Wars," this proposal focused on developing a defence system against ballistic missiles launched from ground, air, or space. The two leaders also set the stage for the Free Trade Agreement negotiations that were soon to follow.

Perhaps the most memorable event of the Summit occurred during the gala held on March 17—St. Patrick's Day. Reagan, Mulroney, and their wives stood at the centre of the stage holding

"We have in many ways a branch-plant economy in certain important sectors. All that would happen with free trade would be the boys cranking up their plants throughout the United States in bad times and shutting their entire branch plants in Canada. It's bad enough as it is."

–Prime Minister
Brian Mulroney, 1983

hands and singing "When Irish Eyes Are Smiling." Some journalists commented that the event reminded them of a story that Mulroney was fond of telling about his experiences as a young boy in Baie-Comeau, Québec. The town was dependent on the paper mill owned by American millionaire Robert McCormick. During McCormick's visits to the mill, he would often ask the young Brian Mulroney—known for his excellent singing voice—to sing Irish favourites such as "Danny Boy" and "Dearie." Afterwards, McCormick would sometimes give Mulroney $50— a large amount in the 1940s. As an adult, Mulroney would tell the story with pride. However, some people thought that it made Mulroney seem as if he had always been at the beck and call of wealthy Americans. Eric Kierans, a former Liberal Cabinet minister turned political commentator, remarked that the singing at the Shamrock Summit gala gave the "impression that our prime minister [had] invited his boss home for dinner." For some Canadians, this perception seemed to stick with Mulroney for the rest of his term in office.

Mulroney was irritated at criticism that he was too friendly with the United States. He addressed such criticism during the Summit: "People who criticize from the bleachers are the same people who for 20 years were in charge of Canadian–American relations, our largest trading partner, friend and ally, treated them like enemies, barraged them with insults, never gave them the benefit of the doubt, and then wondered why we never get along." It was along these lines that much of the debate about the Free Trade Agreement would be fought. Just how close to the United States did Canada wish to be?

The Free Trade Debate

The debate about free trade was not a new one. Wilfrid Laurier lost an election on the issue of freer trade (then called reciprocity) in 1911. As you learned in earlier chapters, after the Second World War Canada tried to protect itself from the overwhelming influence of its southern neighbour. Now, Canadians were being asked to consider entering into an agreement that would make their country's trade relationship with the United States even closer. The free trade debate became one of the most controversial issues for Canadians in the 1980s.

The Mulroney government began negotiations with the United States in September 1985. A deal was reached

"It is my fundamental belief that the challenge to our two countries is to improve and strengthen the mutual benefits from our roles as friends and partners. To this end we must minimize friction, remove needless irritants, and maintain a healthy and vigorous relationship based on mutual understanding, constant and open communications, and a respect for our individual needs and interests."

–Prime Minister Brian Mulroney, speech to the Economic Club of New York, 10 December 1984

Figure 10.5 During the 1988 election debates, John Turner confronted Mulroney about the FTA: "[W]e built this country ... on an infrastructure that deliberately resisted the continental pressure of the US ... For 120 years we've done it. With one signature of a pen, you've ... thrown us into the north-south influence of the United States and reduce[d] us to a colony ... because when the economic levers go, the political independence is sure to follow." But Mulroney and his supporters argued that the FTA would ensure access to American markets and boost trade and investment, guaranteeing more jobs for Canadians.

in October 1987. The main points of the Free Trade Agreement (FTA) included the following:

- *Elimination of tariffs.* The lifting of tariffs on goods and services traded between the two countries would begin on 1 January 1989 and be completed by 1 January 1998. This would allow for open access to the other country's market.
- *Dispute settlement mechanism.* A five-member panel with at least two members from each country would settle disputes that arose between Canada and the United States with regard to trade.
- *Investment.* Restrictions on American investment in Canada would be reduced, but Canada would still have the right to screen and approve takeovers in cultural industries such as publishing and media.
- *Energy.* Canada could not restrict the sales of energy resources to the United States, except in times of shortages. It would then provide the US with a proportional amount of what was available.
- *Agriculture.* All tariffs on agricultural products and processed food would be eliminated over a 10-year period.

When the federal election was called in 1988, the key issue was the FTA. The Liberals and the NDP were against the FTA, as were labour unions. A new lobby group, the Council of Canadians, was formed specifically to oppose the agreement. Opposition was based largely on two beliefs. First, passage of the FTA would lead to a loss of Canadian jobs because American-

owned manufacturing plants would shut down in Canada and move to the United States. Second, because of its increased reliance on trade with the US, Canada would lose much of its independence, especially in the areas of culture and social policies. Critics also argued that Canadian consumers would not really benefit from the small reduction in prices that resulted from the elimination of tariffs.

Figure 10.6 To analyze a political cartoon, carefully consider the different elements. (Refer to the Skill Path in Chapter 5.) Explain what each of the following elements in this cartoon represents and why you think so: the bird, the wall, the people at the conference table. What is the cartoonist's overall message about the debate over free trade?

ISSUES

Free Trade

The issue: Is free trade beneficial or harmful to Canada and its economy?

Since the Second World War, the pursuit of freer trade has been a primary goal in the increasingly globalized economy. The General Agreement on Tariffs and Trade, later to become the World Trade Organization, was established in 1947 with this goal in mind. Organizations such as the European Union, the Association of Southeast Asian Nations, and the Caribbean Community and Common Market also seek to promote this goal regionally.

Arguments For Free Trade	Arguments Against Free Trade
• Economic growth can be achieved by improving productivity. Some countries can produce certain goods more efficiently than others and should therefore specialize in these goods. • When countries specialize in producing certain goods, total world output grows as does the world standard of living. • Small-market countries such as Canada benefit from having easier access to bigger markets such as the United States because producing larger quantities leads to lower costs and therefore lower prices. • Access to bigger markets creates more jobs. • More competition leads to lower prices. • Increased economic interdependence helps to ensure more peaceful relations between countries. • Consumers have the opportunity to choose from a greater variety of products.	• Unemployment increases as more goods are imported. • Production shifts to countries where wages are very low. • Free trade agreements between governments tend to benefit "big business" because these businesses finance the election campaigns of political parties. • Tariffs can help a country develop new industries and diversify its economic activity. • Free trade threatens publicly supported programs such as health care. • Free trade limits Canada's ability to protect its cultural industries such as television, film, and publishing. • Foreign corporations with branches in Canada will move their operations to their home country. • Closer ties to foreign economies threatens a country's political independence. • Production may move to areas with lower environmental protection and worker safety standards.

Figure 10.7 This chart outlines the benefits and drawbacks of free trade. Consider these arguments as you read the opinions about free trade on the following page.

"By removing the tariff on both sides of the border on thousands of items traded between Canada and the United States, we will give Canadian industry new opportunities. It will increase the competitiveness of Canadian exports ranging from petrochemicals to furniture. It will lower costs to Canadian consumers of everything from food and wine to machinery and computers."

Source: Simon Reisman, Canada's chief trade negotiator for the FTA, "Canada's future under free trade." Empire Club of Canada, 16 October 1987.

———————

"Free trade removed virtually all control over foreign investments in Canada, promoted the privatization of public services such as health and education, enshrined the intellectual property rights of corporations, and jettisoned minimal protections for workers, social standards, health and safety measures for the environment. It remains the crowning achievement of the Business Council on National Issues."

Source: Maude Barlow and Tony Clarke, founding members of the International Forum on Globalization, "Canada: The broken promise." *The Nation*, vol. 263, no. 3 (15 July 1996): 23–24.

"You want an example of countries that don't trade with the world—take a look at North Korea and Albania. You like that, terrific! You happen to like better cars, better food, better hospitals and all the rest of it, free trade is the direction."

Source: Bob Crockford, owner of Valley City Furniture, Dundas, Ontario, in *Canada: A People's History*, "Bringing down the barriers." CBC, 1988.

———————

"Head offices are very important to a national economy, because head offices are where the best jobs are. The research and development operations are clustered around the head offices. Where the CEOs and the senior executives live affects how they give to charities … One result of globalization is that companies have tended to shut down branch plant offices and have the whole global company run from the central head office which is typically in the United States or Japan."

Source: Stephen Clarkson, professor of political economy, University of Toronto, "Hoodwinked: The myth of free trade."

Responding

1. Create an I Read, I Think, Therefore organizer similar to the one below. For each quotation above, summarize the main ideas in the "I Read" column and express your opinion in the "I Think" column. In the "Therefore" column, connect the information in the first two columns to this question: How is each of the quotations related to the arguments for and against free trade in Figure 10.7?

I Read	I Think	Therefore

2. How important is trade to you? In a T-chart, list the items you used today in the first column and their country of origin in the second column. What percentage of these items came from another country?

A Free Trade Mandate

The 1988 election campaign was a see-saw battle. At the midpoint of the campaign, it appeared that the Liberals would win as opposition to the FTA grew. In the end, however, the Conservatives won 169 of 295 seats. Mulroney became the first Conservative prime minister to win back-to-back majority governments since Sir John A. Macdonald more than 100 years earlier. Even though more than 50 per cent of Canadians appeared to be opposed to the FTA as indicated by the popular vote, their votes were split between the two major opposition parties. As a result, on 30 December 1988, the FTA was passed by Parliament and took effect on 1 January 1989.

Pursuing NAFTA

Soon after the passage of the FTA in 1988, a new agreement was proposed that would introduce Mexico to the North American trading bloc. Unlike the United States, Canada did not have much interest in negotiating a deal with Mexico. While the total value of trade between the US and Canada was approximately $300 billion, trade between Canada and Mexico was only around $3 billion. However, the geographic position of the US made such an agreement ideal for that country. It could take advantage of cheap Canadian raw materials to the north and inexpensive Mexican labour to the south. Also, Mexico was one of the fastest-growing markets in the world.

Mulroney felt that Canada had little choice but to negotiate. If the United States signed a deal on its own with Mexico, then US trade could take a major shift toward Mexico. Canada

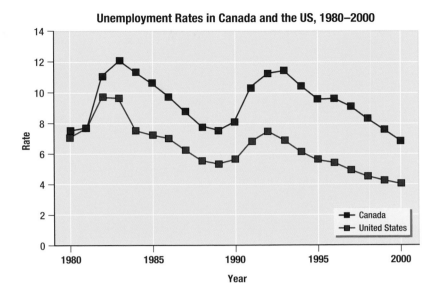

Source: Statistics Canada CANSIM database http://cansim2.statcan.ca, 282-0002; United States Department of Labor.

Figure 10.8 The unemployment rate in both Canada and the US increased in the years after the FTA was signed, but mainly because of a recession in the early 1990s. The rate then fell as the 1990s continued. In the 10 years before the FTA, the average difference between the unemployment rate in Canada and that in the US was 2.1%. In the 10 years after the FTA, this average rose to 3.8%. What does this information suggest about unemployment in Canada since the start of the agreement?

would be left isolated—not just in North America but also in world trade markets. In the 1990s, both the European Union and the Association of Southeast Asian Nations guaranteed their member countries access to a market of 350 million people. A trade agreement between Canada, Mexico, and the United States would create a market of 390 million North Americans, representing the largest trading bloc in the world at that time. While the North American consumer market represented only 8 per cent of the world's total population, it controlled an estimated 31 per cent of the world's wealth.

Learn more about the Free Trade Agreement

PERSONALITIES

Maude Barlow: The "Conscience of Canada"

The election of the Mulroney government and the free trade debate of the 1980s gave rise to a new social justice organization in Canada called: the Council of Canadians (COC). Its goal was the protection of Canadian sovereignty and democracy. One of the founders was Maude Barlow.

Barlow first became involved in social justice movements in the 1970s. She was senior advisor on women's issues for the Trudeau government and ran unsuccessfully for political office in the 1980s. That experience led her to refocus her energy on non-partisan politics and the fight for social justice. Initially, the COC focused on fighting against the free trade negotiations between Canada and the United States, which it considered a threat to Canadian sovereignty.

"Because of our harsh geography and our sparse population, we needed to create national institutions that linked us together, east, west and north, and therefore Canada and the United States developed very different economic systems. Our distinct economy not only has served to foster a different way of life in Canada, but has prevented us from being absorbed into the United States."

Source: Maude Barlow, speech to Empire Club of Canada, 15 November 1990.

In the eyes of the COC, a north–south trade agreement significantly weakened this historical reality. The COC also believed that, because the political system is heavily influenced by big business through their funding of political parties, such trade agreements gave too much power to foreign corporations to challenge our laws and threaten our public institutions.

 Learn more about the Council of Canadians

Figure 10.9 Maude Barlow at a 2006 protest in Charlottetown, PEI, against the privatization of medicine.

Today, Barlow continues her work as the national chair of the COC. Often called the "conscience of Canada," Barlow is co-founder of the Blue Planet Project, which works to prevent the world's water supply from being traded as a commodity for sale. She is also director of the International Forum on Globalization, a research and education institution opposed to economic globalization.

Barlow has received a number of awards for her work in promoting social justice. The author of more than 15 books, her most recent work is *Too Close for Comfort: Canada's Future within Fortress North America*, which focuses on the loss of Canadian sovereignty and the invasion of privacy amidst security measures implemented after the terrorist attacks of 11 September 2001.

Responding

1. Why would Maude Barlow be referred to as the "conscience of Canada"? Explain why you agree or disagree with this idea.

On 17 December 1992, the North American Free Trade Agreement (NAFTA) was signed by the United States, Mexico, and Canada. It was the first negotiated trade agreement between a developing country and a developed country. The agreement, which took effect on 1 January 1994, included these main conditions:

- tariff-free trade by 2008
- no quota limits on imports
- equal access to natural resources
- a provision (called Chapter 11) that allowed companies to sue the countries' governments if legislation hurt their ability to compete
- trade disputes to be handled by a NAFTA panel, although its decisions were not binding

The NAFTA Debate

As the deal removed tariffs from most goods traded between the three countries, its supporters argued that it would make Canada more attractive to global investors because they would use Canada to access the entire North American market. They also argued that NAFTA would make North America more competitive with the Asian and European trading blocs. Because of increasing globalization, Canada needed to secure trading partners as the North American trading bloc could eventually expand to include South America.

Critics of NAFTA worried that it was another step toward the complete domination of Canada by the United States. One fear was that Canadian cultural industries such as publishing and television would be threatened by American corporations' easier access to our markets. It was also feared that industries such as steel, textiles, and automobiles would be vulnerable to the cheaper labour costs in the US and especially in Mexico. This might lead to a reduction in wages for Canadian workers. Opponents also maintained that lower environmental standards in Mexico would result in similar conditions in Canada. In order to compete, Canadian businesses would lobby the Canadian government to relax environmental standards, especially given the provisions of Chapter 11. Finally, it was argued that tax-supported social programs—particularly health care—would be under attack by Canadian businesses. Because businesses funded some of these programs, they had additional costs that US and Mexican businesses did not have to assume. In order for Canada to compete on an even footing, these social programs would be halted.

The Impact of Free Trade on Canada

The effect of free trade on Canada is difficult to gauge since no one can accurately predict what might have happened to Canada's economy without the FTA and NAFTA. However, people on both sides of the debate have claimed they have been proven right. Figure 10.10 on the next page highlights some of these arguments.

"We would like to think we are about to get the best of both worlds—Canadian stability and a more caring society, along with American markets, but what if instead we get their crime rate, health programs, and gun laws, and they get our markets—or what is left of them?"

–Margaret Atwood, Canadian author and opponent of NAFTA

Learn more about the North American Free Trade Agreement

THE IMPACT OF FREE TRADE	
What Supporters Say	**What Opponents Say**
• Since NAFTA became law, the Canadian economy has grown by an average of 3.6% annually. • Canada and Mexico have increased their exports to the United States. More than half of all goods made in Canada go to the US. • Canada's exports account for over 40% of **gross domestic product**. This is higher than for any other **G8** country. • About one in four jobs in Canada is tied to international trade. • About 87% of all the goods Canada exports go to our NAFTA partners. • Close to 2.3 million jobs have been created in Canada since 1994—a 17.5% increase over pre-NAFTA employment levels.	• Between 1989 and 1993 (when the FTA was in effect), 452 major manufacturing plants closed in Ontario. Nearly half were foreign (mainly US) owned, and 65% of these closures were permanent. • A 1996 study of 500 union-organizing drives showed that 62% of employers threatened to close or move their plants rather than negotiate with a union. • Canada lost 255 000 jobs, or 12.8% of its workforce, from 1988 to 1996. This was three times the loss in the US during the same period. • Free trade really only benefits rich people. From 1989 to 2001, family incomes of the wealthiest 20% of Canadians increased by 16.5%; family incomes of the poorest 20% decreased by 7%. • The poverty rate rose between 1989 and 2001, except for Canadians over 65.

Source: International Trade Canada; Council of Canadians; Canadian Centre for Policy Alternatives.

Figure 10.10 One way to help decide which understanding of the impact of free trade is "correct" is to check the source. Was it published by a respected organization? Is it based on sound studies or on opinion? Has important information been left out or misrepresented? Another way to decide which understanding is "correct" is to do more research. Can you find other sources that support or refute the information provided here?

Challenge and Response

1. How was the Shamrock Summit an example of the change in Canadian–American relations under Mulroney's leadership?
2. Imagine you are a Canadian voter during the 1988 election campaign. Write a one-paragraph letter to the editor of your local newspaper explaining why you are for or against the FTA.
3. What do you think are the most convincing arguments for and against the FTA and NAFTA? Explain your response.

International Political Challenges

During Prime Minister Mulroney's time in office, Canada was involved in several international conflicts and disputes. This section explores Canada's changing foreign policy under Mulroney's government—from our stance against apartheid in South Africa to our involvement in the peacekeeping mission in Bosnia-Herzegovina.

Challenging Apartheid

In 1948, the ruling National Party in South Africa created a policy known as apartheid (meaning "apartness" in Afrikaans). Black and white people could not live in the same neighbourhoods, attend the same schools, or swim at the same beaches. Interracial marriages were forbidden, and only white people had the right to vote. The white population was wealthy and controlled the government. The Black population had no power and lived in poverty.

A group known as the African National Congress (ANC), formed under the leadership of Nelson Mandela, fought apartheid. In the early 1960s, Mandela was imprisoned for his efforts. As a result, South Africa became increasingly isolated in the world community during the 1960s and 1970s. The United Nations imposed an arms trade **embargo** on South Africa and the country was barred from participating in international events such as the Olympics.

Shortly after his election in 1984, Mulroney toughened Canada's anti-apartheid stance. He led the world in imposing economic **sanctions** against South Africa in an effort to change its racially based policies. Canada had been encouraging voluntary sanctions since

1978, but this new policy made it much more difficult for Canadian companies to trade with or invest in South Africa. While Mulroney's actions put him at odds with the policies of the United States and Great Britain, it won Canada respect on the international stage. By the end of the 1980s, both the US and Great Britain had finally agreed to such sanctions, and the economic pressure on South Africa increased significantly. In 1990, Mandela was released after spending 27 years in prison. In 1991, the apartheid laws were finally repealed.

The Tiananmen Square Massacre

In April 1989, a million university students held a pro-democracy demonstration in Beijing. They were protesting the abuse of human rights in China. Tiananmen Square was a highly symbolic public space where national celebrations were often held and foreign dignitaries were greeted on their arrival to China. The students occupied the square for two months before the Chinese government sent in the military in June to end the protest. Tanks and armed soldiers cleared the protestors from the square, killing at least 3000—although this number is disputed. Thousands of others were arrested. Some citizens continued to protest. The day after the massacre, a lone student stood in front of a column of tanks, refusing to move when the tanks tried to advance outside the square. The student leaders of the demonstration were publicly executed in July 1989.

In response, the Mulroney government publicly condemned the massacre and initially cancelled a number of minor trade agreements. However, the Chinese market was huge and growing. Imposing economic sanctions such as

Reading Strategy

When you read about an unfamiliar place, locate it on a map, globe, or online atlas. Then think about what you know about the region, country, or continent.

"This institutionalized contempt for justice and dignity desecrates international standards of morality and arouses universal revulsion."

–Prime Minister Brian Mulroney in an address about apartheid to the United Nations, 1985

Learn more about the African National Congress and Canada's fight against apartheid

"Indiscriminate shootings have snuffed out the precious human lives, but they can never snuff out the fundamental urge of human beings for freedom and democracy."

–Prime Minister Brian Mulroney, June 1989

Figure 10.11 A student blocks tanks on the Avenue of Eternal Peace during the Tiananmen Square uprising before being pulled away by bystanders. How would you feel if you were the student in this photograph? What do his actions say to you about the strength of his beliefs?

those imposed on South Africa would have hurt Canadian businesses. In the end, there was little change in the trade relationship between Canada and China. Many Canadians criticized the government's decision.

The Collapse of the Soviet Union

In 1985, Mikhail Gorbachev became the new leader of the Soviet Union. Two of the policies that he pursued were known as glasnost and perestroika. *Glasnost* meant "openness" and signalled a shift in which Soviet society became less secretive. *Perestroika* meant "restructuring"—a move away from the state-organized economy of communism to a free market economy like that in the West.

By the early 1990s, the republics within the Soviet Union had broken up into 15 new countries. To ensure the stability of these new governments, Canada began to adjust some of its foreign aid spending. About $100 million in aid was reallocated from developing countries to help the former communist countries. Critics argued that Canada's aid priorities now seemed to lie in regions with potentially profitable markets rather than in regions in need of humanitarian aid.

The Fall of the Berlin Wall

As the Soviet Union became more open, the countries formerly under its influence began to change as well. Most of these countries had maintained tight control over their economies and

Figure 10.12 Rejoicing Germans destroyed the Berlin Wall in November 1989. How did this symbolize the end of the Cold War?

their citizens. During the fall of 1989, all of this changed with very little warning. Citizens of these Eastern European countries were now allowed to cross the borders into neighbouring countries. In Germany, the Berlin Wall had been built in 1961 to prevent East Germans from crossing the border into West Germany. While television audiences around the world watched, the wall was torn down in dramatic fashion as citizens, some with families that had been separated for decades, climbed on top of it with sledgehammers. After more than 40 years of on-again, off-again tensions between the Soviet Union and the United States and their respective allies, the Cold War had ended.

The 1991 Gulf War

In August 1990, Iraq invaded the small, oil-rich country of Kuwait. The United Nations initially responded to this invasion by imposing economic sanctions against Iraq. Mulroney quickly offered Canada's support in the initiative by sending three ships to participate in the blockade. Iraq's leader, Saddam Hussein, refused to withdraw his troops from Kuwait. The UN then authorized the use of military force in 1991 to end the Iraqi occupation of Kuwait. This type of peacemaking action, first used by the UN in the Korean War, was different from Canada's traditional peacekeeping role. In peacemaking, assigned troops are directly involved in armed

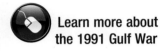

Learn more about the 1991 Gulf War

Learn more about Canada's involvement in Somalia

conflict in an attempt to bring the two sides of a dispute to the peace table.

The multinational force, called Operation Desert Storm, was led by the United States. The force included countries from around the world, including Britain, France, Australia, Saudi Arabia, and Canada. The war was unique in that it was covered almost live by the media, led by the new American 24-hour news network, CNN. Video footage of high-tech, laser-guided aerial weapons making precise hits on their intended targets made for captivating television. The war itself involved 40 days of heavy air attacks followed by only 100 hours of fighting on the ground. Canadian fighter jets were involved in offensive operations, providing air cover and attacking ground targets. The 4500 troops that served in the conflict were the first Canadians to participate in offensive war operations since the Korean War in the 1950s.

The conflict lasted about six weeks and ended with the deaths of more than 120 000 Iraqi soldiers. Casualties in the multinational force totalled approximately 200. A ceasefire was agreed to in February 1991, and Iraq was forced to withdraw from Kuwait. The UN also forced Iraq to destroy huge stockpiles of chemical and biological weapons and manufacturing facilities. These alleged weapons of mass destruction, along with the continued leadership of Saddam Hussein, became the focal point of a second war with Iraq that was fought after the attack on New York's World Trade Center on 11 September 2001.

A National Disgrace in Somalia

In 1990, the country of Somalia, in eastern Africa, was thrown into chaos when

local clans overthrew the government. A violent civil war ensued as competing clans fought for control of the country. By 1992, an estimated 30 000 citizens had been killed. Drought and famine were threatening hundreds of thousands of people.

The United Nations created a peacekeeping mission called Operation Restore Hope. Its goal was to put an end to the civil war by disarming warring groups and providing relief and humanitarian aid to Somalis. As a part of this operation, 900 Canadian soldiers arrived in April 1992 to join an effort involving 20 countries and 30 000 troops. However, the international community was responding to the war without a specific invitation. Because there was fighting between so many different clans, there was no one group that the UN mission represented. Consequently, there was no stable, local organizing force around which it could build support. Ultimately, the mission ended in failure in 1995, although it did manage to alleviate the famine.

For Canada, the Somalia peacekeeping operation will forever be associated with an event that tarnished the image of Canadian peacekeepers. The Canadian Airborne Regiment was disbanded after videos showed questionable initiation practices and evidence of racism. This involved Canadian soldiers killing a number of Somalis under uncertain circumstances, including a 16-year-old Somali boy named Shidane Arone. Captured trying to steal supplies from the Canadian base, Shidane was tied up, beaten, burned, and tortured to death while in custody. One Canadian soldier was convicted and sentenced to imprisonment for his involvement in what became known as the Somalia Affair.

Genocide in Yugoslavia

In 1992, Canada also became involved in the first United Nations-organized, NATO-led peacekeeping operation. With the end of the Cold War, the North Atlantic Treaty Organization (NATO) worked to ensure that countries undergoing the transition from communism could do so in a stable manner. In this way, NATO could protect the interests of its member countries.

The country of Yugoslavia had been created at the end of the First World War from a collection of diverse territories with different languages, religions, and ethnicities. With the fall of communism and the former communist bloc countries asserting their independence, many of the nationalist groups within Yugoslavia wanted to become independent. Croatia, Slovenia, and Bosnia all declared independence within a relatively short period of time. As a result, civil war broke out in 1991. Fighting became centralized in Bosnia-Herzegovina—a state made up of a number of different ethnic groups. Serbian forces committed **genocide** in an attempt to eliminate all Bosnians and Croats from communities they considered Serbian. The mass murders and mass migrations that followed created an international crisis. An estimated 200 000 civilians were believed to have been murdered, while two million refugees were displaced.

At the request of the UN, NATO launched an operation, which included 16 000 Canadian peacekeepers, to monitor a ceasefire and protect civilians in six "safe-haven" towns. This initial effort ultimately failed as Bosnian Serbs attacked both the safe-haven towns and the peacekeepers. NATO forces responded by launching air strikes against Serbian positions. This led to Serbian forces capturing peacekeepers and using them as human shields by chaining them to NATO targets. The conflict escalated until, finally overwhelmed by NATO forces, Serbia signed a peace agreement in 1995. In 2008, the United Nations was still conducting war crimes trials at the International Criminal Tribunal for the former Yugoslavia (ICTY) in The Hague in the Netherlands.

Challenge and Response

1. Compare Prime Minister Mulroney's response to apartheid with his response to the Tiananmen Square massacre. How would you account for the differences?

2. How did the end of the Cold War change Canada's foreign policy? Do you agree with the criticism of those changes? Explain.

3. How can Canadian involvement in Bosnia-Herzegovina be linked to events that started the First World War and to the outcome of the Second World War?

4. Canada was involved in three major military operations during Mulroney's government. Describe how each operation demonstrated changing perceptions of Canada's military and called into question its reputation as a peacekeeping country.

MAP STUDY: The New States of the Former Yugoslavia

Source: Don Quinlan, et al., *Twentieth Century Viewpoints*, 2nd edition, (Don Mills: Oxford University Press, 2003), 229.

Figure 10.13 Eight new states were formed out of the former Yugoslavia. This map shows the ethnic breakdown in each state prior to the 1991 civil war. About 50% of Yugoslavs were Eastern Orthodox Catholic; 30% (for the most part Croats and Slovenes) were Roman Catholic; and 9% were Muslims, living mainly in Bosnia-Herzegovina.

When the communist regime collapsed in Yugoslavia, the various ethnic and religious groups soon sought independence. Competition for territory led to a civil war and genocides. UN troops and later NATO forces stepped into this volatile situation to protect civilians and try to restore order. It was a long and difficult mission.

Analysis and Response

1. Which state does not have a majority ethnic population?
2. Which state is the most ethnically diverse?
3. Why might Kosovo want to join with Albania?
4. Why might it have been very difficult for UN- or NATO-led forces to bring peace and security to this region?
5. Do you think that trying to bring order to divided, war-torn nations is the job of the Canadian military? Explain.

A New Direction for Canada's Economy

At the beginning of his term of office, Prime Minister Mulroney described the four challenges that faced Canada's economy:

- "restore fiscal responsibility" in the government by tackling the debt
- "redefine the role of government itself" and diminish its active involvement in the economy by privatizing Crown corporations and reducing regulations regarding free-market and entrepreneurial activity
- "adopt policies that foster higher investment, greater innovation, and increased international competitiveness"
- convince Canadians that "the changes we are proposing are fundamental to the economic, social, and political structures of our society"

A large part of meeting these challenges was the introduction of the Free Trade Agreement. However, as you will see in this section, there were other important actions that the government took in pursuing a new economic direction for Canada.

The Federal Debt

As you learned in Chapter 8, the public debt grew significantly over the 1970s and early 1980s because the government spent more money on programs than it took in from tax revenues. When this occurs in a particular year, the result is a deficit budget. When all of the yearly deficits are added together, this is known as the public debt.

By 1984, the government owed almost $165 billion to its creditors (the people and institutions that lent it money). The government had to pay interest to these creditors in order to finance the debt. Because of high interest rates in the early 1980s, the government was using almost one out of every three dollars earned in tax revenue to make interest payments on its loans. This amount was larger than the combined federal spending on health care, pensions, social assistance, and family allowances.

Mulroney had campaigned on a promise to get this deficit spending under control. After his election as prime minister, he argued that, because of the size of the debt, Canada could no longer afford to pay well-off Canadians pensions or family allowances. These universal programs were available to all Canadians regardless of their income. The Mulroney government started to cut back some of these benefits. In 1992, family allowance benefits were replaced with a supplement for low-income families. Many Canadians were unhappy with funding cuts to families, pensioners, and unemployed workers, especially at a time of high unemployment.

Tackling the Debt

One way that the Mulroney government attacked the deficit problem was by eliminating indexing—a method used to ensure that government program payments and taxation rise at the same rate as the general level of prices. For example, if a week's worth of groceries costs $100 one year, and increases to $103 the next year, then the price of groceries has increased by 3 per cent. This is also known as inflation. Statistics Canada uses the Consumer Price Index (CPI) to track inflation by measuring the change in prices of consumer goods. If your income is indexed according to the CPI, then your income will rise

"In 1967, when our country celebrated its 100th birthday, our national debt represented $4000 for every Canadian family. Seventeen years later, the national debt represents $24 000 per family. And by 1990—only five years hence—if we do not take action now, the national debt will be the equivalent of every Canadian family owing $54 000."

–Prime Minister Brian Mulroney, speech to the Economic Club of New York, 1984

> "You made promises that you wouldn't touch anything ... you lied to us. I was made to vote for you and then it's 'Goodbye Charlie Brown.'"
>
> –Solange Denis, old age pensioner, confronting Mulroney over OAS payments, 1985

Figure 10.14 Solange Denis and other senior citizens protested on Parliament Hill in 1985. In your opinion, should universal programs be available to all Canadians regardless of income level? Explain.

and you will be able to afford the higher cost of groceries.

Seniors were outraged when the Mulroney government announced that Old Age Security (OAS) payments would no longer be indexed. They descended on Parliament Hill to protest the plan. While the government eventually backed down on its proposal for OAS, it did de-index tax brackets for Canadian taxpayers. This meant that tax revenues increased at a faster rate than inflation as Canadian incomes increased.

In the end, the Mulroney government did little to alleviate the debt problem in Canada. When the Conservatives took over, the deficit was $45 billion. By 1989, it had decreased to $28 billion, but by 1993 it was back up to $42 billion. During the Conservatives' time in power, the debt rose from $128 billion to $471 billion.

The Goods and Services Tax

A manufacturer sales tax of 13.5 per cent had existed in Canada since 1924. Many people believed that it was problematic for a number of reasons. For example, it was an "indirect" tax applied to many goods by manufacturers long before the point of sale. As a result, it was incorporated in the price of goods, and many consumers did not even know they were paying it. Another problem was that it was applied to some goods, but not to others, and it was not applied to any services.

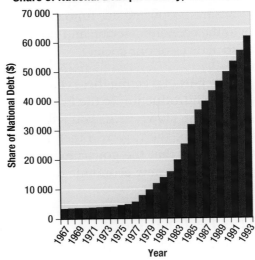

Share of National Debt per Family, 1967–1993

Source: Statistics Canada CANSIM database
http://cansim2.statcan.ca, 385-0010.

Figure 10.15 By 1993, how much was the national debt per Canadian family? By how much did the national debt per family increase between 1967 and 1993? By how much did it increase during Mulroney's term in office? What conclusions can you draw from this information?

ISSUES

The Loonie

The issue: Why was the introduction of the loonie in 1987 controversial?

In 1987, the face of Canadian money changed forever when Canadians were introduced to the loonie. The heavy use of one-dollar bills meant that each one lasted only nine to twelve months before it had to be replaced. It was decided that a coin, which could last 20 years or more, would replace the paper bills. This would save the government over $200 million in replacement costs over the next 20 years.

The coin was to be gold in colour, have 11 sides, and depict an image of voyageurs paddling a canoe. These were the famous French-Canadian fur traders who explored what is now Canada. After the master dies for stamping the design on the coins were created, they were shipped from Ottawa to the manufacturing facility at the Winnipeg Mint. However, they were lost in transit, and a new image for the coin had to be created. An image of a loon was chosen, forever changing how Canadians referred to their money.

On 30 June 1987, $80 million worth of coins were released to Canadians. In order to encourage the use of the loonie, the Bank of Canada immediately stopped printing one-dollar bills and began withdrawing them from circulation in 1989. Some people were outraged that they had to carry a heavy coin instead of paper money. Others praised the idea, especially transit operators and vending machine companies—the coin made it easier for customers to use their products.

"Look at all these ones [one-dollar bills]. It's 150 of these [dollar coins] that I have to carry to the bank … It is truly the worst thing the government has come up with. I hate it."

Source: Michael Borse, hotel manager, "'Toonie' makes its debut." CBC Archives, 1995.

"We're hoping for at least a 15 per cent increase in sales."

Source: Vern Lawrence, vending machine operator, "'Toonie' makes its debut." CBC Archives, 1995.

"To me, dollar bills were getting to be too cumbersome. I was having too many of them all at once … I think the coins are good."

Source: Canadian citizen interviewed on CBC's *The National*, 1987.

"Thank you, Loonie … for wearing out innumerable trouser pockets, causing me to jingle like Santa wherever I go, making me look dorky with bulging pants … Thank you, too, on behalf of my buddy who hauls money for an armoured security company, and who routinely takes out his back by hefting heavy sacks of Loonies."

Source: Henry Allen, quoted in Tavia Grant, "Happy birthday, loonie." Reportonbusiness (*Globe and Mail*) bulletin board, 2007.

"Over the years, the one-dollar coin has become a true Canadian symbol."

Source: Ian Bennett, president and CEO of the Royal Canadian Mint, quoted in Tavia Grant, "Happy birthday, loonie." Reportonbusiness (*Globe and Mail*) bulletin board, 2007.

 Learn more about the introduction of the loonie

Responding

1. In your opinion, was the introduction of the loonie necessary? Provide reasons for your response.

2. In recent years, there have been suggestions for further changes to Canada's currency. Some have proposed a five-dollar coin. Others have argued that the penny should be withdrawn from circulation. Would you support either of these changes? As a class, brainstorm arguments for and against each proposal.

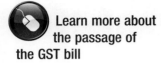

Learn more about the passage of the GST bill

The Mulroney government set out to resolve this confusion by introducing a tax that applied to almost all goods and services—like many other countries were doing. The goods and services tax, more commonly known as the GST, was to be applied at a rate of 7 per cent at the point of purchase. This meant that consumers would be aware that the tax was being collected, making the government more accountable to its citizens for this kind of taxation. Manufacturers welcomed the tax—it made them more competitive internationally because it applied only to goods sold in Canada (including imports). This meant that they were able to sell their goods outside of Canada at a more competitive price.

Reaction to the GST

News of the tax was met with widespread dislike from the public. This uproar led to difficulties for Mulroney in getting the bill passed by the Senate.

The vast majority of senators were Liberal. Six years of Conservative government had still not addressed the imbalance. After the Senate refused to pass the GST bill, Mulroney used a controversial constitutional power to get it passed. He asked the Queen to appoint eight extra senators, which gave the Progressive Conservatives a majority in the Senate and ensured a favourable vote on the GST. The bill was finally passed, and the GST came into effect on 1 January 1991.

The introduction of the GST had a significant impact on the Conservative Party. The change in tax was supposed to be "revenue neutral." In other words, because the new tax was now 7 per cent on most goods and services instead of 13.5 per cent on some goods, it was supposed to provide the government with the same tax revenue and consumers with lower prices. It seemed to consumers, however, that they were paying more in taxes and that prices were not declining as promised. Many analysts say that the introduction of the GST was one of the main reasons for the Conservatives' major loss in the next federal election.

The Collapse of the Cod Fishery

By the early 1990s, a major environmental and economic disaster was looming in Newfoundland. Ever since 1497, when European explorer John Cabot reported on "the schools of cod in the waters off Newfoundland that were so thick that they slowed the ship," cod fishing had been the foundation of Newfoundland's economy.

In 1992, Newfoundland native John Crosbie, the minister of Fisheries in the Mulroney Cabinet, announced a two-year temporary closing of the northern cod fishery. The cod had virtually

Figure 10.16 One of the most popular cod-fishing methods was dragnet fishing. A basket-like net is dragged across the floor of the ocean, scooping up all the fish and anything else in its path. Some have compared this method to strip mining or clear-cutting in forestry—the resource is taken but with extensive damage to the surrounding environment. To what extent could the cod fishery have been managed effectively without destroying Newfoundland's economy?

disappeared, and it was hoped that this closing would allow the fish stocks to recover. Some people suggested that changes in water temperature had led to a shortage of food for the cod. Others suggested that the increasing seal population was eating much of the cod stocks. While these factors might have played a role, there is little doubt that the main factor was overfishing by both foreign and Canadian vessels.

Economists maintained that the cod fishery situation was another example of the tragedy of the commons. This theory holds that when a resource such as water, fish, or air is seen as "common property" because everyone is free to use it, people use as much of the resource as they can for their own personal gain. However, they take little care of the resource because they do not own it. The current issue of global climate change arises from similar concerns. For this reason, many people believe that effective government management of the "commons" is very important. Similarly, when the cod fishery was shut down, the Mulroney govern-

ment faced a great deal criticism for not managing this resource.

When it became clear that the fishery was not going to recover in the short term, the temporary closing was made indefinite in 1993. It was expanded in 1994 to include recreational fishing. This meant that fishers thrown out of work by the closing could not even fish to feed their own families.

The **moratorium** on cod fishing was devastating to the Newfoundland economy. Of course, not everyone in Newfoundland was a fisher, but most had jobs that relied on the fishing industry. There was a direct loss of 40 000 jobs, but the impact on associated jobs went well beyond this—for example, jobs in fish-canning factories, fishing equipment stores, and businesses that served these workers. The federal government provided a $5-billion aid package for those affected. The government of Newfoundland worked to rebuild the economy by diversifying in areas such as tourism, oil and gas development, and the film industry.

 Learn more about the cod fishery

Challenge and Response

1. According to Prime Minister Mulroney, what were the four economic challenges that his government faced?
2. Choose 10 keywords that you would use to summarize the issue of the federal debt during Mulroney's time in office. Beside each keyword, write one sentence to explain its relevance.
3. In your opinion, is the GST a fairer approach to taxation than the manufacturer sales tax that existed before 1 January 1991? Why or why not?
4. What do you think were some other industries that were affected by the moratorium on cod fishing?

Reading Strategy

As you read, make connections to other sections of the chapter or text. For example, what connections can you make between social change in the 1980s and social change in other eras such as the 1920s?

"Without immigration, Canada would not be the culturally rich, prosperous, and progressive nation that it is today ... One could now ask, if immigration had ceased in Canada, what would our population look like today?"

–Cheryl Johnston, Huron Heights Secondary School, 2003

"I will make specific commitments on behalf of the federal government. I look for specific commitments from the provincial and territorial governments and from the representatives of the Aboriginal peoples ... The key to change is self-government for Aboriginal peoples within the Canadian federation."

–Prime Minister Brian Mulroney, First Ministers Conference on Aboriginal Rights, 1985

Social Change in Canada

Many of the social issues of the Trudeau era continued to draw attention during the Mulroney era. These issues included immigration, Aboriginal **self-government**, environmental concerns, violence in Canadian society, and Canadian sovereignty.

Immigration

After the Immigration Act was amended in 1978, a new wave of immigrants came to Canada in the 1980s and 1990s. The majority were from countries such as Jamaica, Vietnam, India, Pakistan, China, Hong Kong, and South Korea. The makeup of Canada was changing—by the 1990s, Canada had become one of the most culturally diverse countries in the world.

The Conservative government decided to pursue an immigration policy that focused on immigrants who would contribute to the growth of the economy. The Business Immigration Program (BIP) allowed people to immigrate to Canada if they were willing to make a business investment of $150 000 to $500 000, depending on where they were settling in Canada. The government believed that this business investment would contribute to the gross domestic product and provide jobs for Canadians. In 1983, business investment from immigrants totalled $821 million. By the end of 1986, it had grown to $1.656 billion. From 1986 to 1990, it is estimated that business investment through the BIP created 82 000 new jobs in Canada. During the Mulroney years, immigration increased from 54 000 people per year to 250 000 per year by the end of 1993.

However, no clear link between business immigration and job creation was ever established. In fact, many people believed that the majority of the jobs created tended to be low skilled and therefore not great contributors to economic growth.

A second criticism of the BIP was that Canada was selling citizenship as a commodity. Although the program was a good way to attract investment from foreign sources when the economy was not doing well, selling Canadian citizenship to immigrants drained resources from other countries. Opponents argued that, because only wealthy people would be able to take advantage of the program, it encouraged a growing gap between developed and developing nations.

Aboriginal Rights

In 1985 Brian Mulroney hosted a First Ministers Conference on Aboriginal Rights. At that meeting, Mulroney called on participants to take Aboriginal concerns seriously. He also indicated a willingness to consider forms of Aboriginal self-government, referring to the fact that Canadians already had forms of self-government through locally elected school boards and municipal councils.

Little progress was made until the early 1990s when the issue of Aboriginal land claims arose once again in one of the most famous standoffs in Canadian history. In 1988, Georges Erasmus, then National Chief of the Assembly of First Nations, had warned Canadians about the potential for violence surrounding the issue of unsettled Aboriginal land claims. It was an eerie prediction of an event that was about to unfold in southern Québec.

Indo-Canadians

Indo-Canadians are one of the largest and fastest-growing cultural communities in Canada. They trace their heritage back to India but their cultural backgrounds are diverse. Indo-Canadians include groups such as Hindus, Muslims, and Sikhs. They speak a variety of languages including Gujarati, Hindi, Punjabi, Tamil, and Urdu. Some Indo-Canadians are immigrants or descendants of immigrants from communities established during British colonial times, including those in East Africa, South Africa, the Middle East, the Caribbean, and Guyana.

Indo-Canadians first arrived during the early part of the twentieth century. The first to arrive were Sikhs who had heard descriptions of Canada from troops returning from service abroad. Shortly after their arrival in British Columbia, Sikhs began to face the same type of discrimination experienced by other Asian peoples in the province. In 1907, the BC legislature took away their right to vote and work in the public service. This right was not returned to Indo-Canadians until 1947. During the *Komagata Maru* incident in

Figure 10.17 This street is in Little India in Toronto. How might a Canadian-born person of Indian descent view Little India? How might a person of another heritage view it? What does the concept of Little India mean to you?

1914, 376 prospective immigrants, mostly Sikh, were denied entry into Canada and confined to their ship for two months before being returned to India.

Despite these initial hardships, the Indo-Canadian community has grown to 713 000 according to the 2001 census and is growing at a rate of 25 000 per year. More than half of the Indo-Canadian population lives in the Greater Toronto Area. Almost 150 000 live in the area surrounding Vancouver. Both of these cities have vibrant Little Indias. Gerrard Street in the east end of Toronto features many restaurants, grocers, clothing stores, and video stores that cater to the various Indo-Canadian communities. The Punjabi Market on Main Street is the centre of cultural and economic activity for Indo-Canadians in the Vancouver area.

Indo-Canadians have made significant contributions to Canadian society in a variety of areas. In the arts, writer Rohinton Mistry and film director Deepa Mehta have both received international acclaim for their work. Ian Hanomansing and Haroon Siddiqui are highly accomplished journalists. In politics, Herb Dhaliwal was the first Indo-Canadian to become a federal Cabinet minister. Ujjal Dosanjh became Canada's first Indo-Canadian premier when he took office in British Columbia in 2000.

"Twenty, thirty years ago, there was a huge pressure to conform to mainstream, white-Canadian lifestyle, to assimilate. As numbers have grown and associations have grown, as [a new] generation is really coming into its own educationally, in terms of occupations and so forth, there is a much greater comfort level in embracing South Asian identity and even religious identity."

Source: Arti Dhand, professor of South Asian Studies, University of Toronto, in Katie Rook, "Party puts the spotlight on Desi culture." *National Post*, 25 October 2006.

One significant concern facing Indo-Canadians is the issue of underemployment—an issue that also challenges other diverse groups. Many people who immigrate to Canada are educated in their countries of origin as nurses, doctors, teachers, engineers, and electricians. However, their credentials are not recognized in Canada, so they must resort to working in low-wage jobs. While the federal and provincial governments have started to address this issue, many Indo-Canadians have undertaken entrepreneurial work running their own businesses.

Responding

1. Do you think most Canadians are aware of the diversity of cultural backgrounds among Indo-Canadians? Explain your response.
2. Write a diary entry in the role of someone who is underemployed—for example, suppose you are trained as a doctor but are forced to take a job at a fast-food restaurant.

The Oka Crisis

Oka is a small town west of Montréal. In April 1989, the town of Oka announced that a local golf course would be expanded from nine to eighteen holes. The expansion of the golf course would use land that was under disputed ownership. The Kanien'kehá:ka (Six Nations Mohawk) believed that the land was a sacred burial ground. Over 200 Kanien'kehá:ka residents of the adjacent reserve of Kanesatake protested the expansion. When further attempts through the court system failed to prevent the planned development, the Kanien'kehá:ka set up a blockade in March 1990 to prevent workers from starting construction. These activists were soon joined by a more militant group known as the "Mohawk Warriors," who saw an opportunity to bring attention to the overall issue of Aboriginal rights. On July 11, 100 police officers stormed the barricade in a failed attempt to end the standoff. In the resulting exchange of gunfire, a police officer was killed.

The Kanien'kehá:ka in Kahnawake, a reserve 30 kilometres south of Oka, supported the Kanien'kehá:ka in Kanesatake by blockading highways that went through their reserve. They also blocked the Mercier Bridge, a major commuter route into Montréal. Commuters who were affected by this blockade became increasingly confrontational, throwing rocks and burning effigies of the Kanien'kehá:ka.

On August 14, 2500 Canadian soldiers were brought in to support the police in ending the standoff. After negotiations with the Kanien'kehá:ka in Kahnawake, the barricade at the Mercier Bridge was removed on August 29. A month later, the Kanien'kehá:ka in Kanesatake decided to remove their barricade as well. The federal government agreed to purchase the disputed land and turn it over to the Kanien'kehá:ka.

Largely in response to the Oka crisis, the Mulroney government established a Royal Commission on Aboriginal Peoples in 1990. The Commission's report recommended that the government spend more than $30 billion in compensation packages and self-government initiatives. Self-government meant that Aboriginal peoples would have control over matters such as education, resource development, social services, justice, and health care.

> "We want to let you know that you are dealing with fire. We say, Canada, deal with us today because our militant leaders are already born. We cannot promise that you are going to like the kind of violent political action we can just about guarantee the next generation is going to bring to our reserves."
>
> –Georges Erasmus, Assembly of First Nations, 1988

 Learn more about the Oka crisis

Figure 10.18 A Kanien'kehá:ka warrior and a Canadian soldier stand face to face during the confrontation in Oka in 1990. The picture came to symbolize the frustration felt during the crisis and the determination of both sides during the standoff. In your opinion, did the Kanien'kehá:ka have any other options besides erecting blockades? Provide sound reasons for your answer.

MAP STUDY: The Oka Crisis

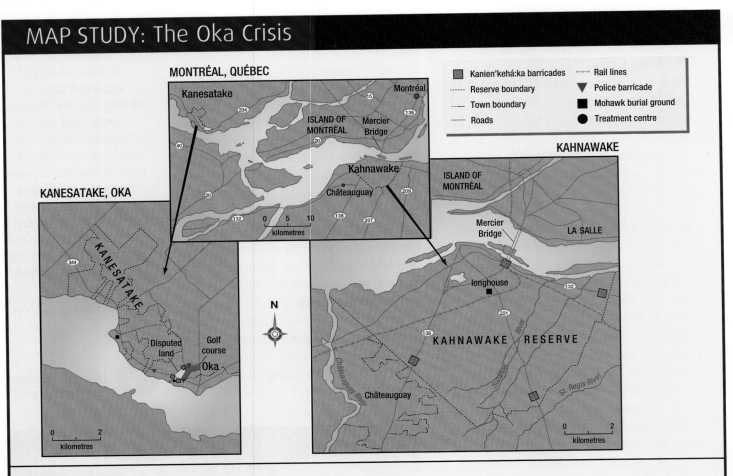

Source: ArtPlus Ltd.

Figure 10.19 When the Kanien'kehá:ka in Kahnawake barricaded the Mercier Bridge, thousand of residents in the nearby community of Châteauguay were affected. The blockade lasted more than a month.

The erection of barricades on highways through Kahnawake and on the Mercier Bridge led to increasing violence between commuters and the Kanien'kehá:ka. As a result, Québec premier Robert Bourassa asked the Canadian army to help the Sûreté du Québec (the provincial police) maintain control in the area around the barricades. When the Kanien'kehá:ka in Kahnawake removed the barricade at the Mercier Bridge, this was a significant setback for the Kanien'kehá:ka in Oka because their barricade on the disputed land had little impact on the general public.

Analysis and Response

1. What impact would the blocking of the Mercier Bridge have on the residents of Châteauguay?

2. As the dispute dragged on, tension increased among people living on the south shore of the St. Lawrence River, many of whom worked in Montréal. Why do you think this was so?

3. Why do you think that support from the Kanien'kehá:ka in Kahnawake was so important for the Kanien'kehá:ka in Kanesatake?

4. Is your own community near a First Nations reserve? How might it be affected should a similar event occur on the reserve?

Air India Flight 182

In the mid-1980s, violence erupted in India as Sikh extremists called for an independent state in India. A base of operations was the Golden Temple in Amritsar. In June 1984, Indian troops stormed the temple in an operation that left 1200 dead. Indian Prime Minister Indira Gandhi was assassinated later that same year.

On 23 June 1985, Air India Flight 182 was travelling from Vancouver to New Delhi with 329 people, including 280 Canadians. As it approached the coast of Ireland, a bomb exploded, sending the plane into the Atlantic Ocean below and killing everyone on board. Just an hour before, another bomb had exploded while baggage from a Canadian Airlines jet originating in Vancouver was being loaded onto another Air India jet at Narita Airport in Japan, killing two workers. The plane was supposed to have been in the air at the time, but the flight had been delayed. Sikh extremists had previously stated that they would make India pay for the raid on the Golden Temple. Now it seemed that they had followed through with their threat.

The Mulroney government was criticized for not responding more quickly and forcefully to the attack. There were accusations that the Canadian Security Intelligence Service (CSIS) and the RCMP were uncooperative and that many aspects of the investigation were mishandled. There were even accusations that the RCMP had been warned of the attack ahead of time, but failed to take action to prevent it and was now trying to cover it up.

In 1988, Inderjit Singh Reyat was arrested for his role in creating the bomb that went off in Japan. He was found guilty and was sentenced to 10 years in prison. In 2000—15 years after the Air India bombing—two suspects were arrested in that case. A two-year trial began in 2003, at a cost of $130 million—the most expensive trial in Canadian history. However, when the suspects were found not guilty, the outraged families of the victims demanded a public inquiry. In 2006, Prime Minister Stephen Harper appointed a Commission of Inquiry into the Air India investigation. The hearings revealed there had been advanced knowledge of potential threats against Air India and that airport security had been lax.

The Polar Sea and Exxon Valdez

In 1969, the *SS Manhattan* navigated through the Northwest Passage, igniting a debate between Canada and the United States over whether the Passage was considered international waters. This debate was reignited in 1985 when the US government sent the icebreaker *Polar Sea* through that same waterway. The US did not ask Canada's permission to use the Passage, although it did notify Canada that it intended to take the route. Mulroney declared that the Passage belonged to Canada "lock, stock, and barrel" and that the United States should request permission to use it.

As a result of this incident, Mulroney announced plans to build a $500-million icebreaker to patrol the Passage and to purchase a fleet of submarines in order to enforce Canada's sovereignty in the Arctic. However, the high costs of these plans, combined with the government's focus on tackling the debt, killed both schemes. In 1988, the United States and Canada signed the Arctic Co-operation Agreement.

"This was not an aviation accident. This was murder, and murder in any justice system requires just that— justice. If this doesn't require a public inquiry, I don't know what does."

–Susheel Gupta, CTV, 17 March 2005

Learn more about the Air India investigation

Jayashree Thampi: Spokesperson for Air India Victims' Families

In 1985, Jayashree Lakshman lost her husband and seven-year-old daughter, Preethi, in the 1985 bombing of Air India Flight 182. In the years following the tragedy, she struggled to put her life back together. In 1988, Lakshman married Venu Thampi, who had lost his wife on Flight 182 and was raising his six-year-old daughter, Nisha, on his own. In 1989 their son, Vivek, was born. For 20 years, Jayashree and Venu Thampi quietly shared their grief while attempting to rebuild their lives.

The attacks on New York's World Trade Center on 11 September 2001 and the outcome of the trial of the two men accused of the Air India bombing changed Jayashree Thampi's way of thinking. She felt that, even though 280 of the 329 victims were Canadian citizens, Canadians did not see the bombing as an act of terrorism.

In observing the Canadian response to the World Trade Center attacks against the United States, Thampi's daughter, Nisha, stated, "It was amazingly fast, the response to an act of terrorism, and the media was saying this was the first act of terrorism in North America. It was like they completely discredited the Air India disaster as an act of terrorism."

In 2005, Jayashree Thampi began working toward the construction of a memorial in Toronto, where most of the Canadian victims had resided. As head of the Air India Victims' Families Association Memorial Committee, she led a project that saw the federal and provincial governments contribute a total of $625 000 to the memorial. The City of Toronto was also approached and donated land in Humber Bay Park East on the shores of Lake Ontario.

The memorial features a sundial, modelled after the one on the Air India Memorial on the coastline of Ireland, where Flight 182 went down. Its base is made from stones obtained from all the provinces and territories of Canada as well as from the countries of the rest of the victims. There is also a wall of black granite on which the names of the victims are inscribed.

> "This memorial acknowledges the bombing of Air India as one of Canada's greatest tragedies ... Above all, this memorial marks a path to eternal life for each one of our loved ones lost. Through our remembrance, on this waterfront, their lives live on forever."
>
> –Jayashree Thampi, "Air India memorial unveiled in Toronto." Public Safety Canada, June 2007.

Figure 10.20 Prime Minister Harper and Jayashree Thampi laid a wreath at the dedication of the Air India memorial on Toronto's waterfront on 23 June 2007, the 22nd anniversary of the bombing.

Responding

1. Why do you think Canada was slow to recognize the Air India bombing as a Canadian tragedy?
2. What do you think other Canadians could learn from the example set by Jayashree Thampi?

state. The spill affected birds, salmon, sea otters, seals and other aquatic life in the area, many of which have yet to recover.

The Montréal Massacre

On 6 December 1989, Marc Lépine entered a classroom at École Polytechnique in Montréal and ordered the women to move to one corner of the classroom. Shouting, "You are all a bunch of feminists, and I hate feminists!" he proceeded to gun down the women. He then wandered the school corridors shooting any woman he encountered before he committed suicide. By the end of the day, 14 female students had been killed and another 13 had been injured in what was the worst mass murder in Canadian history. Prime Minister Mulroney called the incident "a human tragedy of enormous proportions." He ordered the flag on Parliament Hill to be lowered to half-mast.

Evidence collected after the event indicated that Lépine had been raised by a father who demonstrated a lack of respect toward women, including the abuse of his wife. Lépine himself had experienced various failures in life, for which he blamed women—including for being refused admittance to the engineering program at École Polytechnique.

This event was a turning point for Canadians and their awareness of attitudes toward women and violence. Some students affected by the shooting helped to form the Coalition for Gun Control, which successfully fought for an overhaul of Canada's gun laws. Laws passed in 1991 and 1995 obliged purchasers of guns to notify current and former spouses and to wait 28 days before they could complete a purchase.

"Those lost lives were our future ... young minds who wanted to contribute to Canada ... We will never know what gifts of joy or of laughter were extinguished by this act of horror."

–Audrey McLaughlin, leader of the NDP, 1989

Learn more about the Montréal massacre and the Coalition for Gun Control

Figure 10.21 Workers clean the oil off a cormorant caught in the *Exxon Valdez* oil spill.

It established that the US would ask Canada's permission before attempting future voyages. It also stated that the US did not agree that the Passage belonged to Canada. (You will learn more about the issue of Arctic sovereignty in Chapter 12.)

One reason Canada was concerned about international use of the Passage was the potential damage to the fragile Arctic environment should an accident occur, especially if the Passage was used to transport oil. As it happened, on 23 March 1989 the oil tanker *Exxon Valdez* was carrying 200 million litres of oil from Alaska to California. It ran aground and spilled 40 million litres of oil into Prince William Sound off the coast of Alaska.

It was the biggest environmental disaster in American history. Almost $3 billion was spent trying to return Prince William Sound to its previous

Semi-automatic weapons and large-capacity magazines for guns were banned. A centralized gun owner database was also created.

In 1991, December 6 was officially declared to be the National Day of Remembrance and Action on Violence Against Women. During this annual observance in honour of the 14 women at École Polytechnique, Canadians are asked to reflect on violence against women in our society.

Figure 10.22 A memorial service is held each year on December 6 for the 14 women who were killed at École Polytechnique. Do you think Canadian society has become more or less violent in the years since the Montréal massacre? Give reasons for your response.

Challenge and Response

1. a) What significant change did the Mulroney government make to immigration in Canada under the Business Immigration Program?
   b) Do you think the argument that the BIP made citizenship a commodity was fair? Explain.
2. Why do you think the Kanien'kehá:ka felt that they had to resort to erecting barricades? Support for these kinds of tactics is divided even in First Nations communities. Imagine that you are involved in making the decision. Create a PMI chart to show the various aspects of erecting barricades.
3. In your opinion, was the government's response to the bombing of Air India Flight 182 satisfactory? Explain your response.
4. How did the *Exxon Valdez* highlight Canada's concerns about the use of the Northwest Passage?
5. To what extent was the Montréal massacre a turning point in Canadians' awareness of and response to violence against women?

Skill Path:
Making Effective Oral Presentations

To prepare an oral presentation, you need to follow many of the same steps required in preparing an essay: conduct research, use primary and secondary sources, and create an outline to organize your material. Unlike an essay, an oral presentation allows you to use the dramatic elements of your voice and your visuals. Make use of these elements to get the most out of your presentation.

STEP 1: Prepare Your Presentation
- Determine the purpose of your presentation and the intended audience.
- Include relevant and interesting visuals.
- Create overheads or slides displaying primary-source quotations and images.
- Learn the material before your presentation. Rehearse it several times to see if it meets the time limit given by your teacher.
- Practise the pronunciation of unfamiliar names and words so that you will be less likely to stumble over words during your presentation.

STEP 2: Make Your Presentation
- Introduce your topic. Consider using an over-head or a slide to outline what you are going to talk about.
- Explain the purpose of your presentation. Tell the audience what they can expect to learn from it.
- Do not read your material to the audience, except for quotations if necessary.
- Display primary-source quotations and images.
- Speak clearly—neither too quickly nor too slowly.
- Make regular, direct eye contact with the audience to keep members engaged.

- Ensure that the transitions between different parts of your presentation are clear.
- Try to include the audience in your presentation. Questions are one way to encourage participation.
- Ensure that your conclusion is clear and strong.
- After your presentation, ask the audience for comments and/or questions.

STEP 3: Practise Your Skill
Working on your own or in a small group, prepare a presentation on one of the following topics:
- international events that affected Canada during the Mulroney years
- Mulroney's attempts to deal with Québec's concerns
- economic issues during the Mulroney era
- social issues in Canada during the 1980s

Prepare 10 to 20 slides to use in your presentation:
- an introductory slide that outlines the main sections of your presentation
- several visuals that capture significant events or people
- quotations that make important statements about the events
- several slides that develop the key points in each subsection of your presentation
- concluding slides that summarize the facts you have presented
- a slide that provides a question that encourages the audience to reflect further on the topic

Refer to "Making the Best Use of Presentation Software" on the next page.

Making the Best Use of Presentation Software

Presentation software such as Microsoft Power Point, Corel Presentations, and Apple Keynote is a useful tool that can help you make visually powerful presentations. Unfortunately, the technology is not always used to its full advantage. But, sometimes people overuse software capabilities—such as inserting unnecessary bullets, creating too many motion-driven displays, and including distracting sound effects and backdrops—that they weaken the content of the presentation. When using presentation software, keep these tips in mind:

- Do not overcrowd the slides. Use large fonts and no more than 50 to 60 words per slide.
- Structure the slides in logical order. Use the structure of your presentation outline to guide you.
- Use strong visuals such as maps, photographs, and film or video clips. Presentation software enhances the visual potential of a presentation, so take advantage of it.
- Use the motion functions of the software to strengthen the structure and sequence of your presentation.

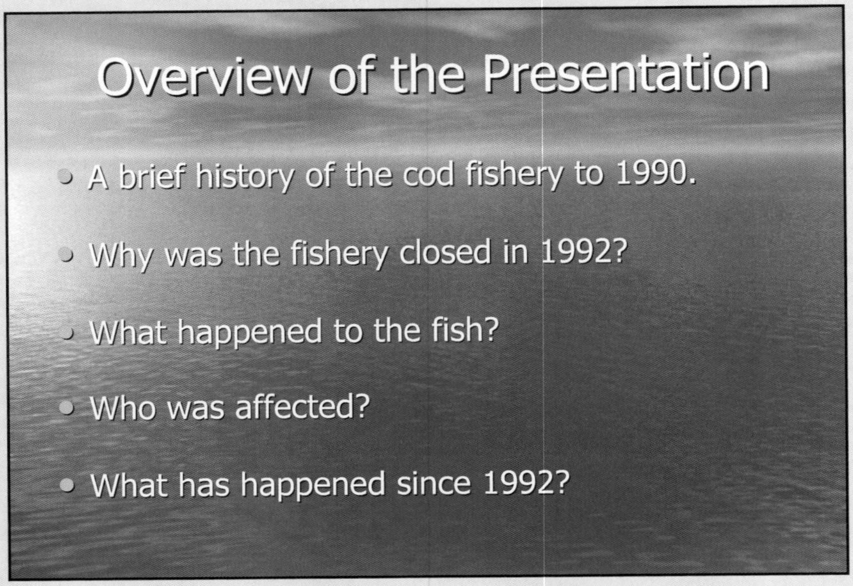

Overview of the Presentation

- A brief history of the cod fishery to 1990.
- Why was the fishery closed in 1992?
- What happened to the fish?
- Who was affected?
- What has happened since 1992?

Figure 10.23 Each of these slides shows an overview of a presentation on the collapse of the cod fishery in Newfoundland. Which slide is more effective? Give reasons for your choice.

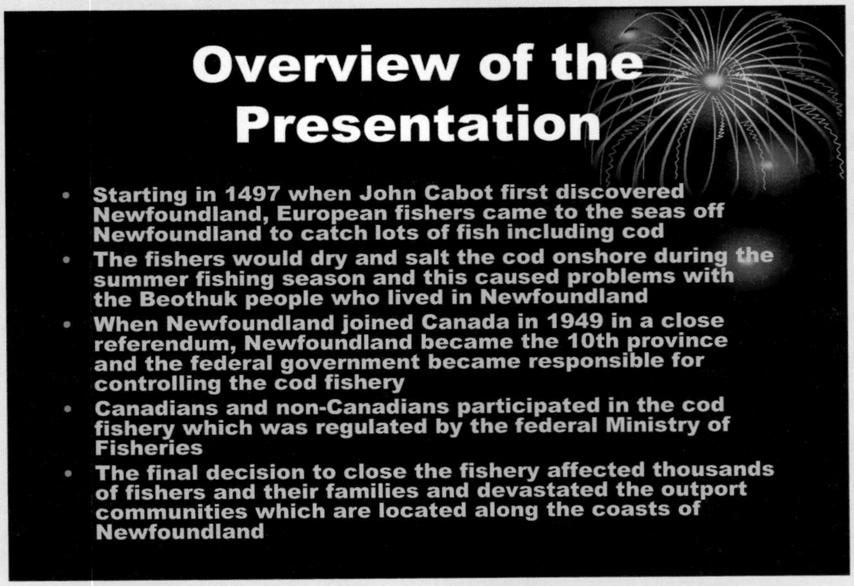

Overview of the Presentation

- Starting in 1497 when John Cabot first discovered Newfoundland, European fishers came to the seas off Newfoundland to catch lots of fish including cod
- The fishers would dry and salt the cod onshore during the summer fishing season and this caused problems with the Beothuk people who lived in Newfoundland
- When Newfoundland joined Canada in 1949 in a close referendum, Newfoundland became the 10th province and the federal government became responsible for controlling the cod fishery
- Canadians and non-Canadians participated in the cod fishery which was regulated by the federal Ministry of Fisheries
- The final decision to close the fishery affected thousands of fishers and their families and devastated the outport communities which are located along the coasts of Newfoundland

National Unity

During Brian Mulroney's campaign for leadership of the Progressive Conservative Party, he claimed that, in order to win power, the party had to win Québec. Mulroney argued that his personal Québec background would help him bring that province into the Constitution with "honour and enthusiasm." He was hoping to realize the dream of virtually every prime minister since John A. Macdonald—achieving national unity.

The Meech Lake Accord

Mulroney's first attempt to bring Québec into the Canadian constitutional was known as the Meech Lake Accord. In April 1987, Mulroney and the 10 provincial premiers met in Meech Lake, Québec, to discuss changes to the Constitution. Each province had its own demands that were largely based on regional complaints. For example, Québec wanted **veto power** over constitutional change, greater power over immigration, and recognition as a distinct society; Alberta wanted Senate reform; and Newfoundland wanted control over its fisheries. After 10 hours of negotiations, an agreement was finally reached. If approved by the provincial governments, it would change the Constitution significantly. Five main changes to the Constitution were proposed by the Meech Lake Accord:

- The provincial governments would have input in the nomination of Supreme Court judges.
- They would have increased power over immigration rules.
- They could opt out of new federal programs but still receive money from the federal government for their own equivalent programs.
- They would have veto power in proposed constitutional amendments.
- Québec would be recognized as a **distinct society**.

Controversy

Critics said the Accord would weaken the power of the federal government to ensure equal services across the country. They also maintained that it gave too much power to the provinces. The most controversial issue, however, was the distinct society clauses. Many Canadians felt that they created two separate Canadas. The concern over how the Supreme Court might end up interpreting the clauses played a significant role in the downfall of the Accord.

Supporters said that the clauses were simply a recognition that a special situation existed in Québec. However, opponents pointed to Québec's use of the "notwithstanding clause" that was included in the 1982 Constitution. In 1988, the Supreme Court of Canada had ruled that some parts of Bill 101—the law that limited the use of languages other than French on signs in Québec—were unconstitutional and therefore void. Québec Premier Bourassa had then introduced new legislation that used the "notwithstanding clause" in order to override the parts that were considered to be unconstitutional. The question for many people was what might Québec be able to do with more constitutional power?

Resistance to the Accord was led by someone who was no stranger to the constitutional debate—former prime minister Pierre Trudeau. He claimed that the distinct society clause was a misleading "no win" situation. By agreeing to its inclusion, Mulroney and the provincial premiers had led Québec to believe that "distinct society"

> "Sir Wilfrid Laurier once said, 'The governing motive of my life has been to harmonize the diverse elements which compose our country.' Surely that is the wish of every member, on all sides of this house. That is our policy. That is our purpose—building a stronger Canada for all Canadians."
>
> –Prime Minister Brian Mulroney, *Report on the First Ministers' Meeting at Meech Lake*, 1987

> "2. (1) The Constitution of Canada shall be interpreted in a manner consistent with...
>   (b) the recognition that Québec constitutes within Canada a distinct society...
> 3. The role of the legislature and Government of Québec to preserve and promote the distinct identity of Québec referred to in paragraph (1)(b) is affirmed."
>
> –Schedule: Constitutional Amendment, 1987

"That bunch of snivelers [the provincial premiers] should simply have been sent packing ... But our current political leaders lack courage. By rushing to the rescue of the unhappy losers, they hope to gain votes in Québec; ... they are only flaunting their ... ignorance of the demographic data regarding nationalism ... Brian Mulroney ... has already entered into history as the author of a constitutional document which ... will render the Canadian state totally impotent."

–Former prime minister Pierre Trudeau's statement on the Meech Lake Accord, 27 May 1987

Figure 10.24 What does the cartoonist think about the relationship between Mulroney and the premiers at the Meech Lake conference?

"But we're a distinct society too, and we've fought for many years for the basic rights that Québec takes for granted, such as participating in constitutional talks."

–Manitoba MLA Elijah Harper, 1987

was the same thing as two nations. If the Supreme Court ruled that way as well, it would lead to Canada's downfall. But if it did not, "Québec will have been tricked, and the howls of protest will strengthen separatism" in Québec. Either way, Canada would lose.

Failure

Part of the problem in getting the Accord ratified was that a number of premiers who attended the Meech Lake conference were voted out of office before the Accord could be ratified by their provinces. Constitutional rules state that the Accord had to be passed within three years of its agreement. When the Québec legislature

ratified it on 23 June 1987, this meant that the other governments had to pass it by 23 June 1990 or it would be dead. As the deadline approached, Manitoba and Newfoundland had not yet passed the Accord. Elijah Harper, an Aboriginal member of the Manitoba legislature, objected to the Accord's failure to address the issue of Aboriginal rights. With the support of Aboriginal peoples across the country, he was addressing what was called "the big lie"—that Canada was made up of two founding nations—English and French. This ignored the fact that Aboriginal peoples were Canada's original inhabitants.

Harper prevented the legislature from debating and voting on the Accord. As a result of Harper's stand, Newfoundland premier Clyde Wells withdrew the Accord from a vote in the Newfoundland legislature. Mulroney's first attempt to bring Québec into the Constitution had ended in failure.

The Charlottetown Accord

Many people in Québec saw the defeat of the Meech Lake Accord as a rejection of the province by the rest of country. Polls showed that two-thirds of Quebeckers now favoured independence. Talk of an independence referendum began to resurface.

Immediately after the failure of the Accord, Mulroney began another pursuit of constitutional change to encourage Québec to sign the Constitution. In the summer of 1991, a Special Joint Committee of the House of Commons and Senate was created to get input from Canadians on constitutional change. The committee travelled across Canada, receiving over 3000 submissions and hearing testimony from over 700 witnesses. The provinces, territories, and Aboriginal groups set up their own public consultations. It was an unprecedented attempt to gain public input in government decision making.

It was only after these consultations that intergovernmental meetings on the Constitution took place in the spring of 1992. On 28 August 1992, after a meeting in Charlottetown, Prince Edward Island, the provincial, territorial, and federal governments, as well as Aboriginal representatives, announced that they had come to a proposed agreement—the Charlottetown Accord. It included proposed changes to the Constitution such as the following:

- *Social and economic issues.* Canadians would be guaranteed programs that protected their universal health-care system, reasonable access to housing and food, publicly funded education, workers' rights, and the environment.
- *The Senate.* A Triple E (equal, elected, and effective) Senate would be introduced, replacing the appointed Senate. It included provisions for equal provincial representation in an elected Senate, with special seats reserved for Aboriginal representation.
- *Québec.* The province would be recognized as a distinct society with its own language, culture, and civil law tradition. It would be guaranteed at least a 25 per cent representation in the House of Commons.
- *Minority rights.* The language rights of English-speaking communities in Québec and French-speaking communities in the rest of Canada would be protected.

- *Aboriginal rights.* The right to self-government for Aboriginal nations was accepted and recognized as one of the three orders of government along with Ottawa and the provinces.

A National Referendum

The Charlottetown Accord was supported by the Progressive Conservatives, Liberals, and the NDP. However, a new political party that had formed in the West, the Reform Party, opposed it. Other opponents included the National Action Committee on the Status of Women, the Parti Québécois, and former prime minister Pierre Trudeau. The "No" side focused on a few points that began to change the minds of many Canadians who had originally supported the Accord. Some argued that "too much" had again been given up to Québec. Others were concerned about the vagueness of the wording "Aboriginal self-government." Still others believed that the Accord did not do enough to address gender inequality issues.

Figure 10.25 In 1992, during a speech in Sherbrooke, Québec, Prime Minister Mulroney ripped a sheet of paper to illustrate how a "no" vote in the Charlottetown Accord referendum would tear apart Québec society. Do you think this was an effective tactic? Explain.

In a national referendum on 26 October 1992, Canadians voted on this question: "Do you agree that the Constitution of Canada should be renewed on the basis of the agreement reached on August 28, 1992?" The majority of Canadians rejected the Charlottetown Accord as 54.4 per cent voted "no." Despite this fact, the results were somewhat positive in one significant way. Among Canadians who voted "no," 54 per cent were those outside of Québec, 56.6 per cent were from Québec, and 62 per cent were First Nations peoples on reserves. The majority of Quebeckers, Aboriginal peoples, and the rest of Canadians said "no" to the Accord, so no one group felt that another was rejecting them.

New Political Parties

Mulroney's attempts to unify Canada had a significant negative impact on the fortunes of his party. During his time in power, two new federal political parties formed that drew support away from the Progressive Conservative Party.

The Reform Party was created in October 1987. Its slogan was "the West wants in" because it believed that Ottawa had a history of ignoring the needs of the Western provinces. It cited examples such as the creation of the National Energy Program and the pursuit of the policy of official bilingualism. (You will learn more about the Reform Party in Chapter 12.)

After the failure of the Meech Lake Accord in 1990, Mulroney faced the creation of a second new party. Lucien Bouchard was a high-profile Conservative MP and Cabinet minister in the Mulroney government. He became increasingly disillusioned with the opposition to the Meech Lake Accord and with the Conservatives' concessions

as they tried to achieve passage of the Accord. Bouchard resigned from the Conservative Party in May 1990 and led a group of other Québec MPs to form the Bloc Québécois. This federal party would have the same aim as the provincial Parti Québécois—the sovereignty of Québec as a nation separate from Canada. Its goal in Parliament would be to look after Québec's interests until independence could be established. In the 1993 federal election, the Bloc Québécois won 54 seats, becoming the official opposition.

Mulroney Retires from Politics

The creation of these two political parties was an unfavourable sign for the Progressive Conservatives. Mulroney had become very unpopular with Canadians, with some polls indicating the support of only 9 per cent of the people. This was the lowest figure for any prime minister in Canadian history. The failure of both the constitutional accords, the introduction of the GST, and an economic recession in the early 1990s left the Conservatives vulnerable in the upcoming election. The Mulroney government had also faced a series of scandals and resignations involving many high-profile Cabinet ministers. In June 1993, Mulroney retired from politics without giving the electorate a chance to vote him out of office.

Kim Campbell was elected the new leader of the Progressive Conservative Party, becoming Canada's first female prime minister. As the party's mandate was about to expire, she called an election for October 1993. After the votes were counted, the Conservatives faced the most shocking turnaround in Canadian political history. They went from holding 169 seats in Parliament

Figure 10.26 How does the cartoonist characterize the Prime Minister's Office that Campbell inherited from Brian Mulroney?

to winning only 2 seats out of 295 in the election. As a result, they lost official party status in the House of Commons. More important, the political scene in Canada had become very regional. Essentially, the West was represented by the Reform Party, Québec by the Bloc Québécois, and Ontario, Manitoba, and the Atlantic provinces by the Liberal Party. It was going to be a difficult task for Jean Chrétien, the newly elected Liberal prime minister, to form a government that united Canada.

Challenge and Response

1. Use a flowchart or fishbone diagram to illustrate the process by which the Meech Lake Accord failed.
2. Why was the distinct society clause in the Meech Lake Accord so controversial? Do you think Québec is a distinct society? Explain.
3. How was the process of creating the Charlottetown Accord different from that of the Meech Lake Accord? Which process seems more logical to you? Explain.
4. Choose one change to the Constitution proposed by the Charlottetown Accord. What would be some possible outcomes of this change?
5. In a concept web, outline the factors that led to the defeat of the Progressive Conservative Party in the 1993 general election. Which factor(s) do you think had the most impact on the party's defeat? Explain.

Profile in Power:

Kim Campbell

Figure 10.27 Kim Campbell (1947–)

"Women of all ages were jubilant … at this historic moment. A woman was going to be prime minister of Canada, and I was that woman. I put aside all my fears about what was to come, and just savoured it.

–Kim Campbell, *Time and Change*, 1996

Avril Phaedra Douglas Campbell was not fond of any of her names, so at the age of 12 she changed her name to Kim. Despite family problems, Campbell did well in school and was voted president of the student council. She later became the first female president of her high school, then the first female freshman president at the University of British Columbia. She was also interested in music and acting. At law school, she wrote, produced, and performed in political satires and skits.

While Campbell was studying law at university, she got involved in local politics. She served four years on the Vancouver School Board before running as a Social Credit candidate in the 1984 British Columbia provincial election. Although she lost, Campbell became a policy advisor to BC premier Bill Bennett. In 1986, she was elected to the provincial legislature. Two years later, she ran as the Progressive Conservative candidate for Vancouver Centre in the federal election and was elected as an MP.

In 1989, Campbell was appointed minister of state for Indian and Northern Affairs and in 1990 became the first female justice minister. In the wake of the 1989 Montréal massacre, Campbell introduced a bill for stricter gun controls. She also drafted a law that protected victims' rights in cases of sexual assault. When Brian Mulroney announced his retirement, Campbell became prime minister in June 1993 after winning the Progressive Conservative leadership.

In the October 1993 election campaign, Campbell's approval rating was high at first. She was seen as clever and assertive, and her campaign was dubbed "Campbellmania." However, she made several public relations mistakes. A Conservative television advertisement seemed to make fun of Liberal leader Jean Chrétien's facial paralysis. Campbell also had to separate herself from Brian Mulroney's unpopularity. The Conservative Party suffered the worst electoral defeat in Canadian history. Because it did not win the minimum requirement of 10 seats, the party no longer had official status. Campbell resigned as party leader. She went on to teach political science at Harvard University and later served as consul general for Canada in Los Angeles.

Responding

1. In your opinion, why do you think Canadians voted so overwhelmingly against the Conservatives in 1993? Give reasons for your response.

Sign of the Times

Figure 10.28 Bryan Adams was recognizable for his raspy voice and combination of pop-rock and ballad songs. He often performed in jeans and a T-shirt, similar to the working-class image portrayed by Bruce Springsteen in the US. He also wrote songs for artists such as Tina Turner, Bonnie Raitt, and Joe Cocker.

International Success

During the 1980s and 1990s, Canadian musicians gained international fame and acclaim. Two of the most successful acts were Bryan Adams and the Barenaked Ladies. Between 1984 and 1992, Adams released three multi-platinum albums, *Reckless*, *Into the Fire*, and *Waking up the Neighbours*, that led to 14 Top 40 international hits. In 1992, Barenaked Ladies released its first full album, titled *Gordon*. With lighthearted songs such as "Be My Yoko Ono" and "If I Had a Million Dollars," it complemented the group's stage performances, which were famous for their comedic improvisations. In many ways, the group redefined the Canadian music scene as one of the first truly successful independent, or "indie," bands.

Figure 10.29 The Barenaked Ladies finally made it big outside of Canada in the late 1990s, breaking into the US music scene with hits such as "One Week," "Brian Wilson," and "Pinch Me." The band became popular with high school and university students after appearances on the hit show *Beverly Hills, 90210* and in theatres and clubs across the US.

Figure 10.30 "Tears Are Not Enough" was performed by a group of well-known Canadian musicians who called themselves Northern Lights. The record sold 300 000 copies and raised $3 million. It was part of an international effort that culminated in an around-the-world concert called Live Aid. It is estimated that this international effort raised around $300 million in aid for Ethiopia. Live Aid was similar in scope to the Live Earth concert series held in July 2007. (See Chapter 12.)

Bryan Adams was also at the forefront of international social activism in the music industry. In the mid-1980s, Ethiopia was in the grips of a devastating drought and famine that claimed the lives of one million people and threatened millions more. Adams co-wrote a song titled "Tears Are Not Enough" to raise funds for Ethiopia. He also took part in Amnesty International's 1986 Conspiracy of Hope Tour, promoting human rights, and in Nelson Mandela's 1988 birthday party concert, highlighting opposition to apartheid in South Africa.

Responding

1. Do you think it would be easier or harder for an independent band to become well known in today's music scene? Why?
2. How did Canadian musicians use music to address social issues during the 1980s? In what other ways has music been used to promote social causes?

Thinking Like a Historian:
Using the Oral Tradition as Historical Evidence

Essential Question: As a historian, how do you find, select, and interpret different types of historical evidence?

Most of the information historians use is found in written documents. For historians, the paper trail is critical in their search for the truth about past events. However, at times they must also rely on oral accounts. For example, interviewing soldiers can reveal much information about life in combat. Popular historian Barry Broadfoot compiled *Ten Lost Years*, his bestselling book on the Great Depression in Canada, using interviews with people who had lived through that era.

Oral accounts may be both primary and secondary sources (see the Skill Path in Chapter 1). Aboriginal oral traditions are now widely accepted in Canada as a rich cultural and literary source. However, when it comes to accepting these traditions in a historical or legal sense, the situation is more complex. In many of the issues that arise between Canadian governments and Aboriginal peoples, oral history is often disputed. Governments tend to focus on evidence contained in written documents. For Aboriginal peoples, however, the evidence lies in oral histories that are passed down from generation to generation.

For example, some land claims disagreements are based on a discrepancy between the government's written record and the Aboriginal oral tradition. Can an oral tradition or history have the same weight as a written document? Written evidence is often based on a non-Aboriginal perspective, while Aboriginal oral traditions are usually primary-source information presented from an Aboriginal perspective.

Since 1997, the Supreme Court of Canada has allowed Aboriginal oral traditions to be used in court cases involving Aboriginal rights and land claims. However, they are subject to being tested by the same rules of evidence as other sources of information. It is important to note that scientists studying global warming in the Arctic find accounts of past weather patterns from Inuit Elders to be a valuable source of information in their attempts to track climate change. The search for historical truth in Canada now generally includes oral traditions and history as well as the written record.

You, the Historian

1. What do you think are the major positive and negative aspects of using oral accounts as historical sources? Create a PMI chart to assess this issue.
2. What are the possible advantages and disadvantages of using oral traditions in legal cases?
3. How would you "test" the validity and reliability of an oral tradition or history?
4. a) Think of one event that has had a major impact on you or your family. Be prepared to share it orally with the class.
   b) Do you think a written account would have more or less impact? Explain.
   c) Would a written version of your story be more or less accurate? Explain.

UNIT 4

Challenge, Change, and Continuity: 1993–2008

IN FOCUS

This unit is different from the other units in this book in an important way. These chapters cover the period in which you were born. The events you are about to discover have affected your ideas about what it means to be Canadian.

In this unit, you will think about the main events in your lifetime that have helped to shape Canada's history. As you do, focus on the following questions:

- What role did the Liberals under Jean Chrétien play in defining Canada at home and abroad?
- How has Canada responded to terrorism in the twenty-first century?
- What impact has the new Conservative Party had on Canada?
- What challenges does Canada face today?
- Which people and events in your lifetime have had the most significant short-term and long-term impact on Canada?

This detail of the painting called *Celebration of Light* was created by Vancouver artist Tiko Kerr in 2006. What do you think are the most important things Canadians have to celebrate in the twenty-first century?

Chapter 11

Canada and the New World Order

Figure 11.1 Federalist forces gathered in downtown Montréal during the 1995 Québec referendum. Federalists claimed this huge cross-Canada outpouring of love for Canada and Québec would encourage the Québécois to vote against sovereignty. Others argued many Québécois would feel it was nothing more than meddling in a provincial referendum and would further the sovereignist cause. In your opinion, would this type of demonstration have helped or hurt the cause of Canadian unity?

Chapter at a Glance

Thinking Ahead

Jean Chrétien spent a lifetime in politics, much of it at the side of Prime Ministers Pearson and Trudeau. After Chrétien became prime minister in 1993, few Canadians expected his decade in power would see such vast transformation. Indeed, a new world order began to take shape during those critical years of challenge and change.

In this chapter, you will examine how the Chrétien government tackled the issues of national unity, the economy, foreign policy, technological innovation, and the environment. As you explore the Chrétien years, focus on these key questions:

- How did Chrétien respond to the separatist challenge from the Bloc Québécois and the Parti Québécois?
- What was the purpose of the Team Canada Missions?
- What was Canada's changing role in the global community?
- Why did Canada stay out of Iraq but go into Afghanistan?

Profile in Power:

Joseph-Jacques-Jean Chrétien

"We believe that Iraq must fully abide by the resolutions of the United Nations Security Council. We have always made clear that Canada would require the approval of the Security Council if we were to participate in a military campaign … If military action proceeds without a new resolution of the Security Council, Canada will not participate."

–Jean Chrétien, speech to the House of Commons, 17 March 2003

Figure 11.2 Jean Chrétien (1934–)

Reading Strategy

Create an organizer on Jean Chrétien with the three headings "Political Challenges," "Accomplishments," and "Influences and Character Traits." Complete the organizer as you read this feature.

Jean Chrétien was the second-youngest child in a family of 19. Eleven of his siblings died in infancy. In recognition of his working-class origins, Chrétien often referred to himself as *le petit gars de Shawinigan* (the little guy from Shawinigan). As a teenager, he hung out in pool halls and often got into street fights.

The Chrétien family placed a priority on learning. Jean attended boarding school for his primary- and secondary-school education. He was teased about his crooked smile, which was the result of a facial paralysis called Bell's palsy. "When I was a kid," he said, "people were laughing at me. But I accepted that because God gave me other qualities, and I'm grateful."

After earning a law degree from Laval University, Chrétien returned to Shawinigan in 1958 and started a law practice. By that time, he was married to Aline Chaîné. They met on a bus when she was 16 years old and married five years later. During his years in politics, Chrétien consulted Aline for both personal and political advice.

Chrétien's father was an organizer for the Liberal Party. As a teenager, Chrétien distributed pamphlets and attended political rallies. At Laval University, he was president of the Liberal Club. By 1960, Chrétien was principal organizer for the Québec Liberal Party. In 1963, he was elected to the House of Commons.

Chrétien's greatest asset as Canada's 20th prime minister was his many years of experience in Parliament. He served with 6 prime ministers, held 12 ministerial positions, and sat in Parliament for 27 years. During his first two years in Ottawa as a backbencher, he worked on improving his English. After the 1968 election, Prime Minister Trudeau made him minister of Indian and Northern Affairs. Chrétien established a separate office for the settling of Aboriginal land claims and created 10 new national parks. He also adopted an Aboriginal child into his young family. In 1980, as minister of Justice, Chrétien was responsible for helping defeat the "Yes" forces in the Québec referendum. Later, he helped to patriate the Constitution and pass the 1982 Charter of Rights.

When Trudeau resigned as prime minister in 1984, Chrétien ran for the Liberal Party leadership against John Turner. His close association with Trudeau—and the Liberal Party's tradition of alternating between anglophone and francophone leaders—led to his defeat. Chrétien resigned from politics in 1986 and returned to his law practice.

When Turner resigned in 1990 after losing two elections, Chrétien became the next Liberal Party leader. Disillusioned with the Mulroney

Figure 11.3 Nunavut Premier Paul Okalik (right) is applauded by Prime Minister Chrétien (centre left) and Governor General Roméo LeBlanc (centre right) during the celebration marking the creation of the new territory on 1 April 1999.

Conservatives, voters turned to the Liberals. On 4 November 1993, Jean Chrétien became prime minister. The country that he inherited was deeply in debt, but by 1997 this was no longer the case.

The challenge from Québec separatists was more difficult. Although Chrétien was criticized for doing very little to win the 1995 referendum, the Québécois narrowly voted to remain in Confederation. In foreign affairs, Chrétien drew attention to African countries in need, signed the Kyoto Protocol on the environment, and refused to participate in the United States' war on Iraq. He established Team Canada Missions to various countries to increase trade and investment opportunities.

When Chrétien retired as prime minister in December 2003, he had served Canada as a Member of Parliament and as prime minister for more than 40 years. He had also won three consecutive majority governments. Jean Chrétien returned to practising law in Ottawa.

Responding

1. What personal qualities did Jean Chrétien have that prepared him for a life in politics?
2. What were Chrétien's major achievements in foreign affairs?

National Unity

> "I don't want to oppose the system—I want to get out of it."
>
> –Québec premier Jacques Parizeau, September 1994

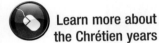 Learn more about the Chrétien years

Almost immediately after winning the federal election of 1993, Chrétien faced a serious challenge to Canadian unity. The failure of both the Meech Lake and Charlotteown accords had moved the issue of national unity to centre stage in Canada. In the 1994 Québec election, a revitalized Parti Québécois—led by long-time separatist Jacques Parizeau—promised to organize a second referendum on Québec sovereignty. Once again, the Québécois faced a divisive campaign about the future of Québec and Canada.

Figure 11.4 In the 1995 referendum campaign, the "Yes" side was led by a coalition of the Parti Québécois (PQ), the Bloc Québécois (BQ), and the Action Démocratique du Québec (ADQ). In this photo, Lucien Bouchard, leader of the BQ (which was the official opposition in Parliament), is flanked by PQ leader and Québec premier Jacques Parizeau on the left and ADQ leader Mario Dumont on the right. Why was it important for the "Yes" side to form a coalition regardless of disagreement among separatists?

The 1995 Referendum Campaign

Before the referendum campaign was launched, it appeared that support for Québec sovereignty was weak. Among separatists, there was disagreement about the most effective way to proceed. Some people were tired of the debate and the whole process of voting in referendums and elections. They were more worried about taxes, jobs, and their day-to-day lives.

However, the federalists—led by Daniel Johnson, leader of the Québec Liberals; Jean Charest, leader of the federal Progressive Conservative Party; and Prime Minister Chrétien—soon found they were losing ground. As the campaign wore on, the separatists appeared to be gaining strength. When Lucien Bouchard became leader of the newly created Bloc Québécois—a federal political party that advocated Québec separatism—the entire province was awakened to the separatist dream. Bouchard had recently survived a life-threatening illness and was viewed as a heroic figure who could be trusted with Québec's future.

What had once seemed a federal runaway victory was now an intense, closely fought race. The province was bombarded with advertisements, announcements, rallies, and parades. In the last days of the campaign, Canadians from across the country got involved. Some made phone calls to people in Québec and others sent postcards urging them to vote "no" and say "yes" to Canada. On the weekend before the vote, federalist forces led by Brian Tobin, federal minister of Fisheries and Oceans, held a huge rally in downtown Montréal at Place du Canada. Canadians poured into Montréal by plane, train, and bus. They were there to demonstrate their love of Québec and their love of a united Canada.

As the province went to the polls, all of Canada was on edge. Throughout the evening, the "No" and "Yes" forces were neck and neck, with the pro-sovereignty forces often having a narrow lead. An incredible 94 per cent of Québécois voters cast their ballots. Finally, the results were tallied: No—50.58 per cent, Yes—49.42 per cent. If 25 000 votes had changed sides, the result would have been a separatist victory. The federalists realized that a less than 1 per cent victory was too close, while the separatists were broken-hearted to have come so close and yet be defeated.

The Reaction

In a speech following the referendum, Premier Jacques Parizeau blamed the defeat on "money and the ethnic vote." This was an attack on the allophone population in Québec—those having a first language other than French, English, or an Aboriginal language. Parizeau's angry outburst stained the separatist cause. His career in ruins and his reputation tarnished, Parizeau soon resigned. He was replaced by the more popular and charismatic Lucien Bouchard.

For the pro-Canada forces, there was both relief and shock. The unity of Canada had almost been lost in an emotional campaign over a complicated question. The reality that the country might be torn apart became painfully clear. Jean Chrétien and his Cabinet took measures to ensure that the unity of Canada would never face such a threat again.

Plan B

To prevent another close call on Canadian unity, Chrétien implemented a strategy known as Plan B.

- In October 1995, Chrétien established a federal sponsorship plan to funnel millions of dollars into Québec. The intention was to heighten recognition of the Canadian government and counter the official position of the governing Parti Québécois. Misuse of this money would later lead to the sponsorship scandal. As you will learn later in the chapter, the Liberal government of Paul Martin came under attack for this misconduct.

- Chrétien also turned to a bright young Québécois, Stéphane Dion—a fearless critic of separatism—to prepare a federal plan for a future referendum. As minister of Intergovernmental Affairs, Dion went to the Supreme Court of Canada for a ruling on the legality of separation. In its careful ruling, the Supreme Court indicated that, while separation was legally possible, it could only come after a democratic referendum where a visible majority of citizens voted on a clear question. (The word *clear* was not specifically defined.)

- In December 1999, the Chrétien government introduced Bill C-20, or the Clarity Act, to regulate any future negotiations with Québec.

The Clarity Act

The Clarity Act gave the federal government a say on the wording of a future referendum question and on the margin needed to win. It stated that any referendum result had to be referred to the House of Commons for debate and prohibited a universal declaration of independence after a referendum vote. These conditions comforted most Canadians.

> "Canadians and Quebeckers would be well advised to fasten their seat belts. The sovereignty train has left the station and is picking up speed. We are lucky we can stay on the sidelines; it is likely to be a rough ride."
>
> –Marie Huhtala, US consul general in Québec, 1995

> "I accuse Lucien Bouchard of having betrayed the population of Québec during last October's referendum campaign. By distorting the political history of his province and of his country, by spreading discord among its citizens with his … rhetoric, and by preaching contempt for those Canadians who did not share his views, Lucien Bouchard went beyond the limits of honest and democratic debate."
>
> –Pierre Elliott Trudeau, February 1996

Learn more about the 1995 referendum

Figure 11.5 At a Parti Québécois policy convention held the year before his resignation, Bouchard told delegates: "Everything depends on our powers of persuasion. The decision to make Québec sovereign will be decided by our ability to convince the Québécois."

Reading Strategy

Create an organizer on Lucien Bouchard with the three headings "Political Role in Québec Sovereignty," "Political Challenges," and "Influences and Character Traits." Complete the organizer as you read this feature.

Lucien Bouchard was perhaps one of the most well-spoken and intelligent leaders of the separatist movement in Québec. His passionate calls for a sovereign Québec brought many Québécois to their feet. Yet he started political life as an avid federalist who helped Brian Mulroney come to power.

In the 1988 federal election, Bouchard won election to the House of Commons. Shortly after, he became minister of the Environment in Mulroney's Cabinet. Later, he became heavily involved in the attempt to win agreement on the Meech Lake Accord. Unhappy with the resistance to Québec's objectives, he resigned from the party in May 1990. In 1991, Bouchard gathered a number of discon-

tented MPs from the Progressive Conservative and Liberal parties to form the Bloc Québécois.

In the 1993 federal election, Bouchard led his party to earning 54 of 75 seats in Québec and 49.3 per cent of the popular vote. From 1993 to 1996, Bouchard's BQ served as the official opposition in Ottawa, the first time a separatist party had held such influence in the House of Commons.

In 1994, Bouchard nearly lost his life to necrotizing fasciitis or "flesh-eating disease." Doctors had to amputate his leg. His illness only increased the admiration and affection that the Québécois felt for him.

When it seemed that support for sovereignty was weak during the 1995 referendum campaign, Bouchard was asked to play a leading role. His arrival electrified the campaign.

"We think that Quebeckers are … different people from the rest of Canada. We have the culture. We have a common language, which is different from Canada's. We have a territory. We have an economy. We have … all the ingredients of a people, of a nation, and … most Quebeckers—either federalists or sovereignists—feel … a distinct collectivity with the flavour and the nature and the aspirations of a people, of a nation."

Source: Lucien Bouchard, *Newshour* interview, PBS, 23 April 1996.

In 1996, Lucien Bouchard was chosen to lead the PQ and assume the office of premier of Québec. While in power, he focused on social and economic issues. He wanted to wait until he was sure "winning conditions" were present before proposing another referendum. This approach disappointed the more extreme members of the PQ. Bouchard resigned as premier in 2001, due to fatigue, frustration, and the long hours away from his family.

Responding

1. In what ways might have Bouchard's career reflected the shifting views of Québécois about their place in Canada?
2. To what extent might Bouchard's resignation from the Progressive Conservative Party have been motivated by political opportunism rather than philosophical differences?

Québec separatists, on the other hand, were incensed and rejected the Clarity Act. Jacques Parizeau even suggested that another Parti Québécois victory should lead to a universal declaration of independence. When André Boisclair was elected leader of the PQ in 2005, he indicated that, if he won the Québec election of 2007, he would move quickly to hold another referendum and simply ignore the Clarity Act. However, the Liberals won 48 seats and 33 per cent of the votes, while the ADQ won 41 seats and 31 per cent of the votes. The once-powerful PQ was reduced to third place with 36 seats and 28 per cent of the votes.

After the 2007 election, Bosclair left politics. He was replaced as PQ leader by longtime PQ activist and fervent separatist Pauline Marois.

Québec now had a minority Liberal government and a powerful ADQ to challenge it. How long the government would last was uncertain. While the PQ was still focusing on separation, the ADQ was attracting voters with talk of **autonomy**. After two tumultuous referendums, the future of Québec within Canada remained unsettled.

Reading Strategy

Referring to your organizers on Chrétien and Bouchard, compare and contrast these individuals as political leaders in a Venn diagram. What characteristics made each one effective as a leader?

Challenge and Response

1. Use a flow chart to illustrate the course of the 1995 referendum. Why do you think the results were so close?

2. One of the major issues in the 1995 referendum was the wording of the referendum question itself:

   "Do you agree that Québec should become sovereign after having made a formal offer to Canada for a new economic and political partnership within the scope of the bill respecting the future of Québec and of the agreement signed on June 12, 1995, Yes or No."

   a) Reread this question and paraphrase it. Share your version with a partner.

   b) Do you think this was a fair question to put before the people of Québec? In a letter to the editor of a national newspaper, explain your response.

3. If Québec were to separate from Canada, speculate on what impact this would have on Québec and on the rest of Canada.

The Deficit and Trade Wars

How long could you or your family keep going if you continued to spend more than you earned? What would your life be like if you had to pay a lot of interest on money you had borrowed in order to maintain your chosen lifestyle? Obviously, you would probably go bankrupt sooner or later and perhaps lose everything you owned. Most of us have to learn to live within our means. It is not possible to have whatever we want, whenever we want it.

Countries have to live under the same set of spending rules and limitations. As you learned in Chapter 10, Prime Minister Mulroney had often criticized Canada's level of indebtedness and tried unsuccessfully to reduce government spending. By the time Jean Chrétien took office, the issue of Canada's debt level was spiralling out of control. People talked about a "debt wall" and worried that future generations would be crippled by the high debts of previous generations. Some commentators even suggested that Canada was like a developing country in terms of debt. Business leaders, financial critics, and the new Reform Party all urged dramatic action, predicting doom and gloom for Canada if it did not get its financial house in order.

The Martin Approach

One of the central themes of the Chrétien era was the struggle to lower Canada's debt and annual deficit. The lead player in this effort was Paul Martin, who had previously been a successful business person. His campaign to lower Canada's deficit was the cornerstone of his political career. As minister of Finance from 1993 to 2002, Martin took quick and dramatic action by

- announcing that the deficit was $46 billion—a staggering $11 billion more than had been suggested by the outgoing Mulroney government.
- setting clear and dramatic targets for debt reduction. However, his critics felt they were unnecessarily harsh and mainly hurt the most vulnerable members of society.
- slashing the size and budgets of federal government departments, making deep job cuts, and overhauling many central programs such as the Canada Pension Plan and employment insurance. At one point, Martin had reduced federal spending to the levels of 1951.
- cutting back federal transfer payments to the provinces. This resulted in an uproar because provincial governments had to either raise their own taxes and/or reduce services to residents.
- initiating a 10-year plan to reduce personal and corporate taxes by $100 billion.
- beginning a series of payments to reduce the national long-term debt.

Learn more about Paul Martin and his handling of the deficit

Figure 11.6 Minister of Finance Paul Martin was generally credited for strengthening Canada's finances during the Chrétien years. He was dubbed the "deficit buster" or the "deficit slayer" by the press. In fact, respect for Martin among observers was such that he was often seen as a rival to the sitting prime minister, Jean Chrétien.

By 1998, Canada started to record the first **budget surpluses** in 27 years. The country quickly earned the approval of world financial leaders and private industry. Although Martin was recognized as a very capable minister of Finance, he was also fortunate that the recession of the later Mulroney years had eased and that interest rates were generally low during his time in office. In addition, the booming American economy contributed to an increase in exports.

The Social Deficit

In reducing the annual deficit, Martin also increased what critics termed the "social deficit." The social deficit was the reduction in the level of social services to Canadians—particularly to children and to those in need. Critics argued that cuts to services such as education, health, public transportation, and welfare were too deep and too fast. For some Canadians, it seemed as if the quality of life was declining, especially in urban areas. In the years since Martin's deficit-fighting work, all levels of government in Canada have been striving to rebuild public services to Canadians.

ISSUES

The Federal Deficit

The issue: Was Paul Martin's approach to tackling the deficit appropriate?

In earlier chapters, you examined the concepts of the federal deficit and the public debt. Before you analyze this issue, review the difference between these two concepts. The federal deficit is the amount by which the federal government's spending exceeds its income each year. When all of these annual deficits are added together, the total amount is referred to as the public debt. This is the amount owed by the federal government.

Although Prime Minister Mulroney promised to balance the books, the annual deficit of the federal government continued to balloon. In fact, most of Canada's tax dollars went toward paying the interest on the public debt and not on federal programs. Prime Minister Chrétien (a former finance minister himself) put Paul Martin in charge of an economic campaign to reduce the deficit, balance the annual budget, and begin the process of reducing Canada's long-term debt—a campaign that divided Canadians.

Arguments For Martin's Approach	Arguments Against Martin's Approach
• Canada would have collapsed economically if government spending had not been brought under control.	• Martin moved too fast and cut spending too deeply. He even raised taxes in the first few years.
• In order to lower taxes, the annual deficit had to be reduced.	• Because of cuts to spending on health care and education, the drive to lower the deficit negatively affected those Canadians most in need.
• Too many Canadian tax dollars had been lost to paying the interest on the debt rather than improving the lives of Canadians.	• Canada's military was allowed to decline and deteriorate.

Figure 11.7 What were the benefits and drawbacks of Paul Martin's approach to reducing the deficit? Should the government have pursued a different strategy? Consider these questions as you examine this chart and the various opinions that follow.

"For years, governments have been promising more than they can deliver, and delivering more than they can afford … This has to end. We are doing it."

Source: Paul Martin, quoted in Alan Freeman, "Budget hits jobs, military." *Globe and Mail*, 23 February 1994.

"There was no choice about the federal government's need to reduce the deficit in the early 1990s. But there were clear choices about how to do it … The fact that Canada's public sector programs were cut … reflected … the deliberate choices of our government … Martin's failure to protect those … programs … even though a clear fiscal opportunity existed to do so … was a major policy failure … "

Source: Jim Stanford, research associate, "Paul Martin, the deficit, and the debt: Taking another look." Canadian Centre for Policy Alternatives, 28 November 2003.

"Martin presented each [Cabinet minister] with a one-page document with three columns, indicating how much the minister would have to cut from [his/her] budget in each of 1995, 1996, and 1997. Some cuts were huge—up to 60 per cent. There was no discussion, no debate, no round table of Cabinet ministers discussing priorities."

Source: Murray Dobbin, author and journalist, "Paul Martin's democratic deficit." *The Tyee*, 16 February 2004.

"It was Martin who brought the huge deficit and the crushing national debt that the Liberals inherited from Brian Mulroney's Conservative government under control, and produced the current Canadian economic miracle of high employment, low debt, and no deficit."

Source: Gwynne Dyer, journalist and historian, "Canada: The master's revenge?", 23 June 2004.

Responding

1. Use a PMI organizer to analyze whether Paul Martin's approach to tackling the deficit was appropriate. What conclusions can you draw from your findings?
2. If you had been in Paul Martin's position, how would you have dealt with the problem of Canada's public debt?

Trade Wars

During the 1993 election campaign, the Liberals attacked Mulroney's Free Trade Agreement (FTA). However, once they were in power, they came to support the FTA and did not make any significant changes to it. In fact, the Liberal government signed the expansion of the FTA to include Mexico. In January 1994, the North American Free Trade Agreement (NAFTA) between Canada, the United States, and Mexico came into effect. NAFTA created a huge North American trading bloc of nearly 440 million people. The Chrétien government hoped to expand its ties throughout Latin America. NAFTA was a positive first step, followed by the Team Canada trade missions. Canada plunged confidently into the world of freer trade, hoping to be one of the major winners in the rise of globalization.

However, Canada has experienced considerable tension with its largest trading partner, the United States.

Three cases in particular have strained relations between the two countries: fish, softwood lumber, and cattle.

Salmon

Fishing stocks are strained all over the world. In Chapter 10, you examined the collapse of the cod fishery on Canada's east coast in the 1990s and the dramatic economic consequences for the region. On the west coast, Canadian fishers were committed to protecting the salmon fishery and their way of life. In 1985, Canada and the United States signed the Pacific Salmon Treaty, which regulated the salmon catch for fishers in British Columbia, Washington state, and Alaska.

By the 1990s, it was clear that the volume of the salmon catch was dropping, possibly because of pollution or overfishing. Since salmon migrated freely across the Canada–US border, it was difficult for the two countries to establish quotas. Fish hatched in Canadian waters might easily grow to maturity and be caught in American waters and vice versa. Each side argued that the other was "intercepting" its fish as they travelled along the west coast of North America. With no quotas in place, fleets from both countries tried to maximize their catch. Government negotiators made little headway in discussions.

In July 1997, talk turned to action when Canadian fishers blockaded an American ferry off the coast of British Columbia. Although harsh words and threats were exchanged, fortunately the "salmon war" never escalated into a full-scale trade war nor any military intervention. However, the action did spur all sides to try to draft an agreement regulating this unstable situation. In 1999, Canada and the US signed a new treaty that established a set of quotas for the salmon fishery. These quotas were to be in effect for a decade. In the future, salmon **aquaculture** is a possible solution for the continued growth of the salmon industry, but important environmental concerns first have to be addressed.

Figure 11.8   Canadian fishers took matters into their own hands and prevented an American ferry from leaving the port of Prince Rupert, British Columbia. This action contributed to heightened tension over the issue of salmon quotas. Do you think that citizens should take direct action on issues being negotiated between their government and another country? Why or why not?

Softwood Lumber

The softwood lumber dispute began as an irritant and escalated into a major political and economic disagreement between Canada and the United States. Both countries share a history of trade disputes over forest products that go back over 100 years. The dispute that broke out in 2002 was particularly heated. It almost set off a trade war and seriously tested the goodwill of citizens and officials on both sides of the border. It lasted throughout the terms of office of three different prime ministers—Jean Chrétien, Paul Martin, and Stephen Harper.

Softwood lumber is wood that is easy to cut. It is used mostly by the construction industry. The softwood lumber industry is vital to many regions of Canada, particularly British Columbia. Canada's forestry industry employs about 280 000 workers and is the backbone of about 300 communities. The US cannot supply enough of its own softwood and relies on Canadian materials for its construction industry. In 2005, this trade was worth $8.5 billion to Canadians.

In May 2002, the United States imposed duties of 27 per cent on Canadian softwood lumber. American officials collected billions of dollars from Canadian producers before their products entered the US. This meant that American producers could sell their domestic softwood (which was more expensive than Canadian softwood) more easily. It also meant an increase in the price of homes in the US.

The duties were imposed because the United States believes that the Canadian government subsidizes the forestry industry through low stumpage fees. Stumpage fees are paid by forestry companies to Canadian governments for the right to harvest wood. Most American forests are in private hands, and the cost to harvest wood is usually higher. Consequently, it was difficult for American producers to compete with Canadian products. On the other hand, the American economy needed Canadian softwood. A constant supply of this product ensured lower prices for American consumers of homes, decks, and other goods.

During the long and increasingly bitter dispute, Canada took the issue to such bodies as the World Trade Organization, NAFTA dispute panels, and the American Court of International Trade. Canada won seven rulings, but the United States insisted on more negotiations rather than dropping the duty fees. The dispute finally ended in September 2006 with the Softwood Lumber Agreement (SLA), signed by the Conservative government of Stephen Harper.

Under the terms of this controversial agreement:

- The United States agreed to return 80 per cent of the over $5 billion in duties it had already collected.
- The US agreed not to launch any new trade actions.
- Canadian-sourced lumber would stay at or below its current (2006) 34 per cent share of the US softwood market.
- Future disputes would be settled by neutral trade arbitrators.
- The SLA would be in effect for seven years with a possible two-year extension.

> "You want gas, you want oil, and you don't want wood. It's too bad, but if you have free trade, you have free trade."
>
> –Prime Minister Jean Chrétien, in a phone call to President George W. Bush, August 2001

> "We can all talk tough, but in the end we have to make sure that we maintain access to our biggest market that represents 90 per cent of our exports to the US."
>
> –Bernard Lord, former premier of New Brunswick, responding to proposed retaliatory trade sanctions against the US, August 2005

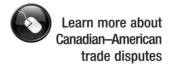
Learn more about Canadian–American trade disputes

Figure 11.9 Cattle farmers protested the US ban on their beef products. In your opinion, did the US overreact to the single case of mad cow disease in 2003? Explain your response.

Banning Beef

Canada's first case of mad cow disease, or BSE (bovine spongiform encephalopathy), was diagnosed in May 2003. As a result, the US closed its borders to all Canadian beef until July 2005. Canadian farmers protested that the US had overreacted—it was only one case and the animal had not entered the food chain. Canada's beef exports total over $2 billion a year. The partial shutdown of the industry led to huge losses for all involved including ranchers and meat packers. After over four years, the US border reopened to older live Canadian cattle and their beef products in November 2007.

Challenge and Response

1. Outline the major economic problem facing the Chrétien government as it assumed office and how the problem was handled.
2. Use a Venn diagram to compare and contrast the salmon and softwood lumber disputes.
3. Review the quotations from Jean Chrétien and Bernard Lord on page 373. From these comments, interpret each politician's position on whether the United States should be bound by the regulations and rulings of NAFTA and the WTO. What is your opinion on this issue?

Aboriginal Issues

After the Oka Crisis and the failed Meech Lake and Charlottetown accords, relations between the federal government and Aboriginal peoples in Canada were often strained. Some of the most complex and difficult issues revolved around unresolved treaty rights and land claims.

Land Claims Settlements

The ownership of land and treaty rights have often been at the centre of disagreements between First Nations and Canadian governments. These claims are in need of being settled for a number of reasons:

- Continued disagreements over ownership and use of lands can lead to conflict and violence.
- The Constitution Act, 1982, specifically recognizes Aboriginal rights.
- Negotiation is more efficient than complex, expensive court cases.
- Aboriginal peoples in Canada have not fared equally in society—settling land claims is a step toward addressing this situation.
- Successful and friendly negotiation might foster more positive relations between Aboriginal communities and Canadian governments.
- Treaties would address existing conflicts over land use, for example, hunting, fishing, logging, and mineral exploration.
- Some lands claims go back well over a century. In these cases, binding legal settlement is long overdue.

The Nisga'a Final Agreement

In 2000, a historic land claims treaty was successfully negotiated with the Nisga'a in British Columbia. The negotiation process had actually started

Figure 11.10 After signing the Nisga'a Final Agreement, Chief Joseph Gosnell explained the significance of the treaty to the Nisga'a Nation: "We're no longer beggars in our own land. We are free to make our own mistakes, savour own victories, and stand on our own feet." Why do you think it would be important to any group or individual to be "free to make our own mistakes"?

in 1887. After nearly a century of inaction, representatives of the Nisga'a, the province of British Columbia, and the government of Canada started formal negotiations in 1990.

The original position of the Nisga'a was that they owned 24 000 square kilometres of land near the Nass River. By 1996, an agreement in principle was reached that formed the basis of the first modern-day treaty in BC. Final negotiations were completed the next year. On 11 May 2000, the Nisga'a Final Agreement came into effect. Among its key provisions:

- Nearly 2000 square kilometres of Crown land were transferred to the Nisga'a Nation.
- Bear Glacier Provincial Park was created.

"Today, the Nisga'a people become full-fledged Canadians as we step out from under the Indian Act—forever. Finally, after a struggle of more than 130 years, the government of this country clearly recognizes that the Nisga'a were a self-governing people since well before European contact. We remain self-governing today, and we are proud to say that this inherent right is now clearly recognized and protected in the Constitution of Canada."

–Chief Joseph Gosnell, on the signing of the Nisga'a Final Agreement, 13 August 2000,

Learn more about the Nisga'a Final Agreement

- The Nisga'a were given the right to control natural resources on their land and to form a local self-government.
- The Nisga'a gave up any future land claims and First Nations tax-exempt status.
- The Nisga'a would receive a series of payments totalling $190 million over 15 years and an additional $66.5 million to implement activities in areas such as fisheries, infrastructure, and training and development.

"I think that one thing we learned was that this was an avoidable situation, that this could have been easily resolved by careful negotiations at the time."

–Don Campbell, defence lawyer, 2 June 1997

Land Disputes and Violence

In spite of the progress in settling many Aboriginal land claims, the issues have not always been resolved through peaceful negotiation. At times, violence has strained land claims issues. A younger generation of Aboriginal activists, inspired by Oka, has been prepared to take more direct steps in what they see as a defence of their land and treaty rights. In 1995, two disagreements between First Nations communities and their neighbours resulted in violence.

Gustafsen Lake, British Columbia

In the summer of 1995, police forces and some members of the Secwepemc First Nation were involved in a land dispute that ended in gunfire and casualties. The dispute was over the use and ownership of land the Secwepemc considered sacred. The Secwepemc held sun dance ceremonies on this land.

When negotiations failed, a major police operation was launched that cost $5.5 million and involved over 400 RCMP officers. The Armed Forces provided personnel carriers and helicopter support. Land mines were planted around the armed camp set up by the Secwepemc. There were exchanges of gunfire—in one tense 45-minute period, thousand of rounds were fired by police and the Secwepemc. Incredibly, no one was killed in this violent confrontation.

The conflict finally ended in September 1995 when the Secwepemc activists surrendered. A long trial resulted in 39 acquittals and 21 convictions on a range of charges. By 2000, conditions had improved to the point where Secwepemc Elders and RCMP leaders were able to meet and take part in cultural and spiritual ceremonies.

Figure 11.11 The National Chief of the Assembly of First Nations, Ovide Mercredi, met with RCMP Staff Sergeant Martin Sarich to reopen communications in an attempt to reach a peaceful settlement to the Gustafsen Lake dispute. Resolution of Aboriginal concerns, especially over land, is often painfully slow. Out of frustration, people sometimes resort to direct action. Canadians have witnessed some violent conflicts involving Aboriginal communities discouraged by delays in government action. In your opinion, are there occasions when it is acceptable to use peaceful civil disobedience or violent protest to end legal disputes or achieve goals? Explain.

Ipperwash, Ontario

Another violent standoff occurred in September 1995 at Ipperwash Provincial Park in Ontario. A land dispute dating back to 1942 resulted in a small group of First Nations protestors occupying the provincial park. They were protesting the slow resolution of their land claims and what they felt was the destruction of a sacred burial ground. When police moved in to remove the protestors, it resulted in much tension and confusion. Shots were fired and Dudley George, a member of the Anishinabek First Nation [a-nih-shih-NAH-bek], was killed. The police claimed the protestors were armed and had fired first. The protestors maintained they were unarmed and the police had used excessive force. The officer who shot George was later convicted of criminal negligence causing death.

In 1998, the original land claim that had been the source of the violence was settled for $26 million. The people of the Kettle Creek and Stoney Point First Nations recovered their land and received individual compensation ranging from $150 000 to $400 000. In 2003, Premier Dalton McGuinty promised an official inquiry into the tragedy. The final report of the Ipperwash inquiry was released in May 2007. It stated that the Ontario Provincial Police, the government of former Ontario premier Mike Harris, and the federal government shared responsibility for the events that led to George's death.

Self-government

A key issue facing political leaders in Canada is Aboriginal self-government. What level of government is most viable for Aboriginal communities? How much should standards and practices vary from other forms of government in Canada? In the case of a dispute, which levels of government should have the final say? The debate is ongoing, but in 1999 a major step forward was taken with the creation of Nunavut, Canada's third and largest territory.

Nunavut

Nunavut means "our land" in Inuktitut, the language of the Inuit, who make up about 85 per cent of the territory's population. The capital is Iqaluit—"place of many fish." The creation of Nunavut was the result of the largest Aboriginal land claims settlement in Canadian history. Today, it is a working example of Aboriginal self-government.

Nunavut's territorial government has several unique features. Everyone over the age of 16 can vote or run for office. Paul Okalik became the first Inuit territorial leader at the young age of 34. The government does not run according to party politics; instead, it tries to resolve issues by **consensus**. Unlike other legislatures, where government and opposition seats directly face one another, government and opposition seats in Nunavut's legislature are set up in a circular fashion to encourage discussion rather than debate.

Nunavut faces major challenges but also has vast resources whose full extent is still being explored. Future development of these resources will help the territory to meet those challenges. In 2002, Nunavut hosted the Arctic Winter Games, welcoming athletes from neighbouring regions such as Greenland, Russia, and Alaska.

"There's a growing number of young people who feel they don't have any hope. And whether that happens in downtown Winnipeg or the Gaza Strip, young angry men are not a good thing to have."

–Maurice Switzer, spokesperson for the Union of Ontario Indians, 2 June 2007

 Learn more about the Ipperwash inquiry

"The immediate cost of conducting relations with Aboriginal people through confrontations and over the barricades is very high. All Ontarians risk even more if we leave long-simmering disputes unsettled until they boil over."

–Justice Sidney Linden, head of the Ipperwash Inquiry, 2 June 2007

 Learn more about Nunavut

MAP STUDY: Nunavut

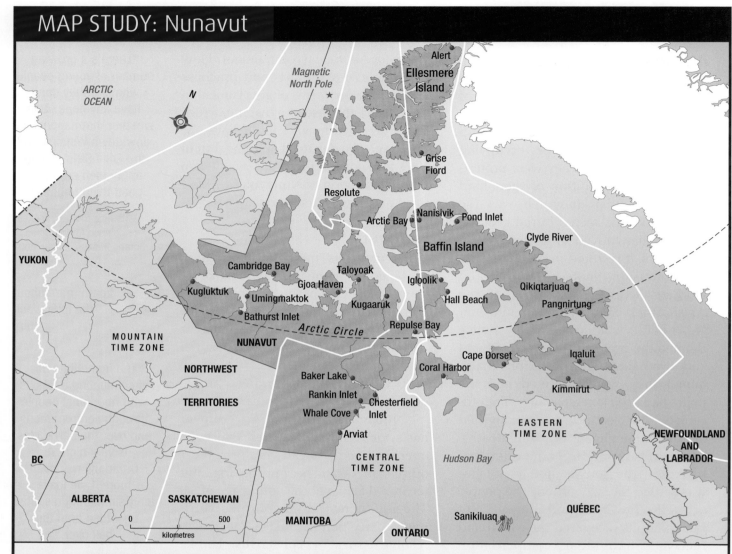

Source: Reproduced with the permission of the Minister of Public Works and Government Services Canada, 2007 and courtesy of Natural Resources Canada.

Figure 11.12   The territory of Nunavut is vast—two million km². It comprises one-fifth of Canada and spans three time zones.

Nunavut is four times the size of France, twice as big as Ontario, and larger than Saskatchewan and Alberta combined. While the physical size of Nunavut is impressive, its population is tiny— about 25 000 people. In fact, it is one of the most sparsely populated places in the world. As there are no main paved roads, the chief modes of travel are snowmobiles, airplanes, and dogsleds.

Analysis and Response

1. Do you think it is possible to effectively govern such a vast and remote area? Explain.
2. Nunavut is rich in minerals and oil and gas reserves. What impact do you think future development of Nunavut's resource wealth will have on the growth and composition of its population?

Abuse at Residential Schools

In Chapter 2, you learned about the federal government's official policy of assimilating Aboriginal peoples—and the residential schools that were part of this policy. Over the years, about 130 residential schools operated across Canada, with approximately 80 000 students attending these schools.

In the 1990s, investigations began into the mistreatment of children at residential schools. Former students spoke out about physical, emotional, and sexual abuse. Many had been physically abused for speaking Aboriginal languages or practising Aboriginal traditions. The result for many children was the loss of their cultures; for some, the loss of their childhood and innocence. By 2003, 12 000 claims of abuse had been made against government and church authorities.

Statement of Reconciliation

In 1998, the Government of Canada issued a Statement of Reconciliation in which it apologized to Aboriginal peoples for many of the abuses of the past, including those related to residential schools. The statement was part of a document called "Gathering Strength: Canada's Aboriginal Action Plan," which was released at a historic ceremony in Ottawa. In her speech, minister of Indian Affairs Jane Stewart included these final comments from the document:

"The Government of Canada recognizes that policies that sought to assimilate Aboriginal people, women and men, were not the way to build a strong country. We must instead continue to find ways in which Aboriginal people can participate fully in the economic, political, cultural and social life of Canada in a manner which preserves and enhances the collective identities of Aboriginal communities, and allows them to evolve and flourish in the future."

The terms of the Action Plan were designed to start a new era in Aboriginal–government relations. They included the establishment of

- an Aboriginal Healing Foundation
- an Independent Land Claims Commission
- an Aboriginal Health Institute
- an alternate dispute resolution process

In 2006, the federal government approved a plan to set aside $1.9 billion to pay residential school victims an initial sum of $10 000 and an additional $3000 for each year of schooling beyond the first year. The agreement was subject to the approval of courts in nine Canadian provinces.

"[T]o those individuals who experienced the tragedy of sexual and physical abuse at residential schools, and who have carried this burden believing that in some way they must be responsible, we wish to emphasize that what you experienced was not your fault … [W]e are deeply sorry."

–Excerpt from the Statement of Reconciliation, 1998

Figure 11.13 Phil Fontaine, National Chief of the Assembly of First Nations, experienced abuse at a residential school in Manitoba. The experience drove him in his fight for redress for Aboriginal peoples.

National Aboriginal Achievement Awards

Despite the challenges confronting Aboriginal communities in Canada, many Aboriginal people have made important contributions to their communities and to Canadian society in general. In recognition of these contributions, the National Aboriginal Achievement Awards (NAAA) were established in 1993 as part of the United Nations International Decade of the World's Indigenous Peoples. These awards "exemplify, encourage, and celebrate excellence in First Nations, Métis, and Inuit communities across Canada."

Each year, a national jury of Aboriginal people selects 12 Aboriginal professionals who have excelled in their careers. The jury also selects one youth and one lifetime achievement award recipient. The award winners are honoured at a nationally televised gala event.

In 2001, Lance Relland, a Métis from Alberta, received the Youth Achievement Award. Five years before, at the age of 16, Relland had been diagnosed with leukemia. At the time, he was a dancer with the Royal Winnipeg Ballet. Relland's best option was to undergo experimental treatment at an American university. However, the Alberta health plan would not pay his costs. He then established a medical foundation, raised over $100 000, and successfully underwent the difficult treatment. Relland learned that less than one per cent of registered bone marrow donors in Canada are Aboriginal. In response, he set up the Aboriginal Bone Marrow Registries Association. Relland went on to study medicine, where he was at the top of his class. As a result of his own experience with a life-threatening illness, Relland has become an activist for patients' rights.

"The Aboriginal community makes significant contributions and participates in diverse ways that many Canadians are not aware of … The National Aboriginal Achievement Awards are highlighting the accomplishments of Aboriginal people and helping to move us closer to our dual goals of increasing education and participation in the Canadian economy."

Source: John Kim Bell, founder of NAAA and classical musician, CBC Arts, 13 January 2004.

Figure 11.14 The NAAA represent "the highest honour the community bestows upon its own achievers." In your opinion, how important is it for people to receive official recognition within their own communities?

Some other past award winners and their achievements include

- 1994: Alanis Obomsawin, Film. One of Canada's foremost documentary filmmakers, Obomsawin has "used film to give an authentic and powerful voice to Aboriginal people in Canada." Her 1971 film Christmas in Moose Factory illustrated the realities of Aboriginal culture to the rest of Canada.
- 1998: Tagak Curley, Business and Commerce. As president of the Nunavut Construction Company, Curley oversaw the building of the infrastructure for the Nunavut government. In his position as community development officer with Indian Affairs and Northern Development, Curley helped organize the Inuit politically and develop their leadership.
- 2007: Monica Peters, Technology and Trades. After relearning her Aboriginal language and regaining her identity as a Kanien'kehá:ka, Peters developed online language translations that could potentially save languages throughout the world that are in danger of becoming extinct.

Responding

1. Referring to the examples of NAAA recipients in this feature, to what extent is it possible to contribute to both your culture and to Canadian society in general?
2. Do you think it is important for young people to have role models within their own communities? Explain.

Challenge and Response

1. What is the connection between land claims and Aboriginal sovereignty?
2. Review the government's apology regarding residential schools in the margin quotation on page 379. What are some possible reasons why students who suffered abuse might have declined or refused to come forward earlier?
3. In Chapter 10, you learned that some Québécois believe Québec should be recognized as a distinct society in Canada's Constitution. Do you think Aboriginal nations are distinct societies in Canada? Explain your answer.

Reading Strategy

Create an organizer with three headings "Organization," "Purpose," and "Benefits for Canada." As you read about the following global organizations, complete the organizer.

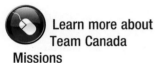

Learn more about Team Canada Missions

Global Connections

Under Prime Minister Chrétien, Canada continued to play a key role in the developing process of globalization. As a major trading country, it was important for Canada to expand its ties with countries throughout the world.

Team Canada

In an effort to increase trade and investment, as well as to create jobs and growth in Canada, the federal government organized a series of Team Canada Missions. Led by Chrétien, these missions involved provincial premiers, territorial government leaders, and private business leaders. They visited various countries with the purpose of highlighting the commercial, political, educational, and cultural links between Canada and these countries. As a result, businesses throughout Canada closed deals with governments around the world. Chrétien led seven Team Canada Missions:

- 1994: China
- 1996: India, Pakistan, Indonesia, and Malaysia
- 1997: South Korea, Philippines, Thailand
- 1998: Mexico, Brazil, Argentina, Chile
- 1999: Japan
- 2001: China (Beijing, Shanghai, and Hong Kong)
- 2002: Russia and Germany

International Organizations

Another way that Canada extended its reach in a rapidly changing world was by actively pursuing its ties with a number of international organizations.

Asia-Pacific Economic Cooperation

The Asia-Pacific Economic Cooperation (APEC) is a group of Pacific Rim countries that meet annually to foster freer trade and investment and to develop greater economic and technical cooperation. In 2008, APEC accounted for 47 per cent of global trade. In 1997, Canada played host to the APEC summit in Vancouver. Protestors demonstrated in the streets to focus attention on the plight of disadvantaged citizens living in APEC countries. (You will learn more about APEC in Looking Ahead.)

Figure 11.15 Critics of APEC argue that, when powerful leaders meet, the concerns of people living in poverty are not heard. To what extent do you think protests at international gatherings are effective? Give reasons for your response.

Arctic Council

The Arctic Council includes eight northern countries and provides for the participation of six indigenous organizations from those countries. These organizations are considered "permanent participants." In Canada, they include the Inuit Circumpolar Conference, the Gwich'in Council International, and the Arctic Athabaskan Council. Norway chaired the Arctic Council from 2006 to 2008; Denmark and Sweden will lead the organization from 2008 to 2010.

The Council is likely to be of great importance in the future because of its focus on economic development and environmental protection in the northern communities of its member countries. One of its continuing, central concerns is the economic, social, and environmental impact of global warming.

Commonwealth of Nations

The Commonwealth of Nations is made up of the countries that were formerly colonies of the British Empire. It is a voluntary association of 53 countries, with a total population of two billion—nearly 30 per cent of the world's population. The Commonwealth works toward improving the life and security of its members through economic and cultural links. Its leaders meet every two years. Canada is one of the Commonwealth's leading advocates and is the largest contributor to its development programs.

La Francophonie

Canada has links with other French-speaking countries around the world through la Francophonie. Created in 1970, la Francophonie is a "cultural and linguistic community of more than 200 million people who use French to varying degrees in their daily lives." It is also an institutional community of 55 states and governments that promotes closer ties among French-speaking countries by encouraging co-operation in education, culture, and technology. Meetings are held every two years to develop policies on politics, economic co-operation, cultural and scientific exchange, justice, and peace and security.

Many of the member countries are former colonies of France. Canada is one of la Francophonie's founding members. The provinces of Québec and New Brunswick (Canada's only officially bilingual province) have special status as participating governments.

Group of Eight

The Group of Eight (G8) is an informal group of the eight major industrial countries: Canada, France, Germany, Italy, Japan, Russia, Great Britain, and the United States. It was previously known as the G7 until Russia became a full participant in 1998. G8 leaders and representatives from the European Union meet at annual summits to discuss economic and foreign policies.

In 2002, Canada hosted a G8 summit in Kananaskis, Alberta. The Chrétien government set three priorities for the group's discussions: "fighting terrorism, strengthening global economic growth and sustainable development, and building a new partnership for Africa's development." In recent years, the summits have addressed health, environmental, and security issues.

Some experts say that the G8 represents the interests of an elite group of developed countries and does not consider the needs of the rest of the world. They point to the fact that countries with fast-growing economies

"In effect, Canada is able to represent both the Commonwealth and [la] Francophonie without being a former colonial power, as are France and Great Britain."

–Michel Tétu, *The Oxford Companion to Canadian History*, 2004

"The world would be much the poorer without the quality of internationalism that has been peculiarly Canada's."

–Shridath Ramphal, Commonwealth Secretary-General, 1975–1990

and large populations, such as China and India, are not included in the G8, nor are African or Latin American countries. During its summits, the G8's promotion of globalization has often resulted in anti-globalization protests. Others argue that the G8 has been instrumental in aiding developing countries. They point to the G8's campaigns to combat disease and to its development programs.

European Union

Created in 1992, the European Union (EU) includes 27 countries (as of 2008). With a total population of nearly 500 million, it is the world's largest and most powerful common market. A common market is the strongest form of regional integration. Common market agreements include the free trade of goods and services and the free movement of capital and labour within the trading bloc. Trading partners outside the bloc are subject to a common set of trade restrictions. While it is not a federation, the EU does have some of the elements common to a federal union: a parliament, a flag, an anthem, a founding date, and a common currency.

Relations with this powerful body are vital to Canada in an increasingly globalized economy. After the United States, the EU is Canada's most important trading partner. Among the EU's trading partners, Canada ranks ninth. EU and Canadian leaders meet regularly at summits to exchange views on a wide range of issues such as climate change and poverty in developing countries.

Figure 11.16   In 1995, minister of Fisheries Brian Tobin ordered Canadian patrol ships to fire shots at a Spanish fishing trawler in international waters off the coast of Newfoundland. The vessel was seized and charged with overfishing and using illegal nets. This disagreement with Spain escalated until it involved all EU countries. Why would the rest of the EU countries have chosen to support Spain in this dispute?

Organization of American States

The Organization of American States (OAS) "brings together the nations of the Western Hemisphere to strengthen co-operation on democratic values, defend common interests, and debate the major issues facing the region and the world." The goal of the OAS is to encourage peace and security in the Americas and to promote the social and economic growth of developing countries within the organization.

Canada's membership in the OAS has given it the opportunity to play a role in Central and South America. The organization meets regularly in Summits of the Americas. Recent summits have focused on freer trade and closer cultural and economic ties, as well as human rights, the drug trade, and terrorism.

World Trade Organization

In Chapter 5, you learned about the General Agreement on Tariffs and Trade (GATT), established in 1947.

The final round of GATT negotiations transformed GATT into the World Trade Organization (WTO) on 1 January 1995. The WTO works to improve trade relations among the countries of the world, especially by removing tariffs and other barriers to trade. Its main purpose is to settle trade disputes among governments and organize trade negotiations and meetings. For example, the softwood lumber dispute between Canada and the United States was taken before the WTO.

The WTO is a voluntary organization of 151 countries (as of 2008). However, it plays a very important role in major world issues because almost all countries in the world are WTO members. Meetings of the WTO have also resulted in anti-globalization protests. Some individuals and groups believe that the WTO and similar organizations favour the interests of developed countries and corporations over those of developing countries and average employees.

"WTO chief Pascal Lamy has acknowledged that free trade hurts some, but he has argued that the majority benefit. He has also said that no poor nation has become wealthy without trading."

–Canadian Press, 15 December 2005

Learn more about Canada's global connections

Challenge and Response

1. Name some significant regions of the world that Canada may be neglecting in terms of exploring trade agreements? Explain.

2. For each organization described in this section, explain how Canada's association with it helps to extend our global links.

3. a) Do you think protestors at meetings of global organizations provide an important alternative understanding of these meetings, or are they simply disruptive? Give reasons for your response.

   b) Considering that the media tend to give more coverage to violent protests, what might this suggest about bias in the media?

"The Rwandan genocide happened because the international community—if I may be brutal, as the genocide was—didn't give one damn for Rwandans because Rwandans don't count. Rwanda is of no strategic value to anybody, and has no strategic resources."

–General Roméo Dallaire, 7 April 2004

"I believe this incident could have been prevented if the UN had stepped in and the peace-keeping troops [had come] early enough ... [M]ost incidents like this could be prevented as long as someone takes the responsibility to step up and try to stop it. Unfortunately, I believe that no one did this in the 1994 Rwanda genocide."

–Rachel D., Southridge School, 2005

"If we want to know peace, if we want to at least heal the wounds, the truth must be known. Justice is important."

–Callixte Kabayiza, Rwandan genocide survivor, 10 April 2007

The New World Order

The end of the Cold War ushered in a "new world order" with only one superpower—the United States. Many Canadians looked forward to greater peace and security and perhaps reduced spending on war materials. However, increasingly brutal regional conflicts and the outburst of extremist activity around the globe shattered that optimistic picture.

Canada gradually moved from a peacekeeping role to a more aggressive peacemaking role in world affairs. Its NATO and NORAD alliances became more active and central to the member countries' concerns. The military was expanded and deployed in a wider and more dangerous mission in Rwanda. Although Canada did not participate in the invasion of Iraq, it did play a leading role in the mission to Afghanistan, as you will discover in Chapter 12.

Rwanda

Rwanda is an African country that has suffered violence and genocide, even while United Nation forces were stationed there. In 1993, a small UN force led by Canadian General Roméo Dallaire was sent to protect the citizens of the country, particularly in the capital of Kigali. Long-term rivalry between the majority Hutus and the minority Tutsis had erupted into civil war. The UN forces were supposed to bring relief supplies of food and aid and help establish a ceasefire in the conflict. Dallaire warned his UN superiors that he feared a major upheaval and did not have a sufficiently large force to prevent a wide-open conflict.

In 1994, a Hutu group, the Interhamwe, began to strike out at the Tutsis in a bloody campaign of rape and murder. *Interhamwe* is a Kinyarwanda word meaning "those who attack together." Within 100 days, the machete-wielding Interhamwe had murdered 800 000 Tutsis. One million people fled the country. Dallaire sent a team of 10 Belgian soldiers to protect the prime minister of Rwanda. The soldiers were seized, tortured, and murdered.

Dallaire asked for a UN rapid-reaction force of about 5000 soldiers to stop the slaughter. The UN debated the request but nothing came out of those talks. The failed UN mission in Somalia had left many countries—particularly the United States—leery of sending troops into violent situations. The UN pulled most of its troops out of Rwanda and even questioned whether the situation was as bad as described. Some critics accused the UN of not caring about Rwanda because it was a poor African country.

In July 1994, a rebel Tutsi army, the Rwandan Patriotic Front, finally drove the Interhamwe out of the country. It then organized a coalition government called the Government of National Unity. In 2003, Rwanda held free elections, but reconciliation is still an ongoing process in the war-ravaged country.

War Crimes

In 1997, the United Nations returned to Rwanda to assist in the establishment of the International Criminal Tribunal for Rwanda. In 1998, this UN tribunal became the first international court to hand down a conviction for genocide.

Roméo Dallaire: Witness to Genocide

Roméo Dallaire seemed destined to a military life. He was born in the post-war Netherlands in 1946 after his father, a Canadian sergeant who had helped liberate the country, met and married a Dutch nurse. As a youth, he was involved in boy scouts and cadets. In 1964, he won admission to Collège Militaire Royal de Saint-Jean in Québec. He was made a lieutenant in 1969 and commanded troops during the October Crisis in 1970.

Dallaire was an artillery officer and continued up the ranks to become a brigadier general in 1989. When the United Nations was trying to settle the Rwandan civil war, it needed a bilingual officer—Rwanda is a francophone country—to serve as force commander in the peace process. Canada was keen to regain world respect as a peacekeeping nation after its disgrace in Somalia. Dallaire was assured he would be leading a textbook UN peacekeeping mission. Within months, that assessment proved tragically inaccurate.

Figure 11.17 In an interview with the CBC News in 2003, Roméo Dallaire said: "I failed, yes. The mission failed. They died by the thousands, hundreds of thousands. That's why [my book is] subtitled *The Failure of Humanity*."

Dallaire returned home in 1994 a broken man. For a time, he was accused of not having been tough enough in Rwanda. He suffered from post-traumatic stress disorder. His career was in shambles. He left the army. His life nearly ended in a suicide attempt. After a period of therapy, Dallaire tried to silence his personal demons by writing about his experiences.

In 2003, his book *Shake Hands with the Devil: The Failure of Humanity in Rwanda* was published. It became a respected bestseller and won the Governor General's Literary Award for Non-Fiction. In 2004, he returned to Rwanda as a witness for the UN's International Criminal Tribunal. He testified for the prosecution in the trial of Colonel Théoneste Bagosora, one of the leaders of the Rwandan genocide.

In 2004, Dallaire ranked 16th in the CBC's *Greatest Canadian* contest. In 2005, Prime Minister Paul Martin appointed Dallaire to the Senate. Dallaire also gives speeches about conflict, stress, and the plight of children in wars. The film *Shake Hands with the Devil*, based on Dallaire's book, premiered at the Toronto International Film Festival in September 2007.

"Almost 50 years to the day that my father and father-in-law helped to liberate Europe—when the extermination camps were uncovered and when, in one voice, humanity said, 'Never again,'—we once again sat back and permitted this unspeakable horror to occur."

Source: Roméo Dallaire, introduction to *Shake Hands with the Devil* (Toronto: Random House Canada, 2003).

Responding

1. Why do you think Roméo Dallaire called the Rwanda mission a "failure of humanity"? Do you agree with his assessment? Explain.

2. Dallaire told CBC News that he felt he, too, had failed. Why might he consider the mission in Rwanda a personal failure? To what extent do you think this is an accurate judgment?

Figure 11.18 Many people are permanently scarred by the images of the twin towers of the World Trade Center collapsing in fire and smoke. The nearly 3000 dead included people from all walks of life and 70 countries, including 26 Canadians. Why do you think the World Trade Center and the Pentagon were chosen as targets?

Canada and War Crimes

In 2000, Canada enacted the Crimes Against Humanity and War Crimes Act to punish people living in Canada who are accused of war crimes. The first person to be tried under this act was Désiré Munyaneza. He arrived in Canada in 1997 following the Rwandan civil war. He was refused refugee status and, in 2005, was arrested and charged with war crimes. In July 2007, Munyaneza went on trial in Montréal for murdering and raping Rwandan women and slaughtering Rwandan men with a machete. At the trial, Dallaire testified about the horrifying scope of the Rwandan genocide. He said at the landmark Canadian war crimes trial that he saw thousands of bodies fill Rwandan rivers and ditches during the turmoil.

The War on Terror

On 11 September 2001, terrorists hijacked four commercial airliners. Two of them were crashed into the World Trade Center in New York, one into the Pentagon near Washington, DC, and the other crashed into a field in Pennsylvania. Canada, along with the other NATO countries, was swift in offering support to its US ally in that country's time of need. Canadian military, police, and intelligence were all put on high alert. In the days following the attacks, planes bound for the United States were rerouted to Canada—particularly Newfoundland and Labrador—because of ongoing security concerns. Local citizens welcomed the displaced passengers.

On 20 September 2001, US president George W. Bush declared a global "war on terror." He spoke of an "axis of evil," referring to Iraq, Iran, and North Korea. Canada's neighbour was wounded and angry and ready to strike hard at those it considered enemies. In a super-heated international environment, Canadian diplomats, politicians, and military leaders had to face difficult choices. For Prime Minister Chrétien, the major question was how closely Canada would tie itself to foreign policy decisions made by the United States and our other allies.

A Renewed NATO

During the Cold War, thousands of Canadians had served on NATO bases in Europe. Over the years, Canadian interest in NATO waned, particularly during the Trudeau era. When the Cold War ended in 1990, many observers felt that NATO was obsolete.

In the 1990s, however, civil war and genocide in the territories of the former Yugoslavia gave the alliance new life and purpose. After many attempts by United Nations peacekeeping forces to protect civilians and monitor weak ceasefire agreements, NATO moved into the region to exert its influence and muscle through direct military intervention. NATO troops enforced peace and protected civilians caught in the crossfire. A heavy, sophisticated bombing campaign forced Yugoslavia to end attacks on Albanians in the province of Kosovo.

With the breakup of the Soviet Union and the end of its influence on other countries in Eastern Europe, NATO saw a vastly changed Europe

and began to adapt. Former enemy countries were clamouring to join the alliance. Between 1999 and 2004, NATO expanded rapidly and took in 10 former Soviet-bloc countries. Many other Eastern European countries are in line to join the alliance.

After 2001, one of NATO's central concerns was the fight against terrorism. NATO sent five aircraft and 200 air troops to patrol the airspace above North America after the September 11 attacks. In 2004, NATO also organized rapid-response units of elite land, sea, and air troops to be sent to crisis areas. By 2007, NATO forces had been active in the Balkans, Afghanistan, Iraq, and Darfur (in Sudan)—far from the original mandate of the alliance.

A New Role for NORAD

Another alliance that seemed to lose its significance after the Cold War ended was the North American Aerospace Defence Agreement (NORAD). Founded in 1957, NORAD's original purpose was to protect North America from Soviet attack, as you read in Chapter 5.

In recent years, however, NORAD's focus has changed. Its mission is aerospace warning and aerospace control. The attacks of 11 September 2001 demonstrated that NORAD was unprepared to defend against an attack from within North America. Today, NORAD monitors domestic airspace and has procedures for shooting down an airplane if it is hijacked. In 2006, NORAD added a maritime mission. It is also involved in monitoring and intercepting smuggling activities—particularly people and drugs.

"The Parties agree that an armed attack against one or more of them in Europe or North America shall be considered an attack against them all…"

–Article Five of the NATO treaty

 Learn more about Canada's military alliances

MAP STUDY: NATO and NORAD

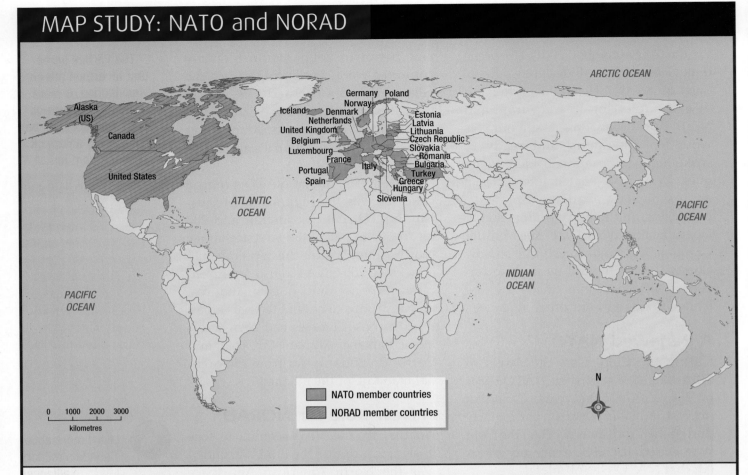

Figure 11.19 These are the member countries of NATO and NORAD as of 2008.

As a member of two military alliances—NATO and NORAD—Canada is committed to being prepared to fight a war. In the past few years, the Canadian Forces have been built up considerably. Canadian troops are stationed far from home not as peacekeepers but as combat soldiers. As you will discover in Chapter 12, Canadians are divided about this new role for the Canadian Forces.

Analysis and Response

1. Which alliance do you think is most important to Canada's interests? Provide reasons for your response.
2. Reread Article Five of the NATO treaty in the margin on page 389. Do you think this alliance is favourable for Canada? Give reasons for your response.
3. Some Canadians believe that Canada should stay out of international conflicts and renounce military alliances. What might be some of the benefits and drawbacks of such a course of action?

Invading Iraq

Although Canada and the United States have generally stayed on good terms, the two countries have not always agreed on important international issues. For example, as you read in Chapter 7, Canada did not support American involvement in the Vietnam War. It has also remained on friendly terms with Cuba, against the wishes of the United States.

In 2003, at the height of the war on terror, the government of Jean Chrétien did not join the US-led "coalition of the willing" in its invasion of Iraq. The coalition's goal was to overthrow Iraqi dictator Saddam Hussein and to locate and destroy alleged weapons of mass destruction (WMDs) that Iraq could use against Israel and its Western allies. The United Nations was divided on the issue of invading Iraq. As a long-time supporter of and contributor to UN missions, Canada was not willing to defy the wishes of this organization.

"[A]re we just following the Americans because we think that they know all the answers? We want Canada to be seen as an independent, strong country on the international scene, but by being followers of the US we aren't asserting our own free-will and independence. So we have to ask ourselves: is the price of war worth it? It's not."

–Matthew Moulton, "The price of war: is it too high?", Historica YouthLinks forum

Learn more about the war in Iraq

Figure 11.20 As the conflict in Iraq worsened, and the death and destruction spiralled out of control, many Canadians were relieved that Canada had not entered this conflict that seemed to be based on a shaky premise and had no obvious end point. Do you think the outcome of the conflict so far justifies the devastation in Iraq? Explain.

ISSUES

Canada and the Invasion of Iraq

The issue: Was Canada's decision not to join the American-led invasion of Iraq justified?

Despite immense pressure from the United States and from our other great ally, Great Britain, Canada refused to participate in the invasion of Iraq in 2003. Canadians were split on the issue—

as were the country's political parties—although the majority supported the decision to stay out of the war. In Québec, most of the population was firmly opposed to sending Canadian troops to Iraq. There were compelling reasons for both joining the coalition and staying out of the war.

Arguments For Joining the Coalition	Arguments For Not Joining the Coalition
• The United States is our closest ally and trading partner.	• The UN was still investigating Iraq for evidence of WMDs and wanted more time before taking military action.
• Our neighbour was attacked on 11 September 2001 and we should therefore have accepted its request for help.	• Canadian officials found no reliable evidence linking Iraq to al Qaeda, the group that had launched several attacks around the world, including those of September 11.
• Saddam Hussein was a brutal dictator who had employed WMDs (in the form of nerve gas) against his own people.	• It was clear that the UN was divided and not likely to approve the invasion. Canada should only have participated in the invasion with UN sanction (approval) and under UN direction.
• Not supporting the US might affect our trading relationship and harm Canada economically.	

Figure 11.21 These are the arguments for and against joining the "coalition of the willing." Which ones are most convincing to you? Why?

"In Iraq, a dictator is building and hiding weapons that could enable him to dominate the Middle East and intimidate the civilized world … This same tyrant has close ties to terrorist organizations, and could supply them with the terrible means to strike this country … The danger posed by Saddam Hussein … must be confronted."

Source: President George W. Bush, in a speech to the American Enterprise Institute, 6 February 2003.

"The price of being the world's only superpower is that its motives are sometimes questioned by others … Not everyone around the world is prepared to take the United States on faith … Therefore it is imperative to avoid the perception of a 'clash of civilizations.' Maximum use of the United Nations will minimize that risk."

Source: Prime Minister Jean Chrétien, in an address to the US Council on Foreign Relations, 13 February 2003.

"Chrétien's decision to keep Canada out of the effort to disarm Iraq is a betrayal of Canadian values, of our national interest, and of our closest allies… "

Source: Former Ontario premier Mike Harris, in an address to the Fraser Institute, 3 April 2003.

"The way to deal with Saddam Hussein is not by killing thousands of Iraqi civilians, any more than the way to deal with American foreign policy was by killing thousands of American civilians on September 11 … We are deeply alarmed that the most powerful nations in the world continue to rely on military force to achieve their global, political, and economic goals while eroding the standard of living, the environment, and the security of people throughout world."

Source: Michael Mandel, law professor, in Rosemary Ganley, "Canada's leaders say 'no' to war." *Catholic New Times*, 20 October 2002.

"The US ... invaded the Middle East without full facts. The US should have backed out when no weapons of mass destruction were found."

Source: Robert R., R.S. McLaughlin Collegiate and Vocational Institute, YouthLinks forum: War in Iraq, 2007.

"A positive point on the war in Iraq is the end of Saddam Hussein's reign. Saddam was a ruthless tyrant and needed to be taken out of power before he killed any more people ... I applaud the United States for ... this great piece of history!"

Source: Justin E., Corner Brook High School, YouthLinks forum: War in Iraq, 2007.

Responding

1. Suggest other arguments that could be used to support either side of the debate on joining the coalition.
2. What role, if any, should Canada have played in the invasion of Iraq? Create a PMI organizer to assess this issue. Based on the results of your PMI organizer, develop and state your position on the issue.
3. Do you think Canada should play a role in Iraq today? If so, describe the type of role. If not, provide reasons for your answer.

Challenge and Response

1. What events moved Canada from a peacekeeper to a peacemaker?
2. What lessons might be drawn from the failure of the UN mission in Rwanda?
3. In a Venn diagram, compare and contrast the current purpose of NATO and NORAD.
4. In your opinion, what is Canada's responsibility toward the United States when it takes pre-emptive, unilateral action against another country? (*Pre-emptive action* means preventing an attack by disabling the enemy; *unilateral action* means involving only one participant.) Explain your position.

Profile in Power:

Paul Edgar Philippe Martin

Figure 11.22   Paul Martin (1938–)

"Three of the highest courts in the land (in Ontario, Québec, and British Columbia) have said that discrimination on the grounds of sex in terms of the definition of marriage is against the Charter of Rights. It is absolutely a question of human rights."

–Prime Minister Paul Martin, June 2004

In 1946, Paul Martin Jr contracted polio and could not speak for a year. His father, Paul Martin Sr, was so distressed he began pressuring the Liberal Party to create a universal health care system for all Canadians. Martin Sr served under four different Liberal prime ministers but never won the party leadership. That fact drove Martin Jr's determination to become prime minister of Canada.

After graduating from law school, Paul Martin worked for Power Corporation of Canada, reviving companies that were not doing well. In 1973, he became president of one of those companies, Canada Steamship Lines, which he later purchased. By the time Martin entered Parliament in 1988, he owned 33 ships and dozens of buildings and companies around the world. When he became prime minister, he relinquished control of his companies to his sons.

In 1990, Martin lost his bid to become leader of the Liberal Party to Jean Chrétien. The two men differed widely on the Charlottetown Accord. Chrétien believed it was flawed and should be abandoned, while Martin thought an amended version would be acceptable. Their rivalry continued throughout Chrétien's time in office. Despite these differences, Chrétien appointed Martin minister of Finance. As you have seen, Martin was one of Canada's most successful Finance ministers. As a result, his popularity and prestige were so great that his dismissal from Cabinet in 2002 caused a crisis in the Liberal Party.

In 2003, Jean Chrétien resigned. Paul Martin became prime minister in December 2003 after winning the Liberal leadership with 93 per cent of the votes. Almost immediately, the Liberals were dealt a crushing blow. In February 2004, the Auditor General revealed that advertising agencies involved in the sponsorship program Chrétien set up in 1995 had wasted or lost millions of dollars and had channelled funds back into Liberal hands. Martin created a Commission of Inquiry to investigate the affair. Before Justice John Gomery had time to report his findings, Martin called a snap election in June 2004, which in effect became a referendum on the Liberal Party. The Liberals were reduced to a minority government.

In November 2005, the Gomery Commission cleared Paul Martin of any wrongdoing in the sponsorship scandal. However, the damage to the Liberal Party's reputation could not be erased. After the opposition parties passed a motion of non-confidence, an election was called for January 2006. The election campaign focused on Liberal corruption. When the Conservative Party won a minority government, Paul Martin resigned as Liberal leader.

Responding

1. Why do you think Canadians voted Martin out of office even though he was cleared of any wrongdoing in the sponsorship scandal?

Disaster Response

Another outcome of increasing globalization and the new world order was the almost instantaneous spread of news of natural disasters and the ability of wealthy developed countries such as Canada to rush emergency assistance to a disaster zone. In the early years of the twenty-first century, Canadian **nongovernmental organizations (NGOs)** and the federal government have been particularly active and effective in this area.

Indian Ocean Tsunami

In December 2004, the world was shocked to learn of the devastation created by a powerful **tsunami** that swept across the Indian Ocean and crashed into regions of Southeast Asia. Within hours, entire communities were swept out to sea or flattened by the rushing waters. More than 150 000 people lost their lives in the first few hours of this disaster.

Prime Minister Martin's government announced that it would match dollar for dollar any funds Canadians donated to NGOs for disaster relief. Canadians and citizens of other countries raised hundreds of millions of dollars for the victims of the tsunami. Canada dispatched its Disaster Assistance Response Team (DART) to Sri Lanka to provide clean drinking water, medical care, temporary shelters, and transportation services. On a per-capita basis, no country was more generous than Canada, which pledged one billion dollars in aid.

"The waves moved so quickly, there was no time to sound the alarm. Walls of water slammed into coastal areas of Indonesia, Malaysia, Myanmar, Thailand, Bangladesh, Sri Lanka, India and—thousands of kilometres away—Somalia in East Africa. The waves destroyed whatever lay in their path: from the built-up tourist resorts of Thailand to isolated fishing villages in Indonesia and Sri Lanka."

—CBC News In Depth,
22 January 2007

Figure 11.23   DART medical technicians attend to a young girl in Sri Lanka following the 2004 tsunami. DART co-ordinated its activities with the government of Sri Lanka and other agencies involved in the relief effort. How did Canadians' response to the disaster reflect a commitment to active global citizenship?

Some individual Canadians travelled to Southeast Asia to offer their help. Other Canadians who had been vacationing in Thailand went to work helping local communities recover. Later on, other Canadians assisted in the creation of a tsunami early-warning network.

Hurricane Katrina

The summer of 2005 was a season of deadly hurricanes in the United States. The most powerful was a Category 5 hurricane named Katrina that hit the central Gulf Coast of the United States. No one was prepared for the complete devastation that resulted from the breaching of the levees (dykes) that surrounded the low-lying city of New Orleans. Sixteen hundred people died in the flooding and tens of thousands were left stranded on rooftops or clinging to debris. The US Coast Guard rescued 33 000 people from the flood waters. Images of distraught people streamed across the globe.

Law and order broke down as police forces almost collapsed. The most powerful country in the world struggled to mount a successful response to the disaster. The United States' disaster relief forces and institutions were almost completely overwhelmed by the scope of the disaster. Some estimates placed the immediate damage at US$75 billion.

Canadians and their government were quick to offer help to their neighbour. Some of the first rescues were made by RCMP teams. The Canadian Forces rushed 1000 personnel and several ships to the scene. Young Canadians volunteered to work with Habitat for Humanity to help rebuild ruined homes. Canadian industrialist Frank Stronach used his resources to

Learn more about Canada's disaster response efforts

build a new community known as Canadaville for some of the displaced people of New Orleans. In Canada, his effort was supported by many donations and volunteers:
- Nineteen Canadian carpenters donated their time and expertise to help build the homes.
- The community was designed by a Toronto-based architectural firm.
- Air Canada provided free flights to the evacuees.
- Other assistance was provided by the Canadian Auto Workers Union, the Canadian Red Cross, St. John Ambulance Canada, and employees of Stronach's companies.

Earthquake in Kashmir

In October 2005, remote areas of Pakistan were struck by a powerful earthquake measuring 7.6 on the Richter scale. Villages and cities collapsed in seconds. The worst damage occurred in isolated mountain communities where it was difficult to send aid. Nearly 79 000 people lost their lives. A year later, almost two million people were still homeless.

Canada donated $79 million for relief supplies, tents, and reconstruction. The 200-member DART was sent to the region to provide emergency water, medical services, and rebuilding assistance. Thousands of individual Canadians sent financial contributions to a range of NGOs including the Canadian Red Cross, Care Canada, World Vision Canada, Oxfam Canada, and UNICEF.

Global Warming

If experts in global warming are correct, countries throughout the world, including Canada, may become increasingly susceptible to natural disasters such as floods, droughts, disease, earthquakes, and tsunamis. Global warming may be a slow process, but the earth's reaction to climate change can be immediate and overwhelming.

Some scientists fear that global warming and climate change may trigger disasters that lead to massive migration and desperate conflict over territory and basic resources such as water and arable land. Canadians may find their generosity and resources tested more frequently in such an uncertain and fragile environment.

Land Mines

There are an estimated 110 million unexploded land mines in the world, scattered throughout 64 different countries. The pressure of a tire, wheel, or human step will cause them to explode. They kill and injure 10 000 to 15 000 people every year, many of them young children. Canada started destroying its land mines in 1997. It has long argued that this form of warfare is barbaric and threatens human life long after the original conflict has been resolved.

Lloyd Axworthy, Canada's minister of Foreign Affairs from 1996 to 2000, lobbied hard for a treaty to end this practice and to develop de-mining programs. In 1996, Canada sponsored a global conference on the issue. In 1997, 122 representatives of the global community came to Ottawa to sign the Convention on the Prohibition of the Use, Stockpiling, Production, and Transfer of Anti-Personnel Mines and on their Destruction. By 2007, 153 countries had signed on. However, there were still some powerful countries that had yet to accept the agreement, including China, Russia, and the United States.

Youth Helping Youth

Many of the world's children live in poverty. Some do not have access to education or medical care. Some live in war zones where they are killed or forced to join armies. Their plight has not gone unnoticed—some young Canadians have stepped up to take action on their behalf.

Free The Children

Many Canadians know about the work of Craig Kielburger and the organization that he founded when he was 12 years old. Free The Children is a non-profit organization that fights child exploitation in regions where children are forced to work in often brutal and dangerous conditions. The organization has raised millions of dollars to defend the rights of children. Some of its accomplishments include building Free The Children schools

> "This will not be the first time people have fought over land, water, and resources, but this time it will be on a scale that dwarfs the conflicts of the past."
>
> –A representative from the Congo in a UN Security Council debate on global warming, April 2007

Figure 11.24 A Free The Children School in Sierra Leone. This is one of more than 500 schools in Asia, Africa, and Latin America providing education to more than 50 000 children every day. Through this program, girls and boys have the opportunity to complete five years of primary education—the minimum required for basic literacy. How does educating children help them to contribute to their communities?

"Unlike any other children's charity in the world, Free The Children is both funded and driven by children and youth. Our mission is to free young people from the idea that they are powerless to bring about positive social change, and encourage them to act now to improve the lives of young people everywhere."

—Free The Children

and delivering more than 202 000 school and health kits to students around the world. In 2007, Kielburger launched the ME to WE project, designed to encourage young people to pursue active volunteerism.

Right To Play

Right To Play uses specially designed sport and play programs to improve health, build life skills, and foster peace for children and communities affected by war, poverty, and disease. Many Canadians serve as high-profile athlete ambassadors for the organization, including Olympic athletes Clara Hughes (speed skating gold medalist), Hayley Wickenheiser (hockey gold medallist), Adam van Koeverden (kayak gold medallist), and Chantal Petitclerc (Paralympic wheelchair racing gold medallist).

Figure 11.25 These children in Dar es Salaam, Tanzania are playing a game called Human Knot in a Right To Play program in February 2007. What impact do you think this opportunity has on their lives?

Challenge and Response

1. When another country suffers a natural disaster, do you think that activism on the part of individual Canadians and NGOs puts more pressure on our government to send humanitarian aid? Explain.
2. Do you think Canadians have a responsibility to play an active role in helping those affected by disasters and in trying to make the world a better and safer place? Discuss this issue as a class or in small groups.

 # Sign of the Times

EARLY TATTOOS

The earliest recorded tattoos were found on Egyptian mummies who were buried in the great pyramids around 2000 BCE. The art of tattooing also existed in the ancient civilizations of Crete, Greece, Persia, Arabia, and China. In Northern Europe, Danes, Norse, and Saxons tattooed family crests on their bodies.

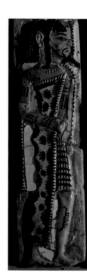

Figure 11.26 The purpose of tattoos has varied from culture to culture and over time. Tattoos have served as rites of passage, as signs of status and rank, as symbols of religious and spiritual devotion, as decorations for bravery, as pledges of love, and as marks of outcasts and convicts. This plaque from the Egyptian Museum is from Libya, circa 1187–1156 BCE.

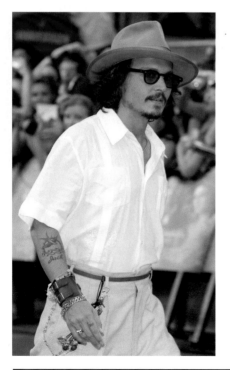

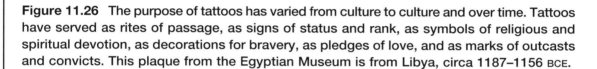 ## CELEBRITIES AND TATTOOS

In North America, tattooing first became popular with sailors during the Second World War. They wore tattoos of their ships and of the women they had left behind to fight overseas. In 1961, an outbreak of infection returned the image of tattooing to a sign of immorality until the early 1970s, when influential rock stars such as the Rolling Stones adopted them to assume a more rebellious image. Today, it is not unusual to see tattoos on rock stars, professional sports figures, ice skating champions, fashion models, and movie stars.

Figure 11.27 Johnny Depp is one of many celebrities who sport tattoos. The cultural status of tattooing has evolved from an anti-social activity in the 1960s to a present-day fashion statement.

Responding
1. What role do you think tattoos play in the expression of personal identity?
2. What is your position on wearing a tattoo yourself? Give reasons for your response.

Skill Path:
Creating Multimedia Presentations

A multimedia presentation is a display of information on a topic that uses a combination of formats—audio, visual, and text. Depending on the creator's imagination, time limitations, and available technology, a presentation may involve several different media such as CDs, DVDs, podcasts, posters, three-panel displays, and brochures. However, it is important that each medium complements the others and enhances the overall presentation.

STEP 1: Determine the Purpose of Your Presentation

Ask yourself what your precise goal is for the presentation.
- Do you want to inform or do you want to encourage a reaction?
- Is your topic narrow or open-ended?
- Who is the specific audience and what information do they need to know?

STEP 2: Select Your Key Points

Since a multimedia presentation involves different means of communicating information through diagrams, photographs, recorded sound, and video clips, for example, it must have a specific focus. Therefore, it is important to clearly define your main points.
- Before deciding on the types of media you will use, draw a blueprint or flowchart of what you intend to present.
- Keep in mind that it will still be possible to change or refine your presentation later on in the process when you are organizing your materials.

STEP 3: Conduct Research

Find and collect relevant information. Your school's teacher-librarian can help you with this task.
- Search the library's computer database for information on your topic. Record the call numbers of sources that are specific to your topic.
- Consult both primary and secondary sources. Refer to the Skill Path in Chapter 1.

STEP 4: Organize Your Information

Gather your research findings and organize them into categories.
- Rank-order these categories from most to least important.
- Determine what information you will use.
- Draw a storyboard that outlines a clear picture of what will happen throughout the presentation.
- Ensure that the information will flow smoothly, without repetition.

STEP 5: Test Your Presentation

In a multimedia presentation, the audience listens, sees, interprets, and perhaps manipulates hardware such as MP3 and DVD players. Ask yourself if you have made the presentation as easy and intuitive as possible for the audience.
- Review the information on presentation software in the Chapter 10 Skill Path.
- Carefully combine the different media in a way that is understandable and useful to your audience.
- Try to create an interesting journey by communicating the information.
- Ensure that the technologies you have used are safely connected and working properly.
- Decide if you will be in charge of all the elements in your presentation or if your audience will be free to view certain elements or the entire presentation on their own.

STEP 6: Practise Your Skill

Choose one of the following topics from the Chrétien years, and organize a plan for creating a multimedia presentation. You do not have to actually create the presentation—just develop a plan for what information you would include and how you would set up your presentation.
- international events
- economic issues
- Québec nationalism
- Aboriginal issues

Thinking Like a Historian:
Making Moral Judgments about the Past

Essential Question: As a historian, how do you make moral judgments about actions that took place in the past?

Historians often need to reflect on past decisions made by countries, groups, or individuals. To truly understand the rationale for those decisions, historians need to be careful about not passing judgment according to the standards of their own time. They also need to avoid judging the decisions purely on the basis of the outcomes.

Canada was twice called on to fight wars in Iraq against Saddam Hussein. In 1991, the Conservative government of Brian Mulroney agreed to send troops as part of a United Nations coalition of forces. In 2003, the Liberal government of Jean Chrétien refused to participate in the United States' invasion of Iraq. What led each of these governments to its decision? What domestic and international factors might have accounted for the difference in response?

You, the Historian

Review the section on the 1991 Gulf War in Chapter 10 (pages 329–330) and the section in this chapter on Prime Minister Chrétien's decision regarding the 2003 invasion of Iraq (page 391). In addition, you might wish to conduct further research.

1. Create an organizer to analyze the decisions made by the Mulroney and Chrétien governments. The example below suggests some criteria for analyzing these decisions.

	Mulroney's Decision (1991)	Chrétien's Decision (2003)
What was happening in Iraq?		
How did other countries respond to the situation?		
How did domestic issues in Canada affect the decision?		
What reason(s) was given for the decision?		

2. Draw conclusions from your analysis. Why do you think each government made the decision it did?
3. Explain your opinion of these decisions in written form. Keep in mind the guidelines historians use for making moral judgments about the past.

Chapter 12

Challenges of the New Millennium

Figure 12.1 After 13 years in the political wilderness, a new Conservative Party, under the leadership of Stephen Harper, ousted the Liberals to form a minority government in 2006. What challenges do you think Harper's government faced?

Chapter at a Glance

Thinking Ahead

As you read in Chapter 10, after Brian Mulroney's success in the 1980s, in 1993 the Conservatives were all but wiped off the political map. For the next 13 years, the Liberal Party ruled the country unchallenged while the Conservatives struggled to regain their identity and their share of public support.

In this chapter, you will discover the twists and turns along the road leading to the rebirth of the new Conservative Party. You will discover the challenges Canada faces in the twenty-first century. As you do, think about these key questions:

- What factors led to the creation of the new Conservative Party?
- What challenges did the Conservative government face?
- Is Canada's commitment to the environment and the Kyoto Protocol achievable?
- Why is Canadian sovereignty in the Arctic an important issue in the twenty-first century?
- Why was Canada's mission in Afghanistan controversial?
- What role should Canada play in the fight against HIV/AIDS?

Profile in Power:

Stephen Joseph Harper

Figure 12.2 Stephen Harper (1959–)

"I think Canadians are always behind our troops wherever they go, and I think the more they understand about the mission ... the more support they'll have for the work we're doing here ... Canada is not an island, we live in a dangerous world, and we have to show leadership in that world. That's what we're doing, and that's what I'm trying to do by going to support our men and women."

–Prime Minister Stephen Harper, "PM makes surprise visit to troops in Afghanistan." CTV, 13 March 2006

Stephen Harper first became interested in politics as a teenager in Toronto, where he joined the Young Liberals. When he was 19, he moved with his family from Toronto to Calgary, where he attended the University of Calgary and earned a master's degree in economics. In Alberta, Harper's strong opposition to Trudeau's National Energy Program prompted him to shift his political loyalties from the Liberals to the Conservatives. However, Harper soon became disillusioned with the party under the leadership of Brian Mulroney. In 1988, he left the Conservatives to join the newly created Reform Party.

Harper had a keen interest in policy issues. He contributed many ideas to the Reform Party's political platform. In 1993, he was elected to Parliament as the MP from Calgary West. His relationship with party leader Preston Manning grew strained over policies and strategies, however. Harper resigned his seat in 1997 and became president of a conservative lobby group called the National Citizens' Coalition.

In 2000, the Canadian Alliance succeeded the Reform Party. When the new party faltered, Harper became leader of the Canadian Alliance. By May 2002, Harper was leader of the official opposition. He continued his climb up the political ladder in 2003 when the Canadian Alliance

joined forces with the Progressive Conservatives to "unite the right" in a new Conservative Party of Canada. Harper won the race for the leadership of the new party just in time to face Canadian voters in the election of 2004. When the votes were counted, the Conservatives had emerged from more than a decade in the political wilderness, finishing second behind the Liberals.

By the end of 2005, the Liberals were struggling under the weight of scandal. Harper was determined to capitalize on their weakness. He campaigned on a promise of government accountability. His strategy worked. On 23 January 2006, Harper and the Conservatives defeated the Liberals to win a minority government. On 6 February 2006, Stephen Harper became the 22nd prime minister of Canada.

Once in office, Harper quickly followed through on many of his campaign promises, including reducing the GST from 7 per cent to 6 per cent. In October 2007, he reduced the GST yet again, to 5 per cent. Harper continued to carve out the new Conservative vision he had for Canada. He used careful political strategizing to achieve many of his goals, including moving Canada away from its long-held commitment to the environmental targets of the Kyoto Protocol. At the same time, however, he upheld Canada's commitment to human rights, including welcoming the spiritual leader the Dalai

Figure 12.3 Harper's first overseas trip as prime minister was to Afghanistan to visit Canadian troops stationed there on a NATO mission. What message do you think this trip sent to the troops in particular and to the military in general? What did it signal about Canada's foreign policy under Harper?

Lama to the Prime Minister's Office in October 2007. The move drew harsh public criticism from the People's Republic of China, who accused Canada of interfering in China's domestic affairs. (China considers the Dalai Lama to be leading the Tibetan separatist movement.)

By the start of 2008, Harper's minority government had successfully remained in office, relatively unchallenged, for two years. It remained to be seen what challenges the future would bring and how long the new Conservatives would maintain their hold on power.

Responding

1. Why do you think Harper changed political parties so many times?
2. Do you agree with Harper's comments about Canadians' attitudes toward our soldiers? Do you think his statement reflects the opinion of the majority of Canadians? Give reasons for your response.

Reading Strategy

Before you begin reading this section, return to Chapter 11 and review the section on the election campaign of 1993.

Learn more about the Reform Party and Preston Manning

"[Manning sent] a signal to traditional party brokers in Ontario and Québec that the West was capable of producing a formidable party … The effort to create the Canadian Alliance was an important step along that road."

—Vancouver Sun,
21 October 2003

Rebuilding the Political Right

A new conservative political party was born in Canada's Western provinces in 1987. The Reform Party, founded by Preston Manning, embraced traditional conservative economic values, such as balanced budgets, social program cutbacks, and deficit reductions. It opposed such liberal social policies as tougher gun laws, abortion, and same-sex marriage.

Reform Strikes a Chord

The Reform Party got off to a slow start. In 1988, when the Conservatives won their second straight majority government, the party failed to elect a single candidate. By 1993, however, Canadians had lost confidence in the Progressive Conservative Party. They delivered them a stunning defeat in the election of 1993, electing only two Conservative MPs across the country. The Reform Party, on the other hand,

had struck a chord with conservative voters—at least in the West. They elected 52 candidates. It seemed that the Reform Party had replaced the Conservatives as the voice of conservatism in Canada.

Manning was determined to build on the party's success. In 1997, after winning 60 seats in the House of Commons, the Reform Party became the official opposition. Yet the party had still failed to win a single seat east of Manitoba. Reform seemed destined to be a Western regional party. Without support in the east, it had little hope of forming the government in Ottawa.

By 2000, Manning realized his party had run its course. A new and broader coalition was needed to unite conservatives across the country. The Reform Party disbanded and re-emerged under the banner of the Canadian Alliance.

The Canadian Alliance

The transition from the Reform Party to the Canadian Alliance was bittersweet for Manning. Although he led the drive to create the Alliance, Manning lost the leadership in July 2000 to Stockwell Day. Like Manning, Day was a social and economic conservative. He was also a popular and media-smart politician. In the early days of his leadership, the Western conservative movement gained new momentum. The Canadian Alliance appeared confident it would surpass the success of the Reform Party in the next election.

Within a year, though, the Canadian Alliance was in disarray. Day hoped to win over moderate conservative voters. Yet his political philosophy, firmly based on socially conservative values, did not appeal to many

Figure 12.4 To many, the success of Preston Manning (shown here speaking with a Toronto commuter) and the Reform Party was as surprising as the collapse of the Conservatives. Why do you think this was so?

Canadians who wanted to maintain Canada's socially progressive policies.

Prime Minister Jean Chrétien decided to capitalize on the Canadian Alliance's troubles by calling an election in the summer of 2000. The Liberals succeeded in portraying the Alliance as a reactionary party that was ill-suited to govern a progressive country like Canada. The Liberals won a majority. The Alliance won 62 seats—two more than Reform had in the previous election. Yet once again they failed to win a single seat outside of Western Canada.

A New Leader

After the election, tensions within the Canadian Alliance mounted as support for Day's leadership crumbled. Several Alliance MPs abandoned the party in protest over Day's leadership. With the party in chaos, Day announced plans to hold a leadership convention to determine his fate.

While Day maintained the support of many social conservatives within the party, economic conservatives had found a new champion—a former Reform MP named Stephen Harper. They believed Harper was more mod-

Figure 12.5 Initially, Stockwell Day was a bright new face in Canadian politics. However, during the election campaign, he made a series of critical errors that made him the subject of ridicule in the media. To what extent do you think the media can influence the way voters view a political candidate?

erate than Day and would attract more voters. They persuaded him to run for the leadership. After winning a decisive victory over Day, Harper took quick action to change the fortunes of the conservative movement in Canada.

"What we've got to do is turn this party into an institution. It's too often been viewed as a popular protest movement or a regional fragment or a leader-centric vehicle or a coalition thrown together for a single election. I think the way to address that is to … build a permanent professional political institution."

—Canadian Alliance leader Stephen Harper after winning the leadership, 2000

Challenge and Response

1. What challenges did the Reform Party face? Why was it unable to overcome them?
2. Why do you think the socially conservative agenda of the Canadian Alliance did not appeal to the majority of Canadians? Explain your response.

A New Party, a New Government

Stephen Harper was determined to "unite the right." In December 2003, he persuaded the new leader of the Progressive Conservative Party, Peter MacKay, to join forces with the Alliance to present a strong and united alternative to the Liberals. The new Conservative Party then had to choose a leader. In 2004, MacKay and Harper both campaigned for the leadership. Harper won.

Figure 12.6   After 13 years of political struggle, Stephen Harper steered the Conservative Party back to power in 2006. With only a minority government, however, there was always the possibility of an early election. What strategies do you think political leaders need to use in minority governments that are different from those they would use if they had a majority?

For the first time in more than a decade, Canada's Conservatives were united under one party and one leader.

The Conservatives Break Through

As Stephen Harper was making his entrance onto the political stage, Prime Minister Jean Chrétien was preparing to make his exit. After he retired in 2003, his successor, Paul Martin, called an election in 2004. Canadians seemed weary of the powerful Liberal Party. After three successive majorities, the Liberals won only enough seats for a minority government. An opportunity was at hand for the new Conservatives.

On 28 November 2005, the Liberal government fell after losing a motion of non-confidence in the House of Commons. Parliament was dissolved and an election was called for 23 January 2006. Harper and the Conservatives relentlessly pursued the Liberals over the so-called "sponsorship scandal" in which members of the Québec wing of the Liberal Party admitted to misusing government funds. Martin and the Liberals were thrown off balance. They appeared to have lost confidence in their ability to pull an election victory out of the sponsorship fire.

The Conservatives, on the other hand, kept the scandal at the forefront of the campaign. They made accountability one of the key issues in the election and assured Canadians that a Conservative government would not tolerate corruption. They also made some campaign promises that appealed to average Canadians, such as reducing the unpopular GST from 7 per cent to 6 per cent, cracking down on crime, and reducing hospital waiting times.

Michaëlle Jean: A Governor General for the Twenty-first Century

"Canada sent a very powerful signal to the world. One reason I accepted [the position of Governor General] is that I knew how much hope a black woman in this office would bring to people who believe in equity and justice."

Source: Governor General Michaëlle Jean, "The people's governor general." *Reader's Digest* (July 2007): 57.

Michaëlle Jean was born in Port-au-Prince, Haiti, in 1957. As a child, she experienced the violence of the dictatorship of François "Papa Doc" Duvalier after her father, a school principal, was abducted and tortured in 1966. In 1968, the family escaped to Canada. They settled in the Québec mining town of Thetford Mines. At school, Jean experienced racism and discrimination, yet she was determined to pursue her education. She earned degrees in languages and literature from the Université de Montréal. Then she earned scholarships to study at three universities in Italy.

In the 1980s, Jean's work at Québec shelters for battered women marked the beginning of a lifelong commitment to prevent violence against women. She frequently returned to Haiti to document the challenges the people in her impoverished homeland faced. This led to a career as a television journalist with Radio-Canada. In 1992, Jean married Jean-Daniel Lafond, a French filmmaker. In 1999, they adopted their daughter, Marie-Éden, from Haiti.

In 2005, the Queen appointed Jean, on the advice of Liberal prime minister Paul Martin, to be Canada's 27th Governor General. Her early days in office sparked some controversy as some people accused her of being sympathetic to separatism. She proved them wrong, however, and adopted a personal motto, *Briser les solitudes* (Break the soli-

Figure 12.7 Her Excellency the Right Honourable Michaëlle Jean, visited the communities of Wunnumin Lake and Mishkeegogamang in northern Ontario in June 2007, in support of literacy education initiatives in Aboriginal communities.

tudes), a reference to the gap that exists between English-speaking and French-speaking Canadians.

Jean quickly became a favourite with both the press and the public. Many Canadians and others she met around the world found her engaging, charming, and charismatic. Jean reflected the "face" of Canada in the twenty-first century: an immigrant of African heritage who spoke many languages—French, English, Italian, Spanish, and Haitian Creole—as well as a working mother. As Governor General, Jean connected with young Canadians as well as with people from across Canada's multicultural population. She reached out to many people in developing countries in Africa and the Caribbean and visited Afghanistan, where she met with Canadian troops as well as with local women and children.

Responding

1. In what ways does a Governor General like Michaëlle Jean reflect Canadian society in the twenty-first century?

2. What signal do you think Canada sent to the world by appointing Jean as Governor General?

Learn more about contemporary Canadian politics

"We'll see what will happen with the government but we know that Canadians don't want elections and we'll continue to do our role as official opposition, explaining why we disagree with the government."

–Liberal leader Stéphane Dion, speaking about the Speech from the Throne, 25 October 2007

Many Canadians were uneasy about Harper and the new Conservatives. They questioned whether they had a hidden agenda to reverse or change the more socially progressive values of Canadian society reflected in legislation. Many others, though, believed the Liberals had been in power long enough. It was time for a change. On 23 January 2006, the Liberals' long hold on power in Ottawa ended.

A Wait-and-See Approach

Yet the election did not produce a clear victory for the Conservatives. They won 124 seats, including 10 in Québec, which had been a political graveyard for the party since the end of the Mulroney era. However, they won only 36 per cent of the popular vote, meaning that two out of three people had supported other parties. The Liberals won 102 seats and the NDP 29. The Bloc Québécois won 51 seats—all, of course, in Québec.

The Conservatives also failed to win seats in Canada's major cities. It seemed that the party's victory was not an endorsement for either Conservative policies or for Stephen Harper. In electing another minority government, Canadians were signalling that they were taking a cautious, wait-and-see approach to the new Conservatives.

The Liberals Choose a Leader

Their election defeat left the Liberals divided and discouraged. A leadership race began almost immediately as Paul Martin announced his resignation. Many high-profile Liberals who were strong candidates to replace Martin as leader surprised people by deciding not to run. The field was wide open for a host of new candidates. By the time of the leadership convention in Montréal in

late November and early December 2006, however, the real contest was down to four people:

- Michael Ignatieff, an internationally known scholar who returned to Canada from his position at Harvard University to run for the leadership
- Bob Rae, the former NDP premier of Ontario who had joined the Liberals in 2006
- Gerard Kennedy, a former education minister in the Ontario Liberal government
- Stéphane Dion, a former Cabinet minister in both the Chrétien and Martin governments

An Upset Victory

The frontrunner going into the convention was Michael Ignatieff. But in a surprising upset, Stéphane Dion won the leadership on the fourth ballot. Since he had been loyal to both Chrétien and Martin, Dion had distanced himself from the bitter rivalry that divided the Liberals. To help rebuild party solidarity, Dion invited his main rivals to be part of a new Liberal "Dream Team." He vowed to restore the tarnished image of the Liberal Party and regain the confidence of Canadians.

However, throughout 2007, Dion had difficulty establishing his credibility as Liberal leader. He failed to make significant gains in public opinion polls. Although voters remained uncertain about many Conservative policies, they did not have confidence in the new Liberal leader.

In October 2007, Harper used the Speech from the Throne to challenge the Liberals to call an election. Dion believed that Canadians did not want a third election in less than four years. As a result, he found himself in a politically

"I know that in politics we have to take perception into account, but you can't let that stop you. You have to look at your own convictions, and I have the conviction that we will win the next election."

–Liberal leader Stéphane Dion, 4 December 2006

Figure 12.8 Stéphane Dion had a reputation as a "come-from-behind" politician who frequently exceeded people's expectations. Do you think there is an advantage to being underestimated? Explain your response.

awkward situation. If he supported the NDP and the BQ in a vote of non-confidence and forced an election, the Liberals might suffer serious consequences at the polls. If they voted with the Conservatives, however, they would be supporting policies they strongly opposed. Dion's solution was to acknowledge his party's opposition to the Throne Speech as well as Canadians' opposition to another election. The Liberals then abstained from the non-confidence vote over the Speech from the Throne. At the beginning of 2008, governing Canada was still a balancing act for politicians in Ottawa.

Challenge and Response

1. Why do you think Canadians did not clearly choose one party over another in the 2006 election? Explain your response.
2. What do you see as the advantages and disadvantages of a minority government? Record your ideas in a T-chart.

The Conservative Government on the Home Front

As prime minister, Stephen Harper knew he had the opportunity to rebuild a lasting foundation for the Conservative Party. During its first months in office, his government moved quickly to implement changes. Harper's political opponents were openly hostile to his plans. They knew, however, that Canadians did not want another election. Instead of challenging the new government, the Opposition reluctantly agreed to compromise.

Campaign Promises

The Conservatives quickly followed through on their election promises, including:

- cutting the GST from 7 per cent to 6 per cent, with promises of further cuts
- restricting political lobbying and limiting political donations from corporations and unions
- creating a family allowance of $1200 a year per child under the age of six
- introducing legislation to deal with violent crime
- initiating discussions with the provinces over health care

Many Canadians supported these initiatives. However, some of Harper's decisions drew sharp criticism from both his opponents and from some members of his own party. When Harper appointed an unelected Conservative party organizer from Québec and a Liberal MP from Vancouver to his Cabinet, critics accused him of violating his party's own position on government appointments. Harper defended his actions by claiming that the government was under-represented in Québec and British Columbia. Therefore, the appointments gave the provinces a greater voice in government.

Broken Promises

On the campaign trail, Harper had promised not to increase taxes paid on **income trusts**. Once in office, however, he reversed his position and increased the taxes. He justified his decision by claiming that the trusts were expanding too quickly and the government was losing much-needed tax dollars. The political fallout was felt across the country, including in the Conservative stronghold of Western Canada. Critics charged that Harper was violating his own pledge of government accountability by reversing a campaign promise. The Toronto Stock Exchange plummeted. Investors suffered massive losses.

Figure 12.9 Harper promised tough new legislation to deal with violent crime, but he opposed tighter gun controls. Following a deadly shooting at Montréal's Dawson College in 2006 and several more shootings across Canada in 2007, more and more Canadians began demanding tighter gun controls. Harper still refused. What do you think governments should do to reduce gun violence?

Harper had also campaigned on a promise to reform the Senate. He wanted to pave the way to create an elected Senate in Canada. Many constitutional experts, however, warned the prime minister that attempting to reform the Senate would open the door to yet another constitutional crisis. After the divisive battles over the Meech Lake and Charlottetown accords, many Canadians did not want to tread into the murky waters of constitutional reform again.

A National Disabilities Act

During the election campaign, the Conservatives promised to introduce a national disabilities act to promote access to medical care and equipment as well as equal opportunities in education, employment, transportation, and housing for Canadians living with disabilities. Once in office, however, the rights of persons with disabilities jostled for priority with other issues on the government's agenda. Groups such as the Council of Canadians with Disabilities (CCD) urged the government to act to address access issues under federal jurisdiction, such as transportation, telecommunications, and new technologies. They appealed to both federal and provincial governments to address other disability issues, such as poverty, unemployment, and housing.

The Rights of Persons with Disabilities

Canada and its disability organizations played a leading role drafting the UN Convention on the Rights of Persons with Disabilities. In December 2006, however, the Conservative government stated Canada would not sign the convention. In response, the Council of Canadians with Disabilities,

Figure 12.10
In July 2007, David Onley, a Toronto television journalist, became the Lieutenant-Governor of Ontario. He pledged to use his position to promote greater accessibility for the 2 million Canadians living with disabilities.

the Canadian Association of Independent Living Centres (CAILC), the Canadian Association for Community Living (CACL), Amnesty International, and over 40 other organizations wrote to the prime minister urging the government to change its position. Their lobbying worked. On 30 March 2007, Canada signed the Convention at the official ceremony at the United Nations. The Convention marks a historic step in ensuring that persons with disabilities can participate fully in society and can contribute fully to their communities.

A Nation within a Nation

On 22 November 2006, Harper surprised both Parliament and the people of Canada when he introduced the following resolution in the House of Commons: "This House recognizes

> "In the developed world, where the life expectancy is 70 years or older, the average person lives eight years of their life with a disability."
>
> —Jim Derksen, CCD, 13 December 2006

> "This historic international human rights document creates a framework for persons with a disability worldwide to dream and to achieve for the betterment of their lives, their family, and their community."
>
> —David Shannon, chair, CAILC Social Policy Committee, 2007

 Learn more about disability issues in Canada

Canadian Paralympians

After the Second World War, sports became a form of therapy to enhance the quality of life for people who sustained injuries, such as the loss of a limb, during the war. An English neurosurgeon organized the first International Wheelchair Games to coincide with the 1948 Olympics. His goal was to establish a global competition for Paralympians to be held alongside the Olympic Games every four years. The first Paralympic Games were held in Rome in the summer of 1960. In 1976, the Paralympics expanded to the Winter Olympic Games when the first Winter Paralympics were held in Örnsköldsvik, Sweden.

Canada has competed in every Paralympic Games since 1968. Today, Canadian athletes have emerged as a powerhouse in the Games. At the Winter Paralympics held in Torino, Italy, in 2006, Canada finished in sixth place. At the Vancouver Winter Olympic Games in 2010, Canadian Paralympic athletes hope to finish in third place—or better!

Paralympic athletes compete in many different sports. The winter games include alpine, slalom, and cross-country skiing, as well as curling and sledge hockey. The summer games include rugby, basketball, swimming, and shooting. Events are organized under five categories—amputee, cerebral palsy, spinal cord injury, visual impairment, and other—to allow athletes to compete regardless of their level of physical functioning.

Canada's Paralympians travel to schools across Canada to motivate, educate, and inspire students not to give up the pursuit of their dreams. They serve as role models for overcoming life's challenges.

Figure 12.11 In 2007, The Royal Canadian Mint issued a 25-cent coin depicting wheelchair curling to commemorate the Vancouver Olympic and Paralympic Games in 2010. It is the first-ever circulation coin issued by a mint in honour of the Paralympic Games.

"Our Canadian Paralympians embody the true spirit of amateur sport. Through sport, the Paralympics empower people with disabilities and enrich their lives."

Source: Dr Gaetan Tardiff, "Celebrating Canada's Olympians." *Toronto Rehab: eMagazine* (Fall 2004).

"True champions continually renew their commitment to excellence, their eyes fixed on new challenges and never content to dwell on past victories."

Source: Canadian Paralympian Chantal Petitclerc, 31 January 2005.

 Learn more about Canada's Paralympians

Responding

1. Why do you think it was significant to commemorate the Paralympic Games?
2. What barriers, either physical or social, are there for persons with disabilities in your school? Identify specific areas in your school where better accessibility is needed and present your findings to the school.

that Québécois form a nation within a united Canada." The move was intended to defuse a motion by the Bloc Québécois calling for the recognition of Québec as a nation. The key difference between the two resolutions was that the Bloc did not include the words *within a united Canada* in their motion.

Harper stressed that the resolution was symbolic and did not give Québec any special political or legal status. The Liberals and New Democrats supported the Conservatives and voted in favour of the resolution. However, the leader of the Bloc Québécois, Gilles Duceppe, maintained that Harper was refusing to recognize Québec for what it was. Nevertheless, he vowed to use the motion to get the federal government to address Québec's concerns.

Figure 12.12 Polls indicated that the majority of Canadians in English Canada do not recognize the Québécois as a nation. Given this opposition, why do you think the Liberals and the New Democrats joined forces with the Conservatives to support the resolution?

The Sovereignty Debate

In June 2007, the issue of sovereignty, which had dominated Québec politics for two generations, appeared to be losing steam. It seemed the people of Québec had grown tired of the debate since the federalists narrowly won the last referendum in 1995. In the provincial election of 2007, the Parti Québécois placed third behind the Liberals and a new conservative party called Action Démocratique du Québec. A poll suggested that 68 per cent of Quebeckers wanted the PQ to drop the issue of independence and focus instead on gaining more power for the province within Confederation. Another poll in June 2007 indicated that the majority of Quebeckers believe that sovereignty is "highly or totally improbable."

Progress and Protest

When the Conservatives took office, many complex Aboriginal land claims disputes were still outstanding. At first, the relationship between the Harper

government and the Aboriginal community did not appear promising. In 2006, the Liberals and Aboriginal leaders had signed the Kelowna Accord. It promised $5 billion over five years for education, housing, and health care in Aboriginal communities. At the time, Harper had denounced the deal. Now that he was in office, Aboriginal leaders were concerned whether he would honour the agreement.

At first, Harper indicated his government accepted the accord in principle. However, he refused to be bound by any terms since few details had been worked out and no measures had been passed by Parliament. When the Conservatives issued their first budget, there was no money allocated to meet the obligations of the Kelowna Accord. Aboriginal leaders responded with disappointment and concern. In March 2007, the House of Commons passed a resolution demanding that the government honour the agreement.

"In Québec, the French word 'nation' means a collectivity bound by a common history, a common language, and a common culture. In English Canada it means a nation-state, an independent country, with a right to sovereignty in international affairs…"

–Errol Mendes, law professor, University of Ottawa, 30 November 2006

"Do Quebeckers form a nation within a united Canada? The answer is yes. Do the Québécois form an independent nation? The answer is no, and will always be no."

–Prime Minister Stephen Harper, 22 November 2006

ISSUES

Québec as a Nation

Reading Strategy

According to *The Canadian Oxford Dictionary*, a *nation* is:
- a community of people of mainly common descent, history, language, etc., forming a state or inhabiting a territory
- the state or territory itself
- a group of Aboriginal people with common ancestry who are socially, culturally, and linguistically united

Think about these definitions as you read this Issues feature and consider the points of view expressed by Canadians.

The issue: Is Québec a nation within Canada?

Many Canadians were unclear about the significance of the government's decision to recognize the Québécois as a nation. They wondered what the declaration might mean for the future of Canada–Québec relations. Canadians from all backgrounds and from all parts of the country expressed their points of view.

"I'm tired of hearing people talk about Québec as just another part of Canada. It is not, we do not share the same history, language, values, religion, ancestry as the rest of Canada. There are more differences between Quebeckers and Canadians than there are between Canadians and Americans. To compare Québec to the rest of the provinces is utterly ridiculous. Why should we be treated differently? Because we are different."

Source: A Quebecker, CTV News Politics Blog, 29 November 2006.

"We should recognize Québec as a unique and distinct nation within our country ... If India can have 800+ languages and every different religion living densely packed in the subcontinent, surely we can survive a couple of unique cultures within our sparsely populated, wide-open spaces."

Source: Giri Puligandla, "Your view." CBC News Online, 23 November 2006.

"I am glad that ... a few people have picked up on the fact that Mr. Harper only mentioned the Québécois, NOT Québec, NOT Quebeckers. I am a Quebecker ... but by no stretch of the imagination do I expect the Québécois to accept me as part of their nation."

Source: Elizabeth Saunders, "Your view." CBC News Online, 24 November 2006.

"Referring to Québec as a 'nation' is ... excluding French Canadians who live all across the country. Should they be left out because they do not live in *la belle province*?"

Source: Drew Adamick, "Your view." CBC News Online, 23 November 2006.

"I don't think that Québec deserves any more recognition than any other distinct culture that exists within Canada. We are a country of immigrants and none deserves to be elevated above others ... There is one Canada, one nation, one people..."

Source: Joey Carr, New Brunswick, CTV News Politics Blog, 23 November 2006.

"There is no satisfactory definition of what makes a 'Québécois.' Can an Arab be a Québécois? A First Nations person? An Asian? ... The answer is no..."

Source: Erik Ruisseaux, Gatineau, Québec, "Your view." CBC News Online, 23 November 2006.

"Under no circumstances should the recognition of the Québécois be achieved by putting the historical and constitutional status of First Nations at risk."

Source: Chief Phil Fontaine, Assembly of First Nations, Canoe, 5 December 2006.

"Nation of Québec—no problem at this end ... Signed the Empire of Alberta."

Source: John Wardrop, Calgary, Alberta, "Your view." CBC News Online, 23 November 2006.

Responding

1. In a T-chart, identify the different arguments presented for and against recognizing the Québécois as a nation. Then, highlight those arguments you agree with. Justify your ideas in an informal class debate.

A Day of Action

On 29 June 2007, Aboriginal leaders organized a National Aboriginal Day of Action. They wanted to protest the government's failure to honour the Kelowna Accord and to focus attention on the long-standing issues between Canada and Aboriginal peoples. The Day of Action was intended as a peaceful protest. However, some people wanted to take more dramatic action by blocking roads and railways. To avoid any violent confrontations, rail service was suspended along the busy Windsor–Québec City corridor. For the most part, however, the Day of Action was limited to peaceful marches and demonstrations. Many Canadians, including unions and university students, showed up to express their support for the rights of Aboriginal peoples.

Figure 12.13 Early in 2006, a prolonged standoff began in Caledonia, Ontario, after a First Nations band took over property it claimed was theirs under an existing treaty. Over several months, there were bitter and sometimes violent clashes between the protestors and non-Aboriginal members of the community. Police approached the standoff cautiously. What might be the consequences if the standoff escalated?

Challenge and Response

1. In a T-chart, weigh the pros and cons of the Harper government in 2006–2007. Then write a newspaper editorial expressing your point of view on the effectiveness of his government.

2. When the Harper government recognized the Québécois as a nation within Canada, one observer said that Pierre Trudeau was "spinning in his grave." Why would Trudeau have opposed this resolution? Recall what you learned in Chapter 9 as you formulate your response.

3. Do you think the Conservative government should have honoured the Kelowna Accord? Give reasons for your response.

"If we were to look at Canada from above today, we would see more than a hundred rallies and marches across the land, and thousands and thousands of people showing their support for a better quality of life for First Nations. Each event and each individual represents a point of hope—hope for a better future for First Nations, and hope for a stronger, more united Canada for all Canadians. We see the support for our cause: more than a hundred thousand strong, and a hundred points of hope."

–Chief Phil Fontaine, Assembly of First Nations, Ottawa, 29 June 2007

ISSUES

Resolving Land Claims

The issue: What is the most effective approach to resolving land claims: negotiation or confrontation?

There are different perspectives on the best way to resolve land claims and other issues between Canada and Aboriginal peoples. Negotiation led to the first treaties between Canada and First Nations, the James Bay Agreement, and the cre-ation of Nunavut. However, confrontations such as the Riel Rebellions and the standoffs at Oka and Ipperwash forced the government to take action. Which approach—negotiaton or confrontation—is more likely to lead to a quality of life for Aboriginal peoples that is equal to that of other Canadians? The arguments below and the quotes that follow express different points of view.

Arguments In Favour of Negotiation	Arguments In Favour of Confrontation
• Canada has always been a peaceful country. • Negotiation has led to important achievements, such as the creation of Nunavut and the residential schools apology. • Negotiation builds bridges with other Canadians.	• The government only listens if violent action is threatened. • Confrontations make Canadians more aware of the injustices faced by Aboriginal peoples. • Living conditions in many Aboriginal communities are themselves a form of violent neglect.

Figure 12.14 These are the main arguments in favour of negotiation or confrontation.

"[Confrontation] does shed a negative light on Aboriginal peoples and we're just here to say that's not the voice of all the Aboriginal population in Canada ... I believe there has to be the same set of rules for all Canadians, Aboriginal or not. When people go this far in disrupting the lives of Canadians, I think that police forces should step in."

Source: Chief Patrick Brazeau, Congress of Aboriginal Peoples, 29 June 2007.

"We feel the concerns and frustration they have. It's a similar frustration we have every day when we drink polluted water and when we bury children who commit suicide. We live a life of disruption. We feel it's only been through these type of actions that First Nations issues have been made a priority for Canadians, and have elevated it in priorities for this government. We'll continue to push this button as long as we have out-standing issues and we'll continue to do it until there's some results."

Source: Shawn Brant, leader of an illegal blockade of rail lines and highways, CBC News, 29 June 2007.

"We don't want to cause a major disruption in the lives of Canadians. We don't want to disrupt the Canadian economy. Canadians are fair-minded people. They know the situation as we've described in our communities is simply unacceptable."

Source: Chief Phil Fontaine, Assembly of First Nations, CBC News, 29 June 2007.

Responding

1. Think about the different arguments and perspectives you have read. What arguments might you add to each side? Which side do you support? Why?

Skill Path:
Keeping Up with the News

If you are like most Canadians, you keep up with current events by watching television or by going online. With modern telecommunications, we can see events unfold from almost anywhere in the world as they happen. Television news usually has less than one minute to present the main idea of the story—that is not enough time to examine an issue in depth. Watching television news is like reading the headlines on the front page of the newspaper. You get the main idea, but you do not know the full story.

To be informed you need to get the story *behind* the headlines. To do this, you need a complete account of the news from a reliable newspaper or newsmagazine. Reading these will keep you informed about current events. When you read a news story, follow these steps to ensure that you are staying current with the news.

STEP 1: Find Out the Facts

You need the facts behind the story presented in a balanced and unbiased way. In a newspaper story, the main issue or event comes first, followed by the most important details and then the lesser or secondary details. For example, this diagram below shows the main issue, the most important details, and then less important details, in a story about the Kyoto Protocol from June 2007.

> **HARPER REFUSES TO COMPLY WITH KYOTO**
>
> Says it is constitutionally impossible
>
> Refusal may spark court challenge
>
> May comply if the Liberals tell them how to meet the targets

STEP 2: Understand the Story

A well-reported news story tells the reader *who*, *what*, *where*, *when*, *why*, and *how*. The *why* is often the most important part of the story. It can help you to understand the story for yourself. In the story about Kyoto, the *why* is that Harper believes it is impossible to meet the Kyoto targets.

STEP 3: Analyze and Interpret the Story

Newspapers go beyond reporting the facts when they provide analysis to explain the issues and offer insights to help readers gain a better understanding. When you read the news about important issues, you need to look for different opinions and points of view that reflect more than one side of the story. Editorials and columns provide analyses and interpretations that may get you thinking about the issue. Remember, though, they only present one side of the story. As a reader, you have to decide for yourself whether you agree or disagree with the writer's point of view by analyzing the facts and deciding whether they support the writer's position. Then you can draw your own conclusions.

STEP 4: Practise Your Skill

1. Choose an important television news story. Find the same story in a national newspaper. Follow the story on television and in print for two or three days. Then create an organizer comparing the information you learned about the story from television news and the newspaper.
2. Using the Internet, track the same news story in three different newspapers from across Canada. Compare the information in a Venn diagram. What different perspectives can you identify?

"I don't believe [the Liberal government] can achieve the targets. I think we need a more balanced approach to cleaning up our atmosphere ... [The] science is still evolving ... Kyoto is never going to be passed and I think we'd be better to spend our time on realistic pollution control measures."

–Conservative leader Stephen Harper, CBC News Online, 9 June 2004

Canada and Kyoto

In 1998, the Liberals signed the Kyoto Protocol and it was ratified in Parliament in 2002. This committed Canada to reduce greenhouse gas (GHG) emissions by 6 per cent below 1990 levels by 2012. (After signing the agreement, however, emissions actually increased by 27 per cent.) Harper was opposed to the Kyoto agreement. As leader of the Opposition, he made it clear that a Conservative government would not implement the Kyoto Protocol.

After the Conservatives were elected, Harper promised an alternative to the Kyoto Protocol. The Conservatives presented a new "made-in-Canada" environmental policy that called for slow changes over several decades. The plan found little support among Canadians. They wanted action to protect the environment—and they wanted it now. Canada also faced severe criticism from many delegates to the annual United Nations Climate Change Conference in Nairobi in November 2006. In response, Harper appeared to reverse his position by

"This government has no intention of adopting measures that would be harmful to the Canadian economy and to jobs."

–Prime Minister Stephen Harper, 22 June 2007

Figure 12.16 P. Bear, the mascot for Greenpeace, went to Parliament Hill in January 2007 to deliver a report produced by Greenpeace and the European Renewable Energy Council. It offered a blueprint for cutting global GHG emissions in half over the next four decades while providing affordable energy alternatives. What action can you take as an individual to make a difference to the environment or contribute to meeting the Kyoto targets?

MAP STUDY: The Kyoto Protocol

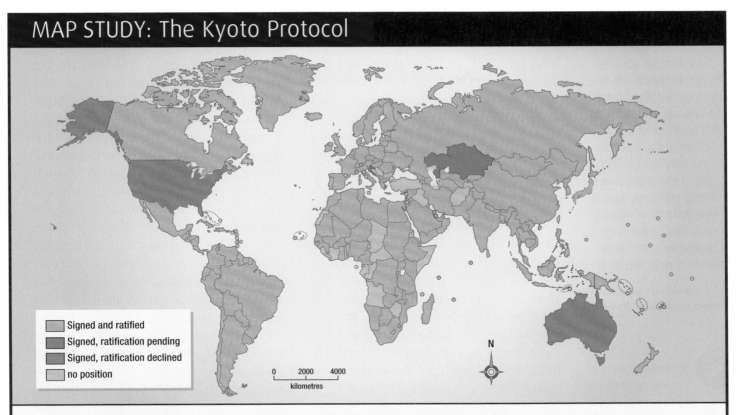

Signed and ratified
Signed, ratification pending
Signed, ratification declined
no position

0   2000   4000
kilometres

N

Source: United Nations Framework Convention on Climate Change, *Kyoto Protocol Status of Ratification*, updated 28 September 2006.

Figure 12.15 The Kyoto Protocol came into effect on 16 February 2005. More than 150 countries have signed the agreement.

Toward the end of the twentieth century, scientific evidence suggested that greenhouse gas (GHG) emissions were dramatically altering the world's climate. Scientists predicted that if emissions continued at their current levels, there would be dire consequences, including

- increasingly violent weather patterns that would create massive floods, scorching heat waves, and devastating hurricanes
- rising sea levels caused by the melting of polar ice caps that would flood lowlands

- droughts that would lead to widespread desertification in many parts of the world

The Kyoto Protocol aims to reduce greenhouse gas emissions in order to curb the effects of climate change. The international agreement set targets for industrialized countries to reduce greenhouse gas emissions by 2012. When Canada signed on, it made a commitment to reduce emissions by 6 per cent below 1990 levels. The Kyoto Protocol is a binding treaty, but it is not law. It is voluntary and, therefore, difficult to enforce.

Analysis and Response

1. Which countries have signed the Kyoto Protocol but have refused to ratify it? What impact do you think this might have on meeting the overall Kyoto targets? Explain your response.
2. Do you think a country has a duty to honour its commitments, even though they may not be legally binding? Express your point of view in a letter to your MP.

"Our federal government's blatantly obvious strategy is to bamboozle Canadians into thinking it's on the ball when it comes to the environment by presenting plans that have one flashy element, which everyone remembers, and then essentially supporting the status quo in everything else."

–David Suzuki, Canadian environmentalist, 1 May 2007

Learn more about the Kyoto Protocol and the most recent environmental developments

adopting policies that supported the environment, such as the Clean Air Act. However, critics charged that these measures were nothing more than smokescreens to divert attention from the fact that Canada would not honour its Kyoto commitment.

In June 2007, a **private member's bill** introduced by a Liberal MP gave the government 60 days to prepare a climate plan to ensure that Canada meets its obligations under the Kyoto treaty. The bill passed in both the House of Commons and the Senate. However, Harper declared it was impossible for Canada to meet its Kyoto targets. His comments set off a debate about whether the government could defy the will of Parliament.

In September 2007, the Harper government announced that Canada had joined a small coalition of countries in the Asia–Pacific Partnership

(AP7). Led by the United States, the partnership includes many of the world's biggest polluters: China, India, Japan, Australia, Korea, and Canada. Together, these countries produce almost half of the world's greenhouse gas emissions. Under AP7, each country voluntarily sets its own goals for reducing GHG emissions; none of the targets are legally binding, however. Critics called the partnership "Kyoto-Lite"—a watered-down version of the Kyoto Protocol, designed more for public relations than for achieving real progress in reducing GHG emissions. However, Harper maintained that by joining AP7 Canada could act as a bridge between some of the world's biggest polluters, such as the United States, and the staunch supporters of Kyoto, such as the European Union.

Challenge and Response

1. Think about the quotations about the government's response to environmental issues in this section. Write your responses to these different points of view. Then, using a Think-Pair-Share reading strategy, discuss your ideas with a partner. Listen to your partner's response and re-evaluate and adjust your original ideas if necessary.

2. Develop a poster, pamphlet, or public service announcement to address the environmental issues in your school, family, or community. Pay close attention to the reduction of GHG emissions in your presentation.

Sign of the Times

LIVE EARTH USA

On 7 July 2007, Live Earth: Concerts for a Climate in Crisis staged concerts around the world. The first concert began in Sydney, Australia. It was followed by concerts in Tokyo, Japan; Shanghai, China; Johannesburg, South Africa; Hamburg, Germany; London, England; and Rio de Janeiro, Brazil, as well as two concerts in the United States—one in Washington, DC, and the wrap-up concert in East Rutherford, New Jersey. The Live Earth concerts brought together 150 musical artists and 2 billion viewers to focus attention on the climate crisis created by global warming.

Figure 12.17 In Canada, CTV broadcast all of the concerts. Coverage began July 6 at 9 PM with the first concert in Sydney and ended July 7 at 11 PM with the final concert in New Jersey. The final act was the Police, shown here. More than 8.3 million Canadians watched some or all of the Live Earth broadcasts.

Figure 12.18 In Montréal, more than 12 000 people gathered in the Old Port for an outdoor concert featuring well-known Québec artists.

LIVE EARTH CANADA

Although there was no Canadian city hosting one of the Live Earth concerts, organizers encouraged all countries to host their own concerts and celebrations. In Toronto, Yonge-Dundas Square displayed eight hours of concert coverage on giant TV screens. In Vancouver, Greenpeace held an all-day concert and information fair on Robson Street to promote local environmental groups.

Responding

1. Imagine you were one of the organizers of Live Earth. Create a poster or another type of media promoting the series of concerts that would appeal to an international audience.
2. Hold a debate on the following: "International events like Live Earth are ineffective in making a difference for the environment. They may draw attention to the issues temporarily, but they have no lasting impact."

Reading Strategy

Before you begin reading this section, return to Chapter 9 and skim the section on Arctic sovereignty. Fill in everything you know in the "Know" column of a K-W-L organizer. Then write down questions you would like to find answers to in the "Wonder" column.

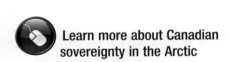

Canadian Sovereignty

Many scientists believe that nowhere will the effects of global warming be more evident—and more devastating—than in the Arctic. In 2002, an RCMP ship navigated through the usually ice-packed Northwest Passage without ever hitting ice. It was a telling sign of the effects of global warming in the Arctic. As the ice floes shrink, it will become easier to navigate through the Northwest Passage. Eventually, these waters will be open to navigation year-round.

What impact will this have on Canadian sovereignty in the Arctic? As you discovered in Chapter 9, not all countries accept Canada's sovereignty in the far North. The Americans maintain that the Northwest Passage is an international waterway outside of Canada's jurisdiction. As it becomes easier to navigate through the Northwest Passage, American and other foreign ships will have more opportunities to challenge Canadian sovereignty in the region.

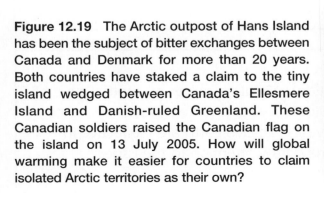

Learn more about Canadian sovereignty in the Arctic

Figure 12.19 The Arctic outpost of Hans Island has been the subject of bitter exchanges between Canada and Denmark for more than 20 years. Both countries have staked a claim to the tiny island wedged between Canada's Ellesmere Island and Danish-ruled Greenland. These Canadian soldiers raised the Canadian flag on the island on 13 July 2005. How will global warming make it easier for countries to claim isolated Arctic territories as their own?

The Economic Impact

The opening of the Northwest Passage has important economic implications. It has accelerated an international race for oil, fish, diamonds, and other resources hidden in the Arctic. Estimates suggest that as much as 25 per cent of the world's undiscovered oil and gas reserves are in the Arctic. As a result, many petroleum companies are now focusing their research and exploration there.

Countries are also competing for control over northern shipping routes. The ability to navigate through the Northwest Passage would reduce the shipping distance between Europe and Asia to 9000 kilometres instead of 16 000 kilometres via the Panama Canal. Experts predict a time-saving route through the Arctic could transform the shipping industry, just as the Suez Canal did in the Middle East in the nineteenth century. It will speed up trade routes and create new ones for Canadian exports as trade goods such as grain are shipped from ports like Churchill, Manitoba on Hudson Bay.

The Environmental and Human Impact

Climate change will greatly affect the environment, the wildlife, and the people who live in the Arctic. For example, it could lead to

- unpredictable weather
- changes in wildlife populations and behaviours
- the melting of permafrost and glaciers
- an increase in forest fires
- a population increase as more people migrate to the region
- the introduction of foreign diseases
- a loss of traditional lifestyles and the displacement of communities

An increase in shipping and oil and gas exploration will only compound these problems in the environmentally fragile Arctic. There will be greater potential for disasters such as oil spills. Oil and gas exploration will disrupt traditional communities and economies.

All of these things will have long-term consequences for the Inuit and the environment on which their livelihood depends. While there may be a few benefits, such as longer fishing, whaling, and sealing seasons, most of the impact of global warming will be negative. The Inuit will no longer be able to predict the weather using traditional methods. This will put them at greater risk of being stranded during bad storms, which scientists say will become more unpredictable because of global warming. Migration and travel routes will be altered. Hunters will have to travel farther to harvest food. Many people will develop a greater reliance on store-bought foods. Already, there is a decrease in the quality and quantity of fresh drinking water. These are just a few of the effects of global warming in the Arctic. As a result, the Inuit expect to be full partners in dealing with the effects of climate and environmental change in their homeland.

Maintaining Sovereignty

To maintain Canadian sovereignty in the Arctic, Harper initially pledged over $5 billion to expand Canada's military presence there, including three armed icebreakers to patrol Arctic waters. In July 2007, however, he announced a change in his government's Arctic strategy. Instead of armed icebreakers, the government would add up to eight patrol vessels for seasonal northern duty. The ships would be operational in 2013 or 2014.

"Forces mostly outside of the Arctic have caused climate change, manifested in the Arctic by changing sea-ice, tundra, and wildlife patterns. And the traditional Inuit way of life is threatened. Inuit must adapt, once again. Inuit are going to have to find new ways to make a living from the land. And whatever form that takes, it will not be what Inuit would have wished for … and it will not be an uninterrupted continuation of the traditional ways."

–Jose A. Kusugak, president, Inuit Tapiriit Kanatami, 2005

 Learn more about global warming and the Arctic

"Canada has a choice when it comes to defending our sovereignty over the Arctic. Either we use it or lose it. Make no mistake, this government intends to use it."

– Prime Minister Stephen Harper, 9 July 2007

"We're going to get ships that aren't really what we need for the Arctic. I'm very worried that the end result will be that we won't have the capability to operate anywhere at anytime in a Canadian Arctic that is drawing huge amounts of attention from commercial operators and nation states."

–Michael Byers, professor specializing in global issues, The University of British Columbia, 9 July 2007

"Chances are slim these ships will do anything more belligerent than fly the Maple Leaf through the Arctic summer. Even so, they are a better choice than the armed icebreakers … Useful on long coasts and even wide rivers, the patrol boats will increase Canada's presence in a place that already looms in the national psyche and is certain to become economically viable."

–James Travers, national affairs columnist, 9 July 2007

Some Canadians supported the decision. They believed that the armed icebreakers were too costly. Since there would only be three ships, the amount of territory they could cover would be limited. Those who opposed the new plan charged that the Conservatives should apply their "use it or lose it" strategy more vigorously by attracting more Canadians to the north. They argue that the greatest threat to Canada's sovereignty comes from the number of foreign scientists and researchers navigating through waters that Canada claims as its own.

Claiming the North Pole

Canada, the United States, Denmark, Norway, and Russia are all working on their own strategies for claiming ownership of parts of the Arctic floor. At stake is a treasure chest of oil and gas reserves potentially worth trillions of dollars. When the Conservatives took office in 2006, they announced plans to step up Canada's efforts to explore and map the Arctic seabed. Canada's potential claims to the Arctic and Atlantic Ocean floors and the resource wealth they may contain amount to 1.75 million square kilometres—roughly the size of Alberta, Saskatchewan, and Manitoba combined. In June 2007, however, Russia raised an international controversy when it became the first country to lay claim to a vast expanse of the North Pole.

In August 2007, Russia dramatically emphasized its claim by using a submarine to plant the Russian flag on the seabed of the North Pole. Canada quickly dismissed the actions of the Russian government. However, critics of the Conservatives demanded that Canada take concrete action to protect its interests in the Arctic.

Challenge and Response

1. Do you think it is important for Canada to assert and maintain its sovereignty in the Arctic? Give reasons for your response.
2. What role do you think the Inuit should play in protecting the Arctic environment?
3. Working with a partner, find out the current status of claims in the Arctic region and around the North Pole. Report your findings informally in a class discussion.

MAP STUDY: Russian-claimed Territory at the North Pole

Source: BBC.

Figure 12.20 The UN is allowing polar countries to stake claims to the Arctic floor. However, the countries involved cannot agree on how to divide the territory. Canada, Denmark, and the UN favour the Median Method, which divides the seabed in proportion to a country's coastline. Russia and Norway favour the Sector Method, which divides the Arctic along lines of longitude.

Polar nations are racing to lay claim to the Arctic sea floor in what many are describing as the earth's "last great land grab." In June 2007, Russia claimed 1.2 million square kilometres of seabed at the North Pole as its territory. Under the UN Convention on the Law of the Sea, a country can claim a piece of the Arctic floor beyond its **economic zone** if it has geological proof the floor connects to its continental shelf. Russian researchers claimed to have found that proof in an undersea mountain chain 1500 kilometres long called the Lomonosov Ridge that is connected to Russia's continental shelf.

Russia's claim may pose one of the biggest challenges yet to Canada's Arctic sovereignty. Canada is preparing claims of its own, but the Law of the Sea places a strict time limit for submitting evidence to support claims. Canada has until 2013 to make its case.

Analysis and Response

1. What do you think countries have to gain by favouring one method of dividing the Arctic over another?
2. Return to the K-W-L chart you started at the beginning of this section. Evaluate what you indicated you knew in the "Know" column. Check off questions in the "Wonder" column that have been answered. Summarize what you have learned in the "Learn" column.

Canada's Global Commitments

In the first decade of the twenty-first century, Canada continued to forge its place in the international community through its NATO commitments and its foreign aid goals. Two of the most important issues during this period were the mission in Afghanistan and the fight against HIV/AIDS in Africa.

The Mission in Afghanistan

Canada backed the NATO-led mission in Afghanistan to hunt down Al Qaeda terrorists responsible for the attacks against the United States in September 2001. Canada agreed to provide a small contingent of soldiers as well as naval support as part of its "Three-D" foreign policy: diplomacy, development, and defence. In 2003, Canada joined NATO's International Security Assistance Force (ISAF) to provide security and stability in the Afghan capital of Kabul. Canadian troops patrolled the city and guarded public works projects.

In 2003, however, Canada's role changed. The US invasion of Iraq forced the American military to divert troops from Afghanistan to Iraq. Canada refused to take part in the Iraq invasion, but agreed to fill the void left by the American troops by expanding Canada's role in Afghanistan to include combat duty.

A Mounting Death Toll

In combat, Canadian troops moved from the relative security of Kabul to the dangerous battlefields of Kandahar province. The province was the former centre of Taliban control and the most dangerous place in Afghanistan.

Figure 12.21 Their knowledge of the territory allowed Taliban insurgents to slip back and forth between Kandahar province and the neighbouring country of Pakistan. How would you describe the terrain of Afghanistan based on this satellite image?

Initially, NATO forces succeeded in driving the Taliban out of the region. Yet **insurgents** kept fighting their way back. NATO troops in Kandahar were under constant attack. NATO forces operating in safer parts of the country were unwilling to send troops to help in Kandahar, though. Canadian, British, Dutch, and American troops were left to fight the insurgents there on their own. By 2006, the death toll among Canadian soldiers began to escalate dramatically as insurgents attacked Canadian troops with **suicide bombs**, land mines, and **improvised explosive devices** (IEDs).

Expanding Canada's Role

Despite the rising death toll, when Stephen Harper took office, he wanted to increase Canada's combat role and to extend the Afghanistan mission to 2009. The Liberals and New Democrats were reluctant to support Harper's plan. They were equally reluctant, though, to defeat the government and force another election. As a result, in May 2006, members of Parliament voted to keep Canadian soldiers in Afghanistan for two more years.

In October 2007, Harper announced the creation of the Independent Panel on Canada's Future Role in Afghanistan. The panel's role was to investigate and make recommendations about the future course for Canadian troops in Afghanistan. In January 2008, the panel issued its findings. The *Manley Report*, named after the commission's chair, former Liberal deputy prime minister and minister of foreign affairs John Manley, recommended that Canada extend its mission under its United Nations' mandate, provided that 1000 soldiers from other NATO forces joined

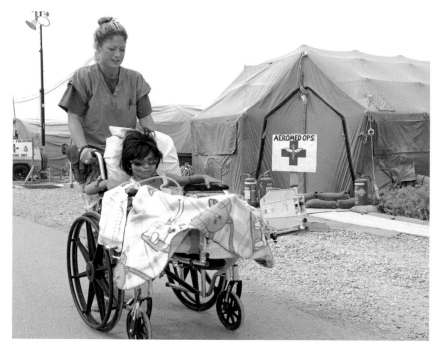

Figure 12.22 Aid workers are in Afghanistan to provide medical assistance and other services. What do you think will be more effective in Afghanistan in the long term—aid projects or military intervention? Give reasons for your response.

Canadian troops by February 2009. Harper accepted the report's recommendations, but the issue of Canada's role in Afghanistan remained a hot political issue.

Aid in Afghanistan

Afghanistan cannot be stabilized through military action alone. Canada is also playing a leading role in the country's economic, social, and political development. Canada has committed $1.2 billion in aid to Afghanistan until 2011. The money is being used to fund such activities as

- reforming the legal system
- strengthening human rights, especially women's rights
- training the Afghan police and army
- organizing free and democratic elections

 Learn more about Canada's role in Afghanistan

"There's a yin and yang here between combat operations and non-combat operations. You just cannot have reconstruction and development unless there's security. It all works together."

–Sean M. Maloney, historian, Royal Military College, Kingston, Ontario, 15 January 2007

MAP STUDY: Afghanistan

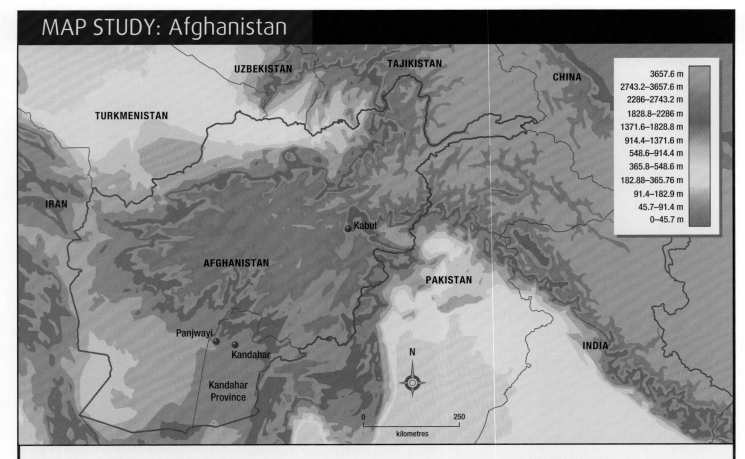

Figure 12.23 The rugged terrain in Afghanistan enabled many Taliban and Al Qaeda operatives to hide out in the mountainous terrain boarding Afghanistan and Pakistan.

Divided by cultural and religious conflicts, Afghanistan has suffered from the ravages of war for decades. In 1996, the **religious fundamentalist** Taliban faction took control of 90 per cent of the country. It provided a safe haven for Al Qaeda terrorists, including their leader, Osama bin Laden.

In 2001, NATO invaded Afghanistan on a mission to hunt down the terrorists and oust the Taliban. Under the Taliban, Afghanistan had become the poorest country in the world outside of the countries of sub-Saharan Africa. Half of the country's 24 million people lived in devastating poverty, surviving on less than one dollar a day. Millions of people fled their homes, seeking refuge in Pakistan and Iran. Thousands more were forced into internal relief camps. There was chaos across the country. Bringing political stability and economic development to Afghanistan was an integral part of NATO's mission.

Analysis and Response

1. What effect do you think the physical geography of Afghanistan has on NATO's efforts to hunt down Taliban and Al Qaeda forces?

2. Other foreign troops have occupied Afghanistan in the past but have been driven out of the country. Do you think NATO forces can succeed where others have failed? Give reasons for your response.

ISSUES

The Mission in Afghanistan

The issue: What were the arguments for and against continuing the mission in Afghanistan?

In July 2007, polls indicated that the majority of Canadians disagreed with the country's role in Afghanistan. Given the high number of casualties, they wanted the government to withdraw Canadian troops. Others argued that Canada was doing its part to fight terrorism and to help Afghanistan move toward peace and democracy. Read the following arguments and points of view about this controversial issue.

Arguments For Staying in Afghanistan	Arguments For Leaving Afghanistan
• The terrorists must be rooted out. • Canada has commitments to both NATO and the United Nations. • Casualties occur in every military conflict. • Canadian troops are committed to completing their mission in Afghanistan. • Canada has a long and distinguished history of combat.	• Canadians are in combat missions so US soldiers can fight in Iraq in a war that Canada does not support. • Canada is neglecting its traditional role as a peacekeeper. • The number of casualties is too high. • It is time for other NATO forces to take on some of the combat duty. • Afghanistan has a long history of war. NATO will fail there as other military forces have before. • The financial and human cost of the mission is too high.

Figure 12.24 This chart highlights the arguments for staying in and leaving Afghanistan. Are there other ideas you could add?

"Given the improving socio-economic situation in Kandahar province, withdrawing now would be like retreating from the beachhead in Normandy immediately after landing. Canada has sacrificed too much to pull out when those incremental measures we've talked about for two years are just starting to have an effect."

Source: Sean M. Maloney, "Winning in Afghanistan." *Maclean's*, (23 July 2007): 26.

"[Canada] is fighting a war against a battle-hardened and determined enemy in one of the most fiercely independent nations on earth … This is a war that Canada and the West cannot win … And Canada will share disproportionately in its ultimate loss in terms of dead and wounded … [with] our international reputation sullied for a long time to come."

Source: Murray Dobbin, "Harper's taste for war." *The Tyee*, 25 September 2006.

"I'm utterly torn on this issue. I believe in honour. Therefore, if we made a commitment to 2009, we should keep it. However, every time I hear of another Canadian death, I have to wonder what's the point of it all. We will not win. That's a given. Nobody's ever won in Afghanistan."

Source: Deborah Burton, "Your view." CBC News Online, 6 July 2007.

"We have to get out of the trap of either/or: that we have to be completely out of Afghanistan or we have to be proud of our [troops] and they have to be fully involved. There's a middle ground."

Source: Chesmak Farhoumand-Sims, assistant professor of conflict studies, St. Paul's University, Ottawa, *Toronto Star*, 17 September 2006.

Responding

1. In your opinion, what are the strongest arguments in favour of Canada's mission in Afghanistan? What are the strongest arguments against it? Give reasons for your responses.

"AIDS kills 6500 people every day in Africa and because of this, there are 14 million children orphaned in Africa ... That number is projected to rise over the next five years to 25 million orphans. Why doesn't the Canadian government step up and lend a helping hand? It would send a good example to other countries if Canada was the first well-off country to make a serious effort to help Africa."

–Daniel Rosario, secondary school student, 2003

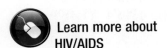
Learn more about HIV/AIDS

- funding small businesses
- building more schools and helping girls (who were not allowed to attend school under the Taliban) get an education

Provincial Reconstruction Teams (PRTs) operated by the Afghan government oversee military and civilian activities. Their role is to establish stability and security and to help non-governmental organizations with reconstruction projects. With greater educational and economic opportunities, there is hope that democracy will survive in Afghanistan and prevent the Taliban from returning to power.

The Fight against HIV/AIDS

In the opening years of the twenty-first century, HIV/AIDS continued to be a global **pandemic**. In August 2006, Canada hosted the 16th International AIDS Conference in Toronto. It brought together more than 20 000 people, including scientists, health-care workers, educators, policy makers, AIDS activists, and people living with HIV/AIDS. The theme of the conference, "Time to Deliver," emphasized the urgent need to provide treatment for people with HIV/AIDS in the world's developing countries. Canada was among other Western countries accused of pledging to help fight the HIV/AIDS pandemic in Africa and Asia, but failing to live up to its promises.

Government Policy

At the conference, Harper was expected to announce the Conservative government's policy statement on HIV/AIDS. At the last minute, however, he decided not to attend, claiming the conference had become too "politicized." He was widely criticized by conference delegates as well as by many Canadians who believed that Canada should play a leadership role in fighting the HIV/AIDS pandemic.

A New Initiative

In February 2007, Harper announced that Canada would work with the Bill and Melinda Gates Foundation to fund the Canadian HIV Vaccine Initiative. Canada committed up to $111 million, with the Gates Foundation providing another $28 million, to support Canadian researchers working to develop new vaccines to fight HIV/AIDS.

Challenge and Response

1. Do you think all NATO members should share combat responsibility and rotate troops through the most hostile regions during a conflict? Give reasons for your response.

2. What obligation do developed countries like Canada have to help developing countries fight diseases such as HIV/AIDS? Discuss your ideas as a class.

3. Keep up with the news on Afghanistan and HIV/AIDS in Africa in major newspapers and news magazines. Create a timeline for each issue to track developments that take place. Place positive developments on one side of the timeline and negative developments on the other side.

PERSONALITIES

Stephen Lewis: Africa's AIDS Activist

Figure 12.25 *Maclean's* magazine named Stephen Lewis "Canadian of the Year" in 2003. In 2005, *Time* magazine listed Lewis as one of the 100 most influential people in the world. Here, he visits with villagers in Zambia in 2006.

Stephen Lewis is one of Canada's most passionate activists. He was born into a socially progressive political family. His father was David Lewis, a founder and former leader of the federal New Democratic Party (NDP). Stephen Lewis followed his father's career path and entered politics. He campaigned for the rights of workers, women, and minorities and captured people's attention with his spellbinding speeches. In 1963, Lewis was elected to the Ontario Legislature. In 1970, he won the leadership of the provincial NDP, a position he held until he retired from politics in 1978.

Lewis's greatest contribution to Canada and the global community came after he left political life. In 1984, he was appointed as Canada's ambassador to the United Nations. From 1995 to 1999 he was deputy director of UNICEF. In 2001, Lewis became the UN special envoy for HIV/AIDS in Africa. This marked the beginning of his ongoing quest to end the HIV/AIDS epidemic that is ravaging the African continent. Today, Lewis is board chair of the Stephen Lewis Foundation. He travels across Africa, visiting communities torn apart by HIV/AIDS. He focuses the world's attention on people infected by HIV/AIDS, particularly the orphans whose parents have died from the disease and who are now raising themselves and their siblings or who are being cared for by their grandmothers.

"Canadians are not known for their boastfulness, but they should break character and be boastful about Stephen Lewis. He has been an extraordinary and relentless one-man band for the world's most poor and vulnerable."

Source: Bono, U2 lead singer and humanitarian.

Lewis is an outspoken critic of the world's wealthiest countries and what he believes is their slow response to the HIV/AIDS crisis. In 2007, he criticized the leaders of the G8 after they pledged to spend US$60 billion to fight the deadly disease in Africa—but without providing any timelines for doing so. He questioned the ethics of the G8 countries, which in 2007 spent $120 billion a year fighting in Iraq and Afghanistan but committed less than half that amount in total to fighting HIV/AIDS.

"I'm weary beyond the definition of weariness at the way in which the G8 plays with figures. So far, they've had an unblemished record of betraying their promises … Yes, there will be more money by 2010. Yes, every penny makes a difference to Africa, and potentially, to lives saved. I'm not so foolish or curmudgeonly as to deny that reality. But spare me the claims of a breakthrough … We have Kilimanjaro to climb before we meet the needs of Africa."

Source: Stephen Lewis, *Race Against Time* (Toronto: House of Anansi Press, 2005), 31–32.

Responding

1. Identify one person who has made a positive difference in the world. Explain what contribution that person has made and describe how he or she made a difference in a Personalities profile.

Skill Path:
Connecting History and Career Opportunities

Sometimes, people continue to pursue their knowledge of history long after they leave school. You learn about history through novels, movies, television, and the Internet. Studying history can be a useful preparation for your future. It can prepare you for job opportunities and volunteer work. Most employers hire people who are motivated, who are able to research and interpret information, and who can offer sound solutions and options. They look for people who can make wise choices and communicate the results of their decisions. The skills of the historian are often the skills of the successful citizen.

Employment specialists and career counsellors identify the following career choices as being of particular interest to students of history:

- business
- government, politics, and public service (including foreign service)
- information technology
- journalism
- law
- non-governmental organizations
- public history, libraries, archives, and museums
- teaching (primary, secondary, and post-secondary)

As you review this list, try to understand what elements in your experience as a history student would provide you with the skills and information you need to succeed in these fields. You might want to review the chapter titles, Skill Paths, and Thinking Like a Historian features in the Table of Contents.

STEP 1: Research the Job Market
When you are looking for a job—even a summer job—you need to review newspaper and online advertisements and visit government, school, and community job centres. Write down all the positions that are of interest to you.

STEP 2: Know the Job Requirements
To get a job, you need to know the skills and information you need to have. If you can show that you truly understand the job requirements and can meet them successfully, it is more likely you will win the position.

STEP 3: Prepare Your Resumé
To apply for a job, you need a resumé outlining your education, achievements, and work experience. Include an opening statement highlighting your personal strengths and qualities. You should consult resumé writing guides to make sure you prepare the most effective document possible.

STEP 4: Apply for the Job
If you are a suitable candidate for the job, your resumé could get you an interview with the potential employer. Prepare for the interview by learning about the company and its products and services and about the position you are seeking.

STEP 5: Practise Your Skill
Read the classified ads in your local newspaper or on a job-posting website. Choose three ads and offer three reasons why a background in history might help you get the job.

Thinking Like a Historian:
Establishing Historical Significance

Essential Question: As a historian, how do you determine why certain events, trends, and issues of the past are important today?

You have now studied the history of Canada from the early twentieth to the early twenty-first century. You have had the opportunity to think about the events, themes, and issues that have shaped the Canadian nation. Yet how do you determine the significance of so many different events? Consider the following questions to help you determine historical significance.

- Are events that affect many people more important than events that affect only a few?
- Are events that threaten to divide or unite the country more significant than those that do not?
- Are events that have long-term consequences more significant than events that do not?
- Are events that reveal emerging or enduring issues more significant than others?
- Are events that are more interesting necessarily more significant than events that are less interesting?
- Are events that affect you personally more significant than events that do not?

You, the Historian

1. Imagine you are preparing a brochure that will introduce new Canadians to the history of Canada since the early twentieth century. You can only describe 10 events. Prepare a list of these 10 events. Justify and defend why you consider them significant.
2. Imagine you are preparing a brochure that will interest elementary school children in studying Canadian history. Choose 10 events you think will interest them. Justify and defend your choices.
3. What are the differences between the two lists you created? Which do you think is a better overview of the significant events in Canadian history? Give reasons for your response.

Looking Ahead
Canada in the Twenty-first Century

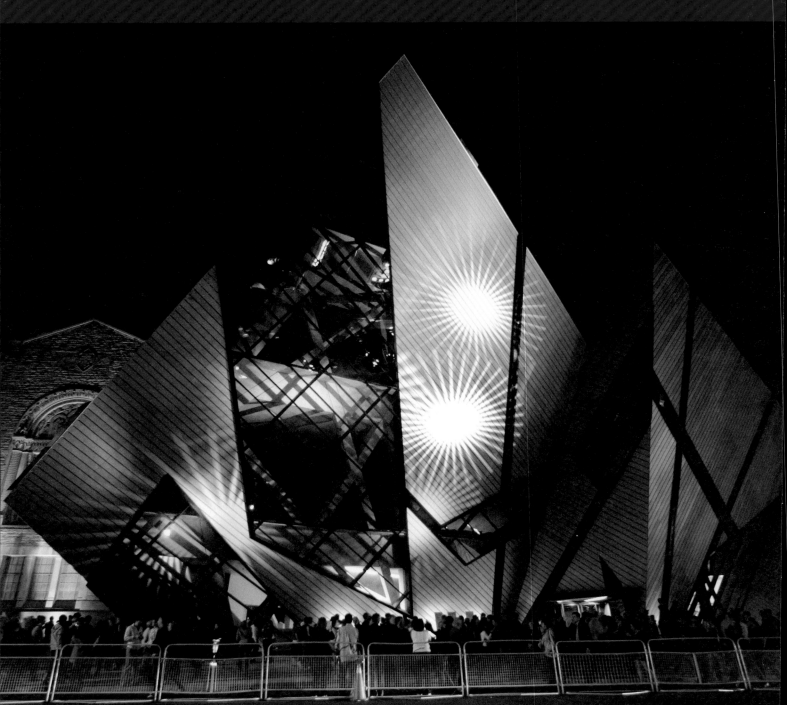

Chapter at a Glance

Thinking Ahead

This chapter is about the future—the years just ahead when you will be adult citizens, with all of the rights and responsibilities of Canadian citizenship. You will earn and exercise the reins of power in your families, your workplaces, your communities, and—for some of you—in your governments.

In this chapter, you have the opportunity to explore some of the issues that you and your peers will face in the future, such as creating equality of life for Aboriginal peoples, overcoming poverty, preserving the environment, meeting the challenges of the military, and establishing rights and responsibilities in a multicultural society. As you explore these issues, keep the following questions in mind:

- What will Canada be like when your generation is in power?
- Who will shape the next chapters of Canadian history?
- What will change and what will remain the same in Canadian society?
- To what extent will Canada be a different place—and will it be a better place?
- What role will *you* play in the unfolding story of *The Canadian Challenge*?

In 2007, this futuristic structure was added to the Royal Ontario Museum (ROM) in Toronto. It is called the Michael Lee-Chin Crystal, in recognition of Lee-Chin's $30-million donation to the ROM. The Crystal was designed to symbolize a bright new future for the museum, for Toronto, and for Ontario. In your opinion, what does the future hold for Canada?

Profile in Power: You

"The opportunity to vote comes with a moral burden to make the most educated and informed decision that you are able to."

–Alia Domino, Valleyview Secondary School, 2003

Congratulations! You are now Canada's newest prime minister. You led your party to a stunning victory. Your enthusiasm, knowledge, vision, and passion inspired people across the country to do their part as citizens and vote. Best of all, you persuaded a record number of young Canadians to make their voices heard about the future of Canada.

Now the campaign is over. It is time to make a difference. You have at least four years to shape your vision of Canada in the twenty-first century. You have to use your new power effectively to prove to Canadians that they were right to entrust you with their future!

You campaigned on a number of important issues, including

- recognizing the rights of Aboriginal peoples and ensuring they share in Canada's prosperity
- reducing family and child poverty
- meeting the challenges of the Kyoto Protocol and reducing Canada's resource consumption
- meeting the challenges of the Canadian military while reflecting Canadian values
- redefining Canadian citizenship and identity in a multicultural society

You have asked members of your government to outline the key points of these five issues for your review during your first days in office. Then you will be meeting with the members of your Cabinet to decide your government's priorities and strategies. Once you have mapped the course for your first session of Parliament, you have the opportunity to tell Canadians about your goals in your government's first **Speech from the Throne**.

"History is to citizenship what mathematics is to science—the key to unlocking competence. For self-governing men and women, to decide where they want to go, they must first know where we have been."

–Thomas Axworthy, "To go ahead, Canada must know its past." *Toronto Star*, 17 June 2007

Responding

1. Identify the positive traits a young politician might bring to the office of the prime minister. What traits might a young politician lack? How could a young politician compensate for any limitations?
2. What qualities would you look for in the members of your Cabinet?
3. At the end of this chapter, you will be preparing your Speech from the Throne. What does your speech need to do to appeal to a diverse society?

Skill Path:
Creating a Plan of Action

Knowing how to create a plan of action is an important skill. You will use this skill throughout your life, whether you are making a plan for your academic future or for your summer vacation. You will also use this skill a number of times in this chapter as you, as prime minister, think about ways to resolve some of the important issues and challenges in Canada today.

STEP 1: Define the Issue

The first step in creating a plan of action is to define the issue or challenge to be resolved. Write down your first thoughts about the issue in three or four simple statements. List all of the ideas you can think of about this issue.

STEP 2: Consider All the Options

Working with a group, brainstorm a list of subtopics related to this issue. Use chart paper to create a concept web to organize your information. When you have completed your brainstorming session, use a jigsaw strategy to conduct further research on the issue. Within your group, divide the subtopics you identified among pairs of students. Each pair is responsible for researching and learning about the assigned subtopic. You and your partner can use newspapers, news magazines, and the Internet to obtain information, but you should also talk to people of diverse backgrounds and experiences to get their ideas and opinions. Be open-minded as you listen to the ideas of others.

STEP 3: Share What You Have Learned

Once you and your partner have completed your research, think about how you will share what you have learned with the other members of your group. Then, present the information you have learned about your subtopic with your group. Be sure to present your information clearly. Take questions from the other members of your group.

Listen carefully and take notes as others present their information. Then discuss everything you have learned about this issue and assess the impact or relative importance of each aspect of the issue.

STEP 4: Identify Solutions

Now that you have your information, you need to refocus your thinking. Discuss the issue again, this time considering all possible solutions. Be an active listener when other members of your group are speaking. Keep an open mind to other points of view and multiple perspectives. Avoid being judgmental. As a group, identify what you believe to be the best solution to resolve the issue. In a T-chart, list the positive and negative aspects of this solution. Then discuss how to minimize the negative effects. Modify your solution if necessary.

STEP 5: Practise Your Skill

Use the steps in this Skill Path to explore the issues and challenges in this chapter and to investigate possible solutions.

Sharing Information in a Jigsaw Strategy

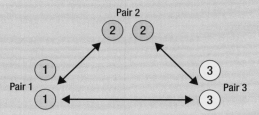

"Despite the resurgence in Aboriginal [self-sufficiency] in the past thirty years, the gap between Aboriginal and general Canadian life opportunities remains disturbingly wide."

–Georges Erasmus, *The LaFontaine-Baldwin Lectures*, 2002

Aboriginal Peoples: The Road to Renewal

Today, Aboriginal peoples in Canada face many challenges, ranging from achieving economic self-sufficiency to settling land claims. Aboriginal leaders are working to guide their communities toward a balance between traditional ways and a better quality of life. In 2005, the Liberal government of Paul Martin signed the Kelowna Accord with Aboriginal peoples. It pledged more than $5 billion to improve housing, health care, and education in Aboriginal communities. By 2008, however, the Conservative government of Stephen Harper had not upheld the agreement.

Standard of Living

Canada's place on the United Nations **Human Development Index** is consistently in the top 10. However, if this ranking were based on statistics for Aboriginal peoples, Canada would plummet to 78th place. Clearly, Aboriginal peoples are not sharing equally in Canada's prosperity. One out of four Aboriginal people lives in poverty—a rate three times higher than that of other Canadians.

One of the consequences of poverty is poor housing. More than 30 per cent of Inuit and First Nations peoples live in substandard housing. Poor housing conditions are associated with many health problems, including the rapid spread of infectious diseases. Extreme poverty leads to poor health, which leads to a lower life expectancy in Aboriginal communities.

Regardless of their standard of living, however, many Aboriginal peoples believe their connections with nature

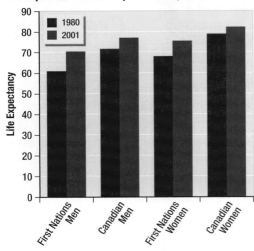

A Comparison of Life Expectancies, 1980 and 2001

Source: Life Expectancy for First Nations People and Canadians, by Gender, Canada, 1980, 1990, and 200, Health Canada, 2004 and Basic Departmental Data 2004. Ottawa: Indian and Northern Affairs Canada, 2004. Adapted and Reproduced with the permission of the Minister of Public Works and Government Services Canada, 2008.

Although the life expectancy for First Nations people in Canada is improving, it is still lower than the life expectancy of other Canadians. The figures are worse for Inuit. Inuit men have a life expectancy of 67.7 years, while Inuit women's life expectancy is 70.2 years. What factors do you think contribute to lower life expectancies among Aboriginal peoples? Why do you think life expectancies are lowest among Inuit?

provide them with a high quality of life. Those who aspire to share the same material benefits as other Canadians are working with the federal and provincial governments to address the causes of poverty rather than the symptoms. Aboriginal leaders are seeking greater control over their lands and resources as well as their fair share of the wealth these resources generate. They want to re-establish self-sufficiency—something they enjoyed for thousands of years before the arrival of Europeans over 500 years ago.

Education

The average level of education among Aboriginal peoples is lower than for other Canadians. As a result, unemployment is higher among Aboriginal peoples, and average incomes are lower than for other Canadians.

Today, however, Aboriginal children and young people are entering schools and colleges in record numbers. Aboriginal education programs promote the revival of Aboriginal languages and traditional practices. Aboriginal communities are seeking greater funding for lifelong learning programs, beginning with early childhood development. They are asking to implement and operate their own

education systems. They are working with the provinces and territories to provide greater skills-training opportunities and to develop joint programs with the private sector to create sustainable economic opportunities that will provide long-term employment.

Restorative Justice

Poverty and lack of employment opportunities often lead to higher crime rates. While Aboriginal peoples represent 4.4 per cent of the Canadian population, they account for 18 per cent of inmates in federal prisons. Today, the Canadian justice system is recognizing that cultural misunderstandings have contributed to this situation.

In 2007, the Chief of the Assembly of First Nations, Phil Fontaine, spoke about the anger and frustration building in Aboriginal communities over the government's slow progress tackling important issues affecting Aboriginal peoples. Although Fontaine does not advocate violence, he warned that violence is a possibility if governments do not take concrete action soon.

"We cannot be a truly multicultural society if we insist on a melting pot for Aboriginal peoples."

–Jose A. Kusugak, president, Inuit Tapiriit Kanatami, 19 April 2004

"Show people who you are, what your tradition is and they'll look up to you because with our changing society people's cultures are being ... diminished. So if [you] keep your tradition and your culture alive, people will probably look up to you."

–Aboriginal youth in *Youth Connecting Youth in Canada*, 23 February 2005

"We ... believe that our own laws are important and need to be respected and applied in our daily lives. Unfortunately, neither Parliament, the legislature, nor the judiciary fully understand our rights and laws."

–Ovide Mercredi, former National Chief of the Assembly of First Nations, November 1999

"Many people ask why First Nations people are so angry. At this point you must realize that we have a right to be."

–Terry Nelson, Chief, Roseau River First Nation, May 2007

"This is discrimination and it's racist. We are held hostage and many First Nations people feel they are second class citizens in this country, our homeland. We have been denied the right to our land and traditional territories. We want to be as others are—independent and making a contribution to our society. We want to stand as equals."

–Phil Fontaine, National Chief of the Assembly of First Nations, 17 April 2007

Aboriginal leaders are working with authorities to develop strategies for greater crime prevention. They want to establish more **restorative justice** programs for Aboriginal offenders and utilize traditional Aboriginal forms of justice that emphasize healing and making amends rather than punishment. They would like more funding for community-based justice programs, including Aboriginal youth justice committees, sentencing circles, and healing lodges that involve the offenders, family members, and community Elders.

Land Claims

Many Aboriginal communities believe that the government has failed to provide them with land to which they are legally entitled. As a result, there are over 800 outstanding land claims across

Canada. Yet in 2008, fewer than 200 of these claims were in negotiations. The process for settling land claims is long and slow. It takes an average of 13 years to settle a claim and only a few claims are settled each year. Half of all land claims are relatively small, involving less than $3 million. Sometimes, there are blockades and standoffs as the rights of Aboriginal peoples come into conflict with the interests of land developers and other business interests.

Today, Aboriginal peoples are asserting their **inherent right** to their traditional lands. They want to settle outstanding land claims in order to expand the land bases of their communities. This would increase the potential to develop and manage natural resource industries within their own jurisdictions.

Reading Strategy

An index is an alphabetical list of topics and concepts found in academic books. It lists the pages where you can find the information you are looking for. Main entries list the general topics. Sub-entries break down the topic to identify specific ideas, issues, and concepts. The index is an effective strategy for finding and reviewing information.

You, as Prime Minister

1. Use the index at the back of this book to help you review what you have learned about Aboriginal issues in Canada in *The Canadian Challenge*. What were the ongoing issues in Canadian–Aboriginal relations over the last century? Which issues are still unresolved today? Which ones will be a priority for your government?

2. Use the jigsaw strategy described in the Skill Path on page 439 to investigate the issues affecting Aboriginal peoples in Canada today. Then share your findings in a Cabinet meeting and brainstorm ways that your government plans to work with Aboriginal leaders and communities to resolve these issues. Make notes to record your ideas. You will need to refer to these notes later on when you write your Speech from the Throne.

The Challenge of Poverty

With its vast wealth of natural resources and relatively small population, Canada has developed into one of the wealthiest countries in the world. The majority of Canadians enjoy a high quality of life. Our government provides us with an abundance of social services, including universal health care, employment insurance, and retirement pensions.

Yet not all Canadians enjoy the benefits of Canada's prosperity. Poverty exists in communities across the country. Estimates indicate that 16 per cent of Canadians live at or below the **poverty line**. Poverty is increasing among youth, unskilled workers, young families, and immigrants. The income gap is widening, as well. Between 1993 and 2004, the average income for the poorest 10 per cent of Canadian families increased by 18 per cent. In contrast, the average income for the richest 10 per cent of Canadian families increased by 46 per cent.

Who Is Poor in Canada?

One of the main reasons for poverty is a lack of jobs that pay decent wages. People who have not had the opportunity to obtain a post-secondary education or skills training find themselves in low-paying jobs or having only seasonal or part-time work. In many cases, labour laws do not apply to these jobs. Therefore, these workers do not have the same job security as others Canadians do. Many new immigrants find that Canadian employers do not recognize their credentials. As a result, they take low-paying jobs or work part-time to support their families while they earn the requirements to practise their profession in Canada.

> "The growing gap between rich and poor is a big problem in Canada ... Inequality weakens our communities; the daily struggle to meet basic needs creates tension and social conflicts ... Polarization results in people no longer understanding each other."
>
> –Vijayata Achatz, Milliken Mills High School, 2007

> "To get an education can be a challenge for the best of us, but add poverty to that mix and it becomes almost impossible. Where does the money come from to buy books and pay tuition fees? It comes out of the grocery money if your hunger for knowledge becomes as consuming as mine has."
>
> –University student, The Urban Poverty Consortium of Waterloo Region, 29 November 2000

Volunteers help to fill orders at a GTA food bank. In November 2007, the United Way of Toronto released a report entitled *Losing Ground: The Persistent Growth of Family Poverty in Canada's Largest City*. It noted that 30% of families in Toronto were poor—up from 16% in 1990. Some newspapers described Toronto as "the poverty capital of Canada." Why do you think poverty is on the rise in cities like Toronto?

Learn more about Campaign 2000

More than half of women who are single parents live in poverty. Many rely on social assistance because a lack of affordable child care prevents them from participating in the labour force. Canadians with disabilities also experience higher rates of poverty than other Canadians do.

Child Poverty

In 1989, the federal government set a goal to eliminate child poverty in Canada by the year 2000. Yet today, almost 1.2 million Canadian children still live in poverty. Children from low-income families are likely to have more health problems than other children do. They are less likely to complete school or to obtain training for jobs in the skilled labour force. As a result, children who grow up living in poverty are more likely to live in poverty as adults.

Strategies to Reduce Poverty

Campaign 2000 is a coalition of over 120 national, provincial, and community organizations across Canada committed to ending child and family poverty. The organization is calling upon Canada to meet a challenge put forth by the United Nations to reduce the national poverty level to below 10 per cent. It has issued a series of recommendations on ways in which governments can meet this target in the 2006 *Report Card on Child and Family Poverty in Canada*.

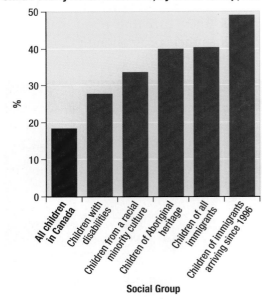

Child Poverty Rates in Canada, by Social Group, 2001

Source: Statistics Canada, Income Trends in Canada, 13F0022XCB, 1980-2001 issue, Released December 22, 2003.

This bar graph shows child poverty rates by social group in Canada. What factors do you think contribute to each of these groups experiencing higher levels of poverty than other Canadian children do?

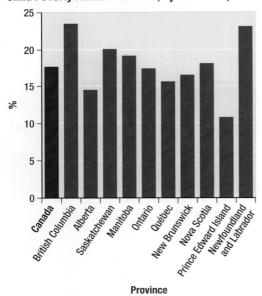

Child Poverty Rates in Canada, by Province*, 2004

*Excludes people living on First Nations reserves and people living in Yukon, the Northwest Territories, and Nunavut.

Source: Printed with permission from Campaign 2000, a cross-Canada network of organizations working to end child and family poverty.

This bar graph shows child poverty in Canada and the provinces in 2004. Why do you think rates vary from province to province?

You, as Prime Minister

1. Recall what you know about poverty in Canada and what actions governments have taken in the past to reduce poverty. Then, write down your ideas about the things governments can do today to reduce poverty.

2. Use the jigsaw strategy described in the Skill Path on page 439 to investigate child and family poverty in Canada today. Then share your findings in a Cabinet meeting. As a group, brainstorm ways that your government plans to reduce poverty in Canada. Make notes to record your ideas. You will need to refer to these notes later on when you write your Speech from the Throne.

Creating a Sustainable Environment

Canada has achieved its wealth and economic development through the exploitation of its vast natural resources. In the process, Canadians have become one of the largest consumers of resources in the world. We consume resources at a rate much higher than almost any other people on earth.

Meeting Kyoto Targets

Opinion polls suggest that Canadians want their government to be a global leader on environmental issues. However, many Canadians believe there is a credibility gap between what Canadian governments have said they will do and what they have actually done, or what is actually being done. Experts say it is impossible for Canada to meet its commitment to the targets set under the Kyoto Protocol. For many Canadians, however, the environment is not a political issue. It is the greatest challenge to our survival on this planet.

While the political debate drags on, scientists continue to point out the effects of global warming and climate change. A report in 2007 from the Intergovernmental Panel on Climate Change (IPCC) warns that in the not-too-distant future Canada will likely face

- a significant increase in the number of forest fires
- the loss of 20 per cent of the Arctic tundra
- significantly lower water levels of the Great Lakes
- increased winter flooding
- extreme heat waves
- more insect plagues

The report concluded that the negative effects of climate change would have the greatest impact on the quality of life of the urban poor and elderly, Aboriginal communities, and resource-based communities.

Reading Strategy

Before reading this section, think of three things you do regularly to contribute to a healthy planet. Share and compare your ideas with a partner. Then generate a list of environmentally sound practices everyone can adopt.

"If we have the political courage to embrace change, there's a new revolution just waiting for us—an opportunity for new industries, new jobs, new potential. This is a huge challenge: bigger than the space race, bigger than the arms race. Call it the Energy Race. I believe we are up to the challenge of this new race, but we have to set the framework of strong targets, new rules, new incentives. If we do this, it will unleash some of Canada's greatest attributes: our inventiveness, our creativity. Imagine the enormous power of our engineers, scientists, technicians, and architects all working toward a common goal."

–David Suzuki, Canadian environmental activist, December 2005

"We are among the world's greatest consumers of energy. This may be attributable in part to our climate; however, other countries with similar climates, namely the Scandinavian countries, manage to consume less energy even though their economy, their lifestyle, and their climate are very similar to ours. We waste a lot and we consume a lot."

–Steven Guilbeault, former Greenpeace Québec director, Culture Online: Made in Canada, June 2004

Canada's Ecological Footprint

The ecological footprint measures the demands people place on nature. It considers all the land and water used to produce all of the resources people consume as well as nature's ability to renew these resources. Then it calculates a figure to tell us what our ecological footprint is. Canada has a huge ecological footprint—83.3 hectares per person. It is one of the largest footprints in the world—making Canadians among the biggest consumers of natural resources on earth.

With more than 6 billion people living on the planet, there is a growing need for Canadians to understand how much of the earth's resources are available to share among all of us. If present trends continue, people will need the resources of three planet earths to sustain our resource consumption. Experts estimate that by 2050, overconsumption of the world's resources will pose a serious threat to human welfare.

Sustainable Development

In order to protect the environment, Canadians need to practise sustainable development. Canadians need to understand the social, environmental, and economic impacts of the way we live our lives and to find ways to sustain our lifestyles in the future.

Many business leaders question whether they can afford the costs of practising sustainable development.

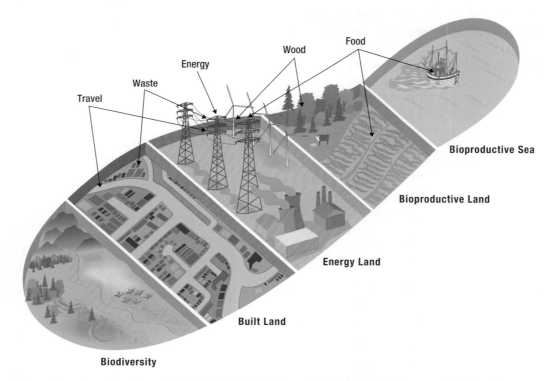

Source: Image based on Figure 4.2 of *Sharing Nature's Interest: Ecological Footprints as an Indicator of Sustainability* (Chambers, Simmons and Wackernagel, 2000), 63. Reproduced with special permission.

The world average ecological footprint is 2.2 hectares. That is still more than the 1.8 hectares scientists believe the earth can support. Why do some people disregard the need to be environmentally conscious? How can your government convince Canadians to adapt their lifestyles to reduce the size of Canada's ecological footprint?

ECOLOGICAL FOOTPRINTS FOR SELECTED COUNTRIES, 2001	
Country	Ecological Footprint (hectares per person)
United States	108.95
Canada	83.3
France	65.82
Britain	62.56
El Salvador	7.57
Ghana	3.23
Vietnam	4.12
Ethiopia	1.56

Source: Dr. John Talberth and Dr. Jason Venetoulis, *Ecological Footprint of Nations: 2005 Update*, (Redefining Progress, 2006).

This table shows the ecological footprints for selected countries. The first four are among the world's most developed countries; the last four are among the world's least developed countries. What patterns can you identify? What does the fact that the footprints for the US and Canada are so much larger than the footprints for France and Britain tell you about the lifestyles of North American consumers?

They warn that the cost of implementing new environmental protection strategies will lead to higher prices for consumers. Environmentalists, on the other hand, question whether we can afford *not* to practise sustainable development. They argue that, through research and development, we can find ways to reduce our consumption of natural resources and find alternative energy sources.

Of course, the responsibility for preserving the environment does not belong only to government and to industry. In the twenty-first century, all Canadians will need to become responsible environmental citizens. Young Canadians today are much more aware of the impact people have on the environment. As the leaders in the twenty-first century, they will have to find new ways to continue to enjoy our economic prosperity while protecting and preserving the very resources that provide it.

"Humanity is living off its ecological credit card. While this can be done for a short while, overshoot ultimately leads to liquidation of the planet's ecological assets, and the depletion of resources, such as the forests, oceans, and agricultural land upon which our economy depends."

–Dr Mathis Wackernagel, The Global Footprint Network, 2007

"Our economic system has made a ... religion out of economic growth, and our god is technology ... No politician is going to run on a platform that requires Canadians or Americans, or anyone else in rich countries, to seriously consider changing their lifestyles."

–William Rees, ecological economist, 12 January 2006

"The successful businesses of tomorrow will be those that rank social and environmental responsibility on the same level with economic profitability."

–Zero Waste Services

"Sustainability means doing things better— not doing without."

–David Suzuki

You, as Prime Minister

1. Use the jigsaw strategy in the Skill Path on page 439 to do further research on environmental issues today, including Canada's compliance with the Kyoto Protocol. Share your findings in a Cabinet meeting. Then brainstorm ways that your government can reduce Canada's ecological footprint. Discuss whether business and industry should practise sustainable development regardless of the cost, and the extent to which you believe Canadians will be willing to absorb the extra costs.

2. In your Speech from the Throne, outline plans to hold a national conference on the environment that involves government, business and industry, and the Canadian public. Include an agenda that highlights the environmental policies and practices your government plans to implement.

 Learn more about Canada's environmental challenges

Reading Strategy

Before reading this section, generate a list of words that you associate with the Canadian military. Share and compare your list with a small group and identify any similarities and differences.

Challenges Facing the Canadian Military

In recent years, the Canadian military has been front-page news more than any time since the Second World War. The challenges facing the military today are the subject of ongoing debate, both in Parliament and in the media. Today, many Canadians are deeply aware of and interested in the Canadian military and its missions.

For more than 50 years, the role of Canada's military was primarily as peacekeepers under the UN. In the early 21st century, that role shifted as the Canadian military became part of strategic NATO defence operations led by the US. What should the international role of the Canadian military be in the 21st century?

Peacekeeping Versus Combat

Beginning in the 1950s, the Canadian military began carving out an international image as one of the world's foremost peacekeepers. Since then, many Canadians have come to expect the role of our military to be one of bringing peace, order, and stability to countries and regions in conflict.

Today, this traditional role has changed with the US-led war on terror. In Afghanistan, Canadian troops became active combatants. At the same time, Canada's role as a leader in international peacekeeping operations faded from public view. In fact, in 2007 Canada was in 50th place among those countries that contributed to peacekeeping missions.

The transition for the military, from peacekeeping to combat, has not been an easy one for many Canadians to accept. Mounting casualties in the war in Afghanistan have led many people to demand a return to peacekeeping,

a role they believe is more in line with Canadian values. Those who disagree with this point of view argue that many recent peacekeeping missions have been as dangerous as the war in Afghanistan.

Other Canadians believe that the focus of the Canadian military should be on our domestic defence. With over 240 000 kilometres of coastline and almost 9000 kilometres of borders to defend, they believe the Canadian military should concentrate on responding to domestic disasters, Canadian sovereignty in the Arctic, and terrorist threats. Others say there is little a conventional military operation can do to prevent a terrorist attack like the one that took place in the United States on 11 September 2001.

The Cost of the Military

Military funding has always been a contentious issue in Canada. Many Canadians believe that funding a standing army should not be a priority. They believe that the billions of dollars needed to maintain the military should be invested in social and environmental programs instead. Others disagree. In 2006, the Harper government pledged billions of dollars to purchase new military vehicles, including transport planes, heavy-lift helicopters, and troop carrier ships. The decision was supported by many Canadians, who believe it is important to maintain a modern military and to commit the financial resources needed to ensure our security.

"Studies on the difference between Canadian and American values frequently conclude that Canada has a much less militaristic political culture than its American neighbour. Canadians consistently put health care, the environment, and the economy at the top of priority lists and defence at the bottom. Even more, Canadians are much more likely to support the United Nations, international law, and diplomacy over military solutions to international conflict."

–Stephen Staples,
Ottawa (X)Press,
13 April 2006

Learn more about the Canadian military

You, as Prime Minister

1. Recall what you know about the role Canada's military has played since the First World War. In your opinion, what is the most important role for the military to play today? Do you think that public opinion should play a part in defining that role? Explain your response.

2. Use the jigsaw strategy in the Skill Path on page 439 to investigate the challenges facing the Canadian military today. Then share your findings in a Cabinet meeting to discuss your government's policy on the role of the Canadian military. Make notes outlining your ideas. Present your government's vision for the role of the Canadian military when you write your Speech from the Throne. Present arguments to convince Canadians that this vision reflects Canadian values.

Redefining Canadian Citizenship and Identity

"The equality of men and women is an overriding right. Of course, people are entitled to their own religious and cultural beliefs, but they must respect the fundamental right of equality between men and women."

–Dyane Adam, former commissioner of official languages, "Women and culture in Canada," April 2005

"You can wave your hands about and prattle about 'equal rights' not being contradictory to religious beliefs, but history has shown the contrary time and again. All current major religions are male dominated. All discriminate against women in some way."

–Lori Masters, "Voices: Women's Rights and Multiculturalism," *Toronto Star*, 29 May 2007

"Don't position women's rights versus multiculturalism ... It should never be either/or. Rather, it should be: how do we protect the rights of women in an inclusive and diverse society?"

–Ratna Omidvar, executive director, the Maytree Foundation, 28 May 2007

Over the years, Canada has opened its doors to immigrants from around the world. In the process, Canadians have come to accept diverse cultures, languages, religions, and traditions. Yet multiculturalism raises some important issues: To what extent should immigrants make a commitment to uphold Canadian values and accept basic Canadian principles of equality? How should the government respond to the challenges of an increasingly multicultural society? To what extent should Canadian society change or stay the same as it attempts to accommodate different cultures?

When Rights Collide

Most Canadians believe in the principles and rights safeguarded in the Charter of Rights and Freedoms. They expect immigrants to accept Canada's democratic principles and our belief in equality for all. In a poll conducted in 2007, 81 per cent of Canadians surveyed believed that immigrants should accept Canadian beliefs about the equality of women. They did not think that the right to religious freedom should override the rights of women. The conflict between some religious beliefs and equal rights has forced governments at all levels to take action to balance these rights in an increasingly diverse society. However, the issue is a sensitive one, with many people holding passionate views on the subject.

Dual Citizenship

Today, people around the world are more mobile than ever before. Canadians in particular are on the move, in part because of our diverse countries of origin. Many people migrate to Canada to attend school or for other reasons. They obtain Canadian citizenship, but later return to their country of origin for business or family reasons. In 1977, Canada changed its citizenship policy to allow Canadians to become dual citizens— that is, to have Canadian citizenship in addition to citizenship from one or more other countries. Statistics Canada says there are more than 4 million immigrants living in Canada who have dual citizenship.

Yet what impact does dual citizenship have on people's rights and responsibilities as Canadian citizens? In 2006, this question was at the heart of a controversial debate that emerged following the outbreak of civil war in Lebanon. At the time, more than 40 000 Canadian citizens of Lebanese origin were living in Lebanon. They retained dual citizenship as both Canadians and Lebanese. When the war broke out, many of these dual citizens were desperate to escape the violence. They turned to the Canadian embassy for help returning to Canada. In response, the Canadian government spent more than $85 million to evacuate 15 000 Canadians living in Lebanon. When the war was over, however, more than 7000 of the evacuees returned to Lebanon.

The situation involving Canadians living in Lebanon raised some important questions about citizenship: Does dual citizenship reduce the value of being a Canadian citizen?

Should immigrants given Canadian citizenship have to renounce their citizenship in other countries? Should people born in Canada and who are granted citizenship in another country have to renounce their Canadian citizenship? What are the rights and responsibilities of Canadian citizenship?

These Canadians of Lebanese heritage were among those evacuated from Lebanon in July and August of 2006. Should Canada be responsible for evacuating Canadians with dual citizenship who do not choose Canada as their permanent place of residence?

"We need to be loyal to one country as far as your citizenship. Your heart can be where you were born, but I think the commitment to Canada has to be strong and I think dual citizenship weakens that."

–Liberal MP Judy Sgro, 21 September 2006

"Dual citizenship in our country is embraced and allowed. It's really shameful that we start questioning people's loyalty."

–Liberal MP Omar Alghabra, 8 December 2006

Learn more about the issue of Canadian citizenship and identity

You, as Prime Minister

1. To what extent do you think that all people in Canada should uphold Canadian values on the equality of women? Outline your position for inclusion in your Speech from the Throne.
2. Working with a group, hold a Cabinet meeting to discuss your government's policy on dual citizenship. Debate the reasons for and against dual citizenship and record your arguments in your notes. Then formulate your policy and your reasons for or against dual citizenship.
3. Now you are ready to write your Speech from the Throne. Compile all of your notes from your Cabinet meetings. Use these notes to help you prepare an outline of the goals your government hopes to achieve as you begin your term in office. Once you have prepared your outline, use the steps in the *Skill Path for Making Effective Oral Presentations* in Chapter 10 as a guide to writing your Speech from the Throne.

Skill Path:
Predicting the Future Based on Evidence from the Past

Have you ever heard the expression "History repeats itself?" Most historians believe that there are patterns in history and that many of these patterns are continuous—that is, that they involve deeply rooted issues that may be passed on from generation to generation. As a result, historians look at historical patterns from the past to make educated predictions about what might happen in the future.

Being able to predict future events and consequences is an important skill to have. You will use this skill in many aspects of your life—when you need to decide what action to take or to predict what the outcome of your actions might be. For example, earlier in this textbook you saw that Prime Minister William Lyon Mackenzie King realized during the First World War that conscription was a bitterly divisive issue that pitted French Canadians against English Canadians. As a result, as prime minister during the Second World War, he went to great lengths to avoid introducing conscription again.

Knowing and understanding history helps *all* Canadians—not just prime ministers and historians—to make decisions and judgments about issues in Canada today. As a student of history, how can you predict the future based on evidence from the past?

STEP 1: Identify the Issue

Identify one issue from Canada's history since 1914 for each of the categories listed in the left-hand column of the chart below. Then identify the potential challenges each issue poses today and any historical patterns associated with this issue.

Type of Issue	Potential Challenges Today	Historical Patterns	Predictions for the Future
Social:			
Political:			
Regional:			
Economic:			
International:			

STEP 2: Summarize the Issue

Write a brief summary of each of the above issues. Be sure to explain each issue using specific examples from both the past and the present. State what you believe are the key causes and consequences of each issue. For each one, make note of the factors that represent continuity and change over time.

STEP 3: Practise Your Skill

Based on your understanding of the evidence from the past, for each issue predict what might happen in the future and record it in the chart. Give reasons to support your ideas. Then, in a class discussion, share your ideas.

Thinking Like a Historian:
Identifying Continuity and Change

Essential Question: As a historian, how do you recognize how things have changed or stayed the same over time?

As you have discovered throughout *The Canadian Challenge*, continuity and change are interrelated. The changes that have happened in Canada have not come about from a single event. More often, they have been the result of a series of related events spread out over time. You have discovered that some of the changes that have taken place in Canada since 1914 have happened quickly, while others have occurred over a much longer period of time. Some changes are still ongoing as we begin our journey through the twenty-first century. You have also discovered that sometimes change is for the better; sometimes it is not. And even as some things change, others remain the same.

You, the Historian

As you complete your study of Canadian history in this course, reflect on how things have changed or stayed the same over time.

1. List and rank in order of importance the five most important social, economic, political, and/or cultural events or issues that have taken place in Canada since 1914. For each one, identify any historical patterns. Then explain to what extent this event or issue has changed or stayed the same over time. Predict whether you think this issue or event will change in the future and, if you believe it will change, in what ways. Give reasons for your response.

2. Create a mind map to identify new challenges facing Canada and Canadians in the twenty-first century.

Glossary

affirmative action: A policy or program that attempts to address past discrimination by taking actions to ensure that women, visible minorities, and people with physical disabilities are represented fairly in workplaces and educational institutions.

alliance: An association of groups, people, or nations that agree to co-operate to achieve a common goal.

allied: States that have formally agreed to co-operate. In the First World War, the alliance led by Great Britain was referred to as the Allies. In the Second World War, the alliance that opposed the Axis Powers.

amend: The act of revising or altering an official document such as a constitution.

anti-Semitism: An attitude of hatred toward Jews or a policy that discriminates against Jews.

apartheid: The legislated separation of the Black majority population from the white minority population in South America.

appeasement: The act of giving bribes of territory to aggressive nations to prevent war.

aquaculture: Farming fish or shellfish under controlled conditions.

arbitration: A process to resolve a dispute between two parties. The decision is made by an impartial referee who both parties agree upon in advance.

armistice: A truce; the agreement that ended hostilities in the First World War.

arms race: A competition between nations where the goal is to develop and accumulate the most weapons and the newest military technology.

Aryan: In Nazi ideology, a person who is of old Germanic heritage.

assimilate: An attempt to integrate members of a minority group into a larger, dominant culture by denying or erasing the culture and traditions of the minority group.

asylum: Protection for refugees.

autonomy: A nation's political independence; the right and ability to self-govern.

Axis: The alliance between Germany, Italy, and Japan during the Second World War.

baby boom: A large increase in a nation's birth rate. Several nations, including Canada, experienced a dramatic rise in birth rates after the Second World War.

biases: Preferences or inclinations that inhibit impartial judgment; prejudices.

Black Tuesday: Tuesday, 29 October 1929, when the stock market crashed in the United States. The stock market crash was a major factor that led to the Great Depression.

branch plant: A factory or business owned and controlled by a larger company that is based in a foreign country.

British Empire: A large number of colonies and territories that were brought under British rule beginning in the late sixteenth century.

budget surpluses: A budget surplus occurs when a government takes in more money than it spends. This is the opposite of a budget deficit.

business cycle: A recurring pattern of increased and decreased financial activity within an economy.

capital punishment: A death sentence as punishment for a crime.

capitalist: A person who supports capitalism.

caricature: An artistic representation in which the artist exaggerates certain visual qualities of the subject, often for comedic or political purposes.

ceasefire: A period of truce or suspension of hostilities.

censorship: A government review of media before public release to eliminate material considered obscene, threatening to national security, or otherwise inappropriate.

cipher: A code used to send secret messages.

civil liberties: A person's freedoms of action and speech, within the bounds of official laws.

civil rights: A citizen's right to political and social freedom and equality.

civil rights movement: In general, a campaign to guarantee all citizens equal rights by preventing discrimination based on race, gender, or disability. In the United States, the campaign by African Americans and others to gain equal rights.

closure: A rule that allows the government to end a debate quickly by limiting the time set aside for discussion.

Cold War: An extended period of hostility between the United States and the Soviet Union following the Second World War. In a cold war, opposing nations attempt to defeat each other by developing better technologies, achieving economic supremacy, and any other means short of military conflict.

collective bargaining: Negotiations between management and a union that represents the workers.

collective security: An agreement among a group of nations to protect other nations from aggressors.

colonial: A resident of a colony; relating to colonialism.

colony: A country or territory that is ruled by a foreign country.

communist: A person who supports communism.

concentration camp: A camp where political prisoners are confined or executed.

conflagration: A great and destructive fire.

conscientious objector: A person who refuses to participate in military service for religious, moral, or ethical reasons.

conscription: A government policy that forces citizens to enlist for military service.

consensus: A general agreement among a group of people; a collective opinion.

co-operative: A business owned and run jointly by members who share the profits.

counterculture: A subculture with values or lifestyles that are in opposition to the conventions of the dominant culture.

Crown corporation: A company owned by the government.

cultural mosaic: A society where people are encouraged to celebrate and promote the coexistence of many different cultures.

decolonization: The process of establishing political independence in a nation that was previously a colony.

defected: To have abandoned one's country or cause in favour of another.

demilitarized zone: An area from which military forces have been intentionally removed, usually as a result of an international agreement. A demilitarized zone is often located on the boundary between two opposing nations.

democratic socialism: A political movement that hopes to achieve socialist aims, including the nationalization of key industries and large-scale government involvement in the economy, in a state governed by democracy.

détente: An easing of a tense relationship between nations.

deterrent: A military action that is intended to discourage an aggressor from attacking.

dictatorship: A state controlled by a ruler with unrestricted authority.

distinct society: An expression used to describe Québec's unique place in Canadian society, based on its Francophone majority, unique character, and reliance on French civil law.

drafted: Forced to participate in military service.

dual citizenship: Having rights of citizenship in two countries at the same time.

economic nationalist: A person who promotes restricting foreign trade and investment in order to promote domestic economic activity.

economic zone: An area just off a country's coastline over which the country has special rights to control exploration and resources. The United Nations Convention on the Law of the Sea grants nations an exclusive economic zone (EEZ) for a distance of 200 nautical miles.

embargo: An act that prohibits countries and other agencies from conducting business with a specific country, usually as a form of political punishment.

enemy alien: A person who is a citizen of a nation that is at war with the country in which he/she lives.

enfranchised: Given rights of citizenship including the right to vote in an election.

entrenched: Firmly established in the constitution.

Establishment: The group of people who hold power and control the major institutions in society.

exchange rate: The ratio at which two currencies are exchanged or traded.

expropriated: Forcibly taken away from its owner.

fascism: A political system characterized by authoritarian nationalism, where the interests of society as a whole are held to be more important than the rights of individual citizens.

filibuster: A long speech given in an official assembly that is meant to slow down progress.

Final Solution: The plan enacted by the Nazis in 1942 to exterminate all Jews in Nazi-controlled Europe.

foreign policy: A country's self-imposed guidelines for interacting with other nations.

G8: The Group of Eight. A group of the world's wealthiest nations that meets every year to discuss common concerns. The member countries are Canada, France, Germany, Italy, Japan, Russia, the United Kingdom, and the United States.

genocide: A planned attempt to eliminate an entire ethnic, racial, or religious group.

global village: A term coined by Marshall McLuhan to describe the world as an interdependent community, where people are linked together through electronic communication.

globalization: The process by which people across the world are becoming more closely connected through trade, communication, transportation, and politics.

Great Depression: A time of economic hardship when many countries experienced a decrease in manufacturing and trade along with high unemployment rates. In the United States, the Great Depression began with the stock market crash on Black Tuesday.

gross domestic product (GDP): The most common way of measuring the size of a country's economy; the value of all goods and services produced within a country in one year.

gross national product (GNP): A way of measuring the economic activity of a nation; the value of all goods and services provided in a country, including those obtained through international trade.

historical empathy: The process of relating to or identifying with people who lived in the past.

Human Development Index (HDI): A United Nations measurement of a nation's general development based on factors such as poverty, literacy, and life expectancy.

immigration: The act of entering a new country to live permanently.

imperialist: A person who promotes a system of governance where one country rules other countries, particularly the British Empire.

Impressionist: A visual artist associated with the artistic movement of Impressionism, which began in the late nineteenth century. Impressionists focus on painting their impression of their subject, rather than what the subject really looks like.

improvised explosive device (IED): An unconventionally prepared bomb, often used by insurgents to fight better-equipped military forces and/or cause widespread human casualties.

income trust: A type of investment that allows corporations to pay fewer direct taxes, so more profit goes directly to the company's shareholders.

Industrialization: The process in which a country adopts industrial methods of production and manufacturing.

inflation: A general rise in the price of goods and services along with a decline in the value of money.

inherent right: A permanent right that cannot be altered or taken away.

insurgents: People who engage in armed conflict against the military forces of an established government.

interest: A payment made in return for a loan of money or goods.

internment: The act of confining or imprisoning someone.

Iron Curtain: A term popularized by Winston Churchill that describes the boundary between communist states of Eastern Europe and democratic states of Western Europe.

isolationism: A country's policy to not get involved with the actions of other countries, often to avoid participating in international conflicts.

isolationist: A person who supports isolationism.

Just Society: Pierre Trudeau's vision of creating a country based on principles of freedom, equality, and compassion.

League of Nations: A global association formed in 1919 to promote peace. It was later replaced by the United Nations in 1945.

left wing: A political term used to describe ideas that favour socialism, such as wanting large scale government involvement in the economy and believing that achieving social equality is more important than achieving personal wealth.

legation: The official residence of a diplomatic representative.

mandate: The act of transferring control of a region to a new government. After the First World War, the League of Nations gave several colonies and territories to Allied nations to manage and develop.

mandatory retirement: An official policy that forces people to retire when they reach a certain age.

manifesto: A public statement of political beliefs.

melting pot: A society where people are encouraged to integrate into the dominant culture rather than celebrate individual cultures and heritages.

merchant mariner: A sailor working on a civilian ship that transports or trades supplies.

middle power: A state with limited military power, but some international political influence.

militarism: A country's policy to maintain a large military that is constantly ready for battle.

minority government: A government in which the ruling political party does not hold more than 50 per cent of the seats.

monetary policy: In Canada, the policy by which the Bank of Canada controls interest rates and the supply of money to increase or decrease economic activity.

money markets: Markets where government bonds and other securities are bought and sold.

moratorium: A temporary suspension of activity.

multicultural: A society made up of individuals with many different cultural backgrounds.

nationalism: A country's policy of maintaining national independence.

nationalist: A person who feels great pride for his or her country.

nationalize: The process of transferring ownership of businesses from individuals to the government.

non-confidence vote: A vote in Parliament to determine whether or not the majority of the Members of Parliament support the party in power.

non-governmental organization (NGO): An organization that does not have official ties to a government. Many NGOs support international aid and development.

notwithstanding clause: Section 33 of the Charter of Rights and Freedoms, which allows Parliament or a provincial government to declare a law valid even though the law may violate some of the rights protected in the Charter.

order-in-council: In Canada, a rule or a command that is decided upon by the Cabinet and formally announced by the Governor General.

pacifist: A person who believes that problems can be solved peacefully, without resorting to violence.

pandemic: An outbreak of a disease across a nation or the entire world.

patriate: To transfer control of a law from the country that originated the law to the country to which the law applies.

patronage: The act of appointing people to government jobs as a reward for past political support.

peacekeeping: Actively keeping the peace between nations or regions through international military and non-military efforts.

plebiscite: A vote on an issue of major national importance in which all eligible voters are asked to participate.

pluralist: A society in which smaller groups maintain their unique cultural identities within the larger society.

poverty line: The minimum level of income required for an adequate standard of living. For a rich country, Canada has many families living close to or below the poverty line.

private member's bill: A proposed law that comes from an individual member of parliament who may or may not be a member of the governing party. Few of these bills become laws because they are not officially sponsored or supported by the individual's party.

racist: A person who believes that one race of people is better than another.

Realism: An artistic movement in which artists try to portray the world in a realistic way, paying particular attention to unidealized scenes of modern life.

recall: A vote through which eligible voters can dismiss an elected official from office.

recession: A temporary period of economic downturn within a country, characterized by a high unemployment rate.

Red Scare: A time when people are afraid that Communists will infiltrate or take over their country.

referendum: A vote on a specific question asked by the government in which all eligible citizens are asked to participate.

refugee: A person who is forced to flee his or her homeland because of a threat of violence or political or religious persecution.

relief: Financial assistance from the government to help support unemployed citizens; today it is called welfare.

religious fundamentalist: A person who holds deep, usually very conservative, religious beliefs. A few fundamentalists turn to violence to defend their views.

reparation: Payment made to a person who has suffered by those who caused the suffering.

residential school: A boarding school for Aboriginal children, often operated by a religious organization in co-operation with the federal government.

restorative justice: A theory of criminal justice where a wrongdoer must repair or make amends for the harm he or she has caused, as an attempt to restore the victim or victims of the crime to their former condition.

sanctions: Military or economic action by a country, or a group of countries, to force another country to conform to an international agreement or standard of behaviour.

sedition: Actions or words intended to provoke rebellion against a government.

self-government: The power of a group of people to make and enforce their own laws. In Canada, this term is typically applied to the right of Aboriginal people to govern their own affairs.

separatism: The political idea that supports establishing Québec as an independent nation.

share: Part ownership of a company.

social dividend: A payment to all citizens based on the wealth or economic health of the country.

social gospel: Using the principles of the Christian gospel to solve social problems and improve people's lives on earth.

social safety net: A set of government programs that provide financial support to those who are sick, elderly, or unemployed.

social welfare: Government programs that are meant to protect Canadians from poverty.

sovereignty: The right for a region to be a self-governing, independent state.

sovereignty-association: The idea that Québec should be politically independent from Canada but still maintain close economic ties, including using the same currency and international trade agreements.

Speech from the Throne: A statement, read by the Governor General at the beginning of a session of Parliament, that sets out the goals the government wants to achieve.

sponsorship: The support given to a political candidate from a business, in the form of money or services.

status: The special rights and privileges assigned to Aboriginal Canadians under the Indian Act.

status quo: The present state of affairs; normal conditions.

stock market: A system that allows stock brokers to buy and sell stocks and shares.

subsidies: Grants of money given by the government to an industry to help the business participate in the economy.

suicide bombs: People who detonate explosions near military areas or other public targets, intentionally killing themselves in the process.

superpower: A country with great political influence and a powerful military, such as the United States and, formerly, the Soviet Union.

sustainable development: Development that fulfills current needs without depleting natural resources or damaging the environment, so that development can continue in the future.

sustainable economy: An economy that is based on sustainable development.

tar sands: A mixture of crude oil and sand. Alberta has many areas covered by tar sands, but the oil must be separated from the sand before it can be used.

tariff: A duty, or tax, on imported products.

total war: A war in which all of a nation's resources are devoted to the war effort.

trading bloc: A region of free trade, defined by a trade agreement. Free trade allows a group of countries to import and export products from each other without paying traditional taxes and tariffs.

Triple Alliance: The alliance formed between Germany, Austria-Hungary, and Italy before the First World War began.

Triple Entente: The alliance formed between England, France, and Russia before the First World War began.

tsunami: A storm-like wave that forms when an earthquake occurs beneath the ocean floor.

universal health care: A government program that provides free health care to all citizens.

urban renewal: The process of redeveloping parts of cities to remove rundown residential, commercial, and industrial areas.

urbanization: The growth and expansion of large cities, which involves large numbers of people moving to the city from a rural location.

VE Day: *VE* stands for "Victory Europe." VE Day represents the day Germany surrendered to the Allied Forces on 8 May 1945.

veto power: The official right, given to a political entity, to single-handedly reject a proposal, forbid an action, or prevent the creation of a law or legislature.

Victory Bond: Savings bonds sold to Canadians to help pay for the cost of the First World War.

War Measures Act: An emergency act created in 1914 that gave the federal Cabinet the power to make quick, unchallenged decisions in times of war.

weapon of mass destruction (WMD): A weapon that can kill a large number of people at once. WMDs are usually nuclear, biological, or chemical weapons, and can greatly damage the natural environment.

Western Front: The land in Europe on which the First World War was fought.

Index

Credits

Photo Credits
t=top; b=bottom; l=left; r=right

Cover: *The Stretcher Bearer Party* by Cyril Barraud, 19710261-0019, Beaverbrook Collection of War Art, ©Canadian War Museum;

2 National Gallery of Canada, Ottawa, Purchased 1956;

4 Glenbow Archives NA-2676-6; **5** Department of National Defence;

8 *Untitled*, Pegi Nicol Macleod, 19710261-5822, Beaverbrook Collection of War Art, ©Canadian War Museum;

10 House of Commons Collection, Ottawa;

12 William James Topley/Library and Archives Canada/PA-028128; **13** Canada. Dept. of National Defence/Library and Archives Canada/PA-000880; **14** The Granger Collection, New York; **15** ©Hulton-Deutsch Collection/CORBIS; **19** ©Irma Coucill; **20** Canada. Dept. of National Defence/Library and Archives Canada/C-006984; **22** Colchester Historical Society Archives; **25** *War in the Air*, Christopher Nevinson, 19710261-0517, Beaverbrook Collection of War Art, ©Canadian War Museum; **26** Library and Archives Canada/C-019951; **28** W.I. Castle/Canada. Dept. of National Defence/Library and Archives Canada/PA-000648; **30** Canada. Dept. of National Defence/Library and Archives Canada/PA-024436; **35 t** Library and Archives Canada/amicus no. 22605683 and amicus no. 23120921, **b** Archives of Ontario, RG 2-43, 4-832; **36** William Rider-Rider/Library and Archives Canada/PA-002162; **40 t** *Dead Horse and Rider in a Trench*, Maruice Cullen, 19710261-0126, Beaverbrook Collection of War Art, ©Canadian War Museum, **b** ©iStockphoto/ Suzanne Carter-Jackson; **42** City of Toronto Archives, Fonds 1244, Item 48.7; **44 t** Toronto Star/The Canadian Press, **b** Library and Archives Canada/ C-024305; **46** Archives of Ontario, F 4436-0-0-0-158; **49** William James Topley/Library and Archives Canada/PA-026987; **52** Aitken Ltd./Library and Archives Canada/C-001690; **54** Provincial Archives of Manitoba/Foote picture # 1696, negative # 2762; **56** Jules A. Castonguay/Library and Archives Canada/C-034443; **58** University of Toronto Archives; **61** Canada. National Parks Branch/Library and Archives Canada/C-036184; **67** Canadian Pacific Railway Company, A.8074; **70** ©Bettmann/CORBIS; **72 t** Topical Press Agency/Hulton Archive/Getty Images, **b** ©Bettmann/CORBIS; **73 tl** ©Condé Nast Archive/CORBIS, **tr** The Granger Collection, New York, **b** ©Condé Nast Archive/CORBIS; **74** Lawren Harris, *Above Lake Superior*, Tom Thomson Art Gallery Permanent Collection, Bequest of Mrs. Norah

Thomson de Pencier; **77 l** A.G. Racey, Montreal Daily Star, 4 March 1926, **r** A.G. Racey, Montreal Daily Star, 27 July 1929; **78** Toronto Star/The Canadian Press; **80** Library and Archives Canada/C-000687; **81** Library and Archives Canada/C-21528; **82** AP/The Canadian Press; **88** Canada. Dept. of National Defence/Library and Archives Canada/PA-036362; **89** Glenbow Archives NA-5416-7; **91** Charles Comfort, *Young Canadian*, 1932, Hart House Permanent Collection, Univeristy of Toronto.; **93** Glenbow Archives NA-3622-19; **94** Glenbow Archives NA-3069-3; **96** The Gazette (Montreal)/Library and Archives Canada/PA-129184; **97** Canada Science and Technology Museum; **98** Library and Archives Canada/PA-122616; **99 t** Everett/The Canadian Press, **b** Pictorial Press Ltd/Alamy; **101** Mary Evans Pictures/The Canadian Press; **103** George Horne Russell (Canadian, 1861-1933) /Library and Archives Canada/C-18713; **104** Prsees-Bild-Zentrale/Library and Archives Canada/PA-119010; **106** Marc Hill/Alamy; **107** ©iStockphoto/ Duncan Walker; **108** Library and Archives Canada/C-027645; **109** Toronto Star/The Canadian Press; **110** Mary Evans Pictures/The Canadian Press; **112** The Globe and Mail; **114** The Canadian Press(Andrew Vaugahn); **115 l** Courtesy of Black Cultural Centre of Nova Scotia, **r** Rick Mahoney; **116** The Canadian Press; **119** Toronto Star/The Canadian Press; **120** *Via Dolorosa, Ortona*, Charles Comfort, 19710261-2308, Beaverbrook Collection of War Art, ©Canadian War Museum; **122** Gilbert A. Milne/Canada. Dept. of National Defence/Library and Archives Canada/PA-116533; **123** The Canadian Press; **124** The Granger Collection, New York; **129** ©John Van Hasselt/COR-BIS SYGMA; **131** National Film Board of Canada. Photothèque/Library and Archives Canada/WRM 2511; **132** True Comics/Library and Archives Canada/MIKAN No. 124362; **133 t** Dime Comics/Library and Archives Canada/C-097252, **b** North Vancouver Museum and Archives, photo no. 728; **134** National Film Board of Canada. Photothèque/Library and Archives Canada/C-024452; **135** City of Richmond Archives, 1998 112 1112, Elsie Esplen Hunter fonds; **136 l** War Poster Collection, Rare Books and Special Collections Division, McGill University Library, **r** Library and Archives Canada, Acc. No. 1983-30-1220; **140** ©A.C. Fine Art Inc./Art Gallery of Hamilton, Gift of Dominion Foundries and Steel Ltd. 1957; **142** ©Bettmann/ CORBIS; **144** Library and Archives Canada/C-10461; **145** ©Bettmann/ CORBIS; **146** Library and Archives Canada/C-021929; **147** AP/The Canadian Press; **148** ©Bettmann/CORBIS; **150** ©Bettmann/CORBIS; **151** Courtesy of the Diefenbunker, Canada's Cold War Museum; **152** Nicholas Morant/National Film Board of Canada. Photothèque/Library and Archives Canada/C-022717; **153 t** by permission of the Marcus family, **b** ©CORBIS; **154** Darryl Evans/©Commonwealth Secretariat; **157** Library and Archives Canada; ©Canada Post Corporation; **158** ©Bettmann/CORBIS; **159** Library and Archives Canada; ©Canada Post Corporation; **160** Topical Press Agency/ Hulton Archive/Getty Images; **163** ©Jerry Cooke/CORBIS; **165** Library and Archives Canada/Gar Lunney/National Film Board of Canada. Photothèque collection/PA-191424; **169** Paul E. Tomelin/Canada. Dept. of National Defence/Library and Archives Canada/PA- 128280; **170** ©Hulton-Deutsch Collection/CORBIS; **171** AP/The Canadian Press; **174** *Maclean's* magazine 17 March 1956/Toronto Public Library; **176** Library and Archives Canada/

National Film Board of Canada Photothèque collection/C-000120; **177** The Canadian Press; **179** Library and Archives Canada/Gar Lunney/National Film Board of Canada. Photothèque collection/e002265645; **181** The Canadian Press; **182** Library and Archives Canada/Credit: Duncan Cameron/Duncan Cameron fonds/PA-113253; **183** Bibliothèque et Archives nationales du Québec; **184** The Canadian Press(Michael Burns); **185** Christopher J. Woods/Canada. Dept. of National Defence/Library and Archives Canada/PA-142289; **189** Glenbow Archives ND-20-234; **194** J. R. Eyerman/Time & Life Pictures/Getty Images; **197** Terry Manzo. Courtesy Stratford Shakespeare Festival.; **198** ©Michael Ochs Archives/CORBIS; **199** Leo Harrison/Toronto Star; **200** ©Michael Ochs Archives/CORBIS; **201** FPG/Taxi/Getty Images; **202 t** Everett/The Canadian Press, **b** ©William Gottlieb/CORBIS; **204** AP/The Canadian Press; **206** York University Libraries, Clara Thomas Archives and Special Collections, Image ASC00018; **207** York University Libraries, Clara Thomas Archives and Special Collections, Image ASC00853; **208** Gone but Never Forgotten: Bob Brooks' Photographic Portrait of Africville in the 1960s—Image No. 200715044; **210** Duncan Cameron/Library and Archives Canada/PA-117093; **212** Paul Horsdal/Library and Archives Canada/PA-130070; **213** National Film Board of Canada. Photothèque/Library and Archives Canada/PA-114838; **215** Nick Nickels/Library and Archives Canada/PA-123915; **217** National Currency Collection, Currency Museum, Bank of Canada; **222** The Canadian Press; **223** Library and Archives Canada/Credit: Duncan Cameron/Duncan Cameron fonds/PA-136153; **224** By permission of the estate of Duncan Macpherson/Library and Archives Canada, Acc. No. 1987-38-316; **226** Reprinted courtesy of L.M. Norris Estate/Library and Archives Canada, Acc. No. 1976-24-4; **227** Library and Archives Canada/Credit: Duncan Cameron/Duncan Cameron fonds/C-036222; **228** Library and Archives Canada/Canadian Corporation for the 1967 World Exhibition fonds/e000995981; **229** The Canadian Press(Chuck Mitchell); **230** Hydro Québec, no. 2007L412; **232** Courtesy UBC Museum of Anthropology, Vancouver, Canada. Photo: Bill McLennan; **233** Courtesy of the family of George Manuel; **234 t** Kenojuak Ashevak (b. 1927)/*The Enchanted Owl* 1960/stonecut on paper/61.1 x 65.7 cm/Purchase 1979/McMichael Canadian Art Collection/1979.10.1. Reproduced with the permission of Dorset Fine Arts, **b** National Gallery of Canada, Ottawa, Gift of the Department of Indian Affairs and Northern Development, 1989. Reproduced with the permission of Dorset Fine Arts.; **234** Photograph by Feheley Fine Arts. Reproduced with the permission of Dorset Fine Arts.; **238** John Reeves/Library and Archives Canada/PA-165118;

242 Daphne Odjig (b. 1919)/*Rebirth of a Culture* 1979/acrylic on canvas/124.5 x 155.5 cm/ Donated by James Hubbard and Dennis Jones in honour of Estella and Stuart Wright/McMichael Canadian Art Collection/1991.14;

244 The Canadian Press(Ted Grant); **246** The Canadian Press(Peter Bregg); **247** The Canadian Press(Peter Bregg); **248** ©Bill Morgenstern/Earth Moods; **251** VISU*TronX*; **253** The Canadian Press; **256** Image I-32427 courtesy of Royal BC Museum, BC Archives; **257** The Canadian Press (Fred Chartrand); **258** Cover of Herold Cardinal, *The Unjust Society: The Tragedy of Canada's Indians*, (Edmonton: M.G. Hurtig Ltd., 1969); **259** The Canadian Press(Bill Brennan); **261** john t. fowler/Alamy; **265** Tannis Toohey/Toronto Star; **266** Reproduced with the permission of Miyuki Tanobe; **268** Toronto Star/The Canadian Press(Frank Lennon); **269** Canadian Olympic Committee/The Canadian Press; **270 t** Toronto Star/The Canadian Press, **b** Pictorial Press Ltd/Alamy; **273** ©Greenpeace/Keziere, Robert; **275** Fumoleau/NWT Archives/N-1995-002:4199; **276** ©Bettmann/CORBIS; **278** The Canadian Press(Peter Bregg); **280** Library and Archives Canada; ©Canada Post Corporation; **281** ©Christopher J. Morris/CORBIS; **282** Time & Life Pictures/Getty Images; **284** KlixPix/First Light; **286** The Canadian Press(Drew Gragg); **287** Toronto Star/The Canadian Press; **290** Glenbow Archives M-8000-716; **293** ©Bettmann/CORBIS; **296** The Canadian Press; **297 t** The Canadian Press (Bill Grimshaw), **b** ©Greenpeace/Ferrero; **299** Canadian Space Agency; **300** ©Pedram Pirnia; **301** Sylvain Pinet/Comité de Solidarité/Trois-Rivières; **302** The Canadian Press(Peter Bregg); **305** Fisheries and Oceans Canada; **306** Department of National Defence; **308** ©Bettmann/CORBIS; **309** The

Canadian Press(Ron Poling); **312** The Canadian Press (Fred Chartrand); **314** ©Christopher J. Morris/CORBIS; **315** The Canadian Press (Bill Grimshaw); **316** The Canadian Press; **319** The Canadian Press (Fred Chartrand); **320** Cartoon courtesy Andy Donato, Toronto Sun; **324** Charlottetown Guardian/The Canadian Press(Brian McInnis); **328** AP/The Canadian Press(Jeff Widener); **329** Wallis/Sipa Press; **334** Wayne Cuddington/Ottawa Citizen; **336** ©Greenpeace/Visser, Robert; **339** ©Salman Ahmed; **341** The Canadian Press(Shaney Komulainen); **344** The Canadian Press (Frank Gunn); **345** ©Gary Braasch/CORBIS; **346** The Canadian Press (Tom Hanson); **350** Cartoon courtesy Andy Donato Toronto Sun; **351** The Canadian Press(Fred Chartrand); **353** ©Adrian Raeside; **354** Denise Grant/Library and Archives Canada/PA-198574; **355 l** ©Neal Preston/CORBIS, **r** ABACA/The Canadian Press; **356** Dimo Safari; **358** Tiko Kerr is a west coast visual artist who enjoys capturing the vitality of his pacific environment.; **360** The Canadian Press (Ryan Remiorz); **362** photo: Jean-Marc Carisse/Library and Archives Canada; **363** The Canadian Press (Tom Hanson); **364** The Canadian Press (Jacques Boissinot); **366** REUTERS/Didier Debusschere; **369** The Canadian Press (Frank Gunn); **372** The Canadian Press (Nick Procaylo); **374** The Canadian Press (Andrew Vaughan); **375** REUTERS/Mike Blake; **376** The Canadian Press (Chuck Stoody); **379** The Canadian Press (Ryan Taplin); **380** National Aboriginal Achievement Foundation; **382** The Canadian Press (Chuck Stoody); **384** The Canadian Press (Jonathan Hayward); **387** ©Christopher Morris/Corbis; **388** AP/The Canadian Press (Jim Collins); **391** AP/The Canadian Press (Wisam Sami); **394** The Canadian Press (Tom Hanson); **395** Department of National Defence; **397** Courtesy of Free The Children; **398** Right To Play; **399 t** The Art Archive/Egyptian Museum Cairo/Alfredo Dagli Orti, **b** REX/The Canadian Press; **402** The Canadian Press (Tom Hanson); **404** PMO photos of the Office of the Prime Minister; **405** Department of National Defence; **406** The Canadian Press (Jeff McIntosh); **407** The Canadian Press (Tom Hanson); **408** The Canadian Press (Jeff McIntosh); **409** The Canadian Press (Thunder Bay Chronicle Journal/Brent Linton); **411** The Canadian Press (Ryan Remiorz); **412** The Canadian Press (Ryan Remiorz); **413** Toronto Star/The Canadian Press (Tara Walton); **414** The Canadian Press (Aaron Harris); **415** The Canadian Press (Jonathan Hayward); **417** The Canadian Press (Nathan Denette); **420** ©Greenpeace/Patrick Doyle; **423 t** ©Lucas Jackson/Reuters/Corbis, **b** ©VAILHE JAN—Focalfix/GAMMA—EYEDEA/PONOPRESSE; **424** Department of National Defence, photo by MCpl David McCord; **428** Property of NASA, available through the Visible Earth; **429** Department of National Defence; **433** ©UNAIDS/Ruben del Prado, 2003; **436** Tara Walton/Toronto Star; **438 t, l-r** Jupiter/The Canadian Press,©iStockphoto/Dan Brandenburg, Photodisc, Photodisc, **b, l-r** Photodisc, ©Alison Wright/CORBIS, ©iStockphoto/Ana Abejon, First Light; **441** The Canadian Press (Fred Chartrand); **443** Tony Bock/Toronto Star; **448 l** The Canadian Press (Tom Hanson), **r** The Canadian Press (Kingston Whig Standard/Micahel Lea); **451** The Canadian Press (Jonathan Hayward).

Text Credits

Statistics Canada information is used with the permission of Statistics Canada. Users are forbidden to copy this material and/or redisseminate the data, in an original or midified form, for commercial purposes, without the expressed permission of Statistics Canada. Information on the availability of the wide range of data from Statistics Canada can be obtained from Statistics Canada's Regional Offices, its World Wide Web site at http://www.statcan.ca, and its toll-free access number 1-800-263-1136.

14 Quoted in Sandra G w y n , *Tapestry of War* (Toronto: HarperCollins Canada, 1992); Patricia Geisler, *Valour Remembered: Canada and the First World War* (Ottawa: Ministry of Supply and Services Canada, 1995); **19** "Francis Pegahmagabow's medals." Canadian Museum of Civilization; Peter Moon, "Building named after Canada's most decorated native soldier." *The Maple Leaf*, 28 June 2006; **20** Robert Fulford, "How the Great War transformed us." *Toronto Star*, 10 October 1992; **21** J.C. McWilliams and R.J. Steel, *Gas! The Battle for Ypres 1915* (St. Catharines: Vanwell Press, 1985), 154–155; Jason Bessey, "The Battle of Ypres 1915." Veterans Affairs Canada, http://www.vacacc.gc.ca/youth/sub.cfm?source=feature/bh_somme2006/bh_youthoverseas/jasonbessey; J.C. McWilliams and R.J. Steel, *Gas! The*

Battle for Ypres 1915 (St. Catharines: Vanwell Press, 1985), 121-122; "Ordeal by fire." *A People's History of Canada*, Episode 12, CBC Television; **22** D.E. McIntyre, "Preface." *Canada at Vimy* (Toronto: P. Martin Associates, 1967); Brent Le Coure, Veterans Affairs Canada, http://www.vac-acc.gc.ca/youth/; **24** "Gervais Raoul Lufbery." World War I: Trenches on the web; **26** Robert Macneil, *Burden of Desire* (New York: Dell Publishing, 1992), 22; **28** Stephen O'Shea, *Back to the Front: An Accidental Historian Walks the Trenches of World War I* (Vancouver: Douglas & McIntyre, 1996), 193; **31** Roger Sarty and John G. Armstrong, "Defending the home front." *Horizon Canada* (1986): 2041; **32** Randy Byrne, "Crisis: Conscription." The Historica Foundation of Canada, 2003; **35** Daphne Read, ed., *The Great War and Canadian Society: An Oral History* (Toronto: New Hogtown Press, 1978), 103; Daphne Read, ed., *The Great War and Canadian Society: An Oral History* (Toronto: New Hogtown Press, 1978), 93; **37** Stephen O'Shea, *Back to the Front: An Accidental Historian Walks the Trenches of World War I* (Vancouver: Douglas & McIntyre, 1996), 186; **39** J.L. Finlay and D.N. Sprague, *The Structure of Canadian History* (Toronto: Prentice Hall, 1989), 290; **40** R. Douglas Francis, Richard Jones, and Donald B. Smith, *Destinies: Canadian History Since Confederation* (Toronto: Harcourt Brace, 1996), 227; **47** Pierre Trépanier, "Groulx, Lionel." in Gerald Hallowell, ed., *The Oxford Companion to Canadian History* (Toronto: Oxford University Press, 2004), 272; David Kilgour, "Two: Down home." Inside outer Canada; **48** Quoted in William Kirby Rolph, *Henry Wise Wood of Alberta* (Toronto: University of Toronto Press, 1950); **49** "Canada and the world: A history." Foreign Affairs and International Trade Canada, http://www.dfait-maeci.gc.ca/hist/canada5-en.asp; **50** Map provided by Dr. Andrew Andersen; **51** Quoted in H. Blair Neatby, *William Lyon Mackenzie King, 1924–1932: The Lonely Heights* (University of Toronto Press, 1963); **54** "Ordeal by fire." *A People's History of Canada*, Episode 12, CBC Television; **56** "Building democracy: J.S. Woodsworth." The Historica Foundation of Canada; **57** Michael Bliss, "Insulin, discovery of." in Gerald Hallowell, ed., *The Oxford Companion to Canadian History* (Toronto: Oxford University Press, 2004), 314; **59** Keith R. Fleming, "Hydroelectricity." in Gerald Hallowell, ed., *The Oxford Companion to Canadian History* (Toronto: Oxford University Press, 2004), 300; **61** Quoted in Douglas Baldwin, *Land of the Red Soil: A Popular History of Prince Edward Island* (Charlottetown: Ragweed Press, 1990); Douglas Leighton, "Automobiles." in Gerald Hallowell, ed., *The Oxford Companion to Canadian History* (Toronto: Oxford University Press, 2004), 57; **62** J. Bradley Cruxton and W. Douglas Wilson, *Spotlight Canada*, 4th edition (Don Mills: Oxford University Press Canada, 2000), 153; **65** Stephen Leacock, *My Discovery of England*, The Literature Network; **66** "Background on the 'persons' case." Information on Bill S-6, http://sen.parl.gc.ca/ckenny/persons.htm; **67** Valerie Knowles, *Strangers at Our Gates: Canadian Immigration and Immigration Policy, 1540–1990* (Toronto: Dundurn Press, 1992); "Advertising in Britain, 1920s." Canadian Museum of Civilization; Rebecca Chowen, "The immigration experience." The Historica Foundation of Canada; **68** "Residential schools: Canada's shame." Teya Peya Productions; Quoted in Celia Haig-Brown, *Resistance and Renewal: Surviving the Indian Residential School* (Vancouver: Tillacum Library, 1993), 84; **69** Quoted in René Fumoleau, *As Long as this Land Shall Last: A History of Treaty 8 and Treaty 11, 1870–1939* (Toronto: McClelland and Stewart, 1975); **71** William Humber, *Diamonds of the North: A Concise History of Baseball in Canada* (Toronto: Oxford University Press, 1995); Quoted in "The road to utopia." Vancouver Art Gallery; Michiel Horn, *The Dirty Thirties: Canadians in the Great Depression* (Toronto: Copp Clark, 1972); **83** "As Tommy Said…" The Tommy Douglas Research Institute; **84** Donald Kerr and Deryck Holdsworth, eds., Geoffrey J. Matthews, *The Historical Atlas of Canada, Volume III: Addressing the Twentieth Century, 1891–1961* (Toronto: University of Toronto Press, 1990); **85** Quoted in Barry Broadfoot, *Ten Lost Years: 1929–1939* (Toronto: Paper Jacks, 1973), 7; **88** Mary Howlett, "Wanted: A new tune." *Maclean's* (1 January 1934); **89** Quoted in Barry Broadfoot, *Ten Lost Years: 1929–1939* (Toronto: Paper Jacks, 1975), 70; Quoted in Beth Brant, *I'll Sing 'til the Day I Die* (Toronto: McGilligan Books, 1995); **90** International, Intergovernmental and Aboriginal Relations (IIAR); **91** Sinclair Ross, *As for Me and My House* (Toronto: McClelland & Steward, 1989), 26; **92** Quoted in Barry Broadfoot, *Ten Lost Years: 1929–1939*, (Toronto: Paper Jacks, 1975); **93** Quoted in Michael Snider, "On to Ottawa trek: Regina Riot." *Maclean's*

(1 July 2002); **97** Quoted in Barry Broadfoot, *Ten Lost Years: 1929–1939* (Toronto: Paper Jacks, 1973), 248; Mitchell MacPhee, The Historica Foundation of Canada, 2007; **102** Quoted in Don Gilmour, *Canada: A People's History*, vol. 2, (Toronto: Canadian Broadcasting Corporation and McClelland & Stewart Ltd., 2001); **103** Quoted in Don Gilmour, *Canada: A People's History*, vol. 2, (Toronto: Canadian Broadcasting Corporation and McClelland & Stewart Ltd., 2001); **117** Daniel Francis, et al., *Canadian Issues*, (Don Mills: Oxford University Press Canada, 1998), 159; **118** Quoted in William Whitehead, *Dieppe 1942: Echoes of Disaster*, (Toronto: Personal Library, 1979); Quoted in *Destined to Survive: A Dieppe Veteran's Story*, (Toronto: Dundurn Press, 1998); **123** Andrew Murray, The Historica Foundation of Canada, 2007; **124** Quoted in Don Gillmor, *Canada: A People's History*, vol. 2, (Toronto: Canadian Broadcasting Corporation and McClelland & Stewart, 2001), 209; Elie Wiesel, *Night*, trans. Stella Rodway, revised edition (New York: Hill and Wang, 2006); **125** Quoted in Don Gillmor, *Canada: A People's History*, vol. 2, (Toronto: Canadian Broadcasting Corporation and McClelland & Stewart Ltd., 2001), 208; **126** Wes Unwin, The Historica Foundation of Canada, 2005; Don Delaplante, "German POW's buried in bleak northern bush." *Globe and Mail*, 12 April 1950; Amir Attaran, "Afghan detainees: Treat 'em right." *Globe and Mail*, 9 March 2007; **131** Jenna Lewis, The Historica Foundation of Canada, 2007; **132** Quoted in Stacey Gibson, "Fairly determined." *University of Toronto Magazine* (Spring 2002); **134** Nick Brown, The Historica Foundation of Canada, 2003; **135** Quoted in Audrey Matheson, "School yard memories." Virtual Museum of Canada; **137** Translated in C.P. Stacey, ed., *Historical Documents of Canada*, vol. 5 (Toronto: Macmillan, 1972), 631; **147** Igor Gouzenko, *This Was My Choice* (Toronto: J.M. Dent & Sons (Canada) Limited), 1948; **150** Joanna Hildebrand, The Historica Foundation of Canada, 2003; **159** Thérèse Casgrain, *A Woman in a Man's World* (Toronto: McClelland & Stewart, 1972); **161** Don Quinlan, et al., *Twentieth Century Viewpoints*, 2nd edition, (Don Mills: Oxford University Press, 2003), 148; **166** Quoted in Robert F. Ladenson, "Ethics case study detail: Case #56, Inuit relocation." The University of San Diego; **167** Quoted in Don Gilmour, *Canada: A People's History*, vol. 2, (Toronto: Canadian Broadcasting Corporation and McClelland and Stewart, 2001), 225; Niall Ohalloran, The Historica Foundation of Canada, 2003; **168** Don Quinlan, et al., *Twentieth Century Viewpoints*, 2nd edition, (Don Mills: Oxford University Press, 2003), 198; **178** Richard Gwyn, *Nationalism with Walls: The Unbearable Lightness of Being Canadian* (Toronto: McClelland & Stewart, 1995); **179** Vincent Massey, *What's Past Is Prologue: The Memoirs of the Right Honourable Vincent Massey, C.H.* (Toronto: Macmillan, 1963); **182** Quoted in Richard Gwyn, *Smallwood: The Unlikely Revolutionary* (Toronto: McClelland & Stewart, 1968); **184** Quoted in "Maurice Richard dead at 78." Canoe, 27 May 2000; **186** "History of the Indian Act (part two)." *Saskatchewan Indian* (April 1978); **190** Rachel Machnik, The Historica Foundation of Canada, 2003; Veronica Strong-Boag, "Canada's wage-earning wives and the construction of the middle class, 1945–60." *The Journal of Canadian Studies* (Fall 1994): 5–25; Adapted from: Statistics Canada, Table "1 B-2", Labour Force Annual Averages, 71-220-XPB, Reference year 1991; **191** Quoted in Veronica Strong-Boag, "Canada's wage-earning wive s and the construction of the middle class, 1945–60." *Journal of Canadian Studies* (Fall 1994); Quoted in Robert Collins, *You Had To Be There: An Intimate Portrait of the Generation that Survived the Depression, Won the War, and Re-Invented Canada* (Toronto: McClelland & Stewart, 1997), 142; **192** Robert Collins, *You Had To Be There: An Intimate Portrait of the Generation that Survived the Depression, Won the War, and Re-Invented Canada*, (Toronto: McClelland & Stewart, 1997), 97; **193** Daniel Francis, et al., *Canadian Issues* (Don Mills: Oxford University Press, 1998), 198; **195** Environment Canada, The National Water Research Institute map at http://www.nwri.ca/threats2full/images/ch1_fig1_l.gif; **196** Quoted in Colin Nickerson, "Cancer, remorse haunts tiny billage." *Boston Globe*, 6 August 1998; **198** Quoted in Alex Barris, *Oscar Peterson: A Musical Biography* (Toronto: HarperCollins, 2002), 122; **203** Ryan Jenkins, "Concepts of a good immigrant, 1890-1990." The Historica Foundation of Canada, 2007; **204** Quoted in Barbara Ladouceur and Phyllis Spence, eds., *Blackouts to Bright Lights: Canadian War Bride Stories* (Vancouver: Ronsdale Press, 1995), 7; **205** Adapted from: Statistics Canada, Age Groups (12) and Sex (3) for

Population, For Canada, Provinces and Territories, 1921 to 2001 Censuses, 97F0003XIE2001002, Released July 16, 2002 and Statistics Canada, Age Groups (13) and Sex (3) for the Population of Canada, Provinces and Territories, 1921 to 2006 Censuses, 97-551-XWE2006005, Released July 17, 2007; **206** Frederick G. Gardiner, "Don of an old dream." *Toronto Star*, 5 December 1999; **212** Quoted in Dean Wood, "Multiculturalism: Appreciating our diversity." *Accord* (November–December 1980); **214** Quoted in Denis Smith, *Rogue Tory: The Life and Legend of John G. Diefenbaker* (Toronto: Macfarlane Walter and Ross, 1995), 230; **215** "The Canadian Bill of Rights." CBC Archives, original broadcast 16 March 1950; **216** Adapted from: Statistics Canada, Native and foreign-born population, 99-517, Volume VII, Part 1, Released in 1965; Statistics Canada, Birthplace, 92-727, Volume 1, Part 3, Released in 1974; Statistics Canada, Population, place of birth, citizenship, period of immigration: Canada, provinces, urban size groups, rural non-farm and rural farm, 92-913, Released in 1984; and Statistics Canada, The Nation: 1996 Census of Population, 93F0020XCB1996004, Released September 18, 1998; **218** Don Quinlan, et al., *Twentieth Century Viewpoints*, 2nd edition, (Don Mills: Oxford University Press, 2003), 157; **219** Quoted in Murray Peden, *Fall of an Arrow* (Stittsville: Canada's Wings, 1979), 128; Lester B. Pearson, *Mike: The Memoirs of the Right Honourable Lester B. Pearson*, vol. 3, (Toronto: University of Toronto Press, 1975), 47–48; Quoted in Murray Peden, *Fall of an Arrow* (Stittsville: Canada's Wings, 1979), 118; **220** "Radio and television report to the American people on the Soviet arms buildup in Cuba." John F. Kennedy Presidential Library & Museum, original broadcast 22 October 1962; Quoted in Peter Newman, *Renegade in Power: The Diefenbaker Years* (Toronto: McClelland & Stewart, 1989), 337; **224** Andrew Coyne, "Columns."; Quoted in Rick Archbold, *I Stand for Canada: The Story of the Maple Leaf Flag* (Toronto: MacFarlane, Walter & Ross, 2002); **227** "Tommy Douglas: The greatest of them all." CBC; Mordecai Richler, *Hunting Tigers Under Glass* (Toronto: McClelland & Stewart, 1968), 36; **231** M. Chaput, *Why I Am a Separatist* (Toronto: Ryerson Press, 1961); **232** Tim Schoulis, John Olthuis, and Diane Engelstad, "The basic dilemma: sovereignty or assimilation." in *Nation to Nation: Aboriginal Sovereignty and the Future of Canada*, John Bird, et al., (Toronto: Irwin, 1992), 23; Quoted in Robert Davidson, *Eagle of the Dawn*, ed. Ian M. Thom, (Vancouver: Vancouver Art Gallery, 1993), 8; **233** George Manuel and Michael Posluns, *The Fourth World: An Indian Reality* (Toronto: Collier-Macmillan, 1974); **235** Quoted in Peter Goddard, "She saw ski-doos, not igloos." *Toronto Star*, 17 February, 2007; **237** Quoted in Robert Davidson, *Eagle of the Dawn*, ed. Ian M. Thom, (Vancouver: Vancouver Art Gallery, 1993), 8; Quoted in Judy Rebick, *Ten Thousand Roses: The Making of a Feminist Revolution* (Toronto: Penguin, 2005), 10; **238** Marshall McLuhan, *Understanding Media: The Extensions of Man* (New York: McGraw Hill, 1964); Marshall McLuhan, *The Gutenberg Galaxy*, (Toronto: University of Toronto Press, 1962); Tom Wolfe, "The all-in-one global village." *Forbes*, (November 1999); **239** Rosemary Brown, *Being Brown: A Very Public Life* (Toronto: Random House, 1989), 85; **249** David Newman, "Canadien assimilation." Suite 101; **250** Scott Reid, *Lament for a Notion: The Life and Death of Canada's Bilingual Dream* (Vancouver: Arsenal Pulp Press, 1993); Adapted from: Statistics Canada, Languages in Canada (Focus on Canada Series: Analytical Products: 1991 Census of Population), 96-313-XPE, Released August 4, 1994; p. 56 and p. 83; **255** Pierre Trudeau, "The values of a just society." in Thomas S. Axworthy and Pierre Elliott Trudeau, eds., *Towards a Just Society*, (Toronto: Penguin Books, 1990), 358; Jacques Hébert, "Legislating for Freedom." in Thomas S. Axworthy and Pierre Elliott Trudeau, eds. *Towards a Just Society*, (Toronto: Penguin Books, 1990), 131; **256** Quoted in Anne Molgat, "Herstory: NAC's first twenty-five years." National Action Committee on the Status of Women; Harold Cardinal, *The Unjust Society: The Tragedy of Canada's Indians*, (Edmonton: M.G. Hurtig, 1969), 1; **259** Kristin Evans, The Historica Foundation of Canada, 2003; **260** Map by Glenn B. Garner 2008; **261** Quoted in "Voices." *Toronto Star*, 30 June 2007; **262** Quoted in Virginia Sauvé and Monique Sauvé, *Gateway to Canada* (Toronto: Oxford University Press, 1997), 89; Zohra Moosa, "Minding the multicultural gap." *Catalyst* (16 March 2007); Lilian To, "Does official multiculturalism unite Canada?" *Vancouver Sun*, 10 April 1997; Neil Bissoondath, "No place like home." *New Internationalist*, Issue 305 (September 1998); Joshua Hergesheimer, "My country, right not wrong." *Catalyst* (15 January 2007);

263 Cheryl Johnston, The Historica Foundation of Canada, 2003; Russ Pichora, The Historica Foundation of Canada, 2003; **264** Manpower and Immigration, Immigration Statistics 1971 and 1981. Citizenship and Immigration Canada. Reproduced with the permission of the Minister of Public Works and Government Services Canada, 2007; **265** Michael Lee-Chin, "Get rich slow." *Forbes* (15 April 2002); **271** Adapted from: the Statistics Canada CANSIM database http://cansim2.statcan.ca, 326-0002; Human Resources and Social Development Canada, "Applied Research Bulletin - The Canada-US Unemployment Rate Gap" Winter-Spring 1997, Reproduced with the permission of Her Majesty the Queen in Right of Canada 2007; **274–275** *Northern Frontier, Northern Homeland: the Report of the Mackenzie Valley Inquiry*. (Ottawa: Minister of Supply and Services Canada, 1977). Reproduced with the permission of the Minister of Public Works and Government Services Canada, 2007; **285** Pierre Elliott Trudeau, *Memoirs* (Toronto: McClelland & Stewart, 1993); **286** Quoted in "Canadians reflect on a quarter century of the Charter." *Toronto Star*, 7 April 2007; Carl Mollins, "The stagnant 70s." *Canadian Business* (August, 2003); Alvin Finkel and Margaret Conrad, *History of the Canadian Peoples* (Toronto: Copp Clark, 2001); **292** Adapted from: Statistics Canada. 1998. The Canada year book. Statistics Canada Catalogue no. 11-402-XPE. Ottawa; Adapted from: the Statistics Canada CANSIM database http://cansim2.statcan.ca, 326-0002; Handbook of Labor Statistics U.S. Department of Labor Bureau of Labor Statistics; Human Resources and Social Development Canada, "Applied Research Bulletin - Unemployment Rate in Canada and the United States, 1948-1995" Winter-Spring 1997, Reproduced with the permission of Her Majesty the Queen in Right of Canada 2007; **298** Marc Garneau, "Viewpoint." Culture Online: Made in Canada; Asaf Rashid, "Space exploration and the bone-chilling streets of Canada." *The Brunswickan* (21 January 2004); **303** APEC Members website (http://www.dfaitmaeci.gc.ca/canada-apec/map-en.asp), Foreign Affairs and International Trade Canada, 2008. Reproduced with the permission of Her Majesty the Queen in Right of Canada, represented by the Minister of Foreign Affairs, 2007; **306** Quoted in Scott Murphy, "Trekking on top of the world." *The Maple Leaf*, 26 July 2006; Quoted in Peter Moon "Patrol overcomes terrain, weather to confirm sovereignty." *The Maple Leaf*, 26 April 2006; **307** Pamela Perry-Globa, et al., *Perspectives on Globalization* (Don Mills: Oxford University Press Canada, 2007), 109; **311** Robert Bothwell, *The Penguin History of Canada* (Toronto: Penguin Group Canada, 2006), 461–462; **320** Quoted in Szandra Bereczky, "Canada's experience with NAFTA: A multimedia competition." Foreign Affairs and International Trade Canada, http://www.international.gc.ca/trade-agreements-accords-commerciaux/agr-acc/nafta-alena/bereczky.aspx; **322** Simon Reisman, "Canada's future under free trade." in *The Empire Club of Canada Speeches 1987–1988* (Toronto: The Empire Club Foundation, 1988); Maude Barlow and Tony Clarke, "Canada: The broken promise." *The Nation*, vol. 263, no. 3 (15 July 1996): 23–24; Quoted in "Bringing down the barriers." Canada, a people's history, CBC; Quoted in Stephen Clarkson, "Hoodwinked: The myth of free trade."; **323** Adapted from the Statistics Canada CANSIM database http://cansim2.statcan.ca, 282-0002; United States Department of Labor; **332** Don Quinlan, et al., *Twentieth Century Viewpoints*, 2nd edition, (Don Mills: Oxford University Press, 2003), 229; **334** Adapted from: the Statistics Canada CANSIM database http://cansim2.statcan.ca, 385-0010; **335** Quoted in "'Toonie' makes its debut." CBC Archives; Quoted in Tavia Grant, "Happy birthday, loonie." *Globe and Mail*, Reportonbusiness, 27 June 2007; **338** Cheryl Johnston, "The Immigration Experience." The Historica Foundation of Canada; **340** Quoted in Katie Rook, "Party puts the spotlight on Desi culture." *National Post*, 25 October 2006; **341** Kristin Evans, "First Nations—first priority?" The Historica Foundation of Canada; **342** ArtPlus Ltd.; **354** Kim Campbell, *Time and Chance: The Political Memoirs of Canada's First Woman Prime Minister*, (Toronto: Doubleday Canada, 1996); **362** Quoted in "Trudeau accuses Bouchard of betraying Quebecers." *The Montreal Gazette*, 3 February 1996; **367** "Canadian disunity." PBS Online Newshour; **370** Quoted in Alan Freeman, "Budget hits jobs, military." *Globe and Mail*, 23 February 1994; Jim Stanford, "Paul Martin, the deficit, and the debt: Taking another look." Canadian Centre for Policy Alternatives, 28 November 2003; **371** Murray Dobbin, "Paul Martin's democratic deficit." *The Tyee*, 16

February 2004; Gwynne Dyer, "Canada: The master's revenge?", 23 June 2004; **376** Quoted in Scott Steele, "Gustafsen Lake standoff: 15 charged." *Maclean's*, (2 June 1997); **378** Reproduced with the permission of the Minister of Public Works and Government Services Canada, 2007 and Courtesy of Natural Resources Canada; **379** "Gathering Strength: Canada's Aboriginal Action Plan." Indian and Northern Affairs Canada, http://www.ainc-inac.gc.ca/gs/pam_e.html; **380** "National Aboriginal Achievement Awards." CBC, 13 January 2004; **383** Michel Tétu, "Francophonie." in Gerald Hallowell, ed., *The Oxford Companion to Canadian History* (Toronto: Oxford University Press, 2004), 237; **385** Helen Luk, "Anti-globalization protesters march on third day of WTO meeting in Hong Kong." The Canadian Press, 15 December 2005.; **386** Rachel D., "Youthlinks Forum." The Historica Foundation of Canada; Quoted in "Rwandans mark genocide as Montreal war-crimes trial continues." *Toronto Star*, 10 April 2007; **387** Roméo Dallaire, *Shake Hands with the Devil: The Failure of Humanity in Rwanda* (Toronto: Random House Canada, 2003); **391** Matthew Moulton, The Historica Foundation of Canada; **392** Quoted in "The Chrétien doctrine and the Iraq crisis." *Canadian Council on International Law*, vol. 29, iss. 1 (Winter 2003); Quoted in Norman Madarasz, "Remember thy neighbor: Canada's opposition to the Anglo-American invasion." *Counterpunch* (5 April 2003); Quoted in Rosemary Ganley, "Canada's leaders say 'no' to war: Leaders resist growing pressure toward new invasion of Iraq." *Catholic New Times*, 20 October 2002; **393** Robert R., "Youthlinks forum." The Historica Foundation of Canada; Justin E., "Youthlinks forum." The Historica Foundation of Canada; **394** Richard Burnett, "Three dollar bill." *Vue Weekly*, Issue 452 (17 June 2004); **395** "Hell, high water and heartache." CBC, 22 January 2007; **397** Quoted in Margaret Beckett, "A threat to global security." *Toronto Star*, 19 April 2007; **398** Free The Children; **404** Quoted in "PM makes surprise visit to troops in Afghanistan." CTV, 13 March 2006; **407** Quoted in Bob Plamondon, *Full Circle: Death and Resurrection in Canadian Conservative Politics*, (Toronto: Key Porter Books, 2006); **409** Quoted in "The people's Governor General." *Reader's Digest* (July 2007): 57; **411** Quoted in Daniel Leblanc, "The master of proving people wrong." *Globe and Mail*, 4 December 2006; **414** Dr Gaetan Tardif, "Celebrating Canada's paralympians." *Toronto Rehab Magazine* (Fall 2004); **415** Quoted in "Is recognizing Québécois only symbolic?" *The Epoch Times*, 30 November 2006; **421** United Nations Framework Convention on Climate Change, Kyoto Protocol Status of Ratification, updated 28 September 2006; **422** David Suzuki, "Our leaders just don't get it." David Suzuki Foundation; **425** Jose A. Kusugak, *Unikkaaqatigii: Putting the Human Face on Climate Change*, (Ottawa: Inuit Tapiriit Kanatami, 2005), 5; Quoted in Bruce Campion-Smith, "PM's vessels 'aren't what we need for the Arctic'." *Toronto Star*, 9 July 2007; **426** Quoted in Bruce Campion-Smith, "PM's vessels 'aren't what we need for the Arctic'." *Toronto Star*, 9 July 2007; James Travers, "Arctic issues make for good politics." *Toronto Star*, 9 July 2007; **427** "Russia plants flag under N Pole." BBC, 2 August 2007; **428** Dorothy Yang, "Invading Afghanistan is not the answer." The Historica Foundation of Canada, 2003; Matthew Houser

and Matt McKeen, "Terrorism: Canada's role." The Historica Foundation of Canada, 2003; Quoted in "Sisters in arms." *Reader's Digest* (April 2007): 94; **429** Peter Goodspeed, "It's going to take time." *The National Post*, 15 January 2007; **431** Sean M. Maloney, "Winning in Afghanistan." *Maclean's* (23 July 2007): 26; Murray Dobbin, "Harper's taste for war." *The Tyee*, 25 September 2006; **432** Daniel Rosario, The Historica Foundation of Canada, 2003; **433** Quoted in "Crusader at the crossroads." The Stephen Lewis Foundation; Stephen Lewis, *Race Against Time* (Toronto: House of Anansi Press, 2005), 31–32; **438** Alia Domino, The Historica Foundation of Canada, 2003; Thomas Axworthy, "To go ahead, Canada must know its past." *Toronto Star*, 17 June 2007; **440** *Life Expectancy for First Nations People and Canadians, by Gender, Canada, 1980, 1990, and 2000, Health Canada, 2004 and Basic Departmental Data 2004*. Ottawa: Indian and Northern Affairs Canada, 2004, Adapted and Reproduced with the permission of the Minister of Public Works and Government Services Canada, 2008; **441** Ovide Mercredi, *The Report of the Aboriginal Justice Inquiry of Manitoba* (Winnipeg: Aboriginal Justice Implementation Commission, 1999); **442** Quoted in Joseph Quesnel, "Aboriginal leader addresses union about First Nation poverty." *First Perspective National Aboriginal News*, 17 April 2007; **443** Vijayata Achatz, The Historica Foundation of Canada, 2007; Quoted in "Let's talk about poverty: Poverty fact sheet #7." The Urban Poverty Consortium of Waterloo Region, 29 November 2000; **444** Quoted in Kerry Gillespie, "Coalition urges raising welfare." *Toronto Star*, 25 May 2007; Sharon Mason Singer and David Hay, "Child poverty is down. No, it's up." *The Tyee*, 2 January 2007; Adapted from: Statistics Canada, Income Trends in Canada, 13F0022XCB, 1980-2001 issue, Released December 22, 2003; Printed with permission from Campaign 2000, a cross-Canada network of organizations working to end child and family poverty; **446** David Suzuki, "Saving the planet." Culture Online: Made in Canada; Steven Guilbeault, "Canadians are becoming more environment-minded." Culture Online: Made in Canada; "Ecological Footprint Model" based on Figure 4.2 from *Sharing Nature's Interest: Ecological Footprints as an Indicator of Sustainability* (Chambers, Simmons and Wackernagel, 2000), 63. Reproduced with special permission; **447** Dr. John Talberth and Dr. Jason Venetoulis, "Ecological Footprint of Nations: 2005 Update", (Redefining Progress, 2006); Mathis Wackernagel, "Living planet report 2006 outlines scenarios for humanity's future." *Footprint Network News*; Quoted in Matthew Burrows, "We create a huge footprint." Straight, Vancouver's Online Resource, 12 January 2006; "Our logo." Zero Waste Services; David Suzuki, "Foreword." in David R. Boyd, *Sustainability within a Generation: A New Vision for Canada*, (Vancouver: The David Suzuki Foundation, 2004), vi; **448** Stephen Staples, "Ready when you are, sir." Ottawa (X)Press, 13 April 2006; **450** Dyane Adam, "Women and culture in Canada." Culture Online: Made in Canada, April 2005; Lori Masters, "Voices: Women's rights and multiculturalism." *Toronto Star*, 29 May 2007; Ratna Omidvar, "When rights collide with freedoms." *Toronto Star*, 28 May 2007.